A Social His...
178

Related titles from Palgrave Macmillan:

Nigel Aston, *Religion and Revolution in France, 1780–1804*
Jarine Garrison, *A History of Sixteenth-Century France, 1483–1598*
David Potter, *A History of France, 1460–1560*
Charles Sowerwine, *France since 1870*
Richard Vinen, *France, 1934–1970*

A Social History of France 1789–1914

Second Edition

PETER McPHEE

First edition published 1992 by Routledge
Second edition published 2004 by
PALGRAVE MACMILLAN
Houndmills, Basingstoke, Hampshire RG21 6XS and
175 Fifth Avenue, New York, N. Y. 10010
Companies and representatives throughout the world

PALGRAVE MACMILLAN is the global academic imprint of the Palgrave Macmillan division of St. Martin's Press, LLC and of Palgrave Macmillan Ltd. Macmillan® is a registered trademark in the United States, United Kingdom and other countries. Palgrave is a registered trademark in the European Union and other countries.

ISBN 0–333–99750–6 hardback
ISBN 0–333–99751–4 paperback

This book is printed on paper suitable for recycling and made from fully managed and sustained forest sources.

A catalogue record for this book is available from the British Library.

A catalog record for this book is available from the Library of Congress.

10 9 8 7 6 5 4 3 2 1
13 12 11 10 09 08 07 06 05 04

Printed and bound in Great Britain by
Creative Print & Design (Wales), Ebbw Vale

Contents

Maps and Tables

Maps

Tables

Abbreviations

Abbreviated titles have been used for periodicals cited in notes more than once:

AdeN	*Annales de Normandie*
AduM	*Annales du Midi*
AHR	*American Historical Review*
AHRF	*Annales historiques de la Révolution française*
AJFS	*Australian Journal of French Studies*
Annales	*Annales: économies, sociétés, civilisations*
BHES	*Bulletin d'histoire économique et sociale*
CSSH	*Comparative Studies in Society and History*
EHQ	*European History Quarterly*
ER	*Études rurales*
ESR	*European Studies Review*
FH	*French History*
FHS	*French Historical Studies*
FPS	*French Politics and Society*
HJ	*Historical Journal*
HR	*Historical Reflections/Réflexions historiques*
HW	*History Workshop*
IH	*Information historique*
JEH	*Journal of Economic History*
JFH	*Journal of Family History*
JIH	*Journal of Interdisciplinary History*
JMH	*Journal of Modern History*
JSH	*Journal of Social History*
MS	*Mouvement social*
P&P	*Past & Present*
RFSP	*Revue française de science politique*
RH	*Revue historique*
RHMC	*Revue d'histoire moderne et contemporaine*
SH	*Social History*
TM	*Les Temps modernes*
T&S	*Theory and Society*

Preface to Second Edition

The invitation from Palgrave Macmillan to produce a second edition of a book first published in 1992 has afforded me the opportunity to integrate the outstanding social history published in the decade since then; at the same time a number of corrections have been made to the earlier text. This edition also extends its chronological span from 1880 to 1914 to cover the 'long nineteenth century' 1789–1914: in political and cultural terms, the nineteenth century began in France (and Europe) with the Revolution of 1789 and ended not on 31 December 1899 but with the declaration of war on 3 August 1914.

PETER MCPHEE
March 2003

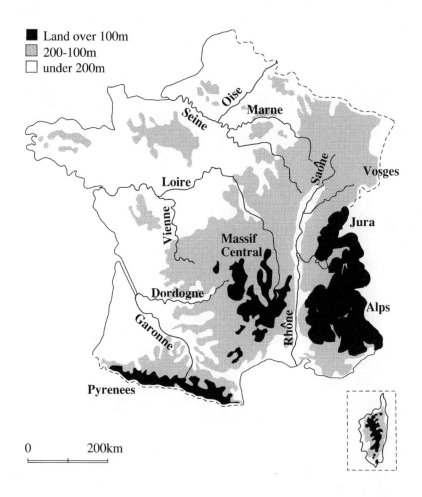

Land over 100m

200-100m

under 200m

Oise

Seine

Marne

Vosges

Saône

Loire

Jura

Vienne

Massif
Central

Alps

Dordogne

Rhône

Garonne

Pyrenees

0   200km

Introduction

When the Provençal poet Frédéric Mistral wrote his memoirs at the end of the nineteenth century he recalled how, as a youth in a southern village, he learnt of the blood-stained memories of the French Revolution which continued to divide his family as well as his community. Disillusioned by republicanism, Mistral later sought calm in the eternal rhythms of nature only to be traumatized by the 'gigantic crabs' which now mechanically harvested crops 'in American style, cheerlessly, in haste, without any joy or singing. . . . That's progress, that's the terrible, inevitable harrow against which nothing can be done or said.' These twin furnaces of change – the French Revolution and later political upheavals, and the mechanization of productive processes – have ever since attracted historians to the period 1789–1914; perhaps no other period of history has been so extensively studied. In recent decades some social historians have suggested that Mistral and other contemporaries were confusing political strife and economic novelty with real social change. Arno Mayer has argued that historians, too, have been preoccupied with change, at the expense of ignoring the continuities in French society. To Mayer, France in this century remained a pre-industrial Old Regime, 'first and foremost a peasant economy and rural society dominated by hereditary and privileged nobilities'. The French Revolution did not undermine their landed power and control of the Church and State, and, while a democratic republic was finally in place by 1880, France remained a traditional peasant and artisan society. Not until the 'general crisis' of the twentieth century, between 1914 and 1945, did the European Old Regime finally die.[1]

The contrasting perspectives of Mistral and Mayer on the 'long nineteenth century', 1789–1914, point to two of the unifying themes of this book. First, they highlight the question of change and continuity: were the political and economic shocks which so struck Mistral more sound and fury than real social transformation? Secondly, the contrasting perceptions of a late twentieth-century American and a Provençal born in 1830 underline the role of hindsight. Do we best understand a past society by listening to the ways in which its inhabitants described it, or are the confusions that they experienced avoided with the benefit of Mayer's detached hindsight? Or, better, do we study the past through a dialogue between its voices and ourselves as individuals living in a society distant in time and culture? For, despite this distance, the experiences of French people in the years 1789–1914 inevitably draw us into dialogue with them, for it was then that the most profound questions were raised about whether poverty was the responsibility of the individual or the state, about what constituted 'legitimate' government and its powers, about the social and environmental effects of industrialization, and about roles and relationships within the family. The answers people gave to these and other questions continue to resonate in our own times.

Any attempt to conceptualize and to write the social history of France across a century – particularly one as highly-charged and often-studied as that after 1789 – also raises methodological issues. The first, and most important, relates to the vexed question of the meaning of 'social history' itself. If social history is not, in G. M. Trevelyan's famous 1942 formulation, 'the history of a people with the politics left out', what is it?[2] Initially coined as a way of describing a history whose concerns contested the primacy of élite, male politics as the object of historical enquiry, the unity social historians share through their concern for all members of society has always been fractured by alternative methodologies and assumptions. At its broadest, social history proclaims the legitimacy of all types of history under its umbrella, and seeks to give proportionate weight to all social groups. At its narrowest, perhaps in reaction to the political disappointments of the 1970s, it has excluded institutionalized politics altogether as somehow 'irrelevant' to people's real concerns.

Whatever the parameters of social history, its concerns obviously range far wider than politics. How then should the social history of a society across a century be ordered into coherent chapters? This is a particularly thorny problem, one which social historians have resolved in diverse ways. Roger Price's detailed overview of the century 1815–1914 adopted a thematic and structural approach, proceeding from the economic and demographic bases of society to a description of major social groups (élites, middle classes, peasants, urban workers) and the major agencies of socialization (religion, education) and, finally, some concluding remarks about politics. Roger Magraw, on the other hand, has preferred a narrative of class struggle between an increasingly dominant bourgeoisie and its opponents: the working class, petits bourgeois, peasants and the 'aristocratic-clerical' right. In contrast, Theodore Zeldin's engaging survey of France 1848–1945 rejected such structural analysis as dehumanizing and simplistic. For Zeldin, social history must be about individuals and their idiosyncrasies: French history is presented by him as a kaleidoscope of stories, ideas and passions but not as a structured society experiencing broad changes and continuities.[3]

This book seeks to draw from the strengths of each of these approaches, but instead sees the social relations of power as its unifying thread. The basis and nature of the exercise of power – politics in its broadest sense – varies according to time and place, and the class, gender and ethnic background of its proponents. But even the intimate relationships of private life, and the distinction between 'private' and 'public', were also a matter of social definition and power. By focusing on social relations of power – the unequal bases from which people acted to change or consolidate their world – the book seeks to avoid one of the weaknesses of much social history writing, its inability to convey any sense of a past which people at the time experienced as the present. The most common focus of social history has been the ways in which societies have been structured; that is, most social history has been concerned with economic structures and their consequent social and occupational formations. Whatever the insights resulting from such an approach, it has been limited by a failure to consider the ways in which people in the past expressed themselves and gave meaning to the confusion and unpredictability of the world in which they lived.

The challenge to long-established chronological divisions in history – in this case the revolutions of 1789, 1830, 1848 and 1870–1 – has come from two directions. In a general way social history has questioned such 'periodization' as privileging the world of élite politics, arguing instead that the rhythms of daily life, and economic and social change move far more slowly and cut across such divisions. Do 'public and private calendars' – the linear progression of political life and the rhythms of the private and familial world – ever move to the same impulses? More particularly, conventional periodization has been charged by feminist historians with being inherently male as well as élitist: that is, the social history of half of the population cannot be understood as a linear chronology which assumes that the political history of men is also the social history of women. If women were denied access to institutional forms of political power, then a social history which is organized around political 'breaks' must necessarily be imposing an interpretative grid which distorts, or even denies, more significant processes in the history of women. While this argument is reflected in the organization in this book, in which most chapters focus on broad periods of change and continuity, a political chronology cannot be totally disregarded. Central to the book is the argument that periods of political and social upheaval involved and affected all French people, though in contrasting ways. In particular, the French Revolution and the Second Republic were years of crisis when women participated in, and were directly affected by, political contestation which went to the heart of their existences.[4]

That is why one of the organizing principles of this book has been chronological, even within the thematic chapters on rural and urban society. In particular, the chapters on the two great social crises of this century – the French Revolution of 1789–95 and the Second Republic, 1848–51 – are concerned to convey the drama and uncertainty in which most people felt intimately involved. While relations of power are always central to a study of society, these were times when huge numbers of people were directly involved in and affected by political processes, when social and political history become inseparable and needed to be fused into a 'social history of politics'. Not to do this would be to deny, in a condescending way, that the political resolution of questions of power can be at the heart of daily life. In Stendhal's great novel about early nineteenth-century society, *Le Rouge et le noir*, completion of which coincided with the Revolution of 1830, he interrupted a chapter about political debate to interpose a conversation with his publisher. 'Politics are like a stone tied to the neck of literature which, in less than six months, will drown it', complained Stendhal; to which his publisher retorted: 'If your characters don't talk politics, then they're no longer Frenchmen of 1830, and your book is no longer a mirror, as you claim.' However, there is no totally satisfactory way of conceptualizing social history. For example, chapters which separately discuss urban and rural society (Chapters 7–8 and 10–11) necessarily imply a division which was far less abrupt in reality. The boundaries between town and countryside were fluid in terms of the occupations and lifestyles of many of their people, just as urban and rural economies were interdependent.

Since about 1960 there has been an extraordinary proliferation of social history: in just one decade, from 1968 to 1978, the proportion of United States history theses on social history subjects leapt from 10.4 to over 27 per cent. This surge of social history has continued into the new century. One important rationale for this book has been the need to synthesize this detailed research into a coherent overview, even if this necessarily reflects my own organizing principles and assumptions. This social history has also been limited by the difficulties of recovering past experience. Despite the extraordinary expansion of the boundaries of social history since 1960 – from fashion and smell to breast-feeding and the colour of eyes – some of the most important and intriguing dimensions of the past are only slowly yielding their secrets. In part this is due to the time-lag in researching the historical background to issues of current concern; for example, remarkably little work has been done on the history of pollution or the rural environment as opposed to the history of economic change. It is also due to a certain urban and male bias in research in social history: the largest single social group, the working women of the countryside, is that which we know least about. Moreover, historians have rarely found, for all their labours, the resources to answer questions about the personal relationships of ordinary people in the past. It is only now that we are starting to learn more of the history of the disabled. The ministerial archives on which historians primarily depend contain a vast body of information of interest to political élites: population censuses, property surveys, economic statistics, tax records, court reports and the like. Very little of this material concerns how the great mass of people made sense of the world and the people around them. Only when they came into contact with the policing bureaucracies of the judiciary, the army and the Church were their attitudes recorded, but then in situations when they were least likely to be frank. Hence we know something of domestic violence extreme enough to be deemed illegal, though regrettably little about sexual abuse, particularly of children. We know a great deal about marriage and fertility patterns, but next to nothing about the ways affection was expressed within most families. In Charles Tilly's words: 'Sad, but true: in the world of history, true love leaves fewer memorials than the sale of a sow.'[5]

But, while most people were unable to read or write the printed word with ease, they were certainly all 'literate' in their capacity to understand and communicate symbolically, literacy in its wider, correct sense. Like all societies, France in the century after 1789 was most often characterized by forms of communication of a non-written kind: the spoken or sung word, the resonant statements made by gesture, buildings, clothing and actions. Most people were 'non-scribal', but they were not 'illiterate' in their capacity to 'read' and convey meanings in these ways. In this sense, social history must also be cultural history. The difficulty for the social historian is that, relying as we usually have to on inscription – the printed word, paintings and drawings – non-scribal forms of communication are often either irretrievable or are transmitted through the written description of others.

These difficulties perhaps account for the taste many social historians have for quantification. Unfortunately, they tend to be uncritical in the use made of statistics generated by the bureaucracy of the time, which are often taken as detached, impartial, and therefore 'factual', statements about social realities. Contemporary statistics are always useful, but need first to be understood as the mental constructs of those who composed them, as the specific way in which a particular group of people ordered the world in which they lived.[6] Similarly, the use of new technologies to construct numerical measures of the past – whether social structures, demographic patterns or economic growth rates – may at times amount to a condescension towards the people ostensibly at the heart of the story, whose understandings of the world in which they lived are rejected in favour of the 'realities' revealed by the computer. Statistics have an undeniable use as a shorthand way of describing society but must be balanced by a sensitivity to personal and group responses to the way the world was perceived. People in the past acted not in response to the way historians – armed with hindsight and the technologies of the statistician – define that world, but in response to the way they deemed it to be.

In recent years historians have developed a more imaginative understanding of the world of politics by placing the practice of power within the context of 'political culture' and the 'public sphere'. That is, they argue, we can best begin to understand the 'social history of politics' only by going beyond formal politics to consider a fuller array of ways in which people thought about and acted out politics. This approach has drawn heavily on the work of the German sociologist Jürgen Habermas, writing in the 1960s in the context of his nation's recent history and emerging knowledge of Stalin's Russia. Recent historians have expanded on Habermas's notions of political culture and public space by going beyond élite intellectual history to the 'spaces' in which ideas were articulated and contested. Most recently, historians have returned to study 'material culture'; that is, the material objects and practices of economic life. They have not done this to repeat older Marxist understandings of intellectual and cultural life as 'reflections' of economic structure; rather, they wish to comprehend the meanings people at the time gave to their world through behaviour as well as in words. Some of the most exciting history being written at present is at the intersection of social and cultural history, but it is precisely because much cultural history starts from the assumption that the world of ideas and the actions of individuals may be studied as somehow 'autonomous' from economic and political context that makes social history still a meaningful approach.[7]

The most effective social history, then, is that which manages to explain the way people responded to the world around them by using the benefits of a longer-term perspective, but without ever losing sight of the fact that the past was the present to those who lived within it. At its best it is broad in its aims, but humble in its claims. Among those historians whose work best exemplifies this social history are Maurice Agulhon, Alain Corbin, Michel Vovelle, John Merriman and Colin Lucas. They have managed, in Le Roy Ladurie's words, to be both 'parachutists' and 'truffle-hunters', always aware of the broad social terrain as they descend to earth in search of their prey, the experiences of real individuals. The author has an important if indirect debt to them and the hundreds of other historians whose researches have informed this overview of the social history of France.

A more direct debt is owed to those who facilitated the preparation of the manuscript in various ways. Grants from the Australian Research Council and the University of Melbourne enabled important bibliographical work to be undertaken. Drafts of the manuscript were subjected to critical and valuable scrutiny by Charlotte Allen, Robert Ewins, Nicole Prosper and Charles Sowerwine, while more specific assistance was offered by Robert Aldrich, David Garrioch, Peter Jones, Emily McCaffrey, John Merriman, Kate Mustafa and Timothy Tackett. Finally, it has been in the process of discussion with students that many of the themes of this book have taken shape. All of these people have contributed in valued ways to whatever positive qualities this book may have; responsibilities for its shortcomings remain with the author.

1
France in the 1780s

On 1 August 1779, Pierre Reynes and his son Mathieu met the royal notary of the small south-western town of Villefranche-de-Lauragais to enter into a contract with the 'high and powerful seigneur' the Marquis d'Hautpoul, through his agent, Jacques Maurel.[1] The farm the illiterate peasants were renting was a considerable one – about 30 hectares – and produced about a hundred *setiers* of wheat (20 *setiers* would feed a family of five) and a wide array of livestock, vegetables and other produce. This was, however, a sharecropping contract: the seigneur took 20 *setiers* in advance – whatever the volume of the crop – and half of the rest; after setting aside seed for the next year, the Reynes would be left with 15 *setiers*, less than their family needed. They were rigidly tied to a three-field system (maize and vegetables, wheat, fallow) and, while the proceeds from livestock were also divided, any extra forage had to be provided by them. Similarly, all the farm implements were the lessees' responsibility. They were to buy young pigs, though the seigneur's agent was to have half; in addition, they were to provide 108 chickens and capons and 600 eggs yearly. The lease was for one year only; should the Reynes not 'do everything necessary' to be good husbandmen (*'bons ménagers et bons pères de famille'*), it would not be renewed.

We will never know what the unfortunate Reynes made of a contract which required them to produce more than enough to feed several households yet left them barely enough to feed themselves. However, the contract hints at many of the essential characteristics of late eighteenth-century France, such as the role of status, wealth and literacy in the exercise of power. Most importantly, it points to the overwhelmingly agrarian basis of this society.

There are no accurate census statistics for eighteenth-century France. The painstaking analysis of parish records undertaken by Jacques Dupâquier and others suggests that approximately 28 million people inhabited the territory of France in 1780, rather more than earlier estimates. Using the later French measure of the 'urban threshold' being 2,000 people – though most towns of up to 10,000 essentially served the surrounding agrarian economy – perhaps two persons in ten lived in an urban centre. The rest inhabited 38,000 rural communities or parishes with on average about 600 residents.[2] These parishes were the smallest unit of an administrative hierarchy which claimed sovereignty over the king's territory. This territory was itself the result of an historical process of conquest, defeat and annexation since the twelfth century, during which 'outside' powers, such as those centred on London, Barcelona and Turin, had been expelled, while others (Rennes, Lille, Strasbourg, Dijon, Lyon, Toulouse, Aix, Perpignan) had been 'provincialized' within it.

The claim of the royal state to its territory was contradicted by ethnic and linguistic diversity. The Reynes were among the several million people of Languedoc who spoke variants of Occitan. The southern border of France since 1659 had incorporated minorities of Basques and Catalans into the country. In the north-west, one million Celts lived in Brittany; the north-eastern border sliced through Flemish-speaking lands. More recently, to the east, Lorraine had been incorporated in 1766, and in 1768 Corsica had been purchased from the Republic of Genoa. On the other hand, the royal state did not include Avignon and the Comtat-Venaissin, papal territory since the fourteenth century, or French-speaking areas in Switzerland or the Austrian Netherlands.

While the monarchy had sought to impose linguistic uniformity 'from above' by requiring priests and those in liberal professions to speak French, and for church registers and public acts to be kept in French, such controls only affected the surface of life in much of France. Most subjects of Louis XVI spoke their own language or dialect and lived within distinctive cultures of perception, language and ritual. Cultural unity across the vast area of the royal state lay essentially in formal adherence to Christianity, though the rhythms of the church year were everywhere grafted onto more ancient regional traditions. The great festivals of community life – in cities as well as the countryside – were the *fête patronale*, one or more days of dancing, singing and worship to honour the local patron saint; Christmas; the great bonfires for the feast of St John in June; Simnel Sunday, the mid-way point of Lent, when fasting restrictions were temporarily lifted; the celebrations associated with personal *rites de passage* such as baptism and marriage; and, above all, Carnival. All of these ritual moments of public life had specific regional forms which coexisted uneasily with church celebrations of Easter, saints' days and the sacraments. For example, depending on the region, the period of Carnival could begin as early as Christmas and climaxed on Shrove Tuesday and Ash Wednesday, with a resurgence on Easter Sunday and Low Sunday (Quasimodo). The essence of Carnival lay in its parody of the constraints of daily life: by inverting and mocking realities, Carnival 'turned the world upside down'. To a world of poverty and restraint was opposed a temporary one of indulgence and excess. To social hierarchy, and laws imposed and enforced by outsiders were opposed egalitarianism, communal autonomy and popular justice; masquerades and transvestism inverted sexual taboos and sex roles. The elaborate rituals culminated on Ash Wednesday with the judgement of the Carnival symbol, the *mannequin* or dummy, and – again depending on the locality – its punishment by drowning, burning, beating or beheading.

It was above all the formal structures of the Catholic Church in its monopoly of public worship which covered France with a grid of relative conformity. Even so, there were some areas, such as the Roussillon, where too few priests spoke French for the Church to enforce what would have been incomprehensible sermons in that language. Those people most likely to understand were officials, professional men and merchants engaged in national administrative and marketing structures, as in Bordeaux, where use of French was a means of

Map 1.1   French provinces in the 1780s, showing principal centres of administration

Note: The identification of the pays d'état is disputable.

stating cultural difference from Gascon peasants. Over much of the royal territory, French was a grid of élite language, as the Abbé Albert, from Embrun in the southern Alps found, when he travelled through the Auvergne in about 1780:

> I was never able to make myself understood by the peasants I met on the road. I spoke to them in French, I spoke to them in my native patois, I even tried to speak to them in Latin, but all to no avail. When at last I was tired of talking to them without their understanding a word, they in their turn spoke to me in a language of which I could make no more sense.[3]

The rural economy was essentially a peasant economy: that is, the labours of the family had a subsistence orientation, a system of polyculture which sought to produce as much as possible of a household's consumer needs. Only in the hinterland of large towns and cities had urban manufacturers conquered what Marx was to describe as the 'home market for capital', where rural producers had to concentrate more extensively on market-oriented agriculture in order to buy the urban commodities – clothes, tools, furniture – which most rural communities produced for themselves. The household was the focus of production as well as reproduction; the household or family economy was the bedrock on which were predicated strategies of survival ranging from the division of labour to patterns of marriage, conception and childraising.

While there remained perhaps half a million serfs, largely in the Franche-Comté and Nivernais, peasants had some control over their means of livelihood and a degree of choice about where and with whom to live. Together they owned perhaps one-third of the land of France, varying sharply from place to place: in three villages of the Morvan, peasant holdings covered 1.2 per cent in La Forêt (where nobles owned 81.8 per cent), 13.5 per cent in Decize (bourgeois owned 63.5 per cent) and 77.6 per cent in La Villette. Everywhere, most holdings – depending on the region, from 60 to 90 per cent – were too small to meet a family's needs. The abandoned terraces of highland France today are testimony to the back-breaking work of the poorer peasantry in an overcrowded countryside. The family economy was sustained by what Olwen Hufton has described as a 'precarious balancing act': like the Reynes, most peasants needed to rent more land, or seek wage-labour, or engage in 'outwork' for urban-based textile manufacturers. Rural people assumed that they would contribute to their household strategy from the time they were old enough to weed vegetables or feed chickens until their strength finally ebbed in old age.[4]

The rural population was commonly referred to as 'paysans'; that is, as 'people of the land *(pays)*'. However, this simple term – like its English counterpart 'peasant' – disguises the complexities of rural society which were revealed in the varied responses of people to the factors affecting their survival. Perhaps 55 per cent of rural producers were peasants in a stricter sense: owners of small plots who supplemented meagre returns by renting, sharecropping *(métayage)* or wage-labour. Above them were the *coqs du village* or rural bourgeois: large tenants (*fermiers* or *tenanciers*) and those landowners *(laboureurs)* needing to employ farm-labourers regularly. Landless labourers, whether hired by the day or as long-term farm servants, made up perhaps 30 per cent of the rural population, ranging from 5 per cent in the Auvergne to 55 per cent around Versailles.

Paradoxical as it may seem, rural France was also the centre of most manufacturing: the textile industry in particular was largely based on women's work in Normandy, the Rouennais, the Velay, and Picardy (where 40,000 women worked part-time in the stocking industry). Rural industry of this type meshed with regional specialities centred on provincial towns: gloves in Millau, ribbons in Saint-Étienne, lace in Dieppe and silk in Lyon. A recent study of rural industry by Liana Vardi focuses on Montigny, in the 1780s a community of about 600 people located in the northern region of Cambrésis, only part of France since 1677.[5] At the beginning of the eighteenth century, its population of essentially subsistence landowners and tenant-farmers had been one-third that size. Throughout the eighteenth century, large owners and tenants monopolized the land, increasingly specializing in corn; the middling and small peasants instead found spinning and weaving linen the answer to poverty and land-hunger. A flourishing if vulnerable rural industry in Montigny was based on merchants 'putting out' spinning and weaving to rural households. In turn, the textile industry provided the incentive for farmers to increase crop yields substantially to feed an increasing population. A key role was played by middlemen, merchant-weavers from places like Montigny who mortgaged small family holdings to join the rush to be affluent. These people remained 'rural' in their personal ties and economic strategies at the same time as they demonstrated a remarkable entrepreneurial ability and enthusiasm.

Farm work was organized around a complex sexual division of labour, but the toil of girls and women was crucial and complementary to that of males. Women's work was especially important in two ways. First, as the majority of the workforce in those stages of textile manufacture 'put out' to the countryside, they earned a major portion of the cash essential to a household for the purchase of necessities produced elsewhere or to pay taxes. Secondly, as scores of thousands of men from highland areas with a long 'dead season' in winter migrated seasonally or for years at a time to look for work, women became the heart of a 'matricentric' household economy in much of the Massif Central and elsewhere. Despite their importance, when women did paid work they were recompensed at only about 40 per cent of male wages: as employers assumed that women were being sheltered by fathers or husbands, they were usually paid only for their food, often as little as would buy two or three pounds of bread. This is one reason why, in the Norman countryside, 66 per cent of widows, compared with 37 per cent of widowers, remarried within two years.[6]

A rural world in which households sought to secure their own subsistence could inevitably expect only low yields for grain crops grown in unsuitable or exhausted soil. In general, seed-yield ratios were as low as 1:6 even in good years. Consequently, most rural communities had restricted 'surpluses' which could be marketed to substantial towns; far more important were nearby small towns or *bourgs* of 2,000–5,000 people, centres of micro-regions whose weekly, monthly or annual market-fairs were as much an occasion for the collective rituals of local cultures as for the exchange of commodities.

The nature of the rural economy was the major reason for the limited extent of urban manufacturing and commerce and of towns themselves: the 'auto-consumption' of so much that rural communities produced and the extraordinary range of productive activities in the countryside meant that towns and cities faced both chronic problems of food supply and a limited rural demand for their goods and services. But although only 20 per cent of French people lived in urban communities, in a European context France was remarkable for the number and size of its towns. Like England at the same time, urban France was dominated by a single city: Paris in 1780 had a population variously estimated as between 550,000 and 700,000. Unlike England, where the next largest centres, Bristol and Norwich, had no more than 20,000 people, France had another large city (Lyon: 145,000), six with 50,000–100,000 (Marseille, Bordeaux, Nantes, Lille, Rouen, Toulouse), 18 with 20,000–40,000 and 50 with 10,000–15,000. The solution to the paradox of how an essentially peasant society could sustain so many substantial towns and cities lies in the functions these provincial centres fulfilled in the eighteenth century. While any provincial town had its large-scale manufacturing sector involved in an international trading framework, most towns were dominated by artisan-type craftwork for the needs of the urban population itself and the immediate hinterland, and by a range of administrative, judicial, ecclesiastical and policing functions. They were provincial capitals: only one person in 40 lived in Paris, and communication between Versailles and the rest of its territory was usually slow and uncertain (travel by coach across the 500 kilometres between Paris and Lyon took five days).

Despite its rapid growth in the decades after 1750, Paris remained a city dominated by craft workshops.[7] Certainly there were a number of expanding, substantial capitalist enterprises: in the *faubourg* Saint-Antoine, Réveillon's wall-paper factory employed 350 people, the brewer Santerre had 800 workers, and 500 employees were concentrated in a glassworks; in the *faubourg* Saint-Denis, substantial textile workshops employed up to 800 people and the Gobelins tapestry workshop, established by Louis XIV, was a major employer in the *faubourg* Saint-Marcel. In all, there were some fifty Parisian 'manufactories' employing between 100 and 800 workers, often under quasi-military discipline. The building industry had boomed in the western neighbourhoods *(quartiers)* of the city, constructing 6,000 new houses for the wealthy fleeing the essentially medieval centre where, above street-level workshops and stores, the various social strata of the population lived in descending layers of wealth in tenement buildings. On the upper floors lived wage-workers such as the stone-mason whose furniture was limited to: 'A poor stove … a very poor cot and trestle-bed, a mattress in a very bad state, two thin woollen blankets, a bolster made of ticking, a butter-pot, a little pottery soup-bowl, a case with four razors, a small box containing old rags and tools.'

Most of the 350,000 people dependent on wage-earning worked in small workshops: the urban equivalent of the rural household economy, these centres of skilled work grouped a master craftsman's family, journeymen (so named for having made their *tour de France*, visiting provincial centres of the craft before submitting their *chef d'oeuvre*), apprentices and labourers. In August 1776, a major reform of guilds by Jacques Necker had undermined the autonomy of masters and transferred regulatory power to the government. Henceforth the *chef d'oeuvre* was no longer strictly necessary and trades were opened to those with the necessary capital, including women, who previously had been restricted to continuing a dead husband's business. Increasingly fractured by the wage-labour relations of the workshop and the difficulty journeymen had in establishing their own workshops, the world of labour nevertheless remained united by the culture, subsistence needs and shared labour skills and routines of the trade and *quartier*.[8]

Paris was an amalgam of neighbourhoods distinguished by topography, social structure and the presence of migrants from particular regions. Inside the new and hated customs walls were *faubourgs* (literally, suburbs) which remained semi-rural, the home of impoverished migrants and noxious industries such as tanning and chemicals. The world of working people was structured through the functions of family, work and neighbourhood, a world that was both intimate and public: three-quarters of the families of the *faubourg* Saint-Antoine lived in one or two rooms. Men relaxed from 14–16-hour days in one of Paris's 3,000 taverns (cafés were considered bourgeois) and women from their paid and unpaid work over cards or in the street; here, too, most disputes were resolved by group pressure. Tolerant of prostitution, gambling, beggars and cohabitation, the 'common people' *(menu peuple)* were hostile to thieves, the officials and ministers they blamed for food-supply problems, and the 140 monasteries and convents which owned one-quarter of the city.

The artisan Jacques-Louis Ménétra was one such Parisian.[9] His memoirs recall his antipathy to nobles, priests and the very wealthy and also his love of reading (he had read Rousseau's *Du contrat social, Emile* and *La Nouvelle Héloïse*), of his workmates' obscene jokes and pranks, and of the pleasures of casual sex, even rape (though some of his exploits were surely apocryphal). An abiding regret was that he 'knew love only as pleasure and not as perfect friendship'. Evident, too, is his love for his son and daughter; two other children had died. Perhaps because his own father had been brutal towards him and his mother had died while he was a child, Ménétra had clear assumptions about the roles father and mother should play: the former as the source of authority, punishment and advice, the latter of affection and imagination.

While Ménétra worked in the glazing trade, where there was a shared knowledge of the entire work process, in others, such as tailoring, there was a clear division of labour. In cities such as Dijon, the geographical mobility of artisans enabled guild recruitment to keep pace with demand, whereas in rapidly changing cities, such as Lyon and Nantes, artisans were united in hostility to the intrusion of large-scale manufacturing. Everywhere in urban France, the horizontal divisions of the workplace, enforced by a judicial system which saw wage-earners as 'servants', existed within a 'corporate idiom' of vertically-segregated trades, each with elaborate forms of brotherhoods *(compagnonnages)*, ritual and controls as defences against mechanization and competition. The trade *compagnonnages* were fiercely competitive, illegal but tolerated associations, often with a provincial network; their complex, often religious, language and rituals, and legendary feuds gave urban life a distinctive flavour.[10]

The world of manual labour in which the *menu peuple*, from masters to labourers, sensed a common if fractured identity, coexisted across a divide of wealth, status and culture with an urban bourgeoisie, at once employer and client. The bourgeoisie of late eighteenth-century France was distinctive in its occupations and other sources of wealth. There were scattered large enterprises in large towns and cities: the textile factories of Lyon, Abbeville (where van Robais had 12,000 employees), Elbeuf and Rouen and a few iron foundries and coal mines (such as at Le Creusot, Niederbronn and Anzin, where 4,000 workers were employed). Here, a distinctively capitalist bourgeoisie was expanding the scale of its enterprises with an uneasy eye across the Channel. An economic boom was occurring in the great ports, especially on the Atlantic coast where a triangular trade linked France with its Caribbean colonies and Africa through commerce in slaves, wines and spirits, sugar, coffee, cotton and indigo. After 1715, the volume of trade grew 4 per cent per annum in Bordeaux, sustaining large shipbuilding, ropemaking, tobacco, sugar and glassmaking enterprises.[11] The colonies accounted for one-third of all French trade. In Saint-Domingue, 31,000 whites ruled 465,500 slaves according to the *Code noir* of 1685, which forbade 'ill-treatment' but denied slaves any legal rights and deemed their children to be the slave-owner's property. In 1785 there were 143 ships actively engaged in the slave-trade: 48 of them from Nantes, 37 each from La Rochelle and Le Havre, and others from Bordeaux, Marseille, Saint-Malo and Dunkerque. In Nantes, the slave-trade represented 20–5 per cent of the traffic of the port in the 1780s, in Bordeaux 8–15 per cent and in La Rochelle as much as 58 per cent in 1786. These slave ships had made more than 3,300 voyages across the century.[12]

However, most middle-class families continued to draw their wealth from a combination of more 'respectable' enterprises: from the practice of law, whether privately or within the judicial bureaucracy of the monarchy, from other professions, from senior positions in administration (in all, there were some 50,000 venal positions in the state apparatus), from investing in secure, low-return government bonds *(rentes)* and from investment in land and seigneurialism. Around Le Mans, 22 per cent of seigneurs were of bourgeois background. A rural bourgeoisie – estate managers for the nobility, capitalist tenant-farmers and the wealthiest peasantry – had sought since the 1760s to emulate English enclosures but, except in some areas of the Paris basin and the north-east, had been thwarted by the collective resistance of the peasantry to techniques which threatened community access to or control of forests, common lands and rights of gleaning.

Distinguished from the *menu peuple* by the fact that their wealth did not come from their own manual labour, the bourgeoisie was also characterized by the exclusion of bourgeois women from both paid work (except in extensive managerial activity in the lace industry) and domestic tasks performed by young women, mostly recent arrivals from embattled rural families. This work, essentially a temporary strategy to accumulate a dowry, also exposed young women to long hours of heavy work, and to sexual pressure or assault. Domestic service, with prostitution, was one of the major sources of urban work for women; in Paris, it also employed many of the 750 blacks and mulattoes, mostly former slaves, from the West Indies and Africa. Literate, skilled and keen to enter the artisanate, these people were the object of racial phobias among the élite, though not, it appears, among the *menu peuple*.[13]

Town and country were also linked by the practice of wet-nursing: a precious resource for rural women in the hinterland of Paris and Lyon was the money earned from suckling the babies of the urban wealthy and of wage-earning women whose work rendered breast-feeding impracticable. (Ménétra's mother had died while he was living with a rural wet nurse.) About half of the 20,000 babies born in Paris each year were sent to *nourrices* in Normandy, Picardy and the Champagne; one-third would die before their mothers saw them again, one of the reasons for the anguish women expressed as they handed over a child.[14]

The central link between town and country was incipient tension over the staple diet of working people: grain, and especially wheat. Master craftsmen and their employees on the one hand and different sections of the rural community on the other necessarily had conflicting interests. The supply of wheat to Paris from the capitalist farms of the Beauce around Chartres was constantly threatened by bands of 'outlaws' patrolling the highway before withdrawing to their impoverished villages.[15] In normal times, the families of masters might spend 30 per cent of their income on flour or bread, while journeymen might thus consume 40 per cent of their wages and labourers 60 per cent. During the frequent years of crop failure, these proportions could rise by one-half, as grain merchants and large farmers speculated on prices. The poorer sections of the peasantry were equally vulnerable; on average, one year in four the size of crops failed to allow what today would be termed a minimum calorific intake.

The vulnerability of urban and rural working people to shortage and hence to disease, and the delicate, complex balancing of resources and hungry mouths underpinned the 'demographic equilibrium' of pre-industrial France. In 'normal' times, the average birth rate was extremely high, about 4.5 for every hundred people, and mortality rates similarly marked, about 3.5 per cent (in many towns and rural areas, only one child in two survived to five years of age). In times of shortage, the rate escalated, as the already physically vulnerable died and infant deaths increased, while fewer births occurred, whether due to miscarriages by malnourished women or to family strategies such as delaying marriage or using contraception (especially withdrawal or coitus interruptus) to minimize births. Once the crisis had passed, birth-rates quickly rose: delayed marriages could occur and, especially with the access to land caused by the death of the elderly, men and women could marry younger than the usual average of 26–9 and 24–7 years respectively. Largely owing to a protracted series of fair to good harvests in the years after 1750, such crises had not been dramatic during this period: by 1780 the population had increased by 3.5 million from perhaps 24.5 million.

The practice of birth control varied widely according to the availability of economic resources, the level of infant mortality, the length of time babies were breast-fed, and the degree of acceptance of the strictures of the Church. In Lourmarin, a mixed Protestant and Catholic village in Provence, women married comparatively young (in their early twenties), had their first child within 12 months, and 19 per cent were already pregnant at marriage. Despite this, most women had fewer than four children, indicating the use of contraception and a degree of religious scepticism. In contrast, 99 per cent of births in Brittany were within marriage and women usually had a baby every 20 months between marrying (on average at age 26) and menopause (age 41–3). Even in evidently devout areas, however, contraception could be used: in the Roussillon, people in Collioure abstained from pre-marital intercourse but married late and births were planned to occur in winter because women's work was so important in the wine and fishing industries in the warmer months. Whereas, in the south-west and Normandy, two-thirds of children survived past the age of ten, in Brittany and Collioure just half could hope to, because of problems of fresh water supply and impoverished diet.[16]

While historians have discerned shifts in articulated attitudes within élites towards marriage and children in the second half of the eighteenth century, the emotional relations between the men, women and children of the people are, except in rare cases, beyond the historian's grasp. There is no reason to suppose, however, that the high numbers of abandoned children in towns or of children who were sent to rural wet nurses for several years was anything other than a grief-ridden response to necessity. The bourgeoisie may have been able to listen to exhortations to breast-feed their children; many working women could not. From birth, the child was also at the centre of a struggle between two practices of health care, the urban male *accoucheur*, concerned with 'modern' forms of medicine and eager for professional respectability, and the rural female midwife calling on the wisdom of regional folklore. In either case, people remained vulnerable to disease; for example, in 1779–80, a dysentery epidemic carried off 175,000 people, mainly in the rural west and Brittany.[17]

The vulnerability of the peasantry was not simply a function of overpopulation, disease, inadequate land or polyculture: given the technology of pre-industrial agriculture, the intensive labour of millions of households was extraordinarily productive. A defining characteristic of peasantries is their 'asymmetrical' relations with powerful outsiders: in eighteenth-century France, rural people were not only vulnerable to the climate, but also underwrote the culture, lifestyles and expenditure of the three pillars of power and privilege, the nobility, the Church and the monarchical state. All three extracted 'surplus' (though the peasantry would never have described it as such), ranging from as little as 14 per cent of what a peasant household might produce in Brittany (8 per cent as tithe, 4 per cent as taxes and 2 per cent as dues) to as much as 40 per cent elsewhere.[18] It is the mode of extraction of this 'surplus' by the nobility and Church in particular which highlights the distinctively pre-capitalist mode of production in rural France.

While feudalism in its 'pure' form, if it ever existed fully, no longer controlled the countryside, the economic power and seigneurial 'rights' fiercely guarded by the nobility were a constant dimension of rural life, especially for provincial nobles *(hobereaux)* resentful of the Versailles élite and unable to afford an expensive education for their children in prestigious church schools or in the military academies in Paris, Angers or Bordeaux. Known as the second 'estate' or 'order' of the realm, the nobility directly owned perhaps one-third of landed property and exercised seigneurial rights over most of the rest *('nulle terre sans seigneur')*. Estimates of the number of noble families vary widely: recent ones suggest about 25,000, their 125,000 members representing no more than one in 200 of the population. Central to the income of most of these families, whatever the considerable variation in wealth and status among them, was control of the land and the people who worked it. Robert Forster has emphasized the role of some nobles in the introduction of capitalist agricultural techniques on their own land,[19] but noble wealth more commonly relied upon restrictive contracts on rented land and regular payment of dues in cash or kind. The importance to nobles of seigneurial dues varied sharply – in the south, from 71 per cent of noble income in the Rouergue to 34 per cent in upper Auvergne and just 8 per cent in the Lauragais – but was everywhere significant. The most important due was regular payment of the *champart* (elsewhere known as the *censive* or *tasque*) on the major crop produced on all land within the *seigneurie*; this was normally one-twelfth or one-sixth, but up to one-quarter in Quercy and the Rouergue.

It was bolstered by other significant 'rights', such as a monopoly *(banalité)* over the village oven, grape and olive press, and mill; irregular payments on land transfers and even marriages; and the exercise of unpaid labour by the community on the lord's lands.

As Anthony Crubaugh has shown, in Aunis and Saintonge, and probably elsewhere, the system of seigneurial justice was far from moribund or atrophied, as many historians have assumed it to be.[20] The royal *sénéchaussée* of Saint-Jean d'Angély, for example, had no fewer than 171 seigneurial justices for its 146 parishes. The system was deeply resented as costly, slow, and preoccupied with the protection of noble privilege and status. In the words of a peasant maxim of the day, 'a bad arrangement is better than a good trial'. Twenty-four cases that Crubaugh studied at Tonnay-Boutonne took an average of 32 months to resolve, with average costs to peasants of 106 livres. When the courts acted on matters of morality, they could be uncompromising and severe: women accused of hiding pregnancy were commonly sentenced to public humiliation and whipping. The courts showed a good deal more alacrity when the prerogatives of the privileged were at stake. Rural folk were under no illusions that the primary purpose of the seigneurial courts was to maintain the property and privileges of the nobility and Church. In Aunis and Saintonge harvest dues were commonly levied at one-sixth or one-seventh and represented about half of the revenues of seigneurs, in one case 87 per cent. Seigneurialism mattered: at least 39 seigneuries in the two regions revised their feudal registers *(terriers)* in the period 1750–89.

In theory, relationships between seigneurs and peasants were based on reciprocity, but *noblesse oblige* had never been an equal exchange for the surplus extracted, and never less so than by the late eighteenth century. The lord's obligation to provide protection, security and assistance in times of crisis had been eroded by the concentration of military force in the hands of the monarchical state, by the purchase of seigneurial rights as an investment by urban bourgeois and by the long-term tendency of the nobility themselves to reside in towns for much of the year. For some seigneurs, the obligations they felt towards those under their direct or indirect control were genuine, and a precious resource for those the nobility themselves had initially made vulnerable; for others, the renting of land and the extraction of seigneurial dues was simply a profitable enterprise.

Whatever the case, the landed wealth and seigneurial control of the nobility and the fragility of the family economy placed peasants in a position of dependence in which social control could be exercised. We cannot know to what extent the deferential behaviour thus required represented a sincere assumption by peasants that such a hierarchy was the natural order of things or whether, in a world of forced obligations, a show of deference gave them precious if restricted room to manoeuvre for seigneurial benevolence. The political culture of the rural world was one which reinforced seigneurial authority at every turn: from the omnipresent statements of power in noble châteaux, dress and overconsumption of food, especially meat and fish, to the reservation of noble space in churches, to the rights to hunt across and feed pigeons on peasant land and to residual powers nobles retained over elected parish councils. Such powers were everywhere resented, as in Provence, where peasants were required to respect a death in the seigneur's family by refraining from public festivals for a year. Here a bereaved noble complained that, on the day of the patron saint's festival at Sausses, 'people had beaten drums, fired muskets and danced the whole day and part of the night, with a remarkable *éclat* and conceit'.[21]

This culture of hierarchy and inequality was sustained by the functions of the second great pillar of the power structure of France in the 1780s: the Church, or first estate. Held together, like the nobility, by its status, rights and 'calling', the Church was itself hierarchical and divided by noble monopoly of position, power and wealth. There were about 170,000 clergy (in all, about 0.6 per cent of the population). The 81,500 'regular' clergy (26,500 monks and 55,000 nuns) of the thousand convents, monasteries and other religious orders of France inhabited institutions which ranged from the moribund to the dynamic, from the contemplative to the socially active (such as the Sisters of Charity in Bayeux, who fed and sheltered 600 women, migrants from the countryside, in their lace workshops).[22] Ministering to the needs of 'secular' society were 59,500 clergy – 39,000 priests *(curés)* and 20,500 curates *(vicaires)* – in all, one cleric for every 470 people. There were several other types of 'lay' clergy. The starkest division within the clergy separated the noble bishops and the canons of cathedral chapters (the Archbishop of Strasbourg had a salary of 450,000 livres and several other royal posts) from the almost exclusively commoner parish clergy of *curés* (whose salary was raised to 750 livres in 1786) and *vicaires* (300 livres). Resentments among the lower clergy were expressed through a banned clerical 'Richerism', based on the writings of a seventeenth-century canon lawyer who had argued that Christ had commissioned not only the 12 apostles as 'bishops', but also the 72 disciples or 'priests' mentioned in Luke. In addition, Dale Van Kley has pointed to the importance of the long-term religious legacy of Protestant and Jansenist notions of political liberty and challenges to ecclesiastical hierarchy dating from the 1730s.[23]

The major source of wealth for the Church as an institution was the tithe, commonly 8–10 per cent of the grain crop of a rural community, and amounting in value to up to 150 million livres annually. In addition, the Church was a powerful landowner in its own right, through the holdings of noble clerics, religious orders (for which dues and rents totalled up to 130 million), or the small plots of most parish clergy. In all, the clergy owned about 7 per cent of the land, varying from less than 2 per cent in parts of the south to 40 per cent in the Cambrésis. Almost everywhere it was located in the most fertile land of the region. Like the nobility, the Church drew its wealth largely from the countryside and yet was essentially urban in the display and expenditure of its worldly power. Central to the life-blood which sustained provincial towns were the opportunities for employment created in a cathedral city; in an important sense, such inland towns were parasitic on the countryside, for the bulk of the seigneurial dues, rents, tithes and fees collected by the first two estates of the realm were spent in urban centres. In the process, domestic servants, skilled artisans and the destitute were placed in a dependent relationship. In Angers, the 600 religious (1.5 per cent of the population) owned some 75 per cent of urban property; clerks, furniture makers, cooks and cleaners depended on them, as did the lawyers who ran the Church's 53 legal courts for the prosecution of rural offenders.[24]

The rituals of the church year were intrinsic to rural life; the spire of the parish church symbolised spiritual power even if not the dominance of the Church's preferred expressions of spirituality. The rich textures of regional cultures were all in a real sense Christian and Catholic: almost everywhere, at least 90 per cent of parishioners attended church regularly, and parents brought children to be baptized well within three days of birth. The only exceptions to this were in the tolerated but geographically-confined Jewish communities of Sephardim in Bordeaux and the Comtat-Venaissin and Ashkenazim in Alsace (in all, some 40,000 persons); and among the 700,000 Protestants, whose public worship was no longer tolerated officially since 1685, in a crescent stretching from Strasbourg in the east via the southern Massif Central to La Rochelle on the Atlantic.[25]

The external exercise of faith – religiosity – suggests an overwhelmingly Catholic society, but the personal importance of such practice – spirituality – is irretrievable for the historian. There are, however, indications of what histori-ans have labelled 'secularization' in the years after 1770. Across the century, the percentage of births outside marriage increased from 2.9 to 4.1 and of pregnant brides from 6.2 to 10.1. Some towns registered an increase in non-attendance at church, paralleled among élites by a trend away from the purchase of religious books and a secularization of their attitudes to death. In Provence, the number of people requesting masses for their souls in their wills declined from 80 to 50 per cent in 1750–89 (46 per cent of men and 67 per cent of women). Nationally, levels of recruitment to the priesthood declined by 23 per cent in 1749–89, and of Benedictine, Franciscan and Augustine monks by one-third in the 20 years after 1770; on the other hand, the number of *congréganistes* (non-cloistered nuns) was increasing.

In general terms, Catholicism was strongest in the west and Brittany, the north and east, the southern Massif Central, the Pyrenees and Basque country, and less so in the centre, the Paris Basin, the south-east and Aunis-Saintonge. Within all of these regions, the most devout were likely to be rural rather than urban, women rather than men, the old rather than the young, and peasants rather than nobles or bourgeois. The authoritarian 'Tridentine' Catholicism the clergy was seeking to inculcate partly explains such contrasts, and was most suc-cessful where the clergy were local and rural in origin, relatively well-off and numerous, as in the west, or where the clergy spoke the local language (Corsica, the Roussillon, Brittany, the Auvergne, the Basque country). Even in such places, the strictures of the clergy about sexual and public propriety may have been resented by men and boys. Both in the lowlands around Bordeaux and in the uplands of the Auvergne there was an increasing preference shown by men for 'profane' Sundays: drinking, dancing and playing *boules*, rather than accom-panying women to church. This was a Catholicism of hell-fire, damnation and fear, taught by a seminary-trained, austere and often 'outsider' clergy (40 per cent of priests were recruited in towns) taught to mistrust the secular and profane. In the 1780s, Yves-Michel Marchais, the priest of a devout western parish, insisted to his congregation:

> The joys, the pleasures, the happiness of life are always dangerous and almost always fatal; the games, laughter, and amusements of the world are like the mark of damnation and are gifts given to us by God in his anger. Whereas tears and suffering are the signs of God's pity and a certain promise of salvation.[26]

However, the message of the Gospels, then as now, was inherently ambiguous: Was it indeed harder for a rich man to enter heaven than for a camel to go through the eye of a needle? Should the meek wait to inherit the earth? And, in the face of the worldliness and opulence of the upper clergy, was not the Bible (especially the books of Daniel and Revelations) replete with warnings to which priests, no less than the congregation, might listen?

The Church offered more than negative answers to the eternal questions: Why is the world as it is? How might it be different? In return for the alms of the faithful, the parish clergy in particular played several crucial roles. The unemployed, old or ill single people, prostitutes and beggars – in all perhaps one-tenth of the urban and rural population even in normal times – resorted individually to an array of expedients to ensure a precarious existence, and none was more important than recourse to the Church. While the capacity of parish priests to dispense charity to the 'deserving poor' was limited by their own poverty and the fact that the tithe was usually accumulated at diocesan level, the Church was the single most important resource for the very poor. Unlike the royal government's assistance, which was inadequate, sporadic and arbitrary, the parish priest was, if usually impecunious, always there; for women who felt an almost sacred obligation to place bread upon the family table, a special dimension was thus added to spirituality. The poor did not have equal access to charity, however, for Church structures were slow to adjust to urban change: the stable populations of Bayeux (10,000) and Angers (34,000) were each served by 17 parishes, while in booming Bordeaux, where the population had increased from 67,000 to 110,000 since 1750, the 14 parishes remained clustered in the inner city, leaving newer parishes with up to 15,000 souls.[27]

Insofar as working people in town and country received instruction, it was the Church which provided the essentials. There are evident difficulties in measuring and describing literacy, but the 47 per cent of males and 27 per cent of females – especially in the north and east – who were at least able to sign their marriage registers in the 1780s are testimony to the Church's efforts. The Church also played a social role as the centre of information and access to outside news; as the most literate person in small communities and as the person who read government decrees as well as sermons at mass, the priest was a key intermediary with the outside. In regions of dispersed habitat, such as Brittany, parts of the west, and much of the Massif Central, Sunday mass was the time when the parish felt its community identity. Peter Jones has argued that in the southern Massif Central the community was indeed a communion of souls, reinforced by mutual mistrust between Catholics and small, concentrated groups of Protestants. In Protestant Pont-de-Montvert, this mistrust drew on memories of an occupation by Catholic troops in 1751–5, and was reinforced daily by the tithes collected by the Catholic Church and dues paid to the absentee seigneur, the Knights of Malta.[28]

Eighteenth-century France was thus a society in which privilege was integral to social hierarchy, wealth and individual identity. At the summit of every form of privilege – legal, fiscal, regional – was the noble élite of the first two estates. Internally united by privileges belonging to their 'corporate' estate, their vision of their social functions and identity, and their relations with commoners, the first two estates in the juridical structure of eighteenth-century France were divided by internal ranking of status and wealth. The ancient and immensely wealthy noble families at the pinnacle of these two orders shared a conception of social and political authority expressed through ostentatious display. The great châteaux and cathedrals of provincial France, beloved of tourists today, were elaborate statements of spiritual and secular power to those who worshipped in or worked near them.

But no more resonant or imposing assertion of divinely-sanctioned worldly power existed than the royal palace at Versailles. The spatial organization of the formal gardens and the sheer size of the 580-metre facade symbolized a royal claim of pre-eminence and authority. The third pillar of the power structure of eighteenth-century France, the monarchy, like nobles and clergy, drew its authority, influence and wealth from its control of its subjects. If its conception of the arena of state intervention was restricted essentially to the conduct of foreign policy, internal policing and the regulation of trade, the size of the state debt and the demands of sustaining the court itself had generated ever-increasing demands for revenue. The ministerial bureaucracy in Versailles was tiny: in all, some 670 staff in the 1780s. Instead, many government functions, including tax-collection, were in private hands.[29] The system of tax-collection was itself an important source of income for the *receveurs de tailles*, the 400 collectors who received a commission on the amount collected from the *taille*, the major direct tax levied on wealth, and for the 40 *fermiers-généraux* who negotiated a down-payment on prospective collections from indirect taxes on salt, tobacco and wine, and kept whatever extra they collected.

In theory based on a clear distinction of power and function between divinely-ordained king, the Church and the nobility, the political culture of the French élite was in reality a world held together by countervailing tensions. Conflicts at court – where noblewomen played an important role – advanced the special claims of factions and corporate bodies for special protection and the spoils of office. In return for the spiritual sanction it gave to kings and their powers within a Gallican tradition, a role carried out at every level from coronation to the *Te Deum* and the reading of royal decrees in parish churches, the Catholic Church expected guarantees of its corporate status, its privileges and its monopoly of public worship and morals. This was inevitably an uneasy relationship. On the one hand, the noble-dominated Assembly of the Church regularly voted only a minimal voluntary contribution *(don gratuit)* towards state expenses. On the other, monarchs directly interfered with church administration: 625 of the 740 monasteries were held *in commendam*, whereby the king's absentee nominee collected one-third of the revenues, and Louis XV had closed 458 religious houses (which had housed just 509 religious in total).

A similarly uneasy interdependence characterized the relationship between monarchy and nobility. In return for their obedience, support and military loyalty, the nobility expected respect for their monopoly of high offices, social pre-eminence and privileges, whether fiscal or honorary. In the 1780s, Louis XVI responded to noble pressures with a series of decrees restricting commoner entry into the officer corps of the army and navy and by reserving certain church positions for poorer nobles. But the pivotal political tension between monarch and nobles remained that between the centralizing or 'centripetal' tendency of the royal state apparatus, and the provincial or 'centrifugal' claims of tradition, autonomy and local authority of the nobility. Such claims, together with other traditions of corporate privilege and the resilience of minority cultures, were the major obstacles to the monarch's absolute authority.

These obstacles were reflected in the institutional structures of eighteenth-century France, as was the reluctance or inability of monarchs to ignore the heritage of exemptions and exceptions through which monarchs had pieced together the territory they ruled. The construction of a map of some 58 provinces and their division into 33 *généralités* for administrative purposes imperfectly coincided with the ethnic and historical realities of the kingdom. Administrative units varied strikingly in size (from sprawling Languedoc to the compact Dombes), in the location of their capitals (Alençon, Rennes and other centres were located in one corner of their *généralité*) and, most importantly, in function and powers. The *pays d'État*, such as Brittany, Languedoc and Burgundy, claimed rights to internal self-government denied to *pays d'élection*. In Brittany, for example, the royal administrator *(intendant)* had direct power only over the highway police *(maréchaussée)*, internal transport and control of beggars.

Cutting across administrative subdivisions was a complex set of internal customs barriers. Much of northern France had formed a customs union in 1664, but was separated from the south, Brittany, the east and Artois by customs houses. Moreover, the eastern provinces traded freely across France's eastern border – though not with the rest of the country – and Dunkerque, Marseille and Bayonne had special claims as 'free ports'. These customs arrangements were further complicated by internal toll-houses belonging to nobles and towns, levying transit charges on goods using roads, bridges and canals. Internal trade was further hampered by variations in the name and values of weights, measures and currency.

Not only were members of the privileged orders largely exempt from state taxation, but the rate at which the *taille* was levied varied significantly between *généralités*: *pays d'État* in particular were more lightly taxed, and several provincial cities had effectively bought themselves immunity from the *taille*. The State's major source of indirect taxation, the *gabelle* on salt, varied even more sharply, with the price for 72 litres ranging from 60 livres 7 sous to 1 livre 10 sous. There were six major divisions for the collection of this tax, with many internal variations. In Brittany, the least taxed province, the smuggling of salt eastwards into the area of heaviest taxation, often by bands of 'pregnant' women, was a precious additional source of income for up to 200,000 families.[30]

Nowhere did administrative and fiscal divisions correspond with the jurisdiction of the 13 *parlements* and four *conseils souverains*, the highest courts of the land. While the *parlement* of Paris had powers over almost half the country, the domain of the *conseils* in Perpignan and Arras was tiny. Moreover, this map of judicial competence improperly matched that of lesser courts, such as the *Chambre des comptes* and the *Cours des aides*. A major division into areas of customary and written law between north and south cut across judicial boundaries, and was immeasurably complicated by the existence of special courts and codes for nobles and clergy and those obligated to them, and of up to 60 regional codes for certain offences. The extraordinary complexity of the administration was matched in the organization of the Church. The archdioceses varied enormously in size, from the massive area of the sees of Tours and Bourges to the small, thinly populated see of Embrun in Provence and other *'évêchés crottés'* or 'muddy bishoprics'. The priests of the Cerdagne in the eastern Pyrenees remained subject to the bishop of Seo-de-Urgel in Spain. Most striking was the contrast in the density of bishoprics, heavily concentrated in the south as a legacy of the fourteenth-century residence of the papacy at Avignon.

The institutional structures of France in the 1780s speak to us of the uneven hold which the royal state apparatus could claim over an area of Europe characterized by geographic, historical and, above all, cultural diversity. Everywhere social divisions of status, wealth and gender were complicated by regional practices, immunities and loyalties of occupation, locale and ethnicity. This complexity of structures and loyalties, underpinned by the micro-regional orientation of the French economy, also explains the distinctive nature of popular protest. Everywhere the targets of popular anger were threats to the household, neighbourhood and community, coming from the king's agents and those who threatened a supply of cheap and plentiful food. To the demands of the State, rural and small-town people, especially in non-French speaking areas, responded by smuggling, forest invasions and, most commonly, by 'sidestepping' state exactions in taxation, conscription and billeting of troops. Most common of all (in 22 of the years 1765–89) was the food riot, when the working people *(menu peuple)* of rural communities or urban *quartiers*, often with the real or involuntary leadership of a mayor, priest or other notable, protected food supplies. This was done in rural areas by preventing large farmers and merchants from taking 'excess' grain from its area of production, and in urban centres by imposing popular price-fixing *(taxation populaire)* on millers, bakers and merchants.[31] Such collective action was characterized by the disproportionate presence of women, explained by their role in food preparation for the family, the relative leniency of the authorities towards women, and the quasi-religious justification for women feeding starving children.

Other forms of protest, by publicists, pushed the regime into a series of liberal reforms in the 1780s: the granting of limited civil rights to Protestants (permitting, for example, the marriage of Protestants before a royal judge), the release of political prisoners, and the abolition of a personal tax on Jews, of serfdom on royal estates, and of pre-trial torture. However, official sanctions against 'deviants' and against attacks on persons and property remained violent and exemplary. In 1783, a Capucin monk was burned alive in Paris, one of 40,000 homosexuals police claimed to have on file. Homosexuals could look neither to the Church nor to doctors for support; while many were prepared to gather publicly in Paris, in the grounds of the Tuileries, they were seen as morally and physically perverted, if not beyond redemption. (In theory at least, 'the crime of women who corrupt one another' was also a capital offence.) The impoverished rural migrants who were forced to turn to prostitution in cities like Montpellier were increasingly singled out for imprisonment, for up to five years, in religious reformatories.[32] Reflecting the on-going struggle of the royal state for control over its subjects, physical punishments were severe and often spectacular: two beggars from the Auvergne were broken on the wheel in 1778 for threatening a victim with a sword and rifle. In all, 19 per cent of the cases before the Prevotal Court in Toulouse in 1773–90 resulted in public execution (reaching 30.7 per cent in 1783) and as many again were sentenced to life imprisonment in naval prisons. Working people often had a contrary notion of 'crime'. Fewer than one-quarter of the cases taken to the *parlement* of Toulouse were for violent assault; most were for outrages to dignity *(honnêteté)* resulting from broken promises, slander, or false accusation, all the worse if the aggressor had insulted the victim in French. However, in the 1780s, men of property were increasingly using the courts – rather than informal community pressures – to enforce their rights, just as in Paris it seems that the State was more frequently intervening in family and work disputes formerly arbitrated by sections of the community.[33]

The protests of urban and rural working people and the campaigns of liberal reformers did not amount to a fundamental challenge to the political and social structures of the established order since they were essentially protests for fairer treatment within that system. However, a series of interrelated changes – economic, social and cultural – was undermining the bases of social and political authority. The limited but highly visible expansion of capitalist enterprise in industry, agriculture and above all commerce, linked to the colonial trade, generated forms of wealth and values discordant with the institutional bases of absolutism, an ordered society of corporate privilege and the claims to authority of aristocracy and Church.

It is true that individual nobles played active roles in agricultural change and mining, and that kings ennobled individuals among the most successful financiers and manufacturers, such as the Bavarian migrant Christophe-Philippe Oberkampf who had established a printed-fabrics factory at Jouy, near Versailles. Similarly, the wealthiest bourgeois sought to buy noble office and title, for they brought with them wealth as well as status in a society they never imagined would end. Claude Périer, a wealthy, textile-factory owner from Grenoble, who also had a sugar plantation in Saint-Domingue, paid one million livres for several seigneuries in 1780. Their return – 37,000 livres annually – was about the same as from alternative investment possibilities.[34] But the social 'fusion' of certain nobles and the wealthiest bourgeois did not bridge a wider gulf of values, privilege and sources of wealth which divided the provincial nobility from most of the bourgeoisie. By no means exceptional was the bourgeois of Montpellier who excoriated noble privileges and 'honours' and their 'scorn' for work in a city where 'possessions and wealth count for everything'. Idleness *(fainéantise)* was for him the epitome of noble uselessness, although, in this pre-industrial society, it was still to agriculture and the professions that he looked for social worth. Dismissive of a clergy that was 'not much esteemed in this city', this bourgeois was no less antipathetic to the boisterous, 'licentious' and Occitan-speaking *menu peuple*. He also marked himself off from noble and artisan by his *'cuisine bourgeoise'*, the private virtues of simplicity in housing and manners. In Paris, too, the discourse of the body reflected bourgeois certainty that the cosmetics and elaborate wigs of the aristocracy denoted degeneracy, 'softness' and idleness in opposition to values of 'nature', practicality and cleanliness. In the 1780s the *Journal de santé* and other periodicals devoted to hygiene and health were launched, calling for schemes to wash the streets and to circulate air: the 'stench' of the urban poor and peasantry, with their belief in the medical value of dirt and urine, was as intolerable as the heavy mix of sweat and perfume of bewigged courtiers.[35]

Coinciding with the articulation of such values and with gradual, long-term and uneven economic change was a series of intellectual challenges to established forms of politics and religion which historians have called the Enlightenment. The relationship between economic change and intellectual life is at the heart of the social history of ideas, and social theorists and historians have always been divided over the nature of such a relationship. In 1939 Georges Lefebvre argued that: 'In the eighteenth century commerce, industry and finance occupied an increasingly important place in the national economy... [the bourgeoisie] had developed a new ideology which the 'philosophers' and 'economists' of the time had simply put into definite form.'[36] On the other hand, those who dispute the correlation of 'enlightened' ideas with a more assertive bourgeoisie have pointed to a number of logical problems in such an argument. First, by 1778 Voltaire and Rousseau were dead and the *Encyclopédie*, the greatest product of the *philosophes*, had been completed. Secondly, the *philosophes* themselves were generally far from radical in their political programme and their work was often patronized and read – even written – by nobles and clergy, such as Mably, Condillac, Raynal and Turgot. Finally, insofar as their work was bought, it was Rousseau's romantic novel, *La Nouvelle Héloïse*, rather than his *Du contrat social*, which seemed to have an audience.

However, such an argument misses the essential interrelation between the central tenets of the new philosophy and the society it was challenging and examining. It is no coincidence that the chief and linked targets of critical writing were royal absolutism and theocracy; in the words of Diderot, 'the rope which holds and represses humanity is made up of two strands: one of them cannot give way without the other breaking'. For most *philosophes*, such a critique was limited by an acceptance of the social value of parish priests as guardians of public order and morality; resigned to what they saw as the ignorance and superstition of the masses, intellectuals similarly turned to enlightened monarchs as the best way of ensuring the liberalization of public life. Such a liberation would necessarily also encourage the unleashing of creativity in economic life: for 'physiocrats' such as Turgot and Quesnay, worldly progress lay in freeing initiative and commerce *('laissez-faire, laissez-passer')*. By removing obstacles to economic freedom – guilds and controls on the grain trade – and by encouraging agricultural 'improvement' and enclosures, the economic wealth would be created which would underpin the 'progress' of civil liberties. Such liberties were for Europeans for, with few exceptions, *philosophes* from Voltaire to Helvétius rationalized plantation slavery as the natural lot of inferior peoples.[37]

In these terms the Enlightenment does appear as a class-based ideology. But what was the social incidence of its readership? It is in this area, of the social history of the Enlightenment, that historians have moved closest to assessing the cultural changes of the 1770s and 1780s. Starting from the premise that publishing is a multi-layered business activity, Robert Darnton has sought, by analysing the clandestine Swiss book trade, to discover what the reading public wanted. In a regime of tight censorship, the cheap pirate editions of the *Encyclopédie* smuggled in from Switzerland sold some 25,000 sets in 1776–89.[38] While the state authorities tolerated the trade in cheap editions of works from the *Encyclopédie* to the Bible, it was the underground trade in banned books which is most revealing, for a whole network of people from printers, booksellers, pedlars and mule-drivers risked imprisonment to profit from public demand. The Swiss catalogues offered readers at every level of urban society a remarkable and socially explosive mixture of philosophy and obscenity: the finest works of Rousseau, Helvétius and d'Holbach jostled with titles such as *The Nun in the Nightshirt, La fille de joie* and *Louis XV's Orgies.* The ribald yet moralistic tone of the latter mocked the Church, nobility and the royal family itself for both degeneracy and impotence, undermining at the same time the mystique of those born to rule as well as their capacity to do so. In provincial towns such as Toulouse, Besançon and Troyes, the *Encyclopédie* and the ribaldry of the literary underground also found a ready market.

The real significance of the Enlightenment, then, is as a symptom of a crisis of authority and deference and as part of a wider political discourse. Well before 1789, the language of 'citizen', 'nation', 'social contract' and 'general will' was articulated across French society, clashing with an older discourse of 'orders', 'estates' and 'corporations'. The same complex relationship between reading public and writer existed in the art world, exemplified in the public reception, if not in the intention, of David's 'Oath of the Horatii' in 1785, with its celebration of civic behaviour perceived as virtuous. The author of *Sur la peinture* (1782) attacked conventional painting and the decadence of the social élite, exhorting art critics to engage 'considerations which are moral and political in character'. Also at variance with the corporate, privileged world of the aristocratic academies were the more open, free-thinking Masonic lodges, a form of bourgeois sociability which proliferated remarkably after 1760: despite injunctions from several popes (which did not prevent 400 priests from joining), there were some 210,000 members in 600 lodges in the 1780s. In some places, nobles established their own, exclusive lodges, but in general the expansion of freemasonry may be understood as an expression of a distinctive bourgeois culture outside the norms of the aristocratic élite. Businessmen, excluded from noble academies, comprised 35–50 per cent of the lodges, which also attracted soldiers, public officials and professional men. Their language of citizenship, rationality and utility is similarly to be found in the claims to status made by junior army officers and the professions, in the *mémoires judiciaires* of popular court cases written by lawyers of the *parlements*, and in the cosmopolitan, unorthodox world of the salons.[39]

While there was no self-conscious class of bourgeois with a political pro-gramme, there was certainly a vigorous critique of the privileged orders and of the allegedly outmoded claims to social order and function on which they rested. The causes célèbres which Sarah Maza has studied through published trial briefs with print runs of up to 20,000 in the 1780s demonstrate a power-ful and more frequent repudiation of a traditional aristocratic world depicted as violent, feudal and immoral and as opposed to values of citizenship, rationality and utility. In the increasingly commercial world of the late eighteenth century, nobles and others debated whether abolishing laws of *dérogeance* to permit nobles to engage in trade would resuscitate the 'utility' of the nobility in the eyes of commoners.[40]

Historians have turned recently to the study of what they call 'material culture': that is, the material objects and practices of economic life. Through this they seek to comprehend the meanings people at the time gave to their world through behaviour and objects as well as words. Colin Jones has estimated that the number of bourgeois increased from about 700,000 in 1700 to perhaps 2.3 million in 1780; even among petits bourgeois a distinctive 'consumer culture' was thriving, apparent in the taste for writing-tables, mir-rors, clocks and umbrellas. The decades after 1750 were a time of a 'clothing revolution', in Daniel Roche's words, in which values of respectability, decency and solid wealth were expressed in clothing across all social groups, but among the 'middling' classes in particular. Bourgeois also marked themselves off from noble and artisan by their *cuisine bourgeoise*, featuring smaller, more regular meals, and by the private virtues of simplicity in housing and manners.[41]

The fevered and contentious world of literature in the 1780s was essentially an urban phenomenon: in Paris, for example, there was a primary school for every 1,200 people and most men and women could read. In rural areas, the major sources of the printed words read aloud to evening gatherings *(veillées)* were the Bible, popular almanachs of festivals and seasons, and the *Bibliothèque bleue*.[42] The latter, cheap and mass-produced paperbacks, offered the rural poor an escape from the misery of daily life into a medieval wonderland of the super-natural, lives of saints, and magic. While there seems to have been a seculariza-tion of the type of information contained in the almanachs, there is no evidence at all that the reading matter peddled through the countryside by *colporteurs* was imbued with 'enlightened' precepts.

Nevertheless, rural France was in crisis in the 1780s and, at least in Burgundy, the discourse through which villages contested seigneurial rights was increas-ingly marked by appeals to social utility, reason and even notions of citizenship. Calonne's edict of June 1787, seeking to impose uniformity on the election, powers and composition of local government, facilitated contention in some areas. Elsewhere, this edict actually reduced the electorate and everywhere enshrined the ex officio powers of clergy and seigneurs. While historians disagree about whether the nobility's 'feudal reaction' of the 1780s also encom-passed dealings with their rural communities, there is abundant evidence of nobles employing lawyers *(feudistes)* to check or tighten the exaction of dues. For example, in 1786, the family of Saulx-Tavanes in Burgundy used their elevation to a duchy to double all dues for a year, resurrecting a practice not used since the thirteenth century. Their investment in farm improvements, never more than 5 per cent of their receipts, shrank to nothing in the late 1780s while rents were doubled in a desperate attempt to pay off debts. A tax official travelling through the south-west was astonished to find nobles enforcing 'rights and dues unknown or forgotten', such as an extraordinary *taille* a noble magistrate in the Toulouse *parlement* exacted every time he bought land. This reaction occurred in the context of long-term inflation, whereby grain prices had outstripped labourers' wages, and short-term harvest failures in 1785 and 1788 which immediately doubled grain prices. Taken together, they explain the escalation of conflict in the countryside: some three-quarters of 4,400 recorded collective protests in the years 1720–88 occurred after 1765, mostly in the form of food riots and anti-seigneurialism.[43]

As the royal state lurched into financial crisis from the mid-1780s, these changes to the economic and cultural structures of French society conditioned conflicting responses to Louis XVI's pleas for assistance. Increasing costs of war, maintaining an expanding court and bureaucracy, and servicing a massive debt impelled the monarchy to seek ways of eroding noble taxation immunity and the capacity of *parlements* to resist royal decrees. The entrenched hostility of most nobles towards fiscal and social reform was generated both by the long-term exigencies of royal state-making and by the challenge to an aristocratic conception of property, hierarchy and social order emanating from a wealthier, larger and socially frustrated bourgeoisie and an openly disaffected peasantry. The unsuccessful attempts of the monarchy to convince or coerce the nobility to acquiesce in its solution to fiscal crisis in the 1780s was to culminate in Louis's decision to convoke an Estates-General for May 1789.[44]

Significantly, even the discourse of entrenched noble interests used the language of the *philosophes*: the *parlement* of Toulouse asserted that 'the natural rights of municipalities, common to all men, are inalienable, imprescriptible, as eternal as nature which forms their basis'. This language of opposition to the royal state, appeals to provincial autonomy in Bordeaux, Rennes, Toulouse, Grenoble and Perpignan, and the vertical bonds of economic dependency generated an alliance between urban working people and local *parlements* in 1788. When the *parlement* of Grenoble was exiled in June 1788 for its defiance towards the ministry's strike at noble judicial power, royal troops were driven from the city by popular rebellion on the 'Day of the Tiles'. In Trévoux in Dauphiné and the Limagne region of the Auvergne there is similar evidence of peasant support for nobles in debates on agrarian reform and provincial autonomy.[45] The self-interest behind noble appeals to 'natural law', 'inalienable rights' and the 'nation' ensured that such an alliance could not last. From a meeting of notables in July 1788 at Claude Périer's recently acquired château at Vizille came an insistent call for the third estate to have double the representation of the others at the Estates-General.

'Revisionist' historians have contested whether there were deep-seated, long-term causes of the political friction which erupted in 1788, and whether there were clear lines of social antagonism. Instead, they have insisted that political conflict was short-term and avoidable, and have pointed to the coexistence of nobles and wealthy bourgeois in an élite of notables, united as property-owners, office-holders and investors, and even by involvement in profit-oriented industry and agriculture. However, within this bourgeois and noble élite was a ruling class of nobles with inherited titles who dominated the highest echelons of privilege, office, wealth and status. Social changes since 1750 had aggravated tensions between this élite and the less eminent majority of the privileged orders while nourishing rival conceptions among commoners about the bases of social and political authority. The specific provisions for the convening of the Estates-General were to focus these conflicting images of a regenerated France with remarkable clarity.

2

The Revolutionary Reconstruction of French Society, 1789–1792

In September 1788, the English agronomist Arthur Young found himself in the Atlantic port of Nantes just six weeks after Louis XVI had announced the convocation of the Estates-General for 1 May 1789. A keen observer and recorder, Young noted in his journal:

> Nantes is as *enflammée* in the cause of liberty, as any town in France can be; the conversations I witnessed here prove how great a change is effected in the minds of the French, nor do I believe it will be possible for the present government to last half a century longer, unless the clearest and most decided talents be at the helm.[1]

As an entrepreneur who found the commercial bustle and civic pride of the great ports the most impressive aspect of French society, it is not surprising that Young should have enthused about the need for the mercantile élite to form part of a rejuvenated rule of the 'talented'. Nevertheless, the alacrity of the Nantais bourgeoisie's response to the invitation to political participation reveals how much further the crisis of absolutist France went beyond friction between nobles and monarch.

The calling of the Estates-General facilitated the expression of tensions at every level of French society, and revealed social divisions which belied the juridical conception of a society of 'orders'. The remarkable vibrancy of debate in the months before May 1789 was also a function of the suspension of press censorship and of Louis's indecision about the procedures to be followed at Versailles. Torn between a loyalty to the established corporate order of rank and privilege and the exigencies of fiscal crisis, the king vacillated on the crucial political question of whether the three orders would meet separately, as when the Estates-General had previously met in 1614, or in a common chamber. In September the *parlement* of Paris had decreed that tradition would be followed in this matter; but Louis's decision on 5 December to double the size of the third-estate representation, while remaining silent on how voting would occur, served only to highlight the crucial issue of political power. By January 1789, a

Swiss journalist had commented: 'the public debate has totally changed in its emphasis; now the King, despotism, and the Constitution are only very secondary questions; and it has become a war between the third estate and the other two orders'.[2]

The journalist, Mallet du Pan, was referring to the rapid polarization of literate opinion expressed through the frenzied pamphlet campaigns of late 1788 and early 1789. It has been calculated that about 1,500 pamphlets on political issues were published between May and December 1788; in the first four months of 1789 they were followed by a flood of more than 2,600 titles.[3]

If Louis's younger brother, Provence, was prepared to countenance increased representation for the third estate, his youngest brother, Artois, and the 'princes of the blood' made their recalcitrance and fear known in a 'memoir' to Louis in December: 'Who can say where the recklessness of opinions will stop? The rights of the throne have been questioned; the rights of the two orders of the state divide opinions; soon property rights will be attacked... already it has been proposed that feudal rights be abolished as a system of oppression, a remnant of barbarism.' At the same time, a 40-year-old priest, Emmanuel Sieyès, son of the postmaster at Fréjus in Provence, was writing the most remarkable of his several pamphlets, titled 'What is the Third Estate?'. Fulminating against the nobility's obsession with its 'odious privileges', Sieyès issued a ringing declaration of commoner capacity:

> Who, then, would dare to say that the Third Estate does not contain everything needed to form a complete nation? It is like a strong, robust man one of whose arms is still enchained. If the privileged order were removed, the nation would not be something less, but something more ... Between liberty and a few odious privileges, they have chosen the latter.[4]

To be sure, Sieyès was no democrat – women and the poor could not hope to represent their fellow citizens – but his challenge articulated a radical intransigence.

Significantly, too, Sieyès wrote of just one privileged order, assuming that the clergy, too, were irrevocably divided between its noble élite and commoner parish priests. This was also recognized by Louis himself: as a way of further pressuring the nobility, and as a mark of his own religious convictions, he announced in January that parish priests (but not curates) would vote individually in the assemblies to elect deputies to Versailles, while monasteries would have only one representative and cathedral chapters one for every ten canons. 'As *curés* we have rights,' exclaimed a parish priest from Lorraine, Henri Grégoire, son of a tailor; 'such a favourable opportunity to enforce them has not occurred, perhaps, for twelve centuries.... Let us take it.' His plea was answered: when the clergy gathered to elect its deputies early in 1789, 208 of the 303 chosen were lower clergy.[5]

Underpinning the polemical fervour of these months were two major manifestations of rapidly changing popular attitudes. First, the reaction of most nobles towards threats to their privilege, focused on the central issue of voting procedures at the Estates-General, alienated the loyalty of many urban working people hitherto supportive of noble resistance to 'ministerial despotism'. But

Louis's renewed image as a benevolent father of his people and restorer of their liberties sat uneasily with the popular conviction that the political claims of the bourgeoisie were those of the entire third estate. Moreover, Parisian working people were making their own connections between the language of élite politics and their economic grievances. In April, a disparaging remark about his employees by a Parisian manufacturer named Réveillon generated an angry riot which confronted troops with slogans redolent of Sieyès's pamphlet: 'Long live the third estate! Liberty, we will not give way!'[6] Réveillon, a prominent member of the local third-estate electoral assembly, was thus being challenged in the terms of his own political discourse.

Secondly, in the spring of 1789, from hamlets and workplaces to regional meetings of clerics and nobles, people all over France were enjoined to formulate proposals for the regeneration of public life and to elect deputies to the Estates-General. The drawing up of *cahiers de doléances* in the context of subsistence crisis, political uncertainty and fiscal chaos was the decisive moment in the mass politicization of social friction. These *cahiers* are an unparalleled resource for the historian. However, their veracity as statements of popular attitudes is often restricted: not only did the number of those participating in their drafting vary widely, in many cases model *cahiers* were circulated through the countryside from towns, even if frequently added to or adapted at a local level. In any case, people were being consulted about reform proposals, not about whether they wanted a revolution.

In rural communities, the economically dependent were also acutely aware of the potential costs of being outspoken about noble privilege: in the impoverished little village of Erceville, north of Orléans, the third-estate meeting was presided over by the local judge employed by the seigneur, a prominent member of the *parlement* of Paris whose holdings covered most of the parish (not surprisingly, his tenants stayed away from the meeting). Neverthless, the peasants, labourers and artisans who drew up Erceville's *cahier* were remarkably blunt, urging that, 'without any distinction of title or rank, the said seigneur be taxed like them', that 'the tithe and *champart* be abolished, or at least converted into an annual payment in money', and – clearly aware of the looming issue of the locus of political power – that all taxes should require 'the consent of the whole Nation assembled in Estates-General'. Here, as everywhere else, the pivotal issues were noble privilege and seigneurialism. A sample of 1,112 of the *cahiers*, 748 of them from village communities, has been the subject of quantitative analysis by John Markoff and Gilbert Shapiro. Their analysis demonstrates that peasants were far more concerned in 1789 with material rather than symbolic burdens, that they largely ignored the trappings of seigneurial status which weighed little in material terms, such as the public display of arms and reserved pews in churches. Inevitably, the composite *cahiers* drawn up by urban bourgeois at the district (*bailliage*) level excised many rural grievances deemed too parochial; nevertheless, 64 per cent of the 666 *cahiers* at this level across France called for the abolition of seigneurial dues. In stark contrast, 84 per cent of noble *cahiers* were simply silent on the whole matter.[7]

The *cahiers* of urban *menu peuple* were variously expressed through meetings of master craftsmen, parish assemblies and, very occasionally, groups of tradeswomen. Most urban working people were too poor to meet the minimal property requirements necessary to participate: in Paris only one in five men over 25 years of age was eligible. Artisan *cahiers*, like those of the peasantry, revealed an overlapping of interests with those of the bourgeoisie on fiscal, legal and political questions, but a clear divergence on economic regulation, calling for protection against mechanization and competition, and for controls on the grain trade. These demands were underscored by subsistence crisis and inflation: in early 1789, Abbeville weavers were spending an estimated 94 per cent of household income on bread. 'Let us not call the rich capitalists egoists: they are our brothers', conceded the hatters and furriers of Rouen, before calling for the 'suppression of machinery' so that 'there would be no competition and no problems about markets'.[8]

The sharpest contrasts in the *cahiers* lay in the polarized world-views of the bourgeoisie and provincial nobles. To the insistence of even small-town bourgeois on a new society characterized by 'careers open to talent', encouragement of enterprise, equality of taxation, liberal freedoms and the ending of privilege, the nobility responded with a utopian vision of a reinforced hierarchy of social orders and obligations, protection of noble exemptions and renewed political autonomy. While 'revisionist' historians have made much of the social and ideological fluidity between bourgeois and nobles before 1789, this uneasy fusion really only embraced the élite of both. To most nobles, seigneurial rights and noble privileges were too important to be negotiable, and from this came the intransigence of most of the 282 noble deputies elected to Versailles. To self-respecting officials, professional men and property owners, such pretensions were simply offensive and demoralizing, reflected in the repeated insistence in *cahiers* at the *bailliage* level that third-estate deputies should refuse to meet separately and, in the words of the bourgeois of the small town of Dourdan, rebuff 'any distinction which might dishonour them'.[9]

As members of a corporate, privileged body, parish priests similarly envisaged a rejuvenated social order under the auspices of a Catholic monopoly of worship and morality. As commoners by birth, however, they were also ominously sympathetic to the needs of the poor, the opening of positions – including the church hierarchy – to men of talent, and to calls for universal taxation. The clergy of Troyes insisted on the traditional distinction of the three orders meeting separately, but made a crucial exception on the matter of taxation: on this issue they urged a common assembly to adopt a tax 'proportionately borne by all individuals of the three orders'.[10]

Indeed, only on two general matters was there widespread agreement across French society. First, there was consensus that the Church was in urgent need of reform to check abuses within its hierarchy and to improve the lot of its parish clergy. Secondly, whatever the undoubtedly sincere protestations of gratitude and loyalty towards the king, his ministers were castigated for their fiscal inefficiency and arbitrary powers. The calling of the Estates-General was everywhere envisaged as a regular, periodic innovation: in a word, it was assumed, albeit implicitly, that absolute monarchy was at an end.

Where nobles and commoners could not agree was about how power was to be expressed within this Estates-General, and to what social and political ends.

Whatever the shared commitment of all three orders to the need for change, and general agreement on a plethora of specific abuses within the Church and State apparatus, the divisions over fundamental issues of political power, seigneurialism and claims to corporate privilege were already irreconcilable by the time the deputies arrived in Versailles.

The indirect system of elections ensured that the great majority of the deputies of the third estate were lawyers, magistrates, officials and men of property. About one hundred were in trade and industry. Reminded of their inferior status from the very opening of the Estates-General, these 646 men, mostly provincial and well-to-do, found together an embracing solidarity of outlook.[11] It was a solidarity which, within six weeks, was to encourage them to mount a revolutionary challenge to absolutism and privilege. Ultimately, Louis's acquiescence in the nobility's demand for voting to be in three separate chambers galvanized bourgeois outrage. On 17 June, the third estate claimed that 'the interpretation and presentation of the general will belong to it.... The name National Assembly is the only one which is suitable.' Three days later, finding themselves locked out of their meeting hall, the deputies moved to an indoor royal tennis court and, with only one dissenting voice, insisted by oath on their 'unshakeable resolution' to continue their proceedings wherever necessary.

The third-estate deputies' resolve was sustained by the steady trickle to their ranks of some of the 208 parish priests who numerically dominated the first-estate representation. The vote to join the third estate taken by 149 clerical deputies (against 137) on 19 June was a decisive turning-point in the political stand-off. Then, on 25 June, 47 liberal nobles, led by the king's cousin, the duc d'Orléans, joined them. Louis's attempt at resolving this challenge by proposing mild reform while maintaining a system of separate orders quickly faded, and by 27 June he had seemed to capitulate. However, despite their assumed mantle of national will, the bourgeois deputies and their allies were soon confronted by a counter-attack from the court. Paris, 18 kilometres from Versailles and the heartland of revolutionary enthusiasm, was invested with 20,000 mercenaries and, in symbolic defiance, Louis dismissed Jacques Necker, his one non-noble minister, on 11 July.

The men of the Assembly were saved by a massive rebellion of Parisian working people. Though largely barred by gender or poverty from participation in the formulation of *cahiers* or election of deputies, from April the *menu peuple* had demonstrated their conviction that the bourgeois deputies' revolt was in the people's name. Pamphlets expressed their anger about exclusion from the political process: 'everything is sacrificed to the owners of property ... it is revoltingly unjust that they alone should be consulted and that disdainful rejection should be the lot of those humble and useful people through whose labours they are able to live without needing to work'. Sustaining this anger was an escalation in the price of a 4lb loaf of bread from 8 to 14 sous, widely assumed to be the result of deliberate withholding of supplies by noble landowners.[12]

The signal for action was the dismissal of Necker. On 12 and 13 July, 40 of the 54 customs-houses ringing Paris were destroyed. Arms and ammunition were seized from gunsmiths and the Invalides military hospital, and royal troops were confronted. The ultimate target was the Bastille fortress in the *faubourg*

Saint-Antoine, for its supplies of arms and gunpowder and as a powerful fortress and awesome symbol of authority. The triumphant seizure of the Bastille on 14 July had two general and revolutionary consequences. First, in political terms, it saved the National Assembly and consecrated a sharp shift in power: on 17 July Louis formally recognised a *fait accompli* by wedding the white of the Bourbon flag to the red and blue of Paris. His brother Artois led the first *émigrés* into exile. The control of Paris by bourgeois members of the third estate was institutionalized by a new city government under Bailly and a bourgeois civil militia commanded by Lafayette with the objective of quelling the violent popular acts of revenge against prominent former office-holders. In provincial centres all over France similar 'municipal revolutions' occurred, as nobles retired or were forcibly removed from office, as in Troyes, or accommodated to an influx of new men, as in Reims.[13]

Everywhere, from Paris to the smallest hamlet, the summer and spring of 1789 was the occasion of a total and unprecedented collapse of centuries of royal state-making. The taking of the Bastille was only the most spectacular instance of popular conquest of local power. While the Assembly moved with remarkable energy and commitment to restructure every aspect of public life, the vacuum of authority caused by the collapse of the Bourbon state was temporarily filled at the local level by popular militias and councils. This seizure of power was accompanied by massive disobedience to the tributary claims of the State, seigneurs and Church; moreover, as royal troops openly fraternized with civilians, the judiciary was powerless to enforce the law.

The municipal revolution was paralleled by the second great consequence of the taking of the Bastille. News of this unprecedented challenge to the might of the State and nobility reached a countryside in an explosive atmosphere of conflict, hope and fear. Since December 1788, peasants had refused to pay taxes or dues or had seized food supplies in Provence, the Franche-Comté, the Cambrésis and Hainaut in the north-east, and the Paris basin, partly in expectation of royal recognition of their plight. This desperate hope was caught again by Arthur Young, on his third tour of France, while talking with a peasant woman in Lorraine on 12 July. This 'furrowed and hardened' woman claimed (in words Young underlined in his journal): 'something was to be done by some great folks for such poor ones, but she did not know who or how, but God send us better, because the taxes and dues are crushing us'.

Fear of aristocratic revenge replaced such hope as news of the Bastille arrived: were bands of beggars roaming through ripening corn in the pay of vengeful seigneurs, or were they 'brigands' fleeing Paris? Hope, fear and hunger made the countryside a tinderbox ignited by glimpses of suspicious strangers. Panics fanned out from five separate sparks as bushfires of angry rumours, travelling from village to village at several kilometres an hour, engulfed everywhere but Brittany and the east. When noble revenge failed to materialize, village militias instead sometimes turned their weapons on the seigneurial system itself, compelling seigneurs or their agents to hand over feudal registers to be burned on the village square. In other places, other targets of local hatred were attacked, such as grain merchants; in Alsace, Jews were singled out. Like the *menu peuple* of Paris, peasants adopted the language of bourgeois revolt to their own ends; on 2 August the steward of the Duke of Montmorency wrote:

> The populace, attributing the high price of grain to the seigneurs of the kingdom, is hostile to all that belongs to them … about three hundred brigands from all the areas connected with the vassals of madame the Marquise de Longaunay carried off the feudal registers of the seigneurie, and destroyed the dovecot: they then gave an acknowledgement of what they had carried off, signed in the name of the Nation.[14]

The panic-stricken response of the Assembly was to abolish feudal dues on 4 August and then, in the succeeding week, to make a distinction between personal servitude (serfdom, *corvées*, seigneurial courts, hunting rights) which were abolished outright, and 'property rights' (dues payable on harvests) for which peasants had to pay compensation before ceasing payment. Similarly, the Assembly announced the end of the tithe and royal taxes – while again insisting that they continue to be paid pending reform – and the end of regional exemptions.

The August Decrees, and the Declaration of the Rights of Man and of the Citizen, which was proclaimed later the same month, represented the end of the absolutist, seigneurial and corporate structure of eighteenth-century France. They were also a revolutionary proclamation of the principles of a new golden age. Laboriously debated at a time of rural rebellion and in the face of noble demands for a 'declaration of duties', the Declaration was an extraordinary document. Universal in tone, resounding in its optimism, this great statement of liberalism and representative government was nonetheless ambiguous in its wording and silences. While proclaiming the universality of rights and the civic equality of all citizens, whatever their social status or residence, the Declaration was above all a statement of bourgeois idealism, ambiguous on whether the propertyless, slaves and women would have political as well as legal equality, and silent on how the means to exercise one's talents could be secured by those without education or property.[15]

As a profoundly revolutionary set of founding principles of the new order, both the August Decrees and the Declaration met with refusal from Louis. Moreover, as the food crisis worsened and evidence multiplied of open contempt for the Revolution on the part of army officers, the victory of the summer of 1789 seemed again in question. For the second time, the *menu peuple* of Paris intervened to safeguard a revolution they deemed to be theirs. This time, however, it was particularly the women of the markets: in the words of the observant bookseller Siméon Hardy, 'these women said loudly that the men didn't know what it was all about and that they wanted to have a hand in things'.[16] On 5 October, some 5,000–6,000 women, belatedly followed by the National Guard, marched to Versailles and compelled the royal family to return to Paris with the Assembly in its wake. By identifying the royal family as 'the baker, the baker's wife and the baker's apprentice', the women were also making explicit the ancient assumption of royal responsibility to God for the provision of food. The key decrees sanctioned, and the court party in disarray, the Revolution's triumph seemed assured; to signify the magnitude of what they had achieved, people now began to refer to the '*ancien* (former) *régime*'.

Jostling with the potent sense of euphoria and unity in the autumn of 1789 was the stark realization of how revolution had been achieved and the magnitude of what remained to be done. The Revolution of the bourgeois deputies had only been secured by the active intervention of the working people of Paris; the deputies' misgivings were expressed in the proclamation of martial law, an enquiry into the 'crimes' of 5–6 October, and the sentencing to death for 'sedition' of Michel Adrien, a labourer. On the other hand, Louis's reluctant consent to change was only thinly disguised by the fiction that his obstinacy was solely due to the malign influence of his court. Most important of all, the revolutionaries' declaration of the principles of the new regime presupposed that every aspect of public life would be reshaped.

Over the next two years, the deputies of the Assembly threw themselves with extraordinary energy into the task of reworking institutions of public life bearing the imprint of the *ancien régime*. The work of 31 committees was facilitated by the preparedness to cooperate of a large number of able, 'patriotic' nobles, by abundant harvests in 1789 and 1790, and above all by the deep reservoir of popular goodwill.[17] Two immediate problems had to be addressed. The first was that the Assembly had inherited the monarchy's bankruptcy, aggravated by popular refusal to pay taxes, and took several measures to meet this crisis. In November 1789, church lands were 'put at the disposal of the nation', nationalized in April 1790, and, from November 1790, sold at auction. These lands were also used to back the issue of *'assignats'*, paper currency which soon began to decline in real purchasing power. Then, in 1791, a new uniform taxation system on property was introduced. Secondly, within the general context of popular sovereignty, the precise forms of the exercise of power had to be detailed. While an English bicameral system was repudiated because of deep mistrust of the nobility, Louis was left with a suspensive veto (though not on finance or the constitution) and extensive executive powers. The ambiguity of the Declaration of the Rights of Man was resolved by excluding women and 'passive' male citizens, those – perhaps 40 per cent of adult men – paying less than three days' labour in taxes, and by imposing sharp property qualifications on those eligible to be electors and deputies.

Every aspect of public life was radically reshaped in line with principles of (limited) popular sovereignty, rationality, uniformity and the 'career open to talents'. The local government law of 14 December 1789 essentially completed Calonne's 1787 legislation by applying a uniform, property-based regime to the whole country. Now, however, the privileged lost their ex officio status and the franchise was radically widened. Local councils were given extensive powers and responsibilities over policing, poor relief, tax collection and education. The inevitable problems created by lack of resources in poor areas and the restricted number of men with the leisure and education to make effective use of complex legislation from Paris were added to by the local contexts into which these new structures and laws were introduced. In many areas the collapse of the royal state had facilitated the emergence of forms of local control which were only reluctantly ceded back to the State; elsewhere, as in the west, the local government law created a puzzling separation of municipality and vestry and excluded many men and all the women used to discussing parish matters after mass.[18]

The 41,000 new 'communes' were the base of a nested hierarchy of cantons, districts and departments (see Map 2.1). The 83 departments announced in February 1790 were designed to facilitate the accessibility of administration (each capital was to be no more than a day's ride from any commune). They also represented an important, pre-emptive victory of the new state over the resurgent provincial identities expressed since 1787. There was usually a valid geographic rationale to each department, but their very names, drawn from rivers, mountains and other natural features, undercut larger provincial and ethnic unities. There was to be no institutional recognition of ancient provinces such as Brittany, Burgundy or Languedoc: the Catalan province of Roussillon would be the department of the 'Eastern Pyrenees', not the *pays Catalan*.

The 60 per cent or more of adult males who were 'active' citizens were the social base of a democratization of political culture. In every aspect of public life – administration, the judiciary, the armed forces, the Church, policing – traditions of corporate rights, appointment and hierarchy gave way to civil equality, accountability, and elections within national structures assuming the common identity of French citizens of whatever social or geographic origin. Such 'fraternity' could also surge from below, as when the Provençal villagers of Lourmarin welcomed: 'the sacrifices that [their] deputies [had] made of the dangerous privilege which isolated this province from the rest of France. To be called a Frenchman is the first and most beneficial of all national rights and the most fertile source of liberty, of equality and of social well-being.' However, the Assembly was also concerned to accelerate 'from above' the coincidence of the new nation of French citizens with use of the French language. The Abbé Grégoire's inquiry of 1790 was sobering for legislators who wrongly assumed that a facility in French was indispensable to be a patriot. Only 15 departments, with three million people, were identified as purely French-speaking; of the 40,000 people of the district of Saint-Geniez in the Aveyron, 10,000 could understand French, 3,000 could read it and 2,000 could speak it. In the Gascon Lot-et-Garonne, priests complained of peasants falling asleep during the reading of decrees from the Assembly, 'because they [did] not understand a word, even though the decrees [were] read in a loud and clear voice and [were] explained'. In consequence, successive assemblies encouraged the translation of decrees into local languages and over much of France the new elements of political life were assimilated through the medium of auto-translation. Elite suspicions developed that the mass of the population who could not understand French were prey to the 'superstitions' and influences of the *ancien régime*.[19]

The old system of royal, aristocratic and clerical courts was swept away, along with regional law codes, in a national system remarkable, too, for its accessibility and humanity. In particular, the introduction of elected Justices of the Peace in every canton was immensely popular. Probably following English and Dutch precedents, the deputies moved to set up a system which, in line with the repeated rural grievances expressed in the *cahiers*, would be accessible to all, cheap and designed to conciliate. Regardless of their social status and wealth, rural people could now seek redress, and did so. Differential forms of execution were removed by the use of the humanitarian proposal of the deputy Dr Joseph Guillotin in all cases. A spirited debate in 1791 sharply reduced the number of capital offences, among them homosexuality. The assumption of individual

Map 2.1 French departments and their capitals

Note: To facilitate reference in other periods, this includes later additions (the two Savoy departments and the Alpes-Maritimes).

1.	Ain	•	Bourg-en-Bresse	11.	Aude	•	Carcassonne
2.	Aisne	•	Laon	12.	Aveyron	•	Rodez
3.	Allier	•	Moulins	13.	Bouches-du-Rhône	•	Marseille
4.	Basses-Alpes	•	Digne	14.	Calvados	•	Caen
5.	Hautes-Alpes	•	Gap	15.	Cantal	•	Aurillac
6.	Alpes-Maritimes	•	Nice	16.	Charente	•	Angoulême
7.	Ardèche	•	Privas	17.	Charente-Inférieure	•	La Rochelle
8.	Ardennes	•	Mézières	18.	Cher	•	Bourges
9.	Ariège	•	Foix	19.	Corrèze	•	Tulle
10.	Aube	•	Troyes	20.	Corse	•	Ajaccio

21.	Côte-d'Or	•	Dijon	56.	Morbihan	• Vannes
22.	Côtes-du-Nord	•	St-Brieuc	57.	Moselle	• Metz
23.	Creuse	•	Guéret	58.	Nièvre	• Nevers
24.	Dordogne	•	Périgueux	59.	Nord	• Lille
25.	Doubs	•	Besançon	60.	Oise	• Beauvais
26.	Drôme	•	Valence	61.	Orne	• Alençon
27.	Eure	•	Evreux	62.	Pas-de-Calais	• Arras
28.	Eure-et-Loir	•	Chartres	63.	Puy-de-Dôme	• Clermont-Ferrand
29.	Finistère	•	Quimper	64.	Basses-Pyrénées	• Pau
30.	Gard	•	Nîmes	65.	Hautes-Pyrénées	• Tarbes
31.	Haute-Garonne	•	Toulouse	66.	Pyrénées-Orientales	• Perpignan
32.	Gers	•	Auch	67.	Bas-Rhin	• Strasbourg
33.	Gironde	•	Bordeaux	68.	Haut-Rhin	• Colmar
34.	Hérault	•	Montpellier	69.	Rhône	• Lyon
35.	Ille-et-Vilaine	•	Rennes	70.	Haute-Saône	• Vesoul
36.	Indre	•	Châteauroux	71.	Saône-et-Loire	• Mâcon
37.	Indre-et-Loire	•	Tours	72.	Sarthe	• Le Mans
38.	Isère	•	Grenoble	73.	Savoie	• Chambéry
39.	Jura	•	Lons-le-Saunier	74.	Haute-Savoie	• Annecy
40.	Landes	•	Mont-de-Marsan	75.	Seine	• Paris
41.	Loir-et-Cher	•	Blois	76.	Seine-Inférieure	• Rouen
42.	Loire	•	St-Etienne	77.	Seine-et-Marne	• Melun
43.	Haute-Loire	•	Le Puy	78.	Seine-et-Oise	• Versailles
44.	Loire-Inférieure	•	Nantes	79.	Deux-Sèvres	• Niort
45.	Loiret	•	Orléans	80.	Somme	• Amiens
46.	Lot	•	Cahors	81.	Tarn	• Albi
47.	Lot-et-Garonne	•	Agen	82.	Tarn-et-Garonne	• Montauban
48.	Lozère	•	Mende	83.	Var	• Draguignan
49.	Maine-et-Loire	•	Angers	84.	Vaucluse	• Avignon
50.	Manche	•	St-Lô	85.	Vendée	• La Roche-sur-Yon
51.	Marne	•	Châlons-sur-Marne	86.	Vienne	• Poitiers
52.	Haute-Marne	•	Chaumont	87.	Haute-Vienne	• Limoges
53.	Mayenne	•	Laval	88.	Vosges	• Epinal
54.	Meurthe	•	Nancy	89.	Yonne	• Auxerre
55.	Meuse	•	Bar-le-Duc			

liberty also extended to prostitution: in July 1791, new municipal regulations removed all reference to prostitution and its policing. While many women were thereby freed from the repressive constraints of religious reformatories such as the Bon Pasteur in Montpellier, it was simultaneously assumed that prostitution and its side effects were an individual choice and responsibility.[20]

The National Guard units of 'active' citizens in every commune chose their leaders but, although officer positions were opened to non-nobles in the armed forces, here the Assembly stalled at applying popular sovereignty to their election. The army in particular was wracked by internal conflict between 'whites' and 'blues', noble officers and soldiers, over control of regimental funds and the role of the army in repressing civilian protests. The stream of departures of nobles, some two-thirds of the 9,000 in the officer corps by 1792, would have a dramatic impact on the social composition of the army. It also added a military dimension to the small, embittered *émigré* communities in exile in Europe, particularly at Coblenz.[21]

The Revolution was, and long remained, overwhelmingly popular: the extent of change in public life cannot be understood except in a context of mass optimism and support. But those who moved to fill the power vacuum left by the collapse of the *ancien régime* and those who were among the major initial beneficiaries of the Revolution were bourgeois. The dramatic reorganization of institutional structures had meant that many thousands of middle-class officials and lawyers lost their positions, venal or not. The 2,700 magistrates of the *bailliage* courts who lost their positions with the radical restructuring of judicial administration in 1790 were enthusiastic supporters of the Revolution: not only did they succeed in being elected to newly created positions but were also compensated for their lost offices (perhaps because one-fifth of the third-estate deputies were from their ranks). Indeed, the final cost of paying compensation to owners of venal offices was more than 800 million livres, necessitating massive issues of *assignats* and precipitating inflation. This compensation came at an ideal time for investment in the vast amounts of church property thrown onto the market from November 1790. Sold at auction and in large lots, this fine property was mainly purchased by urban bourgeois and wealthy peasants, and by a surprising number of nobles. In the district of Grasse, in south-eastern France, for example, where about 7 per cent of land changed hands, it was local bourgeois who dominated the auctions. Three-quarters of the property sold was bought by one-quarter of the buyers; 28 of the 39 largest purchasers were merchants from Grasse.[22]

Just as the bourgeoisie were not alone in their enthusiasm for the Revolution, so nobles and the élite of the Church were not the only ones who regretted the events of 1789–91. Indeed, particular groups within the bourgeoisie must be counted among them. For example, the 605 barristers of the *Ordre des avocats* who had argued cases before the Paris *parlement* responded to their loss of corporate autonomy and prestige by remaining pro-royalist. Those who had invested heavily in offices carrying noble titles or seigneurial rights regretted the demise of the *ancien régime*; so too did those whose wealth was drawn from the slave system as slave-traders or colonial planters. A bitter debate pitted the colonial lobby (the Club Massiac) against the *Société des amis des noirs*, which included Robespierre and Grégoire. Justifications for slavery were articulated, for example, by the wealthy merchant deputy from Le Havre, born in Saint-Domingue, Jacques-François Begouën: not only would abolition be economically ruinous, but slavery was endemic in Africa and those in the colonies were far better treated. The Assembly's decision in May 1791 (granting 'active' status to free blacks with free parents and the necessary property) was far more timid than the action of mulattoes and slaves in Saint-Domingue. It was the latter's rebellion which was responsible for pressuring the Legislative Assembly in April 1792 into extending civil equality to all 'free persons of colour'.[23]

Historians have agreed that, before 1789 and after 1791, issues of foreign policy and military strategy dominated the domestic reform agenda. They generally assume, too, that the two intervening years of sweeping revolutionary change, 1789–91, were a time when radical internal reform preoccupied the Assembly. On the contrary, as Jeremy Whiteman and others have argued, a major impulse for this internal reform was in fact the desire also to 'regenerate' France's capacity to act as the key military and commercial player in Europe and the Caribbean. Central to the reforming zeal of the National Assembly was the belief that the new nation would thereby be 'regenerated' and return to the international status it had enjoyed before the successive foreign-affairs humiliations since 1763. As before 1789, three of the six ministries were War, Navy and Foreign Affairs.[24]

At a local level, resentment towards the Revolution was often occasioned by the loss of status following administrative reorganization, as in Vence (Var), where a vigorous campaign failed to protect its 'city' status (there were only 2,500 inhabitants) or its bishopric, relocated in nearby Saint-Paul. The location of departmental, district and cantonal *chefs-lieux* swamped legislators with a flood of complaints and rivalries which called into question support for the Revolution in towns formerly sustained by the presence of the maze of courts and offices of the Bourbon regime. Where denominational loyalties coincided with class tensions, the Revolution triggered open hostilities. In parts of the Midi, a Protestant bourgeoisie had won religious freedom and civil equality, opening the way to political power, and the Assembly's refusal to proclaim Catholicism the state religion in April 1790 provided the pretext for large-scale violence in Montauban and Nîmes. In the latter, popular Catholic hostility to the political and economic role of wealthy Protestants was bloodily crushed when bands of Protestant peasants from the Cévennes and Vaunage marched on the city and killed 300 Catholics. The seriousness of such religious divisions was made alarmingly clear in the first instance of mass popular disaffection with the Revolution, when in mid-1790 20,000–40,000 Catholic peasants from 180 parishes established the short-lived 'Camp de Jalès' in the Ardèche.[25]

Nevertheless, the popular alliance of the third estate and its allies among the clergy and 'patriotic' nobility continued to draw on a powerful sense of national unity and regeneration well into 1790. This unity was enacted in Paris by the great *Fête de la fédération*, on the first anniversary of the storming of the Bastille; held on the Champ-de-Mars, which had been levelled by voluntary labour, Louis, Talleyrand (former bishop of Autun) and Lafayette proclaimed the new order in front of 300,000 Parisians. This ceremony occurred all over France, the most dramatic example of the use of festivals as an element of revolutionary political culture. In a society rich in religious rituals and displays of royal splendour, the initial forms of enacting revolutionary unity drew on old rituals for style if not for substance or imagery. Conversely, long-established collective displays were not immune from the spontaneous syncretism of regional culture and revolutionary politics. In 1790, following the festivals in Tarascon (Bouches-du-Rhône) in which the powers of the 'Tarasque' monster were dispelled, a local wrote in his diary:

> a long time ago, you had to be a noble to be the *abba* ['captain'] of the Tarasque festival, later, you had to be a *bon bourgeois*, finally it was only given to people of a certain quality. Now at last we have the first year where the rights of man have appeared in this town in the Tarasque being made to flee by peasants not specially dressed for the occasion.[26]

Just two days before Talleyrand and Louis celebrated the union of Church, monarchy and Revolution, the Assembly had voted a reform which was to shatter all three. The widespread agreement in the *cahiers* on the need for reform guaranteed that the Assembly was able to push through the national-ization of church lands, the closing of contemplative orders and the granting of religious liberty to Protestants in 1789 and, the following January, to the Sephardic Jews of Bordeaux and Avignon (by only 374 votes to 280). The Ashkenazim Jews were still excluded.[27]

Mounting clerical opposition to these changes ultimately focused on the Civil Constitution of the Clergy in July 1790.[28] There was no question of separating Church and State: the public functions of the Church were assumed to be integral to daily life, and the Assembly accepted that public revenues would financially support the Church after the abolition of the tithe. It was therefore argued that, like the monarchy before it, the government had the right to reform the Church's temporal organization.

The reallocation of diocesan and parish boundaries might have been accept-able, despite a chorus of complaints from small communities, and half the parish priests stood to benefit from higher stipends. However, in applying popular sovereignty to the choice of priests and bishops, the Assembly clearly crossed the narrow line separating temporal and spiritual life. In the end, whatever the goodwill which existed between parish priests and the Revolution, it proved impossible to reconcile a church based on divinely-ordained hierarchy and dogma and a certainty of one true faith with a Revolution based on popular sovereignty, tolerance and the certainty of earthly fulfilment through the appli-cation of secular reason. Moreover, by applying the practice of 'active' citizen-ship to the choice of clergy, the Assembly excluded women and the poor from the community of the faithful, and theoretically included Protestants, Jews and non-believers. Nor could a compromise be reached, for, with the abolition of corporations in 1789, the Assembly alone could make laws about public life: a church synod could not be consulted.

In the face of the opposition of most clerical deputies, an impatient Assembly sought to resolve the issue by requiring elections to be held early in 1791, with those elected to swear an oath of loyalty to the law, the nation and the king. Ultimately, only a handful of bishops and perhaps half the parish clergy took this oath. Another 10–12 per cent subsequently retracted when, in April 1791, the Pope, also antagonized by the absorption of his lands in southern France into the new nation, condemned the Civil Constitution and the Declaration of the Rights of Man as inimical to a Christian life. Such retractions were concentrated in regions where most priests had already refused the oath: by mid-1791 two Frances had emerged, contrasting the pro-reform areas of the south-east, the Paris basin, Champagne and the centre with the 'refractory' west and south-west, the north and east, and the southern Massif Central.

Everywhere the oath faced parish priests with an agonizing choice of con-science: did the sanction by the king of the Civil Constitution and its associated oath remove anxiety that the oath contradicted loyalty to the Pope and long-established practice? Many priests sought to resolve the dilemma by taking a qualified oath, such as the priest of Quesques (Pas-de-Calais) who took an oath to the nation: 'in everything which belongs to the purely civil and political order, but for that which concerns the government and laws of the church,

I recognise no other superiors or legislators than the pope and the bishops'. The priest's hesitation was mirrored in lay society, as in the case of a Parisian bourgeois whose reaction to the arrest of a woman neighbour in February 1791 for distributing pro-refractory tracts was that 'one would have to be blind to help the priests in their devilish plots. How I pity a people not sufficiently enlightened!' Yet this bourgeois who excoriated priests as 'aristocrats and bigots' remained a devout church-goer.[29] In large cities like Paris, priests who opposed the Civil Constitution risked ridicule. The incisive observer and revolutionary Louis-Sébastien Mercier described how the *curé* of the parish of Saint-Sulpice tried to preach against the Assembly's reforms: 'A universal cry of indignation reverberated through the arches of the church ... . Suddenly, the majestic organ filled the church with its harmonious music and echoed through every heart the famous tune: *Ah! ça ira! ça ira!* ... the counterrevolutionary instigator was invited to sing *ça ira*. He climbed down from his chair, covered with laughter, shame, and sweat.'[30]

The sharp regional contrasts in preparedness to take the oath suggests that it was not only a matter of individual choice, but also of local ecclesiastical culture. In broad terms, the refractory clergy saw themselves as servants of God, while the constitutional clergy saw themselves as servants of the people. To the former, sustained by a strong clerical presence, the Civil Constitution was anathema to the corporate, hierarchical structure of the Church and the leadership of the Pope; to the latter, in areas where the Church had accommodated itself to a weaker temporal role in daily life, it was the will of God's people and reinforced Gallicanism at the expense of the church hierarchy.

Clerical responses must also be seen as a reflection of the attitudes of the wider community. All over France, the oath became a test of popular acceptance of the Revolution as a whole, for only a minority of priests felt sufficiently independent or isolated from their communities to flout public opinion. In the south-east and the Paris basin, where public life had long been relatively 'secularized' and priests were seen as providing only a spiritual service, there was massive acceptance of the Civil Constitution, as of the Revolution in general. The emerging hostility of priests towards the Revolution inspired – but did not alone cause – open hatred: the Parisian glazier Jacques Ménétra dismissed priests as 'immoral men' touting 'fanaticism and superstition' and 'ancient Gothic prejudices', who wanted only to dominate others with 'their dogmas and fabulous mysteries'. In contrast, through most of the west a combination of factors – the wealth and activity of the parish clergy, the commonality of religious and secular community, and popular misgivings about the bourgeoisie's evident monopoly of the Revolution's early fruits – encouraged priests in their wholesale rejection of the oath. In regions with prominent Protestant minorities, such as the Cévennes and Alsace-Lorraine, the oath-taking aroused wider fears about attacks on a way of life to which Catholic ritual and charity was pivotal. In the small southern towns of Millau and Sommières, milling crowds of poor women and children aimed their anger not so much at local Protestants as at pro-revolutionary Catholic administrators deemed to be destroying established forms of religious life: at Millau, women shouted, 'We want to conserve our religion, the religion of Jesus Christ, we want our clergy!'[31] Here, as elsewhere, it was above all women of the people who offered refractory priests support, courage and shelter.

In general, anger at church reform created a large social basis for hostility to the Revolution, and not vice versa. It is only in hindsight that the pre-1791 roots of popular counter-revolution may be discerned. It was the importance of religion in the daily lives of so many people which was to deflect general support for the Revolution into mixed feelings, resentment or open hostility. All over France, church reform remained a lively, even explosive issue as departmental officials, whose administrative zeal was not always matched by a sensitivity to rural practices, implemented laws requiring the election of new priests, the closing of 'surplus' churches and cemeteries, the redrawing of parish boundaries, and the emptying of contemplative religious houses. In some areas, such as the Aveyron and Ardèche, sympathetic administrators sidestepped instructions from Paris for several years, while, in Anjou, the gulf between urban and rural cultures was widened fatally by the alacrity with which officials in Angers upheld the letter of the law.[32]

Whatever the case, the radical decentralization of power created a situation where revolutionary legislation from Paris was interpreted and adapted to local needs. In this process – the social history of administration – the half-million or more men who were elected to local government, the judiciary and administrative positions played the key role in the void that existed between the Assembly's national programme and the exigencies of the local situation. Executing laws which to most people often seemed foreign in content as well as language, and often lacking in resources, these 'active' citizens – professional men, wealthy peasants, businessmen and landowners – made an enormous commitment of time and energy. Where particular legislation was unpopular, especially that concerning the redemption of seigneurial dues or religious reform, this was a commitment which could also earn them isolation and contempt. Everywhere, the birth of new systems of administration within a context of popular sovereignty and hectic legislative activity was part of the creation of a revolutionary political culture.[33]

Electoral participation was only one part of that culture. The voter turn-out at local elections was rarely high because municipal councillors and other officials were more likely to be chosen by public discussion in the streets and fields, at the tavern or after church. Nationally, the protracted electoral process was one reason why participation was also generally low, perhaps 40 per cent for the Estates-General and 20–5 per cent for the Legislative Assembly in 1791 (though reaching 85 per cent in the villages of upper Normandy in 1789 and over 70 per cent around Belfort in 1791). Such figures do not imply apathy; rather, they suggest that voting was only one of the ways by which French people exercised sovereignty. Another was the extraordinary volume of unofficial correspondence which criss-crossed the country, both vertically, to and from constituents and their deputies in Paris, and horizontally, in particular between the Jacobin Clubs (or Societies of Friends of the Constitution) which linked patriots in a web of shared vocabulary and information.

The work of the Assembly was vast in scope and energy. The foundations of a new social order were laid, underpinned by an assumption of the national unity of a fraternity of citizens. At the same time, the Assembly was walking a tightrope. On one side lay a growing hostility from nobles and the élite of the Church angered by the loss of status, wealth and privilege, and bolstered by a disillusioned parish clergy. On the other, the Assembly was alienating itself from the popular base of the Revolution by its compromise on feudal dues, its antipathy to nonjuring clergy, its exclusion of the 'passive' from the political process, and its implementation of economic liberalism.

The Declaration of the Rights of Man had been silent on economic matters, but in 1789–91 the Assembly passed a series of measures revealing its commitment to economic liberalism. With the removal of internal customs houses and controls on the grain trade, it assumed a free national market. By abolishing obstacles to enterprise and individual control of property it sought to encourage initiative. Impediments to freedom of occupation were removed with the abolition of guilds (the d'Allarde law, April 1790) and, most importantly, a free market in labour was imposed by the Le Chapelier law of 14 June 1791 outlawing associations of employers and employees. The Assembly had earlier closed municipal workshops for the unemployed, throwing 31,000 people onto the streets. While these laws were decisive in the creation of a *laissez-faire* economy, they were also aimed at the 'counter-revolutionary' practices of the *ancien régime*, ending, for example, privileged theatres.

The Assembly's commitment to *laissez-faire* and the sanctity of private property brought to the surface divisions within the third estate already articulated in the *cahiers*. Similarly, the tactical hesitation of the Assembly in August 1789 over the full abolition of seigneurialism fuelled ongoing peasant protest. In the four months after December 1789, peasants from 330 parishes in the southwest invaded more than a hundred châteaux to protest against the payment of harvest dues. Further north, in Saintonge, three-quarters of the peasants in the seigneurie of Beaupuis simply refused to pay dues in 1789. Similar protests, whether by violent action or non-compliance, occurred in the departments of the Yonne, Aude, Loiret, Aisne and Oise, and in the Massif Central, Brittany, the Dauphiné and Lorraine. At times, radical priests took the lead, as in Bourgueil (Indre-et-Loire) where Jacques Benoît warned the rich on New Year's Day 1790 that the poor had the right to come, Bible in hand, and demand one-fifth of their wealth.[34]

Finally, on 3 May 1790 a decree set out the value of the redemption of seigneurial rights. For *corvées, banalités*, and those dues paid in money, the rate of redemption was set at 20 times the annual value and, for those paid in kind, at 25 times. It soon became apparent, through agitated reports pouring in from the new departments and from personal correspondence received by deputies, that across most of the country the compromise legislation of May had encountered stubborn and at times violent resistance. This action took two forms. First, since the 1789–90 legislation treated seigneurial exactions as a legal form of rent which peasants could only terminate by compensating the seigneur, many communities decided to pay for legal action to force seigneurs to submit their feudal titles for judicial verification. This legal challenge was often connected with an illegal, second type of action, the refusal to pay feudal dues in the meantime.

This was matched, in sharecropping and tenancy areas, by frustration at the Assembly's protection of property-owners. For example, in December 1790 it decreed that the value of the abolished tithe could now be added to rents, creating what was to be called the 'bourgeois tithe'. Similarly, the increased burden of state taxes was often added to rents; for most peasants, however, the 15–20 per cent increase in taxes was more than offset by the ending of tithes and, ultimately, of dues. In Brittany, on the other hand, where the feudal regime and taxes had been relatively light and tenants had enjoyed considerable security of lease (through the *domaine congéable*), the Revolution substantially increased the burden of taxation and made tenants more vulnerable to expulsion.

The evidently bourgeois conception of property in the Assembly's urban and rural economic legislation was mirrored by a logical inconsistency between the Declaration's universalist proclamation of rights and its decision to limit formal politics to 'active' citizens. In his newspaper *Les Révolutions de France et de Brabant*, Camille Desmoulins denounced the new 'aristocratic system': 'But what is this much repeated phrase "active citizen" supposed to mean? The active citizens are the ones who took the Bastille.'[35] Whereas Jacobin clubs were normally limited to such men, in Paris and elsewhere alternative forums of revolutionary sociability developed for 'passive' men and women. In Paris, the Cordelier Club of Danton and Marat welcomed all-comers, while the Fraternal Society of Citizens of Both Sexes, gathering up to 800 men and women at its sessions, sought to integrate women into institutional politics. The rights of women were also advocated by individual activists such as Olympe de Gouges, the marquis de Condorcet, Etta Palm and Théroigne de Méricourt, and the *Cercle social* urged the vote for women, the abolition of the rights of parents to leave their property to one child, and the availability of divorce. As Gouges averred in 1791: 'Women are now respected and excluded; under the old regime they were despised and powerful.'[36]

Such associational activity was only one of the means through which the struggle over the nature of the Revolution was expressed. In early 1789, there were perhaps 80 newspapers in the whole country; over the next few years about 2,000 others were launched, although four-fifths produced fewer than 12 issues. The newspaper-reading public perhaps trebled within three years. As a corollary, the production of books declined: 216 novels were printed in 1788, but only 103 in 1791. On the other hand, in the same period the number of new political songs increased from 116 to 308, including the *Ça ira*, first sung as the Champ-de-Mars was prepared for the *Fête de la fédération* in 1790. In newspapers, songs, plays and broadsheets, the period 1789–92 was a great age of savage satire, especially licentious attacks on political opponents, because of the ending of political censorship at a time when popular literature was already distinguished by its mix of obscene mockery, anticlericalism and political slander. Royalist writers, such as Gautier, Rivarol, Suleau and Peltier, took this ribald lampooning to extremes, dismissing Bailly as impotent, Brissot as 'black Bis-sot' (a doubly-stupid friend of blacks), Condorcet's wife as 'Madame Con d'or', Pétion as 'Pet-hion' (Donkey-fart), and Théroigne de Méricourt as a prostitute whose 100 lovers a day each paid 100 sous in 'patriotic contributions'.[37] Withering anti-revolutionary mockery was heaped on the homosexual aristocrat the marquis de Villette and the lesbian actress Françoise Saucerotte ('Mademoiselle de Raucourt'), whose political preferences and sexuality were seen to be equally perverse. Much of the ribald mockery took on a sharper edge when applied to women, none more so than Marie-Antoinette, denounced as Austrian, sexually perverted and the emasculator of the king. Louis personified indecisiveness. As Antoine de Baecque has argued, the new man of the Revolution was imagined to be politically and physically virile, the opposite of the mocking image of the aristocracy as physically and morally decadent.[38]

Through such vehicles of expression, millions of people learned the language and practice of popular sovereignty and, in a protracted period of state weakness, came to question the most deeply-engrained assumptions about the sanctity and benevolence of monarchy. Already in 1789, urban *cahiers* had been much more likely to use 'require', 'claim' and 'demand' than the 'pray', 'solicit' and 'beg' of rural people.[39] The dilemma for Louis was how to interpret the contrasting voices of a sovereign people, hitherto his subjects, who were increasingly divided about the changes the Revolution had wrought and the future direction it should take.

This double issue – How to preserve the Revolution from its opponents? Whose Revolution was it to be? – came to a head in mid-1791. Outraged by the changes to the Church and the limitations to his own power, Louis fled Paris early in the morning of 21 June, publicly repudiating the direction the Revolution had taken. In the days after his capture in the eastern village of Varennes, a brief wave of panic, this time fuelled by fear of foreign invasion, swept through frontier regions. Despite Louis's capture and humiliating return, the Assembly reinstated him. For the bourgeois deputies, the issue was clear; in the words of Barnave on 15 July:

> Are we going to end the Revolution, or are we going to start it all over again? ...
> if the Revolution takes one more step, it can only be a dangerous one: if it is in line with liberty its first act could be the destruction of royalty, if it is in line with equality its first act could be an attack on property ... It is time to bring the Revolution to an end.[40]

The following day, the solid citizens of the National Guard opened fire on an unarmed demonstration called to demand Louis's abdication, at the same 'altar of the homeland' on which the *Fête de la fédération* had been celebrated a year earlier. For the first time, open political conflict within the Parisian third estate had resulted in large-scale bloodshed.

In September Louis promulgated the constitution embodying the Assembly's work since 1789, but the issues of his loyalty and whether the Revolution was over were far from resolved. Democrats within the Jacobin Club drew closer to the radical trend of the popular movement, notably the Cordelier Club; outraged by popular militancy, conservatives mockingly disparaged the dress of working people while for these *sans-culottes* (literally, those who wore trousers rather than the knee stockings of the well-to-do) the term became one of pride and identity. Outside France, monarchs expressed concern at Louis's safety, and fears that the Revolution might spread, in threatening declarations from Padua (5 July) and Pillnitz (27 August). Inside France, de Rozoi's royalist *Gazette de Paris* called for 'hostages to the king' to offer themselves in return for Louis's 'freedom'. Some 4,160 letters were received, over 1,400 from Paris and large numbers from Normandy, the north-east, Alsace and Guyenne. From Lourmarin, on the other

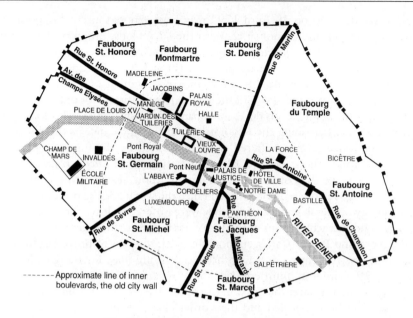

Map 2.2   Paris at the time of the Revolution

hand, the council petitioned the Assembly to hasten to 'banish the monster of feudalism' from what they already called 'the Republic'. The officer corps of the royal army began to disintegrate, with over 2,100 noble officers emigrating between 15 September and 1 December 1791 and 6,000 in all during the year.[41]

As Timothy Tackett has demonstrated by analysing speeches and letters by the deputies, there was a dramatic increase in fears of 'conspiracies' in the months after the king's flight.[42] In turn, the massive rebellion of mulattoes and slaves which erupted in Saint-Domingue in August confronted deputies with the contradiction embedded in the Declaration of Rights and with the international dimensions of the Revolution. It was in this highly-charged context that the new Legislative Assembly, composed of 'new men' following the National Assembly's self-denying ordinance, met in Paris in October 1791. While at the outset most of its members sought to consolidate the state of the Revolution as expressed in the Constitution, the mounting hostility of its opponents inside and outside France focused their concern on the counter-revolution centred on Coblenz. In particular, the followers of Brissot among the Jacobins argued that the Revolution would not be safe until this threat was destroyed. A military strike at Austria and Prussia, logically brief because of the welcome the commoners in those countries would give their liberated brothers, would expose internal counter-revolutionaries in the cauldron of armed conflict between old and new Europe.[43] The 'Brissotins' were encouraged in their optimism by the urgings of political refugees in Paris who, by May 1792, had formed a sizeable force of 54 companies of volunteers. The Scot John Oswald dressed his pikemen in wide black trousers, tricoloured girdles and red caps, and taught them Highland war cries to unsettle the enemy.[44]

The war declared on 20 April 1792 may have exposed internal opposition, but it was neither limited nor brief. With the Civil Constitution of the Clergy, it marks one of the major turning-points of the revolutionary period, both reflecting and influencing the internal history of France for 23 years. Within four months of its outbreak, it had four major consequences. First, it immediately raised the hopes and stakes of the counter-revolution. Not only were there members of the old élite inside France, particularly the court, who looked to defeat as a way of crushing the Revolution, but the initial defeats the disorganized revolutionary armies suffered were aggravated by the urgings of *émigré* nobles and army officers bent on restoring a rejuvenated *ancien régime*.

Secondly, while the counter-revolution could now also aim to be fighting a holy crusade to restore religion, inside France the war made the position of non-juring clergy intolerable: on 27 May they were ordered to leave the country. For the 215 school-teaching nuns of the Ursulines in the north-eastern departments of the Nord and Pas-de-Calais, support for nonjurors was to prove deadly in its consequences. A former priest who had been saying mass for the Ursulines of Lille on 29 April was murdered in angry revenge as revolutionary troops retreated in disarray after their first battle with the Austrians. Within months the Ursulines had been expelled and their order closed; while most slipped across the border into Austrian Flanders, 13 of them whose sense of duty impelled them to stay were later to be guillotined for counter-revolutionary activity in support of the enemy.[45]

A third consequence was that the war revitalized the popular revolution. The political and social demands of working people became more insistent and harder to deny once all men were called to volunteer to fight at a time of worsening inflation. Since 1789 the working people of Paris and elsewhere had repeatedly demonstrated their new assumption of popular sovereignty: could 'passive' citizens now be expected to die for the Revolution? Finally, the war exposed the king. In using his suspensive veto to block critical pieces of legislation (ending pay for nonjurors, ordering *émigrés* to return and nonjurors to leave, seizing *émigré* property and calling volunteers to Paris), the king seemed to be acting in the interests of his wife's nephew, the emperor of Austria. Were not French defeats proof of this, as was his flight in June 1791?

The reception early in August of the Duke of Brunswick's manifesto provoked a panic of anger and fear, threatening as it did summary justice on the people of Paris if Louis was harmed. All but one of the 48 sections of Paris voted to form a Revolutionary Commune to organize insurrection and an army of 20,000 *sans-culottes*. Joined by *fédérés*, volunteers from the provinces on their way to the front, these *sans-culottes* assaulted and took the Tuileries palace on 10 August.[46] Through his own vacillations and the logic of popular politicization at a time of dramatic change and crisis, Louis's decision to consult his people in 1789 had ultimately led to his overthrow. But what was to be done with him? And how could Brunswick's ultimatum be answered?

3
Republicanism and Counter-Revolution, 1792–1795

By overthrowing the monarchy, popular rebellion had effectively issued the ultimate challenge to the whole of Europe; internally, its armed insurrection had dissolved any distinction between 'active' and 'passive' citizens. The Revolution was now armed, democratic and republican. Within a few weeks it would face its greatest challenge. On 2 September word reached Paris that the great fortress at Verdun, just 250 kilometres from the capital and the last major obstacle to invading armies, had fallen to the Prussians. The news generated an immediate, dramatic surge in popular fear and resolve. Convinced that 'counter-revolutionaries' (whether nobles, priests or common-law criminals) in prisons were waiting to break out and welcome the invaders, hastily-convened popular courts sentenced to death about 1,200 of the 2,700 prisoners brought before them. Among them were about 240 priests; their deaths were the final proof for nonjuring clergy that the Revolution had become godless and anarchic. Yet those who 'tried' the prisoners were plainly convinced of the necessity and justice of their actions: one of them wrote home on 2 September: 'necessity has made this execution inevitable .... It is sad to have to go to such lengths, but it is better (as they say) to kill the devil than to let the devil kill you.' Another was himself put to death for the uncivic act of stealing a handkerchief from a corpse's clothing.[1]

The 'September massacres' raise the most disturbing of questions for historians, as they did for contemporaries. Prominent revolutionaries, notably Danton and Marat, excused the killings, as did the Paris Commune. To historians such as Simon Schama, Norman Hampson and François Furet, the escalation of punitive violence was the result of a revolutionary Messianism already discernible in 1789: the counter-revolution was essentially a creation of revolutionary paranoia and popular bloodlust. Such an argument minimizes the extent of the internal and external enemy republicans were facing, and ignores the violent threats made by royalists: before 10 August, the right-wing press had been publishing lists of revolutionaries whom the Prussians would execute, coupled with lurid images of the Seine choked with Jacobins and streets red with the blood of *sans-culottes*. By the summer of 1792, the stakes being fought for in France and western Europe were so high that both pre-emptive and *post facto* punishment seemed to both sides the only way to secure or overturn the Revolution.[2]

A fortnight after the massacres, revolutionary armies won their first great victory, at Valmy, 200 kilometres east of the capital. As news arrived, the new National Convention, elected by universal but indirect manhood suffrage, was convening in Paris.[3] The military crisis was the central issue confronting these 750 deputies, but they also had to resolve the fate of Louis and work towards new constitutional arrangements now that the constitution of 1791 was inoperable. The men of the Convention were united by social background and political assumptions. Overwhelmingly bourgeois by social origin, they remained committed to the desirability of economic liberalism and safeguards for private property. They were also democrats and republicans: immediately on convening on 20 September, they abolished the monarchy and proclaimed France a republic. Their conviction that they stood at the watershed of epochal change was personified by the presence, as elected deputies, of two foreign revolutionaries, Tom Paine and Anarchasis Cloots, and by the decision to give citizen status to other sympathizers, such as Wordsworth, Washington, Hamilton, Kosciuszko, Bentham and Priestley.

It was at this time that Rouget de Lisle's *Chant de guerre pour l'armée du Rhin* became popular. Composed for the king's armies by this royalist army officer in Strasbourg, the song had travelled south and become adopted by republican patriots in Marseille and Montpellier. The soldiers of Marseille brought the song – now known as the 'Marseillaise' – with them to the capital in August. By late September the *Révolutions de Paris* reported:

> The people's spirits are still extremely good ... one must see them, one must hear them repeating in chorus the refrain of the war song of the Marseillaise, which the singers in front of the statue of Liberty in the Tuileries gardens are teaching them every day with renewed success.

> Forward children of the homeland!
> The day of glory is upon us;
> Against us, the bloody standard
> Of tyranny is raised.
> Do you hear these ferocious soldiers
> Bellowing in the fields?
> They come into your very midst
> To slaughter your sons, your wives!
> To arms, citizens, form your battalions,
> March on, march on,
> That impure blood will water our furrows.[4]

Outside Paris, the Marseillaise was used for wider purposes. On 21 October the Jews of Metz in eastern France joined with their Gentile neighbours to celebrate the victory of French armies at Thionville. One of them, Moïse Ensheim, a friend of the Abbé Grégoire, had composed a Hebrew version of the Marseillaise which used biblical imagery to link Jewish history to the Revolution:

> O House of Jacob! You have suffered abundant grief.
> You fell through no fault of your own ...

> Happy are you, O Land of France! Happy are you!
> Your would-be destroyers have fallen to the dust.

In such a way the emancipation of the Ashkenazim Jews of eastern France a year earlier could be celebrated at the same time as a republican victory.[5]

The radicalization of the Revolution also encouraged the government finally to resolve the matter of compensation for seigneurial dues. From the outset of the pre-revolutionary debate, questions pertaining to the control of resources in the countryside and whether they would be unencumbered by seigneurial dues had been central to politics in the countryside. Across most of rural France the response to the National Assembly's prevarication in August 1789 over the final abolition of seigneurialism had been an extension of non-compliance and rebellion against those practices which the Assembly seemed hesitant to abolish. John Markoff has calculated that there were 4,689 protests or 'incidents' between 1788 and 1793, of which anti-seigneurial protests made up 36 per cent of the total. In April 1792 alone, at least a hundred peasant attacks on châteaux were recorded in the department of the Gard. On 25 August, a motion to end seigneurialism was passed by the Legislative Assembly. Seigneurial dues were abolished without compensation, unless they could be proven to be derived from concession of land, with a legally valid contract. In essence, the feudal regime was dead.[6]

The composition of the Convention testifies to the social transformation wrought by the Revolution. There were few former nobles (23) or Catholic clergy (46); instead the Convention was composed of professional men, officials, landowners and businessmen – experienced in local politics and two-thirds under 45 years old – with a sprinkling of artisans and farmers. Municipal councils were more democratic in composition. In major provincial centres, men in commerce and manufacturing were 46 per cent of councillors in Amiens, 41 per cent in Bordeaux, 18 per cent in Nancy and 36 per cent in Toulouse, but artisans and shopkeepers were 18–24 per cent in all four cities.[7] In small rural communities, too, the years 1792–4 were a time of social levelling, with peasants and even labourers represented for the first time on councils.

Despite the considerable consensus in the Convention, in the autumn and winter of 1792–3 it tended to divide into three roughly-equal voting blocs. Paris was dominated by Jacobins (20 of its 24 deputies) of the renown of Robespierre, Danton, Desmoulins and Marat but, like their antagonists, the 'Girondins', they were above all a nationwide political tendency. In social and political terms, Jacobins were somewhat closer to the *sans-culottes*, while the label of 'Girondins' denoted men closer in sympathy to the upper bourgeoisie of Bordeaux, capital of the Gironde, from whence Vergniaud, Guadet and Gensonné had been elected. A large group of uncommitted deputies, dubbed the 'Plain' or 'Marsh', and including Sieyès and Grégoire, swung its support depending on the issue.

It was above all political practice and attitudes on three critical issues which divided republicans. While the deputies present during the king's trial agreed on his guilt, Girondins were particularly likely to argue that his fate should be decided by referendum, that he should not be sentenced to death or that he should be reprieved. The great strength of the Jacobin argument during this dramatic and eloquent debate was that to spare Louis would be to admit his special nature: was Louis Capet a citizen guilty of treason? Robespierre and Saint-Just argued that, as an outlaw, he should simply be summarily executed, but most Jacobins argued for a full trial. On 16–17 January, 361 deputies voted for death, against 360; the Jacobins then successfully defeated the Girondins' final appeal for clemency, by 380 votes to 310.[8] Secondly, the Girondins were further embarrassed by the deterioration of a war they, as followers of Brissot, had urged in 1792. The 'nation in arms' had occupied the Low Countries, the Rhineland and Savoy (which agreed to become a department of France) by Christmas, but the execution of Louis on 21 January expanded the war to include Britain and Spain and altered the fortunes of battle. A series of defeats in the south-east, south-west and north-east resulted in royalist forces crossing well into France by March. Charges that the Girondins were incapable of leading the Republic through military crisis seemed proven by the defection on 5 April of a leading Girondin sympathizer, General Dumouriez, the hero of Valmy.

In 1792 the Girondins had been able to blame Louis for military reverses; whom could they now accuse? The third issue which exposed these 'new conservatives' was their attitudes to their scapegoat, the *sans-culottes* and their economic and political demands. For Vergniaud, 'equality for man as a social being [consisted] solely in the equality of his legal rights'; and Brissot issued a national warning against 'the hydra of anarchy', castigating Jacobins, too, as 'disorganizers who [wished] to level everything: property, leisure, the price of provisions, the various services to be rendered to society'. While Brissot exaggerated the 'levelling' impulses of the Jacobins, they were certainly more flexible in their willingness to place temporary controls on the economy, particularly on the price of foodstuffs.

The Convention responded to the military crisis by ordering a levy of 300,000 conscripts in March. This levy was easily implemented only in the south-east and east – two frontier regions – and around Paris. In the west it provoked massive armed rebellion and civil war, known, like the region itself, as 'the Vendée'. Erupting as it did at a desperate time for the young Republic, and resulting in terrible loss of life, the insurrection left permanent scars on French society and politics, and continues to divide historians. Why 'the Vendée'?[9]

An explanation of the rebellion needs to investigate the region's structures and the specific impact of the Revolution since 1789. The departments south of the Loire where violence flared were in a region of *bocage* (scattered farms separated by high hedgerows), poor communications with the outside, and a mix of subsistence farming and cattle-raising, with textile production based in small village centres (*bourgs*). The large holdings of nobles and religious orders were rented on secure leases to relatively prosperous farmers through bourgeois middle-men, while bourgeois-owned land was rented to poorer tenants. The exactions of seigneurs and the State had been comparatively light. A numerous, locally-recruited and active Tridentine clergy played a pivotal social role, with the wealth to do so; as in other dioceses of the west, only a tiny minority of priests were paid the *portion congrue* instead of directly collecting the tithe.

For the majority of people, Sunday mass was the occasion when, on coming to the *bourg*, the community felt its parochial identity, made decisions and heard news conveyed by the priest.

While the *cahiers* of the area expressed many of the hopes of rural people elsewhere, the Revolution brought them no obvious benefits. Heavier state taxes were collected more rigorously by bourgeois who also monopolized new offices and municipal councils, and bought up church lands in 1791: in the district of Cholet, nobles bought 23.5 per cent of such land, bourgeois 56.3 per cent, but peasants only 9.3 per cent. The collapse of demand for textiles, following the free trade treaty with England in 1786 and the economic difficulties of the revolutionary period, alienated textile workers. Similarly, by assuming the distinctive long-term tenancies of the west to be only one more form of rental agreement, revolutionary governments made the rural middle class more vulnerable rather than recognising them as *de facto* landowners. The hostility of the clergy to the abolition of the tithe, the substantial reduction in their salaries and the imposition of an urban, civic concept of priesthood was bolstered by community disappointment with the Revolution, the attitude of the church hierarchy, and the zealous enforcement of reform by bourgeois officials in Angers, long characterized by their hostility to clerical wealth and values. In the district of La Roche-sur-Yon, for example, administrators had few hesitations about closing 19 of 52 parish churches deemed to be surplus.

The rural community responded to these accumulating grievances in 1790–2 by humiliating constitutional clergy elected by 'active' citizens, by boycotting local and national elections, and by repeated instances of passive or violent resistance to local office-holders. More than anything else, the conscription decree of March 1793 focused their hatreds, for the bourgeois officials who enforced it were exempt from the ballot. Whereas the 'blues' were largely bourgeois, artisans and shopkeepers, the rebels represented a cross-section of rural society. Women played a vital role in the rebellion, as intermediaries between ecclesiastical and secular communities and in sustaining households during the fighting. The slogans of the insurgents expressed support for the 'good priests' as the essence of a threatened way of life, and hatred for bourgeois:

> You'll perish in your towns
> Cursed *patauds* [bourgeois patriots]
> Just like caterpillars
> Your feet in the air

Accordingly, the first targets were local officials, who were assaulted and humiliated, and small urban centres such as Machecoul, where about 500 republicans were tortured and killed in March.

The Vendée was not intially counter-revolutionary so much as anti-revolutionary. However, the subsequent entry of nobles and refractory clergy gave it a counter-revolutionary hue, even if most peasants were unwilling to form an army to march on Paris or to recommence paying dues and tithes. Above all, the vicious cycle of killing and reprisals convinced both sides of the treachery of the other, exacerbated by the nature of the fighting on a terrain suited to guerilla-type ambushes and retreat. Ultimately, the civil war was to claim at least 200,000 lives. The bitterness of the fighting at a time of national military crisis encouraged sweeping repression; when General Westermann reported back to the Convention in December 1793 that 'the Vendée is no more', he admitted: 'I have crushed the children under my horses' hooves, massacred the women – they, at least, will not give birth to any more brigands.'[10]

Some of the structural characteristics of the Vendée resembled those of Brittany, the Beaujolais and the southern Massif Central; there, however, other local features resulted instead in anti-revolutionary activity which either took the form of sporadic resistance by small groups of young men *(chouannerie)* in Brittany or simply lacked mass support. In May, for example, Charrier's 'Christian Army of the Midi' was able to mass only 2,000 followers. A rather more severe body blow to the Republic was the anti-Jacobin insurrection of April in Corsica, important to the Revolution because of Paoli's reputation and the island's long republican tradition.[11]

The civil war in the Vendée, military losses on the frontiers, and the increasingly desperate rhetoric of the Girondins pushed the Plain into supporting Jacobin proposals for emergency wartime measures. Between March and May 1793 the Convention placed executive powers in a Committee of Public Safety, acted to supervise the army through 'deputies on mission', passed decrees declaring *émigrés* 'civilly dead', and instituted public relief and controls on grain and bread prices. The Girondins countered by seeking to impeach Marat, threatening to move the capital to Bourges, attacking the Paris Commune and – like the Duke of Brunswick – warning the *sans-culottes* that, in Isnard's words, 'Paris [would] be annihilated' if insurrection should recur. Such threats, in the context of military crisis and rapid inflation, outraged Parisian working people. Market-women began the call for a purge of such unrevolutionary 'people's mandatories': by mid-April 35 sections had agreed on a list of 22 Girondins to be expelled from the Convention and established a Central Revolutionary Committee. The Paris Commune ordered the formation of a paid militia of 20,000 *sans-culottes* which surrounded the Convention at the end of May and required the reluctant deputies to meet its wishes.[12]

Initially the Convention hesitated – the Girondins had been cowed but at what cost to its own parliamentary independence? – then acted to meet the crisis of a nation in danger of internal collapse and external defeat. In the summer of 1793 the Revolution faced its greatest crisis, at the same time military, social and political. Enemy troops were on French soil in the north-east, south-east and south-west and, internally, the great revolt in the Vendée absorbed a major part of the Republic's army. These threats were aggravated by the hostile response of 60 departmental administrations to the purge of the Girondins. The largest provincial cities (Bordeaux, Lyon, Marseille) fell to a coalition of conservative republicans and royalists, and on 29 August the key Mediterranean naval arsenal of Toulon was handed over by its officers to the English navy blockading the coast.

These so-called 'Federalist' revolts were united only by the coincidence of their timing. However, they all drew on strong regional traditions, as in the hinterland of Marseille, where villages such as Lourmarin followed the example of their local metropolis.[13] Above all, at the heart of Federalism was the anger of the upper bourgeoisie, especially those in commercial towns, at the radical direction the Revolution had taken; the purging of their elected representatives was the last straw. While many leading Federalists were committed republicans, they were doubly compromised: first, because they had repudiated the Convention's authority at a time of the Republic's gravest military crisis; secondly, because the support given them by royalists, nobles and priests tarnished them by association. The immediate targets of the revolts were local Jacobins and militants, reflecting the class-based nature of local divisions. In Toulon the *Comité Général* which seized power included 16 merchants, 8 lawyers, 6 *rentiers*, 11 naval officers and engineers, 3 officials, 3 priests and 3 artisans; it insisted: 'We want to enjoy our goods, our property, the fruits of our toil and industry in peace ... . Yet we see them incessantly exposed to threats from those who have nothing themselves.' In Lyon, too, the Jacobin-Girondin struggle was linked to the political and workplace militancy of silk-weavers, expressed through Jacobin clubs, in the years since 1789. The threat reached the heart of the Convention on 13 July when an enraged Girondin, Charlotte Corday, assassinated Marat. With Le Peletier, murdered by a royalist the night the Convention voted the death of Louis, and Joseph Chalier, the Jacobin leader in Lyon killed by Federalists on 17 July, Marat formed a triumvirate of martyrs for revolutionaries now increasingly antagonistic even to the constitutional clergy.

The Jacobin Committee of Public Safety elected by the Convention on 27 July had as its mission to pass laws and controls necessary to strike 'Terror' into the hearts of counter-revolutionaries.[14] The Convention acquiesced in draconian measures – such as surveillance committees, preventive detention and controls on civil liberties – necessary to secure the Republic to a point where the democratic, libertarian constitution of June 1793 could be implemented. Largely the work of Robespierre, this Constitution was remarkable for its guarantees of social rights and popular control over an assembly elected by direct, universal male suffrage. The results of a referendum on its acceptance (1.8 million 'yes' votes to 17,000) were announced at the *Fête de l'unité* on 10 August, the first anniversary of the overthrow of the monarchy. Participation rates ranged from 17 per cent in the Côtes-du-Nord to 33 per cent in Paris and 50 per cent in the Bas-Rhin; among those who insisted on voting were 343 women at Laon and 175 women and 163 children at Pontoise.

From July to September the Committee of Public Safety took the steps necessary to place France on a war footing and to cement a new third-estate alliance. The Convention had to overcome the odds of fighting on numerous fronts at a time of internal division and civil war, and a good deal of despair: perhaps 35,000 soldiers (6 per cent of the total) had deserted in the first half of 1793, and many others reacted to deficiencies in supplies by stealing local produce. That desertion was cut to a minimum in the year 1793–4 was the result of a mixture of coercion, propaganda and the effectiveness of the Jacobin Committee of Public Safety and its officials in supplying an army of nearly a million men. Sustaining the energies of the Convention and its committees was the demand of the *sans-culottes* that only total mobilization of rich and poor alike could save the Republic: on 23 August all single men of 18–25 years of age were conscripted. National Guard units were charged with hunting down those who evaded conscription or deserted. Conscripts from the same region were given basic instruction in French and scattered through the army to reduce the temptation of collective flight; mass propaganda, such as the *Le Père Duchesne*, was distributed, and 'deputies on mission' from the Convention guaranteed swift retribution to hesitant officers and unwilling rank and file.

This did not prevent endless complaints about ill-fitting uniforms and poor weaponry, but soldiers' letters home were also full of remarks about revolutionary zeal and their commitment to the *patrie*. The political culture of the Republic implied new relationships with authority. In August 1793, Laurent Peyrot, a peasant from Vermenton (Yonne) wrote to the departmental administration asking for financial help because of a wound he had suffered at the battle of Neerwinden on 18 March: this 'defender of liberty' felt 'justly entitled' to aid, and assured the administration: 'the laurel which he has reaped by pouring his blood for liberty will shed its leaves upon your heads'. The language of the officials is similarly revealing, their positive response referring to 'justice' and their 'most sacred duty' towards those 'who have shed their blood for the defence of the *patrie*'. The creation of mass republican armies, with 'line' and volunteer units now fused, had engendered a new military culture which was a microcosm of the 'regenerated' society the Convention anticipated.[15]

The 'Law of Suspects' (17 September) was designed to expose the unpatriotic to detention or to intimidate them into inaction. The arrest of 'suspects' was by no means indiscriminate, and was directed at those who, by word, action or status, were associated with the *ancien régime*. In Rouen 29 per cent of the 1,158 suspects arrested were nobles, 19 per cent clergy and 7.5 per cent former office-holders; such people were arrested because of who they were, coupled with suspicions of '*incivisme*'. The bourgeoisie were 16.8 per cent of 'suspects' and working people 27 per cent. While many of these commoners had worked for the *ancien régime*, those arrested were also charged with anti-revolutionary words and acts; among shopkeepers, such acts often concerned speculation and stock-piling of goods. Significantly, 39.4 per cent of all 'suspects' were women: they were particularly numerous among the nobility and clergy, reflecting the tendency for males in these groups to emigrate, leaving women as the focus of suspicion because of their family name and their support for nonjuring clergy.[16]

Political opposition at a time of war implied the threat of capital punishment for treachery. In October, Marie-Antoinette was followed to the guillotine by the 21 Girondin deputies expelled in June. Whereas, from the inception of the Revolutionary Tribunal in March 1793 until September, only 66 of 260 'suspects' had been found guilty of a capital offence, in the final three months of the year this was the fate of 177 of 395 accused. However, until June 1794, most 'suspects' never appeared before the Tribunal and, of those who did, 40 per cent were acquitted. Those who were not faced the agonies of premature death and farewells to loved ones. Noirette Blancheton, a second-hand-clothes dealer from Coulommiers (Seine-et-Marne) involved in a violent anti-Jacobin riot in May 1793, wrote her last letter to her husband nine months later:

> I must beg you to take very good care of the fruits of our love, our friendship should say enough about this. Give my brother, all my relatives and friends my last good-byes. The strength of my will makes me believe that I will be missed. Accept my embraces, share them with our brothers and be sure of my love until the very end.[17]

The mass mobilization of the whole nation required the Convention to take steps to forge a new unity by positive measures as well as by intimidation. In particular, it was impelled to respond to the waves of rural unrest which had affected two-thirds of all departments since 1789.[18] While diverse in focus and nature, this unrest had as its targets the claims that 'outsiders' (nobles, clergy, bourgeois landowners) exerted over the land or the freeing up of land through sales and division of church and *émigré* property and communal lands, and the subdivision of large estates. The last of these, the 'agrarian law', was made a capital offence in March 1793, but Jacobins later took a series of measures designed to win over the rural masses, the indispensable condition for military success. Final hesitations about the total abolition of feudalism, still present in the Girondin legislation of 25 August 1792, were removed with the annulling of all seigneurial claims on 17 July 1793. On 10 June 1793 the division of common lands was placed in the hands of the commune. However, the cost of surveyors' fees reduced the use made of this law as a way of resolving an issue which had long divided rural people: would the interests of the rural poor best be secured by dividing common lands or by preserving them? Now that the feudal regime was dead, internal divisions began to surface within rural society. From the outset of the Revolution, the friction over the anti-seigneurial legislation of 1789 had also been embedded in more general conflict over ownership and control of the 'wastelands', marginal land which had been used by seigneurs and wealthy peasants to pasture animals and now seized and cleared by the rural poor. The seigneurial regime had finally been abolished, but it was to take far longer to resolve the associated questions of control of collective economic resources, land-hunger and clearances.[19]

With the religious question, the legislators' hesitations about seigneurialism and access to land fuelled rural politics in the years 1792–4, although the precise political orientation of much rural protest is hard to define. The rural revolution had its own rhythms and inner dynamic, generated by the specific nature of the locality. The precise form which rural politics took was a function of perceptions of the benefits and hardships brought by the Revolution, attitudes to the Church, and local social structures. While political attitudes therefore varied across the countryside, underpinning attitudes everywhere was hostility both to the *ancien régime* and to bourgeois concepts of untrammelled rights of private property. To calls for the 'agrarian law' in the north-east corresponded anti-bourgeois risings in the west, Brittany and elsewhere. In Neulisse (Loire), armed youths who gathered for the conscription ballot of 1793 conducted their own choice for the 15 men the commune had to supply: the constitutional priest and 14 bourgeois 'patriots' who had profited most from the Revolution.[20]

Every rural district had its share of ardent Jacobins who read Parisian and local papers or belonged to Jacobin clubs and popular societies. Cérutti's *La Feuille villageoise*, aimed specifically at a rural audience, sold up to 16,000 copies (with an estimated readership of 250,000) in 1793; the administration of the Gers subscribed to a copy for each of its 599 communes. In 1793–4 there were as many as 6,000 Jacobin clubs in provincial France; though they were most common in small towns, in Provence 75–90 per cent of all villages had one, symptomatic of the lively political life of the south-east which also sustained active counter-revolutionaries. From local societies came urgings to the Convention, as from Montmeillant (Ardennes): 'The strength of Hercules with which you are armed and the shield of Minerva which defends you should not leave your hands until the hydra of aristocracy has been reduced to ashes and there is no more trace of its blood on the globe.'[21]

Economically, the plight of wage-earners in particular had continued to deteriorate: by August the purchasing power of the *assignat* had fallen to 22 per cent of its face value, from 36 per cent in June. The Convention now acted to meet the repeated demands of the *sans-culottes* by the 'general maximum' of 29 September which pegged the prices of 39 commodities at 1790 levels plus one-third, and set wages at 50 per cent higher than 1790 levels. In the months between August 1792 and March 1794, the political participation of urban working people reached its peak. While 'revisionist' historians have made much of the fact that only about 10 per cent of men regularly attended section meetings and that many *sans-culottes* militants were bourgeois by occupation, this remains a remarkable level of popular participation at a time of long working days, food queues and worries about survival. It was reflected in an unprecedented levelling in the social composition of local government: in Paris, for example, one-third of the Commune councillors were from the *menu peuple*, as were four-fifths of the 'revolutionary committees' elected in each of the 48 sections of the city. *Sans-culottes* political and social goals were also expressed through more than 40 popular societies (with some 6,000 members of whom 86 per cent were artisans and wage-earners), and above all in local section meetings.[22] Similarly, in Marseille, the Jacobin Club increased in size from 950 in May 1793 to 3,500 after the collapse of Federalism in late August. Skilled workers were now 62 per cent of members (previously 34 per cent); while shopkeepers remained one-fifth, the proportion of bourgeois declined from 28 per cent to 6 per cent, and nobles and clergy had virtually disappeared.[23]

Paris in 1792–4 was the pulsating, tumultuous centre of the Revolution, where huge numbers of civilians and soldiers on the move co-existed uneasily with long-established neighbourhood communities. In the Popincourt section, fewer than one-third were native Parisians; in the central city, 128,000 lodging houses sheltered young male migrants and prostitutes. In such a situation the news spread by 1,000 newspaper street-sellers was embellished by word of mouth, creating a city crackling with a potent mixture of rumour, optimism and suspicion. The Law of Suspects was designed to quell such insecurity; in its implementation, sections and their 116,000 police, drawn from fortnightly service by all able-bodied men, played the grass-roots role. Lies, personal feuds and denunciations found a fertile atmosphere, yet the activities of section authorities were self-consciously legal and 'correct'.[24]

Four years of revolutionary experience, of boundless hopes, sacrifices and anxieties, of living within a revolutionary political culture, generated a distinctive *sans-culottes* ideology in cities and towns. This discourse drew on pre-revolutionary symbolism, often in messianic terms, and on idealized collective practices of the workplace to visualize a new society free of aristocrats, priests and rich men: the vision was of a regenerated France of artisans and smallholders rewarded for the dignity and usefulness of their labour, free from religion, the condescension of the high-born and the competition of entrepreneurs.[25] Club and section meetings drew on religious and bourgeois forms for their organization, but on revolutionary experience for their content. Meetings often began with the singing of the Marseillaise or the *Ça ira* and the reading of letters from the front, followed by discussions of forthcoming anniversaries and processions, the collection of patriotic donations, the denunciation of 'suspects', and orations about 'republican virtues'. To break from a lifetime of induction into the vocabulary of inequality, they sought to impose the familiar use of *tu* in all social dealings (as it was in the Commune and section meetings), dismissing the *vous* formerly required towards their superiors as intrinsically aristocratic. The *sans-culottes* insisted on the pre-eminence of the sections over their 'mandatories' in the Convention. The section was a microcosm of the one and indivisible Republic, reflected in the practice of *publicité*, whereby votes and opinions were delivered openly and orally. Such a practice was as clearly at odds with bourgeois notions of individual rights and representative democracy as was the imposition of price controls with *laissez-faire*.

The place of the Pope and the refractory clergy in the bitter, bloody internal conflict in the west and in the wars being fought on French soil generated a popular response which even called Christianity into question. The Convention's response was a new 'republican' calendar, inaugurated on the first anniversary of the proclamation of the Republic on 21 September 1792 (retrospectively dated the first day of the year I of the republican era). This combined the rationality of decimal measurement (12 months of 30 days, each with three *décadi* of ten days) with a total repudiation of the Gregorian calendar; saints, days and movable festivals were replaced by names drawn from plants, the seasons, work implements and the virtues. The triumvirate of 'martyrs of the Revolution' (Marat, Le Peletier, Chalier) was accompanied by the celebration of the heroism of Bara and Viala, children killed fighting counter-revolution; the great anniversaries of 14 July, 10 August, 21 January and 21 September were ultimately to be supported by 36 national festivals, one each *décadi*.

The popular response to religious counter-revolution was more vitriolic. Marseillais sang a Provençal version of the battle-hymn named after them:

> March on, god's arse
> March on, god's fart
> The *émigrés*, by god,
> Have no more idea of god
> Than old royalist priests.

Popular initiative, at times encouraged by 'representatives on mission', closed churches and pressured the constitutional clergy to abdicate and marry as a sign of patriotism. There were wide variations in the number of such abdications, from only 12 in the Alpes-Maritimes and 20 in the Lozère to 498 in the Saône-et-Loire; in 21 departments of the south-east, there were 4,200–4,500. In all about 20,000 priests abdicated their calling and 6,000 of them married.[26] Some clerics may have felt like the former priest Duffay, who wrote to the Convention in January 1794:

> I listened to the voice of nature and exchanged my old prayer book for a young republican woman … . As I have always regarded the state of priesthood as just as useless as a player of skittles, I have used [my church diplomas] for the fire …. I am labouring in a factory where, despite the exhaustion to which one is subject, I am very happy if my sweat keeps me from poverty.

The Catholic Church was utterly devastated by these months. By 1794 France was a land almost devoid of officiating priests. In the Allier, only 58 of 426 priests did not abdicate, and nationally perhaps only 150 parishes out of 40,000 were openly celebrating mass in spring 1794. Among 3,000 violent clerical deaths in these years were at least 920 clergy who were publicly executed as counter-revolutionaries, and probably 30,000–40,000 (up to 25 per cent) of all clergy emigrated. The former first estate was thereby more directly affected than the nobility: the number of noble *émigrés* (16,431) was about 15 per cent of the second estate.[27]

The dechristianization campaign coincided and was often identified with the activities of 45 *armées révolutionnaires* (in all, about 40,000 men) active in 40 departments in the autumn of 1793.[28] These bands of *sans-culottes* militants, mixed with men on the run and others who simply enjoyed the camaraderie, had as their mission the requisitioning of food for cities and the armies, the payment of taxes, the purging of counter-revolutionaries, the seizure of metals from churches for the war effort, and the maintenance of revolutionary zeal. Their size ranged from small groups of ten to democratically-run armies of up to 7,000 in the Aveyron and Lozère.

The central purpose of the Terror was to institute the emergency and draconian measures necessary at a time of military crisis; however, laws were passed which went well beyond national safety and revealed a Jacobin social vision for a secular and republican education system and a national programme of social welfare. Jacobin education policy, particularly the Bouquier Law of 19 December 1793, foresaw free, compulsory education for children of 6–13 years with a curriculum emphasizing patriotism and republican virtues, linguistic uniformity, the simplification of formal French, physical activity, field-study and observation, and the role of the school in civic festivals. In the first half of 1794, five issues of 'Collections of Heroic and Civic Acts of French Republicans', the third of them in 150,000 copies, were sent to schools to replace catechisms. The Jacobins never had the time or money to implement their education policy, let alone to train lay teachers to replace priests, and few children attended school during the Terror: 128 pupils for the 20,000 inhabitants of Clermont-Ferrand, and five of the enrolled 220 children in Wissembourg (Bas-Rhin).[29]

Jacobin commitment to eradicating poverty similarly foundered because of the financial demands of the war and lack of time. The Ventôse Laws of February-March 1794, which were to use the property of 'suspects' to 'indemnify the poor', and the national programme of social welfare announced on 11 May 1794, were only spasmodically implemented. The Constitution of 1793 had made an unprecedented commitment to social rights and the Convention took several measures to extend the rights of children: on 4 July 1793 abandoned children became a state responsibility and on 2 November 1793 children born outside marriage were guaranteed full inheritance rights. 'Deputies on mission' to departments, such as Bo, Romme, Chabot and Lakanal, took measures to ensure adequate poor relief and distribution of essentials. On the other hand, the Republic was no less hostile than the monarchy to the workshy (*'vagabonds de race'*) and to the rural bands of thieves for whom crime was the basis of a whole subculture left untouched by the Revolution. In prisons, there was a similar continuity in appalling conditions.[30]

Jacobin reforms and popular initiative in the months from September 1792 to March 1794 created one of those rare moments in history when huge numbers of people acted as if they had remade the world. While the term 'cultural revolution' was not utilised until 1922, in the Soviet Union, it is also applicable to these months in France, when the Jacobin—*sans-culottes* alliance, supported in many areas by the peasantry, challenged the most basic meanings of daily life.[31] This cultural revolution drew its intellectual inspiration from ancient Sparta and sought to inculcate 'total regeneration', in Le Peletier's words. Jacobin policy and popular action coincided through official and spontaneous use of festivals, plays, songs, broadsheets, decoration, clothing and leisure. There was, however, a tension between popular symbolic enaction of total change – the physical destruction of religious statuary, paintings, and other signs of the *ancien régime* – and Jacobin concern for what Grégoire called 'vandalism', leading to laws to protect national heritage in September 1792. This coincided with the creation of departmental and national public libraries, archives and museums and the Conservatoire late in 1793.

The cultural revolution was not expressed through books: the number of books printed in 1794 was only 371, compared with pre-revolutionary figures of over 1,000 annually, and in the two years 1793–4 only 36 new novels were published. One exception was the popularity of Rousseau's *Du contrat social*, which went through 13 editions in 1792–5, including a pocket-sized version for soldiers. Similarly, with the constraints on press freedom imposed after the declaration of war and the overthrow of the monarchy, the number of new Parisian papers fell from 134 in 1792 to 78 in 1793 and 66 in the year II. Instead, 1792–4 was the great age of political songs: one estimate is that the number of new songs climbed from 116 in 1789 to 325 in 1792, 590 in 1793 and 701 in 1794. Though most plays were pre-1789 in origin, themes and characters were reworked along revolutionary lines. Others continued to draw their humour from mocking the Church: one of the most popular plays in Paris, running from 1792 to 1794, was Louis-Benoît Picard's *Les Visitandines*, featuring two drunken rogues mistaking a convent for an inn. In January 1794, theatres were subsidized if they gave a free performance each week. In painting, too, the government acted to open the Salon to all artists, and gave 442,000 livres in prizes: 3,000 painters exhibited, compared with about 350 before 1789. In these years, collective display also went through what Michel Vovelle has described as a 'creative explosion', as popular initiatives in organizing festivals and remodelling ancient rituals meshed with the Convention's encouragement of civic commemoration. When news arrived, for example, of Louis's execution or a military victory, whole villages improvised celebrations. Dechristianization ceremonies in particular had a carnival and cathartic atmosphere, often utilizing the *'promenade des ânes'*, used in the *ancien régime* to censure violators of community norms of behaviour.

The certainty felt by revolutionaries in town and country that they were living on the frontier of social change was expressed in the spontaneous changes of name given to communities themselves and to the newborn. Apart from name changes imposed by Jacobin armies after the defeat of counter-revolution, some 3,000 communes themselves acted to erase Christian connotations: Saint-Izague became Vin-Bon, Saint-Bonnet-Elvert became Liberté-Bonnet-Rouge, Saint-Tropez and Montmartre were renamed Héraclée and Mont-Marat, while Villedieu took the name La Carmagnole and Villeneuve-Saint-Georges renamed itself Villeneuve-la-Montagne. It is impossible to estimate how many parents gave revolutionary names to babies in these years: in Poitiers, for example, only 62 of 593 babies born in the year II were named after saints in the *ancien-régime* manner. Instead, given names reflected the contrasting sources of political inspiration: a study of 430 names adopted in the Seine-et-Marne shows that 55 per cent drew on nature or the new calendar (Rose, Laurier, Floréal), 24 per cent on republican virtues (Liberté, Victoire, La Montagne), 12 per cent on antiquity (Brutus, Mucius Scaevola), and 9 per cent on heroes (Le Peletier, Marat). One little boy was called Travail, another Fumier. In the Hautes-Alpes the Lacau parents gave their daughter the name Phytogynéantrope, Greek for a woman giving birth only to warrior sons.

The repudiation of the most fundamental sources of authority in the *ancien régime* inevitably called into question the position of women within the family and society.[32] It is doubtful whether patterns of male violence changed, despite the exhortations of revolutionary legislators to a peaceful, harmonious family life as the basis of the new political order. What did change was the possibility of women protecting their rights within the household. The divorce law voted at the last session of the Legislative Assembly, on 20 September 1792, gave women remarkably broad grounds for leaving an unhappy or meaningless marriage. Revealingly, it was women above all who used this law: in Rouen, 71 per cent of divorce actions were initiated by women, 72 per cent of them textile workers. As skilled workers, these women were more likely to be able to earn a living wage; on the other hand, in the rural areas around Rouen, only 31 marriages ended in these years. Nationally, perhaps 30,000 divorces were decreed under this legislation, especially in towns: in Paris, there were nearly 6,000 in 1793–5.

For every eight marriages in Rouen, one divorce was decreed and an equal number was resolved by family mediation. Although violence was a common cause cited by women, the customary power of men to humble their wives by physical abuse *(correction modérée)* would have been called into question in every household. The divorce law could challenge domestic relationships at a fundamental level. One Rouennais, the 'wretched victim of an abuse authorized by the law', complained that his former wife had divorced him and that his current spouse 'ceaselessly threatens me with divorce when I fail to satisfy all her whims or when I permit myself to make the slightest representation to her'. The nature of the marriage ceremony – as of baptism and burial – also changed, with the priest performing only an optional blessing if indeed a priest was available at all. Religious strictures against marriage in Advent, in Lent, on Fridays and Sundays were now ignored. There were also good reasons – the exemption of married men from conscription – for *de facto* couples to marry and for people to marry younger: compared with a pre-revolutionary annual average of 240,000 marriages, there were over 325,000 in both 1793 and 1794.

The revolutionary armies could not have triumphed – nor could the rising in the Vendée have been so powerful – without the active support of women. In urban centres, the collapse of women's work in luxury industries (especially lace) and domestic service was partly met by the temporary availability of work as scores of thousands of men left for the front. In town and country, women's work became more important than ever before in keeping the household together, though in the years 1792–4 perhaps one family in ten was economically and emotionally drained by the death or wounding of a husband, son or father. Prostitution remained a common last resort for up to 20,000 young women in Paris. Abhorrent to Jacobins as a mark of *ancien-régime* decadence, public soliciting was banned on 4 October 1793 and prostitution itself on 21 Nivôse II (10 January 1794) – to which some prostitutes retorted with a pamphlet: 'Will politics ever offer the same gratification as sex?'. Driven from the streets and pushed towards labour in the war industries, prostitutes nevertheless continued to work.[33]

Throughout the Revolution, there had been a gulf of class and politics between the individual advocates of women's rights, now dead or discredited because of their political conservatism, and the support of urban working women (at times known as *sans-jupons*, those who did not wear petticoats) for the subsistence and military goals of the popular movement as a whole. For six months after May 1793, the Revolutionary Republican Citizenesses, led by Claire Lacombe and Pauline Léon, bridged this gap by organizing as an autonomous women's group and campaigning for women's rights to public office and to bear arms while remaining linked to the radical wing of the *sans-culottes*, the *Enragés*. Several sections began admitting women to their meetings, the *Hommes libres* and *Panthéon* sections acknowledging full voting rights. However, while the Citizenesses attracted 300 women to their meetings, and claimed the active support of 4,000 more, their challenge foundered on the opposition of market-stallholders for whom price controls threatened poverty. On 24 October a group of Citizenesses was severely beaten by market-women, giving the Jacobins and the Convention the chance to move against them.[34]

The ambiguities in men's attitudes to women are evident in revolutionary iconography: images of a serene bourgeois mother teaching her son the Declaration of the Rights of Man contrasted with others of muscular working women giving birth to robust young republicans already fired with military zeal. Similarly, the protective Virgin Mary of *ancien-régime* imagery gave way to the Marianne of the Republic, now in classical garb and liberty cap, but still a feminine allegory watching passively over men. Certainly, with few exceptions, even radical Jacobins were outraged by the political challenge coming from active women. Amar, of the Committee of General Security, justified the banning of the Citizenesses to the Convention on 10 Brumaire II (30 October 1793) by describing men as: 'strong, robust, born with great energy, audacity and courage ... destined for agriculture, commerce, navigation, travel, war ... he alone seems suited for serious, deep thought.... Women are unsuited for advanced thinking and serious reflection ... more exposed to error and an exultation which would be disastrous in public life.'[35]

The smothering of the most militant *sans-culottes* groups revealed the tensions within the popular alliance of the year II, but no less striking were the achievements of this alliance by the end of 1793. By then, republican forces led by a young artillery officer, Napoleon Bonaparte, had recaptured Toulon and foreign armies had suffered major reverses in the north-east and south-east. Though the 'general maximum' had not been fully implemented, the economic slide had been reversed and the purchasing power of the *assignat* stood at 48 per cent. The Vendéan rebellion had been contained and the federalist revolt crushed, both at a huge cost in lives. The most severe retribution for federalism was imposed on Lyon, where Collot d'Herbois ordered 1,667 executions, most by firing squad, to purge the renamed *Ville Affranchie*. While Collot was made a scapegoat for the extent of this killing, it appears that the entire Committee of Public Safety acquiesced in it as the necessary price of an awesome reminder to the provinces.[36] In Nantes, on the other hand, Carrier was not so much acting for the Committee as for furious and vengeful local republicans when he ordered the mass drowning of several hundred people in the Loire.

It was inevitable that the desperate demands of the national mobilization for the war would reverse the decentralization of power of the early years of the Revolution. The civil wars of 1793 had served to underline the dangers of local autonomy, just as the *armées révolutionnaires*, the surge of radical women's demands, and dechristianization highlighted the challenge of local initiatives. The laws of 14 and 16 Frimaire (4 and 6 December) were a direct response to these popular movements, by sharply reducing the independence of local government and the sections, and by asserting the right of religious freedom. Article I of the Law of 14 Frimaire insisted that 'the National Convention [was] the sole centre of government initiative'. The counter-revolution also strengthened Jacobin mistrust of minority languages. In January 1794, Barère (though himself from the Occitan-speaking Pyrenees) inveighed against the 'ignorance and fanaticism' which the foreign coalition manipulated in 'people who are badly instructed or who speak a different idiom from that of public education'. Forgetting the extraordinary sacrifices being made on the borders as he spoke, by patriotic Basques, Catalans, Flemish and Provençaux, Barère assumed that republicanism, civilization and the French language were synonymous. In fact, responses to the Revolution were mediated through the use of minority languages, but not determined by them. Nor were such responses intimidated by the apparatus of the Terror: the mayor of Monbalen (Lot-et-Garonne) was arrested early in 1794 for describing the Convention as composed of 'idiots who did not know what they were doing', and as far as he was concerned they could 'wipe their arses with their decrees'.[37]

It was in this context that a crucial and fateful debate occurred over the continuation and direction of the Terror, when 'moderate' Jacobins such as Danton and Desmoulins urged an end to the controls of the Terror and the implementation of the Constitution of 1793. Others argued that the crisis was far from over. In the south-west, Spanish troops remained in control of French territory; in Saint-Domingue, the offer in June 1793 of freedom to slaves who would fight for the Republic (followed by a general emancipation in July–August, extended to all French colonies by the law of 3–4 February 1794) had not succeeded in defeating the alliance of white planters and the English fleet.[38] In such a situation, the Convention responded by maintaining the committees and their personnel. Despite the turning fortunes of the war, it continued to take an enormous toll: perhaps as many as 200,000 soldiers died in 1794–5, mostly from wounds, and diseases in rudimentary hospitals.

Moreover, to Robespierre and his associates in particular, the Terror had a far higher purpose than simply winning the war. Robespierre's vision of the regenerated, virtuous and self-abnegating society which was, for him, the very *raison d'être* of the Revolution was made explicit to the Convention on 5 February 1794:

> We wish an order of things where all low and cruel passions are enchained by the laws, all beneficent and generous feelings awakened ... where distinctions arise only from equality itself ... where the country secures the welfare of each individual ... where industry is an adornment to the liberty that ennobles it, and commerce the source of public wealth, not simply of monstrous riches for a few families .... We wish in a word to fulfil the course of nature, to accomplish the destiny of mankind.

Ultimately, the political and social divisions within the republican alliance were to prove irreconcilable and explain the deadly politics of 1794. For the majority of the Convention, the goal of the Terror was the attainment of peace, and economic and political controls were but temporary and regrettable impositions to that end: the regular extension of the powers of the Committees was a recognition of its achievements and the continuing war crisis, but not a measure of support for Jacobin ideology. On the other hand, the *sans-culottes* had developed a radically different vision of a society of small farms and workshops created by property redistribution and underpinned by free education, purges of old élites, and direct democracy. The Convention reluctantly supported Jacobin repression of counter-revolutionaries of whatever social class in the name of saving the Republic, but expressed no such doubts about containing the *sans-culottes*. The smothering of the popular movement in Paris and elsewhere, consummated by the execution of the Cordeliers (Hébert, Ronsin, Vincent and their allies) in March and the closing of 39 popular societies, freed the Convention's hand to encourage selling on the open market by lifting profit margins; coupled with the imposition of the wages maximum at September

1793 levels, wage-earners were dealt a severe blow and the *assignat* once again declined, to 36 per cent by July.

Robespierre's followers were treading a narrowing path between their increasingly alienated supporters inside and outside the Convention, and resorted to attempts to mould public opinion in the name of a revolutionary will and morality they claimed to monopolize. In this context, Saint-Just drew on Rousseau's insistence that the 'general will' was not simply an amalgam of opinion but an uncorrupted knowledge of the public interest: in Robespierre's words: *'une volonté une'*. On 26 Germinal II (15 April 1794), Saint-Just expressed his preference for a politics of 'public conscience ... composed of the penchant of the people for the common good'. Unfortunately, this 'penchant' was perverted by the 'evil intent' of former allies: Saint-Just's speech was made only days after the execution of the Cordeliers and the 'indulgents' (Danton, Desmoulins and their supporters), and the day before the arrest of Pauline Léon and Claire Lacombe.

Shortly afterwards, too, Robespierre delivered a report on the organization of public festivals, seeking both to ensure their civically instructive function and to control them. The Robespierrist festival culminated in the 'Festival of the Supreme Being' (7 May), a brilliant display orchestrated by Jacques-Louis David, but a passionless affirmation of Saint-Just's fear that 'the Revolution [had] frozen over'. Similarly, the policing functions of the Terror increasingly sought to control the content of public performances. From late 1793, 150 plays were censored by rewriting or outright banning; by March, Corneille and Racine had disappeared from the stage and 'William Tell' had become a Swiss *sans-culottes*. By April, actors playing noble roles were publicly apologizing before the curtain rose, and finally nobles were simply not depicted at all. Ultimately, Robespierre intervened in May to allow *ancien-régime* plays to be performed intact.

The execution of popular revolutionaries to the right and left of the dominant Jacobins, and the escalation of the Terror at a time of military success, alienated patriotic bourgeois and artisans. In his diary, the wealthy bourgeois Nicolas Ruault castigated what he saw as Robespierre's megalomania and the three 'pitiless demons', Billaud-Varenne, Collot and Amar. For Jacques Ménétra, an active member of a pro-Robespierre section, these months similarly conjured up images of cannibalism, murder, barbarism and unnecessary death.[39] It was above all the battle of Fleurus (26 June) – ending the presence of foreign troops on French soil – which exposed the contradictions in the great alliance of the year II. The removal of the immediate military threat starkly exposed the new purpose for which the Terror was being used: from March 1793 to 10 June 1794, 1,251 people were executed in Paris; following the law of 22 Prairial, which dramatically expanded definitions of 'counter-revolutionary', 1,376 were guillotined in just six weeks. Robespierre's final speech to the Convention on 26 July (8 Thermidor), with its threat to unnamed deputies, provided the motivation for reaction. When he was arrested the following day, he could not look for support to the *sans-culottes* movement, which had been shattered by the Jacobins' own measures, the death of its leaders, and the alienation of wage-earners. A police agent reported that, as Robespierre's head fell on 28 July, a group of brush-makers shouted 'there goes the maximum into the basket' and the next day struck for a one-third increase in wages.[40]

They were not the only people who imagined the end of the Terror would allow the release of popular initiative and the implementation of the Constitution of 1793. Among the 'suspects' released after Thermidor were many *sans-culottes*, including Gracchus Babeuf, who quickly moved to establish the *Tribun du peuple* to focus *sans-culottes* demands. The fall of Robespierre was universally welcomed as symbolizing the end of large-scale executions. Nicolas Ruault regretted only that 'the royalists or aristocrats [had] become rather too insolent. He added: 'Yesterday in the street I was insulted as a patriot by one of these gentlemen who had come out of prison the day before.' However, for radicals of whatever social class, 9 Thermidor was to prove 'a day of dupes'; within a month, about 200 provincial Jacobin clubs had complained angrily about the repercussions of Robespierre's fall. Side by side with the restriction of the scope of the Revolutionary Tribunal, which was finally abolished in May 1795 with the execution of Fouquier-Tinville, public prosecutor in the year II, a bitter social reaction was unleashed. This 'white Terror' was a punitive response of political and social élites to the controls and fears they had undergone. Active Jacobins and *sans-culottes* were arrested in Paris, Jacobins in provincial towns were assassinated, and the club itself, which had been the backbone of the patriotic bourgeoisie's associational life throughout the Revolution, was closed down in November.

The cultural revolution of the year II was over. The well-to-do self-consciously began to use 'Monsieur' and 'Madame' instead of 'Citizen', and older patterns of communication quickly re-established themselves: in 1795 the number of new novels doubled – largely sentimental tales and mysteries – while the number of new political songs declined from 701 to 137. The history of publishing also bears the marks of the new political environment. After their 'emancipation' in 1789 from the controls of the privileged guild of Parisian publishers, authors had enjoyed years of unprecedented liberty of expression until the sharp political curbs of the Terror. With the end of the Terror, authors were again to deal with publishers as free contracting agents; now, however, the regime was to offer subsidies to its literary supporters. Grégoire's report of 17 Vendémiaire III (5 October 1794), which Carla Hesse describes as the 'cultural Thermidor', advocated a deliberate policy of inculcating the right cultural and political values.[41]

The sons and daughters of the well-to-do expressed sartorial contempt for Jacobin 'mediocrity' by parading as *muscadins* and *merveilleuses*, and *jeunesse dorée* patrolled the streets spoiling for the chance to exert physical revenge on *sans-culottes*.[42] The release of social and economic restraints on displays of wealth allowed the re-emergence of prostitutes soliciting wealthy customers at the Palais-Royal and of ostentatious consumption, notably balls at which the wealthy demonstrated their antipathy to the Terror – and symbolised their recent fears – by appearing with shaved necks and thin red ribbons around their throats. The social outlook of the former Girondins and men of the 'Plain' who now dominated the Convention is evident in their education policy, which retreated from Jacobin commitment to universal, free schooling. The Daunou Law of 25–6 October 1795 also envisaged that teachers would be paid from pupils' fees, that girls would be taught 'useful skills' in separate schools, and that there need only be a school in each canton rather than every commune. The Thermidorians were rather more concerned with élite education. In September 1794, the *École Centrale des Travaux Publics* (from September 1795 known as the *École Polytechnique*) was established and linked to specialist engineering and military schools. In October 1795, *ancien-régime* academies, abolished in August 1793 as corporate and élitist, were re-established as the *Institut*.

While the removal of economic controls permitted vengeful displays of wealth, the end of all fixed prices in December 1794 unleashed rampant inflation. By April 1795, the general level of prices was about 750 per cent above 1790 levels. This coincided with a severe winter: the Seine froze over and the soil hardened to a depth of two feet. It was in this context of social and political reaction, and economic deprivation, that the *sans-culottes* made a final desperate attempt to regain the intitiative. The risings of Germinal and Prairial year III (April and May 1795) effectively sought a return to the promises of the autumn of 1793, the epitome of the *sans-culottes* movement. With 'Bread and the Constitution of 1793' pinned to their caps, insurgents shouted for the suppression of the *jeunesse dorée* and the release of imprisoned Jacobins and *sans-culottes*. Women played a major part in these insurrections. In the aftermath of the Prairial insurrection, the Convention decreed, somewhat contradictorily, that they had abused the respect men have 'for the weakness of their sex' and that, unless they immediately respected a curfew, they would be repressed by armed force.[43]

The failure of the May insurrection unleashed more wide-ranging reaction. Over 4,000 Jacobins and *sans-culottes* were arrested, and 1,700 were stripped of all civil rights. Prison camps were established in the Seychelles and French Guiana. Apart from the 'Day of the Black Collars', when *sans-culottes* and some soldiers used the sixth anniversary of the storming of the Bastille to take momentary revenge on *jeunesse dorée*, the Parisian popular movement was silenced. In the Midi, 'Companies of Jesus and the Sun' singled out Jacobins for execution. The determination with which the Convention resolved to end the popular challenge was above all apparent in its constitutional arrangements, for there could now be no question of returning to the egalitarian democracy of the Constitution of 1793. The political agenda of the Convention was made plain by its president, Boissy d'Anglas:

> We should be ruled by the best citizens ... with very few exceptions, you will find such men only amongst those who own some property, and are thus attached to the land in which it lies, to the laws which protect it ... who owe to their property, and to the affluence that it affords, the education which has fitted them to discuss widely and equitably the advantages and disadvantages of the laws which determine the fate of their country.

The Constitution of the year III (August 1795) accordingly restricted participation in electoral assemblies by wealth and education as well as gender, and sharply restricted access to electoral colleges and eligibility by wealth and age. Political life was defined as voting: petitions, clubs and even unarmed demonstrations were banned. Social rights were stripped away. It was plain that only those with an adequate stake in society could be trusted to govern: that is, wealthy, educated, middle-aged and married males:

> 3. Equality is a circumstance in which the law is the same for all … .
> 8. The cultivation of land, all production, every means of labour, and the entire social order are dependent on the maintenance of property.[44]

A subsequent decree required that two-thirds of the incoming legislature were to be chosen from the men of the Convention. In its essentials, this Constitution was a return to the provisions of the Constitution of 1791: France was again to be governed by representative, parliamentary government based on a property qualification and the safeguarding of economic and civil liberties. Equality was to be restricted to equality before the law. In this sense, the Constitution marks the end of the Revolution. To be sure, there were differences between the Constitutions of 1791 and 1795. The regime of the Directory was to be republican, not monarchical, and religious divisions were to be resolved by separating Church and State. Gone, too, was the optimism of the bourgeois idealism of 1791, that with the liberation of human creativity all could aspire to the 'active' exercise of their capabilities: the men of 1795 now appended a declaration of 'duties' to their constitution, exhorting respect for the law, the family and property.

The question remained whether, after six years of conflict, participation and sacrifice, the exclusions and limitations imposed by the chastened republican bourgeoisie could succeed in achieving social and political stability by simultaneously quietening urban and rural working people, and excluding royalists.

4

The Consolidation of Post-Revolutionary Society, 1795–1815

In the late eighteenth century, Collioure was a small, bustling Catalan town, most of whose 2,300 inhabitants survived from wine-growing, fishing and the coastal trade – whether legal or clandestine – within the Mediterranean. Catalans, like the Flemish, Alsatians, Provençaux and Basques of other frontier regions, had directly felt the shattering impact of the Republic's desperate struggle for survival. With the local French garrison, the people of Collioure had resisted a Spanish siege from May to December 1793 before succumbing and being occupied until Jacobin armies recaptured the town in May 1794. In January 1795, the mayor wrote to the Convention of the effects of occupation: 'whether by our brave brothers in arms or by the slaves of the tyrant of Castille. The fury that the latter demonstrated against the poor inhabitants during their six months' stay in the commune was carried to the limit, their countryside ruined, their crops torn out, their houses pillaged or destroyed.'[1] His urgent plea captured the nationwide longing for a politics of reconstruction and, above all, for an end to the exactions of war; he hoped, too, for a resolution of the deadly schism in the Church (Collioure's ten priests and monks had emigrated) and of the problem of the *émigrés* (84 Colliourencs had fled to Spain in May 1794), and perhaps also for the implementation of the Jacobin Constitution of 1793 which had been translated into Catalan and enthusiastically received during the siege.

The devastated townspeople were granted tax relief to help them rebuild their houses and farms and also took their own steps to reconstitute households fractured by death and emigration. In the nine months after July 1794, there were three times as many marriages as in an average year, and the partners were younger than usual. The deeper longings of the community could not be answered, for two general reasons. First, six years of upheaval, sacrifices and internal conflict had left a local legacy of engrained bitterness. Secondly, the class-conscious bourgeois of the Thermidorian Convention and, after October 1795, of the Directory practised a politics of social consolidation which sought to recreate France in their own image. Desperate to avoid the twin perils of royalist counter-revolution and Jacobin popular democracy, the Directory pursued religious, military, economic and social policies which could rely at the local level only on a narrow base of support. The popular response to this 'bourgeois republic' varied widely in form and political content, but was everywhere visceral in its tone.[2]

By excluding royalists and the poor from the political process and by restricting that process to electoral participation, the Directory sought to create a republican regime based on 'capacity' and a stake in society. To avoid a strong executive with its Jacobin taints, there were to be frequent partial elections to the Council of Five Hundred and rotation of executive authority. This combination of a narrow social base and internal instability made the regime resort to draconian repression of alternatives and to a use of military force which was to be fatal. Hence, on the one hand, the regime declared advocacy of the 1793 Constitution to be a capital offence and in March 1796 sharply restricted freedom of the press and association, after calling upon Napoleon Bonaparte to forcibly close the Panthéon Club in Paris which had attracted 3,000 Jacobins. On the other, it called on the military to suppress the attempted royalist coup of 5 October 1795 (13 Vendémiaire An IV), just as it had against the rising of the *sans-culottes* several months earlier.

The mass mobilization for war in 1792–4 had engendered an identification of the Republic and the soldier-citizen; now, in 1795, the military was emerging as a professional army called on to defend a regime with narrow popular support. In the process, the regime further alienated people already outraged by its callousness towards the poor. As Nicolas Ruault wrote to his brother on 14 October: 'The cannon which struck down the royalists and the discontented also killed love of the Republic in a great number of hearts … . The Convention has just made itself dependent on soldiers who will perhaps tomorrow create an *imperator*, a Caesar.'[3] Ruault was prescient, but the royalist coup had also failed because Parisian working people, no matter how resentful towards the bourgeois republic, refused to throw in their lot with royalism. Many working people elsewhere had, however, come to regret the passing of the union of throne and altar, if not of the *ancien régime* itself.

The Directory inherited a massive religious problem.[4] Not only had most priests refused or retracted an oath of allegiance to the Civil Constitution of the Clergy in 1791, but the subsequent exile, imprisonment or execution of these priests had created a vengeful, embittered clerical army on France's borders. In many areas constitutional clergy had been unable to overcome local resentment at the departure of the 'bons curés' and in any case were simply too few to minister to spiritual needs: in 1796, there were only perhaps 15,000 for France's 40,000 parishes. For the men of the Directory, the religious problem was above all one of public order: mistrustful of 'fanaticism' but conscious of a widespread yearning for a reconstitution of the spiritual community, the regime allowed the reopening of churches closed during the Terror (30 May 1795/11 Prairial An III) and allowed *émigré* priests to return (24 August 1796/7 Fructidor An IV), but only on condition that they took a civic oath. Religious observance was to be a purely private matter: no religious displays were permitted outside the church, and the regime continued the Convention's separation of Church and State. The Church was to be sustained by the alms of the faithful.

These years were remarkable for a construction from below of a new Catholicism. This renaissance testifies to the widespread resilience of religious faith, but is no less significant for what it revealed of regional and gender variations. This great surge in populist religiosity was above all the work of women, and was at its strongest in certain rural areas (such as parts of the west, Normandy and the south-west) where huge proportions of priests had emigrated, and provincial cities (Bayeux, Arles, Mende, Rouen, Toulouse) where the collapse of the institutions of the *ancien régime* had left women particularly vulnerable to unemployment and destitution. For example, in Bayeux in April 1796, a crowd of furious women invaded the cathedral – converted into a 'temple of reason' during the Terror – and dashed a bust of Rousseau to the floor to cries of 'When the good Lord was there we had bread!' There was no necessary correlation between this yearning for familar religious rituals and antipathy to the Republic: in the Yonne, for example, the devout insisted that they were republicans exercising constitutional guarantees of religious freedom. The schoolteacher of Souday (Loir-et-Cher) resigned because his attempt to replace religious with republican texts led parents to retort: 'we find our children educated enough and we are taking them from you straight away'; Sister Duffan, on the other hand, wanted her Catholic school to form: 'good Christians and good republicans... for I am far from thinking these two titles incompatible ... . I find in the Gospel the purest maxims of the republican code.'[5]

By 1796, the Catholic Church was irrevocably shorn of its landed wealth, its privileges, its monopoly and much of its social authority. Whatever the reasons for female religiosity, men in general were far less likely to return so passionately to the Church: boys born after 1785 would not have attended parish schools, men born after 1770 had served in secular military units, and the republican calendar itself legitimized an attitude to Sunday as a day like any other. In these ways, a gender-based difference in religiosity, already apparent before the Revolution, was widened. Women, often mistrustful of constitutional clergy and tired of waiting for *émigré* priests to overcome their scruples, expressed a populist religiosity which was profound and self-reliant. Communal authorities were forced to reopen churches, as were those who had bought them as national property, venerable lay people said *'messes blanches'* while midwives baptized the newborn, Sundays were observed as the day of rest rather than the *décadi*, and emptied church treasuries were filled with salvaged relics and venerated non-Christian objects of devotion.

Shaken by the widespread and often violent contestation by devout women of the civic authority of local representatives of the regime, the Directory attempted in 1798 to intimidate 'disloyal' priests into hiding but with negligible impact on a religiosity which was less general but more intense than a decade earlier. Central to the regime's unease at resurgent Catholicism was the continued presence on foreign soil of huge numbers of *émigrés* and unnerving electoral signs that those eligible to vote for deputies were politically open to a return of monarchy. For, while the Jacobin armies had succeeded in expelling counter-revolutionary armies from French soil, the war – and with it the problem of the *émigrés* – continued.[6]

The same men who in 1792 had advocated wars of revolutionary liberation as the solution to foreign animosity and internal division now conducted foreign affairs in an essentially pragmatic and expansionist manner. The army was now smaller (382,000 in 1797 compared with 732,000 in August 1794), and largely composed of conscripts.[7] Lack of adequate supplies led to mutinies in Belgium, Holland and Italy, and to officers turning a blind eye to troops stealing. Whereas the Jacobins of 1793–4 had insisted on the incompatibility of new France and old Europe, the Directory's peace treaties with Prussia (April 1795) and Spain (July 1795), and the commercial and naval treaty signed with the latter in August 1796, were couched in terms which assumed the coexistence of sovereign states. With the creation of 'sister' Republics in the Low Countries in 1795, these treaties signalled the transition from a war of revolutionary survival to one of expansion and negotiation. The welcome extended to 'enlightened' foreigners in 1792 had given way under the Terror to surveillance and suspicion; now a series of laws, such as that of February 1798 empowering officials to expel foreigners from ports, codified the rights of the State over the right of free entry and asylum.[8] Moreover, conflict with Britain and Austria continued: while a peace with the latter was signed at Campo-Formio on 18 October 1797 (27 Vendémiaire An VI), hostilities recommenced in Italy in 1798. This, together with the extension of war with Britain into Ireland and Egypt, convinced the Directory that irregular army levies had to be replaced by an annual conscription of single men aged 20–5 years (the Jourdan Law, 5 September 1798/19 Fructidor An VI).

This law sharply intensified resentment of military service because it increased the numbers of healthy young men removed from the pool of household labour to fight on foreign, often distant, soil and because it introduced a system of 'replacements', whereby wealthy conscripts could buy a substitute from the poor or unemployed who had escaped the ballot. Again, those regions where the hold of the royal state before 1789 had been weakest (such as parts of the Massif Central, Brittany and the west) or which had been incorporated more recently into the state (the Pyrenees, parts of the south-east), particularly resented the deeper intrusion of the State's exactions. Resistance to conscription often became part of a complex of refusal involving religious and ethnic antipathies: in Brittany and the west violent opposition known as *chouannerie* proved to be ineradicable.[9] In areas far from Paris, *insoumission* (refusal of conscripts to join the army) became endemic, often with the tacit approval of most of the community: *insoumis* continued to live and work as before, disappearing only when police appeared. Young men also sought to avoid conscription by self-mutilation or by arranged marriages (for elderly women, the new availability of labour could be an adequate compensation). Occasionally, attempts were made to thwart military bureaucracy by destroying birth records, as on the night of 5 Nivôse An VII (Christmas 1799), when the town hall of Saint-Girons (Ariège) was destroyed by fire, and with it the district's civil registers. Resistance was most durable when it had general community support. In rural areas, where officials and the dwindling number of supporters of the regime were likely to be involved in agriculture, the use of threats, arson, and other destruction of property could intimidate officials into inaction. By 1798, many parts of the west, the Massif Central and the Pyrenees were virtually ungovernable.

The regime's unpopularity and the cynicism with which it had excluded the great majority of people from an effective political voice resulted in a resistance of a different type, that of a refusal to participate: in the national by-elections of October 1795, only about 15 per cent of the 30,000 wealthy voters went to the polls (and elected royalists almost exclusively). The wider electorate for local elections often boycotted polls as a sign of their opposition to the bourgeois republic. This withdrawal of peasants and artisans from formal political life did not, however, represent a hiatus in popular politics. In the Midi, smouldering animosities from the early years of the Revolution and before were ignited by the policies of the Directory into direct attacks on the persons and property of Jacobins or the local agents of the new regime. Here and in the west, up to 2,000 Jacobins were killed by 'white Terror' gangs: the victims were usually wealthy purchasers of nationalized property, and were often Protestants.[10]

Underpinning the interlocking tensions of religious resurgence and ecclesiastical disorganization, desertion and *insoumission*, political abstention and bitter feuds, were the Directory's economic policies. In an economy still on a war footing, the abandonment of price controls in December 1794 had unleashed a massive spurt of inflation. By October 1795, the *assignat's* purchasing power stood at just 0.75 per cent of its face value; by the following February, when the paper currency was abandoned, it was just 0.25 per cent. The difficulties for urban wage-earners created by unchecked price rises were worsened by the harvest failure in autumn 1795. Arguably the worst harvest of the century, and followed by a severe winter, the great subsistence crisis of 1795–6 intensified the volatility of popular responses to the Directory.

Resolutely committed to a *laissez-faire* economy, the regime also sought to impose agrarian individualism and legal hegemony for the rights of private property. No government since 1789 had been willing to confront directly the ancient mesh of communal controls over forest resources, gleaning, commons, use of uncultivated land, and rights of access across private land. Now the Directory acted to legislate for the priority of the rights of the individual owner of private property in forests and on harvested or uncultivated land, and encouraged the sale of common lands by auction. At the same time that political power at the local level was hardening in the hands of the wealthiest, the remaining *émigré* land came onto the market. Earlier sales of such land had often been to the less wealthy, favoured by Jacobin policies allowing subdivision and long-term repayments. Now, rampant inflation and a return to larger-scale sales advantaged those with ready savings. Tenant-farmers and better-off peasants were also able to take advantage of the escalating prices paid for their produce to buy land, clear taxes, and pay off leases. In contrast, subsistence-oriented leasers of small plots faced rising rents as landowners began to reimpose the 'bourgeois tithe', adding the value of the old tithe paid to the Church to the rents they charged.[11] The regime continued the major revolutionary forms of taxation – on land and personal wealth – but added to them a business tax and a tax on doors and windows; the social effects of these new taxes on wealth were more than offset by the reintroduction of indirect taxes on essentials, levied at town gates.

The Directory's search for a viable social basis of support led it to vacillate in its political direction; however, its social policies reveal a far more consistent set of assumptions. In education, its reliance on fees rather than state funding to support primary education restricted the number of children attending state schools and ensured that church schools were more common. In the Year VI, for example, private schools outnumbered state schools by 99 to 11 in the Charente and by 138 to 23 in the Bas-Rhin, and communes without either were in a majority. (However, a recent survey of 259 of these private schools has found that 44 per cent of them, whether run by lay teachers or constitutional clergy, were overtly republican in pedagogical content).[12]

The Directory reversed the Convention's policy of nationalized hospitals and state responsibilities for welfare. In the Year V local boards were given responsibility for hospital administration, and welfare again became based on private charity, despite the pleas of hospitals that they needed state aid because they had lost their pre-revolutionary rights to levy dues on local communities. The regime's philosophy of individual responsibility underscored class antipathies more sharply than at any other period of the Revolution. In sharp contrast to such *laissez-faire* attitudes, however, it reintroduced *ancien-régime* controls over prostitution, as always a last resort for young women migrants to Paris. Prostitutes were placed outside the law but were required to register with police and to work in closed and discreet brothels to control the spread of syphilis and to make public thoroughfares more 'respectable'. No controls were placed on their clients.[13]

The dominant cultural values of these years, symbolized by the construction of a new stock exchange in the capital, were mirrored in literary production. After the hiatus of the Terror, the publication of new books reached pre-revolutionary levels of 815 by 1799; among them were 174 new novels, compared with 99 in 1788 and 16 in 1794. These were predominantly pastoral love-stories, sentimental intrigues and mysteries, but there was also a large number of novels with a specifically religious, educational or moralizing tone. The number of new newspapers declined to 42 (from 226 in 1790 and 78 in 1793) and of political songs to 90 in 1799 and 25 in 1800 (from 701 in 1794). These years also saw the *de facto* end of *tutoiement* as a political form of address, of revolutionary names and even the *décadi* in many areas; on the other hand, the regime's official festivals – for example, that of Old Age – failed to spark popular enthusiasm.[14]

By its religious, military, economic and social policies, the Directory had further alienated large numbers of people already excluded from legal forms of voicing grievances. By 1797, communities, individuals and clandestine movements were utilizing a rich array of illegal forms of protest, ranging from the simple refusal to obey to elaborate programmes for radical change. In Collioure, on 2 April 1797 (13 Germinal An V), a huge crowd of women returning from mass in a nearby village threatened the officer in charge of a grain store located in a former Dominican chapel, demanding both bread and the reopening of the chapel. According to Jacques Xinxet, the mayor and local notary, 'fanaticism, the primary source of all [their] problems', was to blame: 'let's cut the evil at the roots if we want to have internal calm'. The women, poor, devout and hungry, were exhibiting the identification of worship and bread in popular attitudes: 'Give us this day our daily bread'; at the same time, they were expressing a class division between the labouring poor and the bourgeois élite, whose contempt for 'fanaticism' was so evident.[15]

During the same month, hundreds of kilometres to the north, in Vendôme, the trial was taking place of Gracchus Babeuf and 48 of his associates, accused of having plotted to overthrow a lawful government by violent means.[16] The self-educated son of an impoverished Picard tax official, Babeuf had been a radical activist from 1789, whether as a publicist and official in the north-east or as a *sans-culottes* militant in 1793. From his early demands for an income tax, land redistribution (the 'agrarian law'), the full abolition of seigneurial dues, and benefits for soldiers, Babeuf's own intellectual development since 1794 in the Parisian context of economic misery and political repression had led him to advocate a forcible seizure of power to impose the political democracy of the 1793 Constitution and the collectivization of the means of production – indeed, perhaps of work itself. His followers were united more by opposition to the Directory than by revolutionary communism, a programme which in any event had little appeal to *sans-culottes* committed to the redistribution but not social-ization of private property. However, Babeuf's 'Conspiracy of the Equals' was remarkable for the attraction of its political and social radicalism to soldiers, working women and Jacobins.

North-east of Vendôme, property-owners were in the grip of a fear of a different type. Attacks on grain convoys and travellers from the wheat-fields of the Beauce to Paris had always occurred in times of dearth. In 1796–7 this reached spectacular proportions in the *'bande d'Orgères'*, an organised, violent subculture of perhaps 150 men and women of all ages whose 95 forays resulted in 75 murders.[17] Stories of the band's humiliation and violation of their victims and of their subsequent orgies horrified polite society (as did those of the *'chauf-feurs'* of the south, so-called because they burned their victims' feet to extract information). When it was finally broken in 1798, 22 of the band were executed and 24 others sentenced to prison, including 11 women.

What the women of Collioure, Paris and the Beauce might have made of each other we will never know; but all of them, in very different ways, were rebelling against the consolidation of the Revolution in the hands of a distinct class of men prepared to take hard measures to protect their power. The sharp edge of economic deprivation was softened somewhat by several bountiful harvests and a return to metallic currency in 1798, but other sources of antipa-thy remained towards a regime which conscripted poor young men to fight in distant lands while advantaging the well-to-do. Indeed, Donald Sutherland has concluded that most French people were engaged in some form of rebellion against the Republic in these years; however, it was not the Republic as such that was being spurned, but rather the class politics of its self-perpetuating élite.[18] There were, in any case, no organizational or ideological links – other than a hatred for the regime and its bourgeois supporters – between those in opposition in 1795–9: royalist plotters and 'white' terrorists, Babouvists and recalcitrant Jacobins, women protesting for Christ and bread, *chouans*, thieves and deserters from the army.

Despite a good harvest in 1798, the French economy was in tatters: the Bas-Rhin had only 146 master-weavers operating compared with 1,800 in 1790, the Basses-Pyrénées had only 1,200 people employed in the woollens industry compared with 6,000 à decade earlier. Economic resentments and massive popular non-compliance with the demands of the State climaxed in the summer of 1799 in large-scale but uncoordinated royalist risings in the south-west and a resurgence of *chouannerie* in the west in October. Combined with chronic political instability within the narrowing circle of supporters of the regime and Napoleon's successes abroad, the situation was created where some of the great liberals of 1789, such as Talleyrand and Sieyès, were attracted to the promise of a strong executive. On 9–10 November 1799 (18–19 Brumaire An VIII), the Five Hundred were driven out by troops and a decade of parliamentary rule was over.[19] Popular response to the military coup was, in general, one of 'wait and see'. The regime systematically falsified the results of the plebiscite of February 1800 on the coup by doubling the 'yes' votes to over three million and lowering the 'no' votes to 1,500. But within two years of seizing power, Napoleon had met some of the most pressing desires of French people, even if in so doing he created a precedent for the military taking decisive measures when politicians were deemed to be inept.

A decree of 20 October 1800 (29 Vendémiaire An IX) permitted *émigrés* who had not taken up arms to return: then, on 26 April 1802 (6 Floréal An X), the path was opened to all others. While the most intransigent counter-revolutionaries hesitated to acquiesce in the consolidation of a post-revolutionary settlement, the alacrity with which most *émigrés* rushed to return home points to a preparedness to accept the irrevocable demise of the *ancien régime* in return for the chance to rebuild shattered families. Those *émigrés* who refused Napoleon's offer became more intransigent about the conditions on which they would return and – as Napoleon's power was consolidated – more pessimistic about whether this could ever be. The return of the *émigrés* was a highly-charged moment at the local level: not only were many families to which they returned ideologically divided, but every community, no matter how small, contained families who had lost fathers and sons fighting the enemy, now personified by a returning *émigré*. After a decade of exile, noble *émigrés*, for their part, had to face awkward questions from their peers: had it been more courageous to emigrate or to stay? They also had to accommodate themselves to a changed world, the loss of much of their property and social pre-eminence.

With them came the bulk of the nonjuring priests, convinced of the foolishness of the first estate's support for secular reform in 1789 and of the burning need, after ten years of divine retribution, for a purified Catholicism to rechristianize France. Not for the first or last time, Napoleon demonstrated his willingness to accept compromise with the forces of the *ancien régime*, as long as the terms were his: on 15 July 1801 a Concordat was signed with the Papacy, formally celebrated at Easter mass at Notre Dame in 1802. The religious settlement restored the hierarchical basis of clerical appointments under the Pope's authority and recognised Catholicism as 'the religion of the majority of Frenchmen'; at the same time, the re-establishment of state salaries for priests ensured that the regime retained a vital measure of control. Accordingly, in parts of the west in particular, where popular commitment to pre-revolutionary ecclesiastical forms had been central to the massive blood-letting of civil war, the devout refused to accept the compromise and established an untainted *'Petite église'*. In most of the country, however, any hesitation felt towards returning priests because of their desertion of their flocks in 1792 and because of their support for foreign armies was more than overcome by the long-awaited chance to reconstitute parish life.

The Catholic clergy was in a parlous state. Three-quarters of the bishops and priests appointed under the Concordat were refractory clergy, men who were not only embittered by exile but were also aged and often ill-at-ease in the new France. They had to coexist with an energetic female laity and a constitutional clergy shattered by dechristianization, popular disavowal and, now, clerical reaction. The constitutional clergy's experience of the Empire must have been lonely and humiliating: for example, despite his energetic attempts to sustain a church presence in Bayeux during the 1790s, the left-wing cleric Michel Moulland was dispatched to a small parish church in the shadow of the imposing château of Balleroy, from where he wrote self-justifying pleas to his bishop for 25 years.[20]

Above all, Napoleon's early years represented peace. The treaty of Lunéville was signed with Austria on 9 February 1801 (21 Pluviôse An IX) and that of Amiens with Britain on 25 March 1802 (5 Germinal An X). The revolutionary wars, begun as a rapid pre-emptive strike, had lasted one month short of ten years. Their termination offered the chance for deserters and *insoumis* to be amnestied, and for returning *émigrés* and priests to be reintegrated into their communities in a climate of reconciliation. The sunny calm of the summer of 1802 created the perfect conditions for the plebiscite on the new Constitution of the year X, by which Napoleon became Consul for life. The 3.5 million votes cast in its favour were a measure of his popularity at this time. However, from the very outset of his seizure of power three years earlier, it had been evident that the price of stability and reconciliation – indeed, its very strategy – was to be tighter executive authority and centralization, coupled with major concessions to the practices of the *ancien régime*.

Just three months after seizing power, Napoleon had issued a new administrative decree (16 February 1800/28 Pluviôse An VIII) which effectively reduced local government to a rubber stamp: henceforth councils were to restrict themselves to the management of communal finances and resources within rigid formulae of administration. The mayors and deputy-mayors of towns with more than 5,000 people were to be appointed directly by the first Consul, while others were to be named by the prefect of the department. In this way prefects had the powers of *ancien-régime intendants*, and local councils, elected for twenty years on a property qualification, were decidedly less democratic and unfettered than even before the Revolution. The law revealed Napoleon's respect for the social authority of established notables and his mistrust of popular choice. Above all, it demonstrated his conviction that every aspect of public life had to be under the *tutelle* of a hierarchical, unitary system of policing, in both a preventive sense (through public order and surveillance) and punishment.

In establishing his bureaucratic system, Napoleon drew on the experience and powers of the *ancien régime* and Republic, but without the regional diversity of the former or the popular sovereignty of the latter. In other ways, too, Napoleon consolidated the uniformity and universality of revolutionary structures by endowing them with pre-revolutionary authority and hierarchy. Justices of the Peace, one of the most popular of revolutionary innovations, were henceforth to be appointed and their numbers halved, one of the earliest sources of resentment towards the first Consul; moreover, Napoleon's introduction of 'administrative arrest' smacked of *lettres de cachet*. Most importantly, the new parliamentary bodies – the Legislative Corps and the Senate – were essentially consultative chambers, carefully chosen to both reward and incorporate the powerful.[21]

The policing hierarchy of the bureaucracy – its most important internal function – combined the overlapping jurisdictions of the ministries of War, Justice and the Interior. The Minister of the Interior headed a hierarchy in which the most powerful local face of the regime in every department was the prefect, who directed political and civil police and who could also draw on the Minister of War's gendarmerie, 30,000 strong by 1811. The prefect's deputies at the district level were subprefects and, at the bottom of the hierarchy, appointed mayors. Similarly, the Minister of Justice, kept informed about the state of 'public order' by his colleagues, headed a hierarchy of 27 regional *procureurs-généraux* (state prosecutors), a *procureur* in each department and a Justice of the Peace in each canton. These appointed and untenured officials coexisted uneasily with the permanent judiciary who headed a hierarchy of courts from the commune to the national level. Within the ministries, a larger bureaucracy of public officials were emerging as career administrators, fulfilling a function rather than, as before the Revolution, holding office to serve the king. For, despite Napoleon's personal power and directives, one of his legacies was to create a bureaucracy with purposes other than the emperor's will: the development of career structures, permanency of office and the extension of regulations which expressed a distinctive set of assumptions about public order, hierarchy and human nature.[22]

The attitudes of the Napoleonic élite expressed a *mentalité* which assumed a hierarchy of capacity, civilization and race. In 1800, prefectoral responses to a ministerial enquiry into France's regional character and resources resorted to a dualistic imagery, privileging Paris over the provinces, plains over mountains, town over country, bourgeois over peasant, north (except Brittany) over south, French over *patois*, and men over women. To the racial origins of the south ('the people of the Tarn are descended from a mix of races, Gauls, Visigoths, Arabs, Franks and Romans, not to speak of Greeks') were imputed 'character' (the southerner is 'as variable as his climate, he is uncouth, brutal, lively, passionate, lazy or taciturn'). The perceived task of the élite was to eliminate such differences by a combination of 'enlightenment' and order: even the Hautes-Alpes, 'peopled by savages', was capable of being 'civilized'.[23]

The comparative economic and political stability of the Empire facilitated the work of measurers seeking to construct graphic images of the physical, economic and human resources of the new nation. Cartographers and statisticians drew on the Cassini map project aborted early in the Revolution, and on the censuses of 1792–3 and the Year VIII to initiate national registers of property and persons. From 1806 the population was to be enumerated every five years, grouped in lists of families headed by economically active males, categories revealing of élite urban male assumptions. In 1807 the geographer Laprade initiated a cadastral survey of all property in every commune; this massive undertaking, which occupied legions of engineers and technicians until 1850, similarly assumed that, apart from communal property, all land was a privately-owned and used commodity.[24]

The regime also sought to end revolutionary upheaval in the countryside and to halt the environmental degradation accelerated by the Revolution, in particular of the nation's forests. The state of the forests was particularly serious since inhabitants of many highland areas had seized on the overthrow of the Directory, widely perceived as a narrow bourgeois regime, as a pretext for a renewal of illegal tree-felling. The reinforcement of state controls under the Consulate permitted the forest administration to have a series of laws promulgated reorganizing its personnel and re-establishing a centralized forests policy. Forests belonging to communes were placed under the same controls as state forests (law of 9 March 1802/19 Ventôse X), and a year later communes were informed that they had to provide proof of their rights of collective pasturing and wood-collecting in state forests within six months or lose those rights.[25]

The reinforcement of hierarchy in the interests of public order and commerce was mirrored by the deliberate codification of patriarchy in French public life. From the outset of the Revolution women had contested the ambiguity of women's status in the new order: in what senses were they equal citizens, or part of the polity at all? In responding so aggressively towards radical women in 1793, the Jacobins had opened the way for the elaboration of a new ideology of gender, the stereotype of the bourgeois mother of good republican citizens. On the other hand, the extension of some legal rights to women, and above all the use which urban women in particular had made of divorce legislation remained subversive to male power inside and outside the family.

The Napoleonic Code of 21 March 1804, the cornerstone of the regime's administration of civil society, was remarkable for its juxtaposition of the essentials of revolutionary principles with the consolidation of patriarchy. On the one hand, the code assumed a lay society of citizens equal before the law: like the men of 1791 and 1795, those of 1804 imagined a world in which 'talent' would be the rationale of hierarchy and where the exercise of capacity in the use of one's private property was the proof of that talent. On the other, the exercise of talent was to be the preserve of men: married women no longer had the right independently to make contracts or to litigate. They were bound to the authority of fathers, then husbands: henceforth wives could only sue for divorce if their husband's mistress was brought into the marital home. In contrast, a simple act of adultery sufficed for a husband to sue, and the adulterous woman was liable to imprisonment for up to two years.

This ideology of patriarchal authority extended to children, for fathers were authorized to have disobedient offspring imprisoned for one month, if under 16 years, and six months, if 16 to 21. Similarly, the social control employers were able to exercise in the workplace was reinforced by the reimposition of the *ancien-régime* practice of requiring urban workers to carry passbooks *(livrets)* and the strengthening of the Le Chapelier law of 1791 against wage-earners' associations.[26] Building workers who went on strike in 1806 were arrested in their beds, although other workers managed to sustain 90 illegal organizations in Paris during the Empire. The Directory's regulatory regime for prostitutes was tightened: they were now required to attend and pay for medical examinations and to register with the *Bureau des moeurs,* a special section within the Prefecture of Police. Like other workers, they also had to carry cards detailing their identity and place of work.

In social policy, attitudes to leisure and minorities, and the use of public space, the imperial regime expressed its values of social order, hierarchical authority and individual enterprise within the law. Apart from minimal state aid to hospitals and hospices, the Empire continued the Directory's welfare policies, by which the government felt no obligation to the able-bodied unemployed. Such people were left to the care of private and church charities or to their own devices: crime, prostitution and soldiering. As religious teaching orders re-emerged, so the incidence of primary and secondary schooling slowly increased, though not to pre-revolutionary levels: by 1813 there were 35,000 secondary pupils in *lycées*, where they prepared for the *baccalauréat* under military-style discipline, compared with 50,000 before 1789. The Jacobin dream of universal access had long been abandoned through a combination of competitive examinations, fees and fewer scholarships for the poor. Together with specialist colleges and the 60 faculties in Paris and 16 other cities (teaching law, theology, medicine, letters, science and pharmacy), the public secondary schools made up the centrally-controlled Napoleonic 'university'. In 1803 the *Institut* was reorganized, with a return to pre-revolutionary hierarchical organization, and the Academy of Moral and Political Sciences was closed down, symptomatic of the emperor's contempt for 'ideologues'. In the same year, the *ancien-régime* corporate medical system disbanded in 1792–3 was reformed, with tighter controls on permission to practise, a significant step in the professionalization of medicine.[27]

The logical extension of the incorporation of the Church into the regime's hierarchical apparatus of authority and social control was the termination of the revolutionary calendar, at the end of 1805. In this way the attempts of the clergy to recreate the rhythms of the Christian week and year were facilitated, while the particular resonance of revolutionary moments – Ventôse, Thermidor, Germinal – was removed from daily life. Revolutionary festivals were abandoned in favour of commemorations of Napoleon's coronation as emperor (2 December 1804) and his saint's day, on 15 August. In the year VIII, 60 Parisian newspapers were closed down: by 1811 there were only four political papers. In the world of the theatre, too, Napoleon combined a return to the official, élite performance of the *ancien régime* with restrictions on popular expression and dissidence. The great national theatres were subsidized and organized into six specialist functions, while regulations in 1807 permitted only two smaller, tightly-censored theatres to operate from among the 25 formerly catering to more popular audiences. Imperial controls also extended to administrative arrangements for France's 700,000 Protestants and 40,000–50,000 Jews. Lutherans and Calvinists were administratively organized and, from 1804, their ministers were paid by the State. In 1808 'consistories' of rabbis and lay people were appointed (but not paid) by the State to regulate the organization of the Ashkenazim and Sephardic Jews.[28]

Napoleonic reforms of the penal system expressed similar impulses to control and discipline, but less financial restraint: in 1810, eleven million francs was allocated to the prison system and eight new prisons built. Homosexuals were no longer liable to punishment *per se*, but the new penal code exposed them to police harassment through the vague terms of 'offenses against public decency'.[29] The new code also reinstated humiliating punishments, the use of shackles, branding (such as 'R' for recidivists), amputation of a hand, and public exhibition. Political offenders were singled out for transportation, and released prisoners were now to be subject to ongoing supervision. (The consequent discrimination experienced by Valjean, imprisoned throughout the Directory and Empire, who had to carry special identification on release and received half the usual wages as a result, was to be powerfully captured in *Les Misérables* by Victor Hugo, himself a passionate prison-reformer).

Public order, military strategy and assumptions about the ordering of space came together in the Napoleonic creation of a new prefecture for the Vendée, when in 1804 Napoleon decreed that the disordered rubble of La Roche – destroyed by Jacobin armies in 1794 – be restored as the planned town of Napoléonville. The grandiose plan, for a city of 15,000 people, was perfectly rectangular, bisected by wide boulevards and streets leading to three major public spaces: in front of the prefecture, the market, and, largest of all, the place d'Armes for troop reviews. While the town's nomenclature and growth would have a checkered history – in 1851 it still had only 6,000 people – its physical layout was an eloquent élite statement of spatial perceptions of power and the place accorded to administration, commerce and the military.[30]

The peace which had brought such popularity to Napoleon in the early years of his rule had never been total, inside or outside France. In January 1802, 12,000 French troops landed in Saint Domingue to reimpose colonial control: after two years of bloody fighting the first post-colonial black nation – Haiti – was born.[31] Elsewhere, Napoleon reversed the Jacobin abolition of slavery and in 1802 reimposed the *Code noir* of 1685. The code delineated in detail the administration of the selling of slaves 'and other merchandise', sanctioned executions for theft and flight and the removal of children from their mothers, requiring in return only adequate upkeep of slaves while denying them any legal rights. The reintroduction of the code was the sharpest indication of the limitations to the alleged universality of rights proclaimed in revolutionary and Napoleonic legislation.

Popular acceptance that authoritarian rule was the price to pay for peace and economic stability was disillusioned by renewed war with Britain in May 1803, and its rapid extension into an unprecedented military struggle for French *imperium* over a new Europe remodelled along the lines of the Napoleonic Code. (The war was also played out in the Pacific, where Nicolas Baudin's claims to southern Australia, expressed by naming natural features after the

Emperor, could not be contested for years while his English rival Matthew Flinders was detained at Ile-de-France (Mauritius) as an enemy naval officer.) Napoleon's vision of a European order under French hegemony was at the expense of about 900,000 of his own people's lives, and those of probably a greater number of other Europeans who opposed him or who, increasingly, were drafted into his armies. For two million or more Frenchmen who served in the imperial armies, soldiering was a miserable experience: it meant physical exhaustion, fear, boredom, disease and death, overcome only by the romanticized pride at being a survivor. There was also the possibility of plunder, though this was never sanctioned in the way that the removal of art treasures was at the highest level. Soldiering also aroused epidemics of what army doctors described as *'nostalgie'*. This homesickness or *mal du pays* caused many deaths following well-known symptoms: sad appearance, apathy, lack of appetite or sleep, and solitariness. It was particularly common in Egypt in 1799, in the Armée des Alpes in 1800 and in Mayence in 1813–14. While Bretons were notoriously vulnerable, no-one was immune, even while serving in another part of France, as with Burgundians who died in Savoy. Accordingly, imperial officers took pains to pair recruits with a compatriot who also spoke French, to hasten integration and understanding of orders.[32]

Whereas the governments of 1792–4 had appealed to the republican 'virtues', defence of the *patrie* and the common soldier, the Directory and especially the Empire aimed their propaganda at appeals to 'honour', national glory, and the possibilities of promotion and entry into élite corps. For example the *voltigeurs* formed in 1804 (to 'fly about' behind the cavalry) had to be 1.65 m (5′6″) tall and with two years' excellent service, and were excused mundane tasks. A complex system of awards and graded pensions, culminating in the Legion of Honour (first awarded in 1802 for administrative expertise and military prowess), offered the common soldier at least the possibility of status and later security. But for most soldiers – such as the 150,000 on army pensions – life after service, if there was any, was a time of penny-pinching, story-telling and boredom.

The appalling cost of Napoleon's imperial vision was for a long time palatable in France, for the military won an almost uninterrupted series of victories until 1812, and the army and war industries created jobs of a kind for the unemployed. As a former Jacobin who had also been called on to repress street risings, Napoleon knew well the political threat of hungry Parisians and ensured that the capital was adequately provisioned. If urban and rural wage-earners escaped the ballot, they benefited from a shortage of labour which enabled real wages to increase by at least one-quarter under the Empire. There was also an expansion of women's work in mechanized cotton-spinning factories in Paris and material assistance in times of crisis for the 17 per cent of Parisians estimated to be indigent in 1807. In Alsace, too, the continental system, designed to give France economic hegemony over Europe in response to England's naval blockade, was a boon to local industry and commerce until 1813. In inland Normandy and other lace-making areas, distance from the troubled frontiers and the recovery of luxury industries created a durable sense of pride and prosperity. In such areas the emperor personified a heady mix of glory and prosperity.[33]

Napoleon could also call on support from an expanded élite in town and country. While the reimposition of the English naval blockade deepened the difficulties experienced since 1791 by Atlantic and Mediterranean ports, new opportunities were emerging for a *nouvelle bourgeoisie* of military suppliers and for established manufacturers, such as those of Elbeuf, who were prompted to mechanize textile factories. Financial stability was enhanced by the creation in 1800 of the Bank of France (one of whose regents was the former seigneur and then Jacobin, Claude Périer). In rural areas, notables were content with pre-eminence in local affairs and a stable economy, guaranteed by Napoleon's armies being supplied by exactions on foreign lands. Moreover, the system of 'replacement' ensured that notables would never need to be personally exposed to danger. The Napoleonic élite was one which melded material substance through landowning, service to the State through the army and administration, and political reliability. About 28 per cent of mayors were nobles, and 63 per cent of them had fortunes of over 100,000 francs. The new imperial nobility, one-seventh the size of the old, was drawn from the military (59 per cent), officials and notables (39 per cent); only 2 per cent were from the creative arts, commerce and industry. Over one-fifth were already nobles from the *ancien régime*. Similarly, of 281 prefectoral appointees 1800–14, 110 (41 per cent) were *ancien-régime* nobles. Significantly, however, the landed magnates on whom Napoleon drew were increasingly referred to as 'proprietors', rather than nobles or bourgeois, in official discourse: this was to be a unified élite of substance, service and reliability.[34]

This was an élite significantly transformed by the Revolution. In the lower Loire and Rhine regions, old aristocratic families had often remained socially and economically powerful, but now lived within an élite in which political power was shared with new men of bourgeois background. A similar fusing of the hierarchical, ritualized order of the *ancien régime* with the pre-eminence of capacity, efficiency and uniformity of the new order also underpinned the Napoleonic settlement in conquered lands. Napoleon was himself obsessed by the panoply of aristocratic pomp which, for a poor Corsican noble, military triumph alone could never secure. His marriage in 1810 to Marie-Antoinette's niece, Marie-Louise of Austria, was a final repudiation of his republican origins.

Popular resistance to the early years of Napoleonic rule focused on conscription rather than his betrayal of republicanism: from December 1804 to July 1806 alone there were 119 anti-conscription disturbances. But it was above all the invasion of Spain in December 1808 and the inexorable intensification of exactions of men and taxes which generated an 'internal front'. From 1808 the local face of the Empire was frequently the *colonnes mobiles* of gendarmes searching for draft-evaders, and the punitive actions of soldiers and tax-collectors. This was particularly the case in frontier regions, which felt the full force of naval blockades and the passage of troops, and mountain areas resistant to the intrusive demands of the State. Relatives of deserters and *insoumis* were required to pay the costs and wages of a soldier lodged with them; individuals who gave shelter or work to an evader were liable to fines representing six months' pay for a labourer. Families of deserters were required to pay supplementary taxes – in effect to support the *colonne mobile* searching for their young men – or, if delinquent, to see furniture and tools sold at auction, though such auctions were frequently subject to total boycott by small communities. By January 1810, over 267 million francs had been levied in fines, but less than 1 per cent had been collected. From 1808, resistance to the levies of young men and taxes became endemic in much of southern and western France. In 1806–13, officials estimated that there were some 372,000 deserters from the armies and *insoumis*, often in bands who worked, stole and intimidated officials with the complicity of most of the community. At times, a whole commune could declare its resistance, as when the mayor of Larbont (Ariège) publicly burned the birth registers for the period 1751–90 in 1808.[35] Devout Catholics, grateful for the restoration of the Church in 1802, were similarly antagonized in 1809 by the emperor's annexation of the Papal States and virtual house arrest of Pius VII.

The imperial regime depended on territorial expansion for its economic well-being and the continued power of its ruler. At its peak, the Empire consisted of the Low Countries, parts of Germany, the Italian peninsula and Illyrian provinces along the Adriatic, as well as colonial possessions in the West Indies and Indian Ocean. It was buttressed by dependent states (the Grand Duchy of Warsaw, Switzerland and the Confederation of the Rhine) and satellite kingdoms in Italy, Westphalia and Spain. But one of the new Europe's essential weaknesses was the difficulty of successfully responding to Britain's naval blockade: it was their continued trade with Britain which finally led Napoleon to invade Portugal, Spain and Russia and ultimately to overextend the Empire's resources.

As the Empire plunged into the mire of fighting on several fronts, it was forced to rely increasingly on police and censorship: at the peak of the Russian campaign of 1812, Napoleon had to abandon his troops to rush back to Paris to deal with an attempted republican coup. The Russian campaign was ruinous for the regime on both its external and internal fronts. The 422,000 French and foreign soldiers who crossed the Polish border into Russia in June were decimated by the Russian 'scorched-earth' policy and reduced by three-quarters when they took Moscow in September. The return, in temperatures as low as $-30\,°C$, was horrific: no more than 10,000 returned to Poland in December. By the time Napoleon regrouped his forces at Leipzig, in October 1813, morale and discipline was in disarray. Twenty eye-witnesses, who observed the ensuing battle, 'the most shocking sight that eye can ever behold', described how: 'wounded French soldiers crawled to the already putrid carcasses of horses... and greedily regaled themselves with the carrion ... . They even tore the flesh from human limbs, and broiled it to satisfy the cravings of appetite; nay, what is almost incredible, the very dunghills were searched for undigested fragments to devour.'[36] At the same time, in Spain, French troops were being harried by the English army and the Spanish resistance to the foothills of the Pyrenees.

The internal price for these defeats was a further increase in the size of annual and supplementary conscription levies, and the exaction of an extra 11.5 per cent of all taxes, followed by an additional 22.6 per cent on land taxes. In March 1813, Napoleon decreed the sale of common lands, estimated to be worth 370 million francs; however, local resistance meant that only 50 million francs was realized. The cost to Napoleon was that many regions of France again became virtually ungovernable; there is a distinct parallel between 1810–14 and 1797–9.

Some of the opposition was republican: even near Paris, the prefect of the Seine-Inférieure reported in November 1813: 'I have seen children from 12 to 15 dancing to the tune of the "Carmagnole", and young men sing the "Marseillaise".' But, as in 1799, an exhausted country desired nothing more strongly than peace. Napoleon's abdication (6 April 1814) and the first Treaty of Paris (1 May) focused hopes for an end to war and to an inquisitorial regime on a return of the Bourbons under Louis XVIII. Municipal councils rushed to declare their support for their new sovereign in a massive *sauve qui peut* operation, but it was above all the chance to escape from the Empire's exactions of men and money which underpinned the acquiescence of most people in the Restoration. This acquiescence was conditional. The restored monarchy's decision to allow free trade in grain with Europe despite a poor harvest in 1813, its insistence on the continued collection of taxes, and, after an initial amnesty for deserters, renewed searches for draft-evaders from February 1815 quickly took the shine off Louis's return. In Collioure, a band of 40 deserters had taunted former imperial officials in July 1814 with chants of 'You will pay you rogues, you will pay you scum, for the persecution of the poor deserters.' However, in August, a huge crowd of 1,400 men, women and children gathered to prevent the export of grain to Spain, and by December there was nightly singing of the refrain, 'Let's go, comrades, and have done with this damn Bourbon family!'

While councils and notables again moved to transfer their allegiance to Napoleon following his escape from Elba and re-entry into Paris in March 1815, popular fears of renewed military demands were soon realized. A desperate – and unrealized – mobilization now included married veterans and those under 1.57 m in height who were formerly exempt. As if conscious of the alienation of huge numbers of people from his regime since 1803, Napoleon immediately posed as a man of the people, a democrat forced into authoritarian rule by the hostility of Britain and its allies. A referendum proposing democratic reform brought 20 per cent of adult males to the polls, and approved the changes by 1.5 million votes to 5,000. The first elections by manhood suffrage since 1794 were held for local councils on 22 May.

Napoleon's apparent conversion to democracy ultimately meant that, following his final defeat at Waterloo on 22 June, the allies would be far less conciliatory: foreign troops occupied 61 northern, eastern and southern departments, and, at the second Treaty of Paris in November, many of Napoleon's conquests were reversed. Internally, the Second Restoration unleashed a massive purge of administrative personnel: if in 1814 Louis XVIII had accepted the hasty conversion of office-holders as symbolic of their profound royalism, he was now under no such illusions. Some 153 prefects and subprefects were dismissed and 70 transferred, and up to one-third of other officials (perhaps 80,000 in all) were removed at every level down to village mayors. Louis's provincial supporters went even further. News of Waterloo unleashed violent reprisals in coastal cities such as Marseille, Bordeaux and Toulon. In Marseille on 24 June, 50 people were killed, 200 injured and

80 houses and shops burnt down. On 19 August royalists smashed down the doors of the Protestant temple in Saint-Affrique (Aveyron); the church was emptied of its furnishings and the fires from the burning of more than a hundred 3-metre-long benches lit the sky for several nights. Some 6,000 people were sentenced by rapidly-convened courts under the supervision of Count Robert Joseph MacCarthy; in the Midi, where long-standing religious hostilities and the purges after the federalist revolts of 1793 and the fall of the Jacobins in 1794 had fused into angry hatreds, some 2,000–3,000 people were summarily executed.[37]

Louis had not originally been concerned to root out the Napoleonic cancer, convinced as he was that an exhausted and penitent nation would henceforth be united through his person. His Charter of 1814, which was to be the foundation stone of the Restoration, is revealing of his assumption of legitimate right to rule, but at the same time is a statement of the irreversible transformation wrought by the Revolution. On the one hand, the preamble – largely Louis's own work – proclaimed that 'complete authority in France is vested in the person of the king'; the Charter, signed in the 'nineteenth year of our reign', assumed that, despite the nightmare of political turmoil, the divinely-sanctioned crown had passed directly from Louis XVI and the young Louis XVII who had died in prison in 1795. However, the actual text of the Charter – drafted with a committee of politicians – is redolent of revolutionary change. Louis's heart may have been in the *ancien régime* but it was apparent that the most viable basis for political harmony would be a constitutional monarchy, albeit with a stronger executive than that of the early years of the Revolution. The first articles of the Charter proclaimed equality before the law, 'careers open to talent' and the end of privilege. While the old nobility were to reassume their titles and honours, and while the king was to appoint a House of Peers, the Napoleonic nobility was to remain; moreover, any hopes the nobility may have had of resuming the material substance of seigneurialism were dashed. With the Church, *émigré* nobles were to recognize the sale of 'national' lands under the Revolution; the Church was to resume its position as the State religion, but other denominations were to be tolerated and paid for by the State. Louis retained executive powers of veto and appointment, but ultimately would have to govern in harmony with a Chamber of Deputies elected on a narrow property franchise. The radical remaking of the institutional map of France by the National Assembly in 1789–91 was unquestioned.

There is no doubt that in political, ideological and even social terms, Louis regarded the years 1789–1814 as one revolution, and accepted that a return to legitimate royal authority had to be within an historic compromise. Restored France was to be a land in which would be recognised both the virtues of material success and the honour due to the aristocracy; both the forms of constitutional, parliamentary rule and the paternalistic authority of the king; both the claims of a citizenry equal before the law and a hierarchy of property and status. A revolutionary transformation, to be sure, but, in the end, was it no more than the entry, at enormous cost, of a new élite into the old?

5

The Social Consequences
of the Revolution

From the point of view of the working people of town and country, how 'revolutionary' had been the experience of 25 years of Revolution and Empire? To be sure, French people had experienced years of political upheaval and uncertainty but, in the end, was this just a time of dashed hopes and massive sacrifices, whether for national military security or, after 1795, for the territorial dreams of the Directory and Napoleon? Well over one million French people – not to mention those from other countries – had died in internal and external wars between 1792 and 1815: when the bloodshed finally abated, could the survivors only hope to reconstitute the essentials of daily life as they had been in the 1780s?

Responses to these questions go to the heart of important and often acrimonious divisions among historians.[1] For the Marxist historian Albert Soboul, writing in 1962, the Revolution was profoundly revolutionary in its short and long-term consequences: 'A classic bourgeois revolution, its uncompromising abolition of the feudal system and the seigneurial régime make it the starting-point for capitalist society and the liberal representative system in the history of France.'[2] Moreover, argued Soboul, the *sans-culottes* and the Babouvists in particular twice tried to push the Revolution beyond its bourgeois limits, prefiguring a time – and this is the heart of the political acrimony – when industrial expansion would enable a larger, socialist working-class to remake the world in its turn.

Since the mid-1950s, the collapse of the political authority of Marxism has encouraged 'revisionist' historians to dispute long-accepted Marxist certainties about the origins, nature and significance of the Revolution. They have contested the explanation of the Revolution as the political resolution of a long-term and deep-seated social crisis, arguing instead that it was the result of short-term fiscal and political mismanagement; nor do they see the increasing violence of the Revolution as simply a regrettable but necessary response to counter-revolution. Most important of all, they dispute Marxist conclusions that the Revolution was a bourgeois and peasant triumph which cleared the way for the flowering of a capitalist economy. In response, Soboul, Gwynne Lewis and other Marxist historians have dismissed this revisionist or 'minimalist' perspective as born of a political antipathy to the possibilities of revolutionary transformation, in Soboul's words, 'the vain attempts to deny the French

Revolution – that dangerous precedent – its historical reality and its specific social and national character'.

The 'minimalist' approach to the social significance of the Revolution is lucidly articulated by Roger Price: 'In political and ideological terms the Revolution was no doubt of crucial importance, but humanity was not transformed thereby. Most of the population continued to be subject to the age-old constraints of their environment. At the end of all the political upheavals of the Revolution and Empire little had changed in the daily life of most Frenchmen.'[3] From this perspective, fundamental changes to the structures of daily life were simply beyond the reach of political reformers. Across the English Channel, the years 1780–1830 saw a 'revolution' of a different type: there, more gradual but profound transformations to industry and agriculture generated structural changes which left nothing untouched, from the nature of work to demographic patterns, from urban life to crime, protest and family life. Could it not be argued that similarly profound changes in France would have to wait for parallel changes to economic structures in the half-century after 1830?

Certainly, all historians agree that French political culture had been irrevocably transformed, and that the restoration of monarchy could not reverse assumptions of citizenship, even if democratic republicanism could be outlawed.[4] The interaction of a new political language, the search for a symbolism of regeneration and republicanism, and the experience of collective political practices bequeathed a rich legacy of meanings to the idea of citizenship. The years after 1788 unleashed an unprecedented outpouring of the printed word: hundreds of newspapers, perhaps one thousand plays and many thousands of brochures and handbills. Accompanying the heroic canvases of David was a proliferation of popular art in the form of woodcuts, prints and paintings. Writing and painting as forms of revolutionary action were paralleled by the uses made of the decorative arts and festivals, bringing together sculpture, dress, architecture, singing and dancing, and with the populace as actor. Collective practices, from national assemblies to thousands of clubs, section meetings and 40,000 local councils, introduced millions of people to the language and forms of popular sovereignty. Malcolm Crook has estimated that about three million men had been involved in voting across the revolutionary decade; indeed, there were so many elections (several per year), and such lengthy voting procedures, that a certain lassitude developed.[5]

The meaning of this new political culture varied by class, gender and region; it also left a legacy of contrasting ideologies, none of which could claim to represent the aspirations of a majority of French people. Those liberal nobles and the great mass of parish priests who had thrown their weight behind the third estate in 1789 had experienced a protracted nightmare, one which made them deeply antipathetic towards secular, democratic, egalitarian ideas throughout the ensuing century. While Bonapartism and Jacobinism claimed the mantle of popular sovereignty, both were ambiguous about the forms democratic government should take. The memory of Napoleon cast a shadow of the strong man who could slice through the vacillation and verbiage of politicians, if needs be with the army. The Jacobin tradition of militant republicanism remained vague about the role of a strong executive, the rights of insurrection in the name of the people, and, above all, about the relationship between Paris and the 82 other departments. Memories of the Terror, the civil war in the Vendée, and of mass conscription and war were etched deep into the memories of every individual and community.[6] The discovery of masses of bones in Lucs-Vendée by the parish priest in 1860 was to result in another myth, still potent today, of the 'Bethlehem of the Vendée', according to which 564 women, 107 children and many men were massacred on a single day, on 28 February 1794.[7] French people were to remain divided about the political system best able to reconcile authority, liberty and equality. Was economic freedom a necessary corollary of – or inimical to – civil liberties? Could these liberties be reconciled with social equality? And how was 'equality' to be understood: as equality before the law, of political rights, of social status, of economic well-being, of the races, of the sexes?

Whatever the importance of these changes to political culture, 'minimalists' have argued that the essentials of daily life emerged largely unchanged: patterns of work, the position of the poor, social inequalities, and the inferior status of women. First, most French people in 1815 remained, like their parents, owners of small plots, tenants and sharecroppers. As in part a victory for peasant landowners, the Revolution has been seen by historians of all shades as retarding the transition to agrarian capitalism.[8] The 1790 partible inheritance law, further codified by Napoleon, ensured that farms would be constantly threatened by subdivision (*morcellement*). Decisions taken during the Terror, finally to abolish compensation due to nobles for the end of feudal dues and to make *émigré* land available in small plots at low rates of repayment, encouraged small owners to stay on the land.

In urban areas, too, work continued in small workplaces, where masters worked side by side with three or four skilled journeymen and apprentices. It could be argued that the urban *menu peuple* had sacrificed most and gained least. Not only had their dreams of property redistribution been shattered, like those of the poorer peasantry, but a major grievance in 1789, indirect taxation, had been reintroduced and customs-houses ringing cities and towns had been re-erected. The *laissez-faire, laissez-passer* legislation of the Revolution, notably the Le Chapelier law of June 1791, had if anything left them more vulnerable to the oscillations of a 'free' market and the whims of employers whose authority had been strengthened by the reintroduction of the *livret*. Moments of popular power and hope left potent traces in the collective memories of descendants of *sans-culottes* and sections of the peasantry. Even here, however, it could be argued that such memories stifled peaceful reform for many decades and that, for working people, memories of 1792–4 were to be cold comfort for dashed expectations of real social change. The descendants of the radicals of the 1790s had to wait many decades for the realization of such hopes: until 1848 for the abolition of slavery and the implementation of manhood suffrage (for women not until 1944), until 1864 for the right to strike and 20 years more for the right to form unions, until the 1880s for free, secular and compulsory education, and until the early twentieth century for an income tax and social welfare provisions for the sick, the elderly and the unemployed.

Secondly, whatever the grand schemes and principles of the Jacobins, the destitute continued to constitute a major urban and rural underclass swollen in times of crisis by poorer labourers and workers. The realization by the National Assembly that poverty was not simply the result of the church's charity, and that local government could simply not cope with poor relief, had generated a series of work schemes and temporary relief measures which were always piecemeal and never adequately financed by governments preoccupied with war. The hungry years after 1794, when the collapse of economic regulation coincided with harvest failure, exposed the poor to a starvation against which the charity of parish clergy with fewer resources could never be adequate protection. Only in the care of abandoned children was there an ongoing assumption by the State of responsibility for social welfare. Artisans could respond to threats posed by free enterprise by new organizations – in 1803 the glove-workers of Grenoble created the first mutual-aid society in France – but the poor remained particularly vulnerable.[9]

Thirdly, France in 1815 remained a sharply inegalitarian, hierarchical society, one in which most *ancien-régime* nobles continued to be eminent. According to Donald Greer, 13,925 noble males over 12 years of age had emigrated; in all, 1,158 noble men and women were executed during the Terror. But even if one accepts Chaussinand-Nogaret's low estimate of a total of some 125,000 nobles in the 1780s, it is clear that the Revolution was not a holocaust of nobles.[10] The rhythm of the Revolution may be encapsulated in the struggle over the meaning of 'equality', but in the end was restricted to equality before the law. In the new France, most nobles retained the bulk of their property and remained wealthy and powerful, sustained by a bitterly anti-revolutionary clergy and a new élite literature of 'romanticism' which emphasized the forces of emotion and tradition and the poverty of secular rationalism.

In the colonies, too, the pre-revolutionary hierarchies of race were reimposed, with one exception. In January 1802, 12,000 French troops landed in Saint-Domingue to reimpose colonial control; after two years of bloody fighting the first post-colonial black nation – Haiti – was born. Elsewhere, however, Napoleon reversed the Jacobin abolition of slavery in 1794 and in 1802 reintroduced the *Code noir* of 1685, which denied slaves legal recourse and assumed their children to be the slave owner's property. The slave trade would not be abolished until 1815–18, slavery itself not until 1848.

Finally, 'minimalists' argue that the status of women emerged little changed, despite the role of women as the lynch-pin of the family economy and the extraordinary strength they had injected into the early years of the Revolution. Only the right to inherit equally and to sign legal contracts survived the Empire. The 1792 divorce laws were sharply curtailed by Napoleon and finally abolished in 1816; Napoleon also abolished the single mother's right to identify and make claims upon the father of her child. The exhortation of revolutionaries to a harmonious and peaceful family life could not erode a tradition of domestic violence *('correction modérée')* to which men resorted. The bourgeois image of the republican mother, developed under Napoleon into a model of frail femininity governed by laws of 'nature', was both a contradiction of the imperatives of survival for working women and a direct repudiation of the practice of participation in 1790–3. Many noblewomen, too, shunned the pre-revolutionary public world of the salon and adopted the domestic ideal as the price to be paid for consolidating shattered families and restoring social authority by moral example.

The ambiguities in men's attitudes to women – drawing on engrained assumptions about 'women's nature' – are also evident in revolutionary iconography: the serene Virgin Mary of *ancien-régime* imagery gave way to the Marianne of the Republic, now dressed in classical garb and liberty cap, but still a feminine allegory watching protectively but passively over active men. Lynn Hunt, Joan Landes and others have argued that despite, or because of, the political challenge of radical women, the transition from absolutism – under which all were subjects of the king – to a republican fraternity of male citizens had in fact reinforced the subordinate political position of women.[11]

The corollary of this 'minimalist' view of the significance of the Revolution is that those few changes it made to French society were simply not worth the cost: the Revolution was unnecessary in the first place and its political reforms were thin return for shattered lives. For example, William Doyle's survey of the Revolution begins with Montesquieu's aphorism – 'Is the evil of change always less than the evil of suffering?' – and concludes by dubbing the Revolution 'in every sense a tragedy'. The fatal legacy of the Revolution according to Simon Schama was the violent and naïve certainty that 'connected social distress with political change'; the Revolution was 'doomed to self-destruct from overinflated expectations'. For him, the only significant social change was the death of the innocent at the hands of unscrupulous demagogues and brutish mobs.[12]

Such a 'minimalist' view of the significance of the French Revolution cannot do justice to the social importance of this protracted upheaval. This is not so much for the continuities it stresses as for the changes it ignores. Inevitably, the way historians of every generation understand the past is a function of the times in which they live; their own assumptions about politics and society inform the way they investigate and listen to voices from the past. But no French adult alive in 1815 was in any doubt that they had lived through a revolutionary upheaval, and a consideration of the social significance of the Revolution from a longer-term perspective suggests that this was no illusion.

The series of revolts which erupted in the spring and summer of 1789 occurred in a society characterized by the primacy of regional diversity within a state system and territory over which the absolute monarchy had limited hold. Economic structures which sought to meet the needs of the household within a regional or micro-regional market underpinned the vibrancy of regional cultures and minority languages and dialects. The gradual extension of Capetian and Bourbon control over the territory of France had not eroded primordial loyalties of kin, region and ethnicity: indeed, the cost to the royal state of establishing institutional hegemony had been a patchwork of regional and local immunities, exemptions and prerogatives. The institutional structures of public life – in administration, customs and measures, the law, taxation and the Church – everywhere bore the imprint of privilege and historical accretion.

In 1789–91, revolutionaries reshaped every aspect of institutional and public life according to bourgeois assumptions of rationality, uniformity and efficiency. Underpinning this sweeping, energetic recasting was an administrative system of departments, districts, cantons and communes. These departments were henceforth to be administered in precisely the same way within an identical structure of responsibilities, personnel and powers. Diocesan boundaries coincided with departmental limits, and cathedrals were almost always located in departmental capitals. The uniformity of administrative structures was reflected, too, in the imposition of a national system of weights, measures and currency, strikingly 'rational' in its decimal basis (the department of the Lot-et-Garonne encompassed an area where before 1789 there had been 65 different ways of measuring length and 26 measures of grain). These evident benefits to business and commerce were accentuated by the abolition of tolls *(péages)* and internal customs: henceforth, too, governments legislated on the basis of free trade within this national market. All French citizens, whatever their social background and residence, were to be judged according to a single uniform legal code, and taxed by the same obligatory proportional taxes on wealth, especially landed property: there is here a tangible measure of 'fraternity' and 'national unity'.

Such unity was not only at the expense of the exemptions and prerogatives possessed by privileged social orders, occupations and localities, but also superimposed an assumption of centralized uniformity on the complex ethnic reality of France. For successive governments in the years after 1789, effective citizenship was to be predicated on French as the language of liberty. Politicians, officials and army officers from French-speaking areas, and their counterparts from among ethnic minorities – those most likely to have needed a facility in French under the *ancien régime* – shared this prejudice. The suspicion that 'fraternity' signified French was accentuated by the knowledge that priests spoke the language of their parishioners in counter-revolutionary areas.

While popular attitudes to the Revolution among the ethnic minorities who together made up a majority of the 'French' population varied from enthusiasm to outright hostility across time and place, the Revolution and Empire everywhere had a profound impact on collective identity, on the *francisation* of the citizens of a new society. This jump in collective consciousness was in part a function of the repeated call to participation in elections and referenda within a national context; while participation rates were generally low, the unprecedented opportunity for large numbers of adult males to elect national deputies created a radical shift in assumptions about the nature of political power, as did the obvious revolutionary change in the basis of legitimacy, from divinely-ordained monarch to popular sovereignty, however defined. Significantly, electoral participation was consistently highest in small rural communities. Similarly, in the years of revolutionary and imperial wars, millions of young men were conscripted to fight for the Republic, glory or their own survival. Mixed with other young citizens within a French national military bureaucracy, such men were exposed to the language of France, *patrie* and nation.

The increase in the powers and claims of the State was the more dramatic because, for the first time, the State was invested with the resonance of being the institutional form of a more emotional entity, 'the nation'. While the term 'nationalism' only appeared from Balzac's pen in the 1830s, this is an example – as are 'feminism' and 'socialism', which were first coined at the same time – of a *post facto* term for an older set of attitudes. The Revolution brought 'state' and 'nation' together, and baptised the union in wars of revolutionary defence and national glory.[13] 'Nationalism' implies, in Benedict Anderson's term, an 'imagined community' – in France's case, of a sovereign people. The years of Revolution and Empire had dramatically increased and intensified administrative unity, sustained by a new political culture of citizenship and the celebration of national heroes drawn from antiquity or the revolutionary struggle itself. Revolutionaries used 'patriotism' to describe the twin virtues of love of one's country and support for the Revolution. Just as 'patriot' was a political term of pride or denigration, so 'patriotism' pointed to the tension between the *pays* or region and the *patrie* or nation. In the Year III, General Kléber asked that his Alsatian compatriot Ney accompany him in the Army of the Rhine 'so that … I can at least speak immediately with someone who knows my language'. Napoleon, who himself was not fully at ease in French, perhaps had them in mind when he supposedly quipped: 'let these courageous men have their Alsatian dialect; they always fight in French'.

Three times – in the summer of 1793, in 1797–9 and in 1810–14 – a combination of political hostility and massive resistance to the exactions of the State had threatened the new nation with disintegration. However, there was never an organized, articulated repudiation of the idea of nation itself; protest at the politics and claims of the centre unconsciously adopted the conceptual framework of French institutions even as it fought against them. Similarly, social élites among linguistic and ethnic minorities accepted the necessity, even the virtue, of a facility in French. From the Périgord, a reply to Grégoire's 1790 questionnaire noted that 'twenty years ago, it was a ridiculous thing to speak French; we used to call it *francimander*. In the towns today, all the bourgeois speak only French.' In his memoirs, the eminent Catalan noble Jaubert de Passa, two of whose close relatives had been guillotined, recalled nostalgically the years before 1789 when he 'was completely ignorant of the French language and … even felt a lively enough revulsion towards it'.[14] But his memoirs were written in fine French.

Whether or not speakers of minority languages were enthusiastic or hostile towards revolutionary change, the years 1789–1815 represented an acceleration of the process of *francisation*, whereby they came to perceive themselves as citizens of the French nation as well as Bretons, Occitans or Basques. However, this 'double identity' was limited to an acceptance of national institutions and a French political discourse: there is little evidence that popular cultures and minority languages were thereby eroded. French remained the daily language of a minority and France a land of great cultural and linguistic diversity.

This diversity was contradicted by institutional uniformity and the new assumption that the primary nexus in public life was that between the individual and the State. Before 1789, the major form of redistribution of wealth or surplus extraction had been the payment of 'tribute' of various types to the State, the Church and seigneurs. By 1815 the claims of the privileged orders were irredeemably lost; now wealth was appropriated from its producers by the State and through relations of production (through rent, markets and labour).

The State alone could levy tribute of taxes, men and obedience, indicating its growing power and pre-eminence as an agent of social control.[15]

Accordingly, the new state had a more pressing need for reliable, precise information about human and physical resources and political attitudes. The extreme difficulty which historians have had in calculating the number of nobles in pre-revolutionary France – estimates range from 110,000 to 400,000 – is a telling indication of this fundamental shift in the nature of the State. After 1800 in particular, a uniform, hierarchical apparatus of administration provided the vehicle through which an internal army of civil engineers, military officers, statisticians and bureaucrats described, measured and counted. Their population censuses, economic surveys, topographical descriptions and land registers are prized by quantifying historians, but they also furnish an insight into the *mentalité* of senior officials who decided what they needed to know and how to categorize it. For example, the land registers commenced in 1807 were predicated on the assumptions of mathematical exactitude and private property: every metre of the country was to be owned by an individual, a commune or the State, and its tax liability assessed according to its productive value. A land of enormous diversity in resource use and culture became thereby a socially constructed map of individuals and private property uniformly measured, taxed and valued.

The dominance of the nation-state in the collection of taxes and information and in the policing of its citizens was reflected in the number and remuneration of its officers. From less than a thousand in the 1780s, the central bureaucracy in Paris swelled to 25,000 by 1810, with salaries ranging from 12,000 francs for a departmental head to 2,000 for a third-class clerk. The prefect of a rural department was paid 20,000 francs, an inspector in the Ministry of Public Works 12,000, while a chief engineer had a salary of 5,000 francs and a subprefect 4,000. This expanded élite of functionaries compared more than favourably with another bureaucracy, that of the Church, in which archbishops received 15,000 francs, bishops 10,000 and parish priests 1,500.[16]

The abolition of privileged corporations also created a space in which could be advanced the claims of occupational groups to professional status and control of membership by requirements of expertise. In turn, a close relationship developed between professions and the new state. In the case of medicine, this transition was accelerated by protracted wars.[17] In pre-revolutionary France, the treatment of illness was highly personal and extraordinarily varied by region as well as class. From nobles who discussed their symptoms and cures with privileged physicians to the rural poor who used long-established local practices and substances prescribed by the family or neighbourhood midwife or *sage-femme* (less commonly a country *chirurgien-barbier*), illness was perceived as individual in its origin, meaning and remedies. The experience of warfare on an unprecedented scale accelerated revolutionary changes in the diagnosis and treatment of illness and injury. Dealing with a massive number of horrific war wounds forced on the small band of military surgeons a more interventionist, drastic and 'detached' mode of treatment. Initially such changes were confined to the army and navy, and it was to be many decades before their social and medical impact was felt throughout French society; however, together with the reorganization of the medical profession in 1803, the stage was set for a protracted struggle between 'professional' and popular medicine in the nineteenth century.

Central to the 'minimalist' perspective on the significance of the Revolution is the argument that, as a victory of the land-owning peasantry and because of the lost decades of trade expansion due to protracted warfare, these years actually retarded the transition to capitalism. It has thus been claimed that Soboul's identification of the Revolution with bourgeois triumph and capitalist transformation is no more than Marxist wishful thinking. In the words of François Furet, the most prominent French revisionist: 'The Marxist vulgate of the French Revolution actually turns the world upside down: it makes the revolutionary break a matter of economic and social change, whereas nothing resembled French society under Louis XVI more than French society under Louis-Philippe [1830–48].'[18]

Certainly, a capitalist transition of the French economy – to one based on the extraction of surplus value from labour by owners of the means of production in order to make a profit from market-oriented specialization – did not occur abruptly during these years. France in 1815 was not a capitalist society in a global sense any more than it had been a fully feudal society in 1789, but a revolutionary change had still occurred: those institutional, legal and social changes creating the environment within which capitalist industry and agriculture would thrive.

One of the defining characteristics of the 'minimalist' approach is a lack of interest in rural society. This has downplayed the magnitude of change in the countryside. Profit-oriented farm enterprise was facilitated by a series of legislative changes and the relative consistency with which successive regimes after 1789 upheld the primacy of private ownership and control over collective usages and community decisions. Only the strength of the attachment to communal lands by the poorer members of rural communities (although in some areas wealthier peasants also valued such lands for grazing animals) prevented a thoroughgoing change to total private control of rural land.

Research on the extent and social incidence of land sales during the Revolution remains piecemeal, but there is no question that it was significant in most areas. The most detailed estimate is that over 10 per cent of land changed hands as a result of the expropriation of the Church and *émigrés*.[19] Church land in particular was usually of prime quality, sold in large lots by auction and purchased by urban and rural bourgeois – and more than a few nobles – with the capital to thus expand pre-existing holdings. In all, there were up to 700,000 purchasers – at least one family in ten bought some land. Ecclesiastical property in and around Angers was auctioned on the first possible day, and the eager Angevin bourgeoisie paid 8.5 million livres for it, 40 per cent above its estimated value. While most nobles kept their lands intact (Robert Forster estimates that about one-fifth of noble holdings were seized and sold), their method of surplus extraction of necessity changed fundamentally. The final abolition of feudal dues in 1793 implied that nobles' income from property would henceforth be based on rents charged to tenants and sharecroppers or on direct exploitation of noble holdings by farm managers employing labourers.

Accordingly, rents charged by nobles increased by an average of 50 per cent in the years 1800–20 as they sought to compensate for the loss of seigneurial rights: apart from those able to take advantage of the rampant inflation of 1795–7 to buy their way out of leases or to purchase land, tenants and share-croppers experienced limited material improvements from the Revolution.

Like every other group in the rural community, however, they had been affected by seigneurial *banalités* and *corvées* and, with rural labourers, had been those most vulnerable to the arbitrary sanctions of the seigneur's court. As Anthony Crubaugh has stressed, the institution of the system of Justices of the Peace was an extraordinary success in meeting a widespread rural demand for a system of mediation that was accessible, cheap, prompt and able to resolve some of the minor but nagging irritations of rural life. Whereas the seigneurial judge of Jonzac (Charente-Inférieure) had commonly adjudicated only 7–10 cases per year, his successor as Justice of the Peace made 144 judgements in 1792 and 125 in the Year II. To be sure, perhaps two-thirds of cases could not be resolved by Justices of the Peace to the satisfaction of both parties, but the thousands of grievances great and small that rural people took to them is witness to the relevance of the institution.[20]

The abolition of seigneurialism and the shift in the nobles' relation with the land underpinned a revolutionary change in rural social relations, articulated in political practice after 1789. Social authority in the rural community was now based on personal esteem and direct economic power rather than on claims to deference due to a superior order of society. With the disappearance of the seigneurial dues collector from the little village of Le Mesnil-Théribus near Beauvais went some of the social standing of the seigneur, Jean d'Ivery. In 1792, popular hostility forced him to withdraw from the mayoral contest despite his backing from the village wealthy and the priest. Nor was Napoleon's reinforcement of notables' power at the local level meekly accepted: as the prefect of the Aisne wrote to him in 1811, 'the principles subversive of all public order which were popular during the Revolution cannot be easily erased'.[21]

Certainly, those peasants who owned their own land were direct and substantial beneficiaries of the Revolution. As a result of land sales, the total of such peasant holdings increased from perhaps one-third to two-fifths of the total (from 31 to 42 per cent in the Nord), and was no longer subject to tithe or seigneurial exactions. The weight of such exactions had varied enormously, but a total weight of 20–5 per cent of the produce of peasant proprietors (not to mention the *corvée*, seigneurial monopolies and irregular payments) was common outside the west of France. Their removal had two direct consequences. First, producers retained an extra portion of their output which was often directly consumed by a better-fed population: in 1792, only one in seven of the army recruits from the impoverished mountain village of Pont-de-Montvert (Lozère) had been 1.63 m (5′4″) or taller; by 1830, that was the average height of conscripts. The retention of a greater share of produce also increased the safety margin for middling and larger peasant landholders and facilitated the contemplation of the risks of market specialization. This was also made more likely by a second consequence: collections of tithes and dues had usually been in kind, especially wheat, but now peasant proprietors were able to use their land for their own purposes. In the countryside around Bayeux, the heavy, damp soils were quickly converted to cattle-raising once the Church ceased exacting a fixed tithe in grain. Gilles Postel-Vinay has estimated that, despite the absence of able-bodied men drafted into the army, rural producers responded to these incentives by slightly increasing wheat production and producing one-third more wine by 1812 compared with the years before the Revolution.[22]

Using the massive database of the *Institut National d'Etudes Démographiques*, Paul Spagnoli has demonstrated that there was a decisive decline in mortality and an increase in life expectancy from the 1780s to the 1820s: for women from 28.1 to 39.3 years and for men from 27.5 to 38.3 years. In searching for an explanation of a phenomenon unique in Europe, he concludes that it was directly linked to the consequences of the Revolution in the countryside: land sales, fiscal equity, the removal of seigneurial dues and the tithe, higher wages for agricultural labourers, and greater incentives to increase production.[23]

The example of Bayeux points to a crucial dimension of the impact of the Revolution: a watershed in rural-urban relations. In many ways the provincial centres of *ancien-régime* institutions had been parasitic on the countryside: cathedral chapters, religious orders and resident nobles extracted 'surplus' from peasants which was expended in provincial towns such as Bayeux, Dijon and Angers through direct employment of domestic servants, indirect maintenance of skilled trades, especially in luxury goods, and in provision of charity. The population of Bayeux declined by 15 per cent by 1830, leaving administrators, those involved in the rich cattle and dairy industries, farm suppliers and an impoverished artisanate who could never hope to return to the days when they serviced a numerous and wealthy noble and clerical élite. In the countryside around Angers, the Benedictine abbey of Ronceray had formerly owned 5 manors, 12 barns and wine-presses, 6 mills, 46 farms and 6 houses, bringing into the town 27,000 livres annually. Some of it employed – and was collected by – lawyers in the 53 courts and tribunals charged with ensuring that the countryside met its obligations. As a direct result of the Revolution, the countryside largely liberated itself from towns, leaving marketing and administration as the remaining links. It was this which aggravated the suffering of the destitute in such towns after 1789 and the impoverishment of those directly or indirectly dependent on expenditure by clerical and noble élites. The Trappist monastery of Bonnecombe in the Aveyron had distributed annually 300,000 livres' worth of bread to the destitute, paid for from the tithe collected in the countryside; after 1789, the peasantry consumed that part of their produce and the urban destitute were in an even more precarious situation.[24]

Indeed, rather than assuming the expansion of small-scale agriculture to have been a brake on capitalism in the countryside – as 'anglocentric' economic history has done – the Soviet historian Anatoli Ado has identified it as capable of responding productively to marketing opportunities.[25] Instead, argues Ado, the real obstacle to a more rapid transition to agrarian capitalism was the survival of large 'retrograde' property rented out in small plots on restrictive leases. Agrarian change was limited by the failure of peasant attempts to break up these large estates rather than by the survival of the peasantry and many of its collective rights. Where small peasants felt greater security about producing for the market, the results could be dramatic. In the southern department of the Aude, for example, the ending of seigneurial and church exactions, coupled with the collapse of the textile industry, encouraged peasants to turn to wine as a cash crop. Across the 30 years after 1789, the estimates provided by mayors for the area under vines in the department showed an increase of 75 per cent, from 29,300 to 51,100 hectares. The volume of wine produced in the department may have trebled to 900,000 hectolitres across these years. James Livesey has seen in the associated language of the market across rural France a 'commercial republicanism' which was fundamental to the shift towards a democratic public culture.[26]

This 'peasant route' to capitalism was only one of the ways in which the Revolution facilitated agrarian economic change. It also occurred through large-scale ownership or renting of land and the employment of labour. For example, in 1786 the Thomassin family of Puiseux-Pontoise (Seine-et-Oise, today Val-d'Oise) owned 3.86 hectares and rented 180 more from the seigneur, the marquis de Girardin. They then bought up large amounts of nationalized property seized during the Revolution from the abbey of Saint-Martin-de-Pontoise, the Sisters of Charity and eight other ecclesiastical landowners: by 1822 they owned 150.64 hectares, 27.5 per cent of the land in the commune, including much of the marquis's estate. This land was used for commercial grain-growing and, finally, for sugar-beet and a sugar distillery.[27]

There were, however, many bourgeois for whom the Revolution and Empire were economically difficult. This was particularly the case in the great coastal towns where the uncertainties caused by wars and blockades and the temporary abolition of slavery hit overseas trade hard: by 1815, French external trade was only half the 1789 volume and did not regain pre-revolutionary levels until 1830. Between 1790 and 1806, the down-turn in trade caused the population of Marseille to fall from 120,000 to 99,000, that of Nantes from perhaps 90,000 to 77,000 and that of Bordeaux from 110,000 to 92,000.

In contrast, the cotton, iron and coal industries were stimulated by France's role in the continental system and protection from British imports. The manufacturing bourgeoisie of the small Norman textile town of Elbeuf was quite specific about its grievances in its *cahier* of 1789, fulminating against: 'the inefficient administration of finances … these constraints, these impediments to commerce: barriers reaching to the very heart of the kingdom; endless obstacles to the circulation of commodities … representatives of manufacturing industries and Chambers of Commerce totally ignored and despised; an indifference on the part of the government towards manufacturers.'[28] This budding industrial bourgeoisie achieved its goals, including the recognition of its own importance: in the Year V, it was asked for the first time its opinion on a number of commercial treaties, and in the Year IX the advisory role of Chambers of Commerce was formally institutionalized. While Elbeuf felt the full brunt of trade blockades and food shortages, the period 1789–1815 marks an important phase in the mechanization and concentration of the textile industry in the town rather than in rural piece-work. By 1815 the population had increased some 50 per cent, and the number of enterprises had doubled; power remained in the hands of manufacturers adept at protecting their control from challenges from workers as well as from *ancien-régime* élites.

If the Revolution had created the institutional foundations on which capitalism could thrive, to what extent did it also represent the coming to power of a new class? At first glance, the continued economic prominence of the old nobility is remarkable: despite the loss of seigneurial rights and, for *émigrés*, land, nobles remained at the pinnacle of landholding, and landholding remained the major source of wealth in France. Across half of the country, a majority of the 12 wealthiest landowners surveyed in 1802 were nobles, and they dominated the wealthiest areas, such as the Paris basin, the valley of the Rhône, Burgundy, Picardy, and Normandy.[29]

Nevertheless, the wealthy survivors of the landholding élite of the *ancien régime* were now only part of a far broader élite which included all of the wealthy, whatever their social background, and embraced notables in agriculture, business and administration drawing their wealth from a combination of state employment and business. The new male fashion, beginning in the late 1790s, of short hair and *habits* modelled on the English business suit, is one revealing example of 'the language of clothes'. David Garrioch describes the Parisian bourgeoisie which emerged from the Revolution as far more powerful than before: indeed, he has argued that the Revolution 'created' the bourgeoisie as a self-conscious class.[30] More than in the 1780s or 1790s, the ruling class in the early nineteenth century represented the coincidence of economic, social and political power. Those who took the initiative in creating this new regime were the bourgeoisie, whether professional, administrative, commercial, landowning or manufacturing. For them, the Revolution represented the changes to political structures and dominant social values necessary to recognize their importance in the life of the nation. The Revolution was their triumph.

Exemplifying this post-revolutionary amalgam of wealth and status, landed estates and urban enterprise, family name and social mobility, was the great Dauphinois notable Claude Périer. This textile magnate, who had invested in a *seigneurie* in 1780, augmented his massive fortune by purchasing national lands during the Revolution. In 1792, citizen Périer supported the Girondins then, on winning a contract to supply rifles to the army, became a staunch Jacobin. The years of the Empire were good to Périer and he expanded and mechanized his silk-printing works, housed in his great château at Vizille. At the same time, this almost stereotypical *grand bourgeois* required from his dependent tenant-farmers a maze of exactions limiting their control over land use in a neo-feudal way.[31]

No less than Napoleon, Louis XVIII recognized that this new social élite was based on the primacy of wealth. What changed in 1815 – as in 1799 – was the composition of one section of the political élite. In 1810 Napoleon's prefects compiled lists of 1,000 notables in each of the 110 departments of the Empire: these were men chosen for their political reliability as well as local standing and drawn, in roughly equal terms, from the civil service, trade and industry, law, and agriculture. Under the Constitution of 1814, Louis would similarly use his prerogative to appoint loyal peers to the upper house, but nothing could alter the fact that the more powerful Chamber of Deputies was elected from the wealthiest men in France, regardless of occupation or opinion. France remained a distinctly hierarchical society in terms of wealth, power and opportunity, but the basis of political legitimacy had changed radically. For the privileged orders of the *ancien régime* the decade after 1789 had been politically and personally traumatic: long after the Revolution, the Catalan noble Jaubert de Passa was haunted by 'memories which swirl round in my head like a leaden nightmare'.

While most nobles were pragmatic enough to withdraw from public life and accept, however begrudgingly, the institutional changes of the Revolution, their resumption of former titles under the Empire disguises the magnitude of their losses. Robert Forster's judgment, though based on scattered and contrasting case-studies, is that, in real terms, an average provincial noble family's income fell from 8,000 to 5,200 francs. Seigneurial dues had represented as little as 5 per cent of noble income near Bordeaux, while immediately to the north, in Aunis and Saintonge, they amounted to 63 per cent. While many noble families survived with their lands intact, some 12,500 – up to one-half – lost some land, and a few virtually all. Overall, perhaps one-fifth of noble land changed hands. To an extent, the losses of lands and dues were compensated for by charging higher rents to tenants and sharecroppers but, whereas 5 per cent at most of noble wealth was taken by state taxes before 1789, thereafter the uniform land tax was levied at approximately 16 per cent.[32]

Moreover, nothing could compensate for the loss of judicial rights and power – ranging from seigneurial courts to the *parlements* – or the incalculable loss of prestige and deference generated by the practice of legal equality. The *émigré* noble returned to a transformed world, of litigation by creditors and peasants, the collapse of mystique and the exigencies of running an estate as a business. Looking back in 1820 on the abolition of feudalism during the Revolution, Lucy de La Tour du Pin remembered:

> This decree ruined my father-in-law and our family fortunes never recovered.... It was a veritable orgy of iniquities.... Since then, we have been forced to contrive a living, sometimes by sale of some of the few possessions remaining to us, sometimes by taking salaried posts.... And so it is that, inch by inch, over a long period of years, we have gradually slid to the bottom of an abyss from which we shall not emerge in our generation.

The loss of feudal dues, rents and tolls (one of which brought in 12,000 francs per year) was enormous: the marquise estimated that her family had lost 58,000 of its original annual income of 80,000 francs.[33]

Even when a noble survived the Revolution with landholdings intact, social relations underwent a major change. In the Provençal village of Lourmarin, Jean-Baptiste Jérôme de Bruny, a former councillor in the *parlement* at Aix, retained his extensive property but became the largest taxpayer, assessed for 14 per cent of all taxes payable by the community. His *tasque* (one-eighth of harvested grain and olive oil), *banalités* and other dues were gone. The estimated annual value of his *seigneurie* had been about 16,000 livres, but by 1791 the taxable revenue from his lands was estimated at only 4,696 livres, a fall of about 70 per cent. Relations between him and the village were henceforth those of

property, labour and rent, suggested by the speed with which locals began litigation with 'citizen Bruny' after 1789. In the decades after 1800, they fought
a protracted, successful battle with Bruny over his attempts to ignore ancient
collective rights in his woods, 'dealing not with their seigneur but simply with
another French citizen'.[34]

One reason for the enthusiasm with which Lourmarinois supported the
Revolution – though dividing during the 'federalist' revolt of 1793 – was that
some 80 per cent of them were Protestants. Though there seems to have been
a decline in religiosity during the eighteenth century, oral memories of earlier
religious atrocities were kept alive within the community. The construction of
a Protestant church in 1805 was to be a tangible reminder of the significance
of the Revolution for religious minorities. But religious authority seems to have
collapsed further after 1789. Lourmarinois had long practised sexual relations
before marriage but the number of first-born children conceived before
marriage escalated from 19.1 per cent in 1781–90 to no fewer than 34.4 per
cent in 1791–1800 (they also practised birth control, and fewer children
overall were born in the 1790s).

Lourmarin was by no means typical of rural communities: in the devout
Norman parish of Crulai, only 3 per cent of children were born before eight
months of their parents' marriage. However, a startling demographic change
there points to one of the clearest indications of the impact of the Revolution
on daily life: an unprecedented – and permanent – decline in the birth rate, from
42.5 per thousand in the 1780s to 36.6 in the following decade. Nationally the
decline was from 38.8 per thousand in 1789 to 32.9 in 1804; the average inter-
val between births increased from about two years to above three years, a
further indication of deliberate limitation of family size. In 1789–1824 there
was a 22.6 per cent fall in female fecundity. In part this change may have been
due to the absence and death of huge numbers of young men after 1792,
although this may have been offset by an increase in the marriage rate as young
men sought to avoid conscription. (In six parishes around Thoissey-en-Dombes
(Ain), over 30 per cent of the widows who married young bachelors were aged
over 40.) In any case, the total population of France increased by 2.5 million in
the 25 years after 1789, despite heavy war losses. Most likely, the collapse or
absence of clerical authority over birth control facilitated the response of the
peasantry to the Revolution's inheritance laws of 1790 and 1793 requiring children to inherit equally. Given the desire and need to keep small family holdings
intact, rural people responded by deliberately limiting family size, usually by
coitus interruptus, but also by using knowledge of the fertility cycle, abortion,
douching, abstinence, and occasionally infanticide.[35]

Although Napoleon modified the partible inheritance law to allow parents a
'disposable share' to bequeath to the child of their choice, no government – not
even the Restoration – tampered with the principle of equal inheritance. It
seems that in many areas, such as the southern Massif Central and the Pyrenees,
inheritance patterns continued, whereby sons ultimately received the family
holding, so that daughters must either have been cajoled into renouncing their
share or were compensated in other ways. In Marlhes (Haute-Loire), for example, parents adopted a strategy to ensure that every child was provided for while

preserving the household's wealth intact. This was done most commonly by agreement between the children after their parents' death, on whether to divide the farm or whether some siblings should leave and be materially compensated. The historian of Marlhes, James Lehning, has concluded that the revolutionary and Napoleonic legislation marked 'an important shift of control towards heirs', including daughters. On the other hand, because parents were able to transfer their property at any time, they retained an important measure of control over their offspring, even if they could no longer threaten to disinherit them, for example, over the choice of a marriage partner. Whatever the case, the social consequence of this legislation was to focus attention on children's rights as well as on the family estate, especially in regions where pre-revolutionary law had allowed complete testamentary freedom to parents. A study of 83 court cases in Caen over wills contested between siblings between 1790 and 1796 shows that 45 were won by sisters. The citizeness Montfreulle stated to the court in 1795: 'I was married in 1773 "for a bouquet of roses", to use the Norman expression. That was how girls were married then. Greed was in the air and one often sacrificed the daughters for the happiness of one son.' In and around Montauban, the inheritance law did not abruptly change patterns of passing on the family holding to the eldest son, but there was a perceptible – and requisite – concern to meet the rights of his siblings, and a shift in values which saw the material needs of widows being expressly met in wills. In countless households after 1790, the rights of daughters became a family issue – just as the divorce law empowered wives – and in this may lie the most significant shift in the status of women in these years.[36]

While the Revolution had challenged the most basic assumptions about hierarchy and social order, male attitudes to 'women's place' could bridge political divisions. When in Ventôse Year II (February 1794), the great republican paper *Les Révolutions de Paris* ceased publication, it addressed itself to future generations who would have 'only roses to pick; your fathers will have had nothing but the thorns'. It warned of the dangers of factionalism, detention without trial, economic inequalities and the 'military spirit'. Integral to this Jacobinism was another warning:

> For too long we have allowed women to leave their homes to be present at the deliberations of the legislators, at the debates of the popular societies. You will recall their true, their unique vocation, and not permit them to deviate from it any more. They will continue to adorn the national feasts, but they will no longer interfere in public affairs.

In future, the *patrie* would be 'neither a vixen nor a stepmother'; rather the Republic would be 'a good mother of her family' which every citizen would love 'as his mistress'. Despite – or because of – the challenges of women of all social classes and political persuasions, the new male élite had articulated an ideology of gender which sought to separate the 'public', male sphere from the 'private' and female.

This revealing statement of gender politics and sexual attitudes was written in response to the challenge by radical women at the peak of the Revolution.

Similar sentiments were expressed by the vicomte de Bonald, *émigré* and theo-rist of theocratic monarchy, at the peak of royalist reaction in 1816, during the debates which led to the abolition of divorce. He warned that, just as political democracy 'allows the people, the weak part of political society, to rise against the established power', so divorce, 'veritable domestic democracy', allows the wife, 'the weak part, to rebel against marital authority'. Thus, 'in order to keep the state out of the hands of the people, it is necessary to keep the family out of the hands of wives and children'.[37] With extraordinary frankness, de Bonald had thereby dissolved the distinction between private and public life; like the rights of working men and women of town and country, those of women within the family were henceforth at the heart of debates about the social order. As Carla Hesse has argued in an important challenge to feminist historiography which understands the Revolution simply as the masculinist assertion of hege-mony over the political domain, the repeated strictures about 'women's place' must be understood as a prescriptive reaction to women's activities rather than as a simple reflection of gendered actuality. The proportion of women writers in print doubled in the years 1789–1820.[38]

The Revolution marks the end of the near-universal practice of church-going in France, especially among men who had experienced life in the army and years free of church education and the presence of a priest. This decline in the social authority of the Church was reflected in changes to the seasonality of marriages. During the eighteenth century, only about 3 per cent of marriages occurred in the months of December (Advent) and March (Lent). There was a sharp increase during the Revolution (to 12.4 per cent in 1793–9), and while pre-revolutionary patterns re-emerged thereafter, they were never so marked: in 1820–9, 7.5 per cent of marriages occurred in these two months (in towns the figures were a few per cent higher).[39]

The Catholic Church emerged from Revolution without its extensive prop-erty, internally divided, and with several thousand of its clergy prematurely dead. Consequently, most priests – and many of the devout – were to be implacably opposed to republicanism and secularism, even if they finally had to accept the priests' new reliance on state salaries and the end of corporate autonomy. Yet the laity – especially women – had proved their religious commitment in large areas of the countryside; from women, too, would come a widening stream of recruits to religious orders. Nevertheless, the Catholic Church's claims to a monopoly of worship and morality, so vigorously expressed in 1789, could not be repeated: for Protestants and Jews, the legislation of 1789–91 represented legal emancipation, civil equality and the freedom to worship. The civil eman-cipation of Jews facilitated the Dreyfus family's rise from itinerant pedlars in Alsace in the 1780s to wealthy, confident textile magnates in the 1860s, and imbued in them an ineradicable love of a France which symbolized civil liberty, equality of opportunity, and fraternity between Jews and Christians.[40] For revolutionaries, too, religious freedom exemplified their achievements: in a 1790 version of 'snakes and ladders' the emancipation of Jews was represented to children as one of the ladders leading to the new France.

Ultimately, the social changes wrought by the Revolution endured because they corresponded to some of the deepest grievances of the bourgeoisie and peasantry in 1789: popular sovereignty (however short of democracy), civil equality, careers open to 'talent', and the abolition of the seigneurial system. Whatever the popular resentments expressed towards conscription and church reform in many regions, there was never a serious possibility of mass support for a return to the *ancien régime*. Louis XVIII was well aware of that. The question remained whether the political compromises put in place in 1814–15 could create stability as the social and economic consequences of the revolutionary upheaval unfolded.

6

The World of Notables and Bourgeois, 1815–1845

Charles-Maurice de Talleyrand-Périgord was the consummate survivor of the pre-revolutionary nobility. Bishop of Autun before 1789, then a prime mover in the nationalization of church property and the Civil Constitution of the Clergy; ambassador to London in 1792, then an *émigré* before becoming Foreign Minister under the Directory; a key organizer of Napoleon's coup in 1799 and again Foreign Minister until 1807, Talleyrand then played a central role in the negotiations of 1814–15 which brought Louis XVIII to the throne. Despite his chequered political career, Talleyrand remained a great landowner. The village of Limanton, in the south-east of the department of the Nièvre, where he owned 450 hectares, furnishes an example of the disproportionate control of rural wealth which was the basis of élite power.[1] While as many as 240 of the 777 inhabitants of Limanton in 1820 owned some land, 98 of these individuals possessed a combined total of 42 hectares; in contrast, the seven largest proprietors owned 2,851 hectares between them. The largest landowner was the marquis Bruneau de Vitry; however, most of the large proprietors were bourgeois, whether local men or from nearby Moulins-Engilbert. Nobles and bourgeois leased their holdings to other rural bourgeois who in turn leased the land to tenants in substantial farms of 30–60 hectares. These sharecroppers, many in the large multiple families (*communautés*) characteristic of the Morvan region of the Nièvre, furnished half their crops as rent, as well as paying rent for farm buildings and the State's land taxes.

Every rural community resembled Limanton in its sharp polarities of wealth and its social complexities, whatever the individual characteristics which varied markedly across regions. It was predominantly from such communities that the post-revolutionary élites of nobles and bourgeois extracted the wealth which underwrote their lifestyles and sustained their social and political dominance, whether at a local, regional or national level.

The world of the great landed magnates (*grands notables*) was diverse, ranging from the quasi-seigneurialism of inland Brittany to the capitalist agriculture of Normandy and Picardy. It was the common bond of owning substantial property which held élites together, despite internal divisions of social background and ideology which a generation of revolution and war had engrained into the meanings given to the world of the Restoration. On the basis of a study of Larochemillay, 15 kilometres from Limanton,[2] Jean-Claude Bontron has helpfully schematized the forms of power exercised by great magnates:

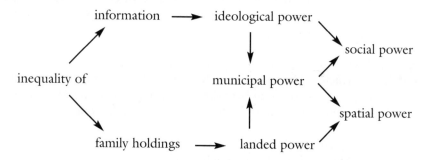

If, following André-Jean Tudesq, we define these *grands notables* as those who paid more than 1,000 francs in tax, two points are apparent: first, the predominance of nobles among them, and, secondly, their concentration in the wealthiest agricultural areas (Normandy, the Paris basin, the north-east, the Lyonnais, Burgundy, the Gironde, and the Midi lowlands from Toulouse to Marseille). But to be a landed magnate involved far more than the possession of exceptional wealth: it was also a function of family standing and the exercise of power, the world of the 'haves' in the broadest sense. In Tudesq's words: 'The great magnate *has* possessions, *has* knowledge, *has* connections, *has* a family, *has* an office which gives him part of public authority...he *has* a name and often a title, he is a notable as a function of what he *has*.'[3] The 'patron–client' relations such inequalities sustained were described by patrons as, and sometimes were, 'patrimonial' (an interaction of deference and benevolence). But all such relations were based on sharp inequalities in economic, social and political power.

In cities, the decades of Revolution and Empire had had a mixed impact on large-scale business, exposing it to the vicissitudes of war and political volatility while creating institutional changes in line with its wishes and advantages for army suppliers. The peace treaties of 1814–15 and the end of the continental system also created opportunities as well as difficulties for French commerce and industry. Trade in particular took a long time to recover. Bordeaux's merchants welcomed the Restoration as the golden reapparition of the expansive times of the eighteenth century, but colonial splendour could never return; Saint-Domingue was now an independent Haiti, and the sugar-cane importing and processing industries were threatened by French sugar beet. The Congress of Vienna had placed restrictions on the slave trade, and on 15 April 1818 Louis XVIII's government banned the trade, though not slavery, altogether. A French corvette which arrived in Martinique with 227 Africans in March 1822 had its cargo freed; the Ibos' celebratory dance may have been a contributory cause to a huge slave revolt in October, after which 37 were whipped and branded, 22 hanged and 7 decapitated.[4]

Away from the coasts, French entrepreneurs proved remarkably resilient and adaptable to changes of regime, none more so than Guillaume Ternaux. Son of a small textile manufacturer, Ternaux had been an enthusiastic early supporter of the Revolution, but had emigrated in 1794. Returning to his native Sedan in the Ardennes in 1798, he was able to rebuild his woollen industry because of the opportunities created by war supplies and the English naval blockade (the Revolution also gave him the opportunity to divorce twice). By 1818 he had 20,000 employees in scattered factories of 100–50 workers across the north and east and was also developing forms of 'vertical integration' by directly importing merino wool from Spain and by opening retail outlets such as 'The Merino Sheep', 'Le Bonhomme Richard' and 'The Cashmere Fleece'. In 1825 he also opened a bank which, in the familial way distinctive of French business, was run by his brother, sons, nephews and cousins. The composer of the Marseillaise, Rouget de Lisle, wrote a *Marseillaise des industriels* in his honour:

> Honour to you, pillar of industry!
> Honour, honour to your noble works!
> Arouse your rivals by your career,
> And live a long time, for them and for the country.[5]

In terms of national politics, the years 1815–30 were dominated by a tenuous balance between the undeniable transformations wrought by the Revolution and the demands of resurgent *ancien-régime* élites for a wider realization of the restoration of 'legitimate' authority.[6] Louis XVIII's Charter had sought to recognize the essentials of the Revolution (representative government, an end to institutionalized privilege and the claims of birth, and legal equality within a uniform structure of administration) while reassuring the Catholic Church of its special role as state religion and the ancient nobility of their social pre-eminence, embodied in the Chamber of Peers. Power in the Chamber of Deputies sanctified the importance of wealth; by limiting the vote to males over 30 years of age paying at least 300 francs in taxes (in all, some 72,000 men or about 0.25 per cent of the population) – and eligibility for office to those over 40 years paying 1,000 francs – Louis sought to formalize a hierarchy of landed substance, whether noble or bourgeois. At the local level, the tiny number eligible to vote (as few as 40 in Corsica) created an élite fusing political power, family ties and official positions. Only in larger and wealthier departments – such as the Seine, where 12,000 men could vote – were elections free of intense personal pressure.

Ancien-régime and Napoleonic nobles and urban and rural bourgeois were united by the claims which substantial property-owning gave to social and political pre-eminence. However, the politics of this diverse élite were fraught with the ideological divisions of the decades before 1815. The arbitrary measure of political worth by taxable wealth alienated the poorest nobility and large numbers of bourgeois accustomed to a life-time of eligibility to vote. Few bourgeois wanted the franchise lowered to include those beneath them in occupational status or wealth, but some of the most militant 'legitimists', as supporters of the Bourbons were known, called for manhood suffrage, secure in their belief that the chastened mass of decent folk *(honnêtes gens)* shared their nostalgia for a full return of noble prerogatives under an absolutist and clerical ruler.

Bourgeois opposition to the Bourbon regime was centred in the army, clandestine and legal organizations, and the world of letters. Initially disaffected in 1814 by the forced retirement on half-pay of 12,000 Bonapartist officers and the reintroduction of the royal symbols of the fleur-de-lis and white flag, bourgeois officers and non-commissioned officers found inactive garrison life the occasion for political protest and nostalgia for the Empire (captured by Stendhal, himself an army officer in 1806–13, in his unfinished novel *Lucien Leuwen*). The terms of the peace treaties and the warmth with which Louis welcomed to the Tuileries the British friends he had made in exile gave the Restoration a lasting identification with the Metternich system of an external balance of power between monarchies and of internal resistance to reform.

Within the narrow parliamentary world, division centred on the claims of Church and king. In reaction to the purges unleashed in 1815 by an ultra-royalist Chamber of Deputies (in which 176 of the 381 deputies were *ancien-régime* nobles), the electorate chose large numbers of liberal constitutional monarchists from 1816 to 1820. One such liberal, a former army officer from the Charente-Inférieure, used his 1819 election manifesto to call for greater civil liberties and an end to the paternalistic pretensions of the Church and monarchy:

> I distrust pious hypocrites who, while very often causing us unhappiness in this world, show too ardent a zeal for making us happy in the next. I believe that governments should have no other function than that of ensuring the safety of persons and property and of securing for everyone much greater freedom in their work and in the pleasures that result from it.[7]

The political exclusiveness of old noble-family networks, in the civil service, the armed forces and the Church, alienated what Alan Spitzer dubbed 'the generation of 1820'. These highly educated, ambitious young bourgeois (such as Armand Carrel, the Cavaignac, Hugo and Scheffer brothers, Auguste Comte, Eugène Delacroix and Prosper Mérimée), born between 1792 and 1803 and connected by education, values and personal contacts, found this exclusivity and political reaction stultifying and personally disadvantageous. To young historians like Augustin Thierry, François Mignet, Adolphe Thiers and François Guizot, who saw the Revolution of 1789–91 both as a bourgeois triumph and as 'progress', the suspension of Victor Cousin's popular course of lectures at the Sorbonne in 1820 was final proof. Cousin was no revolutionary, but he had fired the imagination of his audience with his description of the 1789 Declaration of the Rights of Man as 'the finest, the holiest, the most beneficent, document to have appeared on earth since the Gospel'.[8]

In this struggle within the bourgeois and noble élite about whether the meaning of the Charter of 1814 implied liberalism or the guiding hands of throne and altar, the assassination by a Bonapartist in February 1820 of the childless king's nephew and successor, the duc de Berry, was a major turning-point. The regime's prime target was the '*Carbonari*', a clandestine organization of perhaps 50,000 liberals and democrats dedicated to the overthrow of the regime, although dogged by disagreement over the acceptability of violence to that end.[9] The *carbonari* were predominantly soldiers (40 per cent) and bourgeois (36 per cent), but also included many students and workers. By 1823, the organization had been repressed and ten leaders executed. The parallel surge in the popularity of Rousseau and Voltaire – in 1821–5 their collected works sold up to 58,000 copies – was symbolically rebuffed by the removal of their remains from the Panthéon. However, as Sheryl Kroen has shown through her multi-layered readings of the popularity of Molière's *Tartuffe* – with its theme of the unmasking of a religious hypocrite – the regime's attempt to smother opposition in the theatre and on the streets ultimately succeeded in embedding the democratic political culture the regime feared.[10]

In June 1820 the 23,000 wealthiest electors were given a double vote to increase the influence of the nobles. Tighter censorship of the press was added to the introduction of bond money and a stamp tax (1822); the Church's *petits séminaires* were accorded full recognition as secondary schools, a dozen professors were dismissed from the Sorbonne and a priest installed as rector; and in 1823 a revolt led by liberal army officers in Spain was crushed by French troops. Reaction reached its peak with the accession to the throne in 1824 of Louis's younger brother, the comte d'Artois, who had fled the Revolution as early as July 1789. The count lavished six million francs on his coronation as Charles X in Reims, the traditional site of *ancien-régime* crownings. A phial of sacred unction, said to have been used since the fifth century but smashed by a Jacobin in 1793, was found miraculously restored; after anointment, Charles laid hands on the scrofulous (revealingly, only 120 sufferers arrived, compared with 1,200 at Louis XVI's coronation in 1774). The greatest poets of the age, Hugo and Lamartine, both recently granted membership of the Légion d'honneur, eulogized the new king. In 1825, Charles moved to indemnify those *émigrés* who had suffered property losses. While no attempt was made to seize land sold during the Revolution, this *milliard des émigrés* was an enormous boost to noble families seeking to reconstitute landed estates. The same year, a draconian law was passed threatening capital punishment for sacrilegious acts, and an attempt to restore primogeniture in aristocratic families was only narrowly defeated in Parliament.

The 1820s also saw the flowering of the Church's attempts to rechristianize a country perceived to be both penitent and demoralized after being purged of its revolutionary blindness. But these were new blooms on old stock: the Restoration's 96 nominations to the episcopacy were all elderly, *ancien-régime*, counter-revolutionary clergy, and 76 of them were nobles. Similarly, some two-thirds of the 36,000 parish clergy in 1815 were at least 60 years of age, men on whom the past weighed heavily in a mixture of personal bitterness and resolute conviction. It took years for the clergy to adapt to the compromises it had to make with the Revolution: in the early years of the Restoration this battle was fought out at parish level, as many bishops circulated catechisms insisting on the payment of the tithe on pain of sinning. The clerical élite had rather more success in their attempts to revivify Christian life, particularly in regions where the faith of the laity had re-emerged so strongly after 1795: extensive missions and pilgrimages were organized, culminating in the erection of huge expiatory crosses, illuminated religious pageants at night, and the burning of irreligious literature.[11]

Bourgeois fears of clerico-noble resurgence were paralleled by a belief that, as before 1789, their own economic and social importance was being denied political recognition. The most articulate statement of this alienation and of a utilitarian ideology of social worth – a 'What is the third estate?' for the 1820s – was made by Saint-Simon in the years before his death in 1825. After listing France's 3,000 leading men in business, the professions and creative arts – 'contributing the most to its glory and advancing its civilization as well as its prosperity' – Saint-Simon compared them to the 30,000 members of the élite of nobles, clerics and landowners 'who contribute nothing directly' and whose loss would be negligible. The national wealth must be 'administered by the men most fitted for the job... namely, the most important industrialists'. It was he who had requested Rouget de Lisle to compose his patriotic hymn of praise to Guillaume Ternaux. Saint-Simonianism was to provide an important vehicle through which the 'generation of 1820' could articulate a renewed confidence in the principles of 1789.

Until 1827 royalist majorities supported the throne's attempts to rid France of the evils of liberalism; but finally a majority of the tiny enfranchised élite also became convinced that Charles's agenda was a full restoration of theocratic absolutism. From 1827 to 1830 liberal or constitutional majorities in the chamber confronted a monarch steadfast in his commitment to autocracy. Tensions were aggravated in 1829 by his appointment to the ministry of three nobles (Polignac, Bourmont and la Bourdonnaye) closely identified with the *ancien régime* and the White Terror of 1816. Polignac, for example, was the son of Marie-Antoinette's notorious courtier, and had refused to take the oath of loyalty to the regime in 1815 because the Charter was seen by him as an intolerable concession to liberalism. Legal opposition was voiced in the late 1820s by associations formed to support liberal candidates: *'Aide-toi, le Ciel t'aidera'*, led by Guizot, and Chateaubriand's Society of the Friends of the Freedom of the Press. Such associations were also linked with mounting dissatisfaction among writers. Hugo, too, had quickly become disenchanted with the Restoration, and his hastily-written *Hernani* in February 1830 used romantic genre to aim a barb at the regime. Established liberal newspapers such as *Le Constitutionnel* and *Le Journal des débats* became more assertive despite press restrictions, and were joined in 1829–30 by others such as *Le National, La Tribune* and the students' *La Jeune France*.[12]

Violent showdown was ultimately provoked by Charles's draconian responses to a critical address to the king voted by 221 liberal deputies in March 1830.[13] The Restoration had finally alienated many of those who had directly benefited from the return of peace in 1815. The textile magnate Emile Oberkampf, whose father had been ennobled by Louis XVI and who himself was made a baron in 1820, was among the 221, as was Guillaume Ternaux, who was furious with the government's high protection duties on imports and erosion of political freedoms. After a more decisive liberal electoral victory in July, when all but 19 of the 221 opposition deputies were returned, Charles introduced severe controls on the press and announced new elections on a franchise which excluded all but the 25,000 wealthiest men in France. Stung into action by Charles's attempted coup and pressure from angry working people with their own reasons for hostility to the regime (see Chapter 7), small groups of journalists and liberal deputies called for resistance. Charles's abdication and the triumph of liberal constitutionalism was repeated in the provinces; in 47 of the 50 largest cities, provisional committees of liberal bourgeois also took over local and departmental power.

There are two images commonly evoked by the *Trois Glorieuses*, the three days of fighting which ended the Bourbon regime. The first of these is Delacroix's *Liberty at the Barricades*, painted shortly after the Revolution. The Goddess of Liberty, now given a romantic form rather than the austere classical portrayal common in the 1790s, leads a popular alliance of artisans, liberal bourgeois and street urchins across a barricade and the bodies of martyrs fallen in the struggle to defend the people from reaction. The second image is of the Hôtel de Ville on 31 July: Lafayette, the hero of the American Revolution and of the early years of the French Revolution, embraces Louis-Philippe and thereby legitimizes a new, more constitutional monarch. A former general in the Convention's armies, Louis-Philippe had not fled the Revolution until April 1793 and seemed thereby to offer guarantees of respect for liberal, constitutional rule and reform.

The implication of both images is that the Revolution of 1830 was a popular victory until it was stolen from the people by the bourgeoisie in the months which followed, symbolised in the retort of the Chief Minister, Casimir Périer, in March 1831: 'the trouble with this country is that there are too many people ... who imagine that there has been a revolution'. It is true that the revolution resulted directly only in limited, if significant, political reform, symbolized in the appointment of the 76-year-old Talleyrand as once again ambassador to Britain. The Orléanist regime's revised charter offered guarantees against infringement of press and religious freedoms, restored the tricolour as the national flag and asserted the primacy of the Chamber of Deputies. An electoral reform in 1831 lowered the tax qualification for deputies from 1,000 to 500 francs and for voters from 300 to 200 francs, increasing the electorate from 100,000 to 167,000 (one adult male in fifty).

It is also true, however, that the consolidation of the Orléanist or July Monarchy was only achieved after a prolonged and often violent struggle in which huge numbers of urban and working people mobilized to push the regime in more populist directions before an enlarged propertied élite finally succeeded in crushing such action in 1834. The final acts of this repression were a law on associations (10 April 1834), requiring authorization for all meetings of more than 20 people, and a new press law (9 September 1835) prohibiting insults to the king or calls for a republic, and reintroducing strict censorship and bond money. In 1835, 30 republican newspapers were closed, including *La Tribune*, which had earlier undergone 111 trials and 20 convictions.

From this perspective, it would seem that Casimir Périer was right: 1830 represented no more than the triumph of a slightly enlarged electorate and constitutional monarchy over the rival claims of clerical autocracy and popular democracy. Certainly, the composition of the Chamber of Deputies had changed somewhat – the proportion of *ancien-régime* nobles had declined from two-fifths to one-sixth, and bourgeois were now 65 per cent rather than 35 per cent – but was this simply a shift within a ruling élite of notables? This argument of continuity within the élite across the Revolution of 1830 is conceptually linked to the 'minimalist' argument about the French Revolution: that is, that nobles and well-to-do bourgeois were already fused before 1789 and that this élite endured through all the upheavals of 1785–1835. In contrast, contemporaries as diverse in their views as Louis Blanc, Balzac, Alexis de Tocqueville and Karl Marx (who lived in Paris in 1843–5) agreed that the new regime was in some way 'a bourgeois monarchy', in sharp contrast to the Restoration. The critical issue about the Revolution of 1830 is thus whether the apparently minor political reforms of 1830–1 cloak genuine change in the social composition and political economy of the ruling élite.

In social terms, the Revolution represented a subtle but significant shift in the electorate, which now included a wider range of urban and rural bourgeois (often, those who owned only 30–50 hectares of good land). For example, in the Calvados, voters whose wealth was drawn from industry and commerce increased from 16.7 per cent of the electorate in 1830 to 25.9 in 1847 while landowners fell from 66 to 57.6 per cent (those in the liberal professions remained stable). Nevertheless, the urban electorate remained closely linked to the countryside as merchants and farm suppliers, and especially through its own-ership of land. Even in the capital, Caen, the richest bourgeois drew half of their wealth from land: in 1837 only 187 voters paid more in the *patente* (a business tax) than in land tax.

This subtle shift in the regime's electoral base was reinforced by an 'internal emigration' of legitimist nobility in the 1830s. This was due both to Louis-Philippe's purge of senior administrators and to a deliberate withdrawal from political life of those nobles for whom Louis-Philippe's alleged theft of his cousin's throne in 1830 replayed his father's vote in the Convention in 1793 for the execution of Louis XVI. The new regime dismissed 92 per cent of prefects, 87 per cent of generals and 89 per cent of regional state prosecutors. Half the Chamber of Peers and 120 deputies resigned or had their elections invalidated. At the local level, 112 mayors, 33 of them nobles, resigned in the Dordogne; in the Maine-et-Loire only 134 of 386 mayors did not resign or were not dismissed.

Nevertheless, landed wealth remained the basis of political power under the July Monarchy: 55 per cent of electors were primarily landowners. The nobility also retained its disproportionate position in the élite of wealth. The average tax paid by voters was 497 francs, but 64 per cent of titled nobles and 33 per cent of other nobles paid more than 1,000 francs; conversely, just 7 per cent of bour-geois electors were this wealthy. On average, nobles owned 776 acres (the titled about 2,000) and about 10 per cent of all land, as much as 22.7 per cent of the Loir-et-Cher, 16 per cent of the Pas-de-Calais and 17 per cent of the Calvados. While this was a marked decline from the 25–30 per cent that nobles had owned in 1789, nobles were powerful everywhere. At a national level, 266 of the 387 richest men in France, paying over 5,000 francs in tax, were nobles. Nobles regrouped at the local level during the July Monarchy, for example through the new *Conseils généraux*, elected to advise prefects by the 50 wealthiest tax-payers in each canton. Even at the national level they were re-emerging: by 1846, 25 per cent of deputies were *ancien-régime* nobles and 20 per cent nobles from the Empire.[14]

In these terms, then, the Revolution of 1830 represented only a bourgeois shift in the composition of the electorate which did not significantly alter the on-going pre-eminence of great landed magnates, many of them noble. Historians have made much of this continuity of noble and landed élites, but this disguises essential changes in the economic roles and values of élites in city and country. If in 1840 two-thirds of the 13,000 wealthiest men in France were great landowners, they also drew on business and office-holding for their income. The 165 directors of France's 15 largest companies were not only landowners (24.4 per cent), but were also bankers and merchants (37.7), manufacturers (10.3), professional men (10.9), and officials (15.7). Of the 311 notables in the Chamber of Peers, 83 had shares in insurance, railway or mining companies or were company directors, and 230 were also senior officials (as were 184 of the 459 deputies). De Tocqueville and Marx's vitriolic dismissal of the parliament of the July Monarchy as a stock exchange for the spoils of business and office was based on a social reality.[15]

The Revolution of 1830 was the triumph of 'the generation of 1820'. The élite of the July Monarchy was based on the legitimacy of all forms of wealth and the values of individual improvement and it is no coincidence that structural changes to the economy accelerated at the same time. The Revolution of 1830, by ending the political monopoly of one section of the notables, can thus be understood as the completion of the bourgeois revolution of 1789, and it is not surprising that the regime felt a political affinity with the constitutional monarchy of 1789–91 and placed itself within the march of historical progress. The new government encouraged historical paintings at the annual Salons; Guizot quickly moved to implement his project of preserving and publishing historical documents, institutionalized in the founding of the Société de l'histoire de France and a commission for historical monuments in 1833.[16]

The political economy of the regime marked a decisive break with the past and generated an interrelated series of changes which were to have profound effects on French society. From the outset, Casimir Périer, the son of the Dauphinois capitalist Claude Périer, reassured business that the regime meant external peace and internal order to stall 'the falling off of productivity' and 'injury to private interests': 'our ambition is to re-establish confidence'. His insistence that 'France [would] never exhort the world to liberty except by peaceful example' dashed republican hopes that armed aid would be given to revolutions in Belgium, Italy and Poland. Instead the regime developed a new set of administrative policies to deal with the 6,000 Spanish, Italian and Polish refugees, isolating them in towns well away from the border.[17]

The regime's concern to avoid foreign conflict was not applied to Algeria, where the July Monarchy expanded the Restoration's initial conquest into a long and murderous war of annexation. A bombardment of Tangier and Essaouira in 1844 forced Morocco to accept the French presence in North Africa. Disappointed at missing out on the south island of New Zealand – settlers at 'Port-Louis-Philippe' on Banks Peninsula arrived a few months too late – the regime also prepared to acquire control of Polynesia. The population of the Marquesas Islands was devastated by European diseases and by military retribution for resisting the invaders, whose power was symbolically enacted in the bizarre choice of 3 pm on Good Friday 1845 for the execution of Chief Pakoko.[18]

The historian of the Parisian bourgeoisie, Adeline Daumard, has discerned an appreciable shift in the locus of business and professional activities as these men, now more confident about their dominance and the political environment, expanded their sphere of enterprise to a national scale.[19] The nature and range of the July Monarchy's economic intervention was an important departure in the direction of state-stimulated capitalism. To Marx and de Tocqueville, the Chamber of Deputies conducted itself like a board of directors. However, they were confusing the eagerness of deputies to urge state spending in their electorates and to speculate in a booming share market with the source of economic change, for most deputies continued to be preoccupied with their local constituency and grandiose election promises, made notorious by the fierce satire of Le Charivari and Daumier. Instead, it was the national and tech-nocratic concern of key departments, such as Public Works, which had a vision of rivalling Britain economically even if the foreign policy of the regime preached peace at any price. Bureaucrats such as B.-A. Legrand, trained in administration under Napoleon and now applying 'national interests' to the economy, combined with reforming ministers such as Guizot to push through plans for a social, financial and communications infrastructure. This was espe-cially the case in the railway construction of the 1840s, where the State bought the land and built the lines, while private firms supplied the rolling stock and management. The July Monarchy also increased the construction of all-weather roads threefold, to 1,326 kilometres per year.

The regime's encouragement of urban enterprise spurred a marked increase in the urban population. While France's population grew 8 per cent in 1831–46 (from 32.57 to 35.4 million), Paris grew by 33.5 per cent, Marseille 26 per cent and Lyon 33 per cent. Other established cities experienced major industrial expansion (Rouen, Lille, Strasbourg) or commercial booms (Bordeaux, Le Havre, Nantes); while smaller towns dominated by one or two industries grew dramatically: Le Creusot (metallurgy), Roubaix, Elbeuf, Mulhouse (textiles), Limoges (paper and porcelain), Saint-Etienne (metallurgy and textiles). Overall, industrial production was 30 per cent higher in 1835–44 than in the previous decade.[20]

Throughout the July Monarchy policies were pursued to smother workers' organizations and to hold wages down, to favour large enterprises against smaller rivals, to expand a banking network while removing restrictions on bankrupts returning to business, to create a special bureau of national statistics within the Ministry of the Interior, and to maintain protective external tariffs and internal free trade. Two particularly important pieces of legislation were passed in 1833. First, a law on compensation for land appropriation by the State for railways was pushed through, representing a significant, revealing victory of a concept of land as a commodity whose value was simply its market price against those who argued in vain for a concept of land having a *valeur d'affection* for those who had worked it for generations. Then, in the same year, Guizot's pri-mary-education bill clearly laid down a vision of a skilled, obedient and 'civilized' labour force. Children were to be taught the skills of literacy and numeracy within a Christian moral framework; they were to be ranked by merit and disciplined by a code of sanctions rather than by corporal punishment.

The deputies of the July Monarchy were divided ideologically, between the majorities who supported Guizot's *juste milieu* and angry minorities of legitimists, democrats and reformist liberals who agitated for various degrees of electoral reform, a more assertive foreign policy, and action on the stark evidence of urban poverty aggravated by the refusal of the regime to countenance effective measures on child labour, piece-rates or wages. Whatever the internal conflicts within the regime, however, the deputies and their electorate all agreed on two things: the need to keep workers in line and to encourage agricultural productivity.

Gwynne Lewis has furnished a rich example of the changed context for large-scale enterprise. Since the 1770s the Norman entrepreneur Pierre-François Tubeuf, who had discovered a rich seam of coal at La Grand' Combe near Alès, had been dogged by the noble Castries family, recalcitrant local peasants and workers, and state indecision about below-surface mining concessions on private land. Only after 1830 was a regime in place with a political economy which encouraged large-scale mining leases. By then, both the Tubeufs and Castries had sold their mines to two local bourgeois, Jean-Jacques Puech and Pierre Goirand, who formed the La Grand' Combe company, backed by the prominent politician Odilon Barrot. In 1837 the July Monarchy granted them a loan of six million francs and opened one of the country's first railway lines, from the mine to Beaucaire on the Rhône.[21]

In Limanton, where this chapter began, the 1830s and 1840s were a watershed in agricultural and attitudinal change among notables, symbolized in the sale in 1841 of the largest estate, of the marquis Bruneau de Vitry, to a retired army officer, Antoine Boussaraque.[22] The opening of the Nivernais Canal in the late 1830s and consequent access to markets was the stimulus to large landowners to reorient production on the rich soils of the Aron valley towards cattle farming. In two decades artificial meadows increased from 25 to 368 hectares, as clover was sown on fallow, and natural meadows from 500 to 722 hectares; communal herds grew from 920 to 1,583 head. The substantial investments being made by landowners required far closer supervision of tenants for whom future gains would be at the expense of present subsistence; in the words of a local agronomist, 'the proprietor will be the head, the sharecropper (*métayer*) the arms, but arms which are loyal and obedient to all commands'. Inevitably, sharecropping itself came under question as landlords turned to money leases (*fermage*) to shift incentives to tenants; now they would simply provide cash rent in return for land, tools and animals. Within ten years, from 1836 to 1846, the proportion of *fermage* to *métayage* leases changed from 19 : 81 to 46 : 54. A world of change is encompassed in this transformation of soil resources into a productive commodity and of peasant sharecroppers into market-oriented farmers.

One of the paradoxes of these years is that the 'internal emigration' of legitimist landowners resulted in them paying far greater attention to their local estates. This was a time of 'agromania', reflected in the proliferation of agricultural improvement societies, often dominated by legitimists or other great magnates. Under the Restoration there had been about a hundred such societies at the departmental or district level and just ten cantonal committees (*comices agricoles*); by 1844 there were up to 300 of the former and 800 of the latter. Adolphe de Bourgoing is an example of such a legitimist improver. On his 170 hectares at Mesves-sur-Loire, near Limanton, he had by 1840 introduced the Dombasle and Rozé ploughs, threshing machines, lucerne, sainfoin and clover. He was remarkably active in local public life, and in 1849 was the founding president of the Cosne *comice agricole*. Of course, the speed and extent of these economic changes should not be exaggerated: in many parts of the Nièvre subsistence polyculture and sharecropping remained predominant for decades. Over much of France, many absentee landowners remained uninterested in agricultural change and continued to enforce stultifying tenancy contracts. This was particularly so in the sharecropping regions of the Armagnac, the Bourbonnais and parts of Provence, where crop-sharing and the 'bourgeois tithe' (requiring tenants to contribute to the landlord's taxes) endured throughout the century.[23]

A corollary of changes wrought to the urban and rural economy by the State, the bourgeoisie and 'progressive' nobles was a paternalistic liberalism in social attitudes. The *mentalité* underpinning Guizot's education laws pervaded Orléanist attitudes to the 'social question': ways had to be found of encouraging hard work, abstinence, thrift and self-help through selective assistance, firm policing and moral example. While the cotton-mill owner Grivel, of Auchy-lès-Hesdin (Pas-de-Calais) sought to 'moralize' his 2,500 workers by providing housing, separating the sexes at work, and paying them monthly, the doctrine of individual responsibility more commonly allowed unchecked exploitation. One of 'the generation of 1820', Charles Dunoyer, who, like so many of his peers, became committed to the Orléanist philosophy of economic liberty, individual self-help and public order, argued in 1835 that state-funded social welfare simply 'denuded the good plants for the sake of the weeds': 'Is there any difficulty in pointing out thousands of men, who, by their idleness and licentiousness and above all by the criminal abuse they make of their reproductive powers, behave as if on purpose to aggravate their own misfortune? ... Society owes everybody justice and protection: it owes nobody lucrative employment, education or bread in default of work.'[24] While the July Monarchy was content to follow Dunoyer's assurances, the stark evidence of misery and crime in industrial towns combined with popular protest to keep the social question before its eyes. Official enquiries generated a plethora of reports on crime, health and industrial conditions and maps linking demography, education and health with social problems (including one correlating diet, topography and the incidence of hernias). The work of Villermé, Parent-Duchâtelet and other 'hygienists' combined a lively awareness of the extent of working-class misery with a refusal to concede that it was not simply the result of individual failings.[25]

This assumption particularly informed Parent-Duchâtelet's survey of Parisian prostitutes: despite his graphic evidence of the misery driving young women to sell sexual gratification, he insisted on seeking physiological and moral explanations for 'their crime'. To him prostitution was a question of public health in its widest sense, because of the risk of contamination of bourgeois families by venereal disease, just as were the sewers and slaughter-houses on which he had previously written reports. Parent-Duchâtelet was a fervent exponent of the 'regulatory' system developed under the Directory and Empire, requiring 'a vile trade' to be controlled by police and doctors and paid for by the prostitutes themselves: 'a girl spreads a subtle poison through society which attacks the principles of life at their source; by this trade she commits an offence against society; now it is recognized that the one who commits the offence should pay the costs of repression of this offence and its effects'.[26] Prostitutes who refused to submit to the regulatory controls were incarcerated in separate prisons built in 1801, 1826 and finally Saint-Lazare in 1836, and were encouraged to seek rehabilitation in religious reformatories.

The regime's attitude to the penal system – as to education and prostitution – manifested a distinctive combination of concern for public order and moral rehabilitation as the twin solution to social ills. In 1832, the same year that the Academy of Moral and Political Sciences – abolished by Napoleon – was reopened as part of the *Institut*, the regime abolished shackles, branding and amputation as punishments. Similarly, the regime required prison teachers to be trained and prisons to have a library. Concerned about the nefarious influence of public punishment, the regime shortened the street procession to the guillotine (1832) and in 1836 abolished the chain gang for hard-labour sentences, removing the spectacle of *bagnards* in iron collars struggling along the roads to Brest, Toulon and Lorient. However, extensive prison rioting in the years after the Revolution of 1830 also convinced it of the need for greater prison discipline. This combination of discipline and rehabilitation was evident in the new prison for juveniles in Paris, the Petite Roquette, where young offenders were kept in cellular isolation and subjected to a strict regime of manual and academic work.[27]

The coincidence in 1832 of the outbreak of cholera and the insurrection following General Lamarque's funeral (the climax of Hugo's *Les Misérables*) convinced conservatives that the fevers of revolution and epidemics were inextricably linked. In the complex of issues pertaining to prostitution, disease, crime, living conditions and public order which hygienists collapsed into 'public health', male medical professionals claimed an expert role. Doctors sought to protect and extend their prestige by a vigorous campaign to control *officiers de santé* (less trained and less expensive medical officers in poorer areas) and to regulate the training and internal discipline of their profession. Concerns about professional expertise and public order coincided with mistrust of the clergy in the July Monarchy's 1838 law on 'insane asylums'. Doctors appointed by the State now claimed the 'consoling' as well as the supervisory role of the Church and the punitive function of the judiciary. The *'aliénistes'* among psychiatrists sought a monopoly of moral and scientific treatment, though their claims were always juxtaposed with the belief of Guizot, Royer-Collard and other politicians that psychological disorder was a symptom of popular political unrest and lack of personal restraint. Many rural departments were forced to continue to maintain church asylums because of the cost of replacing them but at the same time encouraged them to move to the periphery of towns. The presence of the insane – as of noxious industries and executions – was deemed to be offensive to the well-to-do and unedifying for the masses.[28]

The July Monarchy coincided with the expression of a distinctive bourgeois culture in the nature of personal relations, the place of women and children, the style and function of clothing, furniture and food, and the practice of leisure and manners. Already evident before the Revolution of 1789, this culture now emerged as dominant; significantly, the disparaging term *'vivre bourgeoisement'*, which aspiring bourgeois had once so eagerly tried to escape, became less common as noble and bourgeois culture melded into a lifestyle of 'notability'. A bourgeoisie confident of its abilities but profoundly uneasy about its political security – had not the perils of 1792–4 narrowly been averted in 1831–4? – placed a primacy on public endeavour and private modesty. This endless search for affluence, respectability and the quieting of anxiety was what most intrigued and repelled Flaubert, Stendhal and Balzac about this bourgeois world they understood so intimately. The king himself personified this culture, with his home-centred, ordered family routine, his bourgeois dress and 'moderation': to de Tocqueville, he was 'chief of the bourgeoisie', orderly, sober, intelligent, and modest in all things except his passion for industry and wealth.

While in economic and political terms the Orléanist bourgeoisie felt itself all-powerful, it remained caught between the old nobility's genealogical certainties on the one hand and the unsettling social question on the other. The deepest anxieties about its social legitimacy were expressed in personal and sexual relations, that conflict between freedom and control Peter Gay sees as the heart of all *mentalités*. 'The anarchic charm of infatuation' was controlled behind the façade of privacy by an unending search for suitable marriage partners, particularly for daughters, and family sanctions against misalliances and 'impropriety'. Central to the gender stereotyping elaborated by bourgeois men was anxiety about the male line: if noblemen had ancient codes which guaranteed 'honour', how was a bourgeois eminence based on work and wealth to be protected from filial deviation? Such fears underpinned both the regular harassment of homosexuals and prostitutes and the tighter legislation of April 1832 against 'paedophilia'. Just as bourgeois men of all ages were exhorted to enact a natural 'maleness', so women were expected to perform certain 'natural' roles. The medical publicist J. J. Virey, widely read from the Restoration to the 1860s, described this complementarity in *De la femme*, a book for men about women, the source of 'the delights and the torments of man'. For Virey, the ideal, natural union was of:

> the most female woman and the most virile man, when a dark, hairy, dry, hot and impetuous male finds the other sex delicate, moist, smooth and white, timid and modest. The one must give and the other is constituted to receive ... to welcome, to absorb, out of a sort of need and feeling of deficit, the overflow of the other in order to establish equality and reach fullness.[29]

Anxiety about 'order', expressed in the male world through tighter controls on crime, prostitution and deviance, was expressed in the home through the popularity of manuals on manners and child-rearing. Mme de Celnart's *Manuel complet de la bonne compagnie* described in detail the restrictions of age, sex and class on offering or requesting shelter during a rainstorm: 'it would be out of place to offer assistance to persons from the lower classes, though if such a person asks you, you must agree graciously'. Manuals written by Claire de Rémusat, Eliza Guizot (the mother and wife of prominent Orléanist politicians), and Aimé Martin stressed the roles of mothers as inculcators of public virtues and private morality. This was one reason why the practice of sending children to rural wet nurses began to decline, as bourgeois parents became more scornful of peasant customs and were subjected to a literature which emphasized early socialization by a complex of rules and non-corporal discipline governing behaviour. Similar views crossed the political spectrum, from legitimist bishops to Michelet, though Michelet's second wife, Athénaïs Mialaret, recalled the greater freedom and affection she had experienced until the age of four with her wet nurse in the south-west. The domestic virtues of 'the mistress of the house' closely involved with children were also adopted by many noblewomen. Unlike smaller bourgeois families, nobles now had twice as many children as in the late eighteenth century and kept them at home until the age of seven. Convinced, like the clergy, that the evils of the Revolution had been partly due to their own social order's corruption and excess, noblewomen saw ordered domesticity as the source of social harmony and the esteem of their inferiors.[30]

Pivotal to the sexual discourse of Virey, Michelet and other male publicists was a sharp dimorphism which theoretically resulted in the perfect union of virility and docility, public and private, science and nature, man and woman. But this complementarity was in no sense an equality and echoed the reasons given by men for excluding women from political rights in the 1790s. It also furnished the increasingly male and professionalized urban medical expert with a domestic space to control, though birth remained the domain of the midwife and many women brought wet nurses into their homes. The medical construct of the ideal female body and its desires became more prestigious after 1830, even though medical treatment for 'hysterical attacks' could range from lime-blossom tea to the application of leeches to the vulva. Psychiatrists began to win judicial respect with their claims that female criminals were suffering from 'menstrual psychosis' or 'menopausal mania'.[31]

Certainly, the distance between the prescriptive messages of such literature and the actuality of women's lives may have been great. The Parisian bourgeoise Stéphanie Jullien insisted to her father that she could not be with someone that she did not love:

> that I am to marry for reason's sake, in order to give myself *a lot in life* … . How could I hold onto him, if I do not love him and desire him? … It is a feeling without which marriage would be hell, a feeling that cannot be born of esteem, and which to me, however, seems to be the very basis of conjugal happiness.

But Stéphanie accepted the contrast 'between the destiny of man and the destiny of woman', and few bourgeois women bridged the widening gap between the public and private domains of the sexes. Some were successful businesswomen, and others, driven by the tension between their gender roles and their abilities, became active writers and painters (George Sand, Louise Colet, Rosa Bonheur, Marie d'Agoult) or, like Eugénie Niboyet, joined working-class women in the feminist organizations of the early 1830s.[32]

At the same time that élite men were wearing simplified 'business suits' as a sign of serious activity, shunning the jewellery and lace of the *ancien régime*, women's dress was increasingly complicated and fussy, a 'language' with multiple meanings: their husband's wealth, the titillating modesty of narrow bodices and flounced skirts, and of women's inactivity in tight corsets and full dresses. Sex-role differentiation extended to cooking: the July Monarchy saw the proliferation of élite restaurants run by male chefs and publicized by male connoisseurs, while domestic cooking was the task of female servants. The new domesticity also increased the emphasis on water's cleansing powers: in the 1830s Paris was equipped with new systems for supplying clean water and evacuating waste. While most Parisians took baths only rarely – public baths were used a total of two million times by a population of one million in the year 1850 – or swam in the Seine in summer, the well-to-do had begun to install bathrooms with hot water, while following Mme de Celnart's injunction to keep their eyes closed while washing their genitals. Hot water was not only seen as sexually stimulating, but also as enervating, particularly if the hair was washed. In contrast, as Alain Corbin has revealed, new medical certainties about the curative properties of cold seawater drew middle-class visitors to growing beach resorts from Deauville to Arcachon. Corbin has also discerned a heightened bourgeois conviction that workers – like peasants, prostitutes, and even Jews and homosexuals – carried overpowering, unhealthy smells with them; the bidet and the vase became essential items of domestic propriety.[33]

The primordial values of privacy and politeness among the well-to-do were expressed similarly in new expressions for appreciating beauty. Whereas, for example, eighteenth-century audiences at concerts chatted, moved and commented loudly on the performance, James Johnson has discerned the victory by the 1830s of the values of silent appreciation. Etiquette manuals reminded those eager to learn the lessons of good taste that talking during performances or leaving early risked opprobrium; warned the *Journal des débats* in 1847, 'the bourgeoisie isn't a class, it's a position. You acquire it, you lose it.'[34]

The corollary of bourgeois gender stereotyping and the desire for domestic propriety and small families was that both sexes found other outlets for their needs for sociability. To the male *cercle* or club, places of leisure and learning, corresponded women's attraction to church organizations, a refuge from isolation and male dominance of the home. The Church could also offer moral approval of women's personal sacrifices and charitable good works, while men found solace with their peers or prostitutes. A police officer in the Midi criticized 'the roughness and lack of consideration shown to women' by bourgeois men; married women live 'generally in a very great reserve. Their husbands, occupied in côteries of men or with chasing prostitutes, oblige[d] them to seek happiness in the home or with their children, or in assiduous attendance at church.' Many men simply abstained from worship: in the town of Cahors

(Lot), only one bourgeois took Easter Communion in 1845, and factories in Rouen and Marseille stayed open on Sundays.

This feminizing of church practice mirrored other changes in religious life. For political reasons, only 12 of the 77 bishops nominated by the July Monarchy were nobles, and by mid-century most of the episcopate was from bourgeois and even artisan and peasant backgrounds. Religious minorities, too, were affected by changes in cultural values: rabbis complained about deserted synagogues and the disappearance of Hebrew in bourgeois homes as well-to-do Jews sent their children to state schools. Perhaps, as Philippe Ariès has suggested, even attitudes to death altered among the bourgeoisie, as the decline in the impact of church teachings and the greater stress on affective relations within the bourgeois family popularized the 'beautiful death' commemorated in the ostentatious tombs of the period.[35]

The July Monarchy was a great age of bourgeois sociability and written culture across the country, despite the regime's tight censorship and control of public gatherings. When sales of *Le Constitutionnel* slumped to 3,600 in 1844, the new publisher, Louis Véron, emulated *Le Siècle* and *La Presse* by combining cheap subscriptions, a large format and serialized novels *(feuilletons)*. Véron paid Eugène Sue 100,000 francs for the rights to *Le Juif errant* and thereby boosted sales to 25,000 by 1846. Between 1834 and 1846, not only did provincial subscriptions to Parisian papers double to over 95,000, but the provincial press grew rapidly. Many sales were by subscription to the 2,000 officially-licensed bourgeois *cercles* (with 121,858 members in 1843) and smaller gatherings with fewer than 20 members which did not need a permit. Small country towns such as Nantua (Ain), Bourganeuf (Creuse) and Château-Thierry (Aisne) all had a weekly for fewer than 5,000 inhabitants, and Dinan (Côtes-du-Nord) had two for 7,600. Most of these papers were conservative information sheets, but some were openly critical in their political outlook, such as the thinly-disguised republicanism of *L'Union de l'Yonne*, launched in Auxerre in 1844, or the anti-Orléanism of *L'Indépendant des Pyrénées-Orientales*, founded in 1846 by a coalition of legitimists and republicans united in their contempt for the materialism of the Parisian élite.[36]

The serialization of novels is one reason why book sales also grew rapidly in these decades. Sales also boomed because of cheap Belgian editions and the growth of reading rooms and lending libraries frequented especially by bourgeois women. As Martyn Lyons has shown, however, this did not represent a sharp break in the reading public's taste: the three best-sellers in both 1821–5 and 1841–5 were La Fontaine's *Fables* (sales of 88,000–125,000 in 1841–5), Fleury's *Catéchisme historique* (80,000–100,000) and Fénelon's *Télémaque* (82,000–98,000). Also popular in the early 1840s were the reprinted histories of France by Saint-Ouen and Anquetil and a proliferation of romantic novels by Walter Scott, Daniel Defoe and Alexandre Dumas. Balzac and Stendhal were nowhere in the top 30 best-sellers, which were dominated by a durable current of classical and religious literature.[37]

What did the French bourgeoise read when she opened an illustrated magazine such as *Le Magasin pittoresque*? She was offered illustrated stories on exotic places (Majorca, Greece) and animals, a good deal of classical and medieval history (the game of chess in Charlemagne's time), folklore (the festival of Saint-Jean in Brittany), and useful information, for example on the taxation system (criticizing only the state lotteries 'which have corrupted the inferior classes ... by distracting them from work, thrift and order, the primary means of self-improvement'). The magazine was intensely nationalistic: 'the French nationality is the most beautiful of the continent' and its language a marvel of beauty and clarity, despite the persistence of *patois* in 'the most backward rural areas'. It was also wishfully optimistic: 'the Revolution of 1789 put the final seal on the political unity of this illustrious people!', and, now that 'the smoke of combat has dissipated, peace has returned, and internal order is re-established'.

Like any other regime, the July Monarchy was convinced that its policies represented the 'national interest', 'progress', indeed 'society' itself. When Henri-Joseph Gisquet, a former employee and protégé of Casimir Périer who became Paris Prefect of Police in the early 1830s, published his lengthy memoirs in 1841, he concluded by defining his political philosophy: to him, the July Monarchy, 'wisely liberal, always in harmony with the country's needs', was the ideal regime to ensure 'public order, the development of the intelligence and education of the masses'. His commitment was to constitutional government, in the hands of 'pure and able' men of 'merit and honesty'. Above all, Louis-Philippe's regime was seen as a bulwark against the twin evils of legitimism and republicanism: 'I want neither the commotions nor the popular excesses of a republican government; nor do I want this divine right which claims France as its patrimony, and which wants to smother the progress of reason with the tyranny of aristocracy and absolutism.'

Gisquet's affirmation was a direct response to the crisis of 1839–40 which nearly toppled the regime.[38] In May 1839 a clandestine republican organization ('The Society of the Seasons') tried to seize power and two days of fighting, and 100 deaths, were necessary to repress it. In August 1840, Napoleon's nephew Louis Napoleon landed at Boulogne hoping to foment a Bonapartist rising. Like that at Strasbourg in 1836, this was an ignominious failure, but Louis Napoleon was a living reminder of a regime which grew more attractive to the disenfranchized with the passing of time. Louis-Philippe's attempt to profit from and undermine Bonapartist memories by bringing Napoleon's ashes from St-Helena to the Invalides in December simply allowed freer rein to nostalgic comparisons with the July Monarchy's lack of glory and a founding principle. In 1840, too, *Le National* launched a series of banquets calling for electoral reform. This coincided with a wave of food rioting following poor harvests; in one incident in Foix (Ariège), 13 protesters were killed. The same year, another of the 18 attempts on Louis-Philippe's life was made. Further political storms erupted with the decision to construct new fortifications around Paris and to make concessions to British interests in the Middle East and Tahiti.

In October, Louis-Philippe appointed the Guizot-Soult government, which was to give the regime six years of unprecedented stability, fuelled by a speculative boom in industrial and railway shares. Guizot's ideology of the 'golden mean' *(juste milieu)* stemmed from his horror of both republicanism (his father had been guillotined during the Terror) and legitimism (fellow Protestants in the Gard had been massacred in 1815). As the July Monarchy seemed to become more stable and durable in the 1840s, increasing numbers of notables of all political persuasions were prepared to acquiesce in its institutions. Nevertheless, the twin evils which Gisquet and Guizot were so keen to avoid, legitimism and republicanism, remained as constant alternatives because, unlike the July Monarchy, they could call on claims to past glory and the popular will. Guizot's injunction to those who called for a widening of the suffrage that they should work to meet the property franchise (*'enrichissez-vous'*) seemed specious. As Jo Burr Margadant has argued, the assumption that only individual merit justified public honour was inherently destabilizing for the July Monarchy, particularly in the context of continuing vilification and caricature by its opponents of the lack of 'honour' in the royal family.[39]

'Honour' was a watchword of these years. Robert Nye has analysed the survival and codification of the duel as a symbol and practice of masculinity. Whereas duelling disappeared in Britain and the United States before 1848, in France there were at least one hundred per year, one-third of them fatal.[40] The July Monarchy made repeated and unsuccessful efforts to reduce the duel to one more form of criminal assault. Instead, the duel was assimilated into bourgeois codes of appropriate, codified behaviour whose existence was seen as evidence of political virility. For journalists, many of whom fought duels, the tension between private interest and public function was particularly acute, caught as they were between notions of honour and the exigencies of employment for the political press. One resolution was found in the ceaseless cascade of scorn for those seen to have compromised honour in public life, none more so than the king himself. For example, in 1840, the major liberal opposition daily, *Le National*, castigated the government for its obsequious surrender of Beirut to the British in these terms: 'Honour, that dear, sacred treasure of nations whose hearts soar, honour rejects all compromise, all trickery; honour has been too often attacked to go without vengeance. Are we the sons of our fathers, or have we aged and degenerated, as they now dare to claim in the councils of our enemies?'[41]

Legitimists in contrast sustained a world apart in the regions they dominated (Brittany, the west, the Midi). In these regions nobles drew on popular antipathy to the 'bourgeois monarchy' as they awaited a full Bourbon restoration under the comte de Chambord as Henri V (the 'miracle child' born to the duchesse de Berry after her husband's assassination in 1820). Basic to legitimist ideology was an analogy between the patriarchal family and an idealized agrarian, Catholic, hierarchical and monarchical state. In contrast to Orléanist liberalism, which saw society in terms of individuals and their rights within the State, legitimists had an understanding of society as an organic whole, in which every aspect of life had a moral unity. It was such a *mentalité* which informed the social concerns of men like Bourgoing and Villeneuve-Bargemont and explains their image of the July Monarchy as morally corrupt, materialistic, godless and selfish. After his dismissal as Prefect of the Nord in 1830, Villeneuve-Bargemont wrote a scarifying account of poverty in industrial Lille, calling for a return to Christian values and state intervention as the only possible solution (as director of a railway company, he was implacably opposed to strikes). On their great estates, legitimist landholders continued to practise – at least in theoretical terms – an appropriate form of paternalism *(patronage)* towards those dependent on them. As the legitimist paper *La Quotidienne* defined it admiringly in 1844, *patronage* is 'an exchange of affection and recognition which tempers and consecrates, by softening its harshness, the providential inequality of the human condition'.[42]

Instances of great landowners being republicans are far rarer. One, recalled by Ernest Lavisse from his childhood in Nouvion-en-Thiérarche (Somme), had two prized engravings: one of Bailly and the Tennis Court Oath of 1789, the other of the representatives of the 13 American colonies signing the Oath of Independence. Much more commonly, republicanism within the élite was urban and outside the world of Parliament, where erstwhile republicans such as François Arago, Garnier-Pagès, Marie and even the radical Ledru-Rollin seemed to have accepted the legitimacy of the July Monarchy in the 1840s. Disaffected journalists clustered round *Le National* and the social democratic *La Réforme* (founded in 1843), whose editor Ferdinand Flocon was described by a contemporary as having the 1793 Declaration of the Rights of Man 'constantly in his head and his pocket'.[43]

To most members of the élite, republicanism was simply an anathema, just as legitimism was equated with obscurantism. When the liberal noble d'Alton-Shée referred to the National Convention of 1792 in the Chamber of Peers in January 1848, he was drummed into silence by the banging of paper-knives on tables.[44] It was rather from the world of urban and rural working people that was to come a stronger challenge to constitutional monarchy.

7
The World of Urban Working People, 1815–1845

> This high price of corn [the highest for 15 years] was the cause of the unrest which spread amongst the people and of the disturbances which broke out at the beginning of the winter. During the first few days of November there was quite a serious insurrection at Toulouse; people refused to buy corn at the price fixed and tried to steal it from the markets. Order was only restored with difficulty, after the disturbance had gone on for several days.[1]

This report by the Minister of the Interior on the harvest failure of 1816 and the food rioting which subsequently erupted in many cities and towns could have been written in similar terms during earlier crises, in 1775 or even 1709. In refusing to accept high prices, working people in Toulouse were manifesting age-old hostility to merchants and revealing the primacy of food prices in matters of survival. Similarly, the regime's responses to the crisis – prohibiting exports and making large purchases overseas – were of a long-established type. Louis exhibited 'his continual goodness and his truly fatherly concern for his subjects' by dispensing charity in Lyon and placing a special order for silk for royal palaces. His officials also employed the *ancien-régime* tactic of using police agents to identify troublesome workers, supplemented by legislation from the Revolution and Empire prohibiting strikes and 'coalitions'.

Two years later, a very different type of protest erupted. In February 1819, the royal prosecutor in the town of Vienne, to the south of Lyon, reported a furious attack by textile workers on a new machine brought into the town by their employers. Cases of machinery were flung into the river Gère and smashed with the tools of trade, as weavers shouted 'We'll do for the machine all right', 'It's not the bloody machine that wants smashing' and 'Get rid of the machine.' Skilled artisans at the time of the Revolution had also been hostile to machinery, but such direct attacks were rare until after 1815. Such protest, while sporadic and geographically specific, points to the gradual but dislocating changes affecting urban France under the Restoration.

The political economy of the regime also reflects these unsettling changes: the Revolution had facilitated a more rapid process of urban industrialization which could not easily be accommodated within the Restoration's paternalistic ideology of responsible, hierarchical social control. It was one thing to regard urban workers as above all a matter of public order whose occasional rumblings were to be met by a combination of strict repression and selective indulgence. But the regime found it difficult to incorporate innovating entrepreneurs who did not share such sentiments of responsibility and who were beginning to reshape the world of urban work.

The population of France grew by 16 per cent (from 30.5 to 35.4 million) in the years 1821–46, disproportionately in towns; the urban population, defined as those living in centres with more than 2,000 people, grew 0.7 per cent annually in 1811–31, then by 1 per cent per annum over the next 20 years. The raw figures of population growth disguise an endless variety within the structures of urban France: of stable, long-established administrative and trading centres (Bordeaux, Nantes), of old cities where new industries unleashed a rapid spurt of social change and population increase (Limoges, Saint-Etienne), of declining towns marooned by administrative reorganization or economic collapse during the Revolution and Empire (Beaucaire, Autun), of new, mono-industrial factory cities (Decazeville, Le Creusot, Roubaix, Montceau-les-Mines). Every town and city remained tied to its hinterland by a nexus of administrative, military and economic functions and through its workforce: in 1820, some 17 per cent of Perpignan's 12,500 inhabitants were agricultural labourers and market-gardeners. In makeshift suburbs *(faubourgs)* on the semi-rural edges of expanding cities such as Paris and Reims congregated the increasing numbers of migrants who aroused in élites a morbid fear of 'marginals', seen as semi-urban and semi-civilized.[2]

In Limoges, the ancient topographic opposition of the *quartiers* of the château and the *cité*, reflecting the social polarity of bourgeoisie and clergy, was swamped by new working-class suburbs as the city grew from 20,000 in 1801 to 38,000 in 1846.[3] The discovery in the eighteenth century of a fine white clay had made Limoges a centre of porcelain manufacturing, though the business was as risky for businessmen as it was hazardous to the health of skilled workers. Industrial and urban expansion occurred within the framework of an *ancien-régime* city. Limoges was notorious for its crowded, dirty streets, none more so than the rue de la Boucherie. Here, long-established clans of butchers were legendary for their large patriarchal families, fervent religiosity and enthusiastic support for the Bourbon monarchy, as they were for the packs of dogs, raucous noise, blood and stench which pervaded their street. In 1828, an army officer found that 'their clothes, their habits, the saints who protect them, their church, their language, indeed, everything is unique to them. They delight in the most excessive filth.'

South-east of Limoges, across the Massif Central, Louis XVIII's former prime minister, the duc de Decazes, founded in 1826 a coal-mining company headed by bankers, aristocrats and businessmen.[4] By 1840 this was the fourth largest industrial enterprise in France, and the tiny village of 'Decazeville' had become a settlement of 8,000 people living in makeshift houses which might have been called a town 'had the municipal authorities taken the trouble to align the houses and to build roads'. This was a violent, industrial 'frontier' town in the heart of rural France. The miners of Decazeville were a mixture of skilled, full-time miners (many from Britain) and semi-skilled workers who alternated their industrial labour with agricultural work in nearby villages.

For every Limoges or Decazeville there were other towns and cities which continued to be based on small-scale, artisanal production. By 1831 the teeming medieval quarters of Paris were housing 43 per cent more people than in 1801 (an increase from 547,000 to 786,000). Such an influx was not due mainly to work opportunities in new industries, for Paris remained a city of artisanal workplaces, apart from a few heavy industries and, later, railway workshops in the northern suburbs of Saint-Denis and La Chapelle. Paris's growth was partly due to the collapse of rural and provincial networks for the poor with the expropriation of the Church and the decline in noble wealth, forcing the economically vulnerable to migrate to the capital in search of work. Other towns actually declined in economic vitality. The great medieval fair-town of Beaucaire on the lower Rhône never recovered from the wars of 1792–1815, although the brief peace of 1800–3 saw a temporary resumption of its former activity, with 217 boats, largely from Spain and Italy, and sales of 46 million francs at the fair of 1802. By 1815, however, the Mediterranean trade circuit was in disarray and the locus of commerce had shifted to Atlantic ports for cotton imports from the United States and wool from Argentina and Australia; the construction of better roads and finally the railway from Lyon to Marseille were the final blows to Beaucaire's proud past.[5]

The Restoration élite assumed that sprawling towns nourished the twin social vices of crime and revolution, but the arbitrary and sporadic benevolence of the monarchy could never be an adequate response to the unprecedented growth of Paris and Lyon which placed overwhelming strain on living and working conditions. Skilled workers instead sustained their own work routines and conditions in defiance of employers and the law. The National Assembly in 1791 had banned all workers' associations or 'coalitions' and had reinforced existing laws against strikes and other obstacles to the functioning of the labour market as a set of individual contracts. In defiance of this, skilled workers had invested their journeymen's brotherhoods (*compagnonnages*) with the function of controlling wages and work as well as being a forum for popular sociability. By 1823, there were 160 such illegal, but tolerated, associations in Paris, with 11,000 members. Such highly-ritualized, semi-clandestine organizations could group a number of trades (the *Enfants de Maître Jacques* in Paris had members from 20 occupations) or neighbourhoods (the *Enfants de Salomon* and the *Enfants de Père Soubise* opposed the carpenters of the two banks of the Seine). Agricol Perdiguier, a *compagnon* joiner from the Vaucluse who worked in Paris, recalled the negotiations with masters over the price of labour or of a task as the two parties manoeuvred between threats of a strike or of informing the police. He also recalled the male world of ritualized and often bloody celebration and brawling between *compagnonnages* at funerals, patron saints' festivals and other gatherings.[6]

The Empire and the Restoration sought to undermine *compagnonnages* and inculcate individual responsibility by encouraging the establishment of mutual-aid societies, voluntary organizations to distribute sickness benefits to contributing members. These could be transformed into trade associations to control entry into jobs. In Marseille, for example, only four of 47 skilled trades were without one. The police in Lyon described the association of skilled hatters:

> [It] places the journeyman, fixes the number of hats each worker can make per day; workers who are strangers to the city cannot be admitted without paying a fee; the apprentice is obliged to pay what they call the *'béjaune'* [a levy to enter the trade]…the workers impose fines of which they themselves are the arbiters, and until a worker has paid the fine inflicted upon him, he is excluded from work.

Occasionally, workers' actions were more open. Jacques-Etienne Bédé, a furniture-maker who had migrated to Paris from Tours in 1811, recalled how in 1820 he and other workers refused to work for an employer who paid piece-rates as well as expecting unpaid work (revealingly, dubbed the *corvée* by workers). Ultimately the stoppage was successful, but only after some of the strikers had been imprisoned for forming a 'coalition'.[7]

The Restoration had strong appeal for large sections of the urban population who had suffered from the insecurities of the Revolution and Empire, and for working people, such as the butchers of Limoges and the textile workers of Nîmes, whose Catholicism was deeply embedded in a traditionalist popular culture. However, the regime's attempts to purge France of the scourge of revolution had limited success. In 1816, not only were republican and Bonapartist slogans and chants made liable to prison terms for up to five years, but a frenzied attempt was made to eradicate revolutionary symbolism. Mayors were ordered to seize and destroy cockades, busts, flags and other political mementos; monuments were replaced and streets renamed (and Napoléonville became Bourbon-Vendée). Napoleonic festivals such as 15 August (Bonaparte's saint's day) and 2 December were replaced by, for example, a day of mourning on 21 January (the anniversary of Louis XVI's execution), when public servants were instructed to dress in black and attend expiatory church services. But the intrusiveness of this cultural counter-revolution only served more deeply to engrain selective memories of the triumphs of 1789–1815 and assumptions of popular sovereignty. From the Seine-Inférieure, police in the 1820s reported tricolour ribbons, ties, embroidery, even swimsuits.[8] When law and medical students protested in 1820 against changes to the electoral system benefiting the wealthiest rural notables, resulting in the shooting of one of the students, Parisian workers joined in the huge demonstration of 5 June, shouting revolutionary slogans. In a situation where political rights of association were sharply curtailed, working people instead used legal gatherings, such as funerals, to voice their antipathy to the Restoration. When, in 1825, the death occurred of General Foy (a prominent liberal deputy in the Chamber who had been an army officer, wounded fourteen times during the revolutionary and imperial wars, before being demoted by the Restoration), 100,000 Parisians followed the funeral cortège to the Père Lachaise cemetery to hear the oration by Casimir Périer. Two years later, 150,000 attended the funeral of the liberal deputy Jacques-Antoine Manuel and listened to eulogies by Lafayette, the banker Laffitte and the popular Bonapartist poet Béranger.

In such ways a tenuous but genuine alliance in opposition to the Bourbons was created between skilled workers and disaffected liberal sections of the middle classes. The corollary in the surge of a liberal newspaper press hostile to Charles X was the anger of printing workers who printed these papers: linked by antipathy to the Restoration, they were divided by attitudes to mechanization, but in the climate of political and economic crisis in the late 1820s, such differences were suppressed. When opposition newspapers were closed down in July 1830, liberal calls for resistance to Bourbon autocracy meshed with the grievances of unemployed printers. A concrete manifestation of resistance to the royalist coup was the appearance of barricades on 27 July, for the first time since the seventeenth century; in the ensuing fighting 2,000 insurgents and soldiers were killed. The liberal opposition to Charles X was impelled further by collective action, as a massive crowd of Parisians marched to Rambouillet and forced the former king to flee the country.

The skilled workers who mobilized against Charles X and in the tumultuous months that followed did so with specific hopes and animosities in mind. In economic terms they demanded work, with higher pay and shorter hours, government intervention to lower consumption taxes and to regulate prices and wages, and protection from foreign workers, machinery and large enterprises. In social terms they expected an end to the regime of priests and nobles; in foreign affairs an intervention to support independence movements in Europe and thus to reverse the humiliation of 1815. Linking all of these demands was their call for 'liberty' and defence of the Charter: to workers, 'liberty' meant freedom from competition and respect for the dignity of skilled work while Article IX of the Charter offered 'the sacrifice of property [did this include machines?] on account of a legally established public interest'. The liberal notables who assumed power in July had diametrically-opposed interests and imputed different meanings to the slogans of 'liberty' and 'defence of the Charter': this was a classic case of 'elective affinity', in which both sides read what they desired into common slogans. Anti-Bourbon unity and euphoria quickly dissolved into mutual suspicion and, ultimately, conflict. Across a gulf of class and ideology, the tenuous alliance of liberal bourgeois and skilled workers quickly degenerated into 'a dialogue of the deaf'. Appeals to the new power-holders for 'liberty' – from competition, machinery and repressive laws – were repudiated by the Prefect of Police as 'in opposition to the laws that have consecrated the principle of the liberty of industry'.[9]

In September groups of skilled workers, conscious of the need for mouthpieces which would articulate workers' attitudes and grievances, established three newspapers written and published by themselves, *L'Artisan*, *Le Journal des ouvriers* and *Le Peuple*. These short-lived papers were above all the voice of master craftsmen and skilled artisans – *Le Journal* would have been satisfied had the franchise been lowered to 100 francs – but defined themselves as 'the most numerous and the most useful class of society…the class of workers'. The editors of *L'Artisan* warned:

we are no longer in a time where the workers were serfs that a master could sell or kill at his ease…. Three days have sufficed to change our function in the economy of society, and we are now the principal part of that society, the stomach, which spreads life into the superior classes, now returned to their true functions as servants. Cease then, oh noble bourgeois, to repulse us from your breast, for we too are men and not machines.

In this plea, the skilled workers' outrage at the deskilling impact of mechanization is evident, as is the mixture of acceptance of and scorn for 'the superior classes'.

Through such journals, skilled workers articulated an ideology of the dignity of manual labour, international solidarity towards movements for national independence in Belgium and Poland, and retribution towards the clerical and noble élites of the Restoration (though many other workers wanted simply to outlaw or destroy machinery and to expel foreign workers). Central to popular ideology were the layered meanings of 'association'. Initially used under the Restoration to express the right of skilled trades to negotiate collectively with employers or to withhold labour, 'association' also came to mean a form of cooperative production through which workers would themselves own mechanized workplaces. In the words of *L'Artisan*: 'who is to prevent us from uniting a hundred workers, and, taking from our daily earnings a small sum incapable of affecting our real needs, why do we not form a capital sufficient to exploit our industry ourselves?' This is what skilled workers understood by 'socialism' (significantly, a word first used in the 1830s), an ideology generated by the changing conditions of the workplace, and developed by skilled artisans themselves. In the words of Philippe Buchez, an historian and publicist:

> We have conversed with these men in their aprons and heavy shoes, with their rude speech, their simple language, about things which would certainly have been unintelligible to many men of the salons. Better than that, we have received memoirs from several of them, written in bad French, to be sure, but filled with ideas that would make the fortune of an economist.[10]

The Revolution of 1830 followed two years of economic crisis and popular – as well as parliamentary – discontent, and its implications were only resolved after four years of rapidly shifting conflict interrelated with protracted economic uncertainty and unemployment, reflected in the leap in the number of suicides in Paris – from 250 to 800 annually – between 1825 and 1835. It was also a national revolution, whose urban face depended on the specific character of provincial towns. In Béziers (Hérault), for example, new power-holders quickly found themselves confronted by rival popular movements. On 7 February 1831, the new Orléanist mayor reported that 'a group of republicans, chanting and shouting, set off to the place de la Madeleine and planted a liberty tree there, with two flags, a model of a rooster, and a liberty cap, symbols of a defunct republicanism which cannot be tolerated under a constitutional monarchy'. Here, and in other towns of the Hérault and Gard, where there were long traditions of Catholic-Protestant conflict, the replacement of the Restoration's local élite by bourgeois Protestants also encouraged the resurgence of a populist, anti-Protestant royalism. Its supporters, called legitimists or 'whites', scuffled with republicans on the streets and at the festivals and markets of the towns of Lower Languedoc. In September 1831 a group of republicans who seized and burnt the records and furniture of the tax-collector shouted alternatively 'Down with the *droits réunis*!' (indirect taxes on urban consumer goods), 'Down with the legitimists!'[11]

Two months later, the anger of Lyonnais silk-workers *(canuts)* erupted over the *tarif*, a fixed minimum rate for finished cloth established by Napoleon, which the Restoration, and now the July Monarchy, had not respected.[12] For three days, bloody street-fighting raged between the bourgeois National Guard and silk-workers ranged under the banner 'To live by working or to die fighting'. Master-weavers were involved as well as wage-earners, but the class-based, vengeful nature of the fighting convinced both sides that this was a new type of urban conflict. Marc Girardin, a prominent liberal opponent of the Restoration and Guizot's deputy in the chair of history at the Sorbonne, drew a striking analogy:

> The revolt of Lyon has brought a great secret into the open . . . . Every manufacturer lives in his factory like the colonial planter in the midst of his slaves, one against a hundred, and the subversion of Lyon is a sort of insurrection of San Domingo . . . . The middle class must recognize clearly what the situation is; it must know exactly where it stands. It has beneath it a proletariat which is agitated and disturbed . . . . That is the danger that threatens modern society; that is where the barbarians will come from to destroy it.

The consequence of the hardening of opposition between the former allies of July was the re-emergence of popular republicanism. Initially, there was little support for the small groups of republicans who had tried in July 1830 to push the workers' mobilization further than liberal reform. By 1832, however, a combination of disillusionment with the July Monarchy, the activism of petit-bourgeois republicans, and the experience of political liberation and repression had developed a new mass republicanism among skilled workers. This was expressed through democratic newspapers such as *Le Bon Sens, Le Journal du peuple* and *Le Mayeux*, whose offices provided the opportunity for skilled workers to meet journalists such as Ferdinand Flocon.

The actions of skilled workers after July 1830 highlighted the collective power of working people and was reflected in a widely-shared assumption that inter-trade unity should replace the internecine combativeness of the *compagnonnages*. In the heady autumn of 1830, new organizations appeared with titles such as the Society of Fraternal Amity, Society of Fraternal and Philanthropic Unions, and Fraternal Union of Workers in the Art of Carpentry. By 1833, the Parisian shoemaker Efrahem was voicing a new meaning of 'association', that of a union of all trades as a basis for political power:

> If we remain isolated, scattered, we are feeble, we will be easily defeated and will submit to the law of the masters; if we remain divided, cut off from one another, if we do not agree among ourselves, we will be obliged to surrender ourselves to the discretion of our bourgeois. There must hence be a bond that unites us, an intelligence that governs us, there must be an *association*.[13]

Such a political and social strategy, described as 'republican socialism' by Bernard Moss, differed fundamentally from that of bourgeois reformers in its understanding of 'democracy'.[14] Heirs of the *sans-culottes* of the year II, skilled

workers assumed that organized labour would also name its political representatives who in turn would be subject to popular mandate and the right of recall.
Popular democracy would be permanent and interventionist rather than parliamentary and electoral. However, republican activists were deeply ambivalent
about the legitimacy of insurrection, shown in their hesitant response to calls
for insurrection in the wake of the funeral of the popular General Lamarque in
June 1832. The extent of violence as this rising was suppressed – 70 troops and
80 insurgents were killed in fighting in the cloister of Saint-Méry – severed the
remaining bonds between Parisian workers and the regime they had brought to
power two years earlier.

Until the insurrection of June 1832, the key republican organization had
been the *Amis du Peuple*, though its membership was small (only about a
hundred by 1832) and composed of radical young bourgeois formerly active in
the *Carbonari*. Some of these activists joined the new Society of the Rights of
Man after the *Amis du Peuple* were suppressed in 1832, but by 1833 they had
been swamped by large numbers of skilled workers. Estimates of the Parisian
membership by early 1834 ranged from 2,000 to 4,000, 75–80 per cent of
whom were skilled wage-earners, mostly under 30 years of age: that is, young
tailors, jewellers, painters, luxury-goods workers, shoemakers, and joiners, those
threatened by unemployment and lack of opportunity in these years of
recession.

The Society of the Rights of Man was the vehicle through which an alliance
was formed between radical workers and middle-class republicans, in contrast
to the isolation of the latter during the 1830 Revolution. This alliance was
forged over issues of elected executives, universal suffrage, administrative
decentralization, education, cheaper credit, law reform, a federated Europe, and
the emancipation of labour through producers' cooperatives. To avoid legal
restrictions on political associations of more than 20 people, the society was
organized in a tight but democratic hierarchy of small local sections. The 162
sections in Paris in 1834 had names such as Robespierre, Saint-Just, Montagne,
Fall of the Girondins, Mucius Scaevola, Peace for the Cottages, and Fleurus.
The role of collective memories of the Revolution is further underlined by the
importance of Robespierre's 'Declaration of the Rights of Man and of the
Citizen', from which the society took its name. The growth of the society was
interdependent with a great wave of 72 strikes in 1833, which were marked by
workers setting up cooperatives and launching attempts at national federations
of associations. Many sections of the society were trade-based and provided a
focus for organization and mutual aid. In particular provinces, too, the society
found a ready response: in the Mediterranean department of the Pyrénées-
Orientales alone, there were 300 members in Perpignan in 1832 and about
2,500 in the department as a whole. Provincial branches were linked with the
50 republican papers still surviving across France in 1833.

In February 1834 the Lyon master-weavers' Society of Mutual Duty called
a general strike over rates of pay for finished cloth and were answered by the
law of 10 April 1834, which required police authorization of all associations of
more than 20 people. This was thus far more than a threat to political liberties;
it also went to the heart of workplace relations. In April, on the eve of the bill

being signed by Louis-Philippe, Lyon was again the scene of extensive fighting as insurgents proclaimed: 'the association of labourers is a necessity of our age, that it is a condition of existence'. This time, however, the forces of repression were far more organized; similarly, in Paris, a rising in protest at the law was summarily repressed, culminating in the 'massacre of the rue Transnonain', immortalized by Honoré Daumier's harrowing lithograph. The government's target was the Society of the Rights of Man: with the trial of 164 leading members of the society, and the press controls introduced in 1835, the revolutionary crisis of 1828–34 had been resolved.[15]

One of the most striking changes in the language of the labour movement in the years after 1830 was the relatively rapid transition from occupational to class definition. This transformation, from skilled artisans grouped in exclusive, and often fiercely competitive, trades to an assumption of the commonality of the working-class experience, amounts to a 'making' of the French urban working class. At its simplest, this was a transition from *sans-culottes* to 'proletarians', used interchangeably with *le peuple*. In the words of Balzac: 'The three former estates have been replaced by what are today called *classes*. We have the lettered, the industrial, the upper, the middle classes, etc..... Each industry has its bourgeois Richelieu named Laffitte or Casimir Périer.' Many historians have contested the substance of this linguistic change, arguing that the continuities in urban social structure belie an apparent change in consciousness. Was this language simply the precocious political consciousness of an *ancien-régime*, 'traditional' artisanate, the expression of the exaggerated fears of Balzac and Girardin, or had something changed in the world of work?[16]

The evidence of substantive change is compelling. The development of a distinctive workers' movement and ideology after 1830 varied according to the specific nature of the work process in towns and industries, the degree of trade continuity with pre-revolutionary craft traditions, and the political memories and experiences of urban workers. It drew on a discourse dating back to the *ancien régime* and the *sans-culottes* but infused with new meanings given to the changing urban world of the nineteenth century. It was also a cultural process expressed through the organs of popular sociability: cafés, cabarets, street theatre, trade associations, mutual-aid societies and, increasingly, those adapted from the middle classes, such as newspapers and reading circles.[17]

There were some striking examples of large-scale industrialization and mechanization, such as in the textile towns of Rouen, Lodève and Lille (where there were 15,000 cotton workers in 34 mills); however, the most common changes were within small-scale workplaces and in commerce.[18] The apparent continuity in the size and overall orientation of urban enterprises should not disguise the changes within them. In the 1820s, and increasingly under the July Monarchy, skilled workers in the printing, furniture, metal and leather trades felt their control of the productive process undermined by mechanization, the division of labour and the consequent simplification of tasks. At the same time, male tailors and shoemakers felt threatened by competition from *confection*, ready-to-wear clothing made by poorly-paid process workers, especially women, and *marchandage* (subcontracting to the lowest bidder). Both would have been forbidden by the corporate controls of the *ancien régime*, but were now sanctioned by 'liberty of enterprise'.

Some of the ready-to-wear clothing was sold in new department stores (*magasins de nouveautés*) such as the Ville de Paris which by 1844 had 150 employees and sales of 10–12 million francs. The expansion of these mass-produced consumer goods reflected a division of gender and workplace in the manufacturing process. Women were only 28 per cent of those who worked for 'made to order' tailors, but 60 per cent of the workforce in large clothing works and 71 per cent of those doing piece-work in the home. Women were paid less than half the male wage and their work was consequently opposed by male tailors as inferior, domestic and threatening. Workers' associations were thus to defend men from competition from women as well as from the threat of deskilling by changes to work practices. Similarly, the large spinning factories (*filatures*) which increasingly dominated Rouen employed equal numbers of men, women and children whereas men were at least half the workforce in smaller workplaces. Men earned between 1 fr. 92 centimes and 2 fr. 76 per day, women 1 fr. 08 – 1 fr. 36 and children 0 fr. 50 – 0 fr. 75. Since 44 per cent of all textile workers earned less than their own subsistence costs, there was a constant tension between men's worries about deskilling and competition from women's work on the one hand, and the pressing need for all household members to contribute to the family budget on the other. In such a context, clandestine *compagnonnages* proved increasingly inadequate to defend conditions of entry into trades – and hence family traditions and working-class culture itself – at a time of economic liberalism and mass migration to towns.[19]

In the shifts in the meaning of 'property' and 'labour' to notions of individually owned commodities after 1789, in the transition of artisans from 'artists' to 'workers', lay decisive changes in the urban world. It is not surprising that Marx developed his concept of 'alienation' during his stay in Paris in 1844–5, talking to French socialists similarly preoccupied with the meaning of changing work processes for artisans used to performing the total productive process. However, the 'class consciousness' of skilled workers combined a lively sense of the dignity of labour with a certainty that social reconciliation was possible if employers became more 'moral'. Faced with a world of unprecedented change in work practices and the urban environment, the regenerating vision of total social transformation in the 'utopias' of Cabet, Fourier and others was attractive to many for its promise of cooperation, plenty and harmony in contrast to the social division, misery and individualism of expanding cities.[20]

The most important mouthpiece for skilled artisans was *L'Atelier*, founded in 1840 as the 'organ of the working-class, edited exclusively by workers'. Among its 75 editors were printers, hatters, jewellers and other skilled artisans, such as Alexandre Martin, Anthîme Corbon, and Perdiguier. The paper combined demands for state-financed producers' cooperatives and associations, and a class analysis of relations of production and surplus labour, with a rejection of violence, expropriation, and collective or 'communist' solutions. The paper called for shorter hours and the reorganization of work, for accident compensation and old-age pensions, and for the abolition of subcontracting, *livrets*, child labour, and work in prisons and convents. While anticlerical in tone, the paper emphasized religion as the 'cement of social unity'; in 1837 the printing workers had published a popular edition of the gospels. Above all, it looked to 'organizing agricultural and industrial production on an altogether different foundation from the present, with association instead of fragmentation, and fraternity and solidarity instead of selfishness'.

Whatever the bonds of household, neighbourhood and class to which *L'Atelier* appealed, one central divide among the working people of towns was that of gender. While excluded from men's trade associations and less likely to go on strike, women workers had a less visible but no less important role in protecting the well-being of the household and neighbourhood. Proceeding from the assumption of their special role within the family – domestic chores and child-care as well as paid work – women continued to take the initiative in battles over the price of foodstuffs and rent and in sustaining neighbourhood structures of support and solidarity (Bédé's book on the 1820 strike was dedicated to one of the worker's wives). To many working women, industrial work was a nightmare of fatigue, poor health and miserable working conditions in which only constant ingenuity could construct a dowry which might offer a couple the chance to become independent artisans or to return to the countryside.[21]

Among the most common occupations of single working-class women was prostitution, either because of economic desperation or because the attraction of higher earnings outweighed the dangers of disease and violence. Céleste Vénard, who had lived on the streets of Paris since her mother's lover had tried to rape her when she was fourteen, was befriended by a prostitute and became one herself two years later: 'I saw myself rich, and covered with lace and jewels.' In 1816–31, 12,700 prostitutes were registered in Paris, over one-third natives of the capital and the rest young provincial migrants; about 30 per cent were former servants. In any one year, about 3,800 prostitutes were registered to work in the 180–200 licensed brothels, graded according to 'luxury' and cost. An equal number were unregistered and living in abject poverty and it was from them that the Saint-Lazare prison drew its 500–600 inmates, in separate divisions for those under and over 13 years of age. Increasingly, prostitutes seemed to have resented the attempts of successive monarchies to use the religious *'Maison du bon pasteur'* for *'filles repentantes'* and were known to shout anti-royalist slogans: between 1821 and 1841, the numbers willing to undergo 'moral rehabilitation' in religious houses declined from 350 annually to fewer than one hundred.[22]

Vulnerable in the workplace because *compagnonnages* saw them as low-paid competition and because of harassment by employers and foremen, women were also disadvantaged in the home where domestic chores and child-rearing were assumed to be their responsibility. To Flora Tristan, women's inferior legal and economic position, and men's tendency to transfer their own subordinate experiences at work into domestic relations, meant that there was 'a constant state of irritation between the *master* and the *servant* (one can even say *slave*, for the woman is, so to speak, the *property* of the husband)'. But Tristan was something of a loner, a *déclassée* noblewoman converted by bitter experience into a socialist and feminist. Her great work was *L'Union ouvrière* (1843), based on the idea of a national and international union of workers to ensure education, work and social welfare, which she sought to make a reality by a *tour de France* in 1844, from Auxerre down the Rhône to Marseille and through the Midi to

Bordeaux, where she died. After Tristan's death, her daughter was cared for by Pauline Roland, a feminist socialist of petit-bourgeois Norman background who herself had three children she insisted on raising alone. Roland wrote for the first distinctly feminist French newspapers, *La Femme libre* (1832) and *Le Tribun des femmes* (1833) as well as writing popular histories of England and France. She was one of a number of women who came to articulate a feminism influenced by the social systematizing of Saint-Simon and Fourier, according to women an almost mystical role in creating the reign of theistic and sexual harmony.[23]

It is extremely difficult to generalize about attitudes to love and sexuality among urban working people, however, because they are so rarely recorded, and even then are likely to be so by outsiders distanced by class and culture. Martin Nadaud, a migrant Creusois stonemason who spent much of his life in Paris, remembered the pretty girl, 'so reserved, so gracious, so radiant with youth and beauty', whom he was to marry; while Agricol Perdiguier, a Provençal joiner, recalled of his *tour de France*: 'I loved, I burned, I suffered, I was violent, shaken, pulled in opposite directions by my passion and my conscience.' At the time Nadaud wrote, late in his life, he was a respectable politician; Perdiguier, too, had become part of Parisian literary society. Nevertheless, the feelings they recalled may well have been quite typical. Parisian workers often lived in *de facto* marriages. The *Société Saint François Régis,* which took as its mission the moralizing of the poor by convincing those in *de facto* relationships to marry, carried out 6,543 marriages of couples in the first 15 years of its activities in 1826–41. Some 74 per cent of the couples had been living together for at least one year and 50 per cent for longer than three years. While low wages impelled women towards forming a household, *de facto* relationships may also have given them more freedom. As Marie Adam, a 22-year-old seamstress, insisted when giving evidence against a jealous former partner, 'a woman who is not committed in a marriage is certainly free to change her feelings'.[24]

Similarly, little is known of male or female homosexuality or popular attitudes to it, though it is clear that élite sexual discourse increasingly condemned male homosexuality less as a temporary, sinful aberration and more as a biological deviance. Police were keen to prevent homosexual prostitution and homosexual relationships between prostitutes. Patricia O'Brien has discerned types of homosexual behaviour in prisons, ranging from 'affectional and romantic' relationships between lesbians and men, expressed in love-letters, to violent assaults on young offenders. Outside prisons, pederasty in particular was violently opposed: in 1836, soldiers had to protect a 60-year-old man from an angry crowd of 300 people, and a clergyman was assaulted by a group of students after making sexual advances.[25]

A second basic division among urban workers was between the numerically dominant artisanal workforce and the growing numbers of semi-skilled factory workers in the new, bursting industrial centres. The most vulnerable rural individuals and households were increasingly forced to leave for the unregulated workplaces of new textile industries. Between them and the world of a skilled joiner like Perdiguier was a gulf of occupation, illiteracy and misery. In new, mechanized factories, employers drew on English practices to impose a rigid discipline, a social control reinforced if they also provided rental accommodation, schools, shops and welfare funds. In Bergery's *Economie industrielle ou science de l'industrie*, published at the time of the Revolution of 1830, employers were advised to implement stricter division of labour and the sexes, supervision, silence and punctuality (measured by the construction of factory gates). Industrial workers were also subject to poor ventilation, humidity, noise and harmful chemicals; dampness and cotton-dust in particular wreaked havoc on the respiratory systems of the very young and old alike. Consequently, life expectancy varied sharply between occupational groups: weavers and spinners in the factories of Mulhouse and the Haut-Rhin who had survived the most vulnerable years of infancy could only expect to live on average into their 30s, while domestic servants and shoemakers on average would live into their 40s and 50s.[26]

It is no coincidence that the 1840s, years of rapid, unprecedented urban change in many cities, generated not only working-class and radical bourgeois ideologies to explain and transform this new world, but also a rash of surveys of the 'social problem' by officials and concerned notables. Hence Dr Louis Villermé's report to the Academy of Moral and Political Sciences described the industrial north and east:

> The workshops of Mulhouse alone, in 1835, contained more than 5,000 workers who lodged in the villages round about. These are the least well paid workers. They mostly consist of poor families with a lot of young children.... Among them are large numbers of thin, pale women, walking barefoot through the sludge... and a still larger number of young children, equally dirty and haggard, dressed in rags which are thick with oil that has fallen on them whilst working.

In apportioning responsibility, however, Villermé castigated 'neglect on the part of the parents' and depraved moral standards manifested in expenditure on smart clothes and in illegitimate births. However, different evidence suggests that, after the perceptible increases in urban wages during the Revolution and Empire, the purchasing power of wages declined by up to one-quarter in the decades after 1815. For example, the wages of foundry workers and shoemakers declined 50 centimes to 4 fr. 50 and 3 francs respectively in 1830–47. The great majority of urban workers left little or nothing at death: four-fifths of the 1,672 people who died in Bordeaux in 1824 were penniless; and in Toulouse in 1846, 44.5 per cent left nothing and another 28 per cent less than 100 francs. Across these decades, too, four-fifths of Parisians left less than 500 francs, while the numbers of deceased leaving huge estates, 500,000 francs or more, rose from 0.3 per cent in 1820 to 0.8 per cent in 1847. The total wealth of all these cities increased significantly, more than doubling in Paris, but its social distribution had if anything further polarized.[27]

The causes of death in Paris reflected poor working conditions, diet and housing: in the 1820s almost half of all deaths were due to pulmonary consumption, pneumonia, pleurisy and intestinal complaints (cancer and heart diseases accounted for fewer than 5 per cent, though per capita tobacco consumption was 1 kilogram annually). An 1843 survey of Lille listed 63 per cent of men, 48 per cent of women and 25 per cent of children as ill or infirm. Though urban diets on average included more meat than in the countryside, bread remained the staple, with urban dwellers consuming 450–600 grams daily, and men as much as 800 grams. Except for the petite bourgeoisie, who were more likely to own their dwellings, wage-earners lived in cramped, multi-functional rooms. During the first half of the century, the population density of Paris doubled to 307 persons per hectare; in the *faubourg* Saint-Honoré and Les Halles it was as high as 1,000. In Lille, a single room cost 6–7 francs per month, a week's wages for unskilled workers. The élite's new concern for running water did not benefit the poor, for by mid-century only one building in five was con-nected to the public water supply; for working women in particular, the ardu-ous, time-consuming chore of carting water from fountains was a part of daily life. This water came downstream from where the new sewerage system for wealthier neighbourhoods entered the River Seine. Working people used collective toilets in tenement buildings which were emptied by 2,300 night-soil carts; in Limoges and elsewhere, raw sewage and house refuse simply flowed down gutters.[28]

Medical care varied similarly in its social incidence. Of the 1,231 doctors living in the 20 districts of the capital, 720 were clustered in three wealthy districts of the west, while the large working-class area of the *faubourg* Saint-Antoine had but 46 practitioners. Since 1801 eight hospices for the infirm elderly, orphans and new mothers had been created, and ten hospitals for the seriously ill, but less debilitating illnesses were untreated and there was no state help for those too sick or unable to find work. Workers in parts of eastern France had access to a free medical service, but elsewhere only petit bourgeois shop-keepers and master craftsmen were able to afford adequate insurance through mutual-aid societies. Accordingly, the wealthy neighbourhoods of western Paris had mortality rates of lower than 17 per thousand while in the 8th, 9th and 12th districts they were nearly 30. Similarly, even though the 1832 cholera epidemic carried off Casimir Périer as well as General Lamarque, only one Parisian in every 107 inhabitants died in the wealthy 2nd district, but one in 22 in the 9th.

Infractions against the State's laws and the threat of imprisonment was a central feature of working-class life for, under the July Monarchy, the rate of incarceration reached its peak, with some 43,000 people (or 1.2 in every 1,000) in prison.[29] Élite certainty that this was a time of a 'crime wave' reflected pro-found social fears rather than a reality, a self-fulfilling prophecy because of tighter policing systems and redefinitions of what constituted crime. Prisoners were almost exclusively working-class, disproportionately urban, and – in contrast to élite reasoning – were only unskilled workers or vagrants in 8 per cent of cases. Men were 80–5 per cent of prisoners, above all for crimes against property (71 per cent of the total). Economic links were less obvious in female crimes; rather, they were imprisoned for 'behavioural' crimes, especially within the family, fuelling a discourse within the professions about the irrationality and emotiveness of 'women's nature'. Close surveillance of released prisoners added to the likelihood of recidivism; these repeat offenders also headed internal prison networks of power and a subculture distinctive in its behaviour, slang and use of tattoos and graffiti.

Michel Foucault illuminated the bourgeois *mentalité* which combined the virtues of social order, the image of the factory as disciplined time and space, and the possibility of 'civilizing' miscreants. Prisoners were now to be more closely watched, particularly with the popularity of Bentham's model *Panopticon*, in which they would be constantly observed by invisible guards. However, Foucault exaggerated the magnitude of the break with the eighteenth century and the level of a conscious ideology of a 'disciplinary' society. Instead, the key innovation of the July Monarchy was a commitment to rehabilitation: productive work, rather than hard labour, religion or education was seen as the most likely protection against future law-breaking (as well as a way of paying for a system which required increasing levels of personnel and new buildings). Prisoners could earn up to 60 per cent of wages paid in equivalent trades outside prison walls, generating working-class anger at a time when many trades were also being hit by mechanization.[30]

While juvenile offenders were usually 'acquitted' of a formal criminal offence, they were sent for rehabilitation to a *maison correctionnelle*, to farm schools, or to work in Algeria and Corsica. If imprisoned, they were corrected in the most refined form of controlled activity, isolation and surveillance. Victor Hugo was struck in 1847 by the contrast between over-crowded dungeons and the new system of confinement for the young, which, though permeated with sadness, impressed him with its stress on work and discipline. In his *Journal*, he described the Petite Roquette as: 'a town composed of a crowd of solitary young; nothing but children who don't know each other, who spend years side by side without the sound of steps or voices ... work, study, tools, books, eight hours of sleep, an hour of rest, an hour of play in a courtyard, prayers morning and evening, and always thought'.

The unregulated expansion of manufacturing and urban centres created appalling conditions for proletarian families and their children. By 1839 there were nearly 150,000 children of 7–14 years in the cotton industry. Living and working conditions were reflected in the rejection on medical grounds of young male conscripts from industrial cities. In France as a whole 86 young men were rejected for every 150 accepted, while in Rouen, Mulhouse, Elbeuf and Nîmes the figures were 166, 110, 168 and 147 respectively. Politicians explained child labour and consequent debility as a result of 'vice, excessive debauchery and loose living', but were reluctant to pass legislation out of 'respect for parental authority' and the needs of employers. When legislation was finally passed in 1841 – prohibiting child labour under eight years of age in factories, and restricting that of older children to 8–12 hours – no serious attempt was made to enforce it. Similarly, public welfare during the July Monarchy largely relied on charity and some municipal and state funding administered by *bureaux de bienfaisance* according to a philosophy that discouraged recourse to welfare except in dire circumstances. Unwanted pregnancies placed single women (especially servants) in a particularly invidious position. In Paris in 1846, 12.8 per cent of babies were abandoned (compared with 3 per cent for all of France), almost all of them from among the 32 per cent of children born outside marriage (these startling figures had, however, declined from 22.7 and 39.3 thirty years earlier). Abandoning a baby to the State's care was the only hope for these young women, with the slim chance that it would not be among the two-thirds of foundlings who died while in the care of rural wet nurses. But the decision was inevitably harrowing, and 95 per cent of mothers left their names and the baby's birthdate, hoping one day to return. Notes pinned to the clothing of infants left in the revolving *tours* outside foundling homes convey something of this grief, as when Aimée Barbier left her son in Rouen in 1831: 'It is with the greatest pain that I separate myself from my son, after the great suffering I have gone through to keep him in his present state.... I hope to see him again as soon as I can take him back for good.'[31]

Education for workers' children was a function of whether families could afford school fees and the sacrifice of the child's wages (likely in any case to buy no more than the child's bread), and of whether they lived in an established town with a tradition of mass primary schooling. While in school, children were taught the basics of reading, writing and arithmetic from texts impregnated with the regime's desire to inculcate 'morality' and religiosity. While only a minority of working-class children regularly attended school, however, it should not be supposed that workers were indifferent or even hostile to their children's education. A magistrate recounted to the *Magasin pittoresque* in 1835 how his dying, impoverished father – who had survived by giving guitar lessons until ruined by the popularity of the piano among the middle classes – had taught him to read, arousing an insatiable desire for books. While his mother did sewing piece-work in friends' rooms to save lighting costs, the small boy sold cakes, drawings and finally worked as a letter-writer for the illiterate in order to buy *Robinson Crusoe*, books of fables and fairy-tales, *Geneviève de Brabant* and history books. He was finally befriended by a bourgeois student whose family found him work as a clerk in a lawyer's office.[32] He was an exception. Nor could workers' children have hoped for a secondary education. In 1842, only 1.2 per cent of children were at public or private secondary schools, and the proportion receiving scholarships had fallen from 43 per cent in 1810 to 16.6 per cent in 1830. Moreover, such an education was popularly seen as impractical because of its emphasis on the classics and Latin.

Social polarities in the distribution of wealth, nutrition, health care and education were paralleled by increasing geographical separation between rich and poor. As two pioneering social historians, Louis Chevalier and Adeline Daumard, showed, the well-to-do fled the increasingly overcrowded centre and east of Paris for the newer, larger houses of the west, leaving medieval *quartiers* where the mushrooming population (which grew 34 per cent to 1,054,000 in 1831–46) had to survive in a hopelessly inadequate urban framework. In an environment of poverty, squalor and disease, the élite's certainty that the 'labouring classes' were also the 'dangerous classes' – for social order was seen as a corollary of public hygiene and morality – was reciprocated by working-class images of the bourgeois as fat, lecherous, ugly and self-indulgent, a class gulf that was 'biological' as well as economic. This imagery was expertly personified as Robert Macaire in Daumier's cartoons carried in *Le Charivari*. A noble described a funeral of one of Louis-Philippe's ministers in the winter of 1847 and the reception of the notables and professional men by the onlookers: 'The people laughed and joked. Not a man took off his hat. Suddenly, just as the coffin was passing us, a voice shouted contemptuously: "What a crew of Robert Macaires!" The people clapped and laughed.'[33]

Certainly, the congested popular neighbourhoods of large cities were violent places, in which theft and assault born of misery was juxtaposed with the ritual street battles of workers' fraternities. What is most remarkable about the social history of urban working-people in these decades, however, is the continued resilience of family and trade solidarities in the face of corroding pressures of rapid change, economic uncertainty and deteriorating living and working conditions. Despite the desperate poverty of Limoges workers, who spent on average three-fifths of their wages on bread and as much as possible of the rest in the 155 taverns and cafés of the town, they were as well known for their respect for persons and property as they were to be for their radical politics. In their strategic and attitudinal responses to a changing urban world, a pivotal role was played by the economic élite of *le peuple*, the petite bourgeoisie of shop-keepers and workshop masters who made up perhaps one-fifth of the urban population.[34] Socially mobile, internally divided and interlocked with the world of both the working-class and bourgeoisie, these petits bourgeois were often migrants from the provinces who arrived with some savings to open cafés, retail shops (there were no fewer than 1,966 linen outlets in Paris in 1847) or small workshops. Few of them could aspire to real wealth; on the other hand, the danger of economic failure, and descent into the impoverished world they knew so well, was ever-present. Although owners of small amounts of capital and exploiters of their own labour, an awareness of the deskilling of workers in their own trades and, above all, the threats to their own independence coming from large-scale concentration, made petits bourgeois identify themselves primarily as workers. Underpinning this identity was the importance of their enterprises in the neighbourhood, as centres of consumption and *sociabilité*.

The two most common attitudinal responses to the uncertainties of a changing urban world among petits bourgeois and many wage-earners were a reworked religiosity and varied political ideologies. The Revolution of 1830 in Paris and many provincial towns unleashed popular anticlericalism in response to the fervent proselytizing of the Restoration Church and its identification with the regime itself. Prelates' residences were sacked, priests and members of religious orders publicly humiliated, and symbols of throne and altar torn down. In Paris, the sacking of the Abbey of Saint-Denis in 1831 occurred as the culmination of Carnival, still a potent moment of popular political culture in the 1830s. Anticlericalism was exacerbated in Lyon by convents' preparedness to provide buildings and a closely-controlled workforce of poorly-paid young women for textile magnates. In many urban centres, however, religious practice remained widespread, and the July Monarchy's perceived secularism generated a reaction among Catholics. During the cholera epidemic of 1832, Catherine Labouré, a 24-year-old novice of the Sisters of Charity in Paris, claimed that the Virgin Mary had appeared to warn her of the impending disaster and to instruct her to have a commemorative medal struck. There was an extraordinary response: by 1836, eight million medals were in circulation.[35]

Labouré and the Sisters of Charity were part of a remarkable religious revival – in town as well as country – in the first half of the century. This was especially the work of religious women, disproportionately from urban, petit-bourgeois backgrounds: the numbers of *congréganistes, béates* and *bonnes soeurs* grew from 15,000 in 1815 to 66,000 in 1850. Unlike nuns in religious orders, these pious women were above all concerned with teaching, sick-care and charity and were less constrained by vows, residence and dress. The *catholicisme au féminin* of the Sisters of Charity, the Daughters of Wisdom and the Little Sisters of the Poor contrasted strongly with the asceticism of the secular clergy. Men's orders also expanded, notably the Christian Brothers in working-class neighbour-hoods, and the re-emergent Jesuits, Trappists and Carmelites. Apart from the Jesuits, whose vows and upper-class recruitment made them the target of attacks in the liberal press, Eugène Sue's *Le Juif errant* and Parliament, most orders were recruited from urban petits bourgeois. Like their female counterparts, these orders offered sociability for the single person, a satisfying if difficult vocation, and the care the State refused to provide.

Among religious minorities, too, working people were more likely to sustain religious practice than were the bourgeoisie. Despite contemporary images of Jews as financiers and usurers and of Protestants as industrialists and bankers, the social composition of religious minorities mirrored that of society as a whole. After the Revolution, however, Jews had tended to congregate more markedly in particular urban *quartiers* while Protestants remained predomi-nantly rural. In the first half of the century, the Jewish population grew from 0.16 per cent of France to 0.26 (96,000), divided, like the general urban pop-ulation, into bourgeois (17 per cent), petit bourgeois (9 per cent), skilled work-ers and petits bourgeois (56 per cent) and the indigent (18 per cent). Under the Restoration, there had been a resurgence of explicit anti-Jewish theology, and Jews had lost university teaching positions in favour of Catholic clergy. The July Monarchy restored the equal treatment of Jews in public life and rabbis were first paid by the State from 1831. A few individual Jews succeeded under the July Monarchy: the Nîmois Adolphe Crémieux became a prominent liberal lawyer and opposition politician, and the Rothschilds' wealth attracted a new type of anti-Semitism, towards the 'finance aristocracy'. In Alsace and Paris, however, Jews were disproportionately represented among the very poor.[36]

Everywhere in France responses to the Revolution had been conditioned by the strength of religious affiliation and local identity. In departments such as the Gard, the rise to political dominance of Protestant employers had accentuated denominational and class hatreds which had had bloody consequences. A deeper tradition of accommodation marked religious difference in parts of the east. In the textile town of Sainte-Marie-aux-Mines, on the border of the Haut-Rhin and Bas-Rhin in Alsace, the 6,162 Catholics and 5,112 Protestants were also divided by class (three-quarters of the textile merchant-manufacturers were Protestant, two-thirds of the workers Catholic) and language (workers were mostly German-speaking, their employers bilingual). Only one in eight marriages was interdenominational. Yet, even though Catholics tended to be Legitimist and Protestants either Orleanist or republican, the two communities shared a long tradition of acceptance of difference which minimized overt friction; here, too, workers felt no contradiction between their German heritage and their assumptions that they were French citizens.[37]

Popular religiosity was a common response to what was perceived as a godless, materialistic regime; popular politics was another. Most petits bourgeois and workers had soon became alienated by the July Monarchy's political economy of restricted suffrage, rapid industrialization and peaceful European diplomacy. Instead they were increasingly attracted to the 'republican socialism' of Louis Blanc, Cabet and Fourier, the 'social Christianity' of legitimists such as Villeneuve-Bargemont, or, above all, to a populist Bonapartism. There are elements of all three in the ideology of the worker-poets of these years, who also wrote for *L'Atelier*.[38] Charles Poncy, a Toulon stone-mason, claimed that 'God himself divided earth's treasures among everyone: the land to the farmers, the sea to the sailors.' While Poncy became an intimate of George Sand, others were fiercely working-class: Savinien Lapointe, son of a shoemaker from the Yonne, retorted to Sand's correction of his poetry, 'so you don't like the common people, do you!' Lapointe had been imprisoned following the abortive rising of mid-1832, an experience which convinced him that workers' associations rather than violent insurrection were the route to a juster world. A similarly peaceful vision informed the work of Jules Vinçard, a Parisian ruler-maker:

> Proletarians of all lands
> No more aggressors
> Nor oppressors
> Let us join our voices and our hearts together;
> It is God who is revealing to us
> His decrees for the future,
> It is he who is coming to unite us in a new faith.

Vinçard's internationalism had popular resonance – in 1840, 9,000 Parisian workers signed a petition for the emancipation of the 285,000 slaves in Martinique, French Guiana and Réunion – but working-class ideology was profoundly ambiguous about the imperial legacy. Deep in the popular consciousness of workers in Paris and other inland cities was a refashioned image of Napoleon Bonaparte as a populist democrat forced into war by the intransigent counter-revolution of England in particular, an image contrasting with that of the July Monarchy as a bourgeois paradise of sordid speculation, social callousness and foreign cowardice. The return of Napoleon's ashes in 1840 furnished the occasion for *L'Atelier* to fulminate against a 'shameful peace regime' and to describe Napoleon Bonaparte as it wished:

> It was not the restorer of the nobility, the resurrector of the categories of the old régime, or the ambitious conqueror that the crowd came to salute, but the artillery lieutenant of '93 .... Above all it was revolutionary France, represented at this ceremony by the veterans of the armies of the Republic and Empire, that the people of Paris came to salute, touched by all these memories of our glorious past.

The Napoleonic legend was malleable and the capacity of Louis Napoleon, Bonaparte's nephew, to define it in populist terms created a massive market among skilled workers for his *Napoleonic Ideas*, which had sold 500,000 copies by 1848.

8

Rural Change and Continuity, 1815–1845

The census-compilers of the nineteenth century decided that rural communities were those with fewer than 2,000 inhabitants: in 1831, some 26.35 million people (81 per cent of the total). Such a measure included many people whose occupations were not agricultural (such as artisans, teachers and priests); conversely, many larger places included people who directly worked the land in the surrounding countryside. A more useful, if still arbitrary, measure of 'rural' would be communities of up to 10,000 people. While some small towns were essentially industrial, most were directly dependent on the rural economy. About one-tenth of the national population lived in these country towns. France was essentially a rural society.[1]

Despite the Revolution, rural France remained sharply hierarchical in economic terms. In 1825 almost four-fifths of holdings, totalling only 17 per cent of the land's wealth, were assessed for less than 20 francs in taxes: their owners depended for survival on renting more land, wage labouring, domestic industrial work or a combination of these. In contrast, the largest 100,000 holdings, just 1 per cent of the total, controlled 28 per cent of soil resources (see Table 8.1).

Table 8.1 Landholding in France, 1825

Assessment category (francs)	Number	%	Estimated total value (francs)	%
0–20	8,024,987	77.94	40,365,685	16.99
21–30	663,237	6.44	16,050,335	6.75
31–50	642,345	6.24	24,865,175	10.46
51–100	527,991	5.13	36,589,776	15.41
101–300	335,505	3.26	52,952,754	22.29
301–500	56,602	0.55	21,680,830	9.14
501–1,000	32,579	0.31	22,671,075	9.54
Over 1,000	13,447	0.13	22,362,630	9.42
Total	10,296,693	100.00	237,538,260	100.00

Source: Georges Dupeux, *French Society 1789–1970*, trans. P. Wait (London, 1972), 107.
Note: Because landowners with titles in more than one commune were counted separately for each, the actual number of adults with land was closer to 6.2 million.

An understanding of French rural society in the first half of the nineteenth century has to be political in its broad sense: that is, rural producers (peasants, tenant farmers, labourers and others) generated 'surpluses' which were appropriated by more powerful individuals and institutions. Through rents, taxes and unequal market exchange, landlords, merchants and the State extracted these surpluses which underwrote the cost of living as notables and of administering and policing a large nation. While inextricably linked to urban France and national structures, rural producers must also be understood within their specific local environment, culture and history. It is this interaction between local and national which was at the core of rural society in these decades, and which remains central to historical understanding of the rich variety of this rural society.

All rural communities remained characterized by sharp internal differentiation in terms of landholding, ownership of non-farm property and the roles individuals played in the productive process. Between regions, too, landowning structures varied widely: the proportion of adults owning some land ranged from less than one-third in the Allier to over three-quarters in the Eure-et-Loir and Charente-Inférieure; tiny properties paying less than 20 francs in tax were 94 per cent of all holdings in Corsica while substantial properties paying more than 50 francs were 18 per cent of all properties in the Bouches-du-Rhône. Almost everywhere, however, the common nineteenth-century literary image of a self-sufficient peasant family cultivating its own plot was true only of a minority. Historians, too, have often confused 'rural people' with 'peasants', a misleading term because it conveys an image of homogeneous, subsistence-oriented and closed communities. For example, in the small Mediterranean village of Canet (population 370), the 1822 land register listed 79 local landowners. However, the four largest proprietors, including the former Jacobin *conventionnel* and regicide Joseph Cassanyes, controlled almost half of the locally-owned land, while 49 others owned a total of only 8.2 per cent. But altogether, Canetois owned just 14.7 per cent of their own commune: absentee landlords shared the rest, including the militant legitimist and former seigneur Joseph Lazerme, who exerted patronal control over his dependent labourers and tenants on his 1,000-hectare estate. Canet was a desperately poor and unhealthy place bordering a mosquito-infested lagoon, its inhabitants surviving from a combination of fishing, polyculture and tending the sheep shepherded down from the Pyrenees in winter. But it could not be described as a community of 'peasants'.[2]

Rural communities were also internally differentiated between owners or renters of land and those who drew their livelihoods only indirectly from the soil: priests, teachers, officials, artisans, bourgeois and those involved in rural industry. The poorest of these often worked part-time on the land. This non-agricultural sector varied according to the size of the community: for example, Michel Vovelle's study of 23 Provençal communes distinguished villages (fewer than 500 inhabitants), with 90 per cent of their workforce in agriculture, from *bourgs* (500–2,500), with 60–80 per cent in agriculture, and the small town of Pertuis (3,800) with 62 per cent. Occupational complexity was also reflected in the degree of involvement in commerce: all of the communities with more than 1,000 people had a weekly market as well as an annual fair.[3]

Between regions, too, there were wide variations in the number of rural people engaged in agriculture. France's largest industry, clothing and textiles, was mainly rural and decentralized, and was one reason for the greater population density of the north. Over 40,000 rural workers were engaged in the woollen industry of Champagne; and there were 25,000 textile workers in silk, cotton and linen in a 50-kilometre radius around Saint-Quentin (Aisne). Above all, rural industry involved part-time work by women: some 108,000 in the Nord, 145,000 in the Seine-Inférieure and 40,000 lace-makers in the Calvados. In the village of Auffay (Seine-Inférieure), two-thirds of all women earned money from 'proto-industrial' textile work, especially weaving, which they had taken over from men as spinning became increasingly concentrated in Rouen. Such work was closely integrated into the rhythms of the agricultural year: these women also spent three or four months working on the land. Just as Agricol Perdiguier, a joiner from Morières (Vaucluse), recalled of his family that 'Madeleine and Babet worked with us, like men', so Martin Nadaud, a migrant stonemason from the Creuse, insisted: 'my wife, like all other women of the countryside, was raised to work in the fields from morning till night and she worked no less... after our marriage'.[4] In the south, too, large numbers of women worked as silk-spinners in the rural areas of the Gard and Ardèche; however, most southern industry was artisanal and centred in small towns. In the *bourgs* around Brignoles (Var), there were perfumeries, soap and paper works, and tanneries (15 in Barjols alone). In the upland areas south of Brignoles, there were over 700 cork-makers and hundreds of workers in small lignite mines and forges.

Rural communities were thus characterized by social and occupational complexity reflecting their specific economic base. Every community was on a spectrum ranging from small agricultural hamlets, where non-agricultural work was done by the household itself or part-time artisans, to small industrial centres whose relationship with the surrounding countryside was essentially one of purchasing agricultural produce. All rural communities had relationships with markets, whether for the exchange of 'use values' in essentially subsistence areas, where they were usually held in local *bourgs* and were as much a socio-cultural occasion as a market, or for the buying and selling of commodities within a regional, national or even international market. In the 1820s, rural France was dominated by the local market-fair: some 6,000 small towns held regular days of marketing and sociability. Some networks were more wide-ranging: transport from the Côte-d'Or by cart and canal carried over 200,000 hectolitres of wine 300 kilometres to Paris annually. The low hillsides south of Dijon were already dominated by vineyards: the land surveys of the 1820s showed them covering four-fifths of the land around Beaune. A different type of 'marketing' linked the increasing number of urban women seeking wet nurses for their infants in the rural hinterlands of Paris, Lyon and Marseille.[5]

The spatial structure of the community itself was varied. The habitat of rural people ranged from the bustling *bourgs* and large villages of the south, Champagne and Alsace-Lorraine to the dispersed farms and hamlets of the western *bocage* areas, the Limousin and the southern Massif Central. In the latter area the meaning of community was above all an assumption of spiritual solidarity centred on a parish church, a mental map which often did not corre-spond with the grid of communal boundaries drawn by urban officials. In areas of clustered habitat, on the other hand, a physical sense of community was rein-forced by cooperative agricultural routines, such as the enforcement of the date of the commencement of the harvest, and the practices of *vaine pâture* (send-ing cattle onto private fallow land) and *droit de parcours* (allowing livestock access to forests across private land). Such practices, and the continued existence of common lands, were at the heart of local conflicts between rich and poor and of resistance to attempts by successive regimes to clear away what they saw as obstacles to agrarian individualism and productivity. This tension was expertly captured by Balzac in his great rural novel, *Les Paysans* – in his words, 'the most important of those I've resolved to write' – set in the Yonne in the 1820s. Whatever the specific links which formed a sense of community, it was also the arena in which internal conflicts were resolved, whether informally or through the formal structures of municipal government and the law.

At the most fundamental level, the key unit of the rural community was the household and its claims over the work and behaviour of its members. Depending on the household's occupations and its own life-cycle, its composi-tion varied remarkably in size and type: from the 'nuclear' families of labourers to 'stem' families of three generations or siblings, from the large households, including farm servants, of substantial farmers to the 'joint' families *(commu-nautés)* of 20–30 relatives on leased farms in the Morvan. Everywhere, however, the household was the essential mediator between individual and com-munity and the focus of a collective strategy for survival, labour and reproduc-tion. In Emile Guillaumin's semi-autobiographical novel, *The Life of a Simple Man*,[6] Tiennon, born in 1823, began to look after the sheep at age seven; at age 12 (that of his first communion) he was introduced to ploughing and han-dling oxen; at 16 he was regarded as a man, doing heavy farmwork, and by 20 had left to work as a farm-servant.

Intimate relationships within the rural family only concerned the State's bureaucracies – on whose records social historians most often rely – when they led to serious conflict. This silence has generally been filled by quoting the pejo-rative judgments of urban 'folklorists' or by historians' own assumptions. Accordingly, it has been asserted that relationships between peasant men and women were 'instrumental' (concerned with economic survival rather than love), often brutal, that women and children were subordinate to patriarchy within the rural family, indeed, that there was no peasant concept of 'childhood' at all. Such notions have been challenged by Martine Segalen. On the basis of the complementarity of men and women's work, she has argued that the pre-capitalist family was not patriarchal, and that there had always been love and respect between men, women and children. Certainly, Segalen has demon-strated that rural people did not need to learn about 'affective' relationships from their social betters. Then, as now, a mixture of subtle and open pressures narrowed the range of marriage partners to one's social and geographic neigh-bourhood, but this did not narrow the range of one's feelings. Peasant women's economic and cultural importance may have bolstered their status within the family, but relations varied – as in every social group – from the loving to the

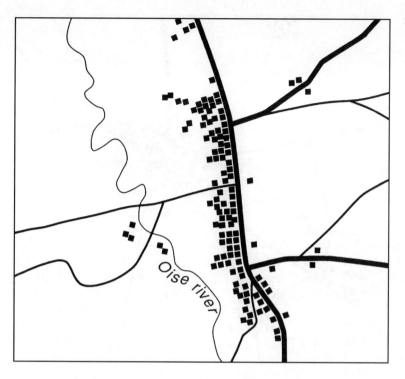

Map 8.1 A Achery (Aisne): Elongated village in a narrow valley

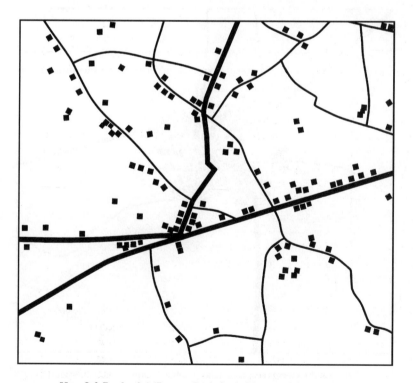

Map 8.1 B Anglet (Basses-Pyrénées): Dispersed farmhouses

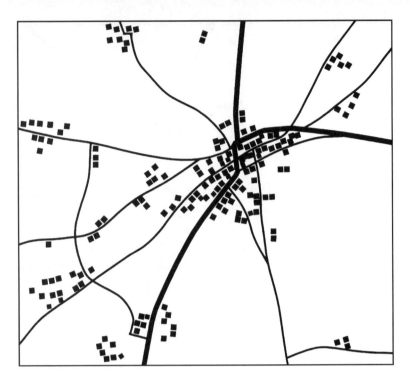

Map 8.1 C   Octeville (Seine-Inférieure): Village with surrounding hamlets and farms

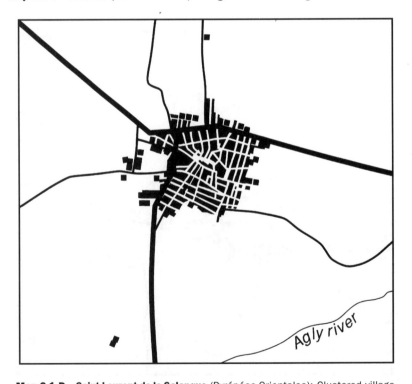

Map 8.1 D   Saint-Laurent-de-la-Salanque (Pyrénées-Orientales): Clustered village

Map 8.1 Types of rural settlement in nineteenth-century France
Source: Adapted from A. Demangeon, *Atlas de la France* (Paris, 1939), p.82.

violent. In the Gévaudan region of the Lozère, there is abundant evidence of domestic violence within rural households, but this may not have been typical.[7]

As Segalen argues, to judge the quality of personal life from the perspective of the individualism – material and sexual – of contemporary society is ethnocentric and ahistorical: instead, the well-being of the rural household as a unit determined the happiness of its members. There were, however, limitations to the picture painted by Segalen. The family relationships she describes cannot be separated from wider patriarchal structures enshrined in the law and political institutions: roles within households were complementary, but this does not imply equality. Moreover, Segalen's key evidence, peasant proverbs (which she claims to be 'the voice of the peasants'), are contradictory, as proverbs always are, and sought to prescribe behaviour rather than to describe it. Hence Breton peasants quipped that 'A dead wife and a living horse make a wealthy man', while for those in Languedoc, 'A dauntless woman in the house is worth more than farm and livestock too', and doubtless there were contrary ones in each region. They also reveal a profound ambiguity about women's sexuality ('One cock is enough for ten hens, but ten men are not enough for one woman' – Pays Basque) and household roles ('The household is going very badly when the hen plays the cock' – Provence).

Of course, these proverbs may instead represent a prescriptive response to women's frequent transgression of gender roles, or the increased powers daughters had within the family because of inheritance rights. In the Morvan region of the Nièvre, for example, customary law before the Revolution gave parents full freedom to dispose of their property. Thereafter, there was a sharp increase in full division of peasant property, passing first to the surviving spouse to ensure security in old age, then to the children to apportion equally. At Larochemillay, 28 of the 42 wills in the years 1821–40 did not bother to use the provision giving parents the right to leave a 'disposable share' to one child, suggesting that children welcomed the inheritance law even if this meant that the number of small proprietors in the Morvan would increase by 46 per cent between 1835 and 1852.[8]

Tenant-farmers seeking to keep large leased property in the family did seek to leave property to one son while compensating other children, as did peasants elsewhere. Such families were more likely to avoid land division by limiting family size, in defiance of the admonitions of a resurgent church. In the village of Meulan (Seine-et-Oise), it has been estimated that contraception was used by 16 per cent of couples in 1765–89, but by 55 per cent under the Restoration. The most common method used was withdrawal, denounced as 'Onanism' by the Church and known elsewhere in Europe as 'the French sin'. According to the priest of Clermont-l'Hérault in the Midi, it was 'encountered daily everywhere'; in 1829 the priests of the diocese of Gap, high in the Alps, claimed that 'the detestable crime of Onan ... has occurred even in peasant huts'.[9]

Even so, the rural population increased significantly, from 23.4 to 26.9 million between 1811 and 1841. The inability of most households to acquire or rent enough land to sustain their members, even with textile work, lay behind the remarkable mobility of the rural population. Up to 500,000 people left their own department each year (many more moved about within departments) to work elsewhere in order to supplement the household budget: 10,000 Savoyards went to factories in Lyon, 25,000–35,000 Creusois trudged to Paris, and 80,000 highlanders from the Pyrenees and Massif Central went grape-picking in the Hérault. Woodcutters and sawyers from the Puy-de-Dôme and Creuse migrated to work in the pine forests of the Landes; 7,000 hemp and linen carders from the Ain went to Alsace-Lorraine; others went mole-trapping around Argentan and Falaise in Normandy (for which they could earn up to 600 francs in ten months). Such departures, which were usually seasonal but could be for years at a time, were part of an ancient economic cycle of temporary migrations which had never been as extensive as in the first half of the nineteenth century and involved one in five rural families.[10]

This rural mobility and increasing contact with 'corrupting' urban centres added urgency to the Church's crusade to recapture its social authority by 'rechristianizing' the countryside through missions, religious education and clerical rejuvenation.[11] Under the Restoration, some 1,200–1,500 missions were conducted, in every diocese except Cambrai and Corsica. Lasting up to six weeks, the missions centred on themes of repentance and renewal. To purge the secular evils of the recent past, calvary crosses were erected in village squares where liberty trees once stood, and books by Voltaire and Rousseau were burned; to resuscitate faith, parishioners were exhorted to return to religious observance. The Church had some success: on average, missions resulted in 250–300 men and twice as many women returning to communion in each department. In Merlimont (Pas-de-Calais), for example, one-third of males confirmed in 1830 were over 22 years of age. By 1830, annual clerical recruitment had reached a post-revolutionary peak of 2,337: in the diocese of Besançon, where there had been only one ordination in 1798–1800, numbers rose from 72 in 1811–15 to a peak of 313 in 1826–30. The evangelizing activities of the clergy were sustained by the energetic devotion of the *béates* ('pious women') who had re-emerged in teaching orders after the Concordat. They took the catechism, practical instruction for both sexes, and a willingness to teach in local languages such as Breton, German and Occitan to the poorest rural areas of perhaps 20 departments.

Whereas priests had been recruited disproportionately from urban bourgeois in the late eighteenth century, they were now mostly peasants and small-town artisans. No doubt, whatever an individual's faith, the priesthood was attractive for pragmatic reasons: priests earned a moderate living (from 700 francs for curates to 1,500 for parish priests) and there were plenty of openings (in the diocese of Besançon, 75 priests, including 12 over 80 years of age, had died in 1812 alone). However, the commitment of recruits should not be underestimated: the seminary of Périgueux rated 59 per cent of its novices as weak or worse in ability, but 97–100 per cent as good or better in application, conduct and character. They had to endure a 'surveillance' system of training, remarkably similar to the regime of the new model prisons, and were constantly supervized and disciplined to produce an obedient, serious priest conscious of his antipathy to the secular world. Above all, a horror of bodily lusts was inculcated, in part to eradicate seminary homosexuality, which also resulted in a 'clerical gynophobia' when priests encountered parishioners.

The renewed Tridentine militancy of the clergy embroiled them in a running battle with the forms of sociability practised in their parishes. Not only were new forms of dancing, such as the waltz and polka, frowned upon, but so too were popular forms of leisure such as the *bourrée* and other dances associated with community festivals, personal ceremonies and work, such as threshing or grape-crushing. The priest of Savigny (Rhône) urged: 'since [peasants] are full of passions, and dancing only enflames these passions, since these gatherings never finish without crime, since a single debauched person can infect those who watch him, and since things are said [at dances] which should not be heard, and things are done which should not be seen, it is prudent for priests to oppose dances altogether'. Exemplifying clerical success was Jean Vianney, the *curé* of Ars, north of Lyon, who used the confessional, refusal of absolution and communion, and his personal example to turn a 'lost' parish into a place of pilgrimage by 1830.[12]

The responses of rural people to an evangelizing church varied sharply, depending on how devout a region had been before 1789 and its responses to the Church's role in the Counter-Revolution. In some areas, such as the Orléanais, Beauvaisis, Burgundy and the south-east, a 'dechristianization' movement had surged in 1793, whereas in Brittany, Alsace-Lorraine, the north-east and the southern Massif Central rural hostility to the Revolution had been inextricably linked to what were perceived to be attacks on religious and therefore community life. Religiosity was everywhere profoundly influenced by history and the Church's missionary zeal after 1815 tended only to reinforce existing attitudes. Similarly, while there was one priest for every 752 people in France by mid-century, this presence ranged from 1 : 1,450 in the Cher to about 1 : 400 in the practising departments of the Manche and the southern Massif Central, where 90 per cent of men and women took Easter mass. Among the 500,000 Protestants, too, there was a reaction against Enlightenment rationalism towards a fundamentalist reading of scripture. Above all, however, the resilience and unity of the Lutherans of eastern France and the Calvinists of the south was based on memories of ancient persecutions revivified, for example, by the killing of about 80 Protestants in the Gard during the White Terror of 1815.[13]

Whatever a *curé*'s popularity and social background, he was everywhere a visible, important local identity. So, too, was the tiny élite of large landowners, noble or bourgeois, who dominated economic resources, social authority and political power. One of the crucial social changes generated by the upheavals of the revolutionary period was a significant shift in the basis and meaning of the deference such large landowners enjoyed. The erosion of the mystique of nobility, the abolition of seigneurial obligations and dues and the practice of popular politics had left economic inequality and dependence as the only basis of deference. Even this did not prevent rural people treating nobles as other citizens. In 1822, the villagers of Rennes (Aude) petitioned the prefect about the pretentions of his appointed mayor: 'The undersigned regard Monsieur de Fleury only as their mayor ... and not as their former seigneur armed with feudal power and arbitrary dispenser of the product of their sweat.' On the other hand, further west along the Pyrenees, nobles – including children – continued to assume social distance by a condescending use of *tu* when addressing peasants. The comte de Comminges later recalled relations between his father and local peasants: 'The peasants were very attached to him, even though he treated them like negroes. Woe to whoever didn't remove his hat while speaking to him, for a blow with his walking-stick soon knocked off the offending headwear. At that time, these dealings were accepted as quite natural.'[14]

Of course, this was simply how a small boy remembered his childhood many decades later: we do not know what the peasants made of such behaviour. Where patronage systems were strongest, as in Corsica, they were not simply a sign of deference but rather a way by which the poor gained access to scarce resources via a wealthy patron. The difficulty in drawing conclusions about social relations between peasants and notables in the countryside, as about responses to a zealous church or relationships within the family, goes to the heart of the most intractable problem in social history. The central difficulty in writing the social history of ideas in the countryside is that the inevitable distance in time, space and culture between the historian and the past is extended by the 'silence' of rural inhabitants in conventional historical sources. The rapidly expanding and hierarchically organized bureaucracy of nineteenth-century France created an enormous body of material recording those elements of rural life important to that bureaucracy: censuses, land surveys, agricultural statistics, and reports on public order. Little of this material relates to how rural people made sense of their world, however, and even less is in their own words. Such a silence has tempted historians to assume that rural people in the 1820s were essentially apolitical, guided only by ancient *mentalités* which were hostile to change, intensely parochial and preoccupied with survival.[15]

More helpful is George Rudé's understanding of popular ideology as a dynamic interplay between perceptions and reality.[16] Like other people, the rural masses viewed the world through a set of 'inherent' and 'derived' perceptions: that is, of attitudes, values and prejudices they had absorbed 'with their mother's milk' as members of particular occupational (and ethnic and gender) groups, which were constantly reinforced and modified by ideas derived from elsewhere, orally or through the written word. Such 'derived' ideas were not simply adopted and assimilated in their original form but were also adapted to particular uses. Nor were such ideas static, for rural people in the first decades of the nineteenth century were living in a changing world which acted to modify or reinforce their perceptions. Such was the weight of the ideological and experiential legacy of the Revolution, however, that popular attitudes after 1815 were everywhere deeply marked by memories, direct or transmitted, of the hopes and disappointments, the triumphs and sacrifices, of the revolutionary period.

In this complex and dynamic process of the making of ideologies, the years around 1830 were also formative. Analysis of the political significance of the Revolution of 1830, once restricted to debates about whether it represented a 'bourgeois triumph', have more recently highlighted the events of July-December as only the Parisian dimension of a nationwide crisis which lasted from 1828 until the last republican and legitimist fires were smothered in the provinces in 1834. The experience of a protracted process of popular mobilization and repression was to generate significant developments in the content of rural politics.[17]

A severe failure of the grain and potato harvests in 1827 developed into a protracted economic slump from 1828; as grain prices rose by 50 per cent, the west, north-west and centre were swept by waves of food rioting to prevent scarce reserves being removed to urban markets. In many areas this crisis coincided with antipathy to the perceived aggression of Charles X and the Church and to a new forest code passed in 1827. The collapse of royal authority in 1830 unleashed a further wave of rural protest, now also aimed at local élites and representatives of the Bourbon regime: in Villesèque (Aude) long-standing friction over access to wooded hillsides culminated in the collective killing of a noble and his son.[18] This was a rare example of extreme violence, but in many areas an explosive coincidence of misery, expectation of radical change, government instability and the liberation of political life generated an escalation of division and conflict. There were in fact many more instances of collective protest in 1832 than in 1830, and it was not until 1834 that the new Orléanist élite succeeded in distancing itself from and repressing those working people of town and country who had assumed 1830 to be their victory.

The Pyrenean department of the Ariège exemplifies the rural phase of this unfolding crisis.[19] Here, the harvest crisis of 1827 was ruinous for upland villagers dependent on buying grain in return for their livestock and already angered by the new forest code which closed state and communal forests to their sheep and goats. At the same time, owners of private forests were closing off access in defiance of ancient customary rights to fuel as wood became a valuable commodity to the expanding metallurgical industry. By October 1829, private forests were regularly being entered by male peasants disguised as women, calling themselves 'demoiselles'. While such disguises no doubt prevented easy recognition by forest guards, they were also symbolic of 'a world turned upside down'. Like many southerners, Ariégeois celebrated Mardi Gras every year with an inversion of worldly restraints on sexuality, dress, obedience, food and drink: the popular justice of seizing forests was a carnivalesque moment symbolised in transvestism. Such protest widened after July 1830 as law enforcers were suddenly unsure about whom they should be obeying. Tax offices were raided, forges destroyed and forests again invaded. The catchword of the parliamentary opposition in Paris had been 'Liberty!' (in political and civil terms); the peasants of the Ariège took up the cry and adapted it to their own cause, as in an anonymous letter to a mayor in August 1830: 'The chief of the regiment of Demoiselles has the honor to tell you that the forges which are near the forests will be completely destroyed, and yours is in that number. Long live Liberty!' Significantly they now discarded their female disguises and began petitioning the new government for reform to the forest code. However, after an initial concession, its response was to send in troops and to support local bourgeois demands for retribution and continued control of forest resources.

In the process of the protracted struggle of the new élite to restrict the Revolution of 1830 to constitutional reform, huge numbers of rural people were alienated. Not all of them responded by commitment to a democratic or republican ideology. In parts of the countryside, notably the north-west and the

Midi, a populist legitimism re-emerged in response to the perceived Parisian and bourgeois nature of the new regime and the resurgence of republicanism. Seeking to capitalize on this, the duchesse de Berry, mother of the young Bourbon pretender (the comte de Chambord or 'Henri V'), landed in Marseille in April 1832 and travelled clandestinely to the royalist heartland in the Vendée. Rural people armed themselves in her support but also to settle old scores: in Mazières-en-Gâtine, insurgents seized taxes, leaving a receipt signed 'Chouans, soldiers of Henri V'. The insurrection was larger and bloodier than historians have realized, requiring the government to place four departments in a state of siege and to quarter troops in some villages until 1845.[20]

Such political mobilizations revealed the resentment in some rural regions that 'legitimate' monarchy had been overthrown in 1830, while elsewhere anger centred on the way a new élite had *'escamoté'* ('spirited away') and stultified a people's revolution. For example the republican Society of the Rights of Man had branches in dozens of departments and hundreds of rural communities, and by 1833, there were 56 republican newspapers in provincial France. Facilitating political mobilization were the 1831 electoral laws which, while they only slightly widened the national electorate, had a stronger impact at the local level. Municipal councils were now to be elected rather than appointed, and in communities of fewer than 1,000 people the wealthiest 10 per cent of the population (approximately 45 per cent of adult males) were to vote. After 30 years politics made a legal and formal reappearance in every village. Some 2,872,000 adult males were eligible to vote for municipal councils, 15 times the number in national elections. By 1837, 37 per cent of councils were categorized as belonging to the 'democratic opposition' in the Dordogne and Landes, 33 per cent in the Allier and Pyrénées-Orientales, and 27–8 per cent in the Ain and Isère.

The subtle change in the composition of the ruling élite, the 'internal emigration' of legitimist nobles and, above all, the political economy of the July Monarchy created a climate and infrastructure for accelerated agricultural change after 1830. Often, as in the case of Limanton (see Chapter 6), such agrarian capitalism was resented by tenants and sharecroppers especially vulnerable to the uncertainties of specialization. In Guillaumin's *The Life of a Simple Man*, set in the neighbouring Allier, Tiennon comments bitterly on a new lease signed in the late 1830s: 'the thing that worried us, and soon seemed unbearable, was the constant presence of the master.... He knew nothing about farming, but mistakenly took his role of managing proprietor seriously. He read books on agriculture, and wanted us to swallow all the theories he found in them.'

Whatever the resistance to change expressed by the most vulnerable, the most significant aspect of agriculture after 1830 was an increase in productivity due to more intensive and specialized agriculture on smallholdings in specific areas. The gradual transition to agrarian capitalism in nineteenth-century France followed this 'peasant route' to 'commodity production' more frequently than it did large-scale capitalist farming. Detailed regional analyses have challenged longstanding anglocentric assumptions that, first, as a triumph for small landowners, the French Revolution retarded the movement towards agrarian capitalism and, secondly, that it was not until the 'modernization' of transport (especially railways) and the mechanization of agriculture and industry after 1860 that a real economic 'take-off' occurred.[21]

Rather than rural France being based on a durable *ancien-régime* type of agriculture in the 1840s, these years witnessed some significant changes. For example, well before the arrival of the railway, the lowland regions of the Bugey (Ain) were specializing in wine, the uplands in timber and stock-raising, as well as in silk, combs (Oyonnax) and *articles de Sainte-Claude*. In the Mayenne, fertilizer from proliferating lime furnaces (from 88 to 200 in 1831–45) permitted a reduction in fallow from 150,000 to 100,000 hectares by 1850 and increased wheat yields from 13 to 14 hectolitres per hectare. In the years 1836–50, the area of sown or artificial pastures in the Doubs increased from 13,000 to 30,000 hectares; the yields of wheat, barley and *méteil* rose by 25 per cent. Specialization in wine, sugar beet and cattle (an increase from 6.7 to 12.2 million head in 1812–52) was facilitated by improved road transport and added to local demand for railways. In 1843 Olivier Le Diouron of Saint-Adrien (Côtes-du-Nord) wrote to the subprefect of Guingamp about the changes he had introduced since 1839: the use on his farm of eight hectares of a new type of plough and the planting of clover had increased his income by 519 francs and his livestock from eight to 12. But only rarely were such changes the result of mechanization or even of the introduction of the scythe to replace the sickle. Increased productivity was due rather to more intensive cultivation, draining of swamps, land clearance, and replacement of fallow with sown pastures.[22]

Of course, such changes should not be exaggerated. By 1840, fallow still covered 21 per cent of farmland and natural pastures and wasteland 23 per cent, while sown pastures were only 5 per cent. In many areas, leases continued to impose long-standing routines and soil use. Nevertheless, specific examples of change have been supported, in global terms, by economic historians using more sophisticated techniques for measuring agricultural output. For example, Toutain and Marczewski have argued that in 1835–44 agricultural output grew at twice the rate of population growth. Despite the fact that the urban population was beginning to increase rapidly and that smallholdings were proliferating in the countryside, more intensive and specialized agriculture in certain areas was enabling farm output to more than keep pace with a rising population.

The 1840s also marked an acceleration of the shift to regional specialization. While rural producers in Bonnières-sur-Seine (Seine-et-Oise) abandoned wine-growing to concentrate on dairy cattle, in the Midi vineyards were replacing sheep and grain on the low hills and plains: in the first half of the century the number of hectares planted in vines almost doubled to 220,000 between Montpellier and the Spanish border. Elsewhere, the contraction of rural industry in the face of urban concentration, overpopulation and depletion of soil resources, and the hope of better opportunities elsewhere quickened the rate of rural emigration. By 1846, the rural population of France had reached its historic peak and in 16 departments – especially in upland areas – a permanent decline had begun.[23]

As a consequence of population increase and more extensive cultivation (from about 16 million hectares in 1789 to 20.6 million in 1840), greater strain was placed on the environment. This was particularly the case in forests and on 'wastelands' which sustained bird and animal life. The greater freedom of owners to use their forests and the increasing demand for charcoal for forges accelerated tree-felling: in the Pyrénées-Orientales, where there were many small *forges catalanes*, the forested area declined from 300,000 to 66,000 hectares in 1730–1830, and by 1850 was at its smallest-ever size. In steep river valleys this led to erosion and ruinous lowland flooding.[24] In upland areas all over France, the first half of the century witnessed a constant, occasionally violent, battle between rural communities and forest wardens contradictorily seeking to exclude peasants from state forests while upholding the rights of private forest owners to use their property as they wished, in line with the forest codes of 1827 and 1846. A similarly revealing ambiguity existed in hunting laws, tightened in 1844 to protect wildlife endangered by the democratization of hunting after 1789 but permitted to those with the money to purchase the requisite licence. On cultivated land, however, peasant polyculture was attuned to the local ecology and conservative of soil resources. A growing population in town and country was fed without recourse to artificial fertilizers and pesticides, virtually all human and animal wastes were returned to the soil, and an endless variety of plant subspecies and local farming practices flourished.

The transition to specialization on owned or leased smallholdings in specific areas generated gradual but fundamental transformations in rural society. In the Nièvre, the trend to specialized cattle-raising in the 1840s was to be the death-knell for sharecropping *communautés* as market-oriented farming under cash leases eroded the need for a large family labour force and held out to tenants the hope of profits and purchase of land. Here, as elsewhere, subsistence-oriented peasants were becoming small farmers dependent on urban markets. The gradual, chequered increase in agricultural productivity was also reflected in a perceptible decline in the mortality rate: even allowing for increasing mortality in industrial towns, nationally there was a decline from 23.5 per thousand in 1816–20 to 22.7 in 1841–5. What such figures hide are the regional impact of specific harvest crises or diseases (though the 1832 cholera epidemic in the Paris basin was grave enough to send the national mortality rate to 28.5 per thousand in that year). Above all, they hide the class differential in the incidence of death, and not just in the higher life-expectancy of the well-to-do. Nationally, there was one discovered infanticide for every 583 live births, but it was the poorest rural women in the poorest regions who felt forced to take this action: in the three departments of the Limousin the rate was 1 : 230–320. It was they, too, who had to resort to the much more common practice of abandoning their babies to the state or church foundling homes.[25]

Awareness that disease and death more often spared the rich than the poor was often explained in rural society by the evil influence and sorcery of the increasing numbers of doctors appearing in the countryside. The conviction of these harbingers of outside cultural systems that they were civilizing primitives was reciprocated by a popular mistrust of their malign powers: 'they have a diploma and that's all; with that they cut, clip, and kill'. Given that it is unclear whether doctors provided more effective treatment than religious orders, local *sages-femmes* (midwives) or unqualified folk-healers (called *charlatans* and *maiges*), it is not surprising that the latter remained more trusted for their local knowledge, oral store of herbal and spiritual remedies, and their humbler origins. They were also more accessible: if Paris had a doctor for every 662 people by 1844, there was only one for every 5,274 Bretons in the Morbihan.[26]

All over rural France, the 1830s and 1840s were a time of changes, though varying regionally in speed, nature and intensity. This was not only the case with economic and demographic structures, but also in cultures and perceptions. The stark contrast between the world of the *grands notables* and of the mass of the rural population is often restated in social history as a dichotomy between 'élite' and 'popular' culture. Such an argument has an implicitly pejorative tone; given the nature of rural social relations and the process by which cultural practices were reproduced and transformed, it is also unhelpful. 'Popular' attitudes and practices were neither discrete nor a vulgarized variant of 'élite' culture; rather, rural cultures were a multilayered and dynamic interplay of both, varying along class, regional and gender lines.

In this context, Maurice Agulhon's analysis of the Provençal back-country of the department of the Var is particularly revealing.[27] This was a land of substantial villages and small towns, clustered round public squares, socially complex, and increasingly linked to urban markets through wine, olive oil, silk and cork production. Economic change, long-standing social resentments, and the geographical typology of the area explain the receptivity of the masses to local bourgeois and petit-bourgeois 'culture brokers'. This can be seen, for example, in wider interest in French literature and education, more general use of the French language, and the imitation of bourgeois salons or *cercles* in the form of popular *chambrées* (in the 83 communities of the districts of Toulon and Brignoles, there were no fewer than 516 of them in 1842). These new cultural forms coexisted with the vibrant, outdoors 'folklore' (in its widest sense) of Provence, evident in the intricate collective ways in which popular politics were expressed.

This process of *francisation* was as much to do with the acceptance of the relevance of French national politics by rural people as it was with the role of cultural intermediaries and the intrusion of the French State. However, rural France remained a land of extraordinary ethnic, cultural and linguistic diversity. Similarly, there were sharp regional variations in levels of religiosity and literacy, insofar as these may be measured with any accuracy. One example of this is in levels of premarital conception, a common measure of acceptance of church authority. The number of first-born children conceived outside marriage in Sainghin-en-Mélantois (Nord) was about 55 per cent; in Biltères d'Ossau (Basses-Pyrénées) it was negligible and lower than in the eighteenth century. In the western dioceses of Laval (Mayenne) and Nantes (Loire-Inférieure), the number of rural people over 14 years of age taking Easter mass in the 1840s was between 74 and 89 per cent, while in rural areas of the diocese of Orléans (Loiret) 67 per cent of girls aged 13–20 attended, but only about 23 per cent of boys, 20 per cent of women and 4 per cent of men. It was about a similar lack of male churchgoing that the bishop of Chartres (Eure-et-Loir) commented in 1842 that 'first communion is at the same time the end of school, the end of catechism, the end of religion: in a word, the end of childhood'. To many priests and bishops, the Revolution of 1830 seemed a return to the dark days of the 1790s, with the élite's materialism being reflected in the collapse of clerical recruitment to 1,100 per annum by 1845, half the 1830 level. Potential recruits may have been concerned about the lack of vacant parishes as well as insecure about the Church's future. From an annual average of 63 ordinations in the diocese of Besançon in 1826–30, the numbers declined to between 14 and 28 in 1841–5.[28]

Though levels of religious observance varied markedly across rural France, in a broader cultural sense the rituals of the Christian year everywhere remained inextricably linked with the seasonal round of agricultural production and the festival cycle of religious cultures (this identification of popular religious beliefs and regional cultures was captured in George Sand's rural novels about the region of the Berry written in 1845–7). The great festivals of rural life – the feast of Corpus Christi, Carnival, the patron saints' feast days – were, like personal *rites de passage*, also religious. These were also the periodic moments of ritualized recreation in villages, apart from ancient ball-games such as 'la soule'.[29]

Edward Berenson has argued that, especially in the southern half of the country, rural people saw the priest's role as limited to that of a celebrant of formal rituals rather than a guide to correct practice. Where priests were doctrinaire or insensitive to local custom, they could expect scorn and isolation. The rituals of populist religion – with their emphasis on singing, dancing, the mocking of taboos, the inversion of hierarchy at Carnival time – were frowned upon by a church at odds with what it saw as the pagan, primitive and threatening dimension of collective celebration. The dilemma for the Church was that the hierarchically ordained structures of formal worship imperfectly corresponded with the Christian dimension of collective beliefs: to whom did Christ belong? As agents of a French national church and hierarchy, parish priests often conflicted with the vibrant and distinctive cultures of ethnic minorities; for example dismissing the *charivari* as 'a provocative din at night' *(tapage injurieux et nocturne)*. They also disapproved of the temporal solutions rural inhabitants found to the problem of survival, either by siding with the administration on questions of law and order or by condemning coitus interruptus as 'conjugal Onanism'. Indeed, one reason for the decline in religious observance and respect in some areas may well be the Church's hostility to contraception as a way of limiting family size.[30]

The Church's battle continued with forms of popular leisure, as it did with ancient lay organizations, such as the *'pénitents'* of Provence or the *'charitons'* of Normandy, which mixed sacred and profane functions, and with church confraternities which had lost sight of their religious goals. In 1837 the *curé* of Balazuc (Ardèche) inveighed against local 'excesses' after a banquet, causing widespread anger culminating in shots being fired at the presbytery, and in his flight from 'savagery'. Despite their ardour to 'moralize' the masses, successful priests had to interact sensitively with their parish; not only were they vulnerable to the episcopacy (only those in canton centres had security of tenure), but even in devout areas they had to conform to collective wishes and tolerate the popular synthesis of church dogma and local cults, shrines and beliefs.[31]

The rapid expansion of primary education after 1830 also confronted the Church with a dilemma for, while the organization of education allowed a measure of continuing church control over teachers and the syllabus included religious education, literacy was feared for the way it created closer access to the written word and threatened patriarchal authority. But only the daughter of a wealthy farmer, like Flaubert's Emma Bovary, could hope for a secondary education, mixing her convent's religious texts with forbidden novels by Walter Scott. The spread of literacy was uneven, and was a function of the level of prosperity (whether children could be spared from household labour), the degree of resistance to French, and whether there was already a tradition of mass education by the Church. By mid-century there were still 2,690 communes without schools, but the number of primary students had increased from 1,937,582 in 1832 to 3,530,135 (62 per cent of whom were boys) in 1847. Most of those schools were rural in every way: children attended school for four or five years after turning six, but only in the winter months when their farm labour was not essential. Greatest emphasis was placed on their ability to read, usually from religious or moral texts, and writing was often taught only subsequently. Teachers were most likely to be someone from a peasant or artisan background, like the priest, but they were paid less (often only 500 francs, much of it from school fees) and often had an enormously difficult task as the lay representative of the State. By the late 1830s there were *Écoles Normales* for training male teachers in most departments, and there were 75,000 teachers across the country, but only in 1838 was the first women's training college opened. A teacher's meagre salary was often augmented by clerical or artisan work: 58 of the 200 teachers in three districts of the Creuse in 1832 worked as farmers, shopkeepers, sacristans, clerks, artisans and café-keepers. Pierre Labrusse, teacher in his native village of Olette in the Pyrenees, supplemented his salary with 100 francs earned as the mayor's secretary. In later life Labrusse recalled his first master at the *École Normale* in 1843: 'a maniac, a freemason, we used to say, a Jacobin, a tyrant!'[32]

Historians of education commonly point to a line running from Saint-Malo to Geneva, highlighted by the work of Louis Maggiolo for the Minister of Education in 1877–9, to indicate a 'literate' north and 'backward' south. It is true that 18 of the 30 departments in which virtually every commune had a school in 1850 were in the north-east, and that those where 15 per cent or more of communities were without were in Brittany and the south-west. This gives only an approximate measure of the spread of literacy, however, for it hides internal contrasts within each department and misses the rapid growth in the south after 1830. For example, by the mid-1840s, 60 per cent of men and 50 per cent of women under 20 years in the canton of Roanne (Loire) could read and write compared with 10–15 per cent of those over 20. Moreover, the great surge in primary school numbers in the south began in the late 1820s: that is, local pressure for access to schooling was at least as important as Guizot's 1833 legislation.

While there were in many areas deep-seated economic and cultural obstacles to schooling, especially for girls, the increased emphasis being placed on a facility in written French had important consequences for minority cultures. In general, these cultures were oral: relatively few people were literate in their own daily language. French was not only the language of the bureaucracy and of

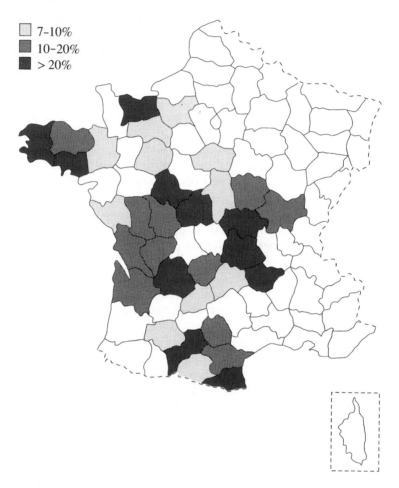

☐ 7–10%
■ 10–20%
■ > 20%

Map 8.2   Commununes in France without primary schools, *c*.1850

Source: Adapted from François Furet and Jacques Ozouf, *Reading and Writing: Literacy in France from Calvin to Jules Ferry* (Cambridge, 1982), p. 266.

social élites, but young rural people in particular were increasingly exposed to French as the language of the written word, and to French national history and geography. The sale by Louis Hachette to the government of one million copies of *L'Alphabet et premier livre de lecture* (1833) was an unprecedented 'best-seller'. Schoolteachers and local élites who established schools had accepted the identity of the French language, national culture and 'progress'. The rules governing the primary school of Olonzac (Hérault) in 1819 declared: '*patois* is forbidden ... it will be recommended to pupils that they speak French at home'. These local councillors had come to see their own language as simply an inferior dialect.

Despite the Church's misgivings about the social impact of literacy, in the 1840s at least there is no doubt that religious brochures and stories were what the rural masses bought, even if it is unclear whether these represented what they wanted to buy or the way they perceived the world. The 3,500 pedlars (*colporteurs*) who carried packs of books on their rural itineraries sold about nine million such volumes each year, and by 1842 the Epinal firm of J.-C. Pellerin was turning out 750,000 religious images annually. The most widely distributed – and probably the most widely read – literature remained the Bible, often read aloud with folktales at *veillées*, evening gatherings of one or more families.[33] Even if most adults were illiterate, men at least had access to the increasing number of provincial newspapers in the 1840s. While most papers in country towns were too expensive for all but urban and rural notables, subscriptions to them and to opposition papers, especially from Paris, were often taken out by proprietors of cafés and taverns. Reading aloud, translation into a local language, and public commentary became a characteristic of male leisure.

Rural France in the 1840s was a complex, changing society whose structure was defined by a network of tensions.[34] The sources of these tensions were as varied as rural society itself, although in general terms it may be said that all over France mounting pressure on and competition for scarce resources was endemic. While agricultural output was increasing substantially, the gains for smallholders and leasers of land were largely cancelled out by increased extraction of surplus through rents and by rising land prices. In the 30 years after 1815, land prices doubled; land taxes rose 53 per cent in 1821–51, reflecting the increase in output, and rents rose 10 per cent in the years 1839–47. From 1820–42 the total of farm mortgages increased by 50 per cent to 13 *milliards*, mostly paid to usurers. In five south-eastern departments studied by Philippe Vigier, land seizures for non-payment of mortgage doubled in the decade of the 1840s. Usurers, who often charged 15–20 per cent for loans, were a key object of popular hatred, as were merchants who offered a minimal security by undertaking to purchase crops in advance, though at low prices, and who then profited from any upswing in markets. While rents were increasing and the price of land becoming prohibitive, wage rates remained low and stable. Male farmservants earned, on top of their keep, an average of 100 francs yearly, and females an average of 75. A male day-labourer could hope to earn 250–300 francs for 250 days work, just enough to keep a family of five in bread, highlighting again the dependence of the rural family on the contributions of all its members.

The first signs were apparent, if only in some regions, of the great transformations which were also to render rural France a different world from that of the 1830s. By mid-century, women outworkers in the Choletais were becoming increasingly 'proletarianized', at the same time enabling male artisans to remain economically independent and in the process represent themselves as the head of the household. Elsewhere, in regions such as the pays de Caux, the cottage textile industries which had employed scores of thousands of women were about to collapse and permanent rural exodus had begun. The evidence of increases in agricultural productivity in the 1840s, coupled with the July Monarchy's road and rail building programmes, created the basis of more 'orderly' and nationally homogeneous marketing structures in which women's collective interventions to protect the 'moral economy' were becoming less important.[35]

Other sources of tension from within and without the rural community were specific to frontier or forest regions, or to areas of rapid changes in the form of production. For example, in highland areas and regions more recently incorporated into the French State, the apparently inexhaustible needs of the State for taxes and conscripts remained charges to be avoided, sidestepped, reduced or even denied wherever possible. In 1844 the commune of La Fage-Montivernont (Lozère) was sheltering 20 deserters and 48 young men who had refused to register. In maritime departments and frontier regions, the efforts of the State to expand the control it exerted over trade and migration were similarly resented and evaded.

One of the great unresolved issues of the revolutionary period, the confrontation between ancient collective rights *(droits d'usage)* to forests, common land and gleaning and the individual property rights sanctified in legislation, was still being played out in the 1840s. Where large landowners sought to profit from the opportunities created by the population growth in urban areas by changing the use of productive resources or by restricting community access to forests or other land, the rural poor responded by every means at their disposal: sabotage, litigation, deception and law-breaking. To meet the need to preserve dwindling forest resources from the inexorable pressures of overuse, the government sought to limit customary usage rights by the poor. In 1846, a revised forest code further restricted wood-gathering and stock-grazing in public forests while offering concessions to entrepreneurs in the timber business. This threatened the viability of thousands of highland communities in the Ardennes, Jura, Alps, Massif Central and Pyrenees.

The responses to such pressures took on a variety of forms. In the mountain region of Couserans (Ariège), where overpopulation was especially acute, the response was to encroach into state forests. In the 1840s, no fewer than 1,750 of the 1,900 households of Massat were prosecuted for this *usurpation*. There were often strong community labour pressures against mechanization, as when labourers in Pézilla-la-Rivière, in the most fertile area of the Pyrénées-Orientales, protested against the introduction of mechanical threshers as being 'totally to the advantage of the large landowners and to the detriment of the workers'. But the most common response to threats to the delicate balancing-act of the household budget was biological, especially when the foe was the most intractable of all, the weather. Despite higher productivity and improved transport links under the July Monarchy, rural France remained vulnerable to vagaries of climate and fluctuations in prices of food staples. Decisions about marriage and conception were closely tied to judgments about trends in grain prices, and there remained a stark correlation between the index of flour prices and the life-expectancy of infants, the elderly and the frail.

A combination of threats to survival, stemming from indebtedness, agrarian individualism and the political economy of a bourgeois regime, and the widening of access to legal political participation at the local level inevitably generated a reworking of political attitudes. Republicanism and, especially, Bonapartism became more attractive with the fading of negative memories of 1789–1815 and in contrast with the barren, self-serving, inglorious image of the July Monarchy. By the mid-1840s, the regime of Louis-Philippe had become identified with the narrow interests of bourgeois notables and was bereft of any popular rural base.

Napoleon's rule came to symbolize employment and national pride. To the 40,000 women lace-makers of the Calvados, exploited by middle-men and paid only one franc per day, the Empire recalled the legendary boom in lace sales. Pierre Joigneaux, born in 1815 in the village of Varennes (Côte-d'Or), remembered: 'when the emperor was talked about, it wasn't to deplore his appalling human butcheries, but to remind we little ones that his eyes were not cold and that for twenty years he gave our enemies rude shocks'. Similarly, Martin Nadaud, born the same year, recalled his father whispering to him after the Revolution of 1830: 'How stupid and foolish these people are! It's not Louis-Philippe whom we need. He is a Bourbon and with the Bourbons it will always be the priests *(la calotte)* who will rule over us. What we need is the son of the great Napoleon.'[36] Joigneaux was from a well-to-do peasant family and became a prominent Parisian journalist. Nadaud, too, went to Paris, but as an impoverished migrant, spending years at a time in the capital before returning home with savings for his family and to see his wife, from whom he had had to part after 17 days of marriage. Both men became republicans in their different occupational milieus, but this was above all an ideology with which the appeal of Bonapartism was commonly mingled.

The vulnerability of most rural people and their alienation from the July Monarchy were both sharply aggravated by the failure of the grain and potato crops in late 1846. In January 1847, Joseph Cassanyes, Mayor of Canet and son of the *conventionnel*, wrote to the local prefect:

> As to the misery that is weighing on the poorest class, I would say without fear of contradiction that in this regard there is no commune worse off than this, because independently of the rigours of the season and the bad harvest of 1846 which have plunged the poor into misery, the population of Canet had to struggle last autumn with a calamitous epidemic.

Cassanyes's letter may have been special pleading, but everywhere the regime was inundated with pleas for help at a time when it had political worries of its own.

9

The Mid-Century Crisis, 1846–1852

In the summer of 1846 Horace Vernet received 25,000 francs from the king to paint 'Louis-Philippe and his sons riding out from the château of Versailles'. Eschewing earlier Orléanist iconography connecting the regime to the Revolutions of 1789 and 1830, and even to Napoleon, Vernet now deliberately linked the idea of a stable dynasty to images of Versailles, the Bourbon fleur-de-lis and a statue of Louis XIV. The serene power of Vernet's imagery was a direct response to – but in sharp contrast with – the social and political context of 1846–7.[1]

Vernet began painting at the very time that wildly erratic weather was ruining grain and potato crops. By early 1847, prices were higher than at any time since 1817, largely because merchants and large farmers deliberately withheld stocks to profit from shortages. High prices hit urban workers already suffering from the collapse of rural demand for manufactures. In 1847, one in every 2.4 Parisians had to apply for emergency relief, one in every 2.6 people in Montauban, one in every 4.2 in the industrial department of the Nord. Belated government relief was inadequate in the countryside.

This protest coincided with a nationwide campaign by the parliamentary opposition, seeking to pressure the regime into electoral reform in the aftermath of the government's comfortable victory in the elections of August 1846. The 60 political banquets held between July 1847 and February 1848 in provincial towns grouped an awkward coalition of the liberal opposition and republicans. The language of the speeches expressed scorn for the regime and called for a new age of purified male political virtue. A celebrated speech at the reform banquet at Châlons-sur-Saône in December 1847 imagined a new regime of men 'purified of all shame, of all cowardice, of all filth, of all degrading passions', men who would be brought to power by universal suffrage and the overthrow of a system based on wealth and private interest.[2]

The banquets failed to achieve their goal, but the final Parisian banquet had unforeseen and fundamental effects. For the first time, delegations of students and workers were invited. An alarmed government banned the gathering, and this attack on the right of free association provided the focus for an array of grievances: to the parliamentary opposition, 'association' meant the right to assemble peacefully; to workers it also meant their rights in the workplace; to students the right to hear recently sacked Sorbonne historians, Michelet, Quinet and Mickiewicz. While leading republicans counselled caution, students, then workers and petits bourgeois, took the initiative and demonstrated on 22 February. Shots fired into angry crowds by nervous troops undercut Louis-Philippe's attempt to calm protests by ministerial changes; on the night of 23 February, barricades were erected all over the city, and it became evident that the middle-class National Guard had deserted the regime. For middle-class guardsmen, whose savings and investments had been eroded by the crisis, the regime's philosophy – *'enrichissez-vous'* – now had too hollow a ring. As crowds descended on the Tuileries, Louis-Philippe snatched up a top hat, an overcoat, his keys and briefcases and fled – in Hugo's words, transformed into an elderly bourgeois.[3]

Ignoring Louis-Philippe's abdication, crowds invaded the Chamber and directly nominated members of a republican provisional government. Apart from a solitary worker, Alexandre Martin or 'Albert' (an editor of *L'Atelier*), this government was drawn from republicans close to the newspapers *Le National* and the more radical *La Réforme*. The journalistic backgrounds of these people – like those of their predecessors in 1830 – point to the role of the press as a locus of opposition under the monarchy. This was not just an ideo-logical counterpoint, but a social one as well, for the men of the opposition press quickly took over key positions at every level of government across the country, as the *commissaires* appointed temporarily to replace prefects, as senior admin-istrators and as heads of government departments.

News of the Revolution was greeted in the countryside with enthusiasm or quiet acceptance, but rarely with dismay.[4] Local notables identified with the regime withdrew from public life, while legitimist nobles and priests rushed to accept the Republic while believing it to be but a stepping-stone to a Bourbon restoration. Was not the Republic a divine punishment for the secular material-ism of the Orléanist *juste milieu*? This support did not prevent the expression of anger in some areas against unpopular priests, but anticlerical outbursts were but one of the responses in the countryside to the collapse of the July Monarchy. The immediate political target was usually an Orléanist mayor or the municipal council composed of better-off inhabitants. The provisional government expected change-over in local councils to await formal elections, but in many areas rural people took matters into their own hands. Just as common was col-lective protest aimed at threats to social and economic well-being, particularly the demands of the State and new productive techniques being introduced by capitalist entrepreneurs. The collapse of political authority in February and the assumption that the new regime was somehow 'the people's' emboldened rural inhabitants to attack the local manifestations of structures of power and wealth which threatened their existence.

Conflict over control and use of forests was especially common in the Pyrenees and the east. Ultimately, the new republican regime had to mobilize more than 48,000 troops to reimpose the forest codes of 1827 and 1846. Attacks were also directed at new techniques in agriculture and transport. Along the Paris-Orléans and Paris-Rouen railway lines, barge-workers, carriage-drivers and innkeepers tore up lines and set stations ablaze. Threshing-machines, scythes and other labour-reducing machinery were destroyed, and recently-sold commons were restored to collective control or redistributed by household. Anger was also aimed at indirect taxes on essential foodstuffs and wine: tax offices were attacked and registers destroyed in southern country towns such as Castres, Prades, Lodève and Bédarieux. In this way rural and small-town inhabitants were hitting at the most onerous and socially discriminatory of the State's revenue-raising methods. From 1816 to 1847, the *quatre vieilles* (four direct taxes) on urban and rural property and businesses had fallen from 74 to 35 per cent of all state revenue. Revenue from indirect taxes on drinks, salt, tobacco and other goods had increased by 450 per cent to a level more important to the State than even under the *ancien régime*. Paralleling such attacks on the system of state taxation and the disproportionate wealth of some individuals were examples of violent protests against persons involved in usury. In the east, in many rural communes around Altkirch (Haut-Rhin), action against usury became entwined with hostility to Jews. Contrasting groups of people took direct action in urban areas: for example, prisoners rebelled against conditions and discrimination against homosexuals in Rennes, Riom and Poitiers; in Paris and Lyon crowds freed prostitutes and military prisoners, and in Grenoble cutlers refused to sharpen the guillotine.[5]

The new government was horrified by such actions: although reformist, its concerns were chiefly in those areas which would 'edify' and politically emancipate the masses. Hence it amnestied only political prisoners and abolished capital punishment but only for political offences. As a sign of its desire to reform public behaviour, it also outlawed the weekly animal fights in Paris between dogs and bulls, bears and wolves, held for 70 years on the place du Combat near the site of the medieval gibbet and the carrion refuse-dump. Politically, the government introduced universal manhood suffrage, freedom of the press and association, and opened the National Guard to all males. In the colonies, slavery was finally abolished (although an independence movement in Guadeloupe was quickly suppressed). The government's concerns were also to alleviate social distress. The salt tax was abolished and the drink tax lowered, an 'enquiry into industrial and agricultural work' initiated, and subsistence was guaranteed to the urban unemployed. To implement the latter, 'national workshops' were opened in Paris, Marseille and other cities. The public works initiated were never adequate to employ the swelling ranks of workers laid off as employers and bourgeois consumers sharply curtailed expenditure: in some luxury trades in Paris, well over 80 per cent of workers were dismissed and industrial production fell by two-thirds in Lille. The government also began investigating the re-organization of work through the 'Luxembourg Commission' and similar bodies in other cities. Beyond generating theoretical discussion of a new economic order based on producers' cooperatives, the Commission also came to play a role in negotiations during industrial disputes, usually imposing regulations favourable to workers.[6]

The democratic republicanism of the Government caught it in a desperate bind. On the one hand, it sought unsuccessfully to reassure employers and prevent a 'strike of capital', while on the other hand political life underwent a spectacular and radical liberation. Within weeks, more than 200 clubs, with up to 75,000 members, opened in Paris. Up to 300 new papers, mostly cheap and ephemeral, appeared in the capital, together printing 400,000 copies by May. Among the most important of these was *La Vraie République*, a militant social-ist mouthpiece calling for political liberties, free and compulsory education, state organization of agricultural, industrial and intellectual work, and the gradual socialization of the means of production. The February Revolution also facilitated an articulation and organization of feminism. Among a dozen news-papers, often published by women printers, the most important was *La Voix des femmes*, founded by Eugénie Niboyet, an experienced journalist from a wealthy, Bonapartist and Protestant background. After the first issue, 400 women, mainly workers, congregated at Niboyet's home and formed a political club. There were correspondents in Brussels, London, Turin, and 13 provincial cities. Like other feminist papers, it stressed the emancipating nature of work, collective action, internationalism, hostility to racism and slavery, religious toleration, radical pol-itics, and demanded women's equality in education, civil rights and divorce. Despite the activism of feminist women in 1848, however, the issue of women's civic rights seems to have troubled men less than in 1793. A women's suffrage bill was perfunctorily discussed and rejected. When the radical republican Ferdinand Flocon argued in the National Assembly in July 1848 that women should not be excluded from political clubs, he was greeted with laughter.[7]

The chief focus of associational and journalistic life was the elections of 23 April, seen as the occasion for the resolution of social tensions already evident in large, angry popular demonstrations in Paris on 17 March and 16 April. Electoral power, hitherto reserved for about 250,000 wealthy bourgeois and nobles, was now in the hands of nine million adult males. While hectic elec-tioneering occurred all over France, in most areas there was little time for alter-native, republican leaders to challenge old élites controlling social and economic power. Almost all of the 851 deputies elected in an 84 per cent turnout claimed adherence to the republic, democracy, and social justice, but most of them were drawn from the 'loyal opposition' to the previous regime. Their propaganda emphasized the virtues of existing family and property structures and was often openly supported by the Church, its role facilitated by the elections being held on Easter Day. The government's decision on 16 March to add an emergency 45 per cent surtax to property taxes in order to fund the urban national work-shops also played into their hands as evidence of urban republican profligacy. Only in specific areas of the east and south and in some cities were republicans able to win. Perhaps 566 of the deputies were former monarchists of various nuances, and only 285 were genuine republicans, including 55 radicals.[8]

The presence of a hostile Assembly in Paris at a time of over 55 per cent unemployment was explosive. The Assembly chose an executive of republicans but ended the Luxembourg Commission and began to seek ways of closing the national workshops; by 15 May, over 113,000 workers and their dependents, by no means all the unemployed, were dependent on them. Draconian laws pro-hibiting street gatherings, consequent mass arrests, and the Assembly's provoca-tive hostility to social reform created a situation electric with anger and fear.

This was precipitated into insurrection by the Assembly's decision on 21 June to close the workshops. For four days an unprecedented civil war tore the city in two. While some workers in the National Guard fought for the government, the geography and social composition of the insurrection supports contemporary observations that this was a class war.[9] Both sides fought for the republic, but between 'family, property, religion' and 'the social and democratic republic' lay a bitter divide of class hostility, terror and desperation. The government lost about 800 troops in securing victory: at least 1,500 (and perhaps 3,000) insurgents were killed and up to 15,000 were arrested, of whom 4,500 were imprisoned or transported. Those overrepresented among the arrested were from industries characterized by large workplaces (the metal, building and leather trades represented 31.7 per cent of the arrests but only 10.1 per cent of the workforce), and included 257 mechanics and 80 railway workers. Those underrepresented were clothing and textile workers (probably only because the authorities were loath to arrest women, who dominated these occupations), those in the luxury goods sector, and students, in contrast to their role in February. The unemployed who were enrolled in the Mobile Guard and fought for the government were mostly young men, with no direct memories of 1830–4 (50 per cent were under 20, compared with the insurgents' average age of 34), and more likely to be shop assistants or from the luxury trades.

The ideology of the insurrection came directly from the workers' movement of the July Monarchy. While many insurgents sought to avoid punishment by pleading innocence or ignorance, others, such as the engineering worker Louis-Auguste Raccari, insisted his aim had been 'the organization of work through association ... to ensure that the worker receive[d] the product of his labour'. Similarly, the state prosecutor at Amiens, north of Paris, heard of local workers saying, 'it is not a question of the Republic, it is a question of combat between masters and workers and we must go and fight for the workers'.[10]

The Parisian insurgents were opposed not only by the army, the Mobile Guard and sections of the National Guard, but also by waves of up to 100,000 volunteers from 53 departments, chiefly royalist landowners and urban bourgeois. There was minimal support for the workers in the provinces (there were rebellions or minor protests in Marseille, Lyon and 20 other cities and towns), and after the civil war large areas of northern and western France were swept by a rural panic about fleeing Parisian *partageux* (socialists), recalling some of the characteristics of the Great Fear of 1789. Cavaignac's publicised telegraph of 26 June to generals and prefects – 'Insurrection completely put down. All rebels have laid down arms or are running away across the countryside' – struck a note of terror in rural areas already tense because of economic and political uncertainty. On the morning of 4 July an elderly woman was disconcerted by two strangers near Vire (Calvados). She reported what she had seen and the news spread like fire through the Norman countryside. By the time the panic reached Caen, there were alleged to be 3,000 'brigands' near Vire, looting, burning and killing. Similar panic spread through the region east of Paris, and even the distant south-west.[11]

In the aftermath of the civil war, the Assembly extended the executive powers of the republican general Eugène Cavaignac which had been voted to him on 24 June, restricted the freedom of association, tightened laws on the press, and maintained a state of siege in Paris for four months. In other cities, too, the June civil war encouraged the government to increase surveillance and a reliable military presence, as in Marseille, where previously conservative dock-workers had been won over to the 'social Republic' by the summer. Between June and December, Cavaignac and his ministers were caught between a republican minority in the Assembly which was increasingly critical of continuing repression and a parliamentary majority of provincial landowners, officials, and businessmen, whose support for Cavaignac stemmed mainly from the efficiency with which he had suppressed the June insurrection. While Cavaignac, with reason, has always been associated with the horrors of June, there is no doubt that he and his ministers were committed to a measure of social reform. Most notable were the financial encouragement of producers' cooperatives which had been central to workers' demands since the 1830s, maximum-hours legislation, and cheap credit for peasants. The last of these was defeated by the Assembly, and a bill to abrogate the law of 8 May 1816 and to reintroduce the right to divorce was similarly doomed in the political atmosphere after June.[12] Cavaignac's greatest triumph was the Constitution of the Republic, promulgated on 12 November. Given the nature of the Assembly, the Constitution was remarkably democratic, liberal, and, for the first time since 1793, the State was to recognize certain social obligations. However, an amendment to insert 'the right to work' was rejected by 596 votes to 187. The president was to be directly elected by the nation, not by the Assembly: given Louis Napoleon's increasing popularity since June, culminating in by-election victories in six departments on 17 September, there were growing fears that a presidency could be a stepping-stone to a new imperial regime.

The repression of the insurrection had crushed the popular movement in Paris, but it was primarily after June that political activity in the countryside began to accelerate. This was fuelled by the reintroduction on 21 June of the indirect taxes on wines and spirits and, especially in the south, anger at the attempts to collect the new 45 per cent surtax. Moreover, the grievances endemic in most rural areas had not been met by the revolution. These problems – indebtedness, the collapse of rural industry, exploitative rents, all aggravated by low prices for produce – were to be at the heart of rural politics for the next four years. Radical republicans, shattered by the electoral disasters of April, responded with a rural-oriented programme and a new organization, *Solidarité républicaine*, formed in November. Its supporters came to be known commonly as *'démoc-socs'* or *'rouges'*.

It was in this situation – with a dominant but politically divided élite in the Assembly, resentment and dashed hopes in the cities, unresolved grievances in the countryside – that the presidential elections of 10 December were held. Most newspapers supported Cavaignac, though a number of influential figures and papers pushed Louis Napoleon forward, apparently as a compromise candidate of divided royalists hostile to the republic. Both candidates sought to appeal to the material interests of virtually every group in French society. Only Ledru-Rollin and Raspail formulated unambiguous, radical programmes, and both had pledged to abolish the presidency. Louis Napoleon won a staggering 74.2 per cent; Cavaignac gathered only 19.5 per cent and Ledru-Rollin, second in eight departments, 5 per cent. Louis Napoleon's lowest votes, from 24 to 54 per cent, were in coastal and frontier departments with sharper memories of the privations of 1799–1815. Like his contemporaries, Karl Marx was stunned by the magnitude of Louis Napoleon's victory and dubbed it 'the insurrection of the peasants'. Not only had people – including urban workers – voted massively for Louis Napoleon in most regions, but they had done so against the urgings of most notables and journalists.[13]

The reasons for the vote were varied, even contradictory: it was not just the glory of a name. Popular opinion often identified Louis Napoleon with radical social change. At Badonviller (Vosges), his victory was celebrated with bonfires and shouts of 'Long live Napoleon! Down with the rich! String up the aristocrats! Long live the guillotine!' However, if the electorate's perceptions of the triumphant candidate were varied, the president soon made his position clear. Late in December, he chose his first ministry, most of whom were drawn from those conservative notables who had supported his candidacy: there was not a republican among them. It soon became apparent that the enemy was no longer socialism, but the Republic itself. Republican prefects and officials were dismissed, and the offices of *Solidarité républicaine* closed down: at the time of its closure, it had offices in 62 departments, 353 branches and an estimated membership of 30,000. In this situation, major republican dailies such as *La République*, which by January 1849 was selling over 56,000 copies, became all the more important as centres of opposition to the president and his supporters.

The immediate focus of political hopes and fears was the impending election on 13 May of a Legislative Assembly to replace the National Assembly, felt to be redundant now that it had completed its task of drafting a constitution. If there was widespread acceptance of the political bankruptcy of Cavaignac's style of 'moderate' republicanism, what was the alternative? The radical social and political consequences of a resurgent left, or an authoritarian regime prepared to take the hard measures necessary to re-establish economic certainty? Never before had French people been confronted with such a stark electoral choice, one made the more urgent by continuing economic stagnation *(mévente)*.

While the right was divided over the most desirable political regime to replace a mistrusted republic (A second Empire? The legitimist pretender Chambord?), it was agreed on the enemy – socialism in all its guises – and conducted an energetic campaign. The 'party of Order', as it was known, distributed some 550,000 brochures before the elections. In Wallon's *Les Partageux*, 'père François' assured his peasant 'children':

> A 'red' is not a man, he's a red, he doesn't reason, he no longer thinks. He no longer has a sense of truth or justice, nor that of the beautiful and good … he's a fallen and degenerate being. His face bears the marks of this downfall. A haggard, brutish, expressionless look; leaden, shifty eyes that never look you in the face and dart about like a pig's.

The concerns of the party of Order illuminate the particular meanings rural notables gave to their world: the identification of 'civilization' with established religion, patriarchal authority in the family, and the sanctity of private property. It was a view of the world profoundly mistrustful of urban congestion, cafés and idleness, of landless and seasonal labourers, and of intellectually or economically independent alternative sources of information in the countryside, such as teachers and café-keepers. Such men threatened a natural order, 'human nature' itself.

The official programme of the left or *'démoc-socs'*, announced by the radical deputies of the new 'Mountain' in April, was wide-ranging and specific. It undertook to turn property from a privilege into a right through cheap credit and a progressive income tax. Education was to be free and military service made compulsory but briefer. Indirect taxes were to be abolished and the State would acquire railways, mines, canals and insurance companies. The right of association was to be added to other liberties. Just as the nature of urban social-ism at mid-century centred on the application of the concept of 'association' (the rights of trade unions, the need for solidarity of class rather than trade, and cooperative forms of production), so the left saw rural socialism as a radical redistribution of taxation, greater access to land and education, and the exten-sion of solidarity through mutual-aid societies to protect the sick, the unem-ployed and political prisoners.

It was in such an atmosphere, of political polarization and continuing socio-economic tension in many regions, that France went to the polls on 13 May. Such was the volatility of politics in early 1849 that only 300 deputies from the National Assembly were re-elected. Candidates of the party of Order won about 53 per cent of the votes nationwide, *démoc-socs* 35 per cent and the marooned 'moderates' 12 per cent. In terms of seats in the new Assembly, the three groups would have about 450, 220 and 80 seats respectively. There were three great areas of success for the party of Order: in the north-east and Normandy, Brittany, and the west. In these areas it won 266 of the 276 seats; 109 of those elected were nobles and 77 per cent were landowners, senior public officials, merchants and manufacturers.[14]

Even though the Legislative Assembly was to be dominated by men of Order, to contemporaries as to historians the most striking outcome of the vote was the surge in support for the left. Despite the crushing of the June insurrection, the deluge of anti-socialist rhetoric, and the massive victory for Louis Napoleon in December, the *démoc-socs* had increased their vote dramatically. Across huge areas of France – the centre, the south-east and parts of the south-west and Massif Central – a 'red' countryside had emerged. In areas such as the Limousin, the results also threw into relief the ambiguity of Louis Napoleon's victory in December, for here the *démoc-socs* did best precisely in those areas where the president's votes had been highest.

In much of urban France, there was a close correlation between voting results and class divisions; in rural France, too, economic misery was endemic and class status keenly felt, but many embattled rural producers voted for the same men of Order as did local notables. Memories, particularly of the Revolution, were a powerful factor in electoral choice. The political geography of mid-century France is best explained through a combination of the economic and social structures of a community or region and the historically conditioned percep-tions its people had of the world in which they lived. This interplay of social structure and history conditioned responses to the ongoing economic crisis and the whittling-away of recently-acquired political freedoms.[15]

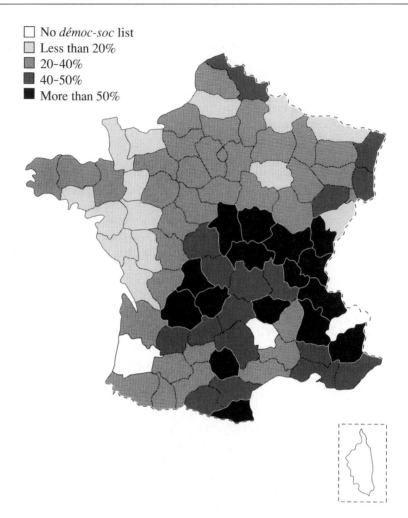

☐ No *démoc-soc* list
▨ Less than 20%
▨ 20–40%
▧ 40–50%
■ More than 50%

Map 9.1 Votes for *démoc-socs*, 13 May 1849
Source: Adapted from Maurice Agulhon, *The Republican Experiment*, *1848–1852*, trans. J. Lloyd (Cambridge, 1983), p. 145.

The rural heartlands of the left were characterized by multifaceted economic activity and links with towns in the production of foodstuffs (such as wine, olive oil, fruit and vegetables), artisanal manufactures (tools, wine barrels, clothing) and raw materials (silk, skins, cork). Such products required a range of urban-rural contact and work processes, united producers with urban consumers in opposition to taxes on essentials *(droits réunis)*, and facilitated popular contestation of the power of local élites. In contrast, regions which produced cattle and grain for urban markets tended to vote for the party of Order. They did not have the same range of contacts with urban populations and were united in their mistrust of towns personified by unscrupulous merchants. In many subsistence areas, too, the programme of the left seemed of little relevance, and notables and priests were able to use their control of information to paint the *démoc-socs* as enemies of the Church, the family and honest toil. Acquiescence of the economically vulnerable in the continued pre-eminence of local élites was reinforced in areas where there was an historic mistrust of republicanism dating back to the religious battles of the French Revolution, nourished by the vigorous campaigns of a renascent church after 1800. In much of the west vivid popular memories endured of religious civil war in the 1790s; similarly, the left did well in areas where the church reform of the Revolution had been accepted, and in pockets of Protestant strength.

In such a context, the propagandizing by journalists, teachers, café-keepers and other republican activists had limited determinative effect, despite the stress historians have placed on their energy. Political choice was much more a function of those economic and historical factors which predisposed voters to respond positively or negatively to party programmes. Other variables which historians have highlighted facilitated rather than determined political choice, and often had contrary effects. The Midi, with its large, clustered, socially complex villages and small towns is often seen as fertile ground for radicalism, yet such communities also nurtured strong popular royalism. Nor was the daily use of a language other than French necessarily an impediment to radicalism: the left may have remained anticlerical, Jacobin and threatening to most Bretons, Basques and Flemish, but many Alsatians, Occitans, Provençals and Catalans eagerly adapted its programme to their own language and culture. As an Occitan, a Protestant, and a rural labourer, it is not surprising that the young Jean Fontane from the village of Anduze (Gard) should have been a *démoc-soc*, though, significantly, he himself imputed it to history: 'If a majority of us were republicans, it was in memory of our beautiful Revolution of 1793, of which our fathers had inculcated the principles which still survive in our hearts. Above all, we were children of the Revolution.'[16]

Contemporary conservatives made no such fine distinctions about regional variations. Convinced as they were of the credulity, avarice and ignorance of the rural masses, they could see no reason why the red tide should not flood north from the Mediterranean and wash away the rights of the propertied and fathers of families, and the religious obedience which bolstered them. One such notable was Marquis Thomas Bugeaud, who had been appointed Governor of Algeria in 1840 by Guizot but then forced to resign in 1847 by repeated allegations of massive loss of life during his punitive raids *(razzias)*. In the aftermath of the civil war of June 1848, Bugeaud had written from his estate in the Dordogne to another former Orléanist deputy, saying:

> the social republic is a gross and dangerous absurdity ... the Republic is transport-
> ing a few wretches; she is leaving the lynxes in the stable; they will not wait long
> to try to devour more sheep ... Goodbye, dear colleague, enjoy the countryside as
> much as you can with the nightmare which is no doubt weighing on your spirit as
> heavily as on mine.

Now, a year later, Bugeaud's rural retreat had also become a nightmare; indeed, he had been defeated in his own canton of Excideuil. Bugeaud had gathered enough votes elsewhere in the Dordogne to be elected to the Assembly, and in the punitive atmosphere following the elections he was elected to one of its committees. Before he could carry out a *razzia* against the left, however, he was carried off by cholera.

The cholera epidemic, which took 19,000 lives in Paris, had other political effects, for it was one of the reasons why Parisian workers did not respond to the calls of the *démoc-soc* deputies for an insurrection against the Government on 13 June. Convinced that, by ordering the army to invade Italy, crush the Roman Republic and reinstate the Pope, Louis Napoleon had violated the constitution, 148 deputies called for open 'resistance'. Workers were not only decimated by cholera and the effects of the repression a year earlier; they also saw little reason to welcome the appeals of republican politicians who had sided with Cavaignac in June 1848. Elsewhere, there were major demonstrations in a score of provincial cities and towns, and armed gatherings in rural areas of the Allier, Saône-et-Loire and Pyrénées-Orientales. This resistance was abruptly crushed: in Lyon, 25 were killed, up to 800 arrested and the city was placed under military rule for three years.[17]

The failure of this rising forced many *démoc-soc* deputies into exile or prison and gave the government the chance to further tighten restrictions on associational activity and the press. Radical activity continued in Paris, but henceforth was tightly constrained by political controls. Some of this activity linked feminism with republican socialism, and was initiated by Pauline Roland and Jeanne Deroin, editors of *L'Opinion des femmes*. After its closure in July 1849, they founded the Fraternal Association of Democratic Socialists of Both Sexes for the Liberation of Women. Their most important work was in the area of workers' cooperatives; in October 1849 a plan for a Union of Workers Associations became a reality when 104 associations accepted their programme and appointed Roland a director. This programme was a remarkably comprehensive plan for a self-regulating society of cooperative production and distribution, leisure and social welfare, which foresaw equality of work between the sexes and the abolition of cash exchanges. On 29 May 1850, 80 police raided Roland's office and she, Deroin and seven other women and 38 men were arrested, and imprisoned until mid-1851.[18]

While the government became increasingly confident that urban opposition could be quietened by repressive laws, police surveillance and an evident economic recovery, the elections of 1849 had dramatically refocused attention. For the next three years, rural France was to be the site of a protracted and angry struggle for the preservation or reshaping of social structures. This struggle occurred within the context of the new agenda announced by Louis Napoleon on the morrow of the rising of 13 June: 'it is time that the good take heart and that the evil tremble'. One of his tactics was the purge of elected local government officials: by February 1851, at least 610 mayors and deputy-mayors and 278 municipal councils had been dismissed in 43 departments.[19]

The response of rural supporters of the left was to take their politics deeper into existing structures of sociability to sidestep restrictions on political clubs: places of leisure, such as cafés and men's societies *(chambrées)*, workplaces and mutual-aid societies became closely identified with particular political opinions. For example, the priest of Vrigny (Loiret) complained that 'the daily gatherings of our woodcutters in their huts are in reality political clubs which are still open'.

In La Garde-Freinet (Var), associational life was particularly remarkable: even before 1848, there had been eight mutual-aid societies and five *chambrées* and these now became, in Maurice Agulhon's words, 'the real cell tissue of the democratic movement'. By 1850, not only had a male workers' association organized a cooperative to control all aspects of the cork-making industry, but women workers had established their own mutual-aid society, and there is evidence of the articulation of a feminist ideology.[20]

This associational activity was fostered by the continued economic slump which showed no signs of abating in many rural areas. In contrast, in most urban areas cheaper foodstuffs were making life easier, together with increasing levels of employment. The Bonapartist regime was also increasingly careful to isolate army garrisons from city populations by rotating companies and maintaining tight surveillance of radical activists. Provincial towns remained key sources for the production of pamphlets and newspapers; however, state attorneys and police waged a constant campaign against the radical press, using tighter press laws to harass and close these mouthpieces. By the spring of 1850, the administration's resolve to remove the apparatus of the *démoc-soc* movement, indeed of republicanism itself, had encompassed not only the press, political clubs and people in public office but was starting to include the public spaces of daily life: cafés, mutual-aid associations, *chambrées* and other occupational or neighbourhood societies. In such a situation, political culture – the substance, forms and locus of political behaviour – became more deeply engrained into popular cultures, both to avoid the tentacles of a repressive state and as a symptom of the urgency and hope felt at the village level.

Rich though the Second Republic was in forms of political action easily recognizable across more than a century – electoral participation, campaign meetings, demonstrations – most political behaviour occurred within highly-charged symbolic intrusions into the collective rituals of community, family and religious life. This had two significant consequences. First, because the locus of political statements became public life in general, as well as the male institutions of clubs, elections and *chambrées*, women became more involved in political contestation. Secondly, the implanting of officially mistrusted, even outlawed, political commitment into rural cultures in certain regions made it a hardier plant that the government was to have extreme difficulty in eradicating. This intertwining of rural radicalism with popular culture occurred, whether deliberately or subconsciously, through the use made of cultural and religious rituals to convey political meaning. In this, the use of symbols – clothing, colours, objects, pseudonyms – was the operative link.

The protracted celebrations of Carnival, with their elaborate parodies and inversions of daily life – 'the world turned upside down' – were particularly suitable for political statements. At Vidauban (Var), the mayor, a royalist or 'white' *(blanc)*, forbade all public gatherings on Ash Wednesday (13 February) 1850. The local state prosecutor reported back to Paris that:

> Contrary to the prohibition made by the communal authority, a farandole, composed in the main of members of a *chambrée* known for its demogagic opinions, went along the main street of this locality. An individual was carrying a rod at the

end of which was a lantern representing a head. Behind came a dummy dressed in white. When the procession arrived at one of the public squares of the village, a sort of tribunal was set up; a man carrying an axe came forward and decapitated the dummy, whose head was then flung into the midst of the crowd who shared it up, uttering the most odious menaces.

In the court case, it was claimed that there had been a bottle of red wine attached to the dummy to simulate blood when broken by the axe blow, and that the dummy was called *'Blanc'*. That is, the dummy was used to symbolise the mayor. There had been shouts of *'Blanc*, you prevented us from dancing the farandole!' The traditional practice in Vidauban was for the Carnival dummy to be burnt, and the fact that this time it had been decapitated signified that *rouges* were evoking the guillotine. The lantern at the end of the rod suggested, at least to the royalists of the community, a head on the end of a pikestaff, again an image fraught with revolutionary implications. The royalist mayor was being tried in a popular court and punished without delay, in the same way that the Carnival dummy was tried and punished every Ash Wednesday.[21]

Political songs became – as in the 1790s – a popular form of celebrating the promise of the future and threatening the demise of the wealthy. Claude Durand, a wealthy peasant from the Deux-Sèvres, struck a popular chord with his 'Song of the Wine-growers', written early in 1850:

> Good villagers, vote for the Mountain:
> They are the gods of poor winegrowers,
> Because with them, good country folk,
> The drink tax will be swept away …
> Free schools there'll also be,
> And money at most at two per cent.

In the same year, in the western and southern foothills of the Alps, peasants side-stepped restrictions on French republican songs by adopting as their own the thyme plant and praising it in Provençal. The potency and hardiness of the plant was used to symbolize the parallel qualities of peasant radicalism in a song which began: 'We will plant some thyme, it will take root, the Mountain will burst into flower.'[22] The 'Song of the Peasants' by the Lyonnais Pierre Dupont also became a favourite of *démoc-socs* because of the yearning and promise of its opening verse:

> It's in two years, scarcely two years,
> That the Gallic cock will crow;
> Incline your ear towards the plain,
> Can you hear what it will say?
> It's saying to the children of the earth
> Who are crushed by their burden:
> Here is the end of misery,
> Eaters of black bread, drinkers of water.

Durand's song was written for the by-election of 10 March to fill the 21 seats in 16 departments left vacant by the exile or imprisonment of those involved in the rising of June 1849. The success of the left in these elections, and others in April, convinced the dominant party of Order in the Assembly to extend the requisite length of residence for voting eligibility from six months to three years. The electoral law of 31 May 1850 was a major turning point in the history of the Second Republic. It had a dramatic impact on the electorate, at one blow reducing it by 30 per cent. While the impact of the law was heaviest in large cities (in Paris the electorate fell from 225,192 to 80,894), it was also marked in specific rural areas characterized by an extensive landless labour force or rural migration. The fervent optimism of the left – and the fears of conservatives – had been focused on the twin elections looming in the spring of 1852: for a new assembly (27 April) and a president (9 May) other than Louis Napoleon, ineligible under the provisions of the constitution. The electoral law of 31 May 1850 was a body blow to a *démoc-soc* movement which had assumed that universal suffrage would inevitably triumph despite restrictions on civil liberties. It also threw the movement into tactical disarray. For how should the left respond? By continuing to organize in the hope that victory was still possible, or by an armed defence of the constitution?

In the summer of 1850 a three-way struggle was being waged for the hearts and minds of French people, between Bonapartists, royalists and *démoc-socs*. On provincial tours Louis Napoleon emphasized that he was a democrat opposed to the Assembly's slashing of the electorate, while appealing for popular support for revision of the constitution to enable him to stand for president again in 1852. Linked to the president by common hostility to the left, legitimists and Orléanists instead campaigned for a royalist coalition to ensure that a king rather than an emperor would rise from the ashes of the Republic. They were thwarted by the legitimist pretender Chambord's repudiation of such a coalition, and by the cleavage between legitimist leadership and rank and file, who had a vision of a populist, paternalistic, authoritarian monarch guided by democratic plebiscites. In Mediterranean France, these populist royalists contested the *démoc-soc* movement in every area of public life and with similar tactics: at La Grand' Combe (Gard), people prided themselves on being 'as white as alabaster' or 'as red as blood'. To statues of Marianne the goddess of the Republic, portraits of Ledru-Rollin, Louis Blanc and Barbès, red flags, red carnations, tricolour cockades and women parading as goddesses of liberty in carnival celebrations, 'whites' responded with statues of Henri V, portraits of Louis XVI or leaders such as de Lourdoueix or de Genoude, white flags, fleur-de-lis, white and green cockades, and young girls dressed in white. Where 'reds' and 'whites' diverged was in the legitimists' commitment to hereditary monarchy and fervent defence of Catholicism.[23]

Similarly, the 'calm patience' counselled by most of the bourgeois leadership of the left was increasingly contested at the local level in republican 'secret societies'. Precisely because these societies were clandestine, the full extent of their existence was invisible to the authorities, and remains so for historians. The most successful attempt to 'uncover' them has suggested that membership totalled 50,000–100,000 in 700 communes. For small-town and village militants, power was to be won in 1852 by insurrectionary democracy: the rural population, legally enfranchised or not, was to vote weapons in hand and impose the triumph of a peasants' and artisans' republic. This was articulated in the 'Song of the Peasants' by the Limoges journalist Alfred Durin:

> In eighteen fifty-two,
> Bring the whole parish,
> Vote bearing arms, two by two,
> Like when you go to a wedding.
> To make all these sluggards flee
> Who make us suffer misery,
> Name as representatives
> Only workers and peasants.[24]

To men of Order, the spring of 1852 loomed as a time when French rural civilization itself – patrimony, the union of spiritual and temporal authority, even the structures of the family – would be put to the torch. In the words of one notable: 'Who knows what will happen to us next year? From one end of France to the other, people are awaiting 1852 in the way that at the approach of the eleventh century people awaited the year 1000 which was to bring the end of the world.'[25] In his best-selling *Le Spectre rouge de 1852*, Auguste Romieu called for 'a total dictator' to make 'blood and tears' flow 'by famine and by bullets'. (Romieu was the author of another best-seller, a manual on domestic propriety: see Chapter 12.)

The crisis was resolved by Louis Napoleon's military *coup d'état* on 2 December 1851. The outcome of extensive clandestine preparations, his actions resulted from the Assembly's refusal to revise the constitution and from pressure by conservatives terrified by 'the red spectre of 1852'. Most people either acquiesced in, or welcomed, the seizure of power by the president as the resolution of a long-term social and political crisis seen to be the root cause of economic uncertainty. However, despite Louis Napoleon's populist bid for support by restoring universal manhood suffrage, in specific areas of France the response to the coup was furious and often violent. Resistance in Paris was small-scale (although 400 people were summarily killed by troops) and there were only peaceful demonstrations in many provincial towns. The most striking characteristic of the resistance to the coup was that it was overwhelmingly rural, because larger towns and cities had been politically quietened by a combination of gradual economic recovery and a closer presence of the army and bureaucracy.[26]

Resistance occurred in 56 departments, although in 26 of these it consisted only of unarmed demonstrations and there were only relatively small-scale armed mobilizations in 17 other departments. Armed resistance centred on four major areas: the centre, the south-west, the Mediterranean littoral and the south-east. According to the judicious estimates in Ted Margadant's exhaustive analysis, about 100,000 people from 900 communes were involved in the resistance: 70,000 of these, from 775 communes, actually took up arms. In the week following 4 December, insurgents established revolutionary administrations in over 100 communes and seized control of an entire department (Basses-Alpes). This resistance typically took the form of armed bands seizing control of their communities (where that was necessary), sending messengers to neighbouring

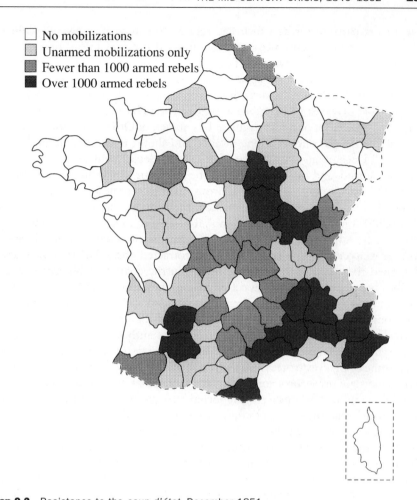

□ No mobilizations
▨ Unarmed mobilizations only
▦ Fewer than 1000 armed rebels
■ Over 1000 armed rebels

Map 9.2 Resistance to the *coup d'état*, December 1851

Source: Adapted from Ted W. Margadant, *French Peasants in Revolt: The Insurrection of 1851* (Princeton, NJ, 1979), p. 22.

communes, and converging on subprefectures and prefectures. Intrinsic to the incidence and style of such activity was the bedrock of republican secret societies which had survived the crackdown of 1850–1 in anticipation of the imposition of insurrectionary democracy in the spring of 1852. In the south-east, resistance was charged with symbolic representations of popular sovereignty, with armed bands led by politically active women dressed as goddesses of the Republic. In few areas were the insurgents able to hold out against the armed forces for more than several days: the failure of urban *démoc-socs* to demobilize army garrisons or to seize departmental capitals allowed army units and the gendarmerie free rein to crush pockets of armed resistance and to imprison about 30,000 insurgents and their sympathizers; in the process up to 100 rebels were killed and about 200 wounded.

Resistance to an illegal seizure of power had created an extraordinary paradox. Whereas a major reason for Louis Napoleon's coup had been the need to act against the party of Order which had refused to extend his powers legally, the extent of provincial resistance pushed frightened notables into supporting him and also served as a *post facto* justification of his actions. The coup was now presented as a pre-emptive strike against the socialist horrors which would have been unleashed in 1852. For the next three months much of rural France was in the grip of what may best be described as state terror, as bureaucrats, magistrates, the army and police, supported by vengeful local men of Order, used the suspension of civil liberties to conduct a long-awaited and almost unchecked purge.[27]

On 20 December – with a state of siege in 31 departments, opposition newspapers silenced, and insurgents still on the run – the electorate was enjoined to go to the polls to give *post facto* approval to the coup in a national plebiscite. While about 1.5 million voters abstained, the coup was approved by a crushing 7,439,000 'yes' votes to 641,000 'no'. There were huge areas of rural France where rich and poor alike acquiesced in a seizure of power beyond their control, or welcomed it as a resolution of a protracted crisis. The state prosecutor described the reaction in rural communes in the district of Nogent-sur-Seine (Aube) as a popular festival: 'In certain communes, music and drums celebrated the counting of the votes; in others they paraded the bust of the Emperor. In one commune where a single 'no' was found in the urn the municipal authority had quickly to destroy the ballot, to save its author from the crowd which was trying to recognize the writing.' In many areas of the countryside, however, some of the 'yes' votes were the result of resignation, intimidation and fear. The same state prosecutor for the Aube, where resistance to the coup had anyway been minimal and peaceful, reported that the 'stupor and fear' of *démocsocs* was such that they were careful to vote 'yes' with their ballot papers open.[28]

Historians have been divided between seeing the resistance as archaic in its violence, the last great peasant rising *(jacquerie)*, or as in defence of the republican constitution, a momentous new commitment to republican democracy.[29] These views have underplayed the insurgents' desire to impose by insurrection a rural form of socialism and a people's republic, foreseen for 1852. In theory, the issue of why these people rebelled should be susceptible to informed analysis: the police, gendarmes and the army began to arrest huge numbers of *démocsocs* early in December and local magistrates began interrogating them. However, for the thousands of peasants, labourers and artisans who found themselves locked away in cold and often improvised prisons in an atmosphere of unchecked administrative and military repression, these interrogations were the occasion for a defensive, *sauve qui peut* response. Put simply, rural insurgents told the judges what they wanted to hear, in order to save their skins.

There were two elements of 'the myth of the peasant' to which rank-and-file insurgents commonly resorted. The first of these was to reinforce the authorities' profound certainty that poor and uneducated rural people were also ignorant, fundamentally stupid, and prone to following the crowd like sheep. Again and again, insurgents 'confessed', 'we marched like a flock of sheep' or 'I acted like everyone else', or simply feigned stupidity and ignorance. Secondly, rural people were aware that the urban bourgeois who were questioning them 'knew' that peasants were too stupid to work things out for themselves and that the real targets of the repression were the middle-class republican activists who were alleged to have subverted them. Accordingly, insurgents 'blamed' their behaviour on the activism of urban radicals and their newspapers.

Occasionally insurgents did admit that their objective was to resist the illegal overthrow of the republican constitution: this was particularly so in the case of well-known leaders of secret societies who knew it would be pointless to feign ignorance. Moreover, admitting a desire to defend the constitution was far less dangerous than admitting something else: a commitment to socialism. The actions of the insurgents when seizing power suggest that the insurrection was as much to impose social revolution as to defend the constitution. For it was not the Cavaignac constitution of 1848 that insurgents fought to defend but, through it, the imposition by insurrectionary democracy of the people's republic, popularly referred to as *la Belle* or *la Rouge*. For example, the 'Democratic Republican Committee' in the village of Beaumont (Basses-Alpes) abolished usury, placed a moratorium on debts, made education free, abolished indirect taxes and moved to share out communal lands. This is what contemporary men of Order knew and feared and explains why their support for repression was visceral and punitive.[30]

The composition of the 27,000 *démoc-socs* tried early in 1852 was already skewed towards activists and those regarded as most 'dangerous'. Rural people and, in particular, women (only 169 were tried) were under-represented. This pattern was accentuated in the punishments meted out, ranging from deportation to prison in Cayenne or to Algeria to being placed under surveillance or freed. Again and again, 'mixed commissions' singled out men of property, education and presumed influence who, as traitors to their own class, merited the most severe sentences. Faced with a massive problem of incarceration if France was genuinely to be cleansed of 'subversive' elements, the authorities fell back on the certainties born of a hierarchical social ideology and decided that the great mass of peasants and labourers had been 'perverted' by their betters. For their part, these rural *démoc-socs* told the judges what they wanted to hear, that they were simple folk who did not really know why they were protesting. Most of them were released or placed under surveillance in their own communities. The authorities could wrap up a more manageable problem of social control; peasants and labourers could go back to their fields. In the end, 'the myth of the peasant' suited both sides and, as a sign of good faith and of the awe the State inspired in them, rural folk voted 'yes' in the president's plebiscite.

For his part, the president's agenda was far from complete: he had far more to achieve than the right to stand for re-election free of a socialist challenge for the fruits of universal suffrage. His new constitution was closely based on that of the year VIII, with initiative concentrated in the executive and the real power of restored universal suffrage reduced to approving the plebiscites of the president if he felt it necessary to appeal to the nation over the heads of querulous politicians. In other ways, the new regime was a regression to the July Monarchy: there were direct references in the constitution to 'Prince Louis Napoleon Bonaparte'; an upper house of up to 150 was reintroduced, composed of marshals, admirals, cardinals (but no Protestants) and Louis Napoleon's personal appointees; and the lower house was reduced in power and size (to 261) and elected from individual candidates rather than party lists.

The prince-president made it plain that the new France would not be one dominated by the rural values of old royalist élites or the 'political classes' of the Republic:

> When a man has made his fortune by his labour, in industry or in agriculture, has improved the lot of his workers and has made an honourable use of his wealth, he is to be preferred to what is nowadays known as a man of politics; for such a man will bring a sense of what is practical to the passing of laws and will support the government in its task of pacification and re-edification.

Similarly, in a speech to the Bordeaux Chamber of Commerce in October 1852, Louis Napoleon outlined a clear agenda for an economic expansion based on state initiatives through the private sector and on a prosperous, orderly workforce. He also seemed ready to assume an imperial mantle with his repeated references to 'Empire'. This mantle was seized in a plebiscite on re-establishment of the Empire held in December 1852 when the firmer grip of the administration, allied with the president's real popularity in many areas, resulted in a huge vote in favour. The Second Republic was dead and with it the hopes of radical social change held by huge numbers of men and women.[31]

Questions of change and continuity are at the heart of any consideration of the significance of a period of conflict and upheaval such as the Second Republic. Certainly these years witnessed the flowering of a powerful workers' movement in Paris, Lyon and some other cities and a commitment to a *démoc-soc* future in large areas of rural France; however, both these challenges to structures of wealth and power were crushed by military force. Moreover, in sharp contrast to the expectations of urban radicals before 1848, the experience of elections by universal manhood suffrage had revealed that most rural people saw provincial notables of various conservative political tendencies as those best able to represent their interests. In the end then, was the sole legacy of the Second Republic the realization by a restored ruling élite that carefully controlled universal suffrage could be used to sustain and legitimize the existing order? The years after 1846 thus might appear to be a time of economic and political crisis to be sure, but above all as a period of political instability rather than real social change.

The mid-century crisis must be seen rather as the dramatic expression of wide-ranging changes occurring in the first half of the century, as a period rich in economic, social and political developments, the watershed of nineteenth-century France. The Second Republic marked the end of royalist regimes in France and the definitive victory of universal manhood suffrage. To follow Maurice Agulhon's apt term, the Second Republic was also a time of a mass 'apprenticeship' in republicanism and, in particular regions, democratic socialism. The Second Republic was also important for the development of an ideological divide between republicanism and Bonapartism. The ambiguity of Bonaparte's Janus-like image – soldier of the Revolution as well as its liquidator – which had been compounded under the July Monarchy by the careful cultivation of the Napoleonic legend and Louis Napoleon's 'socialist' rhetoric, could not survive the illegal seizure of power in 1851 and sweeping repression before and after. For republicans, Louis Napoleon was always to be 'the man of 2 December' and an elective presidency was to be an object of mistrust for over a century.

In many regions, particularly the west and north, tenants, peasants and labourers in general shared with the powerful in their communities a belief that radicalism was the cause of economic uncertainty. By coincidence, the coup occurred several months after a slightly smaller harvest than in preceding years had led to higher prices for wheat and other grains in many areas; the coup itself accentuated these price rises by the confidence it generated among employers and investors. In 1852, the hopes of those who had seen in Order and stability a way out of the rural crisis seemed to be being met. In this emergence of a popular rural base for the party of Order, as well as for Bonapartism, the Second Republic was to have a profound and durable impact on the shape of mass politics in France.

As a period of unprecedented political activity in the French countryside, the Second Republic also marks a transformation in the forms of collective action utilized by rural people as they sought to protect or extend their well-being. The great wave of subsistence protests in 1846–7, and the explosion of forest invasions, occupations and destruction of private property, and anti-tax rebellions in 1848 were to be the last outbreak – at least on a large scale – of forms of protest described by Rudé as 'pre-industrial' and by Tilly as 'reactive' responses to state centralization and capitalist economic structures. From 1848 they were juxtaposed with a remarkable proliferation of demonstrations, mass electoral rallies and associational political activity epitomized in secret societies and resistance to the coup in 1851: collective action best described as 'modern' or 'proactive'.[32]

The political conflicts of the Second Republic and the way in which they were resolved also had social consequences which went well beyond the confines of institutionalized politics. As the following chapters will discuss, the mid-century crisis was to have important repercussions on the nature of social relations of production in urban workplaces, in demographic patterns and social structures in the countryside, on education, and on the ideologies through which people made sense of the troubled world in which they lived. Less dramatic and violent than the French Revolution, the mid-century crisis was nonetheless a watershed in the social history of nineteenth-century France.

10
The Transformation of Urban France, 1852–1880

Until the 1840s Argenteuil had been a rural village nine kilometres from Paris, combining agriculture with local crafts such as the production of plaster of Paris; other people lived from inn-keeping, ferrying goods and people across the Seine, and looking after towpath horses. By the 1870s the tentacular arms of Paris had incorporated it as an industrial outer suburb, with factories, docks and a skyline dominated by a huge railway bridge. Just fifteen minutes from the new Gare Saint-Lazare, Argenteuil's broad reach of the Seine was also an ideal place for a leisurely Sunday, with boating clubs and rentable villas. Among those it attracted was Claude Monet, who lived there from 1872 to 1878, and whose paintings were a personal response to the extraordinary spread of urban, industrial life.[1]

The precipitate growth of Paris – from 1,053,000 in 1851 to 2,269,000 three decades later, an increase of 115 per cent – is the most familiar example of a national phenomenon. All over France, these years were a time of unprecedented growth and importance of large towns: the total urban population (communes of at least 2,000 people) grew by 44 per cent to 13.1 million in these 30 years, but that of the largest cities virtually doubled. See Table 10.1.

Table 10.1   Population of major cities in France, 1851 and 1881

	Population in '000s		% increase
	1851	1881	
Paris	1,053	2,269	115
Lyon	234	376	61
Marseille	198	360	82
Bordeaux	131	221	69
Rouen	100	106	6
Nantes	96	124	29
Toulouse	94	140	49
Lille	75	178	137
Saint-Etienne	56	123	120
Reims	45	93	107
Roubaix	34	91	168
Le Havre	28	105	275

The acceleration of urbanization also has to be seen in the context of a slow increase in the total French population, from 35.8 million in 1851 to 37.7 million three decades later, an increase of just 5 per cent.[2]

The chief source of urban expansion was migration from the countryside. This reflected long-standing economic and personal ties, as rural people chose to go to places where they had family links; however, they often had to look for work in new occupations. In Nîmes, where the silk industry declined rapidly after 1850, migrants from the Cévennes and Mediterranean lowlands now sought work as clerks and seamstresses or on the new railways. Often migration occurred in stages, as impoverished or ambitious rural people from the Massif Central, for example, spent a few years in the textile workshops of a small *bourg* like Marlhes (Loire) before going on to the factories of Saint-Etienne. Similarly, Norbert Truquin, born in the village of Rosières (Somme) in 1833, was sent by his widowed father to be an apprentice wool-carder in Amiens; in 1847 he left there for Paris and, after having been involved in the June Days, migrated to Algeria in 1851. After working as a servant to army officers, he returned in 1855 to a series of jobs on the mainland, only finally settling as a silk-worker in Lyon.[3]

Paris was the strongest magnet for migrants: in 1866, 61 per cent of its inhabitants had been born in the provinces and another 6 per cent outside France. While there were large industries on the city fringes – the Cail and Gouin engineering works at Vaugirard and Batignolles employed up to 2,000 workers – most migrants were drawn to Paris in the hope of work in commerce and small manufacturing. Just as Paris had its particular mix of artisanal and large-scale industry and commerce, so the national urban economy was characterized by distinctive regional capitalisms, as in Rouen-Le Havre, the north-east, Lyon-Marseille and Alsace. By the 1860s, these regional distinctions were starting to diminish as banking and communications networks expanded: during the Empire deposits in private savings banks trebled (to 632 million francs), as did the volume of freight, almost entirely owing to the spread of railways. Among the new banks were the Crédit Mobilier, founded in 1852 by Emile and Isaac Pereire, Sephardic Jews from Bordeaux profoundly influenced by Parisian Saint-Simonianism in the 1820s, the Crédit Lyonnais (1863) and the Société Générale (1864). The railway construction booms of 1853–6 and 1860–4 generated rapid expansion in coal production and metallurgy, with the employers' *Comité des forges* (1864) protecting the interests of the dominant iron and steel producers. In general terms, the decades after 1850 were boom years for French businessmen, even if the enthusiasm of railway constructors, financiers and luxury export manufacturers for the free-trade treaties of the 1860s was not universally shared.[4]

The expansion of the French economy was fuelled by a more committed policy of colonial expansion, in partnership with Catholic mission activity. In 1856, a treaty was signed with Bangkok to protect missionaries, but also to secure trading rights, for the clergy acted as couriers, translators and negotiators for merchants. After the invasion of Saigon in 1859, Cambodia was colonized to act as a buffer against British influence in Siam. In New Caledonia, Kanak attacks on French missionaries gave Paris the pretext formally to annex the island in 1853, unleashing a stream of colonists who steadily seized native lands despite governors' hesitant attempts to regulate expropriation. The regime was

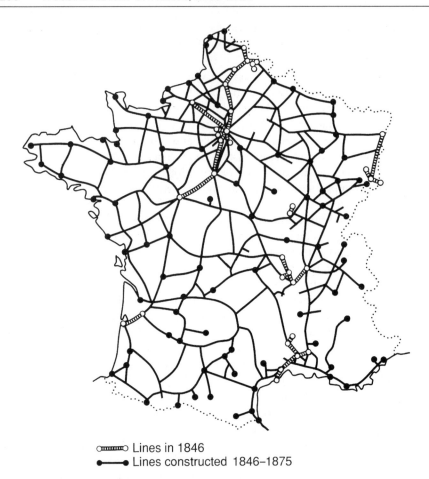

o▭▭▭o Lines in 1846
●———● Lines constructed 1846–1875

Map 10.1 Railway construction in France, 1846–1875

Source: Adapted from Roger Price, *An Economic History of Modern France*, 1730–1914 (London, 1975), p. 24.

also pressured to colonize by mercantile élites. Following the withering of the Caribbean trade, Bordeaux's merchants turned to West Africa for nuts and gums; by 1869, trade with Senegal alone totalled 37 million francs. Marseille's merchants played a similar role in North Africa, while by 1877 42 per cent of Lyon's silk was being imported from East Asia. This closer attention paid to Africa and south-east Asia was also due to the ignominious failure of the attempt to create a satellite state in Mexico (1861–7).[5]

With its corollary, the beginnings of the rural exodus, urbanization was to transform the daily lives of French people. It is this which explains why historians – like contemporaries – have tended to highlight the most dramatic examples. But there was and is no archetypal French city. Not only was French urban growth gradual within a northern European context, but the spectacular surge in cities like Paris, Roubaix and Saint-Etienne was atypical; indeed, the experience of ancient southern textile centres such as Lodève, Bédarieux and Castres was rather one of decline.[6] Urban France in 1881, as in 1801, was still predominantly a slowly changing world of country towns and regional centres. Half of the urban population lived in towns of fewer than 10,000 people, essentially *agro-villes* with artisanal small industry, which serviced the rural hinterland as administrative, marketing and cultural centres.

The rapid growth and economic activity of cities like Châtellerault (Vienne), Toulon (Var) and Saint-Etienne (Loire) could throw into sharp relief the relative stagnation of their prefectoral towns (Poitiers, Draguignan and Montbrison); though a modest growth was sustained by the arrival of the railway in Poitiers and an important garrison in Draguignan, Montbrison lost its prefecture status in 1856. Even in departments where little industrial growth occurred (Vendée, Landes, Haute-Saône), their capitals expanded as a result of the increasing presence and intrusiveness of the State. Centralization of decision-making and power in Paris paralleled the capital's own expansion, but in prefectures and subprefectures all over France the functionaries of a hierarchically ordered bureaucracy were increasingly present, administering, collecting information, judging and policing. By 1870, there were 700,000 public employees at a state, departmental and municipal level.

Urban growth was most spectacular in 'new' towns or in established cities whose growth was accelerated by industry and transport. Essentially one-company or one-industry towns mushroomed near accessible resources. Elsewhere, urban sprawl incorporated outlying agricultural villages as dormitory suburbs or centres of industry – such as Argenteuil and Belleville in Paris – or generated new suburbs on the outskirts of large cities, such as La Guillotière in Lyon or the Faubourg de Paris in Limoges. The unplanned and teeming popular suburbs on the outskirts of cities were further advantaged – at least for entrepreneurs – by being near new railway stations and cheap factory land, for which older urban centres were too expensive and crowded. One general characteristic of rapidly expanding, established cities was that the socially mixed neighborhoods still common in the Paris of Balzac and Stendhal were increasingly polarized into a geographical, class segregation: in Paris, for example, the essential social division between wealthy west and poorer east and north. Such a transformation also implied a new social use of space, as the well-to-do frequented the Bois de Boulogne rather than the Bois de Vincennes or the Parc des Buttes-Chaumont. This segregation was never sharp in the inner city because shopkeepers and luxury-goods craftworkers continued to live and work near their clients; but it was rigid in the new suburbs. The 'dangerous classes' in the heart of old Paris, Lyon and Marseille in the 1830s were now more likely to surround the old cities in new, shabbily constructed industrial suburbs.

A combination of feelings of social obligation and fear of employee militancy often resulted in employers using paternalistic methods ranging from the provision of housing and insurance funds to almost monastic controls on workers. When successful, such concern encouraged workers to identify themselves as 'Schneider's man' at Le Creusot or 'Japy's man' in the watch-making factory at Beaucourt (Belfort). In Saint-Chamond (Loire), workers created their own distinctive culture but in general were politically quiescent because of their debilitating working conditions and the interventionist, legitimist clergy and employers who felt an obligation to protect their charges. At an extreme, the Bonnet silk factory at Jujurieure (Ain) employed nuns to supervise constantly the 400 young girls working to save dowries. However, few employers felt that industrial safety and working conditions were their responsibility. In the five years after 1863, the Nord railway company reported that about 18 per cent of its engine drivers and 29 per cent of its firemen had had industrial accidents; at about the same time, well over 3,000 cases of lead poisoning, mostly in the paint-making industry, were treated in hospitals within five years.[7]

The working-class experience of these decades of rapid urbanization and industrialization varied according to the nature of the city or town and the worker's particular occupation. In Carmaux (Tarn), attempts by management to define precise tasks and hours of work had little effect on peasant-miners who insisted on combining mine-work with seasonal rural labour. Small, artisanal trades in cities such as Saint-Etienne or Toulouse co-existed with large-scale industries, but were increasingly incorporated into their forms of production. The durability of small trades has led some social historians to question Marx's paradigm of the development of a large, industrial working class, arguing instead that the workforce remained a mixture of skilled artisans and disorganized, unskilled factory proletarians. Such an argument misses important changes in the average size of workplaces, in the division of labour within them and, most importantly, that wage-earners of whatever type of skill identified themselves primarily as workers.[8]

Just as importantly, the working-class experience varied according to gender. Women's paid work in towns was constrained by more limited occupational choices and more keenly felt – or imposed – family responsibilities. Of urban women in the paid workforce in 1866, 28 per cent were in domestic service, 21 per cent in garment-making and 20 per cent in textiles; however, while this suggests a remarkable continuity in the nature of women's work, these bald statistics hide important changes.

The decades after 1850 saw an acceleration of the 'feminization' of domestic service: where equal numbers of men and women had been in domestic employ under the *ancien regime*, a century later over 70 per cent of the one million servants were women. In Paris, 92 per cent of servants were poor migrants, often with a priest's reference for an employment bureau which would place them in homes where they often worked from 6 am to 10 pm daily. The lot of the servant was dependent on the individual employer, whose prerogative it was to grant them a day off, to decide what pay, food and lodging to give them, what privacy to allow them, and whether to treat them with courtesy or as menial prey to the whims of the *maîtresse de maison* or the sexual pressures of the *maître*. The hierarchical world of large bourgeois households and the virtual constancy of demands on servants created a domestic world of suspicion and tension, in which bourgeoises bemoaned the erosion of the imaginary harmony of earlier employer-servant dealings. But servants, despite being increasingly demanding and critical, and higher-paid, remained vulnerable; by 1880, one-third of the 6,800 known non-registered prostitutes and of mothers of abandoned children were former domestics, and behind these figures were harrowing individual stories of sexual exploitation by employers or the loneliness of young rural migrants whose search for affection had resulted in pregnancy and dismissal.[9]

Since so many prostitutes refused to be part of the regulated policing system, or worked sporadically, it is impossible to say with certainty how many women wholly or partly survived in this way. However, important changes were occurring in the nature of this work. Despite the rapid increase in the urban population, the number of registered prostitutes nationwide declined from 16,239 in 1851 to 15,047 in 1878; in Paris, the number of brothels fell from 240 in 1840 to 140 in 1880. Increasingly, these brothels catered to more specialized, expensive 'tastes'; some houses charged 100 francs, providing *tableaux vivants* of lesbian love-making, sado-masochism, and so on. Working-class prostitution usually involved independent women using streets or cafés to meet clients who were charged as little as 50 centimes. To Alain Corbin, such changes were the result of the profound 'sexual misery' of bourgeois men and of workers' hostility to regulation, which smacked of the Empire's policing role in the workplace.[10]

Industrial work for women was confined to a narrow range of poorly-paid, unhealthy tasks (73 per cent of women industrial workers were in textiles and clothing). Whether in factories or doing domestic piece-work, women were especially vulnerable proletarians. Industrial work was likely to be taken on only sporadically depending on the demands of parents and children and on their partner's work. By the 1870s mechanization in clothing and textiles was relocating work increasingly in factories. This female factory work was the preserve of girls and young women without children. In the northern textile-factory town of Roubaix, 81 per cent of single women over 15 years of age did paid work compared with 17 per cent of married women. Norbert Truquin described with horror the recruitment, with the help of priests, of 15-year-old country girls on four-year contracts to the Lyon silk industry: 'Working seventeen hours a day in unhealthy workshops, where there's never a ray of sunshine, half of the girls get chest illnesses before the end of their contract ... my boss swore that most of those who left the shops took the road, not to their homes, but to the cemetery.'[11]

The most important turning-point in the history of urban working women – the separation of home and work, with the consequent trend to domesticity among married women with children – was a gradual experience in France. The pre-industrial household economy dominant in urban and rural France until the mid-nineteenth century did not disappear as soon as the home ceased to be the centre of production as well as reproduction. Instead, most urban families adopted a strategy described by social historians as the 'proto-industrial' or 'family wage' economy in which household members all continued to contribute in various ways, by wages as well as unpaid labour, and in which mothers worked only part-time or sporadically outside the home. In industrializing towns such as Saint-Chamond, married women found it increasingly difficult to contribute to the family budget and instead used contraception and abortion to limit family size. This became more of an imperative as the State restricted facilities for abandoning unwanted children. Not that single mothers did not care for their children; as a 27-year-old textile-factory worker from Amiens, already caring for one child, explained in 1857: 'Why do I send this little child to the [foundling] hospital; because I am without any resources ... but I don't want him to be lost for good ... I beg you to have the kindness to keep him there, so I can see him again when I can, because I am not married.'[12]

Many single women continued to sustain a rural-based family economy by sending cash home, although, as temporary migration became permanent, there was a tendency for women to cut all economic ties with their families. Willingly or not, working-class families were experiencing a more rigid division of labour, at work and in the household. Men who went on strike in the 1860s to protest against threats to their employment from low-paid women workers found in the concept of the 'family wage' for men the ideal solution to the expense of private child-care arrangements and of wet-nursing. But, whatever the increased constraints which young children placed on mothers in urban nuclear families, women played a crucial role in the family and neighbourhood. If the mutual-aid society and café were male spaces, then communal laundries and streets were women's and it was here that solidarities of gender enabled women to contest high rents and prices, to find new economic strategies, or to seek support in domestic difficulties.[13]

Debate among historians centres on the consequences of such changes for women's status and self-esteem. To what extent did working-class women see paid work as in some sense liberating? In 1877, 1,946 Parisian girls about to leave primary school were asked about their intended jobs; while a skewed sample, because only a minority of girls completed primary education, the results were clear. Overwhelmingly, work expectations were a function of family background and pressure, and work was seen primarily as a way of supplementing the family budget. About 72 per cent expected to do manual work (especially in the clothing industry), 6 per cent sales or office work, 8 per cent planned to work in business and 12 per cent in the professions (above all, teaching). These hopes reflected family background, although about 10 per cent of the girls from working-class and artisan families hoped to be teachers and postal employees. However, it was much more likely that middle-class girls would cite the desire for personal independence as a reason for career choice.[14]

In 1867 Victor Duruy revised the 1850 education laws to require girls' schools in communes of more than 500 people, but most girls continued to be taught by poorly-trained teachers or in church schools which sought to inculcate piety rather than facility with ideas. Parental attitudes to their daughters' education – wanting religious rectitude and supervision as well as instruction – was also reflected in their choice of school, and by 1867 55.2 per cent of girls attended church schools compared with one-fifth of boys. While it was claimed that 90 per cent of school-age children were attending classes in the 1860s, education officials admitted that perhaps one-third did not do so. National conscription levies under the Empire indicated that four-fifths of conscripts were 'literate', but at least one-fifth of these were regarded by school authorities as unable to read a book or write a letter. Urban literacy rates varied according to the rate of urban growth and access to schools. Few urban children (only about one in 50) went on to secondary school, but among petit-bourgeois families, the *lycée* or Catholic *collège* was often seen as a means of social advancement: in 1868, 28 per cent of secondary pupils were from such backgrounds.[15]

Historians also disagree about whether there was some sort of 'sexual revolution' among working-class people. Some have pointed to increasing illegitimacy rates as a gauge of sexual activity and 'freedom' (which, no doubt, would surprise the young women in question). The premise of this argument is flawed, since the percentage of children born outside wedlock in Paris actually declined, from 36 in 1815 to 24.5 in 1880. How widely accepted among male workers was Proudhon's 1846 imperative that women were either 'housewives or harlots'? One problem in answering this question is that urban working people have very rarely had their views recorded. Another is that Proudhon's dichotomy between work inside and outside the home – let alone that between paid work and sexual probity – would have been meaningless to working-class women, who moved from one to the other depending on family need and job opportunity. Certainly, however, working-class families were less constrained by bonds of polite respectability and property contracts than the well-to-do: young workers commonly lived together in '*unions libres*', marrying only when children arrived (indeed, *bourgeoise* meant 'wife' in workers' slang). Others such as the Parisians François P__ and Marie J__, piece-workers in the garments trade, refused to marry when they had children because, in their startled interviewer's words, religion was seen as 'a hypocritical means employed to limit the freedom of the workers and to dominate them by superstition'. Despite the couple's heavy work (Marie worked 12 hours every day as well as doing the household chores) and François's love of the tavern, the interviewer had to admit that Marie was 'well treated' by him and 'the children receive[d] care and affection'. Free unions also protected women from courts which continued to fine and imprison adulterous wives.[16]

The combined effects of gradual transformations in the nature of the workplace and the household economy were expressed in the strategies single women and couples adopted to control fertility. The labour of children was less important to working-class families than it had been in rural households or among artisans, especially with the passing of laws restricting child labour. Similarly, the nurturing of a new infant threatened the very survival of single urban women without an extended family. Consequently, despite the fulminations of priests and male doctors about the spiritual and physical evils of preventing conception and birth, couples increasingly practised contraception. Families with five or more children had been 14.2 per cent of the total in 1815–19 but were only 6.7 per cent in 1870–4, and this decline was more marked in urban areas. Given the unreliability of available methods of contraception, to women alone fell the dangers, physical and legal, of aborting pregnancies.

Emphasis on the importance of dramatic, large-scale changes to the urban economy have until recently diverted attention from the far more gradual transformations in the world of the master artisans and shopkeepers. Central figures in urban culture, economic life and politics to 1850, these petits bourgeois have too readily been seen as a shrinking, resentful social residue who turned to right-wing populism as their world changed. On the contrary, in the decades to 1880 – and beyond – they remained a large, diverse social group, whose double-edged economic role as employers and workers was mirrored in their neighbourhood importance. The desire for independence and property which fuelled recruitment into the ranks of the self-employed was always, and increasingly, prone to deception. Master artisans became both more threatened by large-scale competition and more dependent on merchant capitalists from whom they bought raw materials and to whom they sold their products. Shopkeepers, too, were similarly vulnerable and dependent. For them, the equivalent of mechanized textile factories or mass production of clothes, furniture and food was the large retail store. It was among petit-bourgeois women that the tension between work and gender role was felt most acutely. The world of their well-to-do clients was one in which the ideology of separate spheres, child-rearing and domesticity was being articulated and practised more clearly than ever before; on the other hand, women's work was indispensable to the survival of the household economy of the small family business, especially in times of economic difficulty or when a woman was the owner.[17]

The discovery in the 1850s of the link between disposal of sewage, the quality of drinking water, and diseases such as cholera impelled governments and bureaucrats nervous of another link – between insalubrity, 'dangerous classes' and 'criminal classes' – to reshape the medieval ground-plan of swelling cities. It was in the capital that the most dramatic urban reconstruction was undertaken, under the personal supervision of the Emperor and the prefect of the Seine for 1853–70, Baron Georges Haussmann. He had been Louis Napoleon's prefect for the Var, one of the left-wing centres of the Second Republic, and one of the major motivations for slicing wide boulevards through the city was to facilitate troop movements from nearby garrisons and to avoid the military nightmare of manoeuvring through twisting, narrow streets. There were other motives linking public order and glory, illustrating what Walter Benjamin discerned as 'the tendency – common in the nineteenth century – to ennoble technological necessities through artistic ends'. The new Paris was to be a worthy imperial capital, with monuments such as the Opéra, Henri Labrouste's superb reading room of the Bibliothèque Nationale, new markets (Les Halles) and the Gare du Nord symbolizing in a practical way élite culture, commerce and modernity. The financing of new housing, with private entrepreneurs assuming ownership after the State had paid expropriation costs, like the July Monarchy's railways, would also benefit the private sector.[18]

By 1870, 560 of the capital's 805 kilometres of streets had sewers (though their discharge was a hazard to communities further down the Seine). The number of buildings with running water increased from 6,000 to 40,500, but 20,000 remained without, in the poorer eastern, northern and south-eastern *arrondissements*, and many others only had water to ground-floor level. A particular *mentalité* was revealed in the spatial organization of the new city, for the 'language' of the formal gardens, linear street grids, and the façades of apartment buildings betrayed a distinctively bourgeois discourse of order. The emperor also felt that the employment created would undercut revolutionary dissatisfaction; necessarily, however, such quiescence was dependent on continued redevelopment, and mounting criticism of Haussmann – by 1867 the city owed 2.5 billion francs – slowed the rebuilding and antagonized building workers, along with all those who had watched their housing torn down. As Zola was to capture in *L'Assommoir*, the rebuilding of Paris displaced poverty without eradicating it. Haussmann himself estimated that 70 per cent of Parisians lived in poverty; his rebuilding programme had pushed many of them into the northern and eastern suburbs recently incorporated into the city limits and unserviced by improvements to the urban infrastructure.

Where the July Monarchy had coupled an unprecedented level of imprisonment with a concern for 'moral rehabilitation', the Second Empire's prison *mentalité* was characterized more by 'professionalization', in line with the increasingly intrusive and ordered nature of the State. One lasting reform from the Second Republic was the 1850 law on the rehabilitation of juveniles through farm-schools. By 1853, 50 per cent of 6–16-year-old delinquents were sent there to receive religious, occupational and educational training. Private institutions were encouraged to open such schools, as did the monks of La Trappe (Orne), who transformed a monastery previously used to discipline priests guilty of sexual acts or alcoholism into a farm-school for 250 boys which became famous for its religious zeal. By 1873, there were 36 such agricultural 'colonies' across the country, with 6,790 prisoners. However, repression remained the overwhelming concern of the prison system. In 1852 the government closed the notorious *bagnes* in Toulon, Brest and elsewhere and hard-labour inmates were instead sent to Cayenne in French Guiana and, after 1857, to New Caledonia. Not only would such deportation 'cleanse' France of hardened criminals, but they would in turn be cheap labour for expanding colonial settlements.[19]

The Second Empire has long had an image of a tawdry, meretricious regime of *nouveaux riches*, captured in Zola's *La Curée* or Alexandre Dumas's depiction of a *'demi-monde'* of wealthy courtesans.[20] But this was an image drawn from the most famous and fleeting examples of speculators and profiteers, not of the mass of the bourgeoisie, for whom the Empire was a time of considerable wealth and sober confidence, reflected in the substance of their consumption – elaborate, formal meals, heavy domestic ornamentation, large, gilt-framed paintings. A gauge of the bourgeoisie's values were the explosions of outrage and indignation at Flaubert's *Madame Bovary*, Zola's *Thérèse Raquin*, Baudelaire's *Les Fleurs du mal* and Manet's *Olympia*.

As in the years after the Revolution of 1830, the ruling élite fretted about its fragile social and political legitimacy at the same time as it was confidently seeking to remake the world in its own image. The most common theme in proliferating marriage manuals and novels about contemporary society was the idealized bourgeois family and the threats posed to it by adultery, lust and lack of discipline. The most troubling passion was sexual, especially homosexual. In 1857 two influential medical treatises analysed the pathology of 'pederasty': the director of the Saint-Yon asylum, Bénédict Morel's *Traité des dégénérescences* and Ambroise-Auguste Tardieu's *Etude médico-légale sur les attentats aux moeurs*. In the anxious debates about the physical and psychological character of those who committed 'crimes against morality' the word 'homosexual' was used for the first time (1869). Despite the bourgeoisie's fears of its internal decay, those arrested for public homosexuality were in fact a cross-section of the male population and it has been argued that a distinctive 'gay subculture' emerged in the same decade.[21]

The elaboration and idealization of the doctrine of 'separate spheres' in bourgeois families was only one part of a bourgeois ideology articulated in the world of political stability and economic expansion after 1851. This ideology of separate spheres was the corollary of a double standard of morality, insistent upon the imperatives of marriage as the transition from virginity to fidelity for women, while tolerating the sexual urges of boys and men. Certainly there is little evidence for the view of some social historians that the 'modernization' of the family among the bourgeoisie raised the status of women and children in more affectionate and equal partnerships. As before and after, personal relationships within families varied enormously; if anything, the continued importance in bourgeois families of financial advantage through family alliances may have reduced the possibility of happiness. A law allowing legal separation, but not divorce, was used by women in particular (in at least 85 per cent of cases), largely on grounds of domestic violence in middle-class marriages; but, even at their peak of 4,000 per year around 1880, such breakdowns represented only 13 marriages per thousand. Are such statistics a measure of conjugal misery, or rather of the relative happiness of most marriages?

Certainly, the decline of wet-nursing led to a significant change in the nature and intimacy of mother-child relations, for bourgeois children were now more likely to be reared within the family. In the 1780s, the hiring of wet nurses, particularly in the countryside, had been the usual practice among all social groups in Paris; by 1869, 59 per cent of babies were nursed by their mothers, and almost all among the bourgeoisie. Their conviction of the moral correctness of their actions, and alarming statistics about the death-rate among children who were bottle-nursed, convinced the Chamber to pass the Roussel law in 1874 curtailing wet-nursing, in the process creating enormous difficulties for working mothers. Bourgeoises were also likely to have fewer children: between 1853 and 1885 the number of resident children per 100 families in Bordeaux fell from 80 to 53 among the bourgeoisie but rose from 91 to 105 among the working classes. A sharper hostility towards the rape of children explains why the number of court cases increased from 136 in 1830 to 679 in 1880. But children remained vulnerable, even if over 3,300 men were arrested following tighter laws against 'paedophilia' in 1863. Over 1,000 children (two-fifths of them girls) were sentenced each year under the Napoleonic Code to short terms of 'personal correction' in prison: 75 per cent were from Paris, mostly from wealthy families.[22]

The expansive capitalism of the Second Empire accentuated the polarity of gender roles in bourgeois families and the discourse which sought to harmonize difference. Difference could imply exclusive physical spaces: in 1856, the Paris Prefect of Police ordered women to be kept well away from the square outside the Stock Exchange as well as excluded from the galleries.[23] Within the domestic world, however, women created their own female culture of close friendships, charitable works and religiosity. In Lille, bourgeoises established crèches, workshops and recreational groups for the 'deserving' poor; in contrast to the indifference of many of their men, they found in Catholicism a justification and solace for their lives. Certainly, their deepest emotional ties were with other women. In the 1860s diary of Caroline Brame, a Parisian bourgeoise in her late teens whose father was from Lille, a regular expression of grief concerned the marriage of her friends:

> They don't understand that Marie's marriage saddens me … I have to repress all that I feel; how many times have I had to hold back my tears! … Why, my God, don't I have more courage? … I will offer whatever sacrifices you ask of me and I will offer them with all my heart, but permit me to find my gaiety again.[24]

The Catholic Church's approbation of Louis Napoleon's coup of 1851 had reinforced anticlericalism among republicans, but for many other urban people the terrors of the Second Republic had served instead to cement their support for religious and moral order.[25] Despite the increased tension between the Empire and the Church after 1860 – because of the emperor's intervention in Italian politics and his closure of Louis Veuillot's ultramontanist *L'Univers* – these decades confirmed the trends of the early nineteenth century, in particular the 'feminization' of the Church. The extraordinary growth of female religious orders continued: by 1878 they had 135,000 members compared with half that number in 1850 – and compared with 30,000 men, although the number of Jesuits had also increased rapidly, to 3,245 in 1880. In Paris, numbers in religious orders grew by 50 per cent during the Second Empire, and 22 new churches were commenced or completed. While many bourgeois men applauded the regime's distancing itself from the Church and were disdainful of Pius IX's 'Syllabus of Errors' (1860), women of the middle classes remained committed to a church education for their children and flocked to Lourdes once the railway was connected in 1866.[26] Everywhere, the Church represented a pillar of certainty and moral order; in 1857, the Mayor of Rouen, when laying the foundation-stone for a new church to which the council had given 600,000 francs, expressed his delight: 'two edifices created for the same purpose, that of the moralization of man, rise almost side by side; not far from here the prison where infractions of the social order will be expiated is nearing completion, and here we see this church rise from the ground, a pious refuge open for preservation from misdeeds'.

In towns where there had been a strong *démoc-soc* movement under the Second Republic, the role of the Church was not forgiven by the working class. In eight parishes in the northern suburbs of Paris only 25 men in a population of 13,000 took Easter communion in the mid-1860s, compared with a figure of 15–16 per cent of the total population of Paris. However, anticlericalism and religious indifference was not a generalized aspect of working-class life. In Decazeville, 47 per cent of men took Easter mass in 1868; in the towns of Picardy, the energetic campaigns of Bishop Parisis had some success; and, where employers were Protestants, as in Nîmes, Mulhouse and Mazamet, churchgoing among Catholic workers was part of a class culture of opposition.

The decades from 1850 to 1880 were unprecedented in the nature and rate of change in larger urban workplaces, with an acceleration of transformations to artisanal work which had occurred under the July Monarchy and with the development of large-scale mechanization. However, any explanation of the link between these changes and worker militancy has to go beyond the resentment of deskilling to investigate the impact of these changes on families and culture in working-class communities. The nature of working-class politics was rich and varied, drawing as it did on regional traditions, collective memories and the particular nature of the town and industry. A crucial factor was the extent to which workers retained control over entry to their occupation, linking family and community. Hence in Bezons, Lodève and some northern textile towns, a continuity of the household economy, now of an industrial type, mitigated the sense of uncertainty and outrage intrinsic to the surge of socialist thinking in Marseille, Toulouse and Paris.[27]

In the first decade of the Second Empire, officials worked to create an image and reality of popular docility and devotion to the emperor, of economic stability and prosperity. They also did this by assiduous surveillance of workers, but historians have too readily accepted the image of workers' passivity in these years, which distorts the experience of the urban workforce. One of the few open rebellions in the early Second Empire was in an area of the west 'quiet' under the Second Republic and hence more lightly policed: in 1854 the impoverished slate-workers of Trélazé, near Angers, organised a protest using a secret society dubbed the 'Marianne' (like those of the Yonne and south-east three years earlier). The example of Lille illustrates ways in which working-class communities more commonly sustained a culture of opposition – as well as highlighting the conditions in which that culture managed to survive.[28] Using inventories of possessions left at death in the years 1856–8 and 1873–5, Félix-Paul Codaccioni found a dramatic increase in the wealth of this expanding city. While the population increased 40 per cent in these years, the average value of wills grew by 135 per cent; at the same time, however, the number of adults leaving wills declined from 32 to 25 per cent. There were startling and sharpening contrasts between social classes. In 1856–8 the ruling class (industrialists, large property-owners, the professions) accounted for 8.1 per cent of deaths and 89.9 per cent of wealth; the middle classes (artisans, white-collar workers, public servants) 32.4 per cent of deaths and 9.5 per cent of wealth; and the working class 59.4 per cent of deaths and 0.4 per cent of wealth. By 1873–5, the working class accounted for 67.6 per cent of deaths but only 0.2 per cent of wealth; the number of workers leaving anything at all had fallen from 18.2 to 5.6 per cent. An industrialist left as much as 10,000 workers in 1856–8 and as much as 20,000 workers 17 years later.

These stark statistics cannot convey the notorious misery in which Lillois textile-workers lived and worked. A damp, cold city, Lille under the Empire was without a drainage system or open spaces, a place where most families lived in single rooms or even in 'caves', lined with stones and open to the streets (chillingly described in Victor Hugo's *Les Châtiments*). Civic and business élites blamed this poverty on workers themselves, citing the existence of one alcohol outlet for every 70 people and a rate of extra-marital births of 20.7 per cent. However, Lillois refused to see themselves as demoralized proletarians seeking refuge in cheap alcohol; instead the cabaret was at the heart of a remarkably rich working-class culture. In the words of one textile worker who wrote to a local paper in 1868:

> Those who reproach the worker for the cabaret might themselves be reproached for theatres, concerts and balls…I read [*Le Courrier populaire*] to the whole house, and tomorrow I will give it to the *chambrée* at Fives…this doesn't mean that you can't also have fun and honestly learn at the cabaret; we'll always go to the cabaret because we like a good glass of cold beer and some games and jokes.

This culture drew on ancient artisanal traditions in Lille and on the regional cultures of the north-east from where most workers had migrated, but was also informed by a sharp class-awareness expressed in places of work and leisure.

In a workplace milieu in which the hopeful cooperative experiments of 1848 had given way to an invigorated policing in the interests of employers, wage-earners could only contest unequal relations of power by semi-clandestine 'manoeuvring', designed to provoke and frustrate employers and to relieve the tedium of mechanical routines. In Lille, *batteurs* (labourers who opened up compressed cotton in imported bales) set out to engage in petty sabotage, dubbing a workmate 'the little soldier' for refusing to go along with them; outside the workplace, too, labourers frequented puppet theatres – dubbed, again, the 'imperial theatre' – characterized by audience interjection, impromptu political allusion and ironic mockery of bourgeois society. But the wily dissimulation of the *batteurs* of Lille also points to the tight constraints on open opposition in the 1850s, particularly where the authorities were on their guard. When the textile industry slumped with the news of an impending free-trade treaty with England, workplace manoeuvring quickly dissipated.

Despite – or because of – the regime's mistrust of democratic politics, the Second Empire is of central importance in the history of the labour movement, as it is in the shaping of urban France. These decades were the great age of mutual-aid societies, although their existence dates back to the *ancien régime*. Between 1852 and 1869, their numbers increased from 2,438 to nearly 6,000, with about 800,000 members from a broad cross-section of workers. Similarly, the cooperative experiments of the Second Republic resurfaced more strongly in the more liberal years of the late 1860s, corresponding as they did to workers' deepest desires for independence, comradeship and control of the work process. In 1867 delegates from 120 Parisian trades formally approved of them as the surest means of eradicating capitalism. The Empire tried unsuccessfully to undermine their contestatory role by offering state subsidies, and to create quiescent workers' organisations by tolerating non-political 'unions' in 1868. By July 1870, perhaps 65,000 Parisians (13 per cent of the workforce) belonged to these 'unions', particularly in the hat-making, bronze-working and typographical trades.[29]

Whatever the power of the regime in terms of administrative controls and popular acceptance, it remained based on contradictions. The emperor could draw on deep reserves of support for an imperial regime, but this support was dependent on him being able to sustain economic well-being, being able to reconcile divergent groups (the Church, businessmen, peasants and workers) – and on his own longevity. He was reluctant to create a political party, seeing himself as the personification of *'la France profonde'* as well as the France of the future. The political dilemma of the Bonapartist regime lay in its attempts to translate the official rhetoric of the Empire into reality by liberalizing the means for people to express their support. Once open and covert means of social control began to be relaxed after 1860, political opposition simply moved to occupy the widening opportunities for dissent, a phenomenon common to authoritarian regimes ever since. Napoleon III was to find that liberal concessions encouraged greater demands for change rather than placating opponents. Following the elections of 1863, when official candidates were defeated in 18 of the 22 largest towns, the Emperor conceded the right to strike in an attempt to regain the loyalty of workers which he had hitherto taken for granted. But this attempt to woo the disaffected inevitably alienated employers from the regime, just as subsequent heavy-handed repression of strikers convinced workers that he remained *'le petit caporal'* of 1851.

The liberalization of laws on the press and associations in the 1860s also permitted the resurgence of feminism, for example, through the *Société de la revendication du droit des femmes* and its newspaper, activated by Léon Richer, Maria Desraimes, Louise Michel, André Léo, Paule Mink and others. Their attacks on double standards of bourgeois morality, their demands for greater educational and occupational opportunities for women, and for political and civil rights, including divorce, were supported by opposition politicians such as Ernest Legouvé, Jules Simon and Alfred Naquet. Julie Daubié, the first woman to obtain the *baccalauréat* (1861) and to graduate in Arts (1871), focused attention on working women in *La Femme pauvre au dix-neuvième siècle* (1870).[30]

In 1869, the freest elections for twenty years stunned the regime for, while the emperor could still be guaranteed a docile legislature, opposition candidates won some 42 per cent of the 7.8 million votes. The elections coincided with France's first major industrial economic crisis, in contrast to the harvest failures and food-rioting which animated the electoral campaigns of 1829–30 and 1846. In June 1869, 15,000 workers were on strike in Saint-Etienne, followed by other major actions over the next year at Aubin (Aveyron), Le Creusot and Mulhouse. By that time, however, the new freedoms of organization were facilitating other mass gatherings, as of 100,000 mourners at the funeral in Paris in January 1870 of the journalist Victor Noir, shot by the emperor's cousin. The use of troops to disperse demonstrators after Noir's funeral, as against strikers at Carmaux, Le Creusot, La Ricamarie, and Aubin in 1869–70, suggested that there was an iron fist in the velvet glove of the liberal Empire. The belated decision to remove the right to strike fuelled the anger of more than 5,000 workers' representatives meeting in Lyon in March 1870, and in the following months 30 workers' organizations affiliated to the International.[31]

Napoleon III's desire to override internal social and political divisions by an appeal to imperial glory found its pretext in Bismarck's challenge to French influence over the choice of the next Spanish monarch. Within a fortnight of the declaration of war (19 July), however, an entire French army had surrendered at Sedan and the emperor himself had been captured.[32]

Once the news reached France, opposition groups in Marseille and Lyon, and later Paris, rushed to proclaim the Republic. In the first weeks of September, a 'Revolutionary League of the South', grouping radical republicans from towns in 16 departments, issued a manifesto calling for reform as well as national defence: they demanded the abolition of church schools and separation of Church and State; liberty of the press; a purge of office-holders and confiscation of the property of traitors; and an emergency tax levy on the wealthy. From the outset of the Third Republic, however, a cleavage of class and ideology ruptured a unity among republicans which had formerly rested on opposition to the Empire. Gambetta's 'Belleville Manifesto' for the 1869 elections had fallen far short of Ledru-Rollin's programme 20 years earlier: calls for the nationalization of key industries, cheap credit and the right to work had given way to anticlericalism and vague references to 'the social problem'. The issue of what sort of republic – parliamentary democracy or socialism? – was ultimately to divide republicans.

The combination of the liberation of political life after September, the suffering during the Prussian siege until late January 1871, and anger at conservative national election results in February sustained a vibrant culture of Parisian popular politics. The Assembly's acceptance of crippling peace terms, including a huge indemnity and the cession of Alsace and parts of Lorraine to Prussia created fury in the capital; however, there was far more to this fury – and to Thiers's insistence on disarming Paris – than wounded national pride. When, on 18 March, soldiers were ordered to remove cannons remaining in Paris, popular resistance combined fierce patriotism with a yearning for political autonomy and radical social change. The hasty evacuation of Paris by the army created a power vacuum filled by the election of the Paris Commune a week later.

The drama of the Paris Commune has obscured the parallels with other cities and towns where a programme of workers' control and participatory democracy had a deep resonance; indeed, Marseille and Lyon had established popular 'communes' before Paris. In March, further short-lived communes were established in Le Creusot, Narbonne, Toulouse, Limoges, Saint-Etienne and a score of other towns. Significantly, these were all urban centres which had grown rapidly during the Second Empire and where the 1860s had seen a vigorous popular participation in resurgent left-wing politics, culminating in 1871 in demands for national defence, municipal autonomy and socialist reform.[33]

The significance of the Commune in the history of revolutionary socialism has also led historians to contest Marx's contemporary assertion that this was an unprecedented revolution for a new socialist society in the hands of the working class and its allies. Instead, many historians have seen it as the last episode of the French Revolution, highlighting the constant appeals back to the revolutionary tradition, the failure of the Commune to socialize property – or even to close the Stock Exchange – and the mixed, pre-industrial nature of the Parisian workforce.[34] It is not surprising that people acutely conscious of the history through which they, their parents and grandparents had lived should talk of the 'year 79' of equality or establish a Committee of Public Safety, but to limit the Commune of 1871 to the bounds of the Paris Commune of 1792–3 is to miss the sense in which it was proletarian, socialist and innovative. Huge numbers of Parisians remained in artisanal work but, compared with 1846, the average workplace now had almost eight workers compared with five, and most workers were in far larger enterprises, such as the men and women in the building trades where the ratio of employees to employers was 13 : 1. Over 42 per cent of those later arrested were labourers, wood-workers, stone-masons and metal-workers. They were, and considered themselves to be, skilled proletarians. Similarly, of the 81 members of the governing Council of the Commune, 35 were or had been manual workers and 40 had been involved in the labour movement, many as members of the International.

The socialism of the Commune was an expression of the culture and experience of such workers, drawn from the tradition of 'republican socialism' developed since 1830 and of a fundamentally different type from that later envisaged by Lenin. As Marx noted, the practice of cooperative production came from workers themselves, not from the Council of the Commune. Workers at the huge arms workshop established at the Louvre submitted their regulations to the Council, insisting that the workshop be run by a revocable, elected manager and a council of delegates from each workbench whose membership would rotate between workers each fortnight. As a stone-carver wrote to the Commission of Labour and Exchange, such cooperatives would result in the 'inevitable abolition of the class of employers and of the exploitation of man by man'. Where workers differed was in their contrary views about whether the State should establish or merely encourage such cooperatives.

Like the *sans-culottes* of 1793 and the insurgents of June 1848, the people of the Commune assumed the practice of direct democracy: in the words of the Club Communal, the people 'must never renounce their right to supervise the actions of their mandatories. People, govern yourselves directly.' However, in stark contrast to their ancestors, they claimed to be speaking only for Paris. The Commune envisaged a devolution of all power – except for national defence and planning – to all the communes of France, one reason why its bulletins were seized or rigorously censored by the government at Versailles. This important development in radical ideology was part of a critical re-evaluation of the place of the revolutionary tradition, climaxing in the debate on the establishing of a Committee of Public Safety and the burning of the guillotine in April. While the military crisis decided the Commune in favour of an emergency committee, Gustave Courbet spoke for an important minority: 'The terms *Public Safety, Montagnards, Girondins, Jacobins* cannot be applied to a republican socialist movement. What we represent is the period that has passed between '93 and '71, with our own genius corresponding to our own particular character.' Courbet was also responsible for the formation of an artists' federation, free of government regulation and patronage, to work for 'cultural regeneration, the building of a communal heritage of beauty, the future development of art and the Universal Republic'.

The men of the Commune never seriously contemplated enfranchising women, although they did recognize the equality of common-law marriages and equal pay for women teachers. The popular paper *Le Père Duchêne* admired the 'good citizeness who is educated, who knows what it's all about and doesn't let herself be led up the garden path by the fucking priests', but insisted that 'a true citizeness, in one word, is a good mother'. However, from women's experience under the Second Empire welled up an insistence on their right to control their workplaces to allow diversification of an individual's work 'to counter the harmful effects on body and mind of continually repeating the same manual operation'. Women members of the International also called for 'the abolition of all competition between men and women workers since their interests are absolutely identical'. Significantly, women also demanded cooperative crèches near workplaces to meet their needs of being able to work outside the home while children received care in a stimulating, secure environment: 'all sorts of toys should be available, such as carts, an organ, an aviary full of birds'.

Like all revolutionary moments the Paris Commune was, in Lenin's words, a 'festival of the oppressed', and the content of that festival drew on smouldering historical resentments which reached to the core of working-class experience since 1848. With the total collapse of the imperial state and the flight of the wealthiest one-third of the city's population, working people recaptured the streets and open spaces from which they had been expelled by high rents and rebuilding. One exhilarated participant was Jules Vallès, the son of cobblers he recalled as mean, brutal and ambitious, and whose youthful involvement in resistance to the coup of 1851 led his father to send him to an insane asylum. He described his feelings about the Commune: 'The moment hoped for and waited for since the first cruelty of my father, since the first slap from the usher, since the first day spent without bread, since the first night spent without lodging. Here is the revenge against school, against poverty and against December.' The heady blend of historical tradition and socialist future was symbolized in the destruction of the Vendôme Column, re-erected in 1864 to glorify Napoleon Bonaparte; those fortunate enough received an invitation to the destruction featuring the revolutionary symbol of a liberty cap on a pike, and watched as the red flag of the future was hoisted on the empty pedestal. Similarly, Louis Barron, who left the army to join the Commune, described a concert given by La Bordas, 'magnificent in her flowing robe draped with a scarlet sash … a goddess of Liberty from the popular *quartiers*', singing her best-known song in a 'formidable, brazen voice, with fierce passion and a fury that inflames the soul':

> They're the Rabble! *[la Canaille!]*
> Well – I'm one of them!

By May 1871 the Paris of the Commune was a world away from the Assembly at Versailles. It is debatable whether Marx's comments on the Communards' failure to march earlier on Versailles or inability to communicate with provincial supporters explain adequately the Commune's failure; but by May the Assembly had a conscript army from non-French speaking and anti-socialist provinces primed to eradicate finally 'the moral gangrene that [had] been consuming society for the past twenty years'. This army's actions were primarily the result of orders from their commanders MacMahon, Gallifet and Vinoy. In the 'bloody week' after 21 May, 130,000 soldiers ran riot through Paris, leaving 10,000–30,000 dead, including 1,200 women raped and bayoneted to death. There were another 1,050 women among the 43,000–47,000 arrested: textile workers, laundresses, teachers such as Louise Michel, and prostitutes, women united in their hatred of 'bosses, rich men and priests', together seen as the cause of low pay, sweatshop conditions, bourgeois morality and competition from work done in convents. On average, they were 40–5 years old, women whose youthful hopes had been crushed with the disappointments of 1848 and 1851. Of those arrested, 5,207 served prison sentences and 4,586 were deported to New Caledonia. After the Commune, Parisian prostitutes were particularly singled out by the government of 'moral Order': while up to 10,000 women had been imprisoned annually during the Empire for infractions of the regulatory code: from 1872 to 1877 the annual figures were about 15,000.

The establishment of the Third Republic in the decade of the 1870s began with the crushing of socialist, communalist insurrection in Paris and elsewhere and ended with the amnesty and return of most of the 4,500 Communards exiled to New Caledonia, the more readily because they had fought so valiantly against the first major Kanak rising for independence in 1878. The pivotal point in the tense political history of this decade was the election in February–March 1876 of a clear republican majority in the Chamber for the first time, although the royalist MacMahon continued as president until 1879. The electoral victory of 1876 prompted the government to lift the state of siege imposed on Paris in 1871 and to return Parliament to Paris from Versailles. In 1880, the first official Bastille-Day celebrations were held: the regime was secure, but the means by which the Republic was established and the nature of the regime itself bitterly polarized republicans at the time, and continues to divide historians.[35]

To counterbalance the democracy of the lower house, the constitution of the Third Republic established a president (with powers resembling those of a constitutional monarch across a seven-year term) and a senate with 75 life members elected by the Assembly and another 225 chosen by regional institutions and an electorate of one delegate per commune. The senate was inevitably dominated by local notables and acted as a brake on social reform throughout the life of the Republic. In July 1873, the Assembly approved the construction of the Sacré-Coeur Basilica on the top of Montmartre, in expiation of the crimes of the Communards in executing the generals Lecomte and Thomas on the spot.

To democratic republicans, the social and ideological caution of the 1870s was the only way to prevent royalists and nervous supporters of 'moral Order' from once again using universal suffrage and the army to overthrow the Republic and institute another authoritarian regime, as in 1851. That is, Grévy, Ferry, Gambetta and other republican leaders simply made a prudent assessment of social and political realities: the firm establishment of the Republic by 1880 was a testament to their judgment and to their sincere commitment to democracy. As Thiers put it famously in 1872, the Republic is the regime 'which divides us least' but 'the Republic will be conservative or nothing'. On the other hand, from a left-wing perspective, today closely identified with the work of Sanford Elwitt, the discourse of democratic republicanism, egalitarianism, anticlericalism and attacks on the 'financial aristocracy' was primarily a smokescreen to protect the social order from revolution. By appealing to a constituency of small property-owners – artisans, shopkeepers and small farmers – bourgeois politicians were able to legitimize existing class and property relations; by painting the industrial bourgeoisie and colonial expansion as patriotic, they were able to generate a unitary ideology of capitalist growth and secular advancement.

From this point of view, the Third Republic represented the most complete hegemony yet achieved by the bourgeoisie, hitherto caught between traditional élites and the anti-capitalism of the working classes.

These two arguments proceed from different premises. From the left, few would disagree that the Communards and their provincial allies did not have the strength to mount a successful challenge against social and political élites, nor that the price of a socialist republic would have been a military *coup d'état*, if necessary with German assistance. At the same time, there is compelling evidence of the particular nature of the Third Republic and its social consequences. It may be that, in the words of Gambetta's biographer, 'statesmanship resides largely in successful recognition that politics is the art of the possible', but Gambetta and his allies had a particular vision of what was 'possible' and desirable.

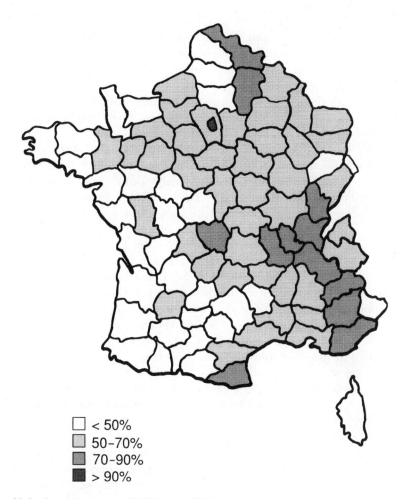

□ < 50%
□ 50–70%
▨ 70–90%
■ > 90%

Map 10.2 Republican votes, 20 February 1876

Source: Adapted from Georges Duby and Armand Wallon (eds), *Histoire de la France rurale*, vol. 3 (1976), p. 373.

In 1872 Gambetta proclaimed that 'there is no longer a social question', thereby reassuring industrialists in cities such as Reims and Saint-Etienne whose liberal politics had helped undermine the Second Empire. An 1874 law banned children under 12 years from any factory or manufacturing work and limited hours to 12 over this age, and women under 21 could not do night-shifts; however, this law was poorly enforced and, by 1880, working conditions were often as bad as in the 1840s. In the 1870s, the republican élite identified the 'social problem' as fundamentally one of lack of education: hence, while state social and medical expenditure remained constant in 1869–79, education expenditure doubled to 46 million francs.[36] This was a regime which understood equality to be access to opportunity through education and the acceptance of civic obligations: in 1872 the invidious practice of *remplacement* by which a wealthy conscript could 'purchase' a substitute was finally ended.

Doctors also found a more receptive audience after the twin disasters of 1870–1 for the introduction of paramilitary gymnastic organizations into schools as a way of preventing further national physical lethargy and moral decay. Dr Jean-Baptiste Barth, whose house had been burnt down during the Commune, organized a temperance society drawing explicit connections between the increased consumption of wines and spirits, criminality and socialism. In 1873, the deputy Roussel – who was to propose the law controlling wet-nursing the following year – successfully moved to make public drunkenness against the law; during the 1881 electoral campaign, Gambetta accused hostile workers in a crowd of being 'drunken slaves'. In the *Annales médico-psychologiques*, doctors wrote of the pathological causes of the Commune, among them alcoholism, and extended their analyses into 'women's nature' which had attracted them to the Commune as it did to violent crimes of passion.[37]

Symbolizing the confidence which business élites drew from the political economy of the Republic – and the ideology of women's ideal roles – were the booming new department stores, serviced by the Compagnie générale des omnibus, which carried 70 million passengers annually down the new boulevards of Paris. Some, such as the Bon Marché, Louvre and Printemps had developed out of earlier *magasins de nouveautés*; they were joined in 1870 by the Samaritaine, 'the cathedrals of modern commerce', as Zola dubbed them in his 1871 novel, *Au bonheur des dames*. The Bon Marché was the first to have a store designed expressly for the purpose (by Gustave Eiffel) and by 1877 its 1,788 employees were totalling sales of 73 million francs. Zola painted an incisive portrait of the contrast between the glamorous world of consumption and the conditions of the sales clerks. These clerks, mostly male, were a tightly-controlled, competitive and vulnerable workforce who sold on commission during a 12–13-hour day; their provident fund only matured on retirement, but 39 per cent of them were fired within five years.[38]

By 1880, a conservative republican regime with business and mass electoral support seemed secure. But the ideological and cultural hegemony of the political élite remained contested in working-class neighbourhoods: in June 1880, Gambetta's own Belleville constituency chose as its member of the Paris municipal council a Communard shoemaker still in exile in New Caledonia.

11
The Peak of Rural
Civilization, 1852–1880

At the same time that Claude Monet had gone north of Paris to Argenteuil to seek to capture on canvas the discordant movements of an industrializing village, Jean-François Millet was completing a lifetime's work south of Paris, near Fontainebleau.[1] Millet settled in Barbizon after the Revolution of 1848 and until his death in 1875 devoted himself to painting and drawing rural life. Describing himself as 'an out-and-out peasant', this son of devout, comfortable landholders from near Cherbourg in Normandy left a rich and evocative legacy of images of labour, landscape and family life. The peasant household's routines of spinning, caring for livestock, harvesting, baking bread, and carting water and wood are captured in images which resonate with respect for rural toil. Above all, Millet's paintings suggest the continuity of the routines of rural life and are in sharp contrast to the images of changing, bustling and fractious urban centres left by Monet. Millet insisted that his desire was to 'paint nothing that was not the result of an impression directly received from nature'; however, apart from periods in the Auvergne and Normandy, almost all of these decades were spent in Barbizon, where he painted from memory. The central problem in the complex relationship between art and society is in his case especially acute: did Millet simply detail the rural world around him, or did this deeply religious and increasingly conservative man construct an imaginary world, rural France as he wished it to remain?

Millet's sensitive images of the eternal routines of peasant life are mirrored in the judgments made by historians, though the painter's admiration for tradition and tillers of the soil has since given way to anglocentric conclusions about the 'backward' nature of most of rural France. While pointing to improvements in transport, especially railways, and an exodus to the cities as stimuli of change, economic historians have stressed the continuity in rural society until after 1880. More generally, Eugen Weber depicted a rural France south of the Loire and in Brittany where ancient subsistence routines, isolation and archaic cultures were only finally eroded between 1880 and 1914 by the forces of mass education and conscription, railways and economic specialization. Only then, argues Weber, did 'modernization' integrate rural France into the culture and politics of the nation and transform 'peasants into Frenchmen'.[2]

Weber's thesis is contradicted by evidence that economic and social change was accelerating in specific regions south of the Loire during the July Monarchy, and the mass peasant politics of left and right during the Second Republic points to the identification rural people were making between their own well-being and the direction of national politics. A closer analysis of economic and social structures in the decades 1850–80 reveals an interrelated complex of transformation. But rather than searching out an illusory watershed between 'traditional' and 'modern' rural society, an alternative model would describe change as occurring everywhere in rural France but varying in timing, nature and intensity according to region, class and gender.

At first glance, the bald statistics of rural land-owning do suggest the continuity of labour-intensive peasant agriculture. In 1884, holdings smaller than one hectare were 61 per cent of the total (covering just 5.2 per cent of France), and those of 1–5 hectares a further 26.5 per cent (covering 17.5 per cent). Rural society remained dominated by small owners (31 per cent of the agricultural work force) and farm labourers (39 per cent). However, the critical issue in understanding rural social structures is not the size of the unit of production but rather what is done with the land and by whom. In the decades from 1840 to 1880 the use of land changed from essentially subsistence to essentially market-oriented production. Such a change varied in timing and degree from region to region: in some areas (the north-east, the Paris basin, the Bordelais, the Rhône valley) it was well advanced by the 1840s, while in others (parts of the Massif Central and Brittany, the Jura, the Alps and the Pyrenees) subsistence polyculture endured well into the twentieth century. In most regions, however, the decades before 1880 were a time of gradual, transforming changes, accelerating those already evident in 1815–45.[3]

In some areas these changes centred on new farm practices on large holdings: either the transformation from sharecropping to capitalist tenancy on substantial rental leaseholds or the use of new farming techniques. While only 0.87 per cent of the total number of farms in the early 1880s, properties over 50 hectares covered 35.3 per cent of the land. In Bonnières, on the Seine 70 kilometres north of Paris, the transition from polyculture to cattle-farming after the arrival of the Paris-Rouen railway link in 1843 was overshadowed by the development of sugar-beet farming in the 1860s. Here the huge capitalist enterprise of Jules Michaux, together with 19 smaller farmers with 24 hectares or more, produced for a local distillery and superphosphate factory. On large farms more widespread use was made of the deeper-reaching Dombasle plough, of the scythe instead of the sickle, of mechanical threshers (a fivefold increase to 310,000 in 1852–82), and lime, phosphate and seaweed fertilizers. But far more common was an increase and change in production on household-based small and medium-sized holdings in response to new techniques, urban demand and faster, more reliable means of transport. The best gauge of the change in rural productivity is that, if 100 people working in agriculture fed 459 mouths in 1852, by 1882 they were feeding 590. By the 1880s in most regions, households were in a qualitatively different relationship with the land and its produce, labour and markets. This relationship is best understood as market-oriented or specialized commodity production, and in the social transition from peasants to small farmers lay a nexus of transformation which was to render rural France a fundamentally different world.[4]

An important factor in increased agricultural output was the bringing into cultivation of coastal marshes and 'wastelands': the first national cadastral survey, carried out between 1807 and 1850, calculated these at 16.2 per cent of the country, but by 1879 they had receded to 13.5 per cent (a decline of 1.4 million hectares). This was most spectacular in Brittany, where the area of moorland was halved to 500,000 hectares in 1840–80, and the Landes, where 2,500 kilometres of ditches drained 300,000 hectares for pine forests; elsewhere 30,000 hectares of coastal marshes were drained in the Gironde in the decade after 1852 and 9,000 of the 19,000 hectares of swamps in the Dombes in the 1860s. Changes in productivity were also spurred by greater regional specialization. For example, while total wine production increased by 71 per cent in 1850–80, in the Midi, the Charentes and the middle Loire regions the increase was 152, 112 and 137 per cent respectively; on the other hand, there was a decline in wine production in the Ile-de-France, the north-east, Franche-Comté and other regions now more specialized in wheat, livestock and commercial crops.

Specialization for markets was facilitated by national and local expenditure on roads and canals – such as that from Brest to Nantes – as well as railways, which by 1870 formed a grid of 17,500 kilometres, as extensive as a century later. The area now regularly supplying Paris's food needs covered a radius of 250 kilometres, compared with 50 kilometres under the July Monarchy; indeed, the livestock markets of Poissy, Sceaux and La Villette were buying from 40 departments as far away as the Lot-et-Garonne, Lozère, Haut-Rhin and Morbihan. It was not only cash which this trade returned to the countryside: the carts which supplied fodder for the 72,000 horses in the capital in 1874 returned home laden with manure for farms up to 120 kilometres away. The gradual 'nationalizing' of marketing structures is evident from the decline in the differential in wheat prices between regions from 70 to 27 per cent. The lowering of tariffs with all of France's neighbours in a series of treaties between 1860 and 1866 boosted the export of sugar fourfold in 1855–79, of potatoes sevenfold and doubled that of wine (to 32 million litres).

The speed and extent of these changes should not be exaggerated. The work of Pasteur and others was only just starting to be known in disease eradication from sheep and silkworms, in fermenting wine and beer, and in milk transportation. In certain areas, such as inland Brittany, the plateau of Millevaches in the Limousin, and the upper Pyrenees, there were few if any changes to productive techniques by 1880. In some regions a major obstacle to changes in land use remained the 'neo-feudal' tenancy agreements imposed by large proprietors: in the 1870s, sharecroppers around Apt (Vaucluse) were still having to sign leases of less than five years requiring them to share in kind all farm produce, to do a maze of unproductive and unpaid work, and even to forego sowing consecutive crops or using commercial fertilizer. Similarly, the general increase in the taxable value of land in 1851–79 (except for Corsica and three south-eastern departments) hides the essential point that many areas with the lowest increases (the Paris basin, Champagne and the east, Provence) were already intensely cultivated and remained wealthier than regions with the largest increases. In the Ile-de-France and north-east there were two or three mechanical threshers and

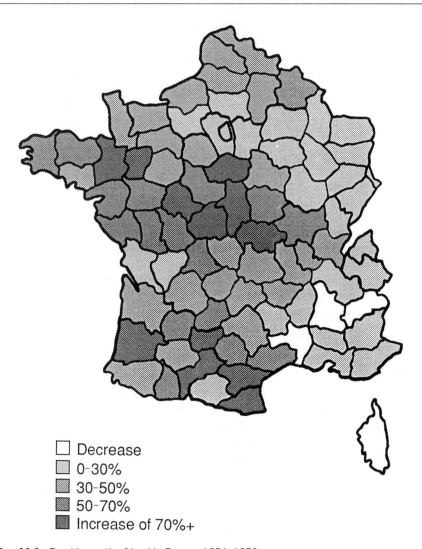

☐ Decrease
▦ 0–30%
▦ 30–50%
▦ 50–70%
▦ Increase of 70%+

Map 11.1 Taxable worth of land in France, 1851–1879

Source: Adapted from Georges Duby and Armand Wallon (eds), *Histoire de la France rurale*, vol. 3 (Paris, 1976), p. 248.

about ten agricultural labourers per 1,000 hectares, but in the Limousin the corresponding figures were 0.16 and 18 and in Brittany 0.16 and 29. The 15 departments with a per capita agricultural revenue in 1864 of above 559 francs (the Ile-de-France, parts of Normandy and Champagne, the Maine-et-Loire, Gers, Hérault and Charente-Inférieure) contrasted with the 23 under 380 francs (Brittany, the Pyrenees, most of the Massif Central and the Franche-Comté).

The transformation of rural economic structures both caused and was itself accelerated by emigration from most of the countryside.[5] A combination of despair at the loss of hope for social change in the countryside after 1851, the concentration of the textile industry in cities and the perceived attractions of urban life underpinned a gradual but important shift in French demographic history: from the 1850s, increasing numbers of temporary migrants became permanent. The years of the Second Republic had been a turning-point, when the rural population had reached its peak and had begun to decline in almost 40 per cent of districts; after 1851, this decline became an exodus which was never to be reversed. In the years 1851–6, the population of rural France declined by 579,000, then by 70,000 annually, and by 1866, 65 departments had experienced an excess of emigration over natural increase. Those who left were overwhelmingly labourers wholly or partly dependent on wage-work: in 1862–82 alone, the numbers of full-time labourers and farm servants declined by over 257,000 and of labourers with small plots by over 407,000. In the tiny, impoverished hamlet of Périllos in the stony Corbières, a sharp break from subsistence agriculture – when 40 of the 140 cultivable hectares were given over to viticulture – coincided with emigration. From its historic peak of 98 in 1856, the population fell to 79 in 1872 and would ultimately abandon the hamlet totally. This rural exodus created a shortage of agricultural labourers in some areas. Of the 4,645 rural people from the Pas-de-Calais recruited by the Marles mining company in 1853–93, 73 per cent were day-labourers; the Flahaut family of large landowners had to increase farm servants' wages threefold in 1858–75 to compete with miners' wages.

Migration from the countryside was never a simple or easy choice and could involve several stages. Jeanne Bouvier was born in the Dauphiné in 1865 to a smallholder and cooper who had also worked on the railways and to a devout, exacting mother with whom she worked in the fields. Ruined by the phylloxera disease in the vineyards, the family moved to Saint-Symphorien-d'Ozon, south of Lyon, and Jeanne was sent to work in a silk factory at the age of 11; there she earned 50 centimes for working from 5 a.m. to 8 p.m. Finally her mother, now separated, succeeded in finding work as a maid for a Parisian brush manufacturer, taking Jeanne with her to find work as an apprentice. In some areas, new opportunities in villages could also attract migrants: in 1856–76 Bonnières's population increased from 714 to 929, including 88 Bretons. But Bonnières was also a departure point, for many migrants stayed only a few years before following many natives to the industrial north of Paris. Seasonal migration continued in many areas: up to 40,000 Creusois continued to walk to Paris to work in the building trades (and, for many, to become involved in the Paris Commune); Auvergnats and Savoyards still spent part of the year in Lyon, hoping, like the wet nurses of the Morvan, to bring back some savings. Thousands of highlanders migrated for the wine harvest along the Mediterranean littoral, though they were increasingly mixed with Spaniards who, too, were more likely to settle permanently.

Almost everywhere, increases in labourers' wages and the incomes of smallholders and tenants outstripped rises in rents and taxes. In global terms, real incomes in the countryside increased by 25–35 per cent in the 30 years after 1851: the consumption per head of flour increased by 34 per cent, of potatoes 40 per cent, of sugar 118 per cent, of meat 40 per cent (but at 22 kilograms per head was only one-third that of urban people) and of wine 21 per cent (though increased consumption of alcohol in distilled form, as in Brittany and

Normandy, had ruinous social effects). Compared with 1839, the number of conscripts exempted for lack of height (less than 1.56 m or 5'2') fell from 16 to 10 per cent. In the years of the Second Empire, average calorific intake rose from 2,480 to 2,875, reaching a minimum adequacy. The mayor of Cormeray (Loir-et-Cher) reported in 1862 that 'everyone has a degree of comfort unknown until now … The people are much better nourished than in the past.'

But this well-being was a function of social class. An enquiry in 1872 reported of 46 departments: 'A single, low room is often the only lodging of a whole family … People eat rye, potatoes, maize, chestnuts. There are people who recount the great story of having eaten meat several times in their life.'[6] Prosperity also varied sharply between regions: the better-fed areas of coastal Languedoc, the Rhône valley, the Ile-de-France and Normandy contrasted with the protein-poor areas of the south-east and centre. The prosperity of many smallholders was also tenuous. Rises in prices received for agricultural produce (overall perhaps 80 per cent) had far outstripped productivity (20–5 per cent), permitting more people to acquire holdings which were therefore smaller: in 1851–82 the number of landholders increased by 15.7 per cent while the size of properties declined 12.1 per cent. In an increasingly commercial economy, these smallholders remained highly vulnerable to price changes and, as the phylloxera beetle began to spread from the Gard in the mid-1860s and cereal prices began to decline from 1873, so did the smallholders' dream of economic independence.

Higher calorific intake was the main reason why rural death rates continued to decline and remained well below those of towns: in 1854–8, 23.1 per thousand compared with 29.8 in towns, in 1879–83, 20.8 per thousand compared with 25.2. But rural people remained vulnerable to infantile diseases and epidemics: in the 1870s, 176 in every thousand infants died compared with 180 in the 1830s. The cholera plague of 1853–4 carried off 143,000 people, up to one in five in parts of the Ariège; while inland swamp-draining ended some diseases, malaria remained endemic on the coasts from the Camargue to the Pyrenees and from the Pyrenees to the Loire. When ill, rural people rarely resorted to doctors; indeed, there were fewer of them in the countryside than 40 years earlier. There was one doctor to 1,425 people in the Alpes-Maritimes, 1,722 in the Hérault and 2,080 in the Gironde (were doctors attracted to sun and wine?), but they were a rare sight in the Morbihan (9,732), Côtes-du-Nord (8,377) and Hautes-Alpes (8,195). Doctors had established their General Association in 1858 – one reason why their numbers had fallen – but by 1880 had still not won a social victory over their rural rivals, the variety of secular and religious healers (and, according to doctors, 'witches') who proliferated in the countryside. These healers were not only far cheaper, but were more tolerant of poverty and patient self-diagnosis, and considered a far wider explanation of ill-health. Moreover, until the new epidemiological understandings of the 1880s, their uses of herbal and spiritual remedies in which patients collaborated were at least as effective as the cures of professional doctors.[7]

Some historians of the family have argued that, after 1850, bourgeois practices of birth control, notions of romantic love and of the idea of childhood began to 'trickle down' to the rural masses. Such arguments are both ethnocentric in their privileging of the urban and 'modern' and incorrect in detail. Forms of contraception had always been practised in those rural communities where smaller families had been economically necessary, and certainly well before feminists and social reformers began explicitly to challenge church teachings in the 1880s. Coitus interruptus had become a widely-used practice, expressed in popular proverbs: 'Do as the miller does: unload the cart at the door', and 'Thresh in the shed but winnow at the door'. In Zola's rural novel, *La Terre*, a young peasant women refers to it as a matter of course. Around Toulouse, grandparents advised abstinence after the birth of a first child: 'You should put your tools away in the attic.' Social historians using a wider array of source material have also argued that rural people had always experienced and expressed love; in Martine Segalen's words, 'a latent sexuality imbued the whole of peasant life'. State laws continued to excuse men who took violent, even lethal, retribution for their wife's adultery but, for example in Corsica, strong codes of female honour often blamed the husband if the wife had an affair. Single women remained sexually vulnerable but few crimes aroused such anger as rape, especially of children.[8]

After the military defeat of 1870–1, doctors inveighed in vain against the lack of virility which had crippled the nation, warning men of the dangers of abstinence and coitus interruptus and of women's 'selfishness'. In this concern they were seconded by the clergy's despair at the practice of 'conjugal onanism'. In 1875, the presence of the Church in the countryside reached its post-revolutionary peak of one priest to every 639 people (compared with 814 in 1821), but the incidence of attendance at Easter mass varied according to region, gender and class.[9] Towards 1880, just 14 per cent of people over the age of 13 went to Easter mass in the diocese of Troyes, while in the rural parishes of the diocese of Strasbourg 94 per cent of those over 14 years attended. In the diocese of Rennes, 90 per cent of men and 97 per cent of women attended, compared with 6 per cent and 29 per cent in the diocese of Orléans. Religious observance was also irregular: in the diocese of Moulins, 64 per cent of the population went to Easter mass, but only 8 per cent took communion monthly, varying from 26.5 per cent among young women to just 0.2 per cent among men. Even in devout areas, there may well have been a connection between clerical antipathy to the practice of contraception and a decline in religiosity.

The social history of religion in the countryside cannot be limited to levels of attendance at formal moments of the church calendar. Instead, religious belief embraced patterns of worship and appeals to supernatural forces which the Catholic Church finally coopted in recognition of their durability and importance. Varying across regions, and even between villages, such beliefs – misleadingly described as 'superstitions' by many clergy, intellectuals and historians – assumed the potency of local saints and rituals as cures, guarantees of good fortune or curses, and constantly challenged the claims to knowledge of the clergy and doctors. While such beliefs were usually centuries old, it had paradoxically been the French Revolution, with its attack on the Catholic monopoly of religious forms, which had emancipated their practice: the nineteenth century was the apogee of popular religiosity. Intimately bound up with the complex cycles of agrarian polyculture, these rituals were far more likely to be

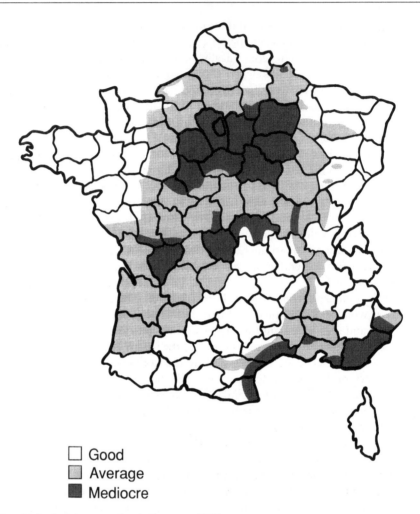

☐ Good
▨ Average
■ Mediocre

Map 11.2   Religious practice in France, c.1880

Source: Adapted from Gérard Cholvy and Yves-Marie Hilaire, *Histoire religieuse de la France contemporaine*, vol. 1 (Toulouse, 1985), from reports of prefects and bishops.

undermined by economic change than by the clergy's invectives or cooption. The Church did succeed, however, in encouraging the proliferation of 'Saint-Sulpice art' – cheap, mass-produced plaster or terracotta statues of beatific, gaudily-painted saints and the Holy Family – to replace the tortured imagery of ancient wood and stone statuary in parish churches.

Anticlericals and republicans – such as Jules Michelet, furious at his exclusion from his mistress's deathbed by a priest – blamed women's greater religiosity on their naturally docile susceptibility to clerical authority. Just as doubtfully, some historians have suggested that ignorance about their bodies' functions predisposed women to religious devotion.[10] Whatever an adequate explanation might be, central to religious life in the decades after 1850 was a struggle between men – priests, husbands, teachers, doctors – for power over women. The heat of this struggle has obscured the ways in which women took their own initiatives to continue to reconstruct a church that was more centred on a god of love than a god of fear, on pious work in health care, education and charity than on formal observance, and on women themselves as active ministers of the faith. The Church and its associated institutions was, for women of the urban middle classes and in many rural areas, a female space in opposition to the café.

The number of women religious (*congréganistes*) continued to increase rapidly in the decades after 1850, and their presence became much more visible in the countryside. By 1861, over 55 per cent of them were based in communes of fewer than 5,000 people; in three-fifths of cases two or three of them worked together in small religious houses, helped by local pious women (*béates*). In the older orders founded or re-established early in the century, bourgeois and artisan women had predominated among recruits, but in newer orders, such as that of Saint-Gildas in Amiens, rural women made up two-thirds of novices. The influence of female orders was an increasingly contentious issue for the Second Empire; similarly, by the late 1860s many clergy had lost their trust in the emperor and were encouraged by Pius IX's rousing repudiation of modernity in the 'Syllabus of Errors' (1864) and his claims to papal infallibility (1870). This could also place an ultramontanist clergy in opposition to a liberal bishop such as Dupanloup of Orléans, who had criticized the notion of infallibility at the Vatican Council, moved his priests too frequently for their liking, and seemed lax in his task of eradicating rural radicalism and 'immorality' (the diocese had one tavern to every 108 people in 1869).

Like the Catholic Church, the 555,000 Calvinists – mainly in the south, but with minorities in the Deux-Sèvres, Paris and the east – were divided between liberal 'modernists' and 'traditionalist' evangelicals. The victory of the latter was in part due to the erosion of communal solidarity in the liberal heartlands of the southern plains by economic change and migration to towns (there were 12,500 Protestants in Marseille in 1872 compared with 3,100 in 1851). However, as among the 270,000 Lutherans of the east, a unity was preserved by a hostility to any perceived pretensions of the Catholic Church and by memories of political conflict and repression revivified in 1851.[11]

Attitudes to education – like religion – remained profoundly influenced by political loyalties, and similarly varied according to region, gender and class.[12] In the struggle between Church and State for the minds of the young, the State had access to 75 per cent of boys but only 45 per cent of girls enrolled in schools. This also suggests that, while men were far less likely to go to church than were women and resented the power of the confessional, they also saw church education as inculcating an appropriate mix of practical skills and religious morality in their daughters, even if two-thirds of teaching nuns had no educational qualifications. This was especially the case in devout areas such as northern Brittany or where there were deep political and denominational loyalties, such as in the middle Rhône valley; as in the eighteenth century, the hold of the church was weaker in the Ile-de-France, Champagne, Burgundy and Touraine.

The State's teachers were an increasing presence in rural France, 111,000 in 1877 compared with 76,000 in the 1840s. They were poorly paid: in the 1860s most men received 600–700 francs and women 400–500, about the same as an urban labourer. The increase to 900–1,200 francs in 1875 was doubly symbolic, of the Republic's commitment to education and of parity for the first time with parish priests. The departmental *Écoles Normales* – of which there were 76 for men and 11 for women by 1869 – charged fees for trainee teachers, but schoolteaching was an increasingly attractive option for the sons and daughters of rural artisans and farmers. Of the 567 teachers trained in the Vosges in 1862–92, for example, 61 per cent were from agricultural backgrounds and 28 per cent from the petite bourgeoisie. Rural youths also made up 12 per cent of the tiny minority who went to secondary schools before entering business or the public service.[13]

In the three decades after 1850 there was an acceleration in the social acceptance of education evident since the turn of the century: more children were sent to school and they attended more regularly. Between 1850 and 1877, while the national population was virtually stable, the number of school pupils increased from 3.3 to 4.7 million (including an increase from 1.5 to 2.3 million girls); of those enrolled, four-fifths rather than two-thirds now attended in summer. While minimal literacy rates increased from 64 to 82 per cent among young men, there were still marked variations, with far lower literacy levels in Brittany, the south-west, and the west and north of the Massif Central. Rather than a symptom of the so-called 'backwardness' of these regions, non-attendance at school was more a function of poverty (met to some extent by increasing provision of free places), the need for children's farm labour, the degree of involvement in the market economy, difficult access in regions of dispersed habitat, and resistance to a French, centralized educational system. According to their interviewer, Patern and Yvonne Le Bihan, devout and hard-working Breton sharecroppers from near Quimper, showed 'great tenderness and solicitude for their children, but they [found] it difficult to make up their minds to entrust them to the schoolmaster … to see them pick up bad habits and to lose respect for their parents'.

Nevertheless, gradual increases in rural standards of living made it possible for more children to attend school. In the impoverished, dispersed settlement of Mazières-en-Gâtine (Deux-Sèvres), where 63 of the 976 people were listed as beggars in 1852, increased interest in education during the Second Empire was attributed by its historian, Roger Thabault, to a series of social and economic changes which made the village more prosperous and 'open'. Among these were an increase in the number of smallholders; the clearing of the gorse, broom and bracken which surrounded the village; the use of lime fertilizer; the growing of beetroot and turnips to feed livestock; better roads (the first commercial coach passed through in 1849); and occupational diversity (the appearance of a road-mender, three grocers, two rural postmen, a shoemaker and six café-keepers).[14]

For many rural households in Mazières and thousands of other villages, the decades after 1850 were a time of comparative prosperity and security, what has been called 'the peak of peasant civilization'.[15] Increases in agricultural productivity first evident in the 1840s and facilitated by the expansion of the railway network played a vital role in alleviating recurrent subsistence crises in the countryside. The shortages and consequent protests in 1853–6 were a pale reflection of those in 1846–7 in northern and western France. Similarly, the departure of many of those whose survival had been most tenuous meant that the centre and south were never again to experience the level of collective protest seen in the spring of 1848 against threats emanating from an increasingly intrusive state and capitalist sector. The exodus of the poorest sections of the rural community eased the pressure on soil resources: while crimes against persons remained relatively constant, crimes against property dropped sharply after mid-century. At the same time, the variety of regional cultures, languages and beliefs endured in a countryside of extraordinary diversity and richness.

In many ways, the decades from 1850 to 1880 were indeed a peak of rural civilization, even if most people remained poor and the benefits of increased agricultural output were unevenly shared according to class and region. At the very moment of its apogee, however, three broad and interrelated changes were occurring which would undermine the rich texture of rural society.

The first broad change was that economic specialization and rural exodus gradually altered the social structure and diversity within rural communities, and much of the social and occupational complexity of agricultural communities began to disappear. Labourers, whether full or part-time, who left the countryside were joined by large numbers of non-agricultural people, artisans, textile workers and professional men, although in larger villages they were replaced by retailers such as bakers, butchers, grocers and dressmakers. Although this process – described by Tilly as 'dedifferentiation' – varied in timing across the face of the countryside, it proved to be inexorable and eroded the social vitality of communal life. The language of 'progress', privileging urban expansion, integration and concentration, hides the experience of rural regions hitherto dependent on small-scale industrial work. By the 1870s, rural France was more 'agrarian' than ever before with whole regions now essentially monocultural and dependent on the urban suppliers for manufactured goods formerly produced within the community. In poorer areas, especially in the highlands, the process was rather one of 'disintegration', as domestic textile work and small local industries collapsed, and these areas became 'pastoralized' and depopulated.[16] The relocation of metallurgy in the half-century after 1830 meant a dramatic 'ruralization' of the countryside as the small rural forges of the Pyrenees, Massif Central, Jura, Ardennes and Normandy were concentrated in cities in the northeast and centre. Similarly, small cotton and wool centres across much of the country, with their dependent outworkers, were now centralized in Lille-Roubaix, Rouen, Lyon, and Saint-Etienne.

These changes were to have profound effects on the nature and meaning of women's work. This was particularly the case in regions which had previously depended on seasonal textile work by women or where subsistence polyculture was being replaced by market-oriented specialization in one or two crops. Of course, such changes were slow, varied from region to region, and were incomplete. Most rural women continued to work outside the home for part if not all of the year (the figure produced by the 1866 census of 25 per cent for the number of women in paid work ignored the unpaid farm work most women continued to do). Moreover, when women migrated, they sought employment in areas which had always been dominated by young rural women, especially domestic work. In Melun in 1872, 54 per cent of domestic servants were rural migrants or foreigners, almost exactly the same proportion as in Versailles and Bordeaux decades earlier. Similarly, these young women long continued to assume they were adjuncts to their rural household, sending wages home themselves or through their employers.[17]

The second, linked change was cultural. Agricultural specialization and rural exodus hastened the abandonment of ancient agrarian routines and, with them, the celebrations and rituals associated with the seasonal routines of agricultural and religious life. Where specialization in labour-intensive production created population growth, rural people were not only in more frequent contact with outside influences, but were also living with migrants from elsewhere. It was these changes, more than 'modernization' by a Parisian bureaucracy which were slowly to erode the relevance of many of the rituals of public life.

Whatever the benefits of a more widespread facility in reading, writing and speaking French, education remained an arena in which the battle between the claims of the centralized nation-state and local ethnic identities was played out. A survey by the Ministry of Education in 1863 reported, conservatively, that most communes were non-French speaking in 21 departments and that significant proportions were in 32 others, in all most of the country (not to mention regional dialects of French). Nevertheless, the twin forces of an increasing state presence, of which teachers were a visible embodiment, and of involvement in national marketing structures were eroding the distinctiveness of local cultures. For example, new, urban, even foreign, dances were being absorbed into regional festivities. It was not that folk dances disappeared: in the 1870s, 80 different dances were reported in just two communes of the Nivernais. But the polka, waltz and schottische were appearing at rural balls and new dance halls, of which there were 104 in the 93 communes of the district of Orléans in 1866. For increasing numbers of people, urban and French signified 'modern': in the 1870s, the young men of Mazières returned from military service – after 1873, increased to five years – determined, as a sign of their worldliness, no longer to speak *patois*.[18]

The process of *francisation* was as old as the French State itself and its acceleration during the decades after 1848 should not be confused with a dichotomy between 'tradition' and 'modernity'. Rural history is dynamic, an unfinished series of complex changes and stages, never 'immobile' nor 'the good old days' for all its inhabitants. As the Bourbonnais sharecropper Emile Guillaumin's novel noted in passing, even *The Life of a Simple Man* from a non-French speaking, dispersed commune was not isolated from the wider world. Under the Second Empire, however, the countryside became more 'open' than before, because of increasing numbers of schools, all-weather roads, railways, and the presence of rural post offices (hitherto mostly in towns and now democratized with the penny-post of 1849). Popular resistance to *francisation* could take the form of non-attendance at school and refusal to speak French, or, as in the Pyrenees, continued infractions of Parisian forest codes or refusal to join the army (in 1841–68, over one-third of all deserters were from the Pyrenees). Paradoxically, a greater awareness of other provinces through schooling encouraged the self-conscious wearing of 'traditional' regional costume on special occasions. But the process of acculturation seemed irreversible and it is no coincidence that in 1854 the Félibrige was founded to safeguard Provençal, nor that in 1859 Frédéric Mistral wrote *Miréio*, a nostalgic homage to the cultural traditions of the Provençal countryside.

The more prevalent assumption of the relevance of French and urban life was revealed in the use of public space. The nineteenth century was a time of proliferation of public monuments, commemorating wars, revolutions and heroes in statues, monumental fountains and other symbolism. While regional forms of collective and personal rituals endured, since the 1840s a new male space, the café or *cabaret*, had challenged the *veillée*. In the Eure, their numbers increased 58 per cent in 1827–51, then by 21 per cent by 1900; in Finistère, their numbers doubled by mid-century, then increased a further 58 per cent by 1900. In general, women were excluded from this space where men assumed that they were making the important decisions with their peers; here, too, French newspapers were available and French spoken depending on the subject and the audience. The polarity of the café (male, non-familial, irreligious, open to French oral and written culture, often left-wing) and the *veillée* (familial, closed, perpetuating a non-French oral, often religious, tradition, praised by the Church) went beyond leisure to symbolize important contrasts of politics, religion and gender.[19]

Hard, repetitious work by the family remained the constant of rural life, but in regions close to large cities the more prosperous farmers began to emulate bourgeois lifestyles. The farmers of the Paris basin who visited the Exhibitions of 1867 and 1878 took home a taste for cast-iron stoves, petrol lamps, commodes, folding tables, ornate beds and bed-linen, and bourgeois clothes for Sundays. In the 1870s, they began drinking coffee in the mornings, wine with dinner and fresh meat several times weekly. Elsewhere, meals remained untouched by urban trends, except for the greater availability of wine. In Brittany, winter meals continued to consist of cauliflower, milk or lard soup with bread or pancakes in the morning; a buckwheat or oatmeal gruel or potatoes at noon; and a combination of these dishes in the evening, washed down with milk more commonly than with cider. Here the Le Bihans's new luxuries were tobacco for Patern and snuff for Yvonne. In the Tarn and Aveyron, a rich soup was eaten twice a day, made of goose fat, potatoes, beans, cauliflower, pork, sausage, ham bones and bread; and in the evening a gruel of chestnuts with potatoes, fresh cheese, lettuce and garlic bread.[20]

Finally, it was in these decades that the rural landscape finally took on the appearance which is now in turn disappearing. Distinctive settlement and field patterns became fixed as the population stabilized and the extension of cultivated land reached its limits. Early in the century, only houses in the Midi were commonly of stone; by the end of the century virtually all were. In the decades 1840–80, the cattle-farmers of the high hamlets of the Cantal and elsewhere in the Massif Central marked their new prosperity and social position by placing lintels with the date, often with the owner's name, above the doors of their solid basalt dwellings. In the 1850s, 20 per cent of houses had thatched roofs, especially in the north-west; by the 1880s, most were tiled. Nevertheless, house design and tiling patterns remained as regionally varied as habitat and field patterns, reflecting topography, soil use, custom and climate.

The ecology of the countryside was also changing within an on-going diversity. A combination of reafforestation following laws passed in 1860 and the decline in the population of beleaguered upland communities permitted the slow, checkered recovery of mountain ecologies. Some areas had been so denuded over the centuries that they were never to recover; however, while this was the result of human pressure, other forest areas had been spared the devastations of fire by the presence of highlanders clearing undergrowth and smothering fires. While the north-east became almost devoid of trees, the first large reafforestation works were undertaken in the Corbières, Larzac and elsewhere. As Tamara Whited has demonstrated, the zeal of the forest administration to rehabilitate 'devastated' forests took little account of the farming practices of highlanders in regions such as the Pyrenees and Savoie and their projects were contested and sidestepped.[21]

Huge new pine forests were planted in the former swamps of the Sologne and Landes. Coastal and inland swamp-draining and the bringing into cultivation of 'wasteland' was, however, to the detriment of the rich fauna and flora of delicate ecologies now 'reclaimed' for human use. In lowland areas, the transition to specialized agriculture, now starting to use chemical fertilizers, was to create long-term problems of soil and water degradation. Peasant polyculture, on the other hand, had generally been conservative of resources and reliant on human and animal manure. The changes in rural society after 1850 thus had, on balance, negative effects on the environment, symbolized by the steady march of the phylloxera beetle through unbroken vineyards: their reconstitution in the 1880s would not only destroy the hopes of small wine-growers, for costs were as high as 2,000 francs per hectare, but would privilege artificial pesticides in the prevention of future catastrophes.

The multifaceted impact of the changes outlined above is evident from specific studies of villages in the Nièvre, Aude and Loire. In the Nièvre, market opportunities, especially for livestock, opened up by urban growth and improved transport were cause and effect of a swing to tenancy leases rather than sharecropping, offering to tenants the lure of keeping profits once a fixed rent had been paid. Although subsistence polyculture and restrictive sharecropping contracts continued in the Morvan region in the east of the department, elsewhere change was rapid. In Limanton (see Chapter 6) the number of sharecroppers among those renting land declined from 22 (53.7 per cent) in 1846 to four (8.7 per cent) in 1876. Across this period, the net revenue from one hectare of meadow land increased by 49 per cent, while leases increased 37 per cent: John Shaffer's estimate is that, on a 50-hectare farm, tenants could make 1,600 francs profit annually after landlords were paid 2,500 francs rent.[22] These decades were a time of relative prosperity for tenant-farmers, evident in their purchases of land and sizable dowries for their daughters. However, while daughters could take more than before to a marriage, in other ways prosperity was accentuating male status, for Nivernais tenants used *sociétés* to sidestep equal inheritance laws. While personal estates were divided among all children, a *société* divided profits from the farm among its members, usually the parents and one son. These changes were paralleled by the decline of extended families: from 1846 to 1876 stem and joint families fell from 31.7 per cent to 13.1 per cent. We cannot know how young women regarded the changes from large extended families working as subsistence sharecroppers to nuclear families working as market-oriented tenant-farmers; whatever the case, male heirs were those who profited most from prosperity.

A parallel experience of 'dedifferentiation' and prosperity occurred in many communities of the Mediterranean plain. In the Occitan village of Cruzy, 30 kilometres north of Narbonne (Aude), the years 1850–80 witnessed a dramatic swing from subsistence polyculture to wine-growing. The high demand for skilled vine-dressers on large capitalist farms pushed wages higher and made hours shorter and enabled workers to acquire their own small vineyards: there were 31 small wine-growers (12 per cent of households) in 1836 and 185 (46 per cent) in 1876. To its historian Harvey Smith, these decades were 'the golden era in the village economy', as its population grew from 1,100 in 1851 to 1,680 in 1881. Side by side with the increase in small wine-growers was the establishment by Alexandre Andoque of a mechanized wine-producing factory on his huge estate just outside the village at Sériège. The simplification of the economic base of Cruzy undermined its occupational complexity, especially for women, and made it particularly vulnerable to harvest crisis and disease; by the late 1870s the phylloxera blight was beginning to devastate Cruzy and its neighbours and would ultimately turn skilled vine-workers and growers into an impoverished agricultural proletariat.[23]

With the 30 other villages ringing the Stéphanois basin, Marlhes was directly affected by changes occurring in Saint-Etienne and other industrial towns. As the ribbon-making industry declined in competition with Germany, Switzerland and the United States, and Saint-Etienne became instead a coal-mining and metallurgical centre, so textile work in Marlhes atrophied: instead of being the domain of women of all ages working at home, it now employed a far smaller number of men and single women in small factories. Larger farms concentrated more on supplying Saint-Etienne with meat, milk and cheese; here women were engaged in cheese-making, while the daughters of the poor migrated to the unhealthy factories of the valley. Marlhes was a devout community, its children educated by Marists: in the years 1861–80, only 2 per cent of births were prenuptial conceptions, and couples limited family size by delaying marriage. The most striking continuity was the survival of the household economy within a changing environment; children agreed on strategies to keep the family holding intact and to care for a widowed parent.

The perceptible concern for the aged in Marlhes raises a neglected issue in social history for, whereas people aged over 60 were only 7 per cent of the French population in 1780, increases in the standard of living meant that they were 12.3 per cent a century later. How accurate is Zola's sad story of old Fouan, who was cajoled and intimidated into giving up his land in the Beauce before his death, abandoned by his offspring, and finally killed? In the late 1850s a social survey described the situation of Anne P___, a 70-year-old who had given her small vineyard near La Rochelle to her daughter when the latter married, was abused by the couple and reduced to sleeping in the granary. Peter

Stearns has argued that the nineteenth century was a time when increasing numbers of elderly confronted a hostile, uncaring environment in which they were seen as burdensome, useless and a hindrance to the hopes of their children. The example of Marlhes contradicts such a view, as does that of the Morvan, where changing inheritance patterns did not undermine the authority of parents. In the Beauce itself, the elderly Jean-Pierre Ménager complained in 1858 of a broken agreement: 'I willed my goods to my son...in return for a yearly rent of 150 francs or the obligation to feed me.' This might recall the story of Fouan, but Ménager's complaint was made in a court of law, suggesting a keen awareness of his rights.[24]

The cumulative effects of these slow and uneven changes – rural exodus and 'dedifferentiation', greater prosperity for most of those who remained, the erosion of regional loyalties and cultures – were to be felt in the nature of political life in the countryside. Paradoxically, the triumph of universal male suffrage had made rural people electorally dominant (as they were to be until the 1930s) at the very time when these changes were beginning profoundly to transform rural life and politics.

After the resolution of the great crisis of mid-century by military *coup d'état*, a powerful combination of authoritarian rule and comparative economic stability undermined the potential for overt political contestation until the late 1860s. The reliance of the Second Empire on a tightly-controlled rural vote made the very word *rural* an object of derision for urban republicans of all shades; similarly, the countryside had become the heartland of all the virtues for conservatives, in stark contrast to their panic 20 years earlier. There are two general reasons why this negative image of reactionary docility needs to be qualified. First, there were very good reasons for rural people to acquiesce in or support the Empire. On the whole, they had never been so prosperous, in part due to the regime's political economy of railway and road construction, draining of swamps, facilitating of exports and provision of free places in schools. The Empire had also given them their longest unbroken experience of universal manhood suffrage. It is not surprising that, when asked in the May 1870 plebiscite whether they approved of the liberal Empire, 7.35 million voters (against 1.54 million) gave their assent. This was an ambiguous choice, however, for a vote in favour of liberal reform implied – as it was designed to – a vote in favour of the Empire as well.

Secondly, the image of rural docility misses the varied ways in which people continued to contest power or to use the politics of the Empire to their own ends. Given the regime's expansion of its repressive forces and willingness to punish left-wing activists – as in a renewed purge of republicans in 1858 – the focus of political life became local government and the insistence by independent small farmers on their local power in confrontation with large landowners, unpopular mayors appointed by the prefect, and intrusive priests. In the Isère and Ain, local priests used the victory of Order in 1851 to embark on an energetic campaign to revivify faith and clerical influence in an area which had had an extensive *démoc-soc* movement. In response, mayors and councils were able to use their control of the communal budget to thwart clerical plans for schools and church maintenance, generating angry opposition of Church and State at the village level. Similarly, in the Loir-et-Cher, one-third of villages witnessed serious clashes between local councils and clergy in 1852–75, generating a virulent anticlericalism: one mayor was accused of describing the Virgin Mary as a prostitute and claiming the sun as his spiritual father, the land as his mother. In the Ille-et-Vilaine, long a royalist stronghold, a militant legitimist noble defeated the Bonapartist candidate for the district of Vitré-Fougères in 1852, only to lose in 1857 when relations between Church and State were at their most cordial. In the elections of 1863, when these relations had sharply deteriorated, rural voters spurned a new Catholic and legitimist candidate to stay with the Bonapartist, the first major act of independence from clerical and noble authority. Paradoxically, the Empire may here have paved the way for republican politics.[25]

In areas like these, the Empire was thus seen as a quasi-republican protection against the pretensions of clergy and nobility, whereas elsewhere it kept its guise of a military regime of Order against the socialist aspirations of 1851. It was this left-wing alternative which was most obviously absent from the political choice open to rural people until the liberal reforms leading up to the elections of May 1869. While the republican vote came disproportionately from towns and cities (only one republican in the Seine-et-Marne and four from the east were from purely rural electorates), a left-wing, or at least republican, constituency had re-emerged (with 3.3 million votes against 4.4 million for official candidates). As in 1849, this was centred on the Mediterranean littoral, the valley of the Rhône and the east; but republicans had gained remarkably in parts of the north and west (Aisne, Côtes-du-Nord, Charente-Inférieure).[26]

In many parts of the countryside, the Empire remained genuinely popular. In the north of the Dordogne, long-standing hatred of nobles (evident in the 'Great Fear' of 1789), mistrust of priests (manifested in a wave of rioting after rumours of a plot to reimpose the tithe in 1868), and hatred of urban radicals (the June Days had caused a panic in the area in 1848) combined with unprecedented prosperity to generate a fervent Bonapartism. The news of the army's reverses in August 1870 reached the drought-afflicted countryside at the same time as the anxious villagers around Hautefaye were attending a market and celebrating Napoleon's saint's day (15 August). A young noble accused of shouting 'Long live the Republic!' was deemed a 'Prussian' and systematically beaten for two hours by a crowd of up to 800 to cries of 'Long live Napoleon!', and was then burned to death.[27]

Elsewhere, the news of the emperor's capture and the proclamation of the Republic on 4 September 1870 was the signal for a myriad of similar proclamations by rural municipal councils, and appointed mayors and Bonapartists were purged from councils. But, despite the enthusiasm for the new Republic in many areas, and easy acceptance of the emperor's fall elsewhere, the national elections of February 1871 were a disaster for republicans, who were only about 200 of the 650 elected, the overwhelming majority being royalists of various nuances. Among those elected were 223 nobles from 72 departments, including 9 princes and dukes, 31 marquises, 68 counts and viscounts and 19 barons: a similar proportion of nobles as in the last legislative body of the Empire. Thiers was elected in 26 constituencies. Like those of April 1848, these elections have been understood by historians, as they were by contemporaries, as typifying conservative, peasant, provincial France: another element in the negative image of the rural vote. In fact, the rural response to the crisis of 1871 was far more complex than that. The victory of royalist notables in February was in part due to the abruptness of the elections; in the space of the one week allowed for campaigning, it was inevitably well-known non-Bonapartist notables who were best placed. More importantly, the Prussian invasion had not only affected Alsace-Lorraine and Champagne, but also Picardy, Ile-de-France, Burgundy and Franche-Comté, and even Normandy and the Orléanais, in all about half the country. Actions of local *francs-tireurs* terrified smallholders because of rumours – and some examples – of Prussian revenge on whole villages. The campaign opposed Gambetta's 'patriotic' republicans to a coalition of 'conservatives' (Ferry's republicans, liberals and royalists) and was effectively a plebiscite on war and peace. In the Aude, for example, a combination of opposition to the emperor's war and republican disorganization resulted in the election of five Orléanists and a legitimist, men respected for their opposition to the Empire but also deemed best able to negotiate a peace.[28]

Little is known of the rural response to the Paris Commune; villages had regained their own municipal autonomy in September 1870 and the Versailles government's censorship and propaganda made accurate news of the Commune impossible to obtain. Certainly, however, the image of rampant peasant reactionaries bent on slaughtering the Parisian working-class – another element in the negative myth of rural politics – is wide of the mark. Indeed, as the crisis wore on, many rural areas became more openly republican and less attracted to Thiers's strident attacks on the Commune, as on 14 May when the republican mayors of 16 departments gathered in Lyon to urge reconciliation. More revealing were the by-elections for the Assembly held in July 1871, in the immediate aftermath of the Commune, for 120 seats made vacant because deputies had been elected for more than one constituency in February. In the Aude, the voters of the Narbonnais, despite the rhetoric of the party of Order after the suppression of Narbonne's own commune in March, gave the republican candidate 58 per cent to fill a seat left vacant by Thiers; across the country 100 of the new deputies were republicans. In a series of by-elections until 1875, republicans consistently won victories, finally enabling the 'Wallon amendment', inserting 'the Republic' into the constitution's founding laws, to be passed by 353 votes to 352.

At a local level, particularly in the south, the years from 1871 to 1877 were a time of protracted conflict between the forces of Order and republicans of various types over the nature of the new regime. As during the Second Republic, supporters of both sides combined electoral campaigns, popular festivals and political symbolism as they disputed victory through the ballot-box and on the streets. In his *Journey to the Red Lands by a Conservative*, François Beslay described how, on the first anniversary of the Republic on 4 September 1871, republicans in Bollène (Vaucluse) found a servant 'with no reactionary prejudices': 'They dressed her in red and placed a Phrygian cap on her head and thus costumed, they paraded her from one café to another through the streets of the town, to the strains of the *Marseillaise*, like a live image of the radical Republic.'

Republicans in Le Muy and Roquebrune (Var) defied the government's banning of 4 September celebrations the following year by holding huge public demonstrations 'legalized' by the fact that this was also a traditional religious feast-day (even if the diocese had the lowest church attendance in France). On 19 May 1873, Lucien Verdet, a municipal councillor in the small industrial town of Oyonnax (Ain) ended a eulogy at a non-religious funeral: 'Dear friend, you won't have had the carnival-style procession ... the banal and venal prayers of a fat curé ... but behind your coffin march free men, who left their work to accompany their free-thinking comrade to his last rest.' Verdet was sentenced to a fortnight's prison for 'religious outrage', but a few years later was elected mayor.[29]

In this protracted political process in 1868–77, paralleling those of 1828–34 and 1846–52, the decisive stand-off was reached on 20 February 1876 when, for the first time, the majority of Frenchmen clearly chose a republican regime as the best guarantee of civil liberties and social progress. Whereas in 1849 the *démoc-socs* had won more than 50 per cent of the vote in just 16 departments, now republicans polled a majority in 51. The west of the Massif Central, the east and the south-east remained their heartlands, but successful inroads had even been made into parts of the north-east (Ardennes, Aube, Doubs) and the west (Deux-Sèvres and Mayenne) where fewer than 20 per cent had voted for the left in 1849. Parties of the right continued to dominate Brittany, Normandy, the west and south-west, and Bonapartist candidates continued to do well in such regions.

The response of the government of 'moral Order' was to counter-attack by dissolving the Assembly (16 May 1877) and unleashing a punitive purge of local officials and associations, as in 1850–1. In 1877, 1,743 mayors were dismissed. Between May and July, 55 *cercles*, clubs and *chambrées* were closed in the Var, and, out of 147 communes, 41 had councils dissolved and 44 had mayors dismissed. In the Pyrénées-Orientales, 68 councils were dismissed at the same time. The Church organized huge pilgrimages to Lourdes and Paray-le-Moniol in an attempt to rally the forces of Order. On 14 October, however, the republican victory of the previous year was repeated, one of the most significant turning-points in French political history. In January 1879, even the senate elections returned a republican majority. These victories were replicated at the local level, symbolized by the bust of Marianne being transferred from the premises of the club to the town hall. In the Ain, once the land of the *curé* of Ars, rural people clubbed together to buy copies of Renan's secular *Life of Jesus* and noisily commemorated the centenary of Voltaire's death in 1878. Elsewhere, across almost half the country, the Republic retained for some time its aura of instability and secularism: in the Vendée, it revivified a century of memories, while in the Calvados narrow republican electoral victories in 1876–81 were followed by a return to the parties of the right, albeit now within a republican spectrum.[30]

The electoral victories of 1876–7 were the strongest evidence for the claim of the 'opportunists' that, by reassuring the propertied classes and proceeding only with political reforms, they had avoided a reaction which might have resulted in a military coup in 1877 rather than another election. However, the political 'settlement' of 1877 was – in parts of the countryside as well as in cities – at the expense of the alienation of the left-wing of republicanism. The signatures of 33 men on a copy of Jules Guesde's socialist programme in the small Provençal town of Cuers in 1879 pointed to the develoment of a socialist electorate with arguably a very different agenda from the *démoc-socs* of 1851.[31]

While the rural response to the protracted crisis of 1868–77 was both more complex and volatile than once thought, many of the acute social tensions and sources of misery which underpinned the violent struggles of the Second Republic had dissipated. The exodus of the poorest sections of the rural community and the transition to market-oriented specialization had defused the explosive class conflicts of mid-century. The majority of rural people were committed to the Republic, but, except in specific areas of the south, this was a republicanism of small farmers, people proud of their economic independence and social dignity, for whom a democratic regime offered guarantees of gradual self-improvement and protection against a return of the time of the notables or the arrival of working-class collectivism. By the late 1860s, and more so by 1880, the countryside appeared to urban élites as a rustic haven from the menace of working-class communities rather than, as in 1851, the primary source of threats to power and property.

In this sense, Jean-François Millet's insistence on timeless rural virtues is most revealing. Millet had always repudiated a political reading of his paintings, though he had welcomed the Republic in 1848 and accepted the Legion of Honour in 1868. During the Second Republic the heavy, menacing lines of *The Winnower* and *The Sower* had outraged nervous notables while Ledru-Rollin bought the former and socialists acclaimed both paintings as expressing their values. By the 1860s, on the other hand, *The Angelus*, with its celebrated peasant couple deep in devotion before resuming honest toil, had begun its long celebration as the epitome of 'the world we have lost' and Millet's favourite biblical phrase: 'in the sweat of thy brow shalt thou eat bread'. In the aftermath of the Paris Commune, his *Peasant Family* captured what he and many of the urban middle class imagined country-folk to be: a sturdy, simple and honest couple grasp their farm tools while between them their child clutches her parents' legs, her arms extended as if to form a crucifix.

In a sense Millet was right: in the years between 1852 and 1880 rural France did indeed represent the peak of rural civilization. A rather more prosperous rural population continued to live within a rich variety of local cultures and ecologies. Their prosperity and changes coming from the outside gave them greater access to education, information and travel, while earlier assumptions about their own citizenship finally coincided with popular sovereignty, however constrained by male suffrage and political élites. At the same time, Millet's nostalgia is revealing: the seeds were sown for the destruction of a civilization which was to prove incompatible with the interrelated forces of state centralization and capitalism. The uniformity of institutional and educational structures and the lure of prosperity through market specialization and urban culture would undermine the local agrarian routines on which regional cultures and the complementarity of men's and women's work had been based, and would erode the variety of human and natural ecologies. This would be, happily, a gradual and incomplete process, but the onset of the long depression in French agriculture in the late 1870s would have a more rapid impact on the fragile prosperity of the countryside.

12

The Social History
of Ideas, 1850–1880:
'The Moralization of
the Masses?'

In 1861 the schoolteachers of lower Normandy declared that 'the population should read more: it should be diverted from certain immoral, revolutionary and socialist books which are passed from hand to hand'. Theirs was thus a double campaign: to encourage the reading of books and, at the same time, to ensure that the right books were being read.[1] All over France, teachers were having marked success in instructing children, especially boys, how to read: the number of totally illiterate conscripts declined from about 40 per cent in 1850 to 18 per cent in 1875, although as many again remained functionally illiterate. The issue was increasingly what people should read, and the teachers' zeal was matched by associations such as the *Société Franklin* and the *Ligue d'enseigne-ment*, which together urged the creation of school and public libraries. By 1870, 15,000 primary schools had tiny libraries of 50–100 books, paralleled by the remarkable surge in public libraries in these decades. Whereas in 1851 there had been 2,428 libraries outside Paris, by 1878 there were 5,086; apart from Brittany and the Massif Central, there was at least one library for every 7,500 people.

Who used these libraries and what did they read? Most readers were male, mainly students and white-collar workers. While women not in paid work accounted for only 10–20 per cent of users of city libraries in Rouen, Pau, Boulogne and Meaux, some women workers were among the wage-earners who comprised up to one-third of library users. On the other hand, clergy were virtually absent, having access to diocesan libraries well stocked with religious works which remained about 14 per cent of all books published. The liberal professions were wealthy enough to buy their own books or to belong to *cercles* with libraries. In these towns and other, smaller urban centres such as Sète (Hérault), Marieux (Somme) and Romilly (Aube), a predominantly petit-bourgeois reading public showed a minimal interest in religion, philosophy, economics, science and the fine arts. Instead, they demanded either history, geography and travel (15–35 per cent of loans), or novels (40–70 per cent).

These lending libraries and the mass production of cheap novels and news-papers flourished at the expense of the 3,000 pedlars who, at mid-century, had sold some nine million publications and images annually. These *colporteurs*, many from the Comminges region of the central Pyrenees, carried in their packs the cheap paperbacks of the *Bibliothèque bleue*: religious tales, catechisms, lives of the saints, practical almanacs, legends (*A Thousand and One Nights, Gargantua*), ribald stories (*The Art of Farting*), and Perrault's sanitized ver-sions of *Sleeping Beauty, Cinderella* and *Little Red Riding Hood*. Under the July Monarchy they had also carried Napoleonic iconography and army stories, but it was the use made of pedlars to carry *démoc-soc* literature after 1848 which moved Napoleon III to act against these free spirits who roamed the roads of rural France. By 1870 a combination of police harassment and competition had reduced their numbers to 500 and their yearly sales to two million volumes.

Their competition came from other sources of print media, especially nov-els and newspapers. Developing from the extraordinary success Eugène Sue's serialized novels had had in newspapers under the July Monarchy, cheaply-produced books flooded provincial France. After 1850, Sue's social criticism and romanticism had little appeal to a bourgeois and petit-bourgeois readership in towns, though it remained popular in the countryside. According to prefects' responses to a ministerial survey in 1866, the popular literature of the provinces was a mixture of tales of the First Empire, obscene and illegal books, long-established classics (*Paul et Virginie, Gil Blas*, the *Fables* of Florian and La Fontaine, the latter also having been the largest seller in 1815–50), and the Bonapartism of Dumas's *Comte de Monte-Cristo*. Above all, the years from 1865 to 1880 belonged to the joint authors Erckmann-Chatrian and to Jules Verne. In the 1870s, Verne's travel novels – *Around the World in Eighty Days, Five Weeks in a Balloon, 20,000 Leagues under the Sea* – poured from the presses in editions of 30,000 (a book's average edition under the Restoration had been 1,500). The great appeal of Verne was his skilful blending of escapism and travel, as in Defoe's fiction but now making use of new or futuristic technol-ogy; unlike Dumas, his stories extolled the virtues of northern Europeans, and were openly racist towards non-whites, misogynist and anti-Semitic. On the other hand, *Le Conscrit de 1813* and *L'Ami Fritz*, by Erckmann-Chatrian, revelled in a bucolic Rhineland of harmony between Jews and Christians, where the virtues of rural and artisanal independence expressed themselves in anti-German patriotism.

Most of all, working people in town and country turned to the cheap daily press. The development of a mass newspaper readership had really begun with Emile Girardin's *La Presse* in 1836, but changes to printing technology – responding to as well as creating popular demand – enabled businessmen to reach a larger clientèle. Jean-Baptiste Dumay, son of a Le Creusot miner who had died seven months before his son's birth, recalled often being in trouble for avoiding school, but 'This passion for missing school was caused by my love of reading. I liked everything: old newspapers, history, novels, travel literature.'[2] By 1869 Polydor Millaud's *Le Petit Journal* was selling 260,000 copies daily, with a combination of scandal, 'human interest' stories, titillating details of crimes, and 'non-political' news, all for five centimes. The early Third Republic saw a further spurt in newspaper sales, aided by the easing of censorship laws in 1881. By 1880, 60 Parisian dailies were selling 1.95 million copies, provincial newspapers well over half a million; significantly, one household in four or five was buying a Parisian paper. For the blind, too, access to print was seen as vital: the technique of Louis Braille (1795–1852), son of a harness-maker from the Seine-et-Marne, was promoted energetically after 1850 and adopted by a world congress in 1878.[3]

To what extent did the popular literature of these decades express the morality, attitudes and politics of its readership? One of the central difficulties in writing the social history of ideas, especially of *mentalités*, is that the inevitable distance in time, space and culture between the historian and the past is here extended by the 'silence' of most people in conventional, written historical sources. Instead, central questions – Which ideas were circulating? Which were listened to? Where did they come from? – are answered for historians by individuals separated from working people of town and country by a gulf of class, and usually of ethnic background and gender as well. The rapidly expanding bureaucracy of nineteenth-century France collected an enormous body of information it deemed important – economic statistics, landholding records, censuses and police reports – but very little of this material relates directly to how working people perceived their world. Instead, it tells us a great deal about the *mentalités* of its compilers.[4]

The Ministries of the Interior, Justice and War, which were all charged with policing ideas and on whose archives historians depend, were organized hierarchically in an urban network descending from Paris to regional and departmental capitals, subprefectures and cantonal centres. Their bureaucrats assumed that ideas were disseminated or diffused in the same way that they transmitted or received instructions. Since historians of ideas necessarily rely on the records compiled by this bureaucratic culture – urban, hierarchical and élite – it has proven difficult to avoid its assumptions about the unilinear, hierarchical diffusion of ideas. Hence the social history of ideas has been written as the 'progress' of schooling and the printed word brought to the masses from above. This diffusion or 'trickling down' model necessarily sees resistance to the values of urban social élites as a sign of 'backwardness', as if books, newspapers and schools (or railways, banks and markets) were a general 'good'. It also misses the ways in which working people of town and country took the initiative in maintaining or changing their own cultures. The increasing sales of books in general retail stores in villages too small to sustain a bookshop was as much a sign of popular demand as it was of changes coming from outside. A social history of ideas then needs to understand attitudes, ideologies or *mentalités* as formed by a complex interplay between historically conditioned beliefs, a changing world and competing new ideas.[5]

Further, because historians most commonly work with the printed word in an urban, bourgeois culture, they have tended to confuse the history of what writers published with the social history of ideas. On the contrary, reading was for all French people a sporadic activity. Nor should it be assumed that the books and newspapers bought or borrowed necessarily influenced how people saw the world around them or even represented what they would have preferred to read. The library of one Parisian carpenter included devotional books, a dictionary, two cookbooks, and books on geography, architecture and French history, but we cannot know which were read most avidly and for what purpose.[6] Similarly, there were often important continuities of *mentalité* under-lying evident changes in reading matter. Just as peasants under the *ancien régime* gathered by the hearth to escape with the *Bibliothèque bleue* from the daily routines of unremitting toil into a medieval world of heroism and the supernatural, so the reading public of the 1870s looked to tales of the Pacific or to a fabulous future of technology and travel. Such *mentalités* – described by Michel Vovelle as the 'collective unconscious' – were resistant to change and are particularly difficult for the historian to discern. The social history of ideas can often do little more than point to trends in reading habits and literary themes while remaining cautious about the extent to which they were moulding or reflecting popular ideas about the world.

Two broad suggestions may be made about the print culture which people bought or borrowed. First, by the 1870s, the dominant themes in novels and the press were republican in the place they gave to Gambetta's 'new society' (*nouvelles couches sociales*), but were also impregnated with the expansionist, often racist ideology of the Third Republic. Above all, they projected a national culture which was in reality bourgeois and Parisian. The pedlars, too, had disseminated a French and written culture, but one which had been readily absorbed into the oral cultures of rural France. Insofar as rural and urban work-ing people read or listened to the mass literature of the 1870s, they were being confronted with a pervasive ideology which was predicated on the desirability of national solidarity, on national, racial and gender stereotypes, and on the honest simplicity of provincial folk.

Secondly, despite the class, regional and gender variations in degrees of con-tact with the written word, the decades 1850–80 represent the triumph of print in the social history of ideas. In these years a massive increase occurred in the production, distribution and consumption of books and newspapers, interde-pendent with the changing techniques and imperatives of a capitalist economy, and with mass literacy. These changes also underpinned an important shift in the social history of reading, for the popular practice of collective reading in cafés and *chambrées*, and at *veillées* gradually gave way to individual, private read-ing: a different relationship between reader and text. In the process, a literary, urban and bourgeois national culture gradually diluted the diversity of regional, oral and working-class cultures.[7]

The nature of the print culture of these decades may also have been both a reflection and a partial explanation of changing ideas and assumptions about the twin processes of external and internal colonization: the acceleration of, first, French colonialism in Africa, Asia and the Pacific, and, secondly, of the *franci-sation* of ethnic minorities.

First, the military defeat of 1870–1 seems to have led to a shift in popular attitudes towards France's overseas empire. Colonial expansion became more purposive than the earlier mix of missionary, military and trade activity. The French naval detachment which took formal possession of New Caledonia in 1853 with hopes of making it 'the Emporium of the Pacific' was certain that

Kanaks were barbarous savages, treacherous and cruel. This was coupled with an admiration for their physical prowess and bushcraft, perhaps drawn from images of warrior societies in the popular novels of Fenimore Cooper (in the 1850s, too, anthropology began to be taught at the Musée National in Paris and the Paris Anthropological Society was founded). This residual admiration was shattered by the rising of 1878, leaving 200 whites and 1,200 Kanaks dead. Among the French occupiers of New Caledonia in 1878 were 4,000 Communards. One of them, Louise Michel, who compiled one of the first collections of Kanak legends, was aware that, as in Paris in 1871, the burning issue was 'liberty and dignity': 'The Kanakas were seeking the same liberty we had sought in the Commune. Let me say only that my red scarf, the red scarf of the Commune that I had hidden from every search, was divided in two pieces one night. Two Kanakas, before going to join the insurgents against the whites, had come to say goodbye to me.' Michel's regret, that 'not all of [her] comrades approved of their rebellion as strongly as [she] did', is an understatement, for most of her fellow-prisoners were enrolled in military units against the Kanaks, and this proof of their commitment to 'civilized' values was an important element in their amnesty in 1880.[8]

The second process, by which ethnic and linguistic minorities in France were incorporated into national administrative and cultural structures, was far more gradual and subtle. The decades after mid-century represented an important acceleration of *francisation* from below, whereby members of minority cultures came to accept, consciously or not, the relevance of French culture as well as national institutions. The increasing centralization and presence of structures of administration, religion and education had slowly transformed collective consciousness of the legitimacy of the nation-state, accelerated by the great political mobilizations after 1789, 1830 and 1848. By 1850, however, ethnic minorities had still not learned to look disparagingly at their language or the 'provincialism' of their values and lifestyles. After 1850 there was a much more concerted attempt to teach ethnic minorities to speak and think in the language and values of the urban middle classes. All children were educated to see themselves as situated within a shared French cultural environment imbued with meanings of 'progress' and 'civilization' which inevitably associated minority languages and cultures with religious superstition and a feudal, 'backward' past.

The impetus for *francisation* did not come simply from above, but just as powerfully came from an acceptance among minorities of French institutions and the very concept of 'nation' itself. This acceptance, already apparent during the French Revolution, was accelerated by the political passions of right and left during the Second Republic. Many Occitans, Provençals, Catalans and others had used their own language and culture to make political statements. This was rarely combined with any conscious statement of the relationship between their ethno-cultural identity and their fervent attachment to French political movements. On the contrary, they assumed compelling reasons why their interests would best be protected by identifying them with those of other republicans, royalists and Bonapartists across the country. In the process, access to French language and culture could become tantamount to 'progress', as the mayor of Gignac (Hérault) assumed in July 1851 when criticizing the local curate for using an Occitan catechism: 'some people think that your use of this language is to indirectly prove to the region how backward it still is'. Conscious defence of a local language could seem nostalgic and politically reactionary: the Provençal Félibrige was founded by disenchanted republicans and clerical conservatives whose anti-Jacobinism masked the absence of an economic or political strategy for an autonomous homeland.[9]

Francisation was thus a process which occurred from below – a change in self-identity – as much as it was the result of the integrating policies of the State and of the capitalist economy. Minorities could also manoeuvre for advantage within state structures. In the Cerdagne (or Cerdanya), a mountain valley high in the eastern Pyrenees, the arbitrary 1659 border between France and Spain across the valley floor did not dissolve deeper links of family and economic structures and culture. However, by the time border disputes between France and Spain were finally settled at the Treaty of Bayonne in 1866–8, Catalans in the French Cerdagne had fought long battles with Spanish communities over land and resource rights and had come to see themselves as French Catalans. A primary school inspector had complained in 1849 that the Catalan 'believes, in good faith, that he forms a people apart, a superior people who in his mind he places above all others'. By the 1870s there would be a greater acceptance of also being French; but this would not totally destroy pride in 'difference' or personal ties (migration, family, political sanctuary) which cut across the border.[10]

From this perspective it could be argued that the 1870s represented the victory of nationalism in ideas of self-identity and assumptions about the nation-state and its prerogatives. Paradoxically, the poverty of many non-French speaking regions would attract young men into the policing bureaucracies of the French state at home and abroad. The schoolroom played an important if indirect role in this victory. Even if a majority of French people commonly used another language or dialect of French, there was by 1880 a near-universal acceptance of the value of primary education in that language.

Love of *la patrie*, the nation and social harmony were not the only virtues schools sought to inculcate. Teachers and their texts taught the values of the family as the basic unit of society, of hard work, cleanliness and politeness, order and self-discipline. Under the Third Republic in particular, there was particular concern with the possibilities of social mobility as the reward for these virtues in a democratic republic. Above all, boys and girls were given potent models of the natural gender characteristics of their sex. Two texts by Zelma Carraud – *Maurice ou le travail* and *La Petite Jeanne ou le devoir* – were adopted for use in 20 departments after their publication in 1852–3. These stereotyped boys as hard-working, loyal, honest, supportive of their employers and 'progress', and committed to the family; girls were similarly shown to be devoted to the family and hard work, but also domestic in their concerns, clean, cheerful and devoted mothers. In other texts for teachers and children – such as Marie Curo's *Etudes morales et religieuses ou éducation pratique des jeunes filles* (1860) and Laurent de Jussieu's *Histoire et causeries à l'usage des jeunes filles chrétiennes* (1856) – girls at both state and church schools were taught that the essential feminine graces were sweetness, modesty and love of order. In Curo's book, the precocious, simpering, joking Louise was contrasted with Cécile: polite, clean, cautious, sweet-natured and somewhat naïve. Mme Paul Caillaud's *Résumé d'éducation pratique* (1873) drew similar conclusions through posing to girls a series of questions: What is the first thing you notice when you enter a house? What do you think of the mistress of the house if everything is in confusion? What is meant by the words: order leads to God?

It may be that there were huge numbers of parents and children in France who accepted such values as natural because they coincided with their own. However, the evidence of these school texts points to another fundamental, perhaps insuperable, problem in the history of ideas: to what extent were such manuals descriptive of widely-shared assumptions about desirable personal and gender-role characteristics, even of behaviour itself? Or were they rather prescriptions for behaviour which particular élites sought to inculcate precisely because it was not common? What did boys and girls make of such texts? One girl, Netty de Boys, recalled of the young Abbé Dupanloup: 'Monseigneur found nothing wrong with me showing passion towards people and things that pleased me. I repeated to him something often said to me about this: "One must try to calm one's passions". He replied firmly: "Never".'[11] Unfortunately, Netty's recollections are a rare example of the young's responses to their socialization.

The values within school texts were those of the ruling bourgeois culture of the decades after 1850. As Jacques Donzelot has argued, family structures were not simply a response to patterns of survival, but were also a matter of constant political intrusion and conflict because of assumptions about their relationship with social and political order. For example, the Empire placed greater stress on the role of the mother and her relatives in child-rearing: in 1857 maternal grandparents were given legal rights of access to the child if the mother died, and unmarried mothers were given state assistance in 1869. There is abundant evidence of changes in attitudes towards children in bourgeois families across the nineteenth century: couples had fewer children and women in particular devoted more time to their nurturing before the age of seven (deemed to be the age of 'reason'). In *Les Pères et les enfants au XIXe siècle*, Ernest Legouvé, also an acknowledged authority on girls' education, encouraged fathers, too, to show greater love, to use the familiar *tu* with their children, and to enjoy family leisure. (Christmas trees first became popular in middle-class families during the Second Empire.)[12]

These values, whether taught in schools or advocated by experts and the State, were essentially those of the bourgeois family; the working people of town and country socialized their children within different contexts of work and household. They did not need to be taught about childhood by their betters, as historians of the family have often assumed. If the meaning of childhood and ways of expressing affectionate parent-child relations were specific to time, place and class, their existence and importance were universal. None of Millet's rural paintings are so evocative in this regard as *First Steps*, *The Child's Candle* and *The Knitting Lesson*. Bourgeois child-rearing sought to identify and develop those qualities which would form proper men and women; but in the country-side, an identifiable *'société enfantine'* of work and games endured through these decades. Bourgeois families may have been encouraged to *tutoyer*, but in the

Aveyron this had long been the practice. In southern Anjou, on the other hand, couples who had used *tu* adopted *vous* after marriage as a sign of mutual respect.[13]

Legouvé's tract on the role of the father and school texts on ideal behaviour for boys and girls were part of a wider discourse within bourgeois society. One of the most striking elements of the social history of ideas in the years 1850–80 is the production and popularity of manuals on domestic propriety and sex roles, both reflecting the bourgeois world and responding to its anxieties. No doubt, as Peter Gay has insisted, many bourgeois marriages were happy, companionable and erotic. Jules Ferry himself, who sought 'to realize humanity without God and without king', was so distraught at a failed romance that he wished for the faith to allow him to become a monk; instead his sensibility focused on his wife Eugénie, crediting her 'sweet influence' for his 'entire philosophy'. Nevertheless, at the very time when the power of the bourgeoisie had never been more wide-ranging, the sales of marriage manuals suggests deep cultural fears and uncertainties. At the core of this social and sexual anxiety was the discordance between the public values of meritocracy, social mobility and individual work and achievement, and a private world which was based on contrary values of demanding sex-role expectations and unequal opportunities.[14]

The watchword of the discourse about ideal social relations was therefore 'order': what were those behaviours which bourgeois men and women should adopt if they were to create domestic harmony and social order? Could the moderate virtues of domesticity create political stability? Marie Dubreuil de Saint-Germain's best-selling *La Femme au XIXe siècle* (1858) extolled the orderly virtues of the bourgeois woman, 'the poetry of the hearth'. Her husband, Auguste Romieu, had 30 years earlier elaborated similar virtues in his *Code civil, manuel complet de la politesse, du ton, des manières, de la bonne compagnie* (1828), which went through 14 editions by 1853 (in 1851 he had also called for Louis Napoleon to become 'a total dictator' to banish '*le spectre rouge*': see Chapter 9. The emperor rewarded him by making him director of the Beaux-Arts in 1852). This example suggests a certain continuity in bourgeois concerns from the 1830s; indeed, in 1860, J. B. F. Descuret articulated a *juste milieu* of the passions, recalling Guizot's *juste milieu* of politics:

Vices or defects	*Virtues or good qualities*	*Vices or defects*
Violence	Strength	Weakness
Anger	Calm	Apathy
Temerity	Courage	Fear
Turbulence	Activity	Nonchalance
Envy	Emulation	Indifference
Prodigality	Economy	Avarice
Study mania	Love of study	Disgust for study
Fanaticism	Religious faith	Incredulity

If Descuret's chart had included sexual passions, no doubt a healthy, procreative heterosexuality would have been centred between lust and impotence. A plethora of marriage manuals for men written by doctors – such as Belliol's

Conseil aux hommes affaiblis, Rauland's *Le Livre des époux* and Roubaud's *Traité de l'impuissance* – sought to resolve their sexual unhappiness, mocked by Zola in *Nana*: '*the poem of male desires*, the great lever that moves the world. There is only arse and religion.'

In one of the best-selling books in nineteenth-century France, Auguste Debay's *Hygiène et physiologie du mariage* (1848; 172 reprints by 1883), 'moderate' sexual pleasure within marriage was seen as essential and desirable for physical well-being and social order. Women were warned that 'the peculiar fancy that some wives occasionally experience' (to lie on top of their husbands) 'disturbs the natural order', and that masturbation would make them anaemic. In acceptance of man's 'natural brutality', they were advised to submit and 'simulate the spasm of pleasure'; men, on the other hand, were urged to use 'caresses and delicious preludes' and to respect their wife's desires lest she seek a lover. Concerns about a proper sexual order recurred in manuals across the century, but they were accentuated after 1870 by public debate linking the military defeat to a lack of virility and numerous healthy offspring. Impotence and masturbation were problems enough (the manuals by Tissot and Rozier on masturbation among men and women were regularly reprinted), but homosexuality in particular was seen as a degenerating psychological weakness due to a lack of 'normal' urges. An excess of such urges also exposed men to the increasing incidence of venereal diseases spread by unscrupulous working-class prostitutes such as Nana, 'who [was] not on heat and [made] fun of the dogs who chase[d] her'. Dr Louis Fiaux blamed the sexual 'passivity' of bourgeois women for their men being forced to frequent diseased brothels (though it seemed natural enough to him that most boys of 17 years had also been). In the literary world of Flaubert, Baudelaire, Daudet and the Goncourts, as well as Zola, morbid fears of sexual licence and physical decay through syphilis added to their social pessimism and alienation.[15]

Fears of domestic and public instability focused on the link between prostitution, the Paris Commune and women's alleged propensity to commit 'crimes of passion' (even though the number of women prisoners had fallen from 17 to 13 per cent of the total by the end of the 1870s). The mass-circulation press and 'men of science' became fascinated and horrified by the female criminal. In part this was a reaction to the role of women in the Commune and the feminist movement of the 1870s, but it also reflected the attempts of criminologists and psychiatrists to stake a claim to professional expertise. In a hotly-debated pamphlet, 'Women who Kill, Women who Vote', the younger Alexandre Dumas called for greater 'protection' (that is, control) of women lest they take revenge on men through crime, the challenging of their natural roles, or even the vote. Women charged with crimes were alternately seen as fatally vulnerable to their emotions, as inherently dangerous because of their vengeful perversity, or as part of a *malaise du temps* in the troubled world of the 1870s. Paradoxically – like peasants resorting to the myth of the simple rustic in courts of law – women charged with crimes of passion were most likely to be acquitted if they entered into the role of the dependent female enslaved by her emotions.[16]

Press interest in women's passions was linked to on-going changes to the classifying concerns of medicine, especially psychiatry. 'Hysteria' became a favoured diagnosis, used for only seven of 648 cases of insanity among women in 1841–2 but, under Jean-Martin Charcot, chief physician at the Salpêtrière prison hospital, for 89 of 500 cases in 1882–3 (the corresponding figures for men were nil and two). In these decades, too, Dr Eugène Dally argued that all criminals were mentally ill, and therefore in need of his help, and Paul Broca applied the principles of phrenology to classify the criminal anatomy. The rise to acceptability of psychiatry, recognized in the creation of a chair in the Faculty of Medicine in 1876, was part of an on-going secularization of the explanation of crime and mental illness against the claims of the Church that these represented sins or spiritual crises.[17]

The resurgent feminism of the 1870s was integral to this discourse. The Paris Commune, like the revolutions of 1789, 1830 and 1848, facilitated an expression of feminist ideas, linked to the political left through individuals such as Louise Michel, Andrée Léo and Paule Mink, and organizations such as the *Société de la revendication du droit des femmes*. Unlike the collapse of feminism with the re-establishment of political order after earlier revolutions, the 1870s witnessed a continuing feminist organization through Léon Richer and Maria Deraismes. In 1878, to coincide with the Republic's Industrial Exhibition, they organized a feminist congress bringing together women from 11 countries; at this congress the more radical Hubertine Auclert and others split with them on the issue of women's suffrage. Unlike their predecessors of 1789–1851, most feminists in the 1870s distanced themselves from collective action and messianic liberation, stressing instead gradualism and women's respectability in order to attract male political support. Feminists campaigned for civil rights, equality of education and opportunity, and the right to divorce; like left-wing men, they were wary of advocating rights to contraception and abortion in a climate of concern about the falling birth-rate and because they were seen only as individual, partial solutions to wider social problems.[18]

The same hierarchies expressed by Napoleon's prefects in their surveys of the French people were reiterated in 1861 by Paul Broca, founder of the Paris Anthropological Society, in his (radically misplaced) certainties about brain size and intelligence: 'in general, the brain is larger in mature adults than in the elderly, in men than in women, in eminent men than in men of mediocre talent, in superior races than in inferior races'.[19] This was a similar belief to the explicitly racist ideology formulated in the 1850s by the legitimist Arthur de Gobineau (whom de Tocqueville had appointed his secretary when Minister of Foreign Affairs in 1849) in his *Essai sur l'inégalité des races humaines.*

Printed ideas in the decades after 1850 thus presented urban and rural working people and their children with potent messages about the nature and role of the nation-state and the separate spheres and appropriate behaviour of males and females. Insofar as the ideas of bourgeois, chiefly Parisian élites had a resonance among those of a different class and culture, this was most likely to be the case where economic change was also eroding an older household economy. As work opportunities declined for married women because of industrial concentration and agricultural specialization, the bourgeois model of the family became more relevant, even desirable. French delegates to the first congress of the International Working Men's Association in 1866 divided sharply over women's right to do paid work, but the majority accepted women's 'natural' role as in the home. Economic change also eroded the seasonal work routines of polycultural agriculture and with them the *raison d'être* of particular cultural rituals, even ancient beliefs about the world. For example, in the impoverished area of the Dombes, north of Lyon, the cult of Saint Guinefort – the 'Holy Greyhound' who had saved a child's life and whose shrine henceforth was a place of pilgrimage for parents with sickly children – had endured from the thirteenth century, and perhaps many centuries earlier. One reason for this was that the stagnant fish-ponds in the region posed a threat to child health: life expectancy in the 1840s was still only 23 years and 90 per cent of conscripts were rejected for health reasons. There was an intellectual scuffle between the Church and secularists over the cult in the late 1870s, but the main reason for the collapse of the cult was that, in the decades after 1850, many ponds were drained and infant health improved. Saint Guinefort had fewer sick children to cure.[20]

Urban élites with secular views of 'progress' felt no regrets about the passing of such quaint 'superstitions', the inevitable price to be paid for what they called 'the moralization of the masses'. During the Second Empire a linked concern about public hygiene and social order received its expression in extensive urban demolition and reconstruction, of which Paris is only the best-known example. The provision of sewers and running water met bourgeois concerns for the cleansing properties of water, reflected also in the construction of more public baths and the provision of showers for soldiers. After the defeat by Prussia, a new urgency was added: personal cleanliness became the mark of a good school-child and caring parents, and therefore almost patriotic. Pasteur's own outrage at 1871 – 'Hatred for Prussia! Vengeance! Vengeance!' – drove his concern for agricultural improvement as well as for his microbiology popularized in the 1880s.[21]

The 'moralization' of the French masses after the social upheavals of the Second Republic and 1871 extended into reforming personal behaviour towards animals, children and health. Following the banning in 1848 of the weekly animal fights on the place du Combat in Paris, the cavalry officer Grammont introduced in 1850 the first law against cruelty to animals in towns, also hoping thereby to lessen the taste for bloodthirsty revolt. The *Société protectrice des animaux*, founded in 1845 and with 3,432 members by 1880, took as its motto: 'For the moralization of the labouring classes, for social progress, and for international union.' It extended Grammont's concerns to the countryside, campaigning against the slow-bleeding of pigs (to produce a better black-pudding), the torturing of animals for sport or their ill-treatment at work: 'for if brutality leads to crime, gentleness of character leads to virtue, resignation, fraternity'. These concerns coincided with a proliferation in middle-class families of domestic pets, especially dogs (for whom railway companies provided special carriages). The *Société protectrice de l'enfance* was established later, in 1866, and by 1882 had 3,486 members in more than 150 towns and villages; in 1872 it proclaimed that if France had had a child protection law, Alsace-Lorraine would not have been lost. One of its prime targets was 'the absurd, barbarous custom' of giving babies 'to a fat, peasant woman ... whose character and morality are unknown' (one of its presidents was Dr J.-B. Roussel, who successfully proposed laws controlling wet-nursing and outlawing drunkennness). The *Société contre l'abus du tabac*, established in 1868 to further 'moral order', succeeded by 1878 in having smoking prohibited, at least formally, in post offices.[22]

The changing urban and political culture of the decades after 1850 was reflected in the creative arts. The most important shift in the social history of painting in the nineteenth century was the twin demise of the *Académie des beaux-arts* as the official arbiter of taste and of the epic religious and historical paintings commissioned by clerical and monarchical patrons. Their place was taken by smaller, cheaper genre paintings and landscapes purchased in huge numbers by the middle classes. The Minister of State, Achille Fould, regretted the demise of 'the lofty and pure regions of the beautiful' (religious and historical paintings and moral allegory) in competition with 'the servile imitations of the least elevated offerings of nature', but, like novelists and journalists, painters needed to survive in a world of new technologies and the development of a mass bourgeois market for *objets d'art*. By the time the Louvre was completed in 1857, the political economy of the Second Empire had reached the world of painting: exhibitions were now to be a marketplace in a privately-run section of a new *Palais de l'Industrie* on the Champs-Elysées, with high admission prices keeping the masses at bay except on Sundays. The government of the Second Empire continued to sponsor the Salon and to include art as part of the Industrial Exhibitions of 1855 and 1867, alongside 'wheelbarrows and warming-pans' as one disgusted critic lamented.[23]

The brilliant stars of the literary and artistic world of nineteenth-century France have long diverted attention away from the galaxy of which they were part. The history of ideas in the creative arts has typically been formulated in terms of the continuing triumph of an avant-garde over moribund 'official' or establishment writing and painting; the shattering of romantic illusions by the civil war of June 1848 has long been posited as the great cultural watershed of the nineteenth century, with its consequent social realism (exemplified in Flaubert's sardonic view of the revolutionaries of 1848 in his 1869 novel, *L'Éducation sentimentale*). New approaches to the social history of art have tended to dissolve such neat distinctions. Not only did artists of whatever 'style' commonly side with governments against popular political challenges, but they moved readily between different styles and inhabited a similar milieu. The most sought-after artists after 1850 were the now-forgotten men Bouguereau, Gérôme, Cabanel and Baudry. While Manet's *Déjeuner sur l'herbe* was provoking outrage or laughter at the *Salon des refusés* in 1863, at the official Salon Cabanel's *Birth of Venus* was triumphing; indeed, Napoleon III bought it for his personal collection. Manet's response for the 1865 Salon, *Olympia*, was similarly shocking, but once again for its contemporary, unsettling reality rather than its style; indeed, he and Bouguereau, an immensely successful painter who once complained: 'I lose five francs every time I have to go and piss', both turned to Raphael and Botticelli for inspiration in their attempts to emulate Cabanel in 1868. When Manet sought official recognition, he successfully approached Cabanel, whose *Birth of Venus* has long seemed to historians the epitome of Second-Empire, tawdry mediocrity. Similarly, impressionism, which had been regarded as shocking in 1873 (when Monet, Renoir, Sisley, Cézanne and Pissarro were rejected from the Salon), was acceptable by the time Manet finally won his medal on Cabanel's recommendation in 1881. In any case, the roots of this style lay in early Dutch and English landscape painting rather than the genius of the avant-garde.

The themes and styles of painting remained a political concern for successive regimes. The Third Republic saw the popularization of 'realism' as a genuinely democratic education. The official report on the Exhibition of 1878 recommended: 'The present government, like that of the First Republic, must regard art as an especially powerful way towards national education and industrial prosperity.... It is simply a matter of propagating art, of cultivating the taste of the people for it, and of putting it in the service of democracy.' The 1878 Exhibition was a major ideological statement of a republican élite confident of the future following the electoral victories of 1877. Its design and exhibits were to be based on competition, in the words of the *Almanach parisien*, 'to bring to this national enterprise the tribute of all the intelligences and talents'. Deliberately larger, 'more grandiose and brilliant' than its 1867 predecessor, it would attract visitors from all over the world to see 'the superiority which, ever since the great century of Louis XIV and Colbert, distinguishes all French products.... And what will make an immense moral impression is that this France, this Paris, that people expected to see in a state of collapse, will be found brilliant in their habitual *éclat*, rich, industrious, more peaceful than ever under the republican regime.'

Doriot's 1880 bust of the Republic, chosen for government buildings, idealized the values of the bourgeois republican élite: this fully-clothed, serene Marianne was crowned with a star and her headband bore the words 'Honour and the Motherland'. Across her breastplate were medallions inscribed Agriculture, Trade, Fine Arts, Education, Justice, Shipping, Science, Industry. This sedate, industrious figure looked back to 1789 rather than 1792 and looked forward to social harmony rather than to social radicalism.

Similar assumptions about progress, science and national destiny were expressed in the first editorial of the major periodical of French history, the *Revue historique*, founded by Gabriel Monod in 1876. Like its counterparts in Britain, Germany and the United States, the new journal celebrated the virtues of secular reason, of history as a science: 'we demand from our contributors strictly scientific methods of exposition, with each assertion accompanied by proof, by source references and quotations'. At the same time, however, this supposedly objective science promoted an ideology of nation and progress: 'we can give to our country the unity and moral strength she needs by revealing her historical traditions and, at the same time, the transformations these traditions have undergone'.[24]

The triumph of the Third Republic was symbolized in 1876–80 by the coincidence of Pierre Larousse's 20,700-page *Grand dictionnaire universel*, official celebrations of the centenary of the deaths of Voltaire and Rousseau, the Industrial Exhibition, and the celebration of the first official Bastille Day in 1880. However, just as the proliferation of professional advice on gender roles, education and 'the moralization of the masses' was prescriptive of orderly behaviour rather than descriptive of a unity of values across French society, so the triumph of the Republic failed to silence opposing ideas about politics and society. As during the Second Republic, the symbolic detail of statues of Marianne represented fundamental divisions among republicans. The more spontaneous reproductions of Marianne among rural and urban working people continued to carry the slogans and symbols of the revolutionary tradition. In particular, the Phrygian cap summarized the opposition of the popular and social against the bourgeois and moderate Republic, as on Bastille Day in 1880, when police removed Phrygian caps from flagpoles. Even decoration of the body was used to make statements about politics, as well as personal virtues and attachments. In 1881 a doctor studied the tattoos on 378 prisoners in military jails: of 1333 tattoos, 344 were decorative and historical emblems, 260 metaphors (such as pierced hearts), 149 military emblems, 111 inscriptions (one, on a forehead, was 'Martyr of Liberty'), 98 occupational emblems, and 91 political and religious emblems (including 34 busts of the Republic; significantly, all of these carried the Phrygian cap).[25]

Inevitably, the bitter disappointments of the 1870s disillusioned many workers about the possibilities of social transformation through producers' cooperatives and democratic republicanism. Workers' congresses in Lyon, Marseille and Le Havre in 1878–80 heard calls for support for Jules Guesde's *Parti ouvrier*, founded in October 1877 with support from the militant textile workers of Artois, to focus instead on a political strategy for the revolutionary seizure of power. At the same time, despair about the efficacy of cooperatives convinced many workers that trade unions were the surest way to defend living standards, and by 1882 some 206 had been formed. The workers congress of 1878 in Lyon heard Marie Finet argue that women 'should work in order to be free, to be independent … to be men's equals'. The delegates applauded, then reaffirmed their opposition to equal pay and, significantly, argued for the family wage (and 'separate spheres') on the grounds that most female workplaces were 'industrial hells', a description with which their wives and daughters would no doubt have agreed. The bloody repression of 1871 created splits and profound ambivalences in the labour movement: juxtaposed with a commitment to defending the rights guaranteed under a republic was a deep class antipathy and political frustration, dubbed the 'internal exile' of the working class. Others, such as Norbert Truquin, chose external exile: after involvement in the Lyon Commune and subsequent imprisonment, he despaired of the possibilities of radical change in France and emigrated to join socialist agricultural colonies in Argentina and Paraguay.[26]

It was not only militants among the working class who failed to share the optimism of republican élites. Among conservatives, the Paris Commune had an impact similar to that of the June 1848 insurrection; this time, however, the temporary success of a socialist alternative generated longer-lasting hostility to working-class radicalism. After all, Archbishop Affre had been accidentally shot during the June 1848 civil war, but his successor Darboy had been deliberately executed by the Communards. The Pope, who denounced the Communards as 'men escaped from hell', was joined by Ernest Renan, author of a secularist *Life of Jesus* in 1863, who now regarded democracy as the source of all France's ills. Hippolyte Taine, a liberal in 1848, was impelled to investigate this source in his *Origins of Contemporary France* (1876), in which the revolutionary crowds of 1789 were dismissed as 'the dregs of society'. Taine's horror at the role of working women in 1871 was reproduced in his description of the women of the October Days in 1789:

> washerwomen, beggars, shoeless women, fishwives enlisted in the last few days with payments in cash ... porters' wives, seamstresses, housewives, and even women of the bourgeoisie. Join with these vagrants, tramps, bandits, thieves, all these dregs that are piled on top of each other in Paris and float to the surface with every violent jolt ... this is the refuse of the street that swirls back and forth with the popular current.

Similarly, the punitive instincts of the men of Order in the National Assembly worked to reclaim the urban space temporarily occupied by the workers of the suburbs. The Hôtel de Ville and the Vendôme Column were rebuilt in exactly the same style, as if the Commune had never happened. In the heart of left-wing Montmartre, the massive white basilica of the Sacré-Coeur was constructed in 'expiation' of the Commune's 'crimes', despite the opposition of the local community. Even the poet Paul Verlaine, a former Communard, turned to clerical reaction, describing Marianne as a 'trollop':

> In the flower of her youth she was a bold young hussy ...
> But now she is a garrulous crone with thin hair and no teeth ...
> Let her be hanged, so that we can see her crazy cross-shaped dance,
> Horizontal in life and vertical in death![27]

The decades after 1848 had a similar effect on Frédéric Le Play, regarded as one of the 'founding fathers' of sociology and admired by social historians for the mass of information he and his followers systematically compiled on urban and rural families in Europe. Himself from a petit-bourgeois background, Le Play had declared himself a 'socialist' in 1848 and joined enthusiastically in the work of the Luxembourg Commission. His subsequent horror at the upsurge of rural radicalism in 1849 attracted him to the paternalistic authority of Louis Napoleon and provided the impulse to undertake the family monographs which would reveal to him the causes of the erosion of patriarchy in the family and politics. He described his idea of ordered, prosperous societies:

> each individual conforms to the duties of subordination fixed by custom. The son obeys the father, the wife the husband, the servant the master, the worker the employer, the soldier the officer, the citizen the civil authorities. All of them, moreover, submit to the united authority of God and the sovereign ... [Since 1789] the constitution of France has rested on three false dogmas: systematic liberty, providential equality and the right to revolt.[28]

The Commune was the affirmation of everything Le Play had feared.

Such a view of the world recalls de Bonald's attack on the divorce law in 1816 (see Chapter 5) and points to a continuity in conservative political thought. Le Play had much in common with the legitimists, who were arguably the dominant group within the Party of Order in both 1850 and 1873 but whose dreams of a Bourbon restoration foundered both times on the comte de Chambord's refusal to compromise with parliamentary democracy and on the divisions within their own constituency about the form a restored monarchy should take. While the legitimist élite recognized that the *ancien régime* was gone forever, its ideology continued to emphasize the need for a landed élite at the head of decentralized institutions as the only remedy for political centralization, godless education, rural exodus and urbanization, and creeping socialism.

The Catholic church's active support for the party of Order under the Second Republic had reinforced old lines of hostility between the clergy and republicans. Legitimist clergy blamed the Second Empire for dashing hopes of a reconciliation with Rome and for permitting the increasing secularization of life which found its expression in the Commune and the anticlericalism of the Third Republic. Louis Veuillot fulminated against a secular tradition he dated to classical Greece in *L'Univers*, avidly read by most parish priests, and welcomed a more aggressive papacy which proclaimed the dogmas of the immaculate conception (1854) and papal infallibility (1870), while condemning in the 'Syllabus of Errors' (1864) 80 'pernicious errors of modern thought'. In marked contrast with the mission campaigns of the Restoration, after 1850 the Church alienated urban workers by negative responses to declining attendance. They had to pay to attend mass, were charged 7 fr. 50 (instead of 2 francs) to register a child born outside marriage because of church pressure on the government, and funerals were refused to those who had 'lived in sin' or who had died violently. Similarly, the extensive charity given to the destitute by the Saint-Vincent de Paul Society was tainted by the society's role in recruiting for the Mobile Guard in 1848 and its links with politicians of the extreme right.[29]

The resolution of the mid-century crisis facilitated the Church's reconquest of urban and rural décor, and the decades of the Second Empire were remarkable for the spate of statues of the Virgin Mary. The most grandiose examples were at Marseille (Notre-Dame-de-la-Garde), Avignon (Notre-Dame-des-Doms) and Le Puy (Notre-Dame-de-France, made from a state gift of 213 guns captured at Sebastopol in 1855). These were replicated in more modest form in rural communities, as in Issirac (Gard) where a petition for assistance to the Empress began: 'Madame, the curé, the mayor, and the councillors for church and communal building earnestly desire to erect in the public square a statue of the Holy Virgin before which they will all come to prostrate themselves to pray for the safety of their Majesties the Emperor, the Empress and the Crown Prince.'[30]

The petition, dated 14 June 1870, was fatally late, and within months a virulent anticlericalism was liberated by the proclamation of the Third Republic. One of the first acts of the provisional commune at Lyon on 4 September 1870 was to arrest magistrates, police commissioners, and priests, assumed to form a naturally reactionary alliance. In turn, as during the Second Republic, the Church's response to the communes in Paris and elsewhere aggravated pre-existing attitudes to it among urban people. In Limoges in 1872 a special train carried 800 people to Lourdes while 1,500 workers followed the funeral of a militant porcelain-worker to a civic burial. One-quarter of the babies born in the radical southern stronghold of Béziers in 1872–82 were not baptized. The Third Republic's reluctance to authorize new religious orders, schools or parishes (by 1877 the average parish in Paris had 16,859 people compared with 5,430 in 1802) created problems for the Church, but it could draw on deep reservoirs of commitment, especially among bourgeois women. It was they whose sons and daughters went to church secondary schools and whose men were now the majority of the episcopate; and it was they who in the 1870s effectively created a network of mass pilgrimages across the country, for this decade was the high point of Marianism, with nine major apparitions.[31]

Many male clergy, however, were convinced that the century past had been a time of sweeping (and regrettable) change in every way. In the nostalgic words of *La Semaine religieuse* of Montpellier in 1877:

> The times are bad … in past times *[autrefois]*, the family was a little world where there was room, work, and pleasures for all … in past times, each province had its costume, varied, but simple and modest … today the country girl knows and wears the exaggerated fashions of the town … in past times, there were as many languages as costumes … in past times, the priest was held in great respect in the countryside … in past times no one read pernicious books in the countryside … in past times there was more joy, more gaiety, you could hear singing everywhere … in past times, there was dancing only on the day of the local festival, today Sunday is no longer the Lord's day but the day of the *bal* … in past times … there was neither café nor billiard-hall … there weren't any newspapers.[32]

No doubt the writer romanticized the 'gaiety' of an idealized Catholic peasant society; on many matters, however, he was acute in his identification of some of the changes through which he had lived. In the very year the editorial appeared, the electoral victories of republicans were to place the Catholic Church in an even more unfriendly environment.

13

The Republican Triumph and its Challenges, 1877–1914

The leadership of the Third Republic was determined to distance itself from the memories of 1793 and 1848. Instead, the new Republic appealed to patriotism and social unity rather than to a radical programme, symbolized in the choice of 14 July (1789) rather than 10 August (1792) as the national day. In the aftermath of the victory of 1876–7, Grévy, Ferry, Gambetta and other leaders of the Third Republic successfully constructed a constituency of small property-owners – artisans, shopkeepers and small farmers, dubbed by Gambetta the 'nouvelles couches sociales' – against both old landed élites and socialist militants.[1] By representing industrial growth and colonial expansion as patriotic endeavours in the aftermath of the national defeat of 1870, they were able to generate wide support for a programme of state investment in infrastructure such as railways, for example through the Freycinet Plan of 1878. Underpinning this economic endeavour was the belief that one reason for the defeat had been industrial weakness; other bodies, such as the Academy of Medicine, instead blamed alcoholism and declining birth-rates.

The consolidation of the Republic after 1877 was reflected in a widening of the social background of members of cabinets. Ministers were now more likely to be from provincial, especially southern, families, and, in 1877–99, 28.7 per cent had fathers who were working-class or petit-bourgeois compared with 13.8 per cent in 1871–7. After 1899 this trend became more pronounced. In universities, too, a greater emphasis on entry qualifications and achievement facilitated the ascension of bright young men – and a few women – from the provinces. The Third Republic thus represented, in Daniel Halévy's phrase, 'la fin des notables' and the triumph of the values of meritocracy and civil equality. Nevertheless, two-thirds of ministers continued to come from backgrounds such as the professions (10 per cent of the National Assembly deputies in 1871–1914 were physicians), the senior public service, urban capitalism and large land-owning, which together represented only 7 per cent of adult males.

The élite of the Third Republic succeeded where their predecessors failed, convincing the great majority of French people that a republican regime would divide society least. For François Furet, the consolidation of the Republic in the late 1870s represented 'a vast transformation in the conditions of French public life': by 1880, with the first official celebration of Bastille Day, the adoption of the Marseillaise as the national anthem, and the return of Parliament to Paris, 'the French Revolution finally entered the harbour'. The central political issues of the early years of the Revolution – What was the basis of legitimate authority? What was popular sovereignty? What was the meaning of civil equality? – had taken 90 years to resolve. Paradoxically, it had been the Second Empire, born of a military *coup d'état*, which had been decisive in consolidating a culture of universal manhood suffrage which even monarchists came eventually to accept.[2]

Republican governments in the early 1880s concentrated on extending civil liberties as the basis of the republican settlement: in 1881, it became easier to open cafés and bars, public meetings no longer required the prefect's authorisation, and censorship and stamp duties were removed from the press. Then, in 1884, the divorce law abolished in 1816 was reinstated after the campaigns of Alfred Naquet, and the Le Chapelier law of 1791 outlawing workers' associations was repealed (the *livret*, however, remained in force until 1890). Nevertheless, this cautious regime had trenchant critics on the right and left. Right-wing opponents of the regime condemned its secularism, and articulated a virulent anti-Semitism and anti-Protestantism: both minorities were seen as 'foreign', 'anti-Christian', disproportionately powerful, and predisposed to revolutionary change. In the search for scapegoats for the military collapse of 1870, the Protestant population also stood condemned as 'German', a mistrust exacerbated by the appointment of Protestants to fill half of the cabinet posts in Waddington's government in 1879.[3] Many of the governments of the Third Republic had large minorities of freemasons, another object of deep mistrust for Catholic royalists.

The political 'settlement' of 1877 also alienated the left wing of republicanism. Despite the dominance of republicans in successive assemblies, most of the social objectives of the *sans-culottes* of the French Revolution remained unrealized. The socialist Jules Guesde hence dismissed the relevance of Bastille Day for workers while finding it quite logical that the bourgeoisie should celebrate the victory of 'the class for whose profit the Bastille was taken'. A group of agricultural labourers from Sigean (Aude) agreed: 'the Republic of the ruling class of today is no different from the monarchies that preceded it'.[4]

Frustration at the attenuated outcomes of political revolution generated support for alternative strategies for social change. Workers' congresses in Lyon, Marseille and Le Havre in 1878–80 heard calls for support for Guesde's *Parti ouvrier français*, with its programme for the revolutionary seizure of power. The POF, like other socialist organizations, remained divided, however, over attitudes to the efficacy of electoral democracy and the desirability of the collectivization of economic resources rather than their redistribution. Disillusionment with the idea of workers' co-operatives, the basis of socialist ideology since the 1830s, convinced many workers that trade unions were the surest way to defend living standards; after they were legalized in 1884, several hundred were soon formed, although fewer than 10 per cent of industrial workers had joined by 1891. Workers' congresses also reaffirmed their opposition to equal pay for women and argued for a 'family wage' for men on the grounds that most female workplaces were 'industrial hells'.

Socialist candidates first emerged strongly in the elections of 1893, garnering 600,000 votes and winning 49 seats, almost as many as the monarchists. Socialist support was strongest in cities such as Limoges with a history of radicalism and labour militancy which had developed further with the city's growth from 38,000 people in 1846 to 85,000 in 1911. Dominated at the start of the century by the clergy and nobility, Limoges was now dubbed '*la ville rouge*'. There was similar expansion of large-scale manufacturing and of the industrial workforce elsewhere in these decades. In the small industrial towns round Saint-Etienne, seasonal migrants from the countryside were increasingly replaced by a permanent labour force, in turn attracted to local socialist politicians who emphasized a programme of increased social security, public education and improved working conditions.

The essentials of the Second Empire's economic policies were continued under the Third Republic. Using an 1867 law which had removed the need for government consent before a joint-stock company (*société anonyme*) could be formed, business corporations proliferated. Across the century the growth of French industry had been gradual but significant, but there were two major periods of increased investment and productivity, in 1840–60 and after 1890. From the mid-1890s, in particular, industrial growth was more sustained, especially in the new industries associated with electricity, chemicals and automobiles. It has been estimated that railways carried 3 billion tonne/kilometres of freight in the decade 1865–74, and seven times as much by 1905–14.[5] By 1907–13, exports, chiefly of textiles and clothing, were estimated at 17 per cent of gross domestic product compared with 11 per cent in 1860.

Despite this industrial expansion, the distinctive French pattern of family firms continued to characterize the industrial sector, and a family business remained the dream of millions: the number of enterprises paying the *patente* or business tax increased from 1.3 million in 1845 to 1.8 million in 1896.[6] In 1885, four-fifths of large firms in Alsace were being run by at least the third generation of the same family, often demonstrating a paternalistic benevolence towards their workforce. In Le Creusot (Saône-et-Loire) the Schneider dynasty sought to create the ideal company town. After 1865, when the population was 23,000, the *patrons* embarked on a programme of constructing employee housing in English-style *pavillons*, carefully ranked in size and external appearance. This attempted social control was further impelled by strike action in 1869–70 and a short-lived 'commune' in 1871. Away to the south-west, in Decazeville (Aveyron), one of Schneider's managers, Alfred Deseilligny, set out to transform cast-iron foundries worked by part-time peasant-workers into steelworks operated by a disciplined workforce. Deseilligny enjoyed popular esteem, being elected deputy (1869) and mayor (1871); not until the great depression of the 1880s and the long strike of 1886 were radical alternatives voiced. By 1914, as in Le Creusot and elsewhere, a distinctive working-class culture had evolved.

Again and again it seemed as though workers were paying the price for the Republic's quest for social peace: troops were used to end strikes at Anzin (Nord) in 1884 and Decazeville in 1886, and killed strikers or their supporters in the Corrèze in 1888 and, most famously, at Fourmies (Nord) in 1891. The deaths of nine strikers at Fourmies, and another strike in his home town of Carmaux (Tarn) the following year, were pivotal moments in the political formation of Jean Jaurès, a brilliant student and lecturer first elected to Parliament in 1885. After defeat in the elections of 1898, Jaurès returned to history, commencing his six-volume *Histoire socialiste de la Révolution française*, the first sustained Marxist analysis of the Revolution. He returned to Parliament in 1902 to play a key role in launching the socialist daily *L'Humanité* in 1904 and the following year the French section of the Second International, the SFIO.[7] By 1914, the SFIO was a formidable and growing force in French politics, in power in some 200 municipalities (including Lille, Lyon and Marseille) and with 102 deputies.

In 1887, the year of his death, a poem by Eugène Pottier was published. Pottier had been a popular cabaret singer and radical who had fled to the United States after the Paris Commune. In 1888, his poem was set to music, and became the anthem of socialism:

> Arise ye workers from your slumbers
> Arise ye prisoners of want
> For reason in revolt now thunders
> And at last ends the age of cant.
> Away with all your superstitions
> Servile masses arise, arise
> We'll change henceforth the old tradition
> And spurn the dust to win the prize.
>
> So comrades, come rally
> And the last fight let us face
> The Internationale unites the human race.
> So comrades, come rally
> And the last fight let us face
> The Internationale unites the human race.

But left-wing politics were not the preserve of industrial cities. By 1914, the Mediterranean littoral had also become a heartland of left-wing politics and unionism. The lowlands had become increasingly monocultural across the century, creating a rural world which was also 'urban' in its labour relations and bustling community life. Access to rail transport and increasing northern demand for wine ensured that all social classes enjoyed a remarkable 'golden age' until the phylloxera louse began its destruction from 1863. Over the next 20 years the area of vineyards shrank from 2.5 to 1.0 million hectares, and production fell from 54 to 29 million hectolitres. The phylloxera crisis not only meant the end of almost all the French root stock, since grafting onto American vines proved the best solution; it also had significant social effects. Even though the price of agricultural land would fall by one-third between 1880 and 1912, the costs of reconstitution were too great for many smallholders. Some of those who could no longer hope for economic independence as small wine-growers joined the flood of migrants to Algeria: there were 272,000 French Algerians in 1872 but 800,000 by 1914. Algerian wines were 10 per cent of total French production by the 1890s.[8]

Two other crises – the 1890s depression and the wine-market crisis of 1900–7 – further advantaged large landholders with the capital to reconstitute and rationalize their vineyards. As if to symbolize their 'modernity' and triumph, these southern bourgeois constructed northern-style 'châteaux' which still dot the Mediterranean landscape. A key social grouping in the south was a distinctive intermediate class between landowners and landless which combined wage-work for large producers with wine-growing on their own smallholdings. Motivated both by a fierce pride in their skills and independence and by an insistence that governments assist them, these increasingly embattled *journaliers-propriétaires* were the class which political parties and union activists alternatively tried to lure into electoral support or away from it into direct action. The wages of women workers were also crucial to the small wine-grower's family budget but, because they formed a huge 'reserve army' of labour paid at about half the rate for men, this also undermined the capacity of men to withdraw their labour. The money value placed on women's work seems to have been widely accepted: even though women had always protested alongside men and went on to form their own unions before 1914, this was done to protect rather than challenge the household economy and women's place in the division of labour. Despite the revolutionary discourse and tactical ploys of union activists, labourers and small-holders made their own pragmatic decisions about when strikes were most likely to succeed and what their objectives should be. Their lively class-consciousness did not extend to a programme for collectivization of the large vineyards.

Continuing increases in agricultural productivity, due to more intensive and specialized land use and limited mechanization, enabled rural producers to supply more essentials to an expanding urban population. The population of France increased by 9.7 per cent from 36.1 million in 1871 to 39.6 million in 1911 – slowly compared to other European countries, but enough to encourage steady increases in agricultural productivity, an average of 0.9 per cent per annum in 1880–1910, slightly higher than the European average. Despite the decline in the percentage of households designated as 'rural' (that is, living in communes with fewer than 2,000 people) from 73 per cent in 1856 to 56 per cent in 1911, France was still primarily a rural society. At the turn of the century, only one person in six lived in a city of more than 100,000 people. In 1911, about four-fifths of French people were still living in the department where they had been born. Yet both these figures were changing inexorably: more people were leaving their *pays* permanently for distant towns and cities.

The greater mobility of French people was matched by the increased presence of foreign-born residents of France. While France had always known waves of migrants, there was an unprecedented surge after the turn of the century. Since 1800, the number of foreigners had increased from about 100,000 to one million by 1880 and three million in the early 1900s; by then Italy had surpassed Belgium as the chief source. Indeed, xenophobia was directed more frequently at Italian migrants than at Eastern European Jews. France remained a magnet for immigrants rather than being a source of emigrants: there were only about 600,000 French nationals living outside France or her colonies by 1911.[9]

The continuity in the size of the rural population hides important long-term changes in the nature of rural society. Across the century after 1815 the department of the Loir-et-Cher, to take one example, underwent many of the changes familiar to historians of rural France and elsewhere. Marketing of agricultural produce was facilitated by the extension of canals, all-weather roads and railways; at the same time this increased accessibility of the outside world was one reason why the rural population started its long decline, accelerated by the phylloxera crisis in viticulture after 1875. Primary schooling became available to virtually all children by mid-century and, after 1882, their attendance was compulsory; the basic literacy of young men conscripted for military service increased from 27 per cent in 1827 to 95 per cent in 1890. The number of Easter communicants fell from perhaps one-half of adults to 10–25 per cent, depending on the locality. This secularisation of public life was matched by a gradual political shift from the dominance of conservative rural notables to democratic republicanism, particularly among the smallholding wine-growers of the valleys. The democratization of village councils was only one expression of collective peasant responses to the threats and opportunities of a changing world. Alan Baker has tabulated the existence of 600 'fraternal associations', an average of two per commune. These associations were of three broad types: the fire-fighting corps which proliferated in 1830–70; livestock insurance and mutual-aid societies; and agricultural and anti-phylloxera syndicates. This density of associations is the more remarkable because Baker limited himself to studying 'instrumental' associations designed to minimise risk and enhance protection for farmers rather than also studying 'expressive' associations such as musical, political and sporting societies. The last third of the nineteenth century was a great age of village sociability across the country. By the end of the century villages of any size had their own band (*fanfare*), shooters' club and *boules* association; there were one thousand of the latter in Anjou by 1900.[10]

Across France, distinctive settlement and field patterns became fixed as the expansion of cultivated land reached its limits. In highland areas in particular, the ecology of the countryside was continuing to evolve. A combination of reafforestation following new laws passed in 1882 and the continuing exodus of people from upland communities permitted the slow expansion of wooded areas.[11] The earliest photographs of most rural communities, taken to meet the huge demand for postcards at the turn of the century, show remarkably denuded landscapes. Nevertheless, between the government surveys of 1878 and 1904–8, the forested area of the five departments of Languedoc-Roussillon increased by about one-seventh, to 475,000 hectares, half its present extent. This increase was largely due to reafforestation in state forests, encouraged by the *Société pour la protection de la nature*, founded in 1901. Some of the reafforestation involved coastal and inland swamp-draining, as in the Sologne and Landes, to the detriment of the rich fauna and flora of vulnerable ecologies now 'reclaimed' for human use. In lowland areas, peasant polyculture had generally been sparing of resources and reliant on human and animal manure. In future, however, more specialized agriculture, increasingly using chemical fertilizers and pesticides, was to create long-term problems of soil and water degradation. This was exemplified by the inexorable march of the phylloxera beetle through vineyards in the 1870s and 1880s: henceforth, artificial pesticides would be commonly used against plant diseases and insects in the reconstituted vineyards.

The term 'rural' had had a sharp pejorative edge around 1870: the appalling torture and murder of a noble accused of being a republican at Hautefaye (Dordogne) in August 1870 and the conservative National Assembly elected in February 1871 had confirmed urban bourgeois in their belief that the country-side was primitive and reactionary. Now, after the political triumph of 1877, 'peasants' were increasingly seen as the sturdy personification of republican virtues. At the same time, as Alain Corbin has suggested, there was even a shift in bourgeois perceptions of agreeable smells: a more prosperous countryside which was seen as the stable base of republican regimes and which was now easily accessible by train seemed less the home of the offensive smells of manure-heap and sweat and more a flowered, simple haven of nature. The still lifes of Monet and the rural scenes of Millet and Corot and legions of lesser painters hence found a ready urban market. This revaluation of rural life was paralleled in the proliferation from the early 1880s of church and municipal *colonies de vacances* which took urban working-class children for extended summer holidays in the fresh country air.[12]

Across the century, the greater presence of national structures of administration, religion and education had slowly engendered a collective acceptance of the powers of the State. In towns and villages all over France, the officials of a hierarchically-ordered bureaucracy were increasingly present, administering, collecting information, teaching, judging and policing. Under the Third Republic, there were 700,000 public employees at a state, departmental and municipal level, including 130,000 primary school teachers. For single women, this expanding public service offered a career as a teacher to 57,000 women by 1906 and as a clerk-typist to 7,000 women in the postal services by 1900.[13]

The village school had become the heart of community identity. The major social reform of the early Third Republic was the Ferry laws of 1879–84, providing for free, secular and compulsory education of boys and girls to 13 years of age by qualified, state-trained teachers. Ferry's reforms were motivated by a political imperative to republicanize a future electorate, rather than by any specific commitment to opportunity for girls, hitherto mostly educated in church schools. His laws were designed to break church control of primary education, but women primary school teachers were to be trained in colleges closely resembling those of Catholic teachers.

Assumptions of a republicanizing, secularizing, even civilizing mission informed Ferry's education reforms: in 1879 he announced to a group of teach-ers: 'the state desires, requires, and will retake possession of its rightful domain'. His laws were designed to break church control of primary education and to implant firmly the civic virtues of the Republic, but also sounded the death-knell for minority languages by establishing French as the sole language of an obligatory instruction prescribed in detailed content in Paris. Similarly, the Sée Law of 21 December 1880, which created lycées and colleges for girls, was not inspired by a quest for women's equality but by the anticlerical project of secularizing the State and consolidating the republican regime. Indeed, Camille Sée's intention was to reinforce the ideal of domesticity, not to destroy it.[14]

Two-thirds of all schoolchildren attended the state schools of the Republic, where they encountered teachers imbued with a professional zeal for their educating mission. (Secondary education remained the preserve of a tiny élite – there were only 128,000 secondary students in 1911, 2.4 per cent of their age group – and university education (42,000 students in 1914) even more so.[15]) Primary school children were required to learn formal French from Larive and Fleury's text: between 1872 and 1889 it sold 12 million copies. The Guizot laws of 1833 had placed emphasis on basic skills of literacy and numeracy within a Christian, moralizing framework; there was little formal attention paid to history and geography before secondary school. Under the Third Republic, far more attention was paid to a deliberate endeavour to inculcate values of patriotism and republican unity, with regional diversity used as a way of celebrating France's natural richness. In G. Bruno's *Le Tour de la France par deux enfants*, which went through 209 printings in 1877–91 and sold eight million copies by 1914, children all over France were presented with an image of their nation as a land of natural beauty and social harmony, a society of peasants and artisans with no sign of class conflict. National heroes – certainly not regional ones – formed a pedigree of greatness culminating in the ideal world of the Third Republic, which boys had a natural duty to defend.[16] Through this pedagogy, the teacher assured girls of their ability through the example of the mathematician Sophie Germain, but stressed that 'a woman's life is entirely interior, and her influence on society occurs in a nearly invisible manner' (like G. Bruno herself, whose real name was Augustine Fouillée).

The assumptions behind the 'republican project', as Charles Sowerwine has dubbed it, were embedded in masculinist certainties of material improvement by the application of reason. Progress was understood to be demonstrably unilinear.[17] These were similar values to those expressed by 'enlightened' élites since the 1780s. What had changed was the pervasiveness of the vehement hostility to 'clericalism', dismissed as obfuscating the march of secular progress through its control of women and its support for the forces of reaction. Central to the Third Republic's educational project was the assumption that republican values could only finally be embedded in French society if the power of the Catholic Church over the minds of the young could be broken. In 1885 the Paris municipal council symbolized this struggle by installing in front of the Sacré-Coeur Basilica in Montmartre a statue of the chevalier de la Barre, executed in 1766 for refusing to remove his hat during a religious procession.

The most obvious target was the many thousands of women in Catholic religious orders. One such order was the *Congrégation de la Mère de Dieu*, founded in 1808 by Madame de Lézeau, daughter of a provincial noble and herself a former nun in Rouen, to teach orphaned daughters of holders of the Legion of Honour. The order concentrated on providing boarding schools for the daughters of public servants, and drew many of its novitiates from daughters of military officers. In 1880 the State commenced public secondary education for women and the following year secularized the Legion of Honour schools. Women teachers from the *congrégations* with only a *lettre d'obédience* from their superior authorizing them to teach were banned from teaching in state primary schools in 1886, then from all teaching institutions in 1904. In this hostile context the superiors of the order, Aimée Halley and Aimée Dejardin, relocated some of its houses in Italy, England and Egypt and revised the school curriculum towards professional and vocational training as more appropriate secondary schooling for middle-class girls than domestic proficiency. As the historian of the order, Rebecca Rogers, notes, the domestic focus of the public secondary schools 'seems retrograde by comparison'; the anticlerical heat of the debate of those decades nevertheless conjured up images of 'backward' and stultifying religious education which would be used to end the nuns' calling.[18]

Mass schooling created the audience for new types of communication. The early years of the twentieth century were a great age of mass readership of newspapers, reflecting both new forms of production and profound cultural changes in the uses of the written word to acquire information and to understand one's identity. In the mid-1830s, perhaps 110,000 copies of newspapers were bought each day in France; this figure had increased to one million by 1870 and three million by 1890, and by 1914 was probably as high as ten million. Polydor Millaud's *Le Petit Journal* sold up to 500,000 copies daily in the 1890s. But industrial concentration was to reduce the diversity of media opinion in this golden age of the cheap popular press. By the early years of the twentieth century, six million Parisian papers were being sold each day, but just four dailies accounted for three-quarters of them.[19]

One of the more popular papers was *Le Petit Parisien*, which specialized in illustrated chronicles of crimes of passion, especially by women driven to murder by their 'natural' propensity for emotional excess. The obverse of the continuing belittling by men of women's political capacity was a denial of their personal responsibility for criminal actions. The law of 30 November 1892 on medical practice completed the virtual monopoly of doctors over diagnosis and healing, in particular of women's propensity to 'hysteria' and the physiological bases of crimes committed by women and the poor. From 1880, as a consequence, there was a marked decline in the most serious punishments – there were only 28 guillotinings in 1898–1907 compared with 95 in 1888–97 – and punishments generally were milder, especially for women. Maximum sentences for serious crimes were inflicted on 34 per cent of men and 18 per cent of women in 1896–1900; by 1910 the figures had fallen to 31 per cent and 11 per cent. Women were 12–13 per cent of prisoners at the turn of the century compared with 16–18 per cent in the 1870s.[20]

One of the major series of textbooks for primary school children was entitled *Tu seras*. The volume *Tu seras soldat* ('You Will be a Soldier') was written by Ernest Lavisse, Professor of History at the Sorbonne. In 1912, Lavisse insisted: 'If the schoolboy does not carry with him the living memory of our national glories, … if he does not become a citizen penetrated with his duties and a soldier who loves his rifle, the teacher will have wasted his time.'[21] The military defeat of 1870 had also led to a shift in attitudes towards France's overseas empire. Hitherto, Tahiti, New Caledonia, Indo-China, North Africa, Madagascar, Senegal and the older colonies of the Caribbean had formed a scattered, often neglected 'empire' based on missionary, military and trade activity; now the Republic pursued a more deliberate colonial policy. In 1881, the colonies were placed under the control of the Minister of Trade rather than the navy. In 1881 Tunisia was made a virtual 'protectorate'. The French Congo was created the next year. The 'protectorate' established over parts of Cambodia in 1863 was expanded to Vietnam in the 1880s and Laos in the 1890s.

A leading exponent of this assertive colonial policy – and of the uniformity of education – was Ferry, republican Mayor of Paris in 1870–1 and Prime Minister in 1880–1 and 1883–5. Underpinning his justification of expansion for reasons of strategic prestige, markets and resources was his belief in France's 'civilizing mission': the 'obligation and duty that are imposed on all civilized people to make the signature of their representatives respected by all barbarous nations'. This ideological imperative was also the bond which united the small but influential colonial lobby; moreover, in Cardinal Lavigerie, the Republic had the support of an influential senior prelate for its colonization of North Africa.[22] Colonialism took on a rehabilitating, 'civilizing' mission for France as well as for its colonial subjects. The Eurocentric assumptions underpinning colonization were not seriously questioned across the political spectrum. Even on the revolutionary left, there was little evidence of a socialist and internationalist critique of external expansion at the expense of non-Europeans. In this sense, the Jacobin commitment to revolutionary wars of liberation in Europe, still popular in 1848, had ossified into a desire for national glory, shattered on the European front in 1870, but unchallenged abroad thereafter.

Despite dissatisfaction on the left and right, the Republic seemed indeed to have entered the harbour of a confident, stable land. The Exhibition of 1889 attracted as many as 175,000 people per day to marvel at the exhibits of the modern world. In all the Exhibition attracted 32 million people, twice the extraordinary record set in 1878. The highlight was Gustave Eiffel's soaring tower, celebrating the centenary of 1789 and the triumph of the Republic over the forces of reaction and, in its use of iron instead of stone, a *chef d'oeuvre* by a railway engineer of the new age.

At the very moment when the centenary of the Revolution was being celebrated, the Republic itself was challenged from within. Successive scandals – such as the Wilson Affair (1887) and the Panama Scandal (1892) – proved to monarchists the illegitimacy and inherent corruption of the Republic. In the context of economic downturn in 1886–7, a scandal involving President Grévy's son-in-law Daniel Wilson, who was effectively selling the country's highest honour, the Legion of Honour, could only enhance the stature of the popular General Boulanger and his vaguely Bonapartist calls for authority and decisive change. The general's popularity reached its apogee in a Paris by-election victory in January 1889. His programme was ideologically ambiguous, but Boulanger's followers exploited campaign songs, pictures and emblems to imply links with the Napoleonic tradition; in turn royalists sought to use him for their own purposes. This time, most people remained immune to the allure of the strong leader: failure in the 1889 elections and the general's flight to Brussels punctured the movement.[23]

By the time of the centenary of the First Republic on 22 September 1892 (celebrated as a public holiday), the Republic seemed to have consolidated its parliamentary power. While many committed Catholics retained their suspicion of or outright opposition to the Republic, Pope Leo XIII issued an encyclical in the same year accepting of those faithful who wished to join the *ralliement* to the Republic. His earlier encyclical (*Rerum novarum* – 'Of new things') had addressed social questions to the point of endorsing the establishment of trade unions. Two immediate consequences of the Pope's actions were the flowering of *Le Sillon*, a journal of social and democratic Christianity founded by the 20-year-old Marc Sangnier in 1894, and the collapse of the monarchist right to 1.5 million votes and 56 seats in the elections of 1893.

The rapprochement of Church and Republic was not to endure. Militant royalists and clericals had never accepted the consequences of the French Revolution: for example, the equal rights to participation in public life of Jews and Protestants. Across the nineteenth century, anti-Semitism in particular remained endemic in French public life, even if no regime after 1830 acted to disadvantage Jews. After 1880, however, the evident triumph of the Republic, the more obvious participation of Jews (as well as Protestants and freemasons) in public life, and widespread unease at the impact of large-scale capitalism on small retailers and producers made the scapegoating of Jews a social force with far more serious political repercussions. After republican political successes in 1882 the editor of a new daily of the Assumptionist Order, *La Croix*, thundered: 'The Jew is the enemy, this has been the Christian cry from Golgotha until today.'[24]

The arrest and banishment of the Jewish Captain Alfred Dreyfus in 1894 served as a focus for the expression of these nationalistic and social resentments. The young Alfred Dreyfus had watched in dismay as German troops occupied his town of Mulhouse in 1870; he felt honour-bound to join the army and, like many other Jews from Alsace, he fled to Paris, where he progressed successfully through élite officer training schools. By the 1880s he was a handsome and wealthy provincial on the eve of a brilliant career and a happy marriage. At the same time, a series of national economic and political crises was to make Jews easy targets to explain uncertainty. Personal jealousies within the officer corps – for Dreyfus's private income was ten times an officer's salary – did the rest. In December 1894, Dreyfus was found guilty of selling military secrets to Germany, and deported to Devil's Island in French Guiana (reopened as a penal colony for recidivists in 1885). Dreyfus served as the ideal whipping-boy in a feverish atmosphere of government instability and financial scandals and at a time of intense international rivalry in the imperial race for Africa. From the outset Dreyfus claimed: 'My only crime is to have been born a Jew.' Anti-Semitism of an unprecedented level was expressed in Alsace-Lorraine and Paris: the capital housed 60 per cent of the 135,000 French Jews.

Dreyfus's plight for long aroused little interest or sympathy in most parts of France; in turn, however, it was the concentration of Jews in specific areas which also explains why most rural people were not attracted to anti-Semitic politics.[25] Three years later, a Parisian stockbroker chanced upon a photograph of the incriminating document and recognised its author as another officer, named

Esterhazy. This was the breakthrough in the campaign of the small, dedicated band of Dreyfus's defenders led by Alfred's wife Lucie and brother Mathieu. The 1898 election campaign was marked by occasional anti-Jewish rioting and the election of several anti-Semites, notably Drumont and Déroulède; the socialist Dreyfusards Guesde and Jaurès lost their seats. Already, however, a majority of the parliament had accepted Dreyfus's innocence. By 1899 he had been repatriated and pardoned. But by then the Dreyfus Affair had become an issue of the reputation of the French officer corps, and of national morale at the time of the great Paris Exhibition of 1900, and not until 1906 was he formally declared innocent and reintegrated into the French army. On his return from French Guiana, Dreyfus was astonished at the new electric lights in Paris and the projection of a moving picture by Georges Méliès, the builder of the world's first film studio. (The 13-minute film, called *The Dreyfus Affair*, was banned by the Government.)

The Dreyfus Affair was one of the turning-points of modern French history, arraying religious minorities, anticlericals and civil libertarians such as Emile Zola (whose open letter *J'accuse* sold 300,000 copies of the newspaper in which it was published) and Sarah Bernhardt against a powerful coalition of nationalists, anti-Semites, and almost all of the media. The discrediting of the anti-Dreyfusards, including much of the Catholic Church, undermined Pope Leo XIII's earlier recommendation that Catholics should abandon their hostility to republican institutions. *La Croix* had reacted to the Dreyfus affair by insisting (and amply demonstrating) that it was the most anti-Jewish journal in France; it sold as many as 170,000 copies per day. In turn, the Dreyfus Affair facilitated the targeting of the Church and the army officer corps by successive Radical governments after 1902, culminating in the separation of Church and State in 1905.

The Law on Associations passed by Waldeck-Rousseau's government on 1 July 1901 permitted citizens to establish associations with few formalities but, since it required them to be composed of French citizens without foreign obligations, all church orders had to change their ties to Rome or face dissolution. Ultimately 12,000 Catholic schools were closed, and 50,000 members of religious orders were dispersed. The consequent inventories of church property, for the laity now controlled it, was the occasion on which popular opposition to the anticlerical measures could be expressed. In many parts of the country there was angry and sometimes violent resistance to the inventorying of sacred objects. Elsewhere, for example in the village of Savines, in the Alpine region of south-eastern France, the reforms were welcomed: there a two-metre-high bronze statue of the Republic was erected in 1906, its right hand brandishing bolts of lightning and the words 'The Rights of Man'. The base of the statue was covered with a litany of republican achievements since 1789, one side listing three key reforms of the Third Republic: the ending of exemptions from compulsory military service, state assistance for the elderly, and the separation of Church and State. The history of France's republics was summarised pithily: 'The First gave us the land, the Second the vote, the Third education.'[26]

A new right-wing movement – Maurras's *Action française* – appeared in 1908, dedicated to nationalism, the expulsion of Jews from France and the end of the Republic. In turn, the condemnation of the socially reformist Catholic movement *Le Sillon* by Pius X in 1910, and his refusal to publicly condemn the *Action française*, thwarted attempts in Brittany and elsewhere to forge a third way between the Catholic Right and republican anticlericalism. Another immediate consequence of the Dreyfus Affair was the flowering of 'popular universities' linking intellectuals and workers; after the first opened its doors in April 1898 there were 230 in 1901, with 50,000 participants. Their decline was almost as rapid, in part provoked by the founder Georges Deherme's invitation to a priest to lecture. Organized labour, too, was suspicious of the academics' 'metaphysics'.

The short-lived universities were one example of new forms of urban sociability which were challenging older patterns of leisure and culture. By the end of the century mass urban culture was increasingly characterized by commercialized leisure in the form of music halls, cabarets, exhibitions, circuses and spectator sports. At the same time, as Carol Harrison has shown, bourgeois men in particular increasingly frequented clubs with interests ranging from music to shooting and horticulture: at the time of the passage of the 1901 law legalizing the freedom of association, there were 45,000 unofficial clubs in existence. Most striking was the proliferation of cycling and football clubs after the turn of the century; workplace football teams in the north and village and school rugby teams in the south fostered a new expression of local identity, often drawing on the violent combativeness of earlier village feuds between young men. Mass urban society created a pool of spectators: football, first developed in Le Havre in 1872 by British maritime companies, supported 2,000 professionals by 1914. The Toulouse rugby team that went undefeated in 1912 was popularly known as *la Vierge rouge* and was represented by the female heroine 'Zézette', perhaps in mimicry of the Virgin Mary, Marianne or even of the Communard Louise Michel. At a national level, Pierre de Coubertin's inspiration of the first Olympic Games in 1896 and Henri Desgranges's organization of the Tour de France in 1903 (building on a national championship established in 1880) celebrated physical exertion and national competition. By 1910 gymnasiums had 200,000 members; as many more were in rifle clubs. Rather more élite in social appeal were 'alpinism' and the new automobiles (held to be less polluting than horses and, like mountaineering, a healthier recreation for urban-dwellers). By 1911 there were 64,000 registered vehicles.[27]

New forms of mass leisure were linked with other forms of mass consumption, for example, through Desgranges's magazine *L'Auto* and the *Guide rouge* issued by Michelin from 1900. The Second Empire had formally gazetted thermal resorts *(villes d'eau)*, and automobiles and trains now gave access to new coastal resorts: Nice, which had had only 1,850 visiting families in 1861–2, welcomed 22,000 people in 1887. Epitomizing this new consumerist world of the Third Republic were the flourishing new department stores in Paris, such as the Bon Marché, Louvre, Printemps and Samaritaine. The world's largest, the Bon Marché, had 4,500 employees and 200 million francs of sales of merchandise by 1906 compared with 1,788 and 73 million in 1877. The department store was the ultimate statement of the bourgeois culture of the Third Republic, with its emphasis on consumption, appearances and respectability. Its mass-produced illustrated catalogues depicted an upper-middle-class life of fine clothing, leisure and family serenity to a middle-class and petit-bourgeois clientèle. By catering to a desire for luxury, modernity and social ascent at cheap prices, the Bon Marché and other stores also created an image of the female consumer sustaining a 'station in life' through the purchase of commodities. New models of sewing machines were advertised as 'modern' and even as sexually attractive.[28]

The Third Republic had 60 governments between 1870 and 1914. For all the political instability of the Republic, however, it was a remarkably durable regime. Frequent ministerial changes hid a continuity in political élites: Aristide Briand was a member of 25 cabinets. Basic to this stability was an 'alliance of iron and wheat', in Herman Lebovics's phrase, of urban and rural producers linked by support for economic protection and hostility to both socialism and labour militancy. The political weight of the farm sector secured tariff measures in the 1890s which protected agriculture from foreign competition. Despite the long dominance of French politics by parties ostensibly committed to reform, however, remarkably little social legislation was enacted. Radical politicians such as Léon Bourgeois and Alexandre Millerand urged a doctrine of 'solidarism' through an income tax to pay for limited accident insurance and old-age pensions, but it was not until 1910 that the latter were implemented, and the income tax was only later introduced as a wartime measure.

In 1906 Georges Clemenceau headed France's first Radical government. It soon had to face the most sustained waves of collective protest since the French Revolution, and responded in much the same way as its predecessors. In March 1906 a massive gas explosion at Courrières (Pas-de-Calais) killed about 1,300 miners, triggering a series of strikes which involved perhaps half a million people by the end of the year. Clemenceau's government did not hesitate to deploy troops, 50,000 in Paris alone. On the vast wine-growing plains of the Mediterranean coastline, a combination of successive abundant harvests, competition from cheap Algerian wines and 'sugared' mediocre wine threatened wine-growers and labourers with impoverishment. In 1907 wine-growers began a series of protests against the collapse in wine prices, due it was believed to the flooding of the market by adulterated, poor-quality wines. The price of a hectolitre of wine fell from 23 francs in 1903 to five francs in 1907. From its origins in the village of Argeliers (Aude) in March 1907, a wave of demonstrations surged from 5,000 people at Coursan, 120,000 at Béziers, 170,000 at Perpignan, 220,000 at Carcassonne, and climaxing at an estimated 500,000 at Montpellier on 9 June. Village and town councils resigned in solidarity: some 258 (76 per cent) of those of the Hérault. A mixture of repression – on 19 June troops in Narbonne killed six demonstrators – and vague government promises undercut the movement.

Whatever the continuities of Third Republic politics, the decades before 1914 seem from hindsight to have been a pinnacle of cultural creativity, evident in the painting of Matisse, Seurat and Cézanne, the music of Debussy, Fauré and Satie, the writing of Zola, Proust and Alain-Fournier, and the scientific brilliance of Marie and Pierre Curie, the physiologist Claude Bernard, Gustave Eiffel, and Louis Pasteur, who first applied a laboratory vaccine against a human disease in the 1880s.[29] However, the notion of living in a 'belle époque' would have seemed odd to industrial workers and to southern wine-growers. In the Midi, as in the valley of the Rhône, the old heartlands of Radicalism were being lost to Jean Jaurès's branch of the Second International, the SFIO, founded in 1905.

Despite the resonance of the chord which the SFIO struck in particular rural and urban communities, of greater significance in the life of urban wage-earners were the *Bourses au travail* or labour exchanges. These were originally established in 1887 by the Paris Prefect of Police Louis Poubelle – who in 1884 had decreed that dustbins (henceforth known as *poubelles*) be used – to control workers waiting for job offers on the place de la Grève in Paris, and developed into centres of working-class meetings and solidarity. Between 1887 and 1902, they were established in 94 towns and cities, and by 1907 there were 157 *Bourses* across the country. These were essentially run by workers themselves and, as the *Confédération générale du travail*, advocated a 'syndicalist' programme of direct action outside parliamentarism. Whereas unions had had a total membership of less than 200,000 in 1890, by 1914 there were about one million members; there were 47 strikes in the Paris building industry alone, and one strike in the underground lasted 11 months.[30]

Trade unions had generally excluded women from their meetings; in Roubaix and Lille women wishing to speak had to present a written request from a male relative. Not until 1899, on the initiative of Marguerite Durand's feminist paper *La Fronde*, were the first women's unions founded for typesetters, typists and cashiers. Durand's justification inevitably offended socialist feminists: 'Working women ... will make the revolution for their bourgeois sisters, but what good are arms which flail about when there are no brains to guide them?' In the same year, the first woman doctor, Madeleine Pelletier, was appointed to the *Assistance publique*. Pelletier habitually dressed in men's clothes and encountered some of the same curiosity and hostility as had working-class lesbians. While the *brasseries de femmes* had become well-known places where lesbians could meet and drink in agreeable surroundings, politically-active lesbians remained an object of mistrust across the political spectrum.[31]

The consolidation of the Third Republic was characterized by the distinctively masculine politics and mission of dominant republican parties, 'sons of the Revolution' in Judith's Stone's phrase. It was also, as Anne-Marie Sohn has dubbed it, 'the golden age of male adultery'; indeed, one president, Félix Faure, had died in 1899 while having sex with a mistress.[32] It also became a golden age of organized feminism. Earlier expressions of feminism, though not using the term, had been consequent to the general liberation of political life after the revolutions of 1789, 1830 and 1848 and the liberalization of politics in the 1860s. Now, in the 1890s, a more organized and reformist feminism emerged in response to the politically stultifying politics of the Third Republic, which encouraged women's education but denied their full citizenship. The largest suffragist organization, the National Council of French Women, claimed 100,000 members by 1914. Madeleine Pelletier, Nelly Roussel, Hubertine Auclert and many others remained divided, however, over the extent to which their social radicalism should be subordinated to the suffrage campaign. In a broader context, this was part of the long debate in France over whether women's futures lay as 'sisters or citizens'; the activities of scores of women's associations were contested by other claims that socialism would end all exploitation.

Working women were separated by a gulf of class and politics from women activists in the *Ligue française pour le droit des femmes*, founded in 1894 to campaign for women's suffrage. While male support for the vote for women had never been stronger, the socially-conservative majorities in the Senate were clearly opposed. Freemasonry was another key vehicle through which activists such as Madeleine Pelletier and Maria Desraimes expressed their feminism and addressed social questions. So, too, were the professions. The first woman medical student in Marseille, Anna-Emilie Hamilton, was appointed director in 1901 of Bordeaux's *Maison de santé protestante*, staffed by trained career nurses (*gardes-malades*), but the professionalization of nursing long encountered opposition not only from conservative politicians and religious orders but also from many women patients.[33]

Women remained vulnerable to the sexual pressure of employers, but now added the strike to their repertoire of protection. In Angers, for example, women in a toy factory went on strike in 1904 over the harassment suffered from a foreman; the strike had extensive local support, but failed. However, trade unions and socialist parties were usually intolerant or unsupportive of the needs of women workers: Renault workers earned in an hour what hundreds of thousands of women clothing workers earned in a day. As economic uncertainty aggravated male sensitivities about job security and appeals were made to the spectre of clerical influence over women, speakers at the SFIO congress in Limoges in 1906 opposed women's suffrage. Only about 3 per cent of the party's 90,000 members were women. Many women workers, for example, in and around Lille, who had earlier been attracted to Guesde's socialist party, now abandoned it.

Catholic organizations were far more successful in attracting women. By 1914 the Patriotic League of French Women had 585,000 members, concerned with disseminating Catholic literature, organizing pilgrimages and promoting the cult of Joan of Arc. (Its political wing, the *Action libérale populaire*, was less successful, winning only 64 seats in 1906.) The energy which huge numbers of women committed to the Church points to a chequered and incomplete, but very significant, transition in religious beliefs. The increasing numbers of women in religious orders and associations, the popularity of Marianism, and the influence of the Italian theologian Ligouri, with his less judgmental ideas about the confessional and coitus interruptus, seems to have tilted the balance towards a Marian 'God of love' in its century-long battle with the Tridentine 'God of fear'. The founder of the Assumptionist Order, Emmanuel d'Alzon, wrote to a young man that 'a single sentiment of love is worth more than 10,000 sentiments of fear'; the Monseigneur de Ségur wrote in 1872 to a young girl that 'even the sadness of contrition is worth nothing, if it is not sweetened and wholly transformed by the confidence of love'.

In most urban areas, however, this transition failed to staunch the secularization of attitudes, particularly among men and the working class. One measure of the erosion of religious authority may be the increase in the proportion of births outside marriage across France, from 2.6 per cent in the 1780s to 8.1 a century later. In Paris, only about 2.3 per cent of marriages in the years 1763–87 were in March, during the period of Lenten abstinence; by 1887–96 almost 7 per cent were. In 1824–8, 81.6 per cent of babies were baptized within seven days; in 1887 just 20.4 per cent were. As Philippe Boutry has argued, there may well have been a subtle but epochal shift in the meaning of religious belief, from an unquestioned part of a culture or *mentalité* to a matter of opinion open to contestation. Despite the dire warnings of the Catholic Church, however, the reintroduction of divorce had not destroyed commitment to marriage: in the 1901 census there were only 53 divorced men for every 10,000 aged 18 to 50 years, and 70 divorced women for every 10,000 aged 15 to 45.[34]

Whatever the depth of disagreement about the policies of the Radical Republic, there was a wider consensus in the discourse of nationalism. Few French people questioned the desirability of strengthening national military capacity after the debacle of 1870 or of an expanding colonial empire. Besides, by the turn of the century, the empire was vastly profitable and the colonial trade was more important than that with Germany: in 1913, the colonies accounted for 9.4 per cent of metropolitan France's imports and 13 per cent of its exports. The Moroccan crises of 1905 and 1911 focused imperial rivalries on antipathy towards Germany. Agreements between France, Britain and Spain had provided for the French possession of Morocco, long assumed to be part of the French 'sphere', but French imperial ambitions were thwarted by Kaiser William II's landing in Tangiers in 1905. Again, in 1911, a German gunboat was sent to the port of Agadir. Only in 1912 was France free to partition Morocco with Spain, and to appoint General Lyautey – a veteran of Algeria, Madagascar and Indo-China – as its *Résident général*.[35] Yet, while the crisis sharpened resentments of German military and economic might, close commercial relations continued. Renault and Michelin subsequently acquired German subsidiaries and trade between the two countries continued to grow.

Franco-German relations deteriorated further within the wider context of concerns about Russia's ambitions in Serbia. In July 1913 the Chamber of Deputies voted to increase the length of military service to three years (in return for the concession to the SFIO deputies of the introduction, for the first time in French history, of an income tax on annual incomes over 5,000 francs to pay the costs of the increased army). Nevertheless, there were signs in 1914 that Franco-German tensions might be easing. Small groups of young socialists and trade unionists were actively opposing calls for military action. In particular, Jean Jaurès, electorally successful and committed to linking the SFIO, the CGT and even the Radical government, refused to accept the inevitability of looming war, even after the assassination of the Austrian Archduke Francis Ferdinand and his wife in Sarajevo on 28 June. On 31 July, however, Jaurès was himself murdered by a right-wing fanatic; he was buried on the morrow of Germany's declaration of war on France on 3 August.

Conclusion – *Plus ça change?*

The 'long nineteenth century' from the French Revolution to World War I has often been described as the 'century of revolution'. Implicit in such a trope is a world of change. In stark contrast, Arno Mayer has emphasized the continuities of social history: France remained 'first and foremost a peasant economy and rural society dominated by hereditary and privileged nobilities'. Mayer's view has found a nuanced echo in that of David Higgs, who has argued that, although the number of *ancien-régime* nobles had declined from about 125,000 before 1789 to fewer than 40,000 after 1870, French society remained dominated by landed wealth and the aristocratic values it underpinned. As late as 1893, 56 per cent of deputies were nobles and wealthy bourgeois. The latter were from the wealthiest 3,000 families in France, with incomes above 100,000 francs.[1]

Robert Forster has argued similarly, that after 1800 a post-revolutionary élite of *capacités* continued to govern the country: an amalgam of *ancien-régime* nobles and new men of substance who drew their wealth from a combination of land-owning, business and official position. Whatever the acrimonious political divisions among them, these men were united by assumptions about the ideal nature of the family, education and social hierarchy.[2] The *Almanach comique* for 1873 joked that the only change from the past was that, whereas men seeking positions for themselves and their sons used to wait for ministers on the stairways of the Tuileries or Versailles, now they lay in wait in first-class railway carriages. It was such notables alone who were able to afford the 30,000–40,000 francs an electoral campaign could cost by 1880, even in the provinces. Typifying them was the Périer family: Claude, a wealthy Grenoble manufacturer who had bought a seigneurie and title in the 1780s, welcomed the Revolution for the business and land opportunities it created; his son Casimir diversified the family businesses and was Louis-Philippe's Chief Minister in 1831–2; in turn Casimir's son Auguste was a deputy under the July Monarchy, the Second and Third Republics, and was Thiers's Minister for the Interior in the 1870s.

Such an argument about the continuities of power misses important changes notables had to make in their self-perceptions and social dealings. Once Louis Napoleon's seizure of power in December 1851 had 'normalized' social relations, pre-1848 notables found that they were holding local office within a regime no longer so dominated at a national level by men from their own milieu. In the short term, this was due to the emperor's deliberate promotion of a new élite of businessmen and entrepreneurs. In the long run, and more corrosively, the consolidation of universal suffrage was to undermine the predominance of great landowners as typical of the national élite, even if they continued to hold disproportionate economic and social power at the local

263

level. The elections of 1849 had altered their style of exercizing power; the pre-eminence of the notables was ratified in most regions, but its popular recognition had to be the result of a politics of persuasion rather than 'natural' deference to their authority. For this reason, André-Jean Tudesq chose to conclude his monumental study of the *grands notables* in 1849, arguing that their power in the first half of the nineteenth century corresponded with the transition from the *ancien régime* to an industrializing society with mass democratic politics. One of Robert Forster's own studies, of the ancient, prestigious and immensely wealthy Saulx-Tavanes family in Burgundy, is a striking example of the collapse of a family unable to come to terms with change. Despite receiving an indemnity of 280,000 francs from the Restoration for their property losses during the Revolution, the Saulx-Tavanes never regained their land or their social influence, even among local people. The octogenarian duchess felt an outsider in a foreign land when she wrote her memoirs in the 1850s: 'All the ties which hold me to life have successively been broken. Only a few traces of what I have known remain. Ideas, opinions, mores have changed; and like the daughters of Jerusalem, I mourn the mysteries of Zion in a strange land.'[3]

The point holds in general terms for the mass of the nobility. In 1830, 266 of the 387 wealthiest families in France had been noble; nobles dominated the parliaments of the constitutional monarchies of 1815–48 based on restricted suffrage. Even during the July Monarchy, however, the social composition of the ruling élite had become less aristocratic and more drawn from business and the professions, while the regime's political economy consistently sought to create a favourable environment for entrepreneurs. Other elements of the state apparatus were also drawing on a wider social pool: by 1850, 70 per cent of army officers had been promoted from the ranks, and the July Monarchy abolished special preferments for nobles, who were now only 8 per cent of officers. The consolidation of the Republic after 1877 was reflected in a widening of the social background of cabinets. Ministers were now more likely to be from provincial and southern families; by the early twentieth century, almost one-third had fathers who were working-class or petit-bourgeois compared with one-seventh 30 years earlier. Certainly, two-thirds of ministers continued to come from bourgeois backgrounds (the professions, senior public service, urban capitalism and large land-owning). But while the early Third Republic thus represented the consolidation of the political triumph of the bourgeoisie, the contrast with 1815 – let alone 1780 – could hardly be more striking.[4] Arno Mayer's view thus seems a partial one.

The electoral triumph of republicanism in 1876–7 was indeed a significant turning-point in French history. Unlike its predecessors, the Third Republic was to grow from its revolutionary origins into the most stable, durable regime of the long century to 1914. The triumph was also much more than a repudiation of traditional notables, which in any case had occurred far earlier in most regions. Across a century, the very meanings which people gave to politics, authority and sovereignty had undergone a revolutionary transformation. The protracted conflicts of 1868–77 between forces of Order and republicans were predicated upon the assumptions that the issue was now the depth of popular support for the new regime and that political legitimacy presupposed popular sovereignty.

The political 'settlement' of the Third Republic was largely due to the commitment a majority of rural and urban working people came to feel to a republican, representative regime with a weak executive. However, there was also an angry, libertarian 'Marianne'. The left was scornful when the marquis de Gallifet, 'butcher' of the Paris Commune during the 'bloody week' of May 1871, was made Minister of the Interior in 1899. A minority of militant workers repudiated the republican settlement as a parliamentary veneer for bourgeois rule; many more regarded democratic republicanism as only a means to an end, for most of the social objectives of the popular movement of the Year II and its successors remained unrealized. By the 1880s demands for free and secular education were being realized, the Le Chapelier law of 1791 had been repealed and divorce reintroduced, but it would be 1913 before the wealthy paid taxes on income as well as property, and later still before the commitment to the sick, elderly and unemployed made in the Jacobin constitution of 1793 was realized.

Among the great political losers of the nineteenth century were the legitimists. Twice – on Louis-Philippe's death in 1850 and with the election of a royalist assembly in 1871 – the comte de Chambord had refused to compromise with other forces of conservatism in the interests of profiting from a favourable political conjuncture. Instead, he insisted on waiting until his people came to their senses and repented, but he died still uncalled in 1883. While probably the numerically-dominant political force at mid-century and still able to call on popular support in parts of the west and north into the 1880s, the legitimists had been marooned by the intransigence of the royal pretender and the notables' profound ambivalence about democracy. While the legitimist élite recognized that the *ancien régime* was gone forever, its ideology continued to advocate the need for a landed élite at the head of decentralized institutions as the only remedy for the evils of Jacobin centralization, secular education, rural exodus and urbanization, and socialism.

The consolidation of the Republic by 1900 – though more evident in hindsight than it appeared to contemporaries – was the culmination of a struggle waged since 1789. The meaning of popular sovereignty as electoral participation had become embedded in mass political culture. Paradoxically, it had been the Second Empire, born of a military *coup d'état* against a Republic, which had embedded a culture of universal manhood suffrage and parliamentary government which even monarchists reluctantly came to accept.[5] Whereas the elections of 1789–95 had attracted only 10–30 per cent of eligible voters to the polls, the percentage of adult males who voted during the Third Republic ranged from 69 to 85. This is not to say that people were afterwards always immune to the attractions of authoritarian regimes and politicians as the price necessary for peace of mind. Three times in the century, in 1799, 1815 and 1851, the seizure of power 'from above' had resolved political instability and social fears, leaving a potent Bonapartist legacy in French public life, the lure of the strong man supported by the army. The major crises in the history of the Third Republic before 1914 – Boulangism and the Dreyfus Affair – had revealed the on-going temptations of this legacy. At its extreme was a new force, the 'revolutionary right', virulently xenophobic and violently hostile to unions, democracy and even the Republic itself. Gyp (Sybille de Martel), who described herself as a professional anti-Semite, pandered to such views with a stream of over one hundred novels (paradoxically published by the Jewish firm Calmann-Lévy). Here and in the writings of Barrès, Drumont and others lay the roots of the anti-republican fascist and royalist parties of the 1930s.

Changes to political culture by 1900 were part of a wider process in the formation of the French nation-state. While the absolutist state of the late eighteenth century had an important presence in law-making and enforcement, the collecting of levies and taxes, this was a contested, sporadic presence and only in the decades after 1789 did the 'nation' become the symbolic legitimation of the State's coercive powers. This legitimation also drew on the attachment of hundreds of thousands of provincial people to whom the State offered employment, depending on their social background, as administrators, teachers, gendarmes, road and rail workers. For example, army officers were disproportionately drawn from the frontier departments and Corsica. Never before had the State had such 'purchase' on the lives and loyalties of French people. The State was now widely perceived as the administrative and political arrangements of an older, deeper universal entity claiming an almost timeless reality. This perception was moulded by decades of involvement in the educational, political, institutional and commercial structures of a territory which since 1789 had elided national identity and citizenship. The first celebration of Bastille Day in 1880 symbolized this national culture at the same time as celebrating the triumph of the Republic, despite the survival of other, provincial cultures and languages as ways of seeing the world.[6]

While historians generally agree on the significance of these gradual but fundamental shifts in the nature of political culture across the 'long nineteenth century', they are less in agreement about social change, especially in rural society. Some have argued that the continuities of daily life, economic structures and social relations need emphasizing instead of the spectacular political upheavals of the century. The gradualism of social change in France seems attested, for example, by the modest increases in population. From 33.6 million in 1836, the total population had increased to only 36.1 million in 1872 and 39.6 million in 1911; the mass of this population continued to live in the villages and small towns of rural France.

The most influential argument for social continuity in the countryside has been that of Eugen Weber, who has contested the substance of what the 'nation' and its politics meant to most rural people by 1880. Weber has argued that peasants south of the Loire and in Brittany lived within resilient, autarchic popular cultures until, in the decades 1880–1910, conscription, education, markets, easier communications and urban values eroded these ancient human environments and created a relatively homogeneous national identity and culture. The French Revolution had thus been largely irrelevant to the deeper structures of rural societies, whatever memories it embedded in popular consciousness. In most of rural France, politics, too, 'remained in an archaic stage – local and personal – into at least the 1880s'.[7] The magnitude of change was thus more perceived than real, more an historian's myth than an accurate assessment of changes to French society.

Weber painted a picture of an archaic countryside by singling out the most extreme examples of 'isolation' as the rural norm and by repeating the horrified reactions of disoriented urban bureaucrats as if they were neutrally describing a 'primitive' France. In fact, the changes to which he points in 1880–1910 were already well advanced almost everywhere. By 1880, virtually all children were receiving primary schooling; two-thirds of them were functionally literate in French. In 1881, 85 per cent of men and 77 per cent of women were at least able to sign their marriage certificate: a century earlier the figures had been 47 and 27. The impulse for mass education came as much from rural people as from the ambitions of educators and governments. In Pont-de-Montvert (Lozère), one of the most inaccessible places for outsiders in all of France, the local council successfully petitioned in 1880 for funds for schools in four hamlets with populations of 120, 66, 46 and 20. In the southern Massif Central, seen as the classic case of 'backwardness', there were no fewer than 852 schools for 24,464 pupils, the highest ratio (1 : 29) in France. The impulse for a veritable mania for new and improved roads similarly came from within the region.[8]

Two-thirds of schoolchildren attended the state schools of the Second Empire and Third Republic where they encountered teachers increasingly likely to be trained and imbued with a professional zeal for their educating mission. They and their school texts taught children a mental map which situated them within a French historical, linguistic and geographical entity. Reactions to the news of the defeats in 1870, in regions far from the eastern frontier, highlight this assumption of 'Frenchness': in the Dordogne a violent crowd of 'patriots' murdered a liberal noble deemed to be a 'Prussian'; in the west, grandsons of the *chouans* of 1793 or 1832 now formed the 'Volunteers of the West' to go and fight.[9]

Nineteenth-century élites, progressively more bourgeois in social composition and ideology after 1815, dominated a state apparatus which gradually widened its spheres of control over public life. By 1880, the State had extended its hegemony over the means of coercion and administration by more wide-ranging techniques of surveillance and record collection. Its concern to use a national prison system to 'moralize' as well as to punish was symbolized in the transformation in the meaning of the guillotine: from a deliberately public display of extraordinary punishment during the French Revolution to one form of punishment among others under the Third Republic. In 1872 the scaffold was abandoned, making the guillotine less of a public spectacle, and executioners were given wage increases within the public servants' scale.

The more confident claims of the professions (medicine, psychology, law) to a monopoly of knowledge about human nature and its deviations were similarly part of a wider bourgeois discourse on the moral and gendered characteristics of a perfectly-ordered society. This was also a discourse of the senses, a 'perceptual revolution' in Alain Corbin's words, which created across the nineteenth century our 'odourless' environment by cleansing cities of the smells of animals, refuse and humans. Taken together, these concerns to 'moralize the masses' created what Michel Foucault called the 'disciplinary' society, the cultural preconditions for twentieth-century forms of authoritarian rule. His influential thesis needs to be qualified by a recognition of an enduring humanitarian, liberal tradition: after 1820 the courts became harsher towards public exhibitions of sexual and bodily functions and the sexual exploitation of children, but more lenient towards the private practice of homosexuality and women accused of adultery. Compared with 1780, those who transgressed élite rules of civil behaviour were no longer tortured or subjected to physical degradation beyond incarceration itself; homosexuals were no longer liable to capital punishment and contrary political opinions were no longer a capital offence; nor were Protestants and Jews subject to constraints on the open practice of their beliefs.[10]

By 1914, the French State had never been so uniform, centralized and uncontested: it could draw on deep reserves of patriotism and obedience. Across the 'long nineteenth century', the claims of the nation-state to loyalty and duty had become embedded in popular identity, even among ethnic minorities. At the farthest extremity from Paris is the small Pyrenean town of Saint-Laurent-de-Cerdans. Here the French Revolution had quickly soured for its Catalan inhabitants with ecclesiastical reforms perceived as an urban, secular outrage against orthodox Catholicism. At the outbreak of war in April 1793, a group of men had gone to the Spanish headquarters to guide troops through the Pyrenean passes, then fired on retreating French volunteers, and several hundred men fought alongside Spanish troops for a year until Jacobin armies retook the area in May 1794. The call to arms in 1914 struck a very different chord. Telling and visible evidence of the change in the nature of personal identity and of the acceptance of the imperatives of the nation-state is to be found outside the chapel of Notre-Dame-de-la-Sort in Saint-Laurent, on the *monument aux morts*. The monument, from which the Spanish border is visible, carries the names of 126 young Laurentins (4 per cent of the entire population) who, rather than slip across the border, had died for *la grande nation* in World War I.

Political élites took the pervasive tenets of their ideology – of commitment to a civilizing mission, national prestige, and self-interest – to their external colonization. Tahiti (once dismissed by Louis-Philippe as 'a few grains of tobacco in the Pacific'), New Caledonia, Indo-China, North Africa, Senegal and the older colonies of the Caribbean formed a scattered and often neglected 'empire' until the 1870s, but by 1914 were administered within the structures of a colonial empire mirroring those of Great Britain and Germany. The crushing of the Kanak rebellion of 1878 opened much of the west and south-west of New Caledonia to white settlement and accelerated the sharp fall in the indigenous population. Convict labour, including that of transported Arab rebels from North Africa, was a valued source of cheap labour in the nascent nickel industry. Elsewhere, colonial policies were more subtle, assuming the potential of colonized people to become full French citizens. Victor Schoelcher, an anti-slavery campaigner and Caribbean deputy since 1848, succeeeded by the early 1880s in winning approval for assimilationist policies, including French education and military conscription.[11]

Changes in the ideology of ruling élites and their supporters and in political institutions were the result of gradual, often subtle, transformations in demographic and economic structures, and the interdependent changes in social relations and perceptions. The specific impact of these changes was a function of social class, and varied between men and women in those classes as well as between and within regions, but no-one was untouched. By the turn of the twentieth century an urban, bourgeois and republican culture had become as hegemonic as had been that of the Church and aristocracy under the *ancien régime*. It is for this reason that the 'long nineteenth century' from 1789 to 1914 has been described by Roger Magraw as the 'bourgeois century'. In the 1780s France was an agrarian, pre-capitalist society in which most of the population, the location of most industry and the sources of power and most wealth were rural; control of land and its producers was the source of the extraction of 'surplus product' by the nobility, clergy, some bourgeois and the State. Across the decades to 1914 an interconnected series of gradual changes altered this society irreversibly, if by no means completely. By the early years of the twentieth century, France was a capitalist society in which market-oriented agriculture and a growing urban industrial economy were the source of the extraction of 'surplus value', by economic élites and the State, from the labour of urban and rural wage-labourers and the self-employed. This was by no means a complete or uncontested process: this was, after all, also a revolutionary century. In 1914 a considerable minority of urban workers espoused socialist ideologies which repudiated the fundamentals of capitalism; in parts of the countryside, languages and cultures survived which spoke of the resilience of peasant societies which did not espouse the same values as urban centres and economies.

France's towns and cities had experienced a series of qualitative changes in their function, size and relationship with the countryside. In the late eighteenth century, a maximum of 20 per cent of the population lived in communities of more than 2,000 people, perhaps 8 per cent in the 75 genuine towns of 10,000 or more. Particular cities such as Lyon, Reims, Marseille, Bordeaux and Nantes were bustling hubs of commerce and manufacturing, and large-scale industry was emerging in centres such as Le Creusot and Anzin. However, most towns and cities were parasitic on the countryside, drawing men and taxes for the State, and rents, seigneurial dues and tithes which noble and clerical élites largely expended within the towns themselves. The retailing and craft industries of these provincial towns, even Paris, focused essentially on the needs of the urban population, including luxury goods for wealthy nobles, clerics and bourgeois.

Revolutionary change after 1789 sharply curtailed the role of provincial towns as centres of noble and clerical consumption, employment and administration, while strengthening their function within a uniform state hierarchy of administration and policing. Many, like Bayeux or Autun, became little more than administrative and service centres for a more commercial agricultural hinterland. Others, such as Rouen, Toulouse, Lyon and Lille, experienced a new revolution in work processes and social relations. Established crafts, such as the clothing, textile and printing trades, were transformed by the introduction of new machinery, the concentration of stages of the work process in larger, urban workplaces, and the division of labour by gender and task. Elsewhere, as in Limoges and Saint-Etienne or in mono-industrial towns like Carmaux, Decazeville and Roubaix, the discovery of new resources and technologies for their processing created distinctively working-class cultures in large-scale capitalist industries. The diversity of this urban, industrial change created a workforce with internal divisions by gender, types of skills and size of workplace. Everywhere, however, the language of labour became the language of class.

In the transition from *sans-culottes* and *menu peuple* to workers and proletarians lay a transformation in the world of urban work, while workers' understandings of their changing world continued to be informed by collective memories and experiences dating back to the *ancien régime*. By 1896, the urban population of France was 39.5 per cent of the total; between 1811 and 1911, the population in towns with more than 3,000 inhabitants increased from 4.2 million to 13.8 millon, while the three biggest cities, Paris, Lyon and Marseille, more than trebled in size.

The corollary of these changes, and greater specialization in the countryside, was that urban entrepreneurs had largely conquered, in Marx's term, 'the home market for capital'. Never before had such a large proportion of the population been dependent on selling its labour or produce in order to purchase the necessities of life. For those with disposable incomes beyond the bare necessities, a mass consumer culture developed in large cities and their environs, exemplified in the new department stores which boomed after 1870. Similarly, the mass production of printed matter, especially novels and newspapers, was integral to urban and industrial life, and one way in which an essentially urban and bourgeois culture established a greater presence within a national culture which coexisted uneasily with other, regional and working-class cultures.[12]

Rather more gradual, but no less significant, were socio-economic changes in the countryside. At first glance, France might seem to have remained a nation of peasant smallholders, tenant farmers and labourers: farms smaller than 20 hectares covered perhaps one-third of the countryside in 1789 and about half in 1884, and the number of people living in rural communities, perhaps 22.5 million in the 1780s, was almost the same a century later. Historians have seen such apparent continuity as evidence of the limited impact of the French Revolution and of the 'backward' nature of the French economy in the nineteenth century. But such simple statistics hide a multitude of changes, both striking and subtle, which varied aross the country in their timing, nature and impact but were nonetheless felt everywhere.

The most important transformation in rural society was that by which peasant polyculture became specialized small farming or 'commodity production'. Market specialization, evident only in the hinterland of large cities in the eighteenth century, was facilitated by the Revolution, which removed the exactions of seigneurs and Church, put up church and *émigré* property for sale, and created the institutional environment for a national market. Small farming coexisted with large-scale, capitalist farming in particular areas, and became more specialized by region across the century. By 1880, most rural people were *paysans* (peasants) only in their attachment to their *pays* and no longer in terms of the way they produced. These changes were paralleled by the disappearance from the countryside of the textile and metallurgical 'proto-industries', which became concentrated in urban centres, and more frequent purchase of urban manufactures, many of them previously produced within rural communities themselves: in countless villages the grocer and dressmaker replaced the charcoal burner and weaver.

By the mid-nineteenth century the population of rural France had reached its historic peak (27 million) and the cultivated land surface its maximum.

A combination of the decline in work opportunities in 'deindustrializing' areas, farm mechanization, and the perceived attractions of the city quickened the exodus of the poorest sections of rural society after 1851. The slight easing of pressure on soil resources is one reason why the years between 1852 and 1880 have been described as 'the peak of rural civilization': never before had so many country folk lived in relative security, and even prosperity for many, nor had such easy access to education, travel and outside ideas. And never again afterwards would rural France be such a diverse human and natural environment in its languages, cultures, fauna and flora, and patterns of production.

At the same time, the signs were evident of the future decay of this great civilization, which was ultimately to prove incompatible with the linked forces of capitalist agriculture and a more intrusive State. Specialized agriculture and the collapse of part-time industrial work narrowed the range of occupations and skills within the community and the household, and would widen the gap in the nature and status of men's and women's work. These changes to complex poly-cultural routines would slowly erode the regional cultures with which they were interdependent at the same time as schooling and retailing were exposing rural people more consistently to a Parisian culture. Changes in resource use, land clearance and reclamation, and monoculture would place greater strain on the environment and reduce the variety of plants and animals. The depopulation of mountain areas permitted the first steps towards reafforestation, but elsewhere the transition from peasant polyculture was to be deleterious to the regional cultures and natural ecologies of the countryside.

The exodus of many young people in search of work opportunities in cities, and the erosion by specialization of the complex household economy within which women's farm labour was crucial, had the effect of reinforcing patriarchal authority. As the complexity of farm work and domestic textile labour receded in the face of specialization and the urbanization of industry, so the importance and range of women's work declined; this was most dramatic in wine-growing areas. The essential characteristic of peasant farming – the household as the unit of both production and 'auto-consumption', dependent on the diverse labours of all its members – was being simplified to an enterprise in which males did most farm work. Where the labour of women became confined to domestic work, child-rearing and the farmyard, the higher status always accorded to men's work became accentuated.

Of course, socio-economic transformations of such magnitude were infinitely varied in their specific nature, timing and intensity across the face of a large, diverse country. Some regions, notably the upland areas of Brittany, the Massif Central and the Pyrenees, remained polycultural, peasant lands into the twenti-eth century, while the collapse of local industries slowly drained people and wealth away. Sawyers who trudged from the Massif Central in the 1890s to spend the winter cutting wood in the Morvan before returning to their farms for the summer harvests were following ancient practices of seasonal migration. But no community lived through the long century to 1914 without major social change: to its population, social structure, economic base, political culture and the collective memories through which its people made sense of the world. This may be illustrated by the example of the Mediterranean village of Canet (see Chapter 8) . Here people remembered the exactions of Jacobin armies and the 'dechristianizing' of 'representatives on mission' in 1793–4 with a horror that made most of them fervent legitimists in the early nineteenth century. A transition from polyculture to viticulture began in the 1830s and surged further in the 1860s with the end of the oidium disease and the arrival of the railway in nearby Perpignan. The population increased from 233 in 1806 to 806 in 1881 as migrants from the Pyrenees settled there permanently; by 1886 only 47 per cent of Canetois were native-born. Canet's population further swelled to 1,215 in 1911 as migrants from the Pyrenees seized on new work opportunities in the vineyards. The transition from polyculture to wine-growing, secular education, and political conflict undermined an earlier devout religiosity. A subsistence economy based on sheep, vegetables and wheat had all but disappeared, and with it older cultural and political assumptions: in 1856, when fields were exposed to drought, a procession was held to appeal to Saint Gauderique, the local patron saint of rain; in the 1880s, when phylloxera threatened the vine-yards, wine-growers and labourers lobbied the government for tax relief and protection from foreign competition, and voted for a radical republican. In 1906, when church property was inventoried after the separation of Church and State, one hundred of the faithful, mainly women, led by a descendant of the former seigneur, barricaded themselves in Canet's parish church for four days; the majority of the men of the village, however, had been voting for left-wing republicans since the 1880s.[13]

These social changes slowly transformed popular perceptions of time and space. Most people in the 1780s were born into a world where the most common way of moving about, even over long distances, was on foot. The rhythms of the day were marked by the sound of distinctive church bells from churches in the neighbourhood and nearby villages. By 1910 city-dwellers in particular were becoming used to motorized transport: 64,000 motor vehicles were registered, and the Paris *Métropolitain* transported hundreds of thousands of people daily. However, even rural people had come to understand and value time and distance in new ways. The remembered appearance of the first bicycle in the western village of Mazières-en-Gâtine in 1890, as in countless other villages, touched a deep chord among people for whom walking great distances had been part of daily life. In the Languedocien village of Gabian, where the arrival of the train in 1879 had promised so much, people soon began com-plaining of the time it took to travel to Béziers: in 1916 the village council peti-tioned for a subsidy for a local bus that could cut the distance and time in half. In the southern Ardèche village of Balazuc, brilliantly studied by John Merriman, locals quipped that the long-awaited railway had arrived just in time, in 1876, for people to catch it as they left the area for good.[14] Here, as every-where, watches and clocks were becoming indispensable personal items. In 1891, Paris time was imposed on the whole of France; Greenwich Mean Time was accepted at a conference in Paris in 1912 as the basis of world time zones; in 1913 the first time signal was transmitted around the world, from the Eiffel Tower. To bring visitors to the 1900 Exhibition (again with a record atten-dance, this time of 51 million) a new station, the Gare d'Orsay, was constructed in the heart of Paris, with clocks six metres in diameter at each end. The

Métropolitain was also opened for the Exhibition, and by 1909 there were 63 kilometres of lines. Railways, already carrying more freight than roads by the 1860s, spread faster under the Freycinet Plan: in 1871 there were 15,632 kilometres of lines, and 40,838 by 1911. Demand for coal, iron and steel trebled accordingly in these decades.[15]

New technologies underpinned a perceptual revolution which slowly transformed the markers of individual and group identities. Following the development of daguerrotypes by Louis Daguerre in 1839, photography slowly became more simple and accessible for ordinary people. By the end of the century the rites of passage in family life – weddings, baptisms, departure for war – were commonly recorded by commercial photographers. Most spectacularly, however, this was the age of the village postcard, after the first illustrated postcard (depicting the Eiffel Tower) had been issued in 1889. Across the country an army of photographers recorded every village from afar, then its church and square cluttered with the local population. By 1907, between 300 and 600 million postcards were being produced annually, about fifty per family. Such postcards – invaluable as an historical source for French society at the turn of the century – performed multiple functions: maintaining contact with those who had left the village, attracting visitors on the trains which serviced tourist resorts, and engraining in individuals a sense of their place in a national mosaic.[16]

Increases in agricultural productivity, due to the emancipation of peasant land from seigneurial and ecclesiastical exactions in 1789–93 and more intensive and specialized land use thereafter, enabled rural producers to supply more essentials to an expanding urban population. Across the nineteenth century there were significant increases in the per capita consumption of food and drink across France as a whole, as Jean-Claude Toutain has calculated. (See Table C.1.) This substantial increase in the average daily calorific intake rather than changes in medical care, housing or public health explains why the national mortality rate declined from 25.3 per thousand in 1816–20 to 18.3 in 1911–13. On average, French men could hope to live to 48 years and women to 52 in 1913 and far longer if they survived infantile diseases, compared with 38 and 41 in 1850; in the late eighteenth century life expectancy was about 28 years for both men and women. People over 60 years of age were 12.6 per cent of the population in 1911, almost double their presence in the 1780s.[17]

These average per capita increases in material standards of living hide stark differences according to class and region. In the 1880s 6 per cent of Parisians were classified as indigent, a far lower figure than a century earlier, but this varied from fewer than 2 per cent in the wealthy 8th *arrondissement* to about 13 per cent in the 20th. In the wealthiest districts of Paris the mortality rate was 11 per 10,000 in 1911–13 but 16.5 in the poorer *arrondissements*. One-third of the young men conscripted in 1872 were unfit for military service because they were under 1.45 m. (4′10″) in height (16.5 per cent of those rejected), syphilitic (4.7 per cent), suffering from rickets or consumption (28 per cent), or other physical ailments caused by malnutrition. Sharp regional contrasts also endured: Parisians had on average three times the disposable income of the Bretons of Finistère, though such material differences were

Table C.1   Food consumption in France per capita, 1781–1913

Daily consumption per capita

	1781–90	1905–13
Bread	552 g	730 g
Sugar	2.2 g	44.1 g
Fish	6.6 g	16.4 g
Animal fats	3.7 g	9.4 g
Vegetable oils	3.2 g	13.6 g
Wine	0.25 l	0.44 l
Potatoes	56.4 g (1803–12)	436.2 g
Milk	117.9 g ⎤ (1815–24)	263.6 g
Cheese	5.5 g ⎦	12.8 g

Yearly consumption per capita

	1789	1905–13
Fruit and vegetables	51 kg (approx.)	111 kg (approx.)
Meat	20 kg (max.)	48 kg (approx.)
Beer	3 l (1781–90)	35.5 l
Cider	26.1 l ⎤	40.2 l
Alcohol	0.9 l ⎬ (1815–24)	6.4 l
Coffee	0.24 kg ⎦	2.7 kg

offset by the consumption of self-produced food and non-material 'cultural goods'. While real wages in Paris increased significantly after 1850, the textile workers of Lille were evidently even poorer in 1880 than in 1850. In an economy increasingly dominated by liquid wealth and commercial exchange rather than landed wealth and 'auto-consumption', the great success of economic élites had been to thwart all attempts to introduce a tax on income instead of land until 1913.

On average, French people were considerably better off in material terms in 1900 compared to 1780, but there is no evidence that differences in wealth had narrowed. On the contrary, the Second Empire in particular had widened the gap between rich and poor.[18] Towards the end of the century, urban working-class families were estimated to be spending two-thirds to three-quarters of their income on food, half of that on bread alone, of which they would eat 2,000 kilograms a year per family. There were minimal workplace protections: an 1898 law limited working hours for children under 18 and women to 11 hours per day. The 1906 census recorded that, of those living in towns and cities of over 5,000 people, 26 per cent lived in dwellings with an average of more than two people to a room.[19]

Compulsory primary education and the gradual increase in material standards of living may be two reasons why there was a significance decrease in trials for murder and serious assault, from 22 cases per 100,000 people in 1820–30 to 8 per 100,000 in 1911–13. The fluctuations in numbers of rape cases may, however, be as much a function of public attitudes and changing laws as of the incidence of sexual assault: the number of cases involving adults increased from 136 in 1830 to a peak of 217 in 1850 and then tumbled to 65 in 1900; cases involving the rape of children increased from 107 in 1830 to a peak of 684 in 1860, then fell to 383 in 1900.[20]

Taken together, the general social trends in France between 1789 and 1914 – urbanization and industrialization, agrarian specialization and capitalism, parliamentary liberalism, the centralized nation-state, mass education, and so on – are often clustered under the umbrella term 'modernization'. The premises of 'modernization' theory have had a powerful but negative impact on the writing of social history: they presuppose that in society and politics, as in the market-place economy, the bourgeoisie of the nineteenth century was the repository of 'modern' values and behaviour taught or diffused to the urban and rural masses through a 'trickling-down' process. Modernization theory also tends to be tele-ological, turning into an inevitable process a whole series of social changes which need to be explained, and assuming that French people were unevenly spaced on an escalator of progress leading to the present day. Logically, if the masses clung to older or different ways of seeing and acting, or even fought against the forces of modernization, they may readily be described as 'backward' or even 'reactionary'. Certainly, the administrative hierarchies, political and literate élites – those who exercised power through their control of the written word and on whose reports, descriptions and images historians depend – judged many of these changes to be 'progress', 'growth' or 'development', terms which have no socially-neutral meaning. Other groups and individuals we have encountered in this book – such as Norbert Truquin, Jeanne Bouvier or the duchess of Saulx-Tavanes – would have found 'modernization' a condescending and mystifying term for the struggle they had to come to terms with and survive in a world with which they were at odds.[21]

Central to the modernization model is the argument that the consolidation of liberal, parliamentary government was the triumph of political modernity over both autocracy and recurrent popular insurrections. Social historians such as Ted Margadant and Roger Price have discerned a transition in the strategy of collective protest after 1850, from violent reactions to the intrusions of the State and capitalism, food and anti-tax riots, to 'proactive' mobilizations through unions, election campaigns, strikes and demonstrations aimed at winning influ-ence and control over national institutions. To Margadant, the key consequence of the failed resistance to the coup of 1851 was 'to prove that armed demon-strations had become an anachronistic form of political dissent'. To Price, acceptance of the values of manhood suffrage and parliamentary democracy, nationalism and theoretical equality of opportunity within an expanding econ-omy brought the age of revolution to an end. Others have argued that the social composition and ideology of urban popular movements changed little if at all across the course of this century, that the Paris Commune was the final act in a pre-industrial *sans-culottes* tradition. Five times, in 1789, 1792, 1830, 1848 and 1870–1, large-scale, popular rebellion had succeeded in overthrowing political regimes; now, with the confidence that popular choice was at last also republi-can, the revolutionary century was over. This argument also draws support from cultural historians who have emphasized continuities in rural life and *mentalités*. Emmet Kennedy has argued that, in the decades before the French Revolution, the Enlightenment drove a wedge between élite and popular cultures; indeed, by relying on Eugen Weber's imagery of a countryside which only began to change in the 1870s, he was able largely to exclude rural people from his *Cultural History of the French Revolution*. The corollary of Weber's argument that after the 1880s northern, bourgeois, urban culture became hegemonic – that the gap between élite and popular cultures closed again – is that popular revolt in the intervening century was the result of a cultural 'lag' in which archaic hatreds of the rich erupted in indiscriminate violence.[22]

This argument is questioned by the on-going existence of revolutionary political organizations and massive popular mobilizations which, in 1907, 1936, 1944 and 1968, almost toppled governments. Most importantly, the victory of parliamentary democracy under the Third Republic was due more than anything else to deeply-held beliefs among working people that popular sovereignty implied manhood suffrage and electoral choice. In the end, this was a victory won by revolution 'from below'. The collapse of the Second Empire lay not only in military defeat but also, as with monarchical regimes in 1789, 1830 and 1848, in widespread resentment at its ruler's claims to personal power. Resistance to the practice of parliamentary democracy came from entrenched élites, not from insufficiently 'enlightened' working people with a predilection for violent protest.

A general 'modernization' model of change is also too crude to accommodate the complexities of past experience. For example, the modernizing forces of urbanization and mass education are seen as inexorably secularizing beliefs about the place of the individual and group in an understanding of humanity, and sapping the habit of religious worship. Certainly, as Philippe Boutry has argued, there may well have been a subtle but epochal shift in the meaning of religious belief, from an unquestioned part of a culture or *mentalité* to a matter of opinion open to contestation. (One measure of the erosion of religious authority may be the increase in the proportion of births outside marriage, from 2.6 per cent in the 1780s to 8.1 per cent a century later.) However, the trends in religious practice after 1780 seem most of all to have reinforced existing patterns which varied according to region, gender and social class. By the late nineteenth century, worship was as generalized in Brittany, the southern Massif Central, the west and Alsace as a century earlier, while in the Ile-de-France, the Beauce, Champagne and parts of the Midi the secularization of public life and decline in church-going only confirmed the clerical despair of the *ancien régime*. Across the century, in Philippe Joutard's words, 'rather than the progress of disbelief, what we see is changes in beliefs and visions of the world, inside religious institutions as well as outside'.[23]

Paradoxically, the decades between 1830 and 1860, painted as years of grasping materialism by Flaubert, Balzac and Sue, were the great age of popular religious revival in much of urban and rural France. After the Revolution's fatal blows to the Catholic Church's wealth, monopoly of religious worship and corporate privileges, the most important religious development was the feminization of religious devotion and activism. In 1780, perhaps four in every one thousand women were *religieuses*, one-third of all clergy; a century later, seven per thousand were entering religious vocations and they were three-fifths of the total. By then there were 222 *congrégations* with more than 100 members: in all some 135,000 women compared with 12,000 early in the century. These women were overwhelmingly in the teaching service, as well as providing the medical and social care which the State and male professions neglected. The feminization of Catholicism may also have brought with it a popular image of a 'God of love', stronger than the authoritarian Tridentine 'God of fear' dominant in the eighteenth century. As a corollary, Claude Langlois and Caroline Ford have argued that, despite the violent protests during the Dreyfus Affair and the separation of Church and State in 1903–5, the public display of punitive bloodshed had lessened sharply compared with the eighteenth century (as had cruelty towards animals).[24]

Just as the activities of women were the essence of Catholic revival in the nineteenth century, so women's labour inside and outside the home was integral to the broad social changes through which all French people lived. Some of these changes – rural exodus, the separation of home and workplace in many industries, monoculture in parts of the countryside – had the effects of distancing women from the supports (or constraints) of the extended family and of making paid work for mothers with young children extremely difficult. Minimal wages offered single women in paid work little chance of an adequate independence. In *L'Ouvrière* (1861), Jules Simon pointed out that a woman earning two francs per day would be left with about 60 centimes for food after paying for lodging (if she could work all year), but that most women earned only about 1 fr. 50 per day. Women responded to changes in the world of work by adjusting decisions about reproduction: while the marriage rate remained fairly constant, at about 15 marriages per thousand people per year, the birth-rate continued to decline, from about 39 per thousand in the 1780s to 25.3 in 1876–80. Adding to the impulse to limit family size – especially through contraception, but also by abortions and occasionally infanticide – was the rural woman's need to balance love of children against the constraints of partible inheritance.

We cannot know to what extent the inheritance rights of daughters and widespread assumptions that women could restrict their fertility without eternal damnation were seen by them as empowering, even 'liberating'. The frenzied public discourse about 'women's place', female criminality and prostitution after the Paris Commune is one gauge of women's ongoing refusal 'to suffer and be still'. However, the energetic efforts of feminists had not successfully challenged idealized gender roles or the assumption that political culture was a male preserve. Whatever their political persuasion, male élites in 1914 no less than in 1794 or 1834 continued to proselytize an ideology of separate spheres which veiled the unhappy reality of many marriages and was a far cry from the exigencies of survival for most women. But women continued to be divided about their own 'nature' and rights; the great-granddaughters of the women of Millau who protested violently against the Civil Constitution of the Clergy in 1791 (see Chapter 2) rioted when the divorce-law campaigner Alfred Naquet came to their town in 1879.[25]

In a commentary headed *Plus ça change*, the English historian Alfred Cobban once characterized the nineteenth century as one of 'stagnation without stability'. Cobban's dismissive conclusion that this century had been 'an unattractive chapter in the history of France' stemmed from his own distaste for what he saw as the irresponsibility of radical ideologues, the 'unorganized horde' of Paris, and Bohemian artists and writers scornful of the meretricious mediocrity of a series of self-serving regimes. This book has instead argued that popular support for revolutionary ideologies was not born merely of despair and ignorance and that painters were more closely integrated into their society than the term 'bohemian' suggests. Among elderly French people at the official celebrations of Bastille Day after 1880, many may have agreed with Cobban that the loss of a loved one through war or disease, of youthful hopes, of pride in a skill, had indeed made the world an unattractive place. None would have agreed with him that, underlying the repeated political upheavals they had witnessed and participated in, little had changed in daily life. The people whom this book has been about would have found this a very odd proposition. Whether from Paris or Limoges, Canet or Bonnières, they would have heard stories from their grandparents of a Napoleonic world of legendary proportions; the elderly would also have handed on their own parents' tales, of a France in the 1780s that must have seemed another world altogether.

These were individual tales of joy and sadness, of a life of work, insecurities and small triumphs, of the politics of the neighbourhood, village and great men. The drama of the long century after 1789 lay in the rich and often conflicting variety of understandings people gave to the changing world around them, a world they often sought to change in their own interests, even if it was too rarely a world of their own making.

Notes

Introduction

1. *The Memoirs of Frédéric Mistral*, trans. G. Wickes (New York, 1986), ch. 9 ('progress' is capitalized in the original); Arno J. Mayer, *The Persistence of the Old Régime: Europe to the Great War* (London, 1981), esp. Introduction.
2. G. M. Trevelyan, *English Social History* (London, 1942), vii.
3. Roger Price, *A Social History of Nineteenth-Century France* (London, 1987); Roger Magraw, *France 1815–1914: The Bourgeois Century* (London, 1983); Theodore Zeldin, *France 1848–1945*, 2 vols (Oxford, 1973–7). Useful discussions of the nature and pitfalls of social history are collected in *JSH* 10 (1976), especially the contributions by Perrot, Fox-Genovese and Genovese, and Zeldin.
4. Different 'calendars' are described in Richard Cobb, *Reactions to the French Revolution* (Oxford, 1972). An example of an alternative structure for the history of women is Bonnie S. Anderson and Judith P. Zinsser, *A History of Their Own: Women in Europe from Prehistory to the Present*, 2 vols (New York, 1988). The argument that political history must be the backbone of social history is well put in articles by Jacques Le Goff and Eric Hobsbawm in *Daedalus*, 100 (1971).
5. Charles Tilly, *The Vendée* (Cambridge, MA, 1964), 83. The paucity of documentation concerning attitudes and feelings, except when manifested in extreme behaviour, renders the project proposed by William Reddy for a 'history of emotions' highly improbable: *The Navigation of Feeling: A Framework for the History of Emotions* (Cambridge, 2001). On the disabled, see Thérèse-Adèle Husson, *Reflections. The Life and Writings of a Young Blind Woman in Post-Revolutionary France*, translated and with commentary by Catherine J. Kudlick and Zina Weygand (New York, 2001). Spirited attacks on the esoterica of social history are Tony Judt, 'A Clown in Regal Purple: Social History and the Historians', *HW 7* (1979), 66–94; Robert Darnton, 'Pop Foucaultism', *New York Review of Books* 9 October 1986, 15–16. The figures for theses are from Robert Darnton, 'Intellectual and Cultural History', in Michael Kammen (ed.), *The Past Before Us* (Ithaca, NY, 1980), 327–49.
6. A revealing discussion of one such statistical survey is Joan Scott, 'Statistical Representations of Work: The Politics of the Chamber of Commerce's *Statistique de l'industrie à Paris, 1847–48*', in Steven L. Kaplan and Cynthia J. Koepp (eds), *Work in France: Representations, Meaning, Organization and Practice* (Ithaca, NY, 1986), 335–63.

7. A brilliant exploration of the 'socio-cultural' dimensions of the political is Colin Jones and Dror Wahrman, *The Age of Cultural Revolutions: Britain and France, 1750–1820* (Berkeley and Los Angeles, CA, 2002).

1 France in the 1780s

1. France in the 1780s Robert Forster, *The Nobility of Toulouse in the Eighteenth Century* (Baltimore, MD, 1960), 193–5.

2. Excellent general overviews of rural France are Daniel Roche, *France in the Enlightenment*, trans. Arthur Goldhammer (Cambridge, MA, 1998), ch. 4; Peter Jones, *The Peasantry in the French Revolution* (Cambridge, 1988), chs 1, 2; and Georges Duby and Armand Wallon (eds), *Histoire de la France rurale*, vol. 3 (Paris, 1976). Population figures are in Jacques Dupâquier, *Histoire de la population française*, vol. 3 (Paris, 1988).

3. Fernand Braudel, *The Identity of France*, trans. S. Reynolds, vol. 1 (London, 1988), esp. 91–7; Peter McPhee, 'A Case-Study of Internal Colonization: The Francisation of Northern Catalonia', *Review* 3 (1980), 399–428. See also the special issue of *TM* nos. 324–325–326 (1973).

4. John W. Shaffer, *Family and Farm: Agrarian Change and Household Organization in the Loire Valley 1500–1900* (Albany, NY, 1982), 48–9. On the household economy, see Olwen Hufton, 'Women and the Family Economy in Eighteenth-Century France', FHS 9 (1975), 1–22; and *The Prospect Before Her: A History of Women in Western Europe, 1500–1800* (New York, 1996), esp. ch. 4; David Troyansky, *Old Age in the Old Régime: Image and Experience in Eighteenth-Century France* (Ithaca, NY, 1989), ch. 6.

5. Liana Vardi, *The Land and the Loom: Peasants and Profit in Northern France 1680–1800* (Durham, NC, and London, 1993).

6. Etienne Gautier and Louis Henry, *La Population de Crulai, paroisse normande: étude historique* (Paris, 1958), 89.

7. For Paris in the 1780s, see Daniel Roche, *The People of Paris: An Essay in Popular Culture in the 18th Century*, trans. M. Evans, (Berkeley, CA, 1987); David Garrioch, *Neighbourhood and Community in Paris 1740–1790* (Cambridge, 1986) and *The Making of Revolutionary Paris* (Berkeley, CA, 2002); Jeffry Kaplow, *The Names of Kings: The Parisian Laboring Poor in the Eighteenth Century* (New York, 1972); Thomas Brennan, *Public Drinking and Popular Culture in Eighteenth-Century Paris* (Princeton, NJ, 1988); Arlette Farge, *Fragile Lives: Violence, Power, and Solidarity in Eighteenth-Century Paris*, trans. Carol Shelton (Cambridge, MA, 1993).

8. Steven L. Kaplan, *La Fin des corporations* (Paris, 2001).

9. Jacques-Louis Ménétra, *Journal of My Life*, trans. A. Goldhammer (New York, 1986). The works of Restif de la Bretonne, particularly *Les Nuits de Paris*, are similarly illuminating.

10. Kaplan and Koepp (eds), *Work in France*, chs 2–9; William H. Sewell, *Work and Revolution in France: The Language of Labor from the Old Régime* to 1848 (Cambridge, 1980), chs 2–3; Michael Sonenscher, *Work and*

Wages: Natural Law, Politics and the Eighteenth-Century French Trades (Cambridge, 1989).

11. Alan Forrest, *Society and Politics in Revolutionary Bordeaux* (Oxford, 1975), ch. 1.

12. Jean-Michel Deveau, *La Traite rochelaise* (Paris, 1990); Roche, *France in the Enlightenment*, ch. 5; James F. Searing, *West African Slavery and Atlantic Commerce: The Senegal River Valley, 1770–1860* (Cambridge, 1993); Robert-Louis Stein, *The French Slave Trade in the Eighteenth Century* (Madison, WI, 1979); Stewart R. King, *Blue Coat or Powdered Wig: Free People of Color in Pre-Revolutionary Saint Domingue* (Athens, GA, 2001).

13. Cissie Fairchilds, *Domestic Enemies: Servants and Their Masters in Old Regime France* (Baltimore, MD, 1984); Sarah C. Maza, *Servants and Masters in Eighteenth-Century France: The Uses of Loyalty* (Princeton, NJ, 1983); Pierre H. Boulle, 'Les Gens de couleur à Paris à la veille de la Révolution', in Michel Vovelle (ed.), *L'Image de la Révolution française* (Oxford, 1989), vol. 1, 159–68.

14. George D. Sussman, *Selling Mothers' Milk: The Wet-Nursing Business in France 1715–1914* (Urbana, IL, 1982), chs 2–4. For the recollections of a middle-class Breton boy placed with a wet-nurse for five years, see Emile Souvestre, *Mémoires d'un sans-culotte bas-Breton* (Brussels, 1843), 11–12.

15. Michel Vovelle, *Ville et campagne au 18e siècle: Chartres et la Beauce* (Paris, 1980).

16. Thomas F. Sheppard, *Lourmarin in the Eighteenth Century: A Study of a French Village* (Baltimore, MD, 1971), ch. 2; Pierre Goubert, 'Legitimate Fecundity and Infant Mortality in France During the Eighteenth Century: A Comparison', *Daedalus* 97 (1968), 593–603; Peter McPhee, *Collioure et la Révolution française, 1789–1815* (Perpignan, 1989), ch. 1.

17. Jean-Louis Flandrin, *Les Amours paysannes: amour et sexualité dans les campagnes de l'ancienne France (XVIe–XIXe siècle)* (Paris, 1975); and *Families in Former Times: Kinship, Household and Sexuality in Early Modern France*, trans. R. Southern (Cambridge, 1979), ch. 4; Philippe Ariès, *Centuries of Childhood*, trans. R. Baldick (Harmondsworth, 1973), ch. 15; François Lebrun, *Se soigner autrefois: médecins, saints et sorciers aux 17e et 18e siècles* (Paris, 1983), ch. 5; and the special issues of *Annales* 32 (1977) and *JSH* 10 (1977).

18. Jones, *Peasantry*, ch. 2; Donald Sutherland, *The Chouans: The Social Origins of Popular Counter-Revolution in Upper Brittany, 1770–1796* (Oxford, 1982), 70.

19. Forster, *Nobility of Toulouse*, esp. chs 2–3 and 'Obstacles to Agricultural Growth in Eighteenth-Century France', *AHR*, 75 (1970), 1600–15. On the size and internal hierarchy of the nobility, see Guy Chaussinand-Nogaret, *The French Nobility in the Eighteenth Century: From Feudalism to Enlightenment*, trans. W. Doyle (Cambridge, 1985), chs 2, 4.

20. Anthony Crubaugh, *Balancing the Scales of Justice. Local Courts and Rural Society in Southwest France, 1750–1800* (University Park, PA, 2001).

21. Alain Collomp, *La Maison du père: famille et village en Haute-Provence aux XVIIe et XVIIIe siècles* (Paris, 1983), 286.

22. Olwen Hufton, *Bayeux in the Late Eighteenth Century: A Social Study* (Oxford, 1967), chs 1, 2, 5. Useful overviews of the Catholic Church are Ralph Gibson, *A Social History of French Catholicism, 1789–1914* (London, 1989), ch. 1; Timothy Tackett and Claude Langlois, 'Ecclesiastical Structures and Clerical Geography on the Eve of the French Revolution', *FHS* 11 (1980), 352–70; Roche, *France in the Enlightenment*, ch. 11; Nigel Aston, *Religion and Revolution in France, 1780–1804* (Basingstoke, 2000), part 1; Philippe Joutard (ed.) *Histoire de la France religieuse*, vol. 3, *Du roi Très Chrétien à la laïcité républicaine XVIIIe-XIXe siècle*, 2nd ed. (Paris, 2001), 11–45; and the outstanding survey by John McManners, *Church and Society in Eighteenth-Century France*, 2 vols (Oxford and New York, 1998).

23. Roche, *France in the Enlightenment*, ch. 11; Dale Van Kley, *The Religious Origins of the French Revolution: From Calvin to the Civil Constitution, 1560–1791* (New Haven, CT, 1996).

24. John McManners, *French Ecclesiastical Society under the Ancien Régime* (Manchester, 1960), chs 1, 6; see also Martyn Lyons, *Revolution in Toulouse. An Essay on Provincial Terrorism* (Bern, 1978), ch. 2; Bernard Bodinier and Eric Teyssier, *L'Evénement le plus important de la Révolution: la vente des biens nationaux en France et dans les territoires annexés, 1789–1867* (Paris, 2000), 333–62.

25. On Protestants and Jews, see Burdette C. Poland, *French Protestantism and the French Revolution: A Study in Church and State, Thought and Religion, 1685–1815* (Princeton NJ, 1957); Zoja Szajkowski, *Jews and the French Revolutions of 1789, 1830, and 1848* (New York, 1970); Marianne Calmann, *The Carrière of Carpentras* (Oxford and New York, 1984); McManners, *Church and Society*, ch. 46; Joutard, *Histoire de la France religieuse*, vol. 3, 46–63.

26. Gibson, *French Catholicism*, 22; Iain A. Cameron, *Crime and Repression in the Auvergne and the Guyenne 1720–1790* (Cambridge, 1981), 230–2. Research into the history of *mentalités* is expertly summarized by Michel Vovelle, 'Le Tournant des mentalités en France 1750–1789: la 'sensibilité' pré-révolutionnaire', *SH* 5 (1977), 605–29 (in English); Robert Darnton, *The Kiss of Lamourette: Reflections in Cultural History* (New York, 1990), ch. 12.

27. Olwen Hufton, *The Poor of Eighteenth-Century France, 1750–1789* (Oxford, 1974); Colin Jones, *Charity and 'Bienfaisance': The Treatment of the Poor in the Montpellier Region, 1740–1815* (Cambridge, 1982), and *The Charitable Imperative: Hospitals and Nursing in Ancien Régime and Revolutionary France* (London, 1989); McManners, *Ecclesiastical Society*, chs 1, 6; Forrest, *Bordeaux*, ch. 1.

28. Peter Jones, *Politics and Rural Society: The Southern Massif Central c.1750–1880* (Cambridge, 1985), ch. 4; Patrice Higonnet, *Pont-de-Montvert: Social Structure and Politics in a French Village, 1700–1914* (Harvard, MA, 1971), ch. 3. On education, see François Furet and Jacques Ozouf, *Reading and Writing: Literacy in France from Calvin to Jules Ferry* (Cambridge, 1982), ch. 2.

29. Clive H. Church, *Revolution and Red Tape: The French Ministerial Bureaucracy 1770–1850* (Oxford, 1981), ch. 2.

30. Hufton, 'Women and the Family Economy', 21; and 'Women in Revolution 1789–1796', *P&P* 53 (1971), 92, 96; Roche, *France in the Enlightenment*, ch. 7, 287–99.

31. George Rudé, *The Crowd in History, 1730–1848* (New York, 1964), chs 1, 13–15; cf. Colin Lucas, 'The Crowd and Politics between Ancien Régime and Revolution in France', *JMH* 60 (1988), 421–57. Among the important studies of protest and the grain trade are Steven Kaplan, *Provisioning Paris: Merchants and Millers in the Grain and Flour Trade during the Eighteenth Century* (Ithaca, NY, 1984); Cynthia Bouton, *The Flour War: Gender, Class, and Community in late Ancien Regime French Society* (University Park, PA, 1993); Judith Miller, *Mastering the Market: The State and the Grain Trade in Northern France, 1700–1860* (Cambridge and New York, 1998); Jean Nicolas, *La Rébellion française. Mouvements populaires et conscience sociale, 1661–1789* (Paris, 2002).

32. Philippe Ariès and André Bejin, *Western Sexuality: Practice and Precept in Past and Present Times*, trans. A. Forster (Oxford, 1985), ch. 6; Robert Aldrich, 'Homosexuality in France', *Contemporary French Civilization*, 8 (1982), 1–19; Michel Rey, 'Du péché au désordre: police et sodomie à Paris au XVIIIe siècle', *RHMC* 29 (1982), 113–24; Antony Copley, *Sexual Moralities in France, 1780–1980: New Ideas on the Family, Divorce and Homosexuality* (London, 1989), 15–20; Colin Jones, 'Prostitution and the Ruling Class in 18th Century Montpellier', *HW* 6 (1978), 7–28; Louis Crompton, 'The Myth of Lesbian Impunity: Capital Laws from 1270 to 1791', *Journal of Homosexuality* 6 (1980–1), 11–25; the chapters by Ragan, Merrick and Sibalis in Jeffrey Merrick and Bryant T. Ragan (eds), *Homosexuality in Modern France* (Oxford, 1996); and the chapters by Delon and Trumbach in Robert P. Maccubbin (ed.), *'Tis Nature's Fault: Unauthorised Sexuality during the Enlightenment* (Cambridge, 1988).

33. Cameron, *Crime and Repression*, 154–75; Nicole Castan, 'Délinquance traditionnelle et répression critique à la fin de l'Ancien Régime dans les pays de langue d'oc', in Michelle Perrot (ed.), *L'Impossible Prison: recherches sur le système pénitentiaire au XIXe siècle* (Paris, 1980); and 'Summary Justice', in Robert Forster (ed.), *Deviants and the Abandoned in French Society* (Baltimore, MD, 1978), 111–56; Yves Castan, *Honnêteté et relations sociales en Languedoc, 1715–1780* (Paris, 1974).

34. The argument that wealthy nobles and bourgeois formed an élite of notables is put by William Doyle, *The Oxford History of the French Revolution* (Oxford, 1989), ch. 1; George V. Taylor, 'Noncapitalist Wealth and the Origins of the French Revolution', *AHR* 72 (1967), 469–96; Chaussinand-Nogaret, *French Nobility*, ch. 5. On Périer, see Bernard Bonnin in Michel Vovelle (ed.), *Bourgeoisies de province et Révolution* (Grenoble, 1987), 61–77. 'Consumer culture' is discussed in the important article by Colin Jones, 'Bourgeois Revolution Revivified: 1789 and Social Change', in Colin Lucas (ed.), *Rethinking the French Revolution* (Oxford, 1991).

35. Robert Darnton, *The Great Cat Massacre And Other Episodes in French Cultural History* (New York, 1984), ch. 3; Georges Vigarello, *Concepts of Cleanliness: Changing Attitudes in France since the Middle Ages*, trans. J. Birrell (Cambridge, 1988), chs 9–11.

36. Georges Lefebvre, *The Coming of the French Revolution*, trans. R. R. Palmer (Princeton, NJ, 1947), 4.

37. The 'undemocratic' and authoritarian aspects of the Enlightenment are stressed by Xavier Martin, *Human Nature and the French Revolution: From the Enlightenment to the Napoleonic Code*, trans. Patrick Corcoran (New York and Oxford, 2001). Current 'postmodern' critiques of the Enlightenment are discussed in Daniel Gordon (ed.), *Postmodernism and the Enlightenment: New Perspectives in Eighteenth-Century Intellectual History* (New York and London, 2001); and Keith Michael Baker and Peter Hanns Reill (eds), *What's Left of Enlightenment? A Postmodern Question* (Stanford, CA, 2001).

38. Robert Darnton, *The Literary Underground of the Old Regime* (Harvard, MA, 1982), and *The Business of Enlightenment: A Publishing History of the Encyclopédie, 1775–1800* (Cambridge, MA, 1979); see also Roger Chartier and Daniel Roche, *Histoire de l'édition française* (Paris, 1984), vols 2 and 3.

39. Thomas E. Crow, *Painters and Public Life in Eighteenth-Century Paris* (New Haven, CT, 1985); Sarah C. Maza, 'Domestic Melodrama as Political Ideology: The Case of the Comte de Sanois', *AHR* 94 (1989), 1249–64; and 'Politics, Culture, and the Origins of the French Revolution', *JMH* 61 (1989), 704–23; Joan B. Landes, *Women and the Public Sphere in the Age of the French Revolution* (Ithaca, NY, 1988), ch. 1; Ran Halévi, *Les Loges maçonniques dans la France d'ancien régime: aux origines de la sociabilité démocratique* (Paris, 1984); Daniel Roche, *Le Siècle des lumières en province: académies et académiciens provinciaux, 1680–1789*, 2 vols (Paris, 1978), vol. 1, 260–78; Jack Censer and Jeremy Popkin (eds), *Press and Politics in Pre-Revolutionary France* (Berkeley, CA, 1987); Dena Goodman, *The Republic of Letters: A Cultural History of the French Enlightenment* (Ithaca, NY, 1994); and Margaret C. Jacob, *Living the Enlightenment: Freemasonry and Politics in Eighteenth-Century Europe* (Oxford, 1991).

40. David Garrioch, *The Formation of the Parisian Bourgeoisie 1690–1830* (Cambridge, MA, 1996), 1; Sarah Maza, *Private Lives and Public Affairs: The Causes Célèbres of Prevolutionary France* (Berkeley, CA, 1993), and 'Luxury, Morality, and Social Change: Why There Was No Middle-Class Consciousness in Prerevolutionary France', *JMH* 69 (1997), 199–229; Jay M. Smith, 'Social Categories, the Language of Patriotism, and the Origins of the French Revolution: The Debate over *Noblesse Commerçante*', *JMH* 72 (2000), 339–74.

41. Jones, 'Bourgeois Revolution Revivified'; and 'The Great Chain of Buying: Medical Advertisement, the Bourgeois Public Sphere, and the Origins of the French Revolution', *AHR* 101 (1996), 13–40. This theme of the development of a commercial, consumer culture is addressed in engaging fashion by Roche, *France in the Enlightenment*, chs 5, 17, 19; and *The*

Culture of Clothing: Dress and Fashion in the 'Ancien Régime', trans. Jean Birrell (Cambridge, 1994).

42. Geneviève Bollème, *Les Almanachs populaires aux XVIIe et XVIIIe siècles: essai d'histoire sociale* (Paris, 1969); Emmet Kennedy, *A Cultural History of the French Revolution* (New Haven, CT, 1989), 38–47. Roger Chartier doubts the extent of the practice of reading aloud in *Cultural History: Between Practices and Representations*, trans. Lydia Cochrane (Cambridge, 1988), ch. 7.

43. Hilton L. Root, *Peasant and King in Burgundy: Agrarian Foundations of French Absolutism* (Berkeley, CA, 1987); Robert Forster, *The House of Saulx-Tavanes: Versailles and Burgundy, 1700–1830* (Baltimore, MD, 1971), ch. 2; Jones, *Peasantry*, 53–8; cf. William Doyle, 'Was There an Aristocratic Reaction in Pre-Revolutionary France?', *P&P* 57 (1972), 97–122; Guy Lemarchand, *Féodalisme, société et Révolution française: études d'histoire moderne, xvie–xviiie siècles* (Caen, 2000).

44. The classic Marxist formulation of the origins of the crisis of 1789 is in Lefebvre, *Coming*, 7–132; and Albert Soboul, *The French Revolution 1787–1799: From the Storming of the Bastille to Napoleon*, trans. Alan Forrest and Colin Jones (London, 1989), 25–113. Their argument is contested by William Doyle, *Origins of the French Revolution*, 2nd edn, (Oxford, 1980); George C. Comninel, *Rethinking the French Revolution: Marxism and the Revisionist Challenge* (London, 1987), chs 1, 2; T. C. W. Blanning, *The French Revolution: Aristocrats versus Bourgeois?* (London, 1987); Jacques Solé, *Questions of the French Revolution: A Historical Overview*, trans. S. Temchin (New York, 1989), chs 1–2. The importance of pre-revolutionary reform is stressed in Peter Jones, *Reform and Revolution in France: The Politics of Transition, 1774–1791* (Cambridge, 1995); Michael Kwass, *Privilege and the Politics of Taxation in Eighteenth-Century France: Liberté, Egalité, Fiscalité* (Cambridge, 2000).

45. Vivian R. Gruder, 'Can We Hear the Voices of Peasants? France, 1788', *History of European Ideas* 17 (1993), 167–90.

2 The Revolutionary Reconstruction of French Society, 1789–1792

1. Arthur Young, *Travels in France during the years 1787–1788–1789* (New York, 1969), 96–7.

2. Soboul, *French Revolution*, 120. For sharply contrasting political histories of 1788–92 see William Doyle, *The Oxford History of the French Revolution* (Oxford, 1989); Simon Schama, *Citizens: A Chronicle of the French Revolution* (New York, 1989). Neither account is able to evoke the social dynamics underpinning politics as effectively as Soboul.

3. Jeremy Popkin, *Revolutionary News: The Press in France* (London, 1990), 25–6.

4. Paul Beik (ed.), *The French Revolution* (London, 1971), 12; Emmanuel Sieyès, *What is the Third Estate?*, trans. M. Blondel (London, 1963);

William Sewell, *A Rhetoric of Bourgeois Revolution. The Abbé Sieyès and 'What is the Third Estate?'* (Durham, NC, 1994).

5. On the clergy in 1789, see John McManners, *The French Revolution and the Church* (London, 1969), 15–23; Ruth Necheles, 'The Curés in the Estates-General of 1789', *JMH* 46 (1974), 425–44; Maurice Hutt, 'The Role of the Curés in the Estates-General', *Journal of Ecclesiastical History* 6 (1955), 190–220.

6. George Rudé, *The Crowd in the French Revolution* (Oxford, 1959), ch. 3.

7. Philip Dawson (ed.), *The French Revolution* (Englewood Cliffs, NJ, 1967), 16–18, 30–2. Seigneurial judges presided over 53 per cent of village assemblies in the Orléanais. On the limitations to and uses of the *cahiers*, see Jones, *Peasantry*, 58–67; John Markoff, *The Abolition of Feudalism: Peasants, Lords, and Legislators in the French Revolution* (Philadelphia, PA, 1996), 25–9. These analyses contrast sharply with the 'revisionist' arguments of George V. Taylor, 'Revolutionary and Nonrevolutionary content in the *Cahiers* of 1789: an Interim report', *FHS* 7 (1972), 479–502.

8. Jeffry Kaplow (ed.), *France on the Eve of Revolution* (New York, 1971), 161–7; Michel Morineau, 'Budgets populaires en France au XVIIIe siècle', *Revue d'histoire économique et sociale* 1 (1972), 203–37. A remarkable children's *cahier* is reproduced in *AHRF* 278 (1989), 476–86.

9. The difficulties of reconciling noble 'reformism' with the intransigence of their deputies in 1789 is reflected in the tension between the 'Afterword' and chs 5, 7 and 8 in Chaussinand-Nogaret, *French Nobility*. The *cahier* of Dourdan is reproduced in John Hall Stewart (ed.), *A Documentary Survey of the French Revolution* (New York, 1951), 76–84.

10. Beik, *French Revolution*, 56–63. On Troyes, see Lynn Hunt, *Revolution and Urban Politics in Provincial France: Troyes and Reims, 1786–1790* (Stanford, CA, 1978), ch. 2.

11. On the elections of 1789, see Malcolm Crook, *Elections in the French Revolution: An Apprenticeship in Democracy, 1789–1799* (Cambridge and New York, 1996), ch. 1.

12. Rudé, *Crowd in the French Revolution*, ch. 4. The continuities in popular protest before and after 1789 are stressed in Lucas, 'Crowd and Politics'.

13. Hunt, *Revolution and Urban Politics*, chs 3–4. On the municipal revolution in general, see Lefebvre, *Coming*, ch. 8; Lynn Hunt, 'Committees and Communes: Local Politics and National Revolution in 1789', *CSSH* 23 (1976), 321–46.

14. J. M. Roberts (ed.), *French Revolution Documents*, vol. 1 (Oxford, 1966), 144–5. The rural revolt is the subject of the classic 1932 study by Georges Lefebvre, *The Great Fear of 1789: Rural Panic in Revolutionary France*, trans. J. White (New York, 1973), and is debated by Peter Jones and Hilton Root in *HW* 28 (1989), 88–110. A recent study is Clay Ramsay, *The Ideology of the Great Fear: The Soissonnais in 1789* (Baltimore, MD, 1992).

15. There is a detailed discussion of the Declaration in Dale Van Kley (ed.), *The French Idea of Freedom: The Old Regime and the Declaration of Rights of*

1789 (Stanford, CA, 1994). See, too, Lynn Hunt (ed.), *The French Revolution and Human Rights: A Brief Documentary History* (Boston, 1996), Introduction.

16. Rudé, *Crowd in the French Revolution*, 69 and ch. 5. An evocative overview of revolutionary Paris is by Richard M. Andrews, 'Paris of the Great Revolution: 1789–1796', in Gene Brucker, *People and Communities in the Western World* (Homewood, IL, 1979), vol. 2, 56–112. For studies of particular neighbourhoods, see Raymonde Monnier, *Le Faubourg St-Antoine: 1789–1815* (Paris, 1981); and Morris Slavin, *The French Revolution in Miniature: Section Droits-de-l'Homme, 1789–1795* (Princeton, NJ, 1984).

17. On the politics of the National Assembly see Alison Patrick, 'Revising the Noble Image: The Second Estate in the Constituent Assembly, 1789–1791', in David Garrioch (ed.), *Two Hundred Years of the French Revolution* (Melbourne, 1989), 63–74; Timothy Tackett, 'Nobles and Third Estate in the Revolutionary Dynamic of the National Assembly, 1789–1790', *AHR* 94 (1989), 271–301. The work of the Assembly is detailed in Jacques Godechot, *Les institutions de la France sous la Révolution et l'Empire* (Paris, 1951).

18. Jones, *Peasantry*, ch. 6; Lawrence Wylie, *Chanzeaux: A Village in Anjou* (Cambridge, MA, 1966), 27–31; Alison Patrick, 'The Approach of French Revolutionary Officials to Social Problems, 1790–1792', *AJFS* 18 (1981), 248–63.

19. Sheppard, *Lourmarin*, 180; Jones, *Peasantry*, 209; Jill Maciak, 'Of News and Networks: The Communication of Political Information in the Rural South-West during the French Revolution', *FH* 15 (2001), 273–306. Grégoire's inquiry is discussed in J.-Y. Lartichaux, 'Linguistic Politics during the French Revolution', *Diogenes* 97 (1977), 65–84; Martyn Lyons, 'Politics and Patois: The Linguistic Policy of the French Revolution', *AJFS* 18 (1981), 264–81; M. de Certeau, D. Julia, and J. Revel, *Une politique de la langue: la Révolution française et les patois. L'enquête de Grégoire* (Paris, 1975).

20. Daniel Arasse, *The Guillotine and the Terror*, trans. C. Miller (London, 1989), ch. 1; Copley, *Sexual Moralities*, 24–5; Jones, 'Prostitution and the Ruling Class'.

21. Jean-Paul Bertaud, *The Army of the French Revolution: From Citizen-Soldiers to Instrument of Power*, trans. R. R. Palmer (Princeton, NJ, 1988), ch. 1; Alan Forrest, *Soldiers of the French Revolution* (Durham, NC, 1990), ch. 2; Samuel F. Scott, *The Response of the Royal Army to the French Revolution: The Role and Development of the Line Army 1787–93* (Oxford, 1978). On the *émigrés* and counter-revolution, see Jacques Godechot, *The Counter-Revolution: Doctrine and Action, 1789–1804*, trans. S. Attanasio (London, 1972); Donald Greer, *The Incidence of the Emigration during the French Revolution* (Cambridge, MA, 1951).

22. Aimé Coiffard, *La Vente des biens nationaux dans le district de Grasse (1790–1815)* (Paris, 1973), 94–103; William Doyle, *Venality: the Sale of Offices in Eighteenth-Century France* (Oxford, 1996). On the provincial support for the 'regeneration' of France: Michael P. Fitzsimmons, *The*

Remaking of France: The National Assembly, the Constitution of 1791 and the Reorganization of the French Polity (Cambridge and New York, 1994); and Philip Dawson, *Provincial Magistrates and Revolutionary Politics in France, 1789–1795* (Cambridge, MA, 1972). Scattered research on the sales of *biens nationaux* is synthesized in Bodinier and Teyssier, *La Vente des biens nationaux*; Jones, *Peasantry*, 154–61. See, too, Georges Lefebvre, *Les paysans du Nord pendant la Révolution française* (Bari, 1959), 431–525.

23. Michael P. Fitzsimmons, *The Parisian Order of Barristers and the French Revolution* (Cambridge, MA, 1987). On slavery, see the chapters by Carolyn Fick and Pierre Boulle in Frederick Krantz (ed.), *History from Below: Studies in Popular Protest and Popular Ideology in Honour of George Rudé* (Montreal, 1985), 243–60; Carolyn Fick, *The Making of Haiti: The Saint-Domingue Revolution from Below* (Knoxville, TN, 1990); Robert Forster, 'Who is a Citizen? The Boundaries of 'La Patrie': The French Revolution and the People of Color, 1789–91', *FPS* 7 (1989), 50–64; David Geggus, *Haitian Revolutionary Studies* (Bloomington, IN, 2002).

24. Jeremy Whiteman, 'Trade and the Regeneration of France 1789–91: Liberalism, Protectionism, and the Commercial Policy of the National Constituent Assembly', *EHQ* 31 (2001), 171–204; Orville T. Murphy, *The Diplomatic Retreat of France and Public Opinion on the Eve of the French Revolution, 1783–1789* (Washington, D.C., 1998); Bailey Stone, *Reinterpreting the French Revolution: A Global-Historical Perspective* (Cambridge and New York, 2002).

25. Gwynne Lewis, *The Second Vendée: The Continuity of Counter-Revolution in the Department of the Gard, 1789–1815* (Oxford, 1978), 31–7 and *passim*; James N. Hood, 'Protestant-Catholic Relations and the Roots of the First Popular Counterrevolutionary Movement in France', *JMH* 43 (1971), 245–75; Ted W. Margadant, *Urban Rivalries in the French Revolution* (Princeton, NJ, 1992).

26. Michel Vovelle, *Les Métamorphoses de la fête en Provence de 1750 à 1820* (Paris, 1976), 71, 103.

27. *Moniteur universel*, no. 46, 15 February 1790, vol. 2, 368–9. The impact of the Revolution on Jews is outlined in Szajkowski, *Jews and the French Revolutions*; Gary Kates, 'Jews into Frenchmen: Nationality and Representation in Revolutionary France', in Ferenc Féher (ed.), *The French Revolution and the Birth of Modernity* (Berkeley, CA), 103–16; Patrick Girard, *Les Juifs en France de 1789 à 1869* (Paris, 1976); David Feuerwerker, *L'Emancipation des juifs en France de la fin de l'Ancien Régime à la fin du Second Empire* (Paris, 1976); and the special issue of *AHRF* 235 (1979). Only during the final sessions of the National Assembly in September 1791 were the Ashkenazim Jews of eastern France granted full civil equality.

28. On the Civil Constitution, see Timothy Tackett, *Religion, Revolution, and Regional Culture in Eighteenth-Century France* (Princeton, NJ, 1986); Aston, *Religion and Revolution*, ch. 7; Jones, *Peasantry*, 191–204. An excellent study of a region of high oath-taking is Tackett, *Priest and Parish*

in Eighteenth-Century France: A Social and Political Study of the Curés in a Diocese of Dauphiné, 1750–1791 (Princeton, NJ, 1977).

29. Raymond Aubert, *En pantoufles sous la Terreur. Réflexions et commentaires sur le 'Journal d'un bourgeois de Paris'* (Paris, 1974), 60–1; Marcel Coquerel, 'Le Journal d'un curé du Boulonnais', *AHRF* 46 (1974), 289. On priests' reactions in general, see Tackett, *Religion and Revolution*, chs 3–4.

30. Laura Mason, *Singing the French Revolution: Popular Culture and Politics, 1787–1799* (Ithaca, NY, 1996), 50.

31. Ménétra, *Journal*, 217–18; Jean-Marie Carbasse, 'Un des premiers cas de résistance populaire à la Révolution: l'émeute du 25 janvier 1791 à Millau', *BHES* 1984–85, 57–72; Timothy Tackett, 'Women and Men in Counterrevolution: The Sommières Riot of 1791', *JMH* 59 (1987), 680–704.

32. Alison Patrick, 'French Revolutionary Local Government, 1789–1792', in Colin Lucas (ed.), *The Political Culture of the French Revolution* (London, 1988), 412–17; Jones, *Peasantry*, 201–2; McManners, *Ecclesiastical Society*, chs 12–15.

33. This 'political culture', one of the most fertile current areas of research in social history, is explored in the four volumes of *The French Revolution and the Creation of Modern Political Culture* (Oxford, 1987–94); Michael Kennedy, *The Jacobin Clubs in the French Revolution: The First Years* (Princeton, NJ, 1982); Mona Ozouf, *Festivals and the French Revolution*, trans. A. Sheridan (Cambridge, MA, 1988); Vovelle, *Métamorphoses de la fête*; Lynn Hunt, *Politics, Culture, and Class in the French Revolution* (Berkeley, CA, 1984); Timothy Tackett, *Becoming a Revolutionary: The Deputies of the French National Assembly and the Emergence of a Revolutionary Culture (1789–1790)* (Princeton, NJ, 1996); and Isser Woloch, *The New Regime. Transformations of the French Civic Order, 1789–1820s* (New York, 1994).

34. Jones, *Peasantry*, 67–85; Jean Boutier, 'Jacqueries en pays croquant: les révoltes paysannes en Aquitaine (décembre 1789-mars 1790)', *Annales* 34 (1979), 760–86; Anatoli Ado, ' "Les Propos incendiaires" du curé Jacques Benoît', *AHRF* 39 (1967), 399–401.

35. Doyle, *Oxford History of the French Revolution*, 124.

36. Dorinda Outram, *The Body and the French Revolution: Sex, Class and Political Culture* (New Haven, CT, 1989), 126. Among the expanding literature on the women's rights movement, see Landes, *Women and the Public Sphere*, 93–129; Gary Kates, *The 'Cercle social', the Girondins, and the French Revolution* (Princeton, NJ, 1985); Paule-Marie Duhet, *Les Femmes et la Révolution, 1789–1794* (Paris, 1971); Felicia Gordon, 'The Gendered Citizen: Marie Madeleine Jodin (1741–90)', in David Williams and Maire Cross (eds), *The French Experience from Republic to Monarchy, 1792–1824: New Dawns in Politics, Knowledge and Culture* (Basingstoke, 2000), 12–27; and Dominique Godineau, *The Women of Paris and their French Revolution*, trans. Katherine Streip (Berkeley, CA, 1998). The development of the popular movement is outlined in R.B. Rose, *The Making of*

the 'Sans-culottes': Democratic Ideas and Institutions in Paris, 1789–92 (Manchester, 1983); and Suzanne Desan, '"Constitutional Amazons": Jacobin Women's Clubs in the French Revolution', in Bryant T. Ragan and Elizabeth A. Williams (eds), Re-creating Authority in Revolutionary France (New Brunswick, NJ, 1992).

37. William Murray, The Right-Wing Press in the French Revolution: 1789–92 (London, 1986), chs 11–12; Kennedy, Cultural History, chs 5, 9–10; Hugh Gough, The Newspaper Press in the French Revolution (London, 1988), Intro., ch. 2; Jack Censer, Prelude to Power. The Parisian Radical Press, 1789–1791 (Baltimore, MD, 1976); Chartier, Cultural History, ch. 7; Jeremy D. Popkin, Revolutionary News: The Press in France, 1789–1799 (Durham, NC, 1990); Laura Mason, 'Songs: Mixing Media', in Robert Darnton and Daniel Roche (eds), Revolution in Print: The Press in France, 1775–1800 (Berkeley, CA, 1989), 252–69; Rolf Reichardt, 'The Politicization of Popular Prints in the French Revolution', in Ian Germani and Robin Swales (eds), Symbols, Myths and Images: Essays in Honour of James A. Leith (Regina, Sask., 1998)

38. Antoine de Baecque, The Body Politic: Corporeal Metaphor in Revolutionary France, 1770–1800 (Stanford, CA, 1997); Merrick and Ragan, Homosexuality in Modern France, chs by Jeffrey Merrick and Elizabeth Colwill. The origins of the vituperative attacks on Marie-Antoinette are studied by Lynn Hunt, The Family Romance of the French Revolution (London, 1992); Chantal Thomas, The Wicked Queen: The Origins of the Myth of Marie-Antoinette, trans. Julie Rose (New York, 2000); Dena Goodman (ed.), Marie-Antoinette: Writings on the Body of the Queen (London, 2003); and Thomas E. Kaiser, 'Who's Afraid of Marie-Antoinette? Diplomacy, Austrophobia and the Queen', FH 14 (2000), 241–71.

39. Michel Vovelle, 'La Représentation populaire de la monarchie', in Keith Baker (ed.), The Political Culture of the Old Régime (Oxford, 1987), 77–96.

40. Cited in G. Michon, Adrien Duport: essai sur l'histoire du parti feuillant (Paris, 1924), 256–7. In 1792–3, Barnave wrote the first class-based analysis of the Revolution: see Emanuel Chill (ed. and trans.), Power, Property and History: Barnave's Introduction to the French Revolution and other Writings (New York, 1971). On this journée, see Rudé, Crowd in the French Revolution, ch. 6. An alternative explanation, emphasizing 'millenarial' ideologies rather than social conflict as the cause of the collapse of consensus, is Norman Hampson, Prelude to Terror. The Constituent Assembly and the Failure of Consensus, 1789–1791 (Oxford, 1988).

41. Murray, Right-Wing Press, 126–8, 289; Sheppard, Lourmarin, 186.

42. Timothy Tackett, 'Conspiracy Obsession in a Time of Revolution: French Elites and the Origins of the Terror', AHR 105 (2000), 691–713.

43. A contrary interpretation, stressing the 'traditional' motivations behind the outbreak of war, is T. C. W. Blanning, The Origins of the French Revolutionary Wars (London, 1986). On the composition and political alignments of the Legislative Assembly, see C. J. Mitchell, The French Legislative Assembly of 1791 (Leiden, 1989).

44. David V. Erdman, *Commerce des Lumières: John Oswald and the British in Paris, 1790–1793* (Columbia, MO, 1986).
45. Elizabeth Rapley, ' "Pieuses Contre-Révolutionnaires": The Experience of the Ursulines of Northern France, 1789–1792', *FH* 2 (1988), 453–73.
46. Rudé, *Crowd in the French Revolution*, ch. 7; Michel Vovelle, *The Fall of the French Monarchy 1787–1792*, trans. S. Burke (Cambridge, 1984), ch. 6.

3 Republicanism and Counter-Revolution, 1792–1795

1. Lucas, 'Crowd and Politics', 438; M. J. Sydenham, *The French Revolution* (New York, 1966), 122. On the massacres, contrast Pierre Caron, *Les Massacres de septembre* (Paris, 1935), with Frédéric Bluche, *Septembre 1792: logiques d'un massacre* (Paris, 1986) and Antoine de Baecque, *Glory and Terror: Seven Deaths under the French Revolution*, trans. Charlotte Mandell (New York and London, 2001). There were small-scale versions of the killings elsewhere, including in eight villages in the Orne, west of Paris, and in Soissons on the eastern front.
2. Schama, *Citizens*, ch. 15; Hampson, *Prelude to Terror*; François Furet, *La Révolution: de Turgot à Jules Ferry, 1770–1880* (Paris, 1989); Darnton, *Great Cat Massacre*, ch. 2, esp. 98. In different ways, the potency of the counter-revolution is stressed in D. M. G. Sutherland, *France 1789–1815: Revolution and Counterrevolution* (London, 1985), chs 4–6; Murray, *Right-Wing Press*, chs 9, 12. See, too, the discussion by Mona Ozouf, 'War and Terror in French Revolutionary Discourse (1793–1794)', *JMH* 56 (1984), 579–97.
3. The identification of political and social tendencies within the Convention has long aroused debate: see Alison Patrick, *The Men of the First French Republic: Political Alignments in the National Convention of 1792* (Baltimore, MD, 1972); Michael Sydenham, *The Girondins* (London, 1961); and the forum in *FHS* 15 (1988), 506–48.
4. Mason, *Singing the French Revolution*, 93–103.
5. Ronald Schechter, 'Translating the 'Marseillaise': Biblical Republicanism and the Emancipation of Jews in Revolutionary France', *P&P* 143 (1994), 128–55.
6. Markoff, *Abolition of Feudalism*, 426, 497–8, ch. 8; Jones, *Peasantry*, 70–4; Anatoli Ado, *Paysans en Révolution. Terre, pouvoir et jacquerie 1789–1794*, trans. Serge Aberdam, Marcel Dorigny et al. (Paris, 1996), ch. 2. According to Markoff, the August decree effectively ended anti-seigneurial protest. On the June decree, see Mitchell, *French Legislative Assembly*, ch. 5.
7. Hunt, *Politics, Culture, and Class*, ch. 5.
8. On the king's trial, see Patrick, *Men of the First French Republic*, chs 3–4; David Jordan, *The King's Trial: The French Revolution versus Louis XVI* (Berkeley, CA, 1979); Michael Walzer (ed.), *Regicide and Revolution: Speeches at the Trial of Louis XVI* (Cambridge, 1974). On Louis himself, see John Hardman, *Louis XVI* (New Haven, CT and London, 1993): Louis is here described as 'fairly intelligent and fairly hard-working' (234). Hardman has recently extended his study in *Louis XVI: The Silent King*

(London, 2000). News of the execution of Louis XVI created deep divisions, even among Frenchmen far away. Bruny d'Entrecasteaux's expedition had been sent to Australia in 1791 in search of the missing explorer La Pérouse. Its leader dead, the malnourished and homesick expedition straggled into Java in October 1793 to learn of events earlier in the year. A violent division emerged between the expedition's new leader, the royalist d'Auribeau, and the naturalist Labillardière, in the 1760s a classmate in Alençon of Jacques Hébert, now a prominent *Enragé*: see Edward Duyker, *Citizen Labillardière: A French Naturalist in New Holland and the South Pacific* (Melbourne, 2003).

9. Among the major studies of the Vendée are Claude Petitfrère, *Les Vendéens d'Anjou, 1793: analyse des structures militaires, sociales et mentales* (Paris, 1981); McManners, *Ecclesiastical Society*, ch. 12–15; Tilly, *The Vendée*; Timothy Tackett, 'The West in France in 1789: The Religious Factor in the Origins of the Counterrevolution', *JMH* 54 (1982), 715–45. A useful review essay is Petitfrère, 'The Origins of the Civil War in the Vendée', *FH* 2 (1988), 187–207.

10. Reynald Secher, *Le Génocide franco-français: la Vendée-vengé* (Paris, 1986) estimated at least 200,000 lives lost on each side, but see Claude Langlois, 'La Révolution malade de la Vendée', *Vingtième siècle* 14 (1987), 63–78. The claim of genocide is contested by Hugh Gough, 'Genocide and the Bicentenary: The French Revolution and the Revenge of the Vendée', *HJ* 30 (1987), 977–88.

11. Sutherland, *Chouans*; T. J. A. Le Goff and D. M. G. Sutherland, 'The Social Origins of Counter-Revolution in Western France', *P&P* 99 (1983), 65–87; Jean Defranceschi, *La Corse française, 30 novembre 1789–15 juin 1794* (Paris, 1980); Jones, *Peasantry*, 217–30.

12. On this *journée*, see Rudé, *Crowd in the French Revolution*, ch. 8; Morris Slavin, *The Making of an Insurrection: Parisian Sections and the Gironde* (Cambridge, MA, 1986).

13. Sheppard, *Lourmarin*, 196–203. Among the many studies of 'Federalism', see Forrest, *Bordeaux*, ch. 5; William Scott, *Terror and Repression in Revolutionary Marseilles* (London, 1973); Paul Hanson, *Provincial Politics in the French Revolution: Caen and Limoges, 1789–1794* (Baton Rouge, LA, 1989); Bill Edmonds, '"Federalism" and Urban Revolt in France in 1793', *JMH* 55 (1983), 22–53; Malcolm Crook, 'Federalism and the French Revolution: The Revolt of Toulon in 1793', *History* 65 (1980), 383–97; David Longfellow, 'Silk Weavers and the Social Struggle in Lyon during the French Revolution', *FHS* 12 (1981), 1–40.

14. The history of the Terror is recounted in Soboul, *French Revolution*, 259–415; and in the classic study by R. R. Palmer, *Twelve who Ruled: The Year of the Terror in the French Revolution* (Princeton, NJ, 1941). These accounts have been contested by François Furet and Denis Richet, *The French Revolution* (London, 1970), chs 6–7; Sutherland, *France 1789–1815*, ch. 6; Schama, *Citizens*; and, at an extreme, Eli Sagan, *Citizens & Cannibals: The French Revolution, the Struggle for Modernity, and the Origins of Ideological Terror* (Lanham, MD, 2001). A judicious

overview is Hugh Gough, *The Terror in the French Revolution* (Basingstoke, 1998).

15. I am grateful to Mrs Josephine Harper for permission to quote Peyrot's letter. Soldiers' experiences are well captured in Jean-Paul Bertaud, *La Vie quotidienne des soldats de la Révolution, 1789–1799* (Paris, 1985); Forrest, *Soldiers of the French Revolution*, chs 4–6. On the army in 1793–4, see Bertaud, *Army of the French Revolution*, ch. 9; John A. Lynn, *The Bayonets of the Republic: Motivation and Tactics in the Army of Revolutionary France, 1791–4* (Urbana, IL, 1984); Scott, *Response of the Royal Army*, ch. 5; and Paddy Griffith, *The Art of War of Revolutionary France, 1789–1802* (London, 1998).

16. Gilles Fleury, 'Analyse informatique du statut socioculturel des 1,578 personnes déclarées suspectes à Rouen en l'an II', in *Autour des mentalités et des pratiques politiques sous la Révolution française* (Paris, 1987), vol. 3, 9–23.

17. Olivier Blanc, *Last Letters: Prisons and Prisoners of the French Revolution, 1793–1794*, trans. Alan Sheridan (London, 1987), 188–91. The standard statistical survey of the Terror remains Donald Greer, *The Incidence of the Terror during the French Revolution: A Statistical Interpretation* (Cambridge, MA, 1935).

18. Ado, *Paysans en Révolution*; Markoff, *Abolition of Feudalism*; Jones, *Peasantry*, chs 3–5.

19. Peter McPhee, *Revolution and Environment in Southern France: Peasants, Lords, and Murder in the Corbières, 1780–1830* (Oxford, 1999); David Hunt, 'Peasant Movements and Communal Property during the French Revolution', *T&S* 17 (1988), 255–83.

20. Jones, *Peasantry*, 225; on this region, see the fine study by Colin Lucas, *The Structure of the Terror: The Example of Javogues and the Loire* (Oxford, 1973). On rural political tendencies, see David Hunt, 'Peasant Politics in the French Revolution', *SH* 9 (1984), 277–99; Jones, *Peasantry*, 206–40; R. B. Rose, 'The "Red Scare" of the 1790s: The French Revolution and the "Agrarian Law"', *P&P* 103 (1984), 113–30.

21. Melvin Edelstein, '*La Feuille villageoise*': communication et modernisation dans les régions rurales pendant la Révolution* (Paris, 1977); Jones, *Peasantry*, 207–17; Colin Lucas, 'The Problem of the Midi in the French Revolution', *Transactions of the Royal Historical Society* 28 (1978), 1–25; Kennedy, *Cultural History*, 304.

22. The classic study of the *sans-culottes* is Albert Soboul, *Les Sans-culottes parisiens de l'An II*, sections of which were translated by G. Lewis as *The Parisian Sans-Culottes and the French Revolution, 1793–4* (Oxford, 1964). The major critiques of Soboul have been by Richard Andrews, 'Social Structures, Political Élites and Ideology in Revolutionary Paris, 1792–1794: A Critical Evaluation of Albert Soboul's *Les Sans-culottes parisiens en l'an II*', *JSH* 19 (1985), 72–112; and Richard Cobb, *The Police and the People: French Popular Protest 1789–1820* (Oxford, 1970), part III.

23. Michael Kennedy, *The Jacobin Club of Marseilles, 1790–1794* (Ithaca, NY, 1973), chs 5–6, appendix I, and *The Jacobin Clubs in the French Revolution: The Middle Years* (Princeton, NJ, 1988).

24. See the important article by Colin Lucas, 'The Theory and Practice of Denunciation in the French Revolution', *JMH* 68 (1996). There is a fine study of changing attitudes towards foreigners by Michael Rapport, *Nationality and Citizenship in Revolutionary France. The Treatment of Foreigners, 1789–1799* (Oxford, 2000).

25. On popular ideology in Paris, see Soboul, *Parisian Sans-Culottes*, chs 1–3; Sewell, *Work and Revolution*, ch. 5; Sonenscher, *Eighteenth-Century French Trades*, ch. 10; and the articles by Cobb and Soboul in Jeffry Kaplow (ed.), *New Perspectives on the French Revolution: Readings in Historical Sociology* (New York, 1965). Steven Kaplan, *La Fin des corporations*, emphasizes that the *sans-culottes'* vision drew on a mythical past of workplace harmony.

26. François Lebrun (ed.), *Histoire des Catholiques en France du XVe siècle à nos jours* (Toulouse, 1980), 260–1; Eugen Weber, 'Who Sang the Marseillaise?', in Jacques Beauroy *et al.* (eds), *The Wolf and the Lamb: Popular Culture in France from the Old Regime to the Twentieth Century* (Stanford, CA, 1977), 163. On 'dechristianization' in general, see the provocative Daniel Guérin, *Class Struggle in the First French Republic: Bourgeois and Bras Nus 1793–1795*, trans. I. Patterson (London, 1977), chs 5–6; Michel Vovelle, *Religion et révolution. La Déchristianisation de l'An II* (Paris, 1976); and the debate between Vovelle and Gérard Cholvy in *AHRF* 233 (1978), 451–70.

27. Serge Bianchi, *La Révolution culturelle de l'an II* (Paris, 1982), 119, and 'Les Curés rouges dans la Révolution française', *AHRF* 54 (1982), 349–92. General discussions of the effects on the Church are Gibson, *French Catholicism*, ch. 2; McManners, *French Revolution*, ch. 10; Aston, *Religion and Revolution*, part III.

28. Richard Cobb, *The People's Armies*, trans. M. Elliott (New Haven, CT, 1987).

29. Kennedy, *Cultural History*, 353–62; R. R. Palmer, *The Improvement of Humanity: Education and the French Revolution* (Princeton, NJ, 1985), chs 4–5; Marie-Françoise Lévy (ed.), *L'Enfant, la famille et la Révolution* (Paris, 1989).

30. Jean-Pierre Gross, *Fair Shares for All: Jacobin Egalitarianism in Practice* (Cambridge and New York, 1997); Alan Forrest, *The French Revolution and the Poor* (Oxford, 1981), chs 5–7; Antoinette Wills, *Crime and Punishment in Revolutionary Paris* (New York, 1981), chs 4–5; Gordon Wright, *Between the Guillotine and Liberty: Two Centuries of the Crime Problem in France* (Oxford, 1983), ch. 2.

31. On the 'cultural revolution', see Bianchi, *Révolution culturelle*, esp. ch. 5; Aileen Ribeiro, *Fashion in the French Revolution* (New York, 1988); Madeleine Delpierre, *Dress in France in the Eighteenth Century*, trans. Caroline Beamish (New Haven, CT, 1997); Kennedy, *Cultural History*, ch. 9, Appendix A; Marvin Carlson, *The Theatre of the French Revolution*

(Ithaca, NY, 1966), ch. 6; Vovelle, *Métamorphoses de la fête*, chs 7–8; Ozouf, *Festivals*, ch. 4.

32. See Cobb, *Reactions to the French Revolution*, 142–8, and *A Sense of Place* (London, 1975), 77–135; Roderick Phillips, *Family Breakdown in Late-Eighteenth Century France: Divorces in Rouen, 1792–1803* (Oxford, 1980), esp. 108–24, 161–2.

33. Hufton, 'Women in Revolution'; Angela Groppi, 'Le Travail des femmes à Paris à l'époque de la Révolution française', *BHES* 1979, 27–46; Jean-Paul Bertaud, *La Vie quotidienne en France au temps de la Révolution (1789–1795)* (Paris, 1983), ch. 10.

34. This most significant episode in the history of women's political participation is discussed by Desan, 'Jacobin Women's Clubs', in Ragan and Williams, *Re-creating Authority*; Scott H. Lytle, 'The Second Sex (September, 1793)', *JMH* 26 (1955), 14–26; Landes, *Women and the Public Sphere*, 140–5, 160–8; Marie Cerati, *Le Club des citoyennes républicaines révolutionnaires* (Paris, 1966); R. B. Rose, *The Enragés: Socialists of the French Revolution?* (Melbourne, 1965), chs 5–6; and *Tribunes and Amazons: Men and Women of Revolutionary France 1789–1871* (Sydney, 1998), 246–8. Rose's argument should be compared with Olwen Hufton, 'Women in Revolution', *FPS* 7 (1989), 65–81; and Madelyn Gutwirth, *The Twilight of the Goddesses: Women and Representation in the French Revolutionary Era* (New Brunswick, NJ, 1992), ch. 7.

35. Bianchi, *Révolution culturelle*, 248. On symbolism, see Maurice Agulhon, *Marianne into Battle: Republican Imagery and Symbolism in France, 1789–1880*, trans. J. Lloyd (Cambridge, 1981), Intro., ch. 1; Hannah Mitchell, 'Art and the French Revolution', *HW* 5 (1978), 122–45.

36. Paul Mansfield, 'The Repression of Lyon, 1793–4: Origins, Responsibility and Significance', *FH* 2 (1988), 74–101.

37. Roger Dupuy, *De la Révolution à la chouannerie: paysans en Bretagne* (Paris, 1988), 7–8; Maciak, 'Of News and Networks', 281. See, too, Lyons, 'Politics and Patois'; Patrice Higonnet, 'The politics of linguistic terrorism and grammatical hegemony during the French Revolution', *SH* 5 (1980), 41–69.

38. Fick, *The Making of Haiti*; D. P. Geggus, *Slavery, War and Revolution: The British Occupation of Saint-Domingue, 1793–1798* (Oxford, 1982), and *Haitian Revolutionary Studies*.

39. Nicolas Ruault, *Gazette d'un parisien sous la Révolution, 1783–1796* (Paris, 1976), 352–55) [some doubts have been raised over the authenticity of these memoirs]; Ménétra, *Journal*, 219–20.

40. Rudé, *Crowd in the French Revolution*, 141 and ch. 9. See, too, Richard Bienvenu (ed.), *The Ninth of Thermidor: The Fall of Robespierre* (Oxford, 1968); Gérard Walter, *La Conjuration du neuf thermidor, 27 juillet 1794* (Paris, 1974); David P. Jordan, *The Revolutionary Career of Maximilien Robespierre* (New York, 1985); Michael Kennedy, 'The "Last Stand" of the Jacobin Clubs', *FHS* 16 (1989), 309–44. The diversity of support for the end of the Terror is stressed by Martyn Lyons, 'The 9 Thermidor: Motives and Effects', *ESR* 5 (1975), 123–46.

41. Carla Hesse, *Publishing and Cultural Politics in Revolutionary Paris, 1789–1810* (Berkeley & Los Angeles, CA, 1991).

42. François Gendron, *La Jeunesse dorée: épisodes de la Révolution française* (Montreal, 1979). The best overview of the Thermidorian period remains Georges Lefebvre, *The Thermidorians*, trans. R. Baldick (London, 1965). See, too, Bronislaw Baczko, *Ending the Terror: The French Revolution after Robespierre* (Cambridge, 1994).

43. On these *journées*, see Rudé, *Crowd in the French Revolution*, ch. 10; Bertaud, *Army of the French Revolution*, ch. 12; Kare Tønnesson, *La Défaite des sans-culottes: mouvement populaire et réaction bourgeoise en l'An III* (Oslo, 1959).

44. Stewart, *Documentary Survey*, 572–612.

4   The Consolidation of Post-Revolutionary Society, 1795–1815

1. McPhee, *Collioure*, 65 and ch. 4.

2. On the Directory, see Georges Lefebvre, *The Directory*, trans. R. Baldick (London, 1964); Denis Woronoff, *The Thermidorian Regime and the Directory, 1794–1799*, trans. J. Jackson (Cambridge, 1984); Martyn Lyons, *France under the Directory* (Cambridge, 1975); Michael Sydenham, *The First French Republic, 1792–1804* (London, 1974), Part II. Recent scholarship has placed more emphasis on the social history of politics in the provinces: Sutherland, *France 1789–1815*, chs 7–8; Gwynne Lewis and Colin Lucas (eds), *Beyond the Terror: Essays in French Regional and Social History, 1794–1815* (Cambridge, 1983).

3. Ruault, *Gazette*, 393. On Vendémiaire, see Rudé, *Crowd in the French Revolution*, ch. 11; Bertaud, *Army of the French Revolution*, ch. 12. The mixture of old and new in diplomacy is engagingly treated in Linda Frey and Marsha Frey, '"The reign of the charlatans is over": The French revolutionary attack on diplomatic practice', *JMH* 65 (1993), 706–44.

4. Useful general surveys of the Church under the Directory are McManners, *French Revolution*, chs 13–14; Olwen Hufton, 'The Reconstruction of a Church 1796–1801', in Lewis and Lucas, *Beyond the Terror*, 21–52, and 'Women in Revolution', *FPS* 7 (1989), 65–81.

5. Suzanne Desan, 'The Rhetoric of Religious Revival during the French Revolution', *JMH* 60 (1988), 1–27; Jean Vassort, 'L'Enseignement primaire en Vendômois à l'époque révolutionnaire', *RHMC* 25 (1978), 625–55; Kennedy, *Cultural History*, 360.

6. On the links between internal and external counter-revolution, see Maurice Hutt, *Chouannerie and Counter-Revolution: Puisaye, the Princes and the British Government in the 1790s*, 2 vols (Cambridge, 1983); William Fryer, *Republic or Restoration in France?, 1794–1797: The Politics of French Royalism* (Manchester, 1965); Harvey Mitchell, *The Underground War against Revolutionary France: The Missions of William Wickham, 1794–1800* (Oxford, 1965).

7. On the army under the Directory, see Bertaud, *Army of the French Revolution*, chs 10–11. The question of how 'liberating' French armies

were divides historians: see Robert R. Palmer, *The Age of the Democratic Revolution. A Political History of Europe and America, 1760–1800*, vol. 2 (Princeton, NJ, 1964); T. C. W. Blanning, *French Revolution in Germany: Occupation and Resistance in the Rhineland, 1792–1802* (Oxford, 1983); Simon Schama, *Patriots and Liberators: Revolution in the Netherlands, 1780–1813* (London, 1977).

8. Rapport, *Nationality and Citizenship*.

9. Alan Forrest, 'Conscription and Crime in Rural France during the Directory and Consulate', in Lewis and Lucas, *Beyond the Terror*, 92–120.

10. Lewis, *Second Vendée*, ch. 3; Colin Lucas, 'Problem of the Midi', and 'Themes in Southern Violence after 9 Thermidor', in Lewis and Lucas, *Beyond the Terror*, 152–94; Cobb, *Reactions to the French Revolution*, 19–62, and *Police and the People*, 85–117; Jones, *Peasantry*, 240–7.

11. On this important, understudied period of rural social relations, see Jones, *Peasantry*, 103, 122–3, 134–7; Gwynne Lewis, 'Political Brigandage and Popular Disaffection in the Southeast of France, 1795–1804', in Lewis and Lucas, *Beyond the Terror*, 195–231; S. Aberdam, 'La Révolution et la lutte des métayers [dans le Gers]', *ER* 59 (1975), 73–91.

12. Palmer, *Improvement of Humanity*, ch. 6; Kennedy, *Cultural History*, 360; Godechot, *Institutions de la France*, 461–8; Maurice Crosland, 'The French Academy of Sciences in the Nineteenth Century', *Minerva* 16 (1978), 73–102.

13. Cobb, *Police and the People*, 234–9; Colin Jones, 'Picking up the pieces: The Politics and the Personnel of Social Welfare from the Convention to the Consulate', in Lewis and Lucas, *Beyond the Terror*, 53–91.

14. Research on 'cultural production' is conveniently tabulated in Colin Jones, *The Longman Companion to the French Revolution* (London, 1989), 260–2. On changes to festivals, see Vovelle, *Métamorphoses de la fête*, ch. 9; Ozouf, *Festivals*, ch. 5.

15. McPhee, *Collioure*, 72–3. The argument that such popular contestation represented deliberate Catalan resistance to the French state is unconvincingly put by Michel Brunet, *Le Roussillon: une société contre l'État, 1780–1820* (Toulouse, 1986).

16. R. B. Rose, *Gracchus Babeuf: The First Revolutionary Communist* (London, 1978); J. A. Scott (ed. and trans.), *The Defense of Gracchus Babeuf before the High Court of Vendôme* (Amherst, MA, 1967); Ian H. Birchall, 'When the Revolution had to Stop', in Williams and Cross, *The French Experience*, 42–57.

17. Cobb, *Reactions to the French Revolution*, ch. 5; Michel Vovelle, 'From Beggary to Brigandage: The Wanderers in the Beauce During the French Revolution', in Kaplow, *New Perspectives*, 287–304.

18. Sutherland, *France 1789–1815*, ch. 8; see, too, Lynn Hunt, David Lansky and Paul Hanson, 'The Failure of the Liberal Republic in France, 1795–1799: The Road to Brumaire', *JMH* 51 (1979), 734–59. Two accessible accounts of Napoleon's rise are Malcolm Crook, *Napoleon Comes to Power: Democracy and Dictatorship in Revolutionary France, 1795–1804*

(Cardiff, 1998); and Robert Asprey, *The Rise of Napoleon Bonaparte* (New York, 2000).

19. Claude Langlois, 'The Voters', in Frank A. Kafker and James M. Laux (eds), *Napoleon and his Times: Selected Interpretations* (Malibar, FL, 1989), 57–65. On the Napoleonic period in general, see Georges Lefebvre, *Napoleon*, 2 vols, trans. H. Stockhold and J. Anderson (London, 1969); Louis Bergeron, *France under Napoleon*, trans. R. R. Palmer (Princeton, NJ, 1981); Jean Tulard, *Le Grand Empire, 1804–1815* (Paris, 1982), and *Napoleon: The Myth of the Saviour*, trans. S. Waugh (London, 1984); David Chandler, *The Campaigns of Napoleon* (London, 1966); Martyn Lyons, *Napoleon Bonaparte and the Legacy of the French Revolution* (Basingstoke, 1994); Robert B. Holtman, *The Napoleonic Revolution* (Baton Rouge, LA, 1981); Geoffrey Ellis, *The Napoleonic Empire* (London and New York, 1991); Philip G. Dwyer (ed.), *Napoleon and Europe* (London, 2001). Critical recent biographies are Alan Schom, *Napoleon Bonaparte* (New York, 1997); and Evangeline Bruce, *Napoleon and Josephine: An Improbable Marriage* (New York, 1995).

20. Hufton, *Bayeux*, 264–80; Claude Langlois and Timothy Le Goff, 'Les Vaincus de la Révolution: jalons pour une sociologie des prêtres mariés', in Albert Soboul (ed.), *Voies nouvelles pour l'histoire de la Révolution française* (Paris, 1978). On the Concordat, see McManners, *French Revolution*, ch. 15; S. Delacroix, *La Réorganisation de l'Eglise de France après le Concordat (1801–1809)* (Paris, 1962).

21. The degree of political opposition within the regime is examined in Irene Collins, *Napoleon and his Parliaments, 1800–1815* (New York, 1979); Isser Woloch, *Jacobin Legacy: The Democratic Movement under the Directory* (Princeton, NJ, 1970); Jean Vidalenc, 'L'Opposition sous le Consulat et l'Empire', *AHRF* 40 (1968), 472–88; Bergeron, *France under Napoleon*, ch. 4.

22. Napoleon's system is conveniently summarized in Howard Payne, *The Police State of Louis Napoleon Bonaparte, 1851–1860* (Seattle, WA, 1966), ch. 1; see, too, Godechot, *Institutions de la France*, 508–44; Bergeron, *France under Napoleon*, chs 1–2; Church, *French Ministerial Bureaucracy*, chs 1, 8; and, for the wider European parallels, Stuart Woolf, *Napoleon's Integration of Europe* (London, 1991).

23. Marie-Noëlle Bourguet, 'Race et folklore: l'image officielle de la France en 1800', *Annales* 31 (1976), 802–23, and *Déchiffrer la France: la statistique départementale à l'époque napoléonienne* (Paris, 1989); Stuart Wolf, 'French Civilisation and Ethnicity in the Napoleonic Empire', *P&P* 124 (1989), 96–120; Chartier, *Cultural History*, ch. 8; Isser Woloch, *Napoleon's Collaborators* (New York, 2001).

24. Josef Konvitz, *Cartography in France, 1660–1848: Science, Engineering, and Statecraft* (Chicago, 1987), chs 1–2; Dupâquier *et al.*, *Population française*, vol. 3, 16–36.

25. McPhee, *Revolution and Environment*, ch. 6.

26. Steven Kaplan, 'Réflexions sur la police du monde du travail, 1700–1815', *RH* 261 (1979), 17–77.

27. Jean-Claude Caron, 'The History of a Renaissance: The French *University* from the Revolution to the Restoration (1792–1824)', in Cross and Williams, *The French Experience*, 107–19.

28. Carlson, *Theatre*, epilogue. A general survey of culture under Napoleon is F. W. J. Hemmings, *Culture and Society in France, 1789–1848* (Leicester, 1987), ch. 3. On Jews, see Girard, *Les Juifs en France*; Feuerwerker, *L'Emancipation des juifs*; and the special issue of *AHRF* 235 (1979).

29. Michael David Sibalis, 'The Regulation of Male Homosexuality in Revolutionary and Napoleonic France, 1789–1815', Merrick and Ragan, *Homosexuality in Modern France*.

30. John Merriman (ed.), *French Cities in the Nineteenth Century* (London, 1982), 28–30.

31. Fick, *The Making of Haiti*; Geggus, *Haitian Revolutionary Studies*. An enduring classic is C. L. R. James, *The Black Jacobins: Toussaint L'Ouverture and the San Domingo Revolution* (New York, 1963).

32. Marcel Reinhard, 'Nostalgie et service militaire pendant la Révolution', *AHRF* 30 (1958), 1–15; Jacques Houdaille, 'Pertes de l'armée de terre sous le Premier Empire, d'après les registres matricules', *Population* 27 (1972), 27–50; Louis Henry and Yves Blayo, 'La Population de la France de 1740 à 1860', *Population* 30 (1975), 71–122. On the Napoleonic army, see John R. Elting, *Swords around a Throne: Napoleon's Grande Armée* (New York, 1988); Isser Woloch, *The French Veteran from the Revolution to the Restoration* (Chapel Hill, NC, 1979); Jean-Paul Bertaud, 'Napoleon's Officers', *P&P* 112 (1986), 91–111; David Gates, *The Napoleonic Wars 1803–1815* (London, 1997). On the question of changing military values, see John A. Lynn, 'Toward an Army of Honor: The Moral Evolution of the French Army, 1789–1815', *FHS* 16 (1989), 152–73, and the subsequent debate, 174–82.

33. Monnier, *Faubourg St-Antoine*, and 'L'Evolution de l'industrie et le travail des femmes à Paris sous l'Empire', *BHES* 1979, 47–60; Tulard, *Myth of the Saviour*, 186–92; Ellis, *Napoleon's Continental Blockade: The Case of Alsace* (Oxford, 1981); Bergeron, *France under Napoleon*, ch. 7; Gilles Postel-Vinay, 'A la recherche de la révolution économique dans les campagnes (1789–1815)', *Revue économique* 6 (1989), 1015–45. Among regional case-studies see Gavin Daly, *Inside Napoleonic France: State and Society in Rouen, 1800–1815* (Aldershot, 2001); Geoffrey Ellis, *Napoleon's Continental Blockade*; Jeff Horn, 'Building the New Regime: Founding the Bonapartist State in the Department of the Aube', *FHS* 25 (2002), 225–63.

34. Jean Tulard, *Napoléon et la noblesse d'Empire* (Paris, 1979); E. A. Whitcomb, 'Napoleon's Prefects', *AHR* 79 (1974), 1089–1118; Bergeron, *France under Napoleon*, ch. 3; Guy Chaussinand-Nogaret, *Une histoire des élites, 1700–1848* (Paris, 1975), part II; Geoffrey Ellis, 'Rhine and Loire: Napoleonic Élites and Social Order', in Lewis and Lucas, *Beyond the Terror*, 232–67. The experiences of an eminent *ancien régime* noble family which returned from exile into official position under the Empire are recalled in Felice Harcourt (ed. and trans.), *Escape from the Terror: The Journal of Madame de la Tour du Pin* (London, 1979), chs 25–30.

35. Forrest, 'Conscription and Crime'; Eric A. Arnold, 'Some Observations on the French Opposition to Napoleonic Conscription, 1804–1806', *FHS* 4 (1965–66), 452–62; Isser Woloch, 'Napoleonic Conscription: State Power and Civil Society', *P&P* 111 (1986), 101–29; Houdaille, 'Pertes de l' armée', 47.

36. Frederic Shoberl, *Narrative of the Most Remarkable Events which Occurred in and near Leipzig*, 2nd edn (London, 1814). See, too, the *Memoirs of Sergeant Bourgogne, 1812–1813* (London, 1997); and Rory Muir, *Salamanca 1812* (New Haven, CT, and London, 2001).

37. Daniel P. Resnick, *The White Terror and the Political Reaction after Waterloo* (Cambridge, MA, 1966); Lewis, *Second Vendée*; and David Higgs, *Ultraroyalism in Toulouse from its Origins to the Revolution of 1830* (Baltimore, MD, 1973), esp. ch. 3. On the resilience of revolutionary commitment, see Peter M. Jones, 'Protestantism and Jacobinism in the Department of the Aveyron, 1789–1815', in Martyn Cornick and Ceri Crossley (eds), *Problems in French History* (Basingstoke, 2000), ch. 2; and R. S. Alexander, *Bonapartism and the Revolutionary Tradition in France: The Fédérés of 1815* (Cambridge, 1991).

5 The Social Consequences of the Revolution

1. Much of this debate has its origins in the positions taken by Alfred Cobban in his 1955 essay, 'The Myth of the French Revolution', in *Aspects of the French Revolution* (London, 1968), ch. 5; and Soboul, *French Revolution*, Introduction and Conclusion. This debate is surveyed in Doyle, *Origins of the French Revolution*, part I; Gregor McLennan, *Marxism and the Methodologies of History* (London, 1981), ch. 9; Maurice Agulhon, 'The Heritage of the Revolution and Liberty in France', *Review* 12 (1989), 405–22; and Comninel, *Rethinking the French Revolution*, ch. 1. Important discussions of the Revolution's significance are Jones, *Peasantry*, ch. 8; Gwynne Lewis, Introduction to Soboul, *French Revolution*; Bill Edmonds, 'Successes and Excesses of Revisionist Writing about the French Revolution', *EHQ* 17 (1987), 195–217; and Colin Jones, 'Bourgeois Revolution Revivified'; these may be contrasted with Doyle, *Oxford History of the French Revolution*, ch. 17, and Schama, *Citizens*, Epilogue. The debates around the bicentenary are expertly surveyed by Steven Laurence Kaplan, *Farewell, Revolution: Disputed Legacies, France 1789/1989* (Ithaca, NY, 1995), esp. 470–86; and *Farewell, Revolution: The Historians' Feud, France 1789/1989* (Ithaca, NY, 1995).

2. Soboul, *French Revolution*, 19.

3. Roger Price, *An Economic History of Modern France, 1730–1914* (London, 1975), xi.

4. Hunt, *Politics, Culture, and Class*; François Furet, *La Révolution: de Turgot à Jules Ferry, 1770–1880* (Paris, 1989). It is also the major assumption behind the contributions to the four volumes of *The French Revolution and the Creation of Modern Political Culture*. Jack Censer, 'The Coming of a

New Interpretation of the French Revolution?', *JSH* 21 (1987), 295–309, is a useful review essay.

5. Crook, *Elections in the French Revolution*.

6. There has been surprisingly little analysis of the importance of collective memories of the Revolution. The outstanding study is Agulhon, *Marianne into Battle*; see also Raymond Huard, 'La Révolution française, événement fondateur: le travail de l'histoire sur l'héritage et la tradition', *Cahiers d'histoire de l'Institut de recherches marxistes* 32 (1988), 54–71; Peter McPhee, 'The Dead Hand of the Past? The Place of the French Revolution in Political Perceptions in Mid-Nineteenth Century Rural France', in Garrioch, *Two Hundred Years of the French Revolution*, 87–102.

7. Kaplan, *Disputed Legacies*, 84–111. In fact, between 300 and 500 of Luc's 2,320 people were killed in all the fighting during the Vendéan insurrection: Jean-Clément Martin and Xavier Lardière, *Le Massacre des Lucs-Vendée 1794* (Vouillé, 1992). On Chanzeaux, see Lawrence Wylie, *Chanzeaux: A Village in Anjou* (Cambridge, MA, 1966).

8. See, for example, Georges Lefebvre, 'The Place of the Revolution in the Agrarian History of France', in Robert Forster and Orest Ranum (eds), *Rural Society in France: Selections from the Annales* (Baltimore, MD, 1977), 31–49; Alfred Cobban, *The Social Interpretation of the French Revolution* (Cambridge, 1964), chs 7, 12, 14; Peter McPhee, 'The French Revolution, Peasants, and Capitalism', *AHR* 94 (1989), 1265–80; Peter Jones, 'Agricultural Modernization and the French Revolution', *Journal of Historical Geography* 16 (1990), 38–50.

9. Kathryn Norberg, *Rich and Poor in Grenoble, 1600–1814* (Stanford, CA, 1985), 294; Cissie Fairchilds, *Poverty and Charity in Aix-en-Provence, 1640–1789* (Baltimore, MD, 1976), ch. 7, Conclusion.

10. Greer, *Terror*, chs 2, 5, and *Emigration*, chs 2, 4; Chaussinand-Nogaret, *French Nobility*, ch. 2; Robert Forster, 'The Survival of the Nobility during the French Revolution', *P&P* 37 (1967), 71–86; Thomas Beck, 'The French Revolution and the Nobility: A Reconsideration', *JSH* 15 (1981), 219–34.

11. Margaret H. Darrow, 'French Noblewomen and the New Domesticity, 1750–1850', *Feminist Studies* 5 (1979), 41–65; Landes, *Women and the Public Sphere*, ch. 6, Conclusion.

12. Doyle, *Oxford History of the French Revolution*, xiii, 425; Schama, *Citizens*, 906, Epilogue.

13. Useful general studies of nation-states and minorities are Benedict Anderson, *Imagined Communities: Reflections on the Origin and Spread of Nationalism* (London, 1983); Anthony D. Smith, *The Ethnic Origins of Nations* (Oxford, 1986), esp. ch. 6. On France, see Robert Lafont, 'Sur le problème national en France: aperçu historique', *TM* 324–325–326 (1973), 21–53; Lyons, 'Politics and Patois'; Higonnet, 'Linguistic Terrorism'; and several of the essays in Pierre Nora (ed.) *Rethinking France: Les Lieux de mémoire*, vol. 1, *The State*, trans. Mary Trouille (Chicago, 2001). The brilliant study by David A. Bell, *The Cult of the Nation in France: Inventing Nationalism, 1680–1800* (Cambridge, MA, 2001) emphasizes the pre-revolutionary roots of nationalism.

14. Gérard Cholvy, 'Société, genres de vie et mentalités dans les campagnes françaises de 1815 à 1880', *IH* 36 (1974), 161; McPhee, 'Internal Colonization'.

15. See the discussion in Eric Wolf, *Europe and the People without History* (Berkeley, CA, 1982), ch. 3.

16. Bergeron, *France under Napoleon*, 137–8; Church, *French Ministerial Bureaucracy*, ch. 8.

17. Matthew Ramsey, *Professional and Popular Medicine in France, 1770–1830: The Social World of Medical Practice* (Cambridge, 1988), esp. ch. 2; David M. Vess, *Medical Revolution in France, 1789–1796* (Gainesville, FL, 1975); Gerald L. Geison (ed.), *Professions and the French State, 1700–1900* (Philadelphia, PA, 1984).

18. François Furet, *Interpreting the French Revolution*, trans. E. Forster (Cambridge, 1981), 24.

19. Bodinier and Teyssier, *La Vente des biens nationaux*, Conclusion.

20. Jones, *Peasantry*, ch. 8; McManners, *Ecclesiastical Society*, 251–2; Crubaugh, *Balancing the Scales of Justice*.

21. Bertaud, *Vie quotidienne*, ch. 12.

22. Hufton, *Bayeux*, ch. 2, Conclusion; Higonnet, *Pont-de-Montvert*, 97; Postel-Vinay, 'Révolution économique dans les campagnes'.

23. Paul Spagnoli, 'The Unique Decline of Mortality in Revolutionary France', *JFH* 22 (1997), 425–61, is important and provocative.

24. McManners, *Ecclesiastical Society*, chs 1, 6; Hufton, 'Women in Revolution 1789–1796', 98. Despite its title, Hufton's article essentially concerns women in provincial cities, those who suffered most from economic dislocation during the Revolution. While the Revolution destroyed the charity networks of the *ancien régime*, these had not always been effective: 80–90 per cent of abandoned children in Paris and Rouen died before their first birthday.

25. Anatoli Ado, 'Bilan agraire de la Révolution française', *Cahiers d'histoire de l'Institut Maurice Thorez* 27 (1978), 42–65. Ado's work is discussed in McPhee, 'Peasants and Capitalism'; Albert Soboul, 'Sur le mouvement paysan', in *Problèmes paysans de la Révolution, 1789–1848* (Paris, 1976), ch. 5; Antoine Casanova and Claude Gindin, 'Réflexions marxistes en mouvement: du modèle à la voie spécifique', in Vovelle (ed.), *L'Image de la Révolution française*, vol. 3, 1823–30.

26. McPhee, *Revolution and Environment*, ch. 7; James Livesey, *Making Democracy in the French Revolution* (Cambridge, MA, 2001). A superb recent case-study is Anne Jollet, *Terre et société en Révolution: approche du lien social dans la région d'Amboise* (Paris, 2000).

27. Albert Soboul, 'Concentration agraire en pays de grande culture: Puiseux-Pontoise (Seine-et-Oise) et la propriété Thomassin', in *Problèmes paysans*, ch. 11.

28. Jeffry Kaplow, *Elbeuf during the Revolutionary Period: History and Social Structure* (Baltimore, MD, 1964), 193–209, and chs 3, 5.

29. Louis Bergeron, Guy Chaussinand-Nogaret and Robert Forster, 'Les Notables du "Grand Empire" en 1810', *Annales* 26 (1971), 1052–75; Bergeron, *France Under Napoleon*, 125–31.

30. Delpierre, *Dress in France in the Eighteenth Century*, David Garrioch, *The Formation of the Parisian Bourgeoisie, 1690–1830* (Cambridge, MA, 1996).

31. See the contributions of Bernard Bonnin, Robert Chagny and Françoise Ours in Vovelle (ed.), *Bourgeoisies de province*.

32. Forster, 'Survival of the Nobility'. Forster later formulated a more 'minimalist' view: see 'The French Revolution and the "New" Elite, 1800–1850', in Jaroslow Pelenski (ed.), *The American and European Revolutions, 1776–1848* (Iowa City, 1980), 182–207.

33. Harcourt (ed.), *Escape from the Terror*, 93–94, 243–4.

34. Sheppard, *Lourmarin*, 211 and ch. 8. Sheppard himself prefers to emphasize the continuities of daily life in Lourmarin.

35. Gautier and Henry, *Crulai*, 119; Dupâquier *et al.* (eds), *Population française*, ch. 7; Alain Bideau, 'A Demographic and Social Analysis of Widowhood and Remarriage: The Example of the Castellany of Thoissey-en-Dombes, 1670–1840', *JFH* 5 (1980), 28–43. Reasons for the change in fertility patterns are discussed in Marcel Reinhard, 'Demography, the Economy, and the French Revolution', in Evelyn M. Acomb and Marvin L. Brown (eds), *French Society and Culture since the Old Régime* (New York, 1966), 20–42; Angus McLaren, *Sexuality and Social Order: The Debate over the Fertility of Women and Workers in France, 1770–1820* (New York, 1983), ch. 1; Etienne van de Walle, 'Motivations and Technology in the Decline of French Fertility', in Robert Wheaton and Tamara K. Hareven (eds), *Family and Sexuality in French History* (Philadelphia, PA, 1980), 135–78; Spagnoli, 'Decline of Mortality'.

36. Suzanne Desan, '"War between Brothers and Sisters": Inheritance Law and Gender Politics in Revolutionary France', *FHS* 20 (1997), 628; James R. Lehning, *The Peasants of Marlhes. Economic Development and Family Organization in Nineteenth-Century France* (London, 1980), ch. 8; Margaret H. Darrow, *Revolution in the House: Family, Class, and Inheritance in Southern France, 1775–1825* (Princeton, NJ, 1989). See, too, Jones, *Southern Massif Central*, 101–4; Louis Assier-Andrieu, 'Custom and Law in the Social Order: Some Reflections upon French Catalan peasant communities', *Law and History Review* 1 (1984), 86–94; Zeldin, *France 1848–1945*, vol. 1, 144–7.

37. Roderick Phillips, 'Women and family breakdown in eighteenth-century France: Rouen 1780–1800', *SH* 2 (1976), 217; Lynn Hunt, 'The French Revolution and Private Life', in Michelle Perrot (ed.), *A History of Private Life*, vol. 4, trans. A. Goldhammer (Harvard, MA, 1989); Elisabeth G. Sledziewski, 'The French Revolution as the Turning Point', in Geneviève Fraisse and Michelle Perrot (eds), *A History of Women in the West: Emerging Feminism from Revolution to World War*, trans. Arthur Goldhammer (London and Cambridge, 1993), 33–47. A provocative discussion of the gender discourse of the Revolution is Dorinda Outram, *The Body and the French Revolution: Sex, Class and Political Culture* (New Haven, CT, 1989).

38. Carla Hesse, *The Other Enlightenment: How French Women Became Modern* (Princeton, NJ, 2001); and 'The Cultural Contradictions of Feminism in

the French Revolution', in Jones and Wahrman, *The Age of Cultural Revolutions*. Hesse's argument is reinforced by Jacqueline Letzter and Robert Adelson, *Women Writing Opera: Creativity and Controversy in the Age of the French Revolution* (Berkeley, CA, 2001).

39. Jacques Houdaille, 'Un indicateur de pratique religieuse: la célébration saisonnière des mariages avant, pendant et après la Révolution française', *Population* 2 (1978), 367–80. Two fine surveys of the state of the Catholic Church in 1815 are Lebrun (ed.), *Histoire des Catholiques*, 275–87; and Gérard Cholvy and Yves-Marie Hilaire, *Histoire religieuse de la France contemporaine*, vol. 1 (Toulouse, 1985), ch. 1.

40. Michael Burns, *Dreyfus: a Family Affair, 1789–1945* (London, 1992).

6 The World of Notables and Bourgeois, 1815–1845

1. Shaffer, *Family and Farm*, 150–3; J. Orieux, *Talleyrand: The Art of Survival*, trans. P. Wolf (New York, 1974).

2. Jean-Claude Bontron, 'Transformations et permanences dans une société rurale: à propos du sud du Morvan', *ER* 63–64 (1976), 141–51.

3. André-Jean Tudesq, *Les Grands notables en France (1840–1849): étude historique d'une psychologie sociale*, 2 vols (Paris, 1964), vol. 1, 457. Two studies by David Higgs explore the world of Restoration nobles at a regional and national level: *Ultraroyalism in Toulouse*, and *Nobles in Nineteenth-Century France: The Practice of Inegalitarianism* (Baltimore, MD, 1987). The Right is well summarised in James Roberts, *The Counter-Revolution in France 1787–1830* (London, 1990).

4. Françoise Thésée, 'La Révolte des esclaves du Carbet à la Martinique (octobre–novembre 1822)', *Revue française d'histoire d'outre-mer* 80 (1993), 551–84; Paul Michael Kielstra, *The Politics of Slave Trade Suppression in Britain and France, 1814–48: Diplomacy, Morality and Economics* (Basingstoke, 2000).

5. Guillaume de Bertier de Sauvigny, 'Un grand capitaine d'industrie au début du XIXe siècle: Guillaume Ternaux 1763–1833', *RHMC* 28 (1981), 335–43; John F. Laffey, 'Municipal Imperialism in Nineteenth-Century France', *HR* 1 (1974), 81–114.

6. The political history of the Restoration is well told in André Jardin and André-Jean Tudesq, *Restoration and Reaction, 1815–1848*, trans. E. Forster (Cambridge, 1983), chs 1–3; Guillaume de Bertier de Sauvigny, *The Bourbon Restoration*, trans. L. M. Case (Philadelphia, PA, 1966); and Pamela Pilbeam, *The Constitutional Monarchy in France 1814–48* (Harlow, 1999). A fascinating insight into these years is offered in the account of a giraffe's journey from Marseille to Paris in 1826 by Michael Allin, *Zarafa* (London, 1998).

7. Translated in the excellent collection by Irene Collins (ed.), *Government and Society in France, 1814–1848* (London, 1970), 27. See, too, Douglas Porch, *Army and Revolution: France 1815–1848* (London, 1974).

8. Alan B. Spitzer, *The French Generation of 1820* (Princeton, NJ, 1987). See, too, Comninel, *Rethinking the French Revolution*, ch. 3; and Stanley

Mellon, *The Political Uses of History: A Study of Historians in the French Restoration* (Stanford, CA, 1958).

9. Alan B. Spitzer, *Old Hatreds and Young Hopes: The French Carbonari against the Bourbon Restoration* (Harvard, MA, 1971).

10. Sheryl Kroen, *Politics and Theater: the Crisis of Legitimacy in Restoration France, 1815–1830* (Berkeley, CA, 2000).

11. Gibson, *French Catholicism*, chs 3, 7; Cholvy and Hilaire, *Histoire religieuse*, chs 2–3; Soboul, *Problèmes paysans*, 156–9.

12. Irene Collins, *The Government and the Newspaper Press in France, 1814–1881* (Oxford, 1959), ch. 6; Claude Bellanger *et al.* (eds), *Histoire générale de la presse française* (Paris, 1969), vol. 2, 91–111. A local study of the resurgence of liberalism is Alan B. Spitzer, 'The Elections of 1824 and 1827 in the Department of the Doubs', *FH* 3 (1989), 153–76.

13. On the Revolution of 1830, see Jardin and Tudesq, *Restoration and Reaction*, ch. 5; David Pinkney, *The Revolution of 1830* (Princeton, NJ, 1972); Pamela M. Pilbeam, *The 1830 Revolution in France* (London, 1991); and the pathbreaking collection edited by John M. Merriman, *1830 in France* (New York, 1975).

14. The outstanding study of the landed élites of the July Monarchy is Tudesq, *Grands notables*. See also Ralph Gibson, 'The French Nobility in the Nineteenth Century – particularly in the Dordogne', in Jolyon Howorth and Philip G. Cerny (eds), *Elites in France: Origins, Reproduction and Power* (London, 1981), 5–45; Gabriel Désert, 'Le Corps électoral du Calvados (1820–1847), *Annales de Normandie* 10 (1960), 265–78, 376–9; Thomas D. Beck, 'Occupation, Taxes, and a Distinct Nobility under Louis-Philippe', *ESR* 13 (1983), 403–22, and 'French Revolution and the Nobility'.

15. Robert Forster, 'The "New" Elite', 199; J. P. Mayer (ed.), *The Recollections of Alexis de Tocqueville*, trans. A. Teixeira de Mattos (Cleveland, OH, 1959), 2–3; Karl Marx, *The Class Struggles in France, 1848 to 1850* (Moscow, 1979), 30–4.

16. Pierre Nora (ed.), *Realms of Memory: The Construction of the French Past*, trans. Arthur Goldhammer, vol. 2 (New York, 1997); Judith Bowen, 'Librarians as Guardians of Memory – the Case of France', in Evelyn Kerslake and Nickianne Moody (eds), *Gendering Library History* (Liverpool, 2000), 231–9; Michael Marrinan, *Painting Politics for Louis-Philippe: Art and Ideology in Orléanist France, 1830–1848* (New Haven, CT, 1988).

17. Gérard Noiriel, *The French Melting Pot: Immigration, Citizenship, and National Identity*, trans. Geoffroy de Laforcade (Minneapolis, MN, 1996); Patrick Weil, *Qu'est-ce qu'un Français: histoire de la nationalité française depuis la Révolution* (Paris, 2002).

18. A useful general overview of French colonialism is Robert Aldrich, *Greater France: A History of French Overseas Expansion* (London, 1996). Specific studies include Aldrich, *The French Presence in the South Pacific, 1842–1940* (Honolulu, 1990); Greg Dening, *Islands and Beaches. Discourse on a Silent Land: Marquesas, 1774–1880* (Honolulu, 1980); Colin Newbury, *Tahiti*

Nui: Change and Survival in French Polynesia, 1767–1945 (Honolulu, 1980), chs 3–5; Charles-Robert Ageron, *Modern Algeria: A History from 1830 to the Present*, trans. Michael Brett (London, 1991); John Ruedy, *Modern Algeria: The Origins and Development of a Nation* (Bloomington, IN, 1992); C. R. Pennell, *Morocco since 1830: A History* (London, 2000). A fascinating account of Moroccan responses to France is Susan Gilson Miller (ed. and trans.), *Disorienting Encounters. Travels of a Moroccan scholar in France 1845–1846: The Voyage of Muhammad as-Saffar* (Berkeley, CA, 1992).

19. Adeline Daumard, *Les Bourgeois de Paris au XIXe siècle* (Paris, 1970), part 2, ch. 3.

20. Note the important article by Christopher Johnson, 'The Revolution of 1830 in French Economic History', in Merriman (ed.), *1830 in France*, ch. 5. See also David Landes, 'Religion and Enterprise: The Case of the French Textile Industry', in E. C. Carter, R. Forster and J. N. Moody (eds), *Enterprise and Entrepreneurs in Nineteenth and Twentieth-Century France* (Baltimore, MD, 1976), 41–86; David H. Pinkney, *Decisive Years in France, 1840–1847* (Princeton, NJ, 1986); Bertrand Gille, *La Banque et le crédit en France de 1815 à 1848* (Paris, 1959).

21. Gwynne Lewis, *The Advent of Modern Capitalism in France 1770–1840: The Contribution of Pierre-François Tubeuf* (Oxford, 1993).

22. Shaffer, *Family and Farm*, chs 8–10.

23. Soboul, *Problèmes paysans*, ch. 7; Peter Simoni, 'Agricultural Change and Landlord-Tenant Relations in Nineteenth-Century France: The Canton of Apt (Vaucluse)', *JSH* 13 (1979), 115–35; Duby and Wallon (eds), *France rurale*, vol. 3, 116–18; Charles K. Warner (ed.), *From the Ancien Régime to the Popular Front: Essays in the History of Modern France in Honor of Shepard B. Clough* (New York, 1969), 96–101; André Thuillier, *Economie et société nivernaises au début du XIXe siècle* (Paris, 1974), ch. 6.

24. Collins, *Government and Society*, 153–4; Tudesq, *Grands notables*, vol. 2, 581. Elite social attitudes are well summarized in Roger Price, *The French Second Republic: A Social History* (London, 1972), 31–56. On Guizot in particular, see Douglas Johnson, *Guizot: Aspects of French History, 1787–1874* (London, 1963).

25. William Coleman, *Death is a Social Disease: Public Health and Political Economy in Early Industrial France* (Madison, WI, 1982); Konvitz, *Cartography in France*, ch. 6.

26. Jill Harsin, *Policing Prostitution in Nineteenth-Century Paris* (Princeton, NJ, 1985); Alain Corbin, *Women for Hire: Prostitution and Sexuality in France after 1850*, trans. A. Sheridan (Cambridge, MA, 1990).

27. Wright, *Guillotine and Liberty*, ch. 3. The repressive elements of this system are stressed in Michel Foucault's influential *Discipline and Punish: The Birth of the Prison*, trans. A. Sheridan (London, 1977).

28. Jan Goldstein, *Console and Classify: The French Psychiatric Profession in the Nineteenth Century* (Cambridge, 1988), esp. chs 1, 8; Robert Castel, *The Regulation of Madness: Origins of Incarceration in France*, trans. W. D. Halls (Oxford, 1988); Robert A. Nye, *Crime, Madness and Politics in Modern France* (Princeton, NJ, 1984), esp. ch. 2; Gérard Bléandonu and

Guy Le Gaufey, 'The Creation of the Insane Asylums of Auxerre and Paris', in Forster, *Deviants and the Abandoned*, 180–212; Louis Chevalier, *Laboring Classes and Dangerous Classes in Paris During the First Half of the Nineteenth Century*, trans. F. Jellinek (London, 1973).

29. Robert A. Nye, 'Honor, Impotence and Male Sexuality in Nineteenth-Century French Medicine', *FHS* 16 (1989), 56; Peter Gay, *The Bourgeois Experience: Victoria to Freud*, vol. 2, *The Tender Passion* (Oxford, 1986), 3 and *passim*. Family relationships are discussed in Daumard, *Bourgeois de Paris*, part 2, chs 4–5; Perrot, *A History of Private Life*, vol. 4, part 2. The politics of sexual discourse are examined in Copley, *Sexual Moralities in France*, ch. 4; McLaren, *Sexuality and Social Order*, ch. 4; and Jacques Donzelot, *The Policing of Families*, trans. R. Hurley (London, 1980).

30. Darrow, 'French Noblewomen'; Maurice Crubellier, *L'Enfance et la jeunesse dans la société française, 1800–1950* (Paris, 1979), chs 1–2; Sussman, *Wet-Nursing Business*, ch. 5. Well-chosen documents have been edited by Hellerstein *et al.*, *Victorian Women: A Documentary Account of Women's Lives in Nineteenth-Century England, France, and the United States* (Stanford, CA, 1981), esp. 24–31, 111–12, 144–9.

31. Ann-Louise Shapiro, 'Disordered Bodies/Disorderly Acts: Medical Discourse and the Female Criminal in Nineteenth-Century Paris', *Genders* 4 (1989), 68–86; Jean Borie, 'Une gynécologie passionnée', and Jean-Pierre Peter, 'Les Médecins et les femmes', in Jean-Paul Aron (ed.), *Misérable et glorieuse: la femme au XIXe siècle* (Paris, 1980).

32. Claire G. Moses, *French Feminism in the Nineteenth Century* (Albany, NY, 1984), ch. 2; Michela De Giorgio, 'The Catholic Model', trans. Joan Bond Sax, in Fraisse and Perrot, *Emerging Feminism from Revolution to World War*, 168–197.

33. Philippe Perrot, *Le Travail des apparences ou la transformation du corps féminin: XVIIIe-XIXe siècle* (Paris, 1984); Stephen Mennell, *All Manners of Food: Eating and Taste in England and France from the Middle Ages to the Present* (Oxford, 1985), ch 6–8; Georges Vigarello, *Concepts of Cleanliness: Changing Attitudes in France since the Middle Ages*, trans. J. Birrell (Cambridge, 1988), chs 12–13; Alain Corbin, *The Foul and the Fragrant: Odor and the French Social Imagination*, trans. M. Kochan *et al.* (Cambridge, MA, 1986), and *The Lure of the Sea: The Discovery of the Seaside in the Western World*, trans. Jocelyn Phelps (Oxford, 1992); Jean-Pierre Goubert, *The Conquest of Water: The Advent of Health in the Industrial Age*, trans. A. Wilson (Oxford, 1989).

34. James H. Johnson, *Listening in Paris: A Cultural History* (Berkeley, CA, 1995), esp. ch. 13.

35. Gibson, *French Catholicism*, chs 3, 7; Daumard, *Bourgeois de Paris*, part 2, ch. 4; Philippe Ariès, *The Hour of our Death*, trans. H. Weaver (London, 1981), ch. 10.

36. Bellanger *et al.*, *Presse française*, 111–46, 173–203; Maurice Agulhon, *Le Cercle dans la France bourgeoise, 1810–1848* (Paris, 1977); Carol E. Harrison, *The Bourgeois Citizen in Nineteenth-Century France: Gender, Sociability, and the Uses of Emulation* (Oxford, 1999).

37. Martyn Lyons, *Le Triomphe du livre: une histoire sociologique de la lecture dans la France du XIXe siècle* (Paris, 1987), chs 3–7; James S. Allen, *Popular French Romanticism: Authors, Readers and Books in the Nineteenth Century* (New York, 1981); D. G. Charlton (ed.), *The French Romantics*, 2 vols. (Cambridge, 1984); Hemmings, *Culture and Society*, ch. 6; Chartier and Roche, *Edition française*, vols 2–3. See too Richard Sennett's historical novel, *Palais-Royal* (New York, 1986).

38. On the political history of the July Monarchy, see Jardin and Tudesq, *Restoration and Reaction*, chs 6–7, 9; H. A. C. Collingham, *The July Monarchy: A Political History of France, 1830–1848* (London, 1988); and Pilbeam, *Constitutional Monarchy in France*.

39. Jo Burr Margadant, 'Gender, Vice, and the Political Imaginary in Postrevolutionary France: Reinterpreting the Failure of the July Monarchy, 1830–1848', *AHR* 104 (1999), 1461–96. On caricature, see Petra ten-Doesschate Chu and Gabriel P. Weisberg, *The Popularization of Images. Visual Culture under the July Monarchy* (Princeton, NJ, 1994); David S. Kerr, *Caricature and French Political Culture 1830–1848: Charles Philipon and the Illustrated Press* (Oxford, 2000).

40. Robert A. Nye, *Masculinity and Male Codes of Honor in Modern France* (Oxford, 1993), 137. See, too, Nye, 'Honor, Impotence and Male Sexuality in Nineteenth-Century French Medicine', *FHS* 16 (1989), 56; Spitzer, *The Generation of 1820*; Gay, *The Tender Passion*. Family relationships are discussed in Adeline Daumard, *Bourgeois de Paris*, part 2, chs 4–5; Perrot, *A History of Private Life*, vol. 4, part 2. The politics of gender discourse are further examined in Anthony Copley, *Sexual Moralities in France 1780–1980: New Ideas on the Family, Divorce and Homosexuality* (London, 1989), ch. 4; Jacques Donzelot, *The Policing of Families*, trans. R. Hurley (London, 1980).

41. William Reddy, 'Condottieri of the Pen: Journalists of the Public Sphere in Postrevolutionary France (1815–1850)', *AHR* (1994), 1552–3. See, too, Reddy, 'Marriage, Honor, and the Public Sphere in Postrevolutionary France: *Séparations de Corps*, 1815–1848', *JMH* 65 (1993), 437–72.

42. Cholvy, 'Campagnes françaises', 155; Tudesq, *Grands notables*, vol. 1, 130–236. Two evocative literary descriptions of legitimism are in Stendhal's novels, *Le Rouge et le noir*, ch. 23, and *Lucien Leuwen*, ch. 11.

43. Ernest Lavisse, *Souvenirs* (Paris, 1912), 76; Frederick A. de Luna, *The French Republic under Cavaignac, 1848* (Princeton, NJ, 1969), ch. 2; Peter McPhee, 'The Crisis of Radical Republicanism in the French Revolution of 1848', *Historical Studies* 16 (1974), 71–88.

44. Victor Hugo, *Journal* (Paris, 1954), 336. Hugo's acerbic memories of the July Monarchy, parts of which have been translated as *Things Seen*, are one of the best introductions to the world of the notables.

7   The World of Urban Working People, 1815–1845

1. For this and other examples of popular protest during the Restoration, see Collins, *Government and Society*, 62–70. On the food riots of 1816–17 see

Nicolas Bourguinat, *Les Grains du désordre. L'État face aux violences frumentaires dans la première moitié du XIXe siècle* (Paris, 2002), 154–61 and *passim*.

2. John M. Merriman, *The Margins of Urban Life: Explorations on the French Urban Frontier* (Oxford and New York, 1991). The diversity of urban France is stressed in Merriman, *French Cities*; Maurice Agulhon (ed.), *Histoire de la France urbaine*, vol. 4 (Paris, 1983); Jean Vidalenc, *La Société française de 1815 à 1848*, vol. 2, *Le Peuple des villes et des bourgs* (Paris, 1973); Dupâquier *et al., Population française*, vol. 3, chs 3–4.

3. John M. Merriman, *The Red City: Limoges and the French Nineteenth Century* (Oxford and New York, 1985), ch. 1.

4. Donald Reid, *The Miners of Decazeville: A Genealogy of Deindustrialization* (Cambridge, MA, 1985).

5. Pierre Léon, 'Vie et mort d'un grand marché international: la foire de Beaucaire (XVIIIe–XIXe siècles)', *Revue de géographie de Lyon* 28 (1953), 309–28.

6. Much of the discussion of the workers' movement and ideology in this chapter draws on William Sewell's important *Work and Revolution*, chs 7–10. For a critique of Sewell, see Lynn Hunt and George Sheridan, 'Corporatism, Association, and the Language of Labor in France', *JMH* 58 (1986), 813–44. See, too, Agricol Perdiguier, *Mémoires d'un compagnon* (Paris, 1964); Alain Faure and Jacques Rancière, *La Parole ouvrière, 1830–1851* (Paris, 1976); Cynthia Truant, 'Solidarity and Symbolism among Journeymen Artisans: The Case of Compagnonnage', *CSSH* 21 (1979), 214–26.

7. Sewell, *Work and Revolution*, 174; Mark Traugott (ed.), *The French Worker: Autobiographies from the Early Industrial Era* (Berkeley, CA, 1993), ch. 1. Michael D. Sibalis, 'The Mutual Aid Societies of Paris 1789–1848', *FH* 3 (1989), 1–30.

8. Kroen, *Politics and Theater*, 43–54, 190–6.

9. Edgar Leon Newman, 'What the Crowd Wanted in the French Revolution of 1830', in Merriman, *1830 in France*, ch. 1, and 'The Blouse and the Frock Coat', *JMH* 46 (1974), 26–59. An excellent overview of the Revolution in 1830, from a national perspective, is Pamela L. Pilbeam, *The 1830 Revolution in France* (Basingstoke, 1991). See too her *Republicanism in Nineteenth-Century France, 1814–1871* (London, 1995); and *French Socialists before Marx. Workers, Women and the Social Question in France* (Teddington, 2000); and Jill Harsin, *Barricades: The War of the Streets in Revolutionary Paris, 1830–1848* (New York & London, 2002).

10. Sewell, *Work and Revolution*, 198–203 and ch. 9.

11. Sylvie Vila, 'Une révélation? Les Luttes populaires dans le département de l'Hérault au début de la Monarchie de Juillet, 1830–1834', in *Droite et gauche de 1789 à nos jours* (Montpellier, 1975), 105–35. See, too, Brian Fitzpatrick, *Catholic Royalism in the Department of the Gard, 1814–1852* (Cambridge, 1983), chs 4–5; James C. Deming, *Religion and Identity in Modern France: The Modernization of the Protestant Community in Languedoc, 1815–1848* (Lanham, MD, 1999).

12. Robert J. Bezucha, 'The Revolution of 1830 and the City of Lyon', in Merriman, *1830 in France*, ch. 4. Girardin's speech is translated in Collins, *Government and Society*, 151–2.

13. Sewell, *Work and Revolution*, 216; Eric Hobsbawm and Joan Scott, 'Political Shoemakers', *P&P* 89 (1980), 86–114.

14. Bernard H. Moss, *The Origins of the French Labor Movement, 1830–1914: The Socialism of Skilled Workers* (Berkeley, CA, 1976), chs 1, 2. Moss places far more stress than does Sewell on the role of republican students and activists.

15. Robert J. Bezucha, *The Lyon Uprising of 1834: Social and Political Conflict in the Early July Monarchy* (Cambridge, MA, 1974).

16. See Tony Judt, *Marxism and the French Left: Studies in Labour and Politics in France, 1830–1981* (Oxford, 1986), ch. 2; R. B. Rose, '*Prolétaires* and *Prolétariat*: Evolution of a Concept, 1789–1848', *AJFS* 18 (1981), 282–99. Balzac's comments are in 'Ce qui disparaît de Paris', *Oeuvres complètes* (Paris, 1869–76) vol. 21, 439.

17. Maurice Agulhon, 'Working Class and Sociability in France before 1848' in Pat Thane, Geoffrey Crossick and Roderick Floud (eds), *The Power of the Past* (Cambridge, 1984). The argument that skilled workers were motivated by love of their work is challenged by Jacques Rancière, *The Nights of Labor: The Workers' Dream in Nineteenth-Century France*, trans. J. Drury (Philadelphia, PA, 1989), and 'The Myth of the Artisan: Critical Reflections on a Category of Social History', *International Labor and Working-Class History* 24 (1983), 1–16 (with discussion on pp. 17–26).

18. Among the many excellent studies of individual towns and cities in the first half of the nineteenth century, see Merriman, *The Red City*; Ronald Aminzade, *Class, Politics and Early Industrial Capitalism: A Study of Mid-Nineteenth Century Toulouse* (Albany, NY, 1981); Maurice Agulhon, *Une ville ouvrière au temps du socialisme utopique: Toulon de 1815 à 1851* (Paris, 1970).

19. Christopher H. Johnson, 'Patterns of Proletarianization: Parisian Tailors and Lodève Woollens Workers', in John M. Merriman, *Consciousness and Class Experience in Nineteenth-Century Europe* (New York, 1979), 65–84, and 'Economic Change and Artisan Discontent: The Tailors' History, 1800–48', in Roger Price (ed.), *Revolution and Reaction: 1848 and the Second French Republic* (London, 1975), 87–114; Joan Scott, 'Men and Women in the Parisian Garment Trades: Discussions of Family and Work in the 1830s and 1840s', in Thane, Crossick and Floud, *Power of the Past*; Francis Démier, 'Les ouvriers de Rouen parlent à un économiste en juillet 1848', *MS* 119 (1982), 3–31.

20. Christopher H. Johnson, *Utopian Communism in France: Cabet and the Icarians, 1839–1851* (Ithaca, NY, 1974). Cabet was particularly popular in Vienne: see the opening of this chapter.

21. Louise Tilly and Joan Scott, *Women, Work and Family* (New York, 1978); Austin Gough, 'French Workers and Their Wives in the Mid-Nineteenth Century', *Labour History* 42 (1982), 74–82; Madeleine Rebérioux, 'L'Ouvrière', in Aron, *Misérable et glorieuse;* Michelle Perrot, 'La femme populaire rebelle', in Christiane Dufrancatel *et al.* (eds), *L'Histoire sans*

qualités (Paris, 1979); Michelle Perrot *et al.* (eds), *Travaux de femmes dans la France du XIXe siècle* (Paris, 1978); Judith Coffin, *The Politics of Women's Work: The Paris Garment Trades, 1750–1915* (Princeton, NJ, 1996). Roger Magraw, *A History of the French Working Class* (Oxford, 1992), vol. 1, offers a fine synthesis and interpretation.

22. Harsin, *Policing Prostitution*; Corbin, *Women for Hire*; Victoria E. Thompson, *The Virtuous Marketplace: Women and Men, Money and Politics in Paris, 1830–1870* (Baltimore, MD, 2000).

23. Moses, *Feminism in the Nineteenth Century*, ch. 2. The study of feminism and gender is one of the most important areas of current historiography: Laure Adler, *A l'aube du féminisme: les premières journalistes (1830–1850)* (Paris, 1979); Joan W. Scott, *Only Paradoxes to Offer: French Feminists and the Rights of Man* (Cambridge, MA, 1996); Michèle Riot-Sarcey, *La Démocratie à l'épreuve des femmes. Trois figures critiques du pouvoir 1830–1848* (Paris, 1994); Geneviève Fraisse, *Reason's Muse: Sexual Difference and the Birth of Democracy*, trans. J. M. Todd (Chicago, 1994); Christine Fauré, *Democracy without Women: Feminism and the Rise of Liberal Individualism in France*, trans. C. Gorbman and J. Berks (Bloomington, IN, 1991); and Susan Grogan, *French Socialism and Sexual Difference: Women and the New Society, 1803–1844* (London, 1992).

24. Gay, *The Tender Passion*, epilogue; Michel Frey, 'Du mariage et du concubinage dans les classes populaires à Paris (1846–1847)', *Annales* 34 (1978), 803–29; Jeffry Kaplow, 'Concubinage and the Working Class in Early Nineteenth Century Paris', in Albert Cremer (ed.), *Vom Ancien Régime zur Französischen Revolution. Forschungen und Perspektiven* (Gottingen, 1978), 349–73.

25. Patricia O'Brien, *The Promise of Punishment: Prisons in Nineteenth-Century France* (Princeton, NJ, 1982), ch. 3; Jean-Paul Aron and Roger Kempf, *Le Pénis et la démoralisation de l'Occident* (Paris, 1978).

26. Michelle Perrot, 'The Three Ages of Industrial Discipline in Nineteenth-Century France', in Merriman (ed.), *Consciousness and Class Experience*; Coleman, *Death is a Social Disease*, ch. 8.

27. Adeline Daumard (ed.), *Les Fortunes françaises au XIXe siècle* (Paris, 1973), and *Bourgeois de Paris*; Coleman, *Death is a Social Disease*, chs 7, 8. Extracts from Villermé's reports are translated in Collins, *Government and Society*, 137–40.

28. Price, *Social History*, ch. 2.

29. O'Brien, *The Promise of Punishment*; Michelle Perrot, 'Delinquency and the Penitentiary System in Nineteenth-Century France', in Forster, *Deviants and the Abandoned*, ch. 7.

30. Foucault, *Discipline and Punish*. Foucault's work is debated by Patricia O'Brien in Lynn Hunt (ed.), *The New Cultural History* (Stanford, CA, 1987), and in Perrot, *L'Impossible Prison*.

31. Rachel G. Fuchs, *Abandoned Children: Foundlings and Child Welfare in Nineteenth-Century France* (Albany, NY, 1984); Colin Heywood, *Childhood in Nineteenth-Century France: Work, Health and Education among the 'Classes Populaires'* (Cambridge, 1988), chs 4–8; Lee Shai

Weissbach, *Assuring the Future Harvest: Child Labor Reform in Nineteenth-Century France* (Baton Rouge, LA, 1989), ch. 1; Katherine A. Lynch, *Family, Class, and Ideology in Early Industrial France: Social Policy and the Working-Class Family, 1825–1848* (Madison, WI, 1988).

32. Ariès, *Centuries of Childhood*, 218–30; Raymond Grew and Patrick Harrigan, *School, State, and Society. The Growth of Elementary Schooling in 19th-Century France: A Quantitative Analysis* (Ann Arbor, MI, 1991). Popular literary tastes are discussed in Lyons, *Triomphe du livre*, chs 5, 8; Allen, *Popular French Romanticism*.

33. Chevalier, *Laboring Classes and Dangerous Classes*, 417; Daumard, *Bourgeois de Paris*.

34. An important essay on this neglected social class is Geoffrey Crossick and Heinz-Gerhard Haupt (eds), *Shopkeepers and Master-Artisans in Nineteenth-Century Europe* (London, 1984), 3–34. See, too, the same authors' *The Petite Bourgeoisie in Europe, 1780–1914: Enterprise, Family and Independence* (London and New York, 1995).

35. Alain Faure, *Paris, Carême prenant. Du Carnaval à Paris au XIXe siècle, 1800–1914* (Paris, 1978); Cholvy and Hilaire, *Histoire religieuse*, 180 and chs 2, 4; Gibson, *French Catholicism*, chs 4, 5; Laura Strumingher, *Women and the Making of the Working Class: Lyon 1830–1870* (St Albans, VT, 1979), chs 1–2. An outstanding study of the 'feminization' of the Catholic Church is Claude Langlois, *Le Catholicisme au féminin: les congrégations françaises à supérieure générale au XIXe siècle* (Paris, 1984).

36. Jay Berkovitz, *The Shaping of Jewish Identity in Nineteenth-Century France* (Detroit, MI, 1989); Christine Piette, *Les Juifs de Paris (1808–1840): la marche vers l'assimilation* (Québec, 1983); Zosa Szajkowski, *Jewish Education in France, 1789–1939* (New York, 1980); Paula Hyman, *The Jews of Modern France* (Berkeley, CA, 1998); Phyllis Albert, *The Modernisation of French Jewry: Consistory and Community in the Nineteenth Century* (Boston, 1977); Barnett Singer, 'The Jews of Vaucluse in the Nineteenth Century', *Jewish Social Studies*, 40 (1976), 159–76; David I. Kertzer, 'The Montel Affair: Vatican Jewish Policy and French Diplomacy under the July Monarchy', *FHS* 25 (2002), 265–93.

37. Rebecca McCoy, 'Alsatians into Frenchmen: The Construction of National Identities at Sainte-Marie-aux-Mines, 1815–1851', *FH* 12 (1998), 429–51.

38. Edgar Leon Newman, '*L'arme du siècle, c'est la plume*: the French Worker Poets of the July Monarchy and the Spirit of Revolution and Reform', *JMH* 51 (1980), Supplement; Sewell, *Work and Revolution*, 236–42; Barbara Ann Day-Hickman, *Napoleonic Art, Nationalism, and the Spirit of Rebellion in France (1815–1848)* (Newark, Delaware, and London, 1999).

8 Rural Change and Continuity, 1815–1845

1. The best overview of rural society in the first half of the nineteenth century is Duby and Wallon, *France rurale*, vol. 3, 59–175. Regional specificities

are stressed in Jardin and Tudesq, *Restoration and Reaction*, part 2; Jean Vidalenc, *La Société française de 1815 à 1848*, vol. 1, *Le Peuple des campagnes* (Paris, 1970). Among the many outstanding studies of particular regions, see Maurice Agulhon, *The Republic in the Village: The People of the Var from the French Revolution to the Second Republic*, trans. J. Lloyd (Cambridge, 1970); Alain Corbin, *Archaïsme et modernité en Limousin au XIXe siècle, 1845–1880*, 2 vols (Paris, 1975); Jones, *Southern Massif Central*; Pierre Lévêque, *Une société provinciale: la Bourgogne sous la Monarchie de Juillet* (Paris, 1983); Christiane Marcilhacy, *Le Diocèse d'Orléans au milieu du XIXe siècle: les hommes et leurs mentalités* (Paris, 1964).

2. Peter McPhee, 'Social Change and Political Conflict in Mediterranean France: Canet in the Nineteenth Century', *FHS* 12 (1981), 68–97. Discussions of the complexities of the term "peasantry" in the French context are Charles Tilly, 'Did the Cake of Custom Break?', in Merriman, *Consciousness and Class Experience*, 17–44; McPhee, 'A Reconsideration of the "Peasantry" of Nineteenth-Century France', *Peasant Studies* 9 (1981), 5–25.

3. Duby and Wallon, *France rurale*, vol. 3, 59–62; Fernand Braudel and Ernest Labrousse (eds), *Histoire économique et sociale de la France* (Paris, 1976), 636–47; Michel Vovelle, 'Villes, bourgs, villages: le reseau urbain-villageois en Provence (1750–1850)', *AduM* 40 (1978), 413–33.

4. Joan W. Scott and Louise A. Tilly, 'Women's Work and the Family in Nineteenth-Century Europe', *CSSH* 17 (1975), 45. See also P. Kriedte *et al.*, *Industrialization before Industrialization* (Cambridge, 1981), ch. 2; Gay L. Gullickson, *Spinners and Weavers of Auffay: Rural Industry and the Sexual Division of Labor in a French Village, 1750–1850* (Cambridge, 1986); Tessie Liu, *The Weaver's Knot: The Contradictions of Class Struggle and Family Solidarity in Western France, 1750–1914* (Ithaca, NY, 1994); Duby and Wallon, *France rurale*, vol. 3, 68–74; Colin Heywood, 'The Rural Hosiery Industry of the Lower Champagne Region, 1750–1850', *Textile History* (1976), 89–111, and *Childhood in Nineteenth-Century France*, chs 1–2.

5. Braudel and Labrousse, *Histoire économique*, 275–304; Robert Laurent, *Les Vignerons de la Côte d'Or au XIXe siècle*, 2 vols (Paris, 1957–8), vol. 1, 19–25; Sussman, *Wet-Nursing Business*, 309–28.

6. Trans. E. Weber, (London, 1983), first published 1904.

7. Martine Segalen, *Love and Power in the Peasant Family: Rural France in the Nineteenth Century*, trans. S. Matthews (Oxford, 1983); Elisabeth Claverie and Pierre Lamaison, *L'Impossible mariage: violence et parenté en Gévaudan, XVIIe, XVIIIe et XIXe siècle* (Paris, 1982); Perrot, *A History of Private Life*, vol. 4, parts 2, 4. Examples of a 'negative' view of the peasant family are Patricia Branca, *Women in Europe since 1750* (London, 1978), 17–24; Edward Shorter, *The Making of the Modern Family* (London, 1976); Michael Mitterauer and Reinhard Sieder, *The European Family: Patriarchy to Partnership from the Middle Ages to the Present* (Oxford, 1982), chs 2, 5, 8. They may be contrasted with the evidence of 'affective'

relationships centuries earlier in Emmanuel Le Roy Ladurie, *Montaillou: Cathars and Catholics in a French Village, 1294–1324*, trans. B. Bray (London, 1980), chs 8–14.

8. Shaffer, *Family and Farm*, 22–3, 69–73, 95–104. See, too, Flandrin, *Amours paysannes*, ch. 2; Dupâquier *et al.*, *Population française*, vol. 3, chs 7–8.

9. Cholvy, 'Campagnes françaises', 158. Elite attitudes to contraception are well analysed in McLaren, *Sexuality and Social Order*.

10. Abel Chatelain, *Les Migrants temporaires en France de 1800 à 1914: histoire économique et sociale des migrants temporaires des campagnes françaises au XIXe et au début du XXe siècle*, 2 vols (Lille, 1977); Duby and Wallon, *France rurale*, vol. 3, 71–7.

11. Gibson, *French Catholicism*, ch. 3; Cholvy and Hilaire, *Histoire religieuse*, chs 2, 4; Yves-Marie Hilaire, 'La Pratique religieuse en France de 1815 à 1878', *IH* 25 (1963), 57–69; Gérard Cholvy, 'Une école des pauvres au début du 19e siècle: 'pieuses filles', béates ou soeurs des campagnes', *HR* 7 (1980), 125–41; Paul Huot-Pleuroux, *Le Recrutement sacerdotal dans le diocèse de Besançon de 1801 à 1960* (Besançon, 1966), 58–98.

12. Michael R. Marrus, 'Modernization and Dancing in Rural France: From "La Bourrée" to "Le Fox-Trot"', in Beauroy *et al.*, *Popular Culture in France*, 141; Gibson, *French Catholicism*, 100–2; Pierre Boutry, *Prêtres et paroisses au pays du curé d'Ars* (Paris, 1986).

13. Cholvy and Hilaire, *Histoire religieuse*, 35–43; D. Robert, *Les Eglises réformées en France, 1800–1830* (Paris, 1961); Joutard (ed.) *Histoire de la France religieuse*, vol. 3, 293–320.

14. Forster, 'Survival of the Nobility', 85, and 'The "New" Elite', 200; André Armengaud, *Les Populations de l'Est-Aquitain au début de l'époque contemporaine: recherches sur une région moins développée (vers 1845–vers 1871)* (Paris, 1961), 91.

15. The fullest statement of this position is Eugen Weber, *Peasants into Frenchmen: The Modernization of Rural France 1870–1914* (Stanford, CA, 1976). It may be contrasted with James R. Lehning's probing *Peasant and French: Cultural Contact in Rural France during the Nineteenth Century* (Cambridge, 1995). On Corsica, see Stephen Wilson, *Feuding, Conflict and Banditry in Nineteenth-Century Corsica* (Cambridge, 1988).

16. Rudé, *Crowd in History*, ch. 14; and *Ideology and Popular Protest* (New York, 1980), ch. 2.

17. Merriman, *1830 in France*; Duby and Wallon, *France rurale*, vol. 3, 151–9; Vila, 'Les Luttes populaires dans le département de l'Hérault'; Jardin and Tudesq, *Restoration and Reaction*, 93–116. A brilliant study of food-rioting and the State's responses is Bourguinat, *Les Grains du désordre*.

18. McPhee, *Revolution and Environment*, ch. 8.

19. John M. Merriman, 'The Demoiselles of the Ariège, 1829–1831', in Merriman, *1830 in France*, 87–118; Peter Sahlins, *Forest Rites: The War of the Demoiselles in Nineteenth-Century France* (Cambridge, MA, 1994).

20. Roger Thabault, *Education and Change in a Village Community: Mazières-en-Gâtine 1848–1914*, trans. P. Tregear (London, 1971), ch. 3. A challenging revision of the significance of the duchess's 'adventure' is by

Jo Burr Margadant, 'The Duchesse de Berry and Royalist Political Culture in Postrevolutionary France', *HW* 43 (1997), 23–52.

21. See, for example, Roger Price, *Economic History*, ch. 2; Hugh D. Clout, *Agriculture in France on the Eve of the Railway Age* (London, 1980), chs 6, 12. These views are challenged by Ted W. Margadant, 'Tradition and Modernity in Rural France during the Nineteenth Century', *JMH* 56 (1984), 667–97; McPhee, 'Reconsideration of the Peasantry'; Edward Berenson, *Populist Religion and Left-Wing Politics in France, 1830–1852* (Princeton, NJ, 1984), 3–18; Duby and Wallon, *France rurale*, vol. 3, 107–41; Jacques Mulliez, 'Du blé, "mal nécessaire": réflexions sur les progrès de l'agriculture de 1750 à 1850', *RHMC* 26 (1979), 3–47; Colin Heywood, 'The Role of the Peasantry in French Industrialisation, 1815–1880', *Economic History Review* 34 (1981), 359–76; Robert Aldrich, 'Late-comer or Early Starter? New Views on French Economic History', *Journal of European Economic History* 16 (1987), 89–100.

22. 'Progrès agricole d'un simple fermier', *Histoire et Société Rurales* 17 (2002), 209–17; Jean-Claude Toutain, *Le Produit de l'agriculture française de 1700 à 1958*, 2 vols (Paris, 1961); Jean Marczewski, 'Some Aspects of the Economic Growth of France, 1660–1958', *Economic Development and Cultural Change* 9 (1961), 369–86; William H. Newell, *Population Change and Agricultural Development in Nineteenth-Century France* (New York, 1977), 43–84; Patrick O'Brien and Caglar Keyder, *Economic Growth in Britain and France, 1780–1914: Two Paths to the Twentieth Century* (London, 1978); George W. Grantham, 'Divisions of Labour: Agricultural Productivity and Occupational Specialization in Pre-Industrial France', *Economic History Review* 46 (1993). Regional diets are analysed in Clout, *Agriculture in France*, ch. 11.

23. Evelyn B. Ackerman, *Village on the Seine: Tradition and Change in Bonnières, 1815–1914* (Ithaca, NY, 1978); Duby and Wallon, *France rurale*, vol. 3, 80–5.

24. Hugh D. Clout, 'Agricultural progress and environmental degradation in the Pyrénées-Orientales during the nineteenth century', *Bulletin de la Société royale de géographie d'Anvers* 83 (1972–3), 31–53.

25. Corbin, *Archaïsme et modernité*, vol. 1, 520; Patrice Bourdelais and Jean-Yves Raulot, *Une peur bleue: histoire du choléra en France 1832–1854* (Paris, 1987); Richard Evans, 'Blue Funk and Yellow Peril: Cholera and Society in Nineteenth-Century France', *EHQ* 20 (1990), 111–26; Rachel Fuchs, *Abandoned Children*.

26. Ramsey, *Professional and Popular Medicine*, 283 and chs 3–6; Jacques Léonard, *La Médecine entre les pouvoirs et les savoirs: histoire intellectuelle et politique de la médecine française au XIXe siècle* (Paris, 1981); Judith Devlin, *The Superstitious Mind: French Peasants and the Supernatural in the Nineteenth Century* (New Haven, CT, 1987), chs 2, 8.

27. Agulhon, *Republic in the Village*, esp. ch. 8.

28. André Armengaud, *La Population française au XIXe siècle* (Paris, 1971), 15; Marcilhacy, *Diocèse d'Orléans*, 488–91; Hilaire, 'Pratique religieuse', 62; Huot-Pleuroux, *Diocèse de Besançon*, 65–72.

29. Jean-Claude Farcy, 'Le Temps libre au village (1830–1930)', in Alain Corbin (ed.), *L'Avènement des loisirs 1850–1960* (Paris and Rome, 1995), 230–74.

30. Berenson, *Populist Religion*, 64; Theodore Zeldin, 'The Conflict of Moralities: Confession, Sin and Pleasure in the Nineteenth Century', in *Conflicts in French Society: Anticlericalism, Education and Morals in the Nineteenth Century* (London, 1970), 13–50. The classic work on popular festivals is Arnold van Gennep, *Manuel de folklore français contemporain*, 9 vols (Paris, 1937–58). Among George Sand's rural novels written in 1845–7, see *Le Péché de M. Antoine, Le Meunier d'Angibault, François le Champi* and *La Mare au diable*.

31. John M. Merriman, *The Stones of Balazuc: A French Village in Time* (New York, 2002), 174–5; Gibson, *French Catholicism*, 57–8; Devlin, *French Peasants and the Supernatural*, ch. 1.

32. Furet and Ozouf, *Reading and Writing*, chs 3, 4, 7; Grew and Harrigan, *School, State, and Society*; Jean-Yves Mollier, *Louis Hachette (1800–1864): le fondateur d'un empire* (Paris, 1999); Mary Jo Maynes, 'Work or School? Youth and the Family in the Midi in the Early Nineteenth Century', in Donald N. Baker and Patrick J. Harrigan, *The Making of Frenchmen: Current Directions in the History of Education in France, 1679–1979* (Waterloo, Ont. 1980); Robert Gildea, *Education in Provincial France (1800–1914): A Study of Three Departments* (Oxford, 1983); Philippe Rosset, 'Pierre Labrusse, instituteur', *AduM* 91 (1979), 509–23; Cholvy, 'Campagnes françaises'.

33. Berenson, *Populist Religion*, 59–73; Lyons, *Triomphe du livre*, 152–60, and 'Oral Culture and Rural Community in Nineteenth-Century France: The *veillée d'hiver*', *AJFS* 23 (1986), 102–14. Cf. Chartier, *Cultural History*, ch. 7.

34. Magraw, *The Bourgeois Century*, 106–19; Braudel and Labrousse, *Histoire économique*, 739–67; Philippe Vigier, *La Seconde République dans la Région alpine: étude politique et sociale*, 2 vols (Paris, 1963), vol. 1, 38–40; Soboul, *Problèmes paysans*, 283–84, and 'The French Rural Community in the Eighteenth and Nineteenth Centuries', *P&P* 10 (1956), 78–95; Jean-François Soulet, *Les Pyrénées au XIXe siècle*, vol. 2, *Une société en dissidence* (Toulouse, 1987), 149–71, 502–15; Armengaud, *Est-Aquitain*, 564–69.

35. Duby and Wallon, *France rurale*, vol. 3, 59–175; Peter McPhee, *The Politics of Rural Life: Political Mobilization in the French Countryside 1846–1852* (Oxford, 1992), chs 1–2; Gullickson, *Spinners and Weavers of Auffay*, ch. 10; Cécile Dauphin *et al.*, 'Women's Culture and Women's Power: Issues in French Women's History', in Joan W. Scott (ed.), *Feminism and History* (Oxford, 1996).

36. Pierre Joigneaux, *Souvenirs historiques*, 2 vols (Paris, 1891), vols 1, 9; Martin Nadaud, *Mémoires de Léonard, ancien garçon maçon* (Paris, 1976), 99. See, too, Balzac's *Le Médecin de campagne* and the novels of Eugène Le Roy, notably *Jacquou le Croquant* and *Le Moulin du Frau*.

9 The Mid-Century Crisis, 1846–1852

1. Marrinan, *Painting Politics for Louis-Philippe*, 17–19, part V. The crisis of 1846–7 and popular responses to it are surveyed in detail in Roger Price, *The Modernization of Rural France: Communications Networks and Agricultural Market Structures in Nineteenth-Century France* (London, 1983), 134–93; Bourguinat, *Les Grains du désordre*; Ernest Labrousse (ed.), *Aspects de la crise et de la dépression de l'économie française au milieu du XIXe siècle, 1848–1851* (La Roche-sur-Yon, 1956). See, too, George Sand, *Correspondance*, 22 vols (Paris, 1964–87), vol. 7.

2. Quoted in *La Réforme*, 9 January 1848. The failure of the July Monarchy – most commonly explained by the coincidence of political ineptitude and socio-economic crisis – has been reconfigured in challenging fashion by Jo Burr Margadant, 'Gender, Vice, and the Political Imaginary in Postrevolutionary France'.

3. John J. Baughman, 'The French Banquet Campaign of 1847–1848', *JMH* 31 (1959), 1–15; John G. Gallaher, *The Students of Paris and the Revolution of 1848* (Edwardsville, IL, 1980). The best general introduction to the Revolution of 1848 and the Second Republic is Maurice Agulhon, *The Republican Experiment, 1848–1852*, trans. J. Lloyd (Cambridge, 1983). More detailed studies are Ronald Aminzade, *Ballots and Barricades: Class Formation and Republican Politics in France, 1830–1871* (1993); David Barry, *Women and Political Insurgency. France in the Mid-Nineteenth Century* (Basingstoke, 1996); Harsin, *Barricades*, chs 13–15; Magraw, *A History of the French Working Class*, vol. 1, 131–85. Price, *French Second Republic*, is a detailed critique of Marx's two classics, *The Class Struggles in France 1848 to 1850 (1850)* and *The Eighteenth Brumaire of Louis Bonaparte (1852)*. Two durable French studies are Paul Bastid, *Doctrines et institutions politiques de la Seconde République*, 2 vols (Paris, 1945); Charles Seignobos, *La Révolution de 1848, le Second Empire (1848–1859)* (Paris, 1921). The mood of Paris in 1848 is captured in Flaubert's *Sentimental Education* and Daumier's lithographs.

4. The Second Republic has been the focus of some of the most outstanding regional studies in French social history. See, for example, Agulhon, *Republic in the Village*; Corbin, *Archaïsme et modernité*; Pierre Lévêque, *Une société en crise: la Bourgogne au milieu du XIXe siècle* (Paris, 1983); Marcilhacy, *Diocèse d'Orléans*; Vigier, *Région alpine*; Jean-Luc Mayaud (ed.), *1848 en provinces*, special issue of *Cahiers d'histoire* 43 (1998). This work is synthesized and interpreted in McPhee, *Politics of Rural Life*.

5. Ackerman, *Village on the Seine*, 86–9; Soboul, *Problèmes paysans*, chs 12, 13; Michelle Perrot, '1848: Révolution et prisons', in Perrot, *L'Impossible Prison*; Mary Lynn Stewart-McDougall, *The Artisan Republic: Revolution, Reaction, and Resistance in Lyon, 1848–1851* (Montreal, 1984), 42–8.

6. Sewell, *Work and Revolution*, ch. 11; Rémi Gossez, *Les ouvriers de Paris*, vol. 1, *L'Organisation, 1848–1851* (La Roche-sur-Yon, 1967); Lawrence C. Jennings, *French Anti-Slavery: The Movement for the Abolition of Slavery in France, 1802–1848* (Cambridge, 2000). A sympathetic discussion of the

provisional government is O. E. Heywood and C. M. Heywood, 'Rethinking the 1848 Revolution in France: The Provisional Government and its Enemies', *History* 79 (1994), 394–411.

7. Scott, *Only Paradoxes to Offer*, 64, 81; Peter Amann, *Revolution and Mass Democracy: The Paris Club Movement in 1848* (Princeton, NJ, 1975); Jacques Godechot (ed.), *La Presse ouvrière, 1819–1850* (La Roche-sur-Yon, 1966); Adler, *A l'aube du féminisme*; Moses, *Feminism in the Nineteenth Century*; Judith DeGroat, 'The Public Nature of Women's Work: Definitions and Debates during the Revolution of 1848', *FHS* 20 (1997); Peter McPhee, 'The Changing Contours of 1848', in Robert Aldrich and Martyn Lyons (eds), *The Sphinx in the Tuileries and Other Essays in Modern French History. Papers presented at the Eleventh George Rudé Seminar* (Sydney, 1998).

8. George W. Fasel, 'The French Election of April 23, 1848: Suggestions for a Revision', *FHS* 5 (1968), 285–98; de Luna, *Cavaignac*, 100–18; Tudesq, *Grands notables*, vol. 2, 1028–72.

9. On the June Days, see de Luna, *Cavaignac*, ch. 6; Donald C. McKay, *The National Workshops: A Study in the French Revolution of 1848* (Cambridge, MA, 1933), chs 5–6; Mark Traugott, *Armies of the Poor: Determinants of Working-Class Participation in the Parisian Insurrection of June 1848* (Princeton, NJ, 1985); Pierre Caspard, 'Aspects de la lutte des classes en 1848: le recrutement de la garde nationale mobile', *RH* 511 (1974), 81–106; Charles Tilly and Lynn H. Lees, 'The People of June, 1848', in Price (ed.), *Revolution and Reaction*, 170–209; Robert Bezucha, 'The French Revolution of 1848 and the Social History of Work', *T&S* 12 (1983), 469–84; and two contemporary classics: Mayer, *Recollections of de Tocqueville*, 140–206; and Marx, *Class Struggles*, ch. 1.

10. Quoted in the fine collection of documents edited by Roger Price, *1848 in France* (London, 1975), 111–12.

11. On the provincial response to the June Days, see Price, *French Second Republic*, 189–92; Lefebvre, *Great Fear*, 54–56; Jean Vidalenc, 'La Province et les journées de juin', *EHMC* 2 (1948), 83–144.

12. William H. Sewell, 'Uneven Development, the Autonomy of Politics, and the Dockworkers of Nineteenth-Century Marseille', *AHR* 93 (1988), 604–37; de Luna, *Cavaignac*, especially chs 10, 12; William Fortescue, 'Divorce Debated and Deferred: The French Debate on Divorce and the Failure of the Crémieux Divorce Bill in 1848', *FH* 7 (1993), 137–62. There were still some 190 co-operatives in existence in Paris in December 1851.

13. On the presidential elections, see Price, *French Second Republic*, 208–25; Marx, *Class Struggles*, ch. 2; de Luna, *Cavaignac*, ch. 15; André-Jean Tudesq, *L'Election présidentielle de Louis-Napoléon Bonaparte, 10 décembre 1848* (Paris, 1965).

14. On the elections and ideologies of the parties, see Agulhon, *Republican Experiment*, 75–7, ch. 4; Price, *French Second Republic*, 225–45; Tudesq, *Grands notables*, vol. 2, 1212–26; Jacques Bouillon, 'Les Démocrates-socialistes aux élections de 1849', *Revue française de science politique* 6 (1956), 70–95.

15. Among the many attempts to explain voting patterns, see Agulhon, *Republican Experiment*, 105–9; Edward Berenson, 'Politics and the French Peasantry: The Debate Continues', *SH* 12 (1987), 219–29; William Brustein, *The Social Origins of Political Regionalism: France, 1849–1981* (Berkeley, CA, 1988); Ted W. Margadant, *French Peasants in Revolt: The Insurrection of 1851* (Princeton, NJ, 1979), chs 2–4, 7; Price, *Revolution and Reaction*, 38–51; Leo A. Loubère, 'The Emergence of the Extreme Left in Lower Languedoc, 1848–1851: Social and Economic Factors in Politics', *AHR* 73 (1968), 1019–51; McPhee, *Politics of Rural Life*, ch. 5; D. M. G. Sutherland, 'Chouannerie and Popular Royalism: The Survival of the Counter-Revolutionary Tradition in Upper Brittany', *SH* 9 (1984), 351–60. Such 'structural' explanations are contested by Jones, *Southern Massif Central*, chs 8, 10; Eugen Weber, 'The Second Republic, Politics, and the Peasant', *FHS* 11 (1980), 521–50.

16. On the role of collective memories, see McPhee, 'The Dead Hand of the Past?'; Raymond Huard, 'Souvenir et tradition révolutionnaires: le Gard (1848–1851)', *AHRF* 258 (1984), 565–87. The work of activists is stressed by Berenson, *Populist Religion*, ch. 5; Roger Magraw, 'Pierre Joigneaux and Socialist Propaganda in the French Countryside, 1849–1851', *FHS* 10 (1978), 599–640; Loubère, 'Lower Languedoc'.

17. Bernard Moss, 'June 13, 1849: The Abortive Uprising of French Radicalism', *FHS* 13 (1984), 390–414; Stewart-McDougall, *Artisan Republic*, chs 6–7.

18. Edith Thomas, *Pauline Roland: socialisme et féminisme au XIXe siècle* (Paris, 1956).

19. The outstanding study of this repression is John M. Merriman, *The Agony of the Republic: The Repression of the Left in Revolutionary France, 1848–1851* (New Haven, CT, 1978); note the contrasting conclusion of Thomas R. Forstenzer, *French Political Police and the Fall of the Second Republic: Social Fear and Counterrevolution* (Princeton, NJ, 1981).

20. Agulhon, *Republic in the Village*, chs 4, 11, 12; Merriman, *Agony of the Republic*, ch. 3; Margadant, *Peasants in Revolt*, ch. 7.

21. Agulhon, *Republic in the Village*, 254–60, ch. 5. On the interplay of politics and popular culture, see Robert J. Bezucha, 'Mask of Revolution: A Study of Popular Culture during the Second French Republic', in Price (ed.), *Revolution and Reaction*, 236–53; McPhee, *Politics of Rural Life*, chs 6–7; Merriman, *Agony of the Republic*, 86–101.

22. The text of the Provençal song is included as part of a fascinating recollection of these years by Frédéric Mistral, *Memoirs*, ch. 9. Several other songs of the left are reproduced in Duby and Wallon, *France rurale*, vol. 3, 171, 173.

23. Agulhon, *Marianne into Battle*, ch. 4; Raymond Huard, 'Montagne rouge et montagne blanche en Languedoc-Roussillon sous la Seconde République', in *Droite et gauche*, 139–60; M. R. Cox, 'The Liberal Legitimists and the Party of Order under the Second French Republic', *FHS* 5 (1968), 446–64.

24. Margadant, *Peasants in Revolt*, ch. 6; Corbin, *Archaïsme et modernité*, 1017–19.

25. Marcel Dessal, 'Le Complot de Lyon et la résistance au coup d'état dans les départements du Sud-Est', *1848. Revue des Révolutions contemporaines* 189 (1951), 84; Adrien Dansette, *Louis-Napoléon à la conquête du pouvoir* (Paris, 1961), 313–20. A fine social history of painting in this context is Timothy Clark, *Image of the People: Gustave Courbet and the 1848 Revolution* (London, 1973).

26. The standard treatment of the coup, although too reliant on 'modernization' theory, is Margadant, *Peasants in Revolt*, especially chs 1, 10–12. See too, Dansette, *Louis-Napoléon*; Henri Guillemin, *Le Coup du 2 décembre* (Paris, 1951); Agulhon, *Republic in the Village*, chs 14–17; and Zola's historical novel *La Fortune des Rougon*.

27. On the repression, see Merriman, *Agony of the Republic*, chs 6–8; Margadant, *Peasants in Revolt*, ch. 12; Forstenzer, *Fall of the Second Republic*, ch. 6; Vincent Wright, 'The *Coup d'État* of December 1851: Repression and the Limits to Repression', in Price, *Revolution and Reaction*, 303–33; Price, *1848 in France*, part 5.

28. Price, *French Second Republic*, 321–33. Examples of direct pressure on voters are in Merriman, *Agony of the Republic*, 274–5; Payne, *Police State*, 56–7; Agulhon, *Republican Experiment*, 172–3.

29. This debate is surveyed in Agulhon, *Republican Experiment*, 160–5. An example of the former view is Weber, 'Politics and the Peasant'; of the latter, Margadant *Peasants in Revolt*, ch. 5; Berenson, *Populist Religion*, 221–4.

30. Agulhon, *Republican Experiment*, 159, and *Republic in the Village*, ch. 16.

31. On the political 'settlement' of 1852, see Agulhon, *Republican Experiment*, ch. 7; Seignobos, *Révolution*, 218–38.

32. Rudé, *Crowd in History*, ch. 15; Charles Tilly, 'How Protest Modernized in France, 1845–1855', in William C. Aydelotte (ed.), *The Dimensions of Quantitative Research in History* (Princeton, NJ, 1972), 192–255.

10 The Transformation of Urban France, 1852–1880

1. Paul Tucker, *Monet at Argenteuil* (New Haven, CT, 1982); Robert L. Herbert, 'Industry in the changing landscape from Daubigny to Monet', in Merriman, *French Cities*, ch. 6.

2. For overviews of urban change, see Merriman, 'Introduction', in *French Cities*; *France urbaine*, vol. 4, 18–125. Total population increased with the annexation of Nice and Savoy in 1860 and decreased with the loss of Alsace and parts of Lorraine in 1870. Including the latter, the total population increase was 7.6 per cent, that of towns 48.5 per cent (Dupâquier *et al.*, *Population française*, vol. 3, 122–32).

3. Leslie Page Moch, *Paths to the City: Regional Migration in Nineteenth-Century France* (Beverley Hills, CA, 1983); Lehning, *Marlhes*, ch. 6; William H. Sewell, *Structure and Mobility: Men and Women of Marseille, 1820–1870* (Cambridge, 1985); Michelle Perrot, 'A Nineteenth-Century Work Experience as Related in a Worker's Autobiography: Norbert Truquin', in Kaplan and Koepp, *Work in France*, ch. 10.

4. On the urban economy, see Alain Plessis, *The Rise and Fall of the Second Empire, 1852–1871*, trans. J. Mandelbaum (Cambridge, 1985), ch. 3, and *La Banque de France et ses deux cents actionnaires sous le Second Empire* (Geneva, 1982); Guy Palmade, *French Capitalism in the Nineteenth Century*, trans. G. Holmes (Newton Abbot, 1972), ch. 3.

5. The best general work in English on the French overseas empire is Robert Aldrich, *Greater France: A History of French Overseas Expansion* (London, 1996). More specific studies are Pierre Brocheux and Daniel Hémery, *Indochine: la colonisation ambigue, 1858–1954* (Paris, 1995); Robert Aldrich, *The French Presence in the Pacific 1842–1940* (London, 1990); Nancy Nichols Barker, *The French Experience in Mexico, 1821–1861: A History of Constant Misunderstanding* (Chapel Hill, NC, 1979). The attitudinal response to the French overseas empire from the mid-nineteenth century onwards has been a major recent theme in the historiography of France: see, for example, William B. Cohen, *The French Encounter with Africans: White Responses to Blacks, 1530–1880* (Stanford, CA, 1980); Lewis Pyenson, *Civilizing Mission: Exact Sciences and French Overseas Expansion, 1830–1940* (Baltimore, MD, 1993); Madeleine Dobie, *Foreign Bodies: Gender, Language, and Culture in French Orientalism* (Stanford, California, 2001); Tony Chafer and Amanda Sackur (eds), *Promoting the Colonial Idea: Propaganda and Visions of Empire in France* (New York and Basingstoke, 2002), Robert Aldrich, 'Homosexuality in the French Colonies', in Jeffrey Merrick and Michael Sibalis (eds), *Homosexuality in French History and Culture* (New York, 2002), 201–18.

6. Christopher H. Johnson, *The Life and Death of Industrial Languedoc, 1700–1920: The Politics of Deindustrialization* (Oxford and New York, 1995), part 2.

7. Elinor Accampo, *Industrialization, Family Life, and Class Relations: Saint Chamond, 1815–1914* (Berkeley, CA, 1989), chs 5–6; Price, *Social History*, ch. 6.

8. For a cross-section of different approaches to the nature of class formation, see Aminzade, *Toulouse*, ch. 4; Joan W. Scott, *The Glassworkers of Carmaux* (Cambridge, 1974); Rolande Trempé, *Les Mineurs de Carmaux, 1848–1914*, 2 vols (Paris, 1971); Merriman, *The Red City*, ch. 3; Kaplan and Koepp, *Work in France*, chs 13–16; and the contributions to Merriman, *French Cities*, and *Consciousness and Class Experience*. The Marxist paradigm of proletarianization is contested by William Reddy, *Money and Liberty in Modern Europe: A Critique of Historical Understanding* (Cambridge, 1987); Gérard Noiriel, *Workers in French Society in the Nineteenth and Twentieth Centuries*, trans. H. McPhail (London, 1990).

9. Louise A. Tilly, 'Three Faces of Capitalism: Women and Work in French Cities', in Merriman, *French Cities*, ch. 7; Theresa McBride, *The Domestic Revolution: The Modernization of Household Service in England and France, 1820–1920* (New York, 1976); Fuchs, *Abandoned Children*, chs 1, 3; Pierre Guiral and Guy Thuillier, *La Vie quotidienne des domestiques en France au XIXe siècle* (Paris, 1978); Aron, *Misérable el glorieuse*.

10. Corbin, *Women for Hire.*

11. Tilly, 'Women and Work' in Merriman, *French Cities*; Yves Lequin, *Les Ouvriers de la région lyonnaise (1848–1914)*, 2 vols (Lyon, 1977); George J. Sheridan, 'Household and Craft in an Industrializing Economy: The Case of the Silk Workers of Lyon', in Merriman, *Consciousness and Class Experience*, 107–28; Strumingher, *Women and the Making of the Working Class*; and the special issue of *MS* 1978.

12. R. Burr Litchfield and David Gordon, 'Closing the Tour: A Close Look at the Marriage Market, Unwed Mothers, and Abandoned Children in Mid-Nineteenth Century Amiens', *JSH* 13 (1980), 458–73; Fuchs, *Abandoned Children*, ch. 6; Accampo, *Saint Chamond*, chs 3–4; Scott, 'Parisian Garment Trades', in Thane, Crossick and Floud, *Power of the Past.*

13. Leslie Page Moch and Rachel G. Fuchs, 'Getting Along: Poor Women's Networks in Nineteenth-Century France', *FHS* 18 (1993), 34–49.

14. John W. Shaffer, 'Family, Class and Young Women: Occupational Expectations in Nineteenth-Century Paris', *JFH* 3 (1978), 62–77; Susan Bachrach, *Dames Employées: The Feminization of Postal Work in Nineteenth-Century France* (New York, 1984).

15. On education during the Second Empire, see Furet and Ozouf, *Reading and Writing*, ch. 5; Patrick Harrigan, *Mobility, Elites and Education in French Society of the Second Empire* (Waterloo, Ont., 1980); Crubellier, *L'Enfance et la jeunesse*, chs 6, 13; Gildea, *Education in Provincial France*, chs 3–4, 6; Robert D. Anderson, *Education in France 1848–1870* (Oxford, 1975).

16. Hellerstein *et al.* (eds), *Victorian Women*, 318–23; Fuchs, *Abandoned Children*, 73–4. The argument for 'liberation' is put in Edward Shorter, *The Making of the Modern Family* (New York, 1975); Patricia Branca, *Women in Europe since 1750* (London, 1978), ch. 3. It is contested, for example, by James F. McMillan, *Housewife or Harlot: The Place of Women in French Society, 1870–1940* (Brighton, 1981), chs 1–2. Sharon Marcus, *Apartment Stories: City and Home in Nineteenth-Century Paris and London* (Berkeley, CA, 1999) challenges common interpretations about public and private spheres.

17. Crossick and Haupt, *The Petite Bourgeoisie in Europe, 1780–1914*; and the contributions of Haupt and Alain Faure to Crossick and Haupt, *Shopkeepers and Master Artisans.*

18. Benjamin's remark was made in his brilliant 1935 essay, 'Paris, the Capital of the Nineteenth Century', in *Selected Writings*, vol. 3, *1935–1938*, trans. Edmund Jeffcott *et al.* (Harvard, MA, 2002), 41. On the reconstruction of Paris, see David P. Jordan, *Transforming Paris: The Life and Labors of Baron Haussmann* (New York, 1995); David Pinkney, *Napoleon III and the Rebuilding of Paris* (Princeton, NJ, 1958); Jeanne Gaillard, *Paris, la ville (1852–1870)* (Paris, 1975); Goubert, *Conquest of Water*; Ann-Louise Shapiro, *Housing the Poor of Paris, 1850–1902* (Madison, WI, 1985). Urban reconstruction was also undertaken in cities such as Lyon, Bordeaux, Marseille, Rouen, Cherbourg, Blois, Besançon and Le Havre.

19. O'Brien, *The Promise of Punishment*; Wright, *Guillotine and Liberty*, ch. 4; Perrot, *L'Impossible Prison.*

20. Recent studies of the regime include David Baguley, *Napoleon III and His Regime: An Extravaganza* (Baton Rouge, LA, 2000); and Roger Price, *The French Second Empire: An Anatomy of Political Power.* (Cambridge, 2001). Two examples of recent French revaluation of Napoleon III are Philippe Séguin, *Louis Napoléon le Grand* (Paris, 1990); and Alain Minc, *Louis Napoléon revisité* (Paris, 1997).

21. Pierre Hahn, *Nos ancêtres les pervers: la vie des homosexuels sous le Second Empire* (Paris, 1979); Aldrich, 'Homosexuality'; Merrick and Ragan *Homosexuality in Modern France*, chs by Thompson and Peniston.

22. Georges Vigarello, *A History of Rape. Sexual Violence in France from the 16th to the 20th Century*, trans. Jean Birrell (Cambridge, 2001), ch. 10; Perrot, *A History of Private Life*, vol. 4, part 2; Sussman, *Wet-Nursing Business*, chs 5, 7; Yannick Ripa, *Women and Madness: The Incarceration of Women in Nineteenth-Century France*, trans. C. Menagé (Oxford, 1990); and see note 16 above.

23. Victoria E. Thompson, *The Virtuous Marketplace: Women and Men, Money and Politics in Paris, 1830–1870* (Baltimore, MD, 2000).

24. Bonnie G. Smith, *Ladies of the Leisure Class: The Bourgeoises of Northern France in the Nineteenth Century* (Princeton, NJ, 1981); Michelle Perrot and Georges Ribeill (eds), *Le Journal intime de Caroline B.* (Paris, 1985): the latter is reviewed by Joan W. Scott, 'New Documents on the Lives of Women: The Journal of Caroline B., 1864–1868', *Signs* 12 (1987), 568–72. See, too, *Daughter of Paris: The life story of Celeste Mogador, Comtesse Lionel de Moreton de Chabrillan, told by herself and Charlotte Haldane* (London, 1961); James Smith Allen (ed.), *'In the Solitude of my Soul': The Diary of Geneviève Breton, 1867–1871*, trans. James Palmes (Carbondale, IL, 1994); *Memoirs of a Courtesan in Nineteenth-Century Paris*, trans. Monique Fleury Nagem (Lincoln, NE, 2001); and the brilliant essay 'Backstage' by Alain Corbin in Perrot, *A History of Private Life*, vol. 4, ch. 4.

25. On religion under the Second Empire, see Gibson, *French Catholicism*, chs 3–7; Cholvy and Hilaire, *Histoire religieuse*, esp. ch. 8; Agulhon, *Marianne into Battle*, ch. 5; Yves-Marie Hilaire, *Une chrétienté au XIXe siècle? La Vie religieuse des populations du diocèse d'Arras (1840–1914)*, 2 vols (Lille, 1977); Jacques-Olivier Boudon, *Paris, capitale religieuse sous le Second Empire* (Paris, 2001).

26. Ruth Harris, *Lourdes: Body and Spirit in the Secular Age* (New York and London, 1999) brilliantly reconstructs and contextualizes the origins of the famous shrine. See, too, Raymond Jonas, *France and the Cult of the Sacred Heart: An Epic Tale for Modern Times* (Berkeley, CA, 2000).

27. Leonard R. Berlanstein, 'Illegitimacy, Concubinage, and Proletarianization in a French Town, 1760–1914', *JFH* 5 (1980), 360–74. An excellent general survey of these years is Magraw, *A History of the French Working Class*, vol. 1, 191–275.

28. On Lille, see William Reddy, *The Rise of Market Culture: The Textile Trade and French Society, 1750–1900* (Cambridge, 1984), part 3; Félix-Paul Codaccioni, *De l'inégalité sociale dans une grande ville industrielle: le drame*

de Lille de 1850 à 1914 (Lille, 1976); Pierre Pierrard, *La Vie ouvrière à Lille sous le Second Empire* (Paris, 1965).

29. Madeleine Rebérioux, 'Les Ouvriers du livre', in Chartier and Roche, *l'Édition française*, vol. 3; Price, *Social History*, ch. 6. Matthew Truesdale, *Spectacular Politics: Louis-Napoleon Bonaparte and the Fête Impériale, 1849–1870* (New York, 1997).

30. Moses, *Feminism in the Nineteenth Century*, ch. 8.

31. The Aubin strike informs Zola's *Germinal*, though it is placed at Anzin (Nord) and in the political language of the early 1880s. On Noir's funeral, see Price, *The French Second Empire*; and the innovative study by Avner Ben-Amos, *Funerals, Politics, and Memory in Modern France 1789–1996* (Oxford and New York, 2000).

32. Richard Holmes, *The Road to Sedan. The French Army, 1866–1870* (London, 1984); David Wetzel, *A Duel of Giants: Bismarck, Napoleon III, and the Origins of the Franco-Prussian War* (Madison, WI, 2001).

33. Merriman, *The Red City*, ch. 4; Aminzade, *Toulouse*, ch. 8; Jeanne Gaillard, *Communes de province, commune de Paris, 1870–1871* (Paris, 1971). The desire for self-government is stressed by Louis Greenberg, *Sisters of Liberty: Marseille, Lyon, Paris, and the Reaction to the Centralized State, 1868–1871* (Cambridge, MA, 1971).

34. Karl Marx, *The Civil War in France (1871)*. On the Paris Commune, see Stewart Edwards, *The Paris Commune: 1871* (London, 1971), and his excellent collection of documents, *The Communards of Paris, 1871* (London, 1973); Edith Thomas, *The Women Incendiaries*, trans. J. and S. Atkinson (London, 1967), and *Louise Michel*, trans. P. Williams (Montreal, 1980); Eugene Schulkind, 'Socialist Women during the 1871 Paris Commune', *P&P* 106 (1985), 124–63; Roger L. Williams, *The French Revolution of 1870–1871* (London, 1969); Jacques Rougerie, *Procès de communards* (Paris, 1964), and *Paris libre: 1871* (Paris, 1971); William Serman, *La Commune de Paris (1871)* (Paris, 1986); Robert Tombs, *The War Against Paris, 1871* (Cambridge, 1981), and *The Paris Commune 1871* (Harlow, 1999); Gay L. Gullickson, *Unruly Women of Paris: Images of the Commune* (Ithaca, NY, 1996); Roger V. Gould, *Insurgent Identities: Class, Community and Protest in Paris from 1848 to the Commune* (Chicago, 1995); Philip Nord, *The Republican Movement. Struggles for Democracy in Nineteenth-Century France* (Cambridge, MA, 1995); Ronald Aminzade, *Ballots and Barricades: Class Formation and Republican Politics in France, 1830–1871* (Princeton, NJ, 1993).

35. Important recent contributions to this debate are Sanford Elwitt, *The Making of the Third Republic: Class and Politics in France, 1868–1914* (Baton Rouge, LA, 1975); Agulhon, *Marianne into Battle*, chs 6–7; Aminzade, *Toulouse*, Conclusion; Katherine Auspitz, *The Radical Bourgeoisie: The Ligue d'Enseignement and the Origins of the Third Republic, 1866–1885* (Cambridge, 1982); J. P. T. Bury, *Gambetta's Final Years: 'The Era of Difficulties', 1877–1882* (London, 1982); Judith F. Stone, *Sons of the Revolution: Radical Democrats in France, 1862–1914* (Baton Rouge, LA, 1996); Elinor Accampo *et al.* (eds), *Gender and the Politics of Social Reform*

in France, 1870–1914 (Baltimore, MD, 1995); James R. Lehning, *To Be A Citizen: The Political Culture of the Early French Third Republic* (Ithaca, NY, 2001). On the Kanak rebellion, see Martyn Lyons, *The Totem and the Tricolour: A Short History of New Caledonia since 1774* (Sydney, 1986), ch. 5; Roseline Dousset-Leenhardt, *Colonialisme et contradictions. Nouvelle-Calédonie, 1878–1978: les causes de l'insurrection de 1878* (Paris, 1978).

36. David M. Gordon, *Merchants and Capitalists: Industrialization and Provincial Politics in Mid-Nineteenth Century France* (University of Alabama Press, 1985); Crubellier, *L'Enfance et la jeunesse*, ch. 9; Weissbach, *Child Labor Reform*, ch. 10; Heywood, *Childhood in Nineteenth-Century France*, ch. 10.

37. Susanna Barrows, 'After the Commune: Alcoholism, Temperance, and Literature in the Early Third Republic', in Merriman (ed.), *Consciousness and Class Experience*, and *Distorting Mirrors: Visions of the Crowd in Late-Nineteenth Century France* (New Haven, CT, 1981); Harsin, *Policing Prostitution*, chs 8–9; Ann-Louise Shapiro, *Breaking the Codes: Female Criminality in Fin-de-Siècle Paris* (Stanford, CA, 1996); Castel, *Regulation of Madness*; Joshua Cole, *Population, Politics, and Gender in Nineteenth-Century France* (Ithaca, NY, 2000).

38. Michael B. Miller, *The Bon Marché: Bourgeois Culture and the Department Store, 1869–1920* (Princeton, NJ, 1981). Consumerism is further explored in Leora Auslander, *Taste and Power: Furnishing Modern France* (Berkeley, CA, 1996); Rosalind H. Williams, *Dream Worlds: Mass Consumption in Late Nineteenth-Century France* (Berkeley, CA, 1982).

11   The Peak of Rural Civilization, 1852–1880

1. Robert L. Herbert, *Jean-François Millet* (London, 1976); John Berger, *About Looking* (New York, 1980, 69–78).

2. Weber, *Peasants into Frenchmen*. For a critique of Weber's thesis, see Tilly, 'Did the Cake of Custom Break?', in Merriman, *Consciousness and Class Experience*.

3. The outstanding survey of rural France in these years is the collaborative work by Maurice Agulhon, Gabriel Désert and Robert Specklin, in Duby and Wallon, *France rurale*, vol. 3, 183–381. Overviews in English include Margadant, 'Tradition and Modernity'; Georges Dupeux, *French Society 1789–1970*, trans. P. Wait (London, 1972), 105–18. Among many fine regional studies, see Corbin, *Archaïsme et modernité*; Raymond Huard, *La préhistoire des partis: le parti républicain en Bas-Languedoc, 1848–1881* (Paris, 1982); Jones, *Southern Massif Central*, chs 7–10; Alan R. H. Baker, *Fraternity among the French Peasantry: Sociability and Voluntary Associations in the Loire Valley, 1815–1914* (Cambridge, 1999); Johnson, *Life and Death of Industrial Languedoc*; Raymond A. Jonas, *Industry and Politics in Rural France: Peasants of the Isère, 1870–1914* (Ithaca, NY, 1994).

4. Ackerman, *Village on the Seine*. Changes to agricultural practices are outlined in Duby and Wallon, *France rurale*, vol. 3, 183–253; Hugh Clout (ed.), *Themes in the Historical Geography of France* (London, 1977); Price,

Modernization of Rural France; Cholvy, 'Campagnes françaises'; George Grantham, 'Agricultural Supply during the Industrial Revolution: French Evidence and European Implications', *JEH* 49 (1989), 43–72.

5. On migration, see Moch, *Paths to the City*, esp. ch. 2; Sussman, *Wet-Nursing Business*, ch. 6; Ronald Hubscher, *L'Agriculture et la société rurale dans le Pas-de-Calais du milieu du XIXe siècle à 1914*, 2 vols (Arras, 1979–80). The story of Jeanne Bouvier is from *Mes mémoires, ou 59 années d'activité industrielle, sociale et intellectuelle d'une ouvrière, 1876–1935* (Paris, 1983), 35–65.

6. Plessis, *Second Empire*, ch. 4. Two studies of changing consumption patterns are Gabriel Désert, 'Viande et Poisson dans l'Alimentation des Français au Milieu du XIXe siècle', *Annales* 30 (1975), 519–36; Thierry Fillaut, 'Alcoolisation et comportements alcooliques en Bretagne au XIXe siècle', *Annales de Bretagne* 1983, 35–46.

7. On health care and diseases, see Price, *Social History*, 49–73; Léonard, *Médecine française*; Devlin, *French Peasants and the Supernatural*, chs 2, 8; McLaren, *Sexuality and Social Order*, ch. 3.

8. The 'trickling-down' model underpins the work of Shorter, *Making of the Modern Family*; and Branca, *Women in Europe*. These contrast with Segalen, *Love and Power in the Peasant Family*, 127–32; Wilson, *Nineteenth-Century Corsica*, 120–5; and Lehning, *Marlhes*, ch. 10 (note the description of courting on pp.161–2). A brilliant evocation of attitudes to love and of village life in the 1860s is Gillian Tindall, *Célestine: Voices from a French Village* (New York, 1995).

9. On religion in the countryside, see Gibson, *French Catholicism*, chs 3–8; Cholvy and Hilaire, *Histoire religieuse*, chs 5–7, 9; Marcilhacy, *Diocèse d'Orléans*; Thomas Kselman, *Miracles and Prophecies in Nineteenth-Century France* (New Brunswick, NJ, 1983), and *Death and the Afterlife in Modern France* (Princeton, NJ, 1993); Langlois, *Catholicisme au féminin*, 451–68, ch. 15; Alain Corbin, *Village Bells: Sound and Meaning in the 19th Century French Countryside* (New York, 1998); Nicole Edelman, *Voyantes, guérisseuses et visionnaires en France, 1785–1914* (Paris, 1995).

10. For example, Gibson, *French Catholicism*, 184–5.

11. André Encrevé, *Protestants français au milieu du XIXe siècle: les réformés de 1848 à 1870* (Geneva, 1986); Joutard, *Histoire de la France religieuse*, vol. 3, 346–55, 428–38.

12. On education, see Furet and Richet, *Reading and Writing*, chs 3, 7; Anderson, *Education in France*, esp. ch. 8; Gildea, *Education in Provincial France*, esp. chs 4, 6; Merriman, *The Stones of Balazuc*; Peter V. Meyers, 'Professionalization and Societal Change: Rural Teachers in Nineteenth-Century France', *JSH* 9 (1975–6), 542–58. Catholic nuns are studied by Sarah Curtis, *Educating the Faithful: Religion, Schooling, and Society in Nineteenth-Century France* (DeKalb, IL, 2000).

13. Sharif Gemie, *Women and Schooling in France, 1815–1914: Gender, Authority, and Identity in the Female Schooling Sector* (Keele, 1995).

14. Hellerstein *et al.* (eds), *Victorian Women*, 352–5; Thabault, *Mazières-en-Gâtine*.

15. The phrase is used by the contributors to Duby and Wallon, *France rurale*, vol. 3. On patterns of crime, see A. Q. Lohdi and Charles Tilly, 'Urbanization, Criminality and Collective Violence in Nineteenth-Century France', *American Journal of Sociology*, 79 (1974), 296–318; Jean-Claude Farcy, 'Les Archives judiciaires et l'histoire sociale: l'exemple de la Beauce au dix-neuvième siècle', *RH* 524 (1977), 313–52.

16. Charles Tilly, 'Clio and Minerva', in J. C. McKinney and E. A. Tiryakian (eds), *Theoretical Sociology* (New York, 1970), 434–66.

17. Scott and Tilly, 'Women's Work and the Family'.

18. Marrus, 'Dancing in Rural France', in Beauroy *et al.*, *Popular Culture in France*; Weber, *Peasants into Frenchmen*, ch. 6.

19. Farcy, 'Le Temps libre au village'.

20. On domestic life, see Segalen, *Love and Power in the Peasant Family*; Duby and Wallon, *France rurale*, vol. 3, 307–55; Alain Corbin, *Le Temps, le désir et l'horreur. Essais sur le XIXe siècle* (Paris, 1991), 23–52, 171–83. Monuments are analysed in Agulhon, *Marianne into Battle*, chs 5–7.

21. Tamara Whited, *Forests and Peasant Politics in Modern France* (New Haven, CT and London, 2000). On the neglected history of the environment, see too Duby and Wallon, *France rurale*, vol. 3, 255–305; Andrée Corvol, *L'homme aux bois: histoire des relations de l'homme et de la forêt (XVIIe–XXe siècle)* (Paris, 1987); Clout, 'Environmental Degradation'.

22. Shaffer, *Family and Farm*, chs 8–9.

23. Harvey Smith, 'Work Routine and Social Structure in a French Village: Cruzy in the Nineteenth Century', *JIH* 5 (1975), 357–82.

24. Lehning, *Marlhes*, ch. 8; Farcy, 'Archives judiciaires', 342; Peter Stearns, *Old Age in European Society: The Case of France* (London, 1977), ch. 1; Jean-Pierre Gutton, *Naissance du vieillard: essai sur l'histoire des rapports entre les vieillards et la société en France* (Paris, 1988).

25. Roger Magraw, 'The Conflict in the Villages: Popular Anticlericalism in the Isère (1852–70)', in Zeldin, *Conflicts in French Society*, 169–227; Judith Silver, 'French Peasant Demands for Popular Leadership in the Vendômois (Loir-et-Cher)', *JSH* 14 (1980), 277–94; Duby and Wallon, *France rurale*, vol. 3, 361–3.

26. On the elections, see Louis Girard *et al.* (eds), *Les élections de 1869* (Paris, 1960); Leo Loubère, *Radicalism in Mediterranean France: Its Rise and Decline, 1848–1914* (Albany, New York, 1974), ch. 5.

27. Alain Corbin, *The Village of Cannibals: Rage and Murder in France, 1870*, trans. A. Goldhammer (Cambridge, MA, 1992).

28. Stéphane Audoin-Rouzeau, *1870: la France dans la guerre* (Paris, 1989); Jean Bécarud, 'Noblesse et représentation parlementaire: les députés nobles de 1871 à 1968', *RFSP* (1973), 972–93; Gaillard, *Communes de province*; Christopher Guthrie, 'The Battle for the Third Republic in the *Arrondissement* of Narbonne, 1871–3', *FH* 2 (1988), 45–73.

29. Agulhon, *Marianne into Battle*, chs 6–7; Tony Judt, *Socialism in Provence, 1871–1914: A Study in the Origins of the Modern French Left* (Cambridge, 1979), ch. 6; Huard, *Préhistoire des partis*; Charles Sowerwine, *France since 1870: Culture, Politics and Society* (Basingstoke, 2001), 29.

30. Judt, *Socialism in Provence*, ch. 3; Yves Lecouturier, 'La Pénétration de la république dans le bocage calvadosien (1848–1924)', *AdeN* 28 (1978), 241–57; Boutry, *Prêtres et paroisses*.

31. Judt, *Socialism in Provence*, 68. On the vexed question of whether disenchantment with the Third Republic generated a genuine rural socialism, see the debate between Judt and Roy Sandstrom in *HJ* 21 (1978), 685–95; Yves Rinaudo, *Les Vendanges de la République: les paysans du Var à la fin du XIXe siècle* (Lyon, 1982).

12   The Social History of Ideas, 1850–1880: 'The Moralization of the Masses'?

1. An excellent survey of the book trade is Lyons, *Triomphe du livre*, chs 8–11. See, too, Allen, *Popular French Romanticism*; Auspitz, *The Radical Bourgeoisie*; Graham Keith Barnett, *Histoires des bibliothèques publiques en France de la Révolution à 1939* (Paris, 1987); Chartier and Roche, *Edition française*, vol. 3; J.-J. Darmon, *Le Colportage de librairie en France sous le Second Empire: grands colporteurs et culture populaire* (Paris, 1972); Jean-Pierre Rioux, *Erckmann et Chatrian ou le trait de l'union* (Paris, 1989).

2. Mark Traugott (ed.), *The French Worker: Autobiographies from the Early Industrial Era* (Berkeley, CA, 1993), 313.

3. Claude Bellanger *et al.*, *Presse française*, vol. 2, 327–31; Price, *Social History*, 353–5; Lennard Bickel, *Triumph over Darkness: The Life of Louis Braille* (Sydney, 1988). On the experiences of a young blind woman much earlier, under the Restoration, see Thérèse-Adèle Husson, *Reflections*.

4. There is an outstanding discussion of these problems in Martyn Lyons, *Readers and Society in Nineteenth-Century France: Workers, Women, Peasants* (Basingstoke, 2001), ch. 6.

5. An example of a 'diffusion' model is Furet and Ozouf, *Reading and Writing*, chs 1, 4. The model is discussed in Peter McPhee, 'Historians, Germs and Culture-Brokers: the Circulation of Ideas in the Nineteenth-Century Countryside', and Hamish Graham, 'How did Nineteenth-Century Workers Get into Frédéric Le Play's 'Bad Books'', both in *AJFS* 23 (1986). On *mentalités*, see Michel Vovelle, *Ideologies and Mentalities*, trans. E. O'Flaherty (Oxford, 1990).

6. Graham, 'Le Play's Bad Books'.

7. See the fascinating case-studies in Lyons, *Readers and Society in Nineteenth-Century France*, ch. 5.

8. Colonialism is discussed in Aldrich, *Greater France*; Bury, *Gambetta's Final Years*, ch. 4; Jean Ganiage, *L'Expansion coloniale de la France sous la Troisième République* (Paris, 1968); and Henri Brunschwig, *French Colonialism, 1871–1914: Myths and Realities* (New York, 1966). On New Caledonia, see Lyons, *Short History of New Caledonia*, chs 4–5; Linda Latham, *La Révolte de 1878: étude critique des causes de la rébellion de 1878 en Nouvelle-Calédonie* (Nouméa, 1978); Dousset-Leenhardt, *Nouvelle-Calédonie*; Alice Bullard, *Exile to Paradise: Savagery and Civilization in*

Paris and the South Pacific, 1790–1900 (Stanford, CA, 2000); Bullitt Lowry and Elizabeth Ellington Gunter (eds and trans.), *The Red Virgin: Memoirs of Louise Michel* (University, AL, 1981), ch. 14.

9. Anderson, *Imagined Communities*; Anthony D. Smith, *Ethnic Origins of Nations*, ch. 6; Christian Coulon and Françoise Morin, 'Occitan ethnicity and politics', *Critique of Anthropology*, 13–14 (1979), 105–23. On schooling and patriotism see two outstanding books, by Stephen L. Harp, *Learning to be Loyal: Primary Schooling and Nation-building in Alsace and Lorraine, 1850–1940* (DeKalb, IL, 1998); and Jean-François Chanet, *L'Ecole républicaine et les petites patries* (Paris, 1996).

10. Peter Sahlins, *Boundaries: The Making of France and Spain in the Pyrenees* (Berkeley, CA, 1989); McPhee, 'Internal Colonization'.

11. Yveline Fumat, 'La Socialisation des filles au XIXe siècle', *Revue française de pédagogie* 52 (1980), 45; Françoise Mayeur, *L'Education des filles en France au XIXe siècle* (Paris, 1979), chs 5–6; Laura S. Strumingher, *What were Little Girls and Boys Made Of? Primary Education in Rural France, 1830–1880* (Albany, NY, 1983); Hellerstein *et al.* (eds), *Victorian Women*, 60–8.

12. Donzelot, *Policing of Families*, esp. ch. 2; André Armengaud, 'L'Attitude de la société à l'égard de l'enfant au XIXe siècle', *Annales de démographie historique* (1973), 303–12; Jean-Noël Luc, '"A trois ans, l'enfant devient intéressant...": la découverte médicale de la seconde enfance (1850–1900)', *RHMC* 36 (1989), 83–112; Perrot, *A History of Private Life*, vol. 4, esp. part 2.

13. Assumptions about the ideas of childhood and 'romantic love' 'trickling down' to the masses are particularly evident in Ariès, *Centuries of Childhood*; Shorter, *Making of the Modern Family*. Such views are disputed in Segalen, *Love and Power in the Peasant Family*, chs 1, 4, 6; Crubellier, *L'Enfance et la jeunesse*, ch. 3; and McMillan, *Women in French Society*, ch. 2, though McMillan quickly dismisses unchanging 'peasants' (p. 5).

14. Gay, *The Tender Passion*, ch. 6. On Ferry, see François Furet (ed.), *Jules Ferry: fondateur de la République* (Paris, 1986); Jean-Michel Gaillard, *Jules Ferry* (Paris, 1989).

15. Gay, *The Tender Passion*, 369–70; McMillan, *Women in French Society*, chs 1–2; Nye, 'Nineteenth-Century French Medicine', and *Crime, Madness and Politics in Modern France* (Princeton, NJ, 1984), 132–70; Eric Hobsbawm, *The Age of Capital, 1848–1875* (New York, 1979), chs 13–14; Laure Adler, *Secrets d'alcôve: histoire du couple de 1830 à 1930* (Paris, 1983), 67–99; Roger Williams, *The Horror of Life* (Chicago, 1980); Hellerstein *et al.*, *Victorian Women*, 174–7; Zeldin, *France 1848–1945*, ch. 11; Claude Quétel, *History of Syphilis*, trans. J. Braddock and B. Pike (Oxford, 1989); Corbin, *Le Temps, le désir et l'horreur*, 171–83.

16. Shapiro, *Breaking the Codes*; Joëlle Guillais, *Crimes of Passion: Dramas of Private Life in Nineteenth-Century France*, trans. J. Dunnett (London, 1990).

17. Nye, *Crime, Madness and Politics*, ch. 4; Goldstein, *Console and Classify*, ch. 9; Ripa, *Women and Madness*; Castel, *Origins of Incarceration*, ch. 6; Perrot, *A History of Private Life*, vol. 4, part 4.

18. Charles Sowerwine, *Sisters or Citizens? Women and Socialism in France since 1876* (Cambridge, 1982), ch. 1; McMillan, *Women in French Society*, ch. 4; Moses, *Feminism in the Nineteenth Century*, ch. 7; McLaren, *Sexuality and Social Order*, chs 5, 9; Steven C. Hause, *Hubertine Auclert: The French Suffragette* (New Haven, CT, 1987); Patrick Kay Bidelman, *'Pariahs Stand Up!': The Founding of the Liberal Feminist Movement in France, 1858–1889* (Westport, CT, 1982).

19. Stephen Jay Gould, *The Mismeasure of Man* (New York, 1981), 82–5.

20. Hellerstein *et al.*, *Victorian Women*, 396–400; Jean-Claude Schmitt, *The Holy Greyhound: Guinefort, Healer of Children since the Thirteenth Century*, trans. M. Thom (Cambridge, 1983). Cultural change in the countryside is discussed in Price, *Social History*, 169–80.

21. Vigarello, *Concepts of Cleanliness*, ch. 14; Bruno Latour, *The Pasteurization of France*, trans. A. Sheridan and J. Law (Cambridge, MA, 1988).

22. Kathleen Kete, *The Beast in the Boudoir: Petkeeping in Nineteenth-Century Paris* (Berkeley, CA, 1994); Robert J. Bezucha, 'The Moralization of Society: The Enemies of Popular Culture in the Nineteenth Century', in Beauroy *et al.*, *Popular Culture in France*, 175–88; Eugen Weber, 'Religion and Superstition in Nineteenth-Century France', *HJ* 31 (1988), 399–423. There was a similar attack on alcohol consumption: see Patricia E. Prestwich, *Drink and the Politics of Social Reform: Antialcoholism in France since 1870* (Palo Alto, CA, 1988).

23. Albert Boime, *The Academy and French Painting in the Nineteenth Century* (London, 1971); Robert L. Herbert, *Impressionism: Art, Leisure and Parisian Society* (New Haven, CT, 1988); James Harding, *Artistes Pompiers: French Academic Art in the Nineteenth Century* (London, 1979); Miriam R. Levin, *Republican Art and Ideology in Late Nineteenth-Century France* (Ann Arbor, Michigan, 1986); Patricia Mainardi, *Art and Politics of the Second Empire: The Universal Expositions of 1855 and 1867* (New Haven, CT, 1987), and *The End of the Salon: Art and the State in the Early Third Republic* (Cambridge, 1993); Anne Middleton Wagner, *Jean-Baptiste Carpeaux: Sculptor of the Second Empire* (New Haven, CT, 1986); Philip Nord, 'Manet and Radical politics', *JIH* 19 (1989), 447–80.

24. Fritz Stern, *The Varieties of History* (New York, 1956), 172–4. At Gambetta's funeral in December 1882, Monod marched holding a banner proclaiming that 'History is the key science'.

25. The contested meanings of 'Marianne' and other 'texts' are discussed in masterly fashion in Agulhon, *Marianne into Battle*, chs 6–7; and by the contributors to Nora, *Les Lieux de mémoire*, vol. 1.

26. Sowerwine, *Sisters or Citizens?*, 23; Michelle Perrot, *Workers on Strike* (Newhaven, CT, 1987), and 'Norbert Truquin', in Kaplan and Koepp, *Work in France*, ch. 10; Judt, *Marxism and the French Left*, 96; Eric Hobsbawm, 'Man and Woman in Socialist Iconography', *HW* 6 (1978), 121–38 (and discussion in nos 7, 8).

27. Agulhon, *Marianne into Battle*, ch. 7; David Harvey, *Consciousness and the Urban Experience: Studies in the History and Theory of Capitalist Urbanism*

(Baltimore, MD, 1985), ch. 4. Taine's treatment of the crowd is discussed in Rudé, *Crowd in the French Revolution*, Introduction.

28. Fréderic Le Play, *Les ouvriers européens*, 2nd ed., 6 vols (Tours, 1877–9), vol. 1, 198, 149 and chs 1, 3, 5–7, 16–17. On Le Play, see Graham, 'Le Play's "Bad Books"'; Michael Z. Brooke, *Le Play: Engineer and Social Scientist* (London, 1970).

29. Gibson, *French Catholicism*, ch. 7; Austin Gough, 'Reflections on the Death of an Archbishop', in Eugene Kamenka (ed.), *Paradigm for Revolution? The Paris Commune 1871–1971* (Canberra, 1972), ch. 3; Austin Gough, *Paris and Rome: The Gallican Church and the Ultramontane Campaign, 1848–1853* (Oxford, 1986), and 'The Conflict in Politics: Bishop Pie's Campaign against the Nineteenth Century', in Zeldin, *Conflicts in French Society*, 94–168.

30. Agulhon, *Marianne into Battle*, ch. 5; Gibson, *French Catholicism*, ch. 5.

31. Gibson, *French Catholicism*, 163–4, ch. 7; Merriman, *The Red City*, 133.

32. Gibson, *French Catholicism*, 98, and ch. 8 for a discussion of Marianism; Cholvy and Hilaire, *Histoire religieuse*, chs 5, 9.

13   The Republican Triumph and its Challenges, 1877–1914

1. An excellent introduction to the politics and urban culture of the Third Republic before 1914 is Sowerwine, *France since 1870*, chs 3–7. General surveys of the Third Republic to 1914 include Maurice Agulhon, *The French Republic 1879–1992*, trans. Antonia Nevill (Oxford, 1993), part 1, and *Marianne au pouvoir: l'imagerie et la symbolique républicaines de 1880 à 1914* (Paris, 1989); Robert Gildea, *France, 1870–1914* (London, 1996); Jean-Marie Mayeur and Madeleine Rebérioux, *The Third Republic from its Origins to the Great War, 1871–1914* (Cambridge, 1984).

2. Furet, *La Révolution*, esp. 479, 516–7. Note the argument of Sudhir Hazareesingh, *From Subject to Citizen. The Second Empire and the Emergence of French Democracy* (Princeton, NJ, 1998).

3. Robert R. Locke, *French Legitimists and the Politics of Moral Order in the Early Third Republic* (Princeton, NJ, 1974); Steven C. Hause, 'Anti-Protestant Rhetoric in the Early Third Republic', *FHS* 16 (1989), 183–201.

4. Guthrie, 'Narbonne', 73.

5. A tonne/kilometre is one metric ton carried for one kilometre.

6. Crossick and Haupt, *The Petite Bourgeoisie in Europe*, 41.

7. Harvey Goldberg, *The Life of Jean Jaurès* (Madison, WI, 1962). On the survival of working-class culture, see Michelle Perrot, *Workers on Strike: France 1871–1890*, trans. C. Turner (New Haven, CT, 1987); Lenard R. Berlanstein, *The Working People of Paris, 1871–1914* (Baltimore, MD, 1984).

8. Laura Frader, *Peasants and Protest: Agricultural Workers, Politics, and Unions in the Aude, 1850–1914* (Berkeley, CA, 1994). Among other case-studies are Peter McPhee, 'Social Change and Political Conflict in Mediterranean France: Canet in the Nineteenth Century', *FHS* 12 (1981),

68–97; J. Harvey Smith, 'Work Routine and Social Structure in a French Village: Cruzy in the Nineteenth Century', *JIH* 5 (1975), 357–82.

9. Lehning, *To be a Citizen*.

10. Baker, *Fraternity among the French Peasantry*; Farcy, 'Le Temps libre au village'.

11. Whited, *Forests and Peasant Politics*.

12. Corbin, *Foul and the Fragrant*, esp. 186–95; Laura Lee Downs, *Childhood in the Promised Land: Working-Class Movements and the Colonies de Vacances in France, 1880–1960* (Durham, NC, and London, 2002).

13. Linda L. Clark, *The Rise of Professional Women in France: Gender and Public Administration since 1830* (Cambridge, 2000).

14. James F. McMillan, *France and Women, 1789–1914: Gender, Society and Politics* (London and New York, 2000).

15. Jo Burr Margadant, *Madame le Professeur: Women Educators in the Third Republic* (Princeton, NJ, 1990); Anderson, *Education in France*; Françoise Mayeur, *L'Education des filles en France au XIXe siècle* (Paris, 1979), ch. 5; Antoine Prost, *Histoire de l'enseignement en France, 1800–1967* (Paris, 1968). Sharif Gemie, *Women and Schooling in France, 1815–1914: Gender, Authority, and Identity in the Female Schooling Sector* (Keele, 1995) emphasizes the cultural obstacles to women's acceptance as lay teachers.

16. Meyers, 'Rural Teachers'; Weber, *Peasants into Frenchmen*, ch. 18; Pierre Nora (ed.), *Les Lieux de mémoire*, vol. 1, *La République* (Paris, 1984); and the special issue of *TM* 324–325–326 (1973).

17. Sowerwine, *France since 1870*, ch. 4.

18. Rebecca Rogers, 'Retrograde or Modern? Unveiling the Teaching Nun in Nineteenth-Century France', *SH* 23 (1998), 146–64.

19. On the parallel history of the mass production of cheap books, see the outstanding works by Jean-Yves Mollier, including *L'Argent et les lettres: histoire du capitalisme d'édition, 1880–1920* (Paris, 1988); and *Michel & Calmann Lévy, ou la naissance de l'édition moderne, 1836–1891* (Paris, 1984).

20. Shapiro, *Breaking the Codes*; Guillais, *Crimes of Passion*; Ruth Harris, *Murders and Madness: Medicine, Law, and Society in the Fin de Siècle* (Oxford, 1989), ch. 6.

21. Sowerwine, *France since 1870*, 53.

22. Aldrich, *Greater France*. On French West Africa, see Alice L. Conklin, *A Mission to Civilize: The Republican Idea of Empire in France and West Africa, 1895–1930* (Stanford, CA, 1997); Christopher J. Harrison, *France and Islam in West Africa, 1860–1960* (Cambridge, 1988); A. S. Kanya-Forstner, *The Conquest of the Western Sudan: A Study in French Military Imperialism* (Cambridge, 1968).

23. Michael Burns, *Rural Society and French Politics: Boulangism and the Dreyfus Affair, 1886–1900* (Princeton, NJ, 1984); Jean-Yves Mollier, *Le Scandale de Panama* (Paris, 1991). The social history of politics in these years has been the subject of several excellent case-studies, for example, by Philip G. Nord, *Paris Shopkeepers and the Politics of Resentment* (Princeton, NJ, 1986); Johnson, *Life and Death of Industrial Languedoc*; Jonas, *Industry and Politics in Rural France*.

24. Pierre Sorlin, *'La Croix' et les Juifs (1880–1899)* (Paris, 1967).
25. The Dreyfus family is the subject of a fascinating study by Michael Burns, *Dreyfus: A Family Affair*. Among a vast literature see, too, Eric Cahm, *The Dreyfus Affair in French Society and Politics* (London, 1996); Jean-Denis Bredin, *The Affair: The Case of Alfred Dreyfus*, trans. Jeffrey Mehlman (New York, 1986); Michel Winock, *Nationalism, Anti-Semitism, and Fascism in France*, trans. by Jane Marie Todd (Stanford, CA, 1998). Astonishingly, such was Dreyfus's commitment to France that, despite his degradation at the hands of its army, and the death of family and friends in World War I, he enlisted and served in the artillery throughout the war.
26. Duby and Wallon, *France rurale*, vol. 3, 517. Sanford Elwitt, *The Third Republic Defended: Bourgeois Reform in France, 1880–1914* (Baton Rouge, LA, 1986); Judith F. Stone, *The Search for Social Peace: Reform Legislation in France, 1890–1914* (Albany, NY, 1985); Herman Lebovics, *The Alliance of Iron and Wheat in the Third French Republic, 1860–1914: Origins of the New Conservatism* (Baton Rouge, LA, 1988).
27. Harrison, *The Bourgeois Citizen*; Claire Andrieu, Gilles Le Béguec, and Danielle Tartakowsky (eds), *Associations et champ politique: La Loi de 1901 à l'épreuve de siècle* (Paris, 2001); Philip Dine, *French Rugby Football: A Cultural History* (Oxford, 2001); Stephen L. Harp, *Marketing Michelin, Advertising and Cultural Identity in Twentieth-Century France* (Baltimore, MD, 2001); Georges Vigarello, 'Le Temps du sport', in Corbin, *L'Avènement des loisirs*, 193–221; Whited, *Forests and Peasant Politics* ch. 6.
28. Miller, *The Bon Marché*; Leora Auslander, *Taste and Power: Furnishing Modern France* (Berkeley, CA, 1996); André Rauch, 'Les Vacances et la nature revisitée (1830–1939)', in Corbin, *L'Avènement des loisirs*, 83–117.
29. A superb summary of belle–époque élite culture is Sowerwine, *France since 1870*, ch. 7.
30. An accessible summary of organised labour in these years is Magraw, *A History of the French Working Class*, vol. 2, part V.
31. Francesca Canadé Sautman, 'Invisible Women: Lesbian Working-Class Culture in France 1880–1930', in Merrick and Ragan, *Homosexuality in Modern France*; Sowerwine, *France since 1870*, 79–80; Judith R. Walkowitz, 'Dangerous Sexualities', in Fraisse and Perrot, *Emerging Feminism from Revolution to World* War, 369–98.
32. Stone, *Sons of the Revolution*; Nye, *Masculinity and Male Codes of Honor*; Anne-Marie Sohn, 'The Golden Age of Male Adultery: The Third Republic', *JSH* 29 (1995), 469–90.
33. Charles Sowerwine, *Sisters or Citizens? Women and Socialism in France since 1870* (Cambridge, 1978); Scott, *Only Paradoxes to Offer*; Georges Duby and Michelle Perrot (eds), *A History of Women in the West*, vol. 4 (Cambridge, MA, 1994); James F. McMillan, *France and Women 1789–1914: Gender, Society and Politics* (London and New York, 2000); Katrin Schultheiss, '"La Véritable Médecine des Femmes": Anna Hamilton and the Politics of Nursing Reform in Bordeaux, 1900–1914', *FHS* 19 (1995), 183–214.

34. Anne Martin-Fugier, 'The Actors', in Perrot, *A History of Private Life*, vol. 4, 261–337.

35. Pennell, *Morocco since 1830*, chs 4–5.

Conclusion – *Plus ça change?*

1. Mayer, *The Persistence of the Old Régime*, Intro.; Higgs, *Nobles in Nineteenth-Century France*, 28–30; Dupeux, *French Society*, p. 172.

2. Forster, 'The 'New' Elite'.

3. Tudesq, *Grands notables*, vol. 2, 1230–40; Forster, *House of Saulx-Tavanes*, 201, ch. 5, Conclusion. The adaptation of patronage systems to electoral democracy is discussed in Wilson, *Nineteenth-Century Corsica*, ch. 11.

4. William Serman, *Les Origines des officiers français, 1848–1870* (Paris, 1979) Jean Estèbe, *Les Ministres de la République, 1871–1914* (Paris, 1982), esp. chs 1–2.

5. Hazareesingh, *From Subject to Citizen*.

6. Anderson, *Imagined Communities*; Serman, *Les Origines des officiers français*. An example of the opportunities the bureaucracy created for provincial people is the story of the Corsican Timothée Landry in Bernard Raffalli and Jacqueline Sauvageot, *Une vigne sur la mer: deux siècles en Corse* (Paris, 1980).

7. Weber, *Peasants into Frenchmen*, 241.

8. Jones, *Southern Massif Central*, ch. 9; Furet and Ozouf, *Reading and Writing*, chs 1, 6. A fascinating description of the southern Massif Central, and its new railway, is Robert Louis Stevenson, *Travels with a Donkey in the Cévennes* (1878).

9. Duby and Wallon (eds), *France rurale*, vol 3, 366–7; Corbin, *Village of Cannibals*.

10. Arasse, *Guillotine and the Terror*; Corbin, *Foul and the Fragrant*, Concl.; James Donovan, 'Justice and Sexuality in Victorian Marseilles, 1825–1885', *JSH* 21 (1987), 229–62; Foucault, *Discipline and Punish*. There is an interesting debate between Foucault and Maurice Agulhon in Perrot, *L'Impossible Prison*.

11. Lyons, *Totem and the Tricolour*, chs 5–7; Nelly Schmidt, 'Schoelcherisme et assimilation dans la politique coloniale française: de la théorie à la pratique aux Caraïbes entre 1848 et les années 1880', *RHMC* 35 (1988), 305–40.

12. The resistance of working-class culture to the 'culture of capitalism' is stressed by Reddy, *Rise of Market Culture*.

13. McPhee, 'Canet in the Nineteenth Century'; Jean Anglade, *Le Massif central au XIXe siècle* (Paris, 1971), ch. 16.

14. Thabault, *Education and Change*; Peter McPhee, *Une communauté languedocienne dans l'histoire: Gabian 1760–1960* (Nîmes, 2001), 110; Merriman, *The Stones of Balazuc*, 117, 141–2. On earlier rhythms of time marked by the bells of village churches, see Corbin, *Village Bells*.

15. Donald M. Lowe, *History of Bourgeois Perception* (Chicago, 1982), Corbin, *Le Temps, le désir et l'horreur*, 9–22.

16. Aline Ripert and Claude Frère, *La Carte postale: son histoire, sa fonction sociale* (Paris, 1983).

17. Jean-Claude Toutain, 'La Consommation alimentaire en France de 1789 à 1962', *Economies et sociétés* (1971), 1913–75; and the special issue of *Annales* 30 (1975). Demographic trends are conveniently summarized in Price, *Social History*, ch. 2; and Dupâquier *et al.*, *Population française*, vol. 3.

18. Plessis, *Second Empire*, ch. 4; Adeline Daumard, 'Wealth and Affluence in France since the Beginning of the Nineteenth Century', in W. D. Rubinstein (ed.), *Wealth and the Wealthy in the Modern World* (London, 1980), ch. 2.

19. Sowerwine, *France since 1870,* ; Antoine Prost, 'Public and Private Spheres in France', in Antoine Prost and Gérard Vincent (eds), *Riddles of Identity in Modern Times;* Philippe Ariès and Georges Duby, *A History of Private Life*, vol. 5 (Cambridge, MA, 1991), 54.

20. Vigarello, *A History of Rape*, ch. 10.

21. Critiques of modernization theory within the context of French history are by Tilly, 'Did the Cake of Custom Break?', in Merriman, *Consciousness and Class Experience*; McMillan, *Women in French Society*, ch. 2; Judt, 'Social History and the Historians'; Peter McPhee, 'Electoral Democracy and Direct Democracy in France 1789–1851', EHQ 16 (1986), 77–96; Lyons, *Readers and Society in Nineteenth-Century France*, Conclusion.

22. Margadant, *Peasants in Revolt*, 267; Price, *Social History*, ch. 9; Kennedy, *Cultural History*, 35–57, 380–92; Richard Cobb, *A Second Identity: Essays on France and French History* (London, 1969), ch. 20; R. B. Rose, 'The Paris Commune: The Last Episode of the French Revolution or the First Dictatorship of the Proletariat?', in Kamenka, *The Paris Commune*, 12–29. On changing patterns of collective protest see Tilly, 'How Protest Modernized', and 'Charivaris, repertoires and urban politics', in Merriman, *French Cities*, ch. 3.

23. Boutry, *Prêtres et paroisses*, 649; Gibson, *French Catholicism*, chs 4, 8; Joutard *Histoire de la France religieuse*, vol. 3, 488; Langlois, *Catholicisme au féminin*, 317, 699–733, Conclusion.

24. Langlois, *Catholicisme au féminin*, and 'La Fin des guerres de religion: la disparution de la violence religieuse en France au 19e siècle', FHS 21 (1998), 3–25; Caroline Ford, 'Religion and Popular Culture in Modern Europe', *JMH* 65 (1993), 152–75, and 'Violence and the Sacred in Nineteenth-Century France', FHS 21 (1998), 101–12.

25. Carbasse, 'L'Émeute du 25 janvier 1791'; Michelle Perrot, 'Women, Power and History: The Case of Nineteenth-Century France', in Siân Reynolds (ed.), *Women, State, and Revolution: Essays on Power and Gender in Europe since 1789* (Amherst, MA, 1987), ch. 3; Martin-Fugier, 'The Actors', in Perrot, *A History of Private Life*, vol. 4, 261–337. The origins of the dichotomy of 'public' and 'private' antedate the French Revolution by at least a century: see Roger Chartier, *A History of Private Life*, vol. 3, *Passions of the Renaissance*, trans. A. Goldhammer (Cambridge, MA, 1989), esp. part 3.

A Guide to Further Reading

Simply to list relevant historical writing since 1960 would take many volumes of this size; instead, this brief essay seeks to suggest useful departure points for the main themes of this book. These are in English except where there is no satisfactory alternative to an outstanding but untranslated work in French. Fuller publication details may be located in the footnotes to the relevant chapter. An excellent guide to further reading on many of the themes in this book is in Malcolm Crook (ed.), *Revolutionary France 1788–1880* (2002). The *Bibliographie annuelle de l'histoire de la France* seeks to list every publication in French history, including work in English. The five-part *Historical Dictionary of France* (1985–87) has some useful essays on social history topics. The internet newsletter H-France regularly reviews recent literature.

There have been few attempts to survey social history over the whole period 1789–1914 because the Revolution continues to divide the interests of most historians. Surveys of 1815–1914 which combine a wealth of information with differences of approach are Roger Magraw, *France 1815–1914: The Bourgeois Century* (1983); Roger Price, *A Social History of Nineteenth-Century France* (1987); Sharif Gemie, *French Revolutions, 1815–1914* (1999); Christophe Charle, *A Social History of France in the Nineteenth Century*, trans. Miriam Kochan (1994); Robert Tombs, *France 1814–1914* (1996); Martin S. Alexander (ed.), *French History since Napoleon* (1999). In French, an imaginative, illustrated overview is Yves Lequin (ed.), *Histoire des français XIXe-XXe siècles*, 3 vols (1984); the Hachette series *La Vie quotidienne* includes some outstanding volumes. Altogether different is Theodore Zeldin's idiosyncratic *France 1848–1945* (1973); however, like Gordon Wright's *France in Modern Times*, 3rd edn (1981), it is very readable. Ralph Gibson, *A Social History of French Catholicism 1789–1914* (1989) lucidly and perceptively synthesizes a great deal of recent research and has much to say about French society in general, as does Jacques Dupâquier *et al.*, *Histoire de la population française*, vol. 3 (1988). The relevant volumes of *A History of Private Life* (Roger Chartier (ed.), *Passions of the Renaissance* (1989); and Michelle Perrot (ed.), *From the Fires of Revolution to the Great War* (1990)) are consistently illuminating and engaging, if disproportionately concerned with literate urban élites, as is Geneviève Fraisse and Michelle Perrot (eds), *A History of Women in the West: Emerging Feminism from Revolution to World War* (1993). Of particular richness is the seven-volume series edited by Pierre Nora, *Les Lieux de mémoire*, originally published 1984–92. Three translated volumes were published as *Realms of Memory* (1996–8); four more are being published under the direction of David Jordan as *Rethinking France* (2001–).

The best introduction to eighteenth-century France is Daniel Roche, *France in the Enlightenment*, trans. Arthur Goldhammer (1998). The outstanding survey by John McManners, *Church and Society in Eighteenth-Century France*, 2 vols (1998) has much to say about society in general. Local studies permit a closer approach to French society; among them are Robert Forster, *The House of Saulx-Tavanes: Versailles and Burgundy 1700–1830* (1977); Daniel Roche, *The People of Paris: An Essay in Popular Culture in the 18th Century* (1987); David Garrioch, *The Making of Revolutionary Paris* (2002); Thomas Sheppard, *Lourmarin in the Eighteenth Century: A Study of a French Village* (1971); Olwen Hufton, *Bayeux in the Late Eighteenth Century: A Social Study* (1967); John McManners, *French Ecclesiastical Society under the Ancien Régime* (1960); Peter Jones, *Politics and Rural Society: The Southern Massif Central c.1750–1880* (1985); Patrice Higonnet, *Pont-de-Montvert: Social Structure and Politics in a French Village, 1700–1914* (1971); and Liana Vardi, *The Land and the Loom: Peasants and Profit in Northern France 1680–1800* (1993).

The crucial roles of women in household work strategies are discussed in Olwen Hufton's important *The Prospect Before Her: A History of Women in Western Europe, 1500–1800* (1996). The urban workshop economy is the subject of the difficult but rewarding study by Michael Sonenscher, *Work and Wages: Natural Law, Politics and the Eighteenth-Century French Trades* (1989). A series of excellent essays treating the eighteenth and nineteenth-century world of work is presented by Steven Kaplan and Cynthia Koepp (eds), *Work in France: Representations, Meaning, Organization and Practice* (1986).

Debates on the origins of the Revolution are summarised from a 'revisionist' perspective in William Doyle, *Origins of the French Revolution*, 2nd edn (1980), while Colin Jones synthesizes a mass of recent research into an effective Marxist riposte in Colin Lucas (ed.), *Rethinking the French Revolution* (1991). Increasing attention has been paid to the cultural origins of the Revolution, well summarized in Roger Chartier, *The Cultural Origins of the French Revolution* (1991). Important specific studies are Thomas Crow, *Painters and Public Life in Eighteenth-Century Paris* (1985), and the deservedly influential work of Robert Darnton, *The Great Cat Massacre and Other Episodes in French Cultural History* (1984), and *The Literary Underground of the Old Regime* (1982).

Exemplifying Marxist and 'revisionist' understandings of the origins, course and significance of the Revolution are Albert Soboul, *The French Revolution 1787–1799: From the Storming of the Bastille to Napoleon* (1989) and William Doyle, *The Oxford History of the French Revolution* (1989). D. M. G. Sutherland, *The French Revolution and Empire: The Quest for a Civic Order* (2003) is a detailed, provocative overview which succeeds in viewing the Revolution from a national rather than Parisian perspective but understates popular support for the Revolution. Recent overviews are by Jeremy Popkin, *A Short History of the French Revolution* (1995), Peter McPhee, *The French Revolution 1789–1799* (2002); and David Andress, *French Society in Revolution, 1789–1799* (1999); the last of these includes a superb collection of documents, as does Lynn Hunt (ed.), *The French Revolution and Human Rights: A Brief Documentary History* (1996). Andress integrates women's participation and issues of gender, on which see Dominique Godineau, *The Women of Paris and their French Revolution*, trans. Katherine Streip (1998); Lynn Hunt, *The Family*

Romance of the French Revolution (1992); Joan Landes, *Women and the Public Sphere in the Age of the French Revolution* (1988); Madelyn Gutwirth, *The Twilight of the Goddesses: Women and Representation in the French Revolutionary Era* (1992). More nuanced views of women's participation in and experience of the Revolution are by Carla Hesse, *The Other Enlightenment: How French Women Became Modern* (2001); R. B. Rose, *Tribunes and Amazons: Men and Women of Revolutionary France 1789–1871* (1998), and Margaret Darrow's innovative *Revolution in the House: Family, Class and Inheritance in Southern France, 1775–1825* (1989).

Peter Jones, *The Peasantry in the French Revolution* (1988) is an outstanding complement to Georges Lefebvre, *The Great Fear of 1789: Rural Panic in Revolutionary France* (1973). Of real importance is John Markoff and Gilbert Shapiro, *Revolutionary Demands: A Content Analysis of the Cahiers de doléances of 1789* (1998). On rural resistance to the Revolution, see Charles Tilly's path-breaking *The Vendée* (1964); Donald Sutherland, *The Chouans: The Social Origins of Popular Counter-Revolution in Upper Brittany, 1770–1796* (1982); Lawrence Wylie, *Chanzeaux: A Village in Anjou* (1966); Gwynne Lewis, *The Second Vendée: The Continuity of Counter-Revolution in the Department of the Gard, 1789–1815* (1978); and Claude Petitfrère's useful review essay 'The Origins of the Civil War in the Vendée', *FH* (1988). A study of a pro-revolutionary region is Peter McPhee, *Revolution and Environment in Southern France: Peasants, Lords, and Murder in the Corbières, 1780–1830* (1999).

Apart from the local studies cited earlier, the urban, provincial face of the Revolution is expertly traced in Gail Bossenga, *The Politics of Privilege: Old Regime and Revolution in Lille* (1991); Alan Forrest, *Society and Politics in Revolutionary Bordeaux* (1975); Bill Edmonds, *Jacobinism and the Revolt of Lyon, 1789–1793* (1990); William Scott, *Terror and Repression in Revolutionary Marseilles* (1973); Paul Hanson, *Provincial Politics in the French Revolution: Caen and Limoges, 1789–1794* (1989); Ted W. Margadant, *Urban Rivalries in the French Revolution* (1992); and Richard Andrews' engrossing essay on revolutionary Paris in Gene Brucker (ed.), *People and Communities in the Western World*, vol. 2 (1979).

Nigel Aston, *Religion and Revolution in France, 1780–1804* (2000) is a read-able, perceptive survey of the religious conflicts of the revolutionary period. More specific analyses include Timothy Tackett's illuminating *Religion, Revolution, and Regional Culture in Eighteenth-Century France* (1986); and Michel Vovelle, *La Révolution contre l'église: de la raison à l'être suprême* (1988). Social policy during the Revolution is studied by Colin Jones, *The Charitable Imperative: Hospitals and Nursing in Ancien Régime and Revolutionary France* (1989); Alan Forrest, *The French Revolution and the Poor* (1981); Isser Woloch, *The French Veteran from the Revolution to the Restoration* (1979); Jean-Pierre Gross, *Fair Shares for All: Jacobin Egalitarianism in Practice* (1997). An impor-tant study of the impact of the 1792 divorce law is Roderick Phillips, *Family Breakdown in Late-Eighteenth Century France: Divorces in Rouen 1792–1803* (1980).

The fundamental works on the Parisian popular movement, George Rudé, *The Crowd in the French Revolution* (1959), and Albert Soboul, *The Parisian*

Sans-Culottes and the French Revolution, 1793–4 (1964), have been supplemented by William Sewell, *Work and Revolution in France: The Language of Labor from the Old Régime to 1848* (1980). 'The Revolution armed' has been studied by Jean-Paul Bertaud, *The Army of the French Revolution: From Citizen-Soldiers to Instrument of Power* (1988), Alan Forrest, *Soldiers of the French Revolution* (1989), and, in different guise, by Richard Cobb, *The People's Armies* (1987). Popular political life is the focus of R. B. Rose, *The Making of the 'Sans-Culottes': Democratic Ideas and Institutions in Paris, 1789–1792* (1983), and, nationally, of Michael Kennedy, *The Jacobin Clubs in the French Revolution*, 2 vols (1982, 1988). Particularly useful on the theory and practice of citizenship are Malcolm Crook, *Elections in the French Revolution: An Apprenticeship in Democracy, 1789–1799* (1996) and Michael Rapport, *Nationality and Citizenship in Revolutionary France. The Treatment of Foreigners, 1789–1799* (2000).

The period 1795–1815 remains that most neglected by social historians, despite the fine collection of essays in Gwynne Lewis and Colin Lucas (eds), *Beyond the Terror: Essays in French Regional and Social History, 1794–1815* (1983). There are also relevant chapters in Richard Cobb, *The Police and the People: French Popular Protest 1789–1820* (1970), and *Reactions to the French Revolution* (1972); Denis Woronoff, *The Thermidorian Regime and the Directory* (1984); Martyn Lyons, *France under the Directory* (1975) and *Napoleon Bonaparte and the Legacy of the French Revolution* (London, 1994); Sutherland, *French Revolution*; and Louis Bergeron, *France under Napoleon* (1981). Provincial case-studies include Geoffrey Ellis, *Napoleon's Continental Blockade: The Case of Alsace* (1981); Gavin Daly, *Inside Napoleonic France: State and Society in Rouen, 1800–1815* (2001).

The social impact of the Revolution remains the most contentious issue in the history of the century after 1780. Among the plethora of publications for the bicentenary of the French Revolution in 1989, special issues of *HW, FPS, FHS* and *AHR* surveyed current debates. Among the 'minimalist' overviews are Olwen Hufton, 'Women in Revolution 1789–1796', *P&P* (1971); Robert Forster, in Jaroslaw Pelenski (ed.), *The American and European Revolutions, 1776–1848* (1980) and the conclusions to William Doyle, *The Oxford History of the French Revolution* and Simon Schama, *Citizens: A Chronicle of the French Revolution* (both 1989). These may be contrasted with the concluding chapters of Soboul, *French Revolution*, and Jones, *Peasantry*; and Bill Edmonds, 'Successes and Excesses of Revisionist Writing about the French Revolution', *EHQ* (1987). The impact of the Revolution on 'political culture' is stressed by Colin Jones and Dror Wahrman, *The Age of Cultural Revolutions: Britain and France, 1750–1820* (2002); Lynn Hunt, *Politics, Culture, and Class in the French Revolution* (1984); Carla Hesse, *Publishing and Cultural Politics in Revolutionary Paris 1789–1810* (1991); the contributors to the four volumes of *The French Revolution and the Creation of Modern Political Culture* (1987–94); Timothy Tackett, *Becoming a Revolutionary. The Deputies of the French National Assembly and the Emergence of a Revolutionary Culture (1789–1790)* (1996); Isser Woloch, *The New Regime: Transformations of the French Civic Order, 1789–1820s* (1994); and Emmet Kennedy, *A Cultural*

History of the French Revolution (1989). These are largely concerned with literate, urban culture: more wide-ranging is Mona Ozouf, *Festivals and the French Revolution* (1988). The Revolution's musical expression is studied by Laura Mason, *Singing the French Revolution: Popular Culture and Politics, 1787–1799* (1996). The Revolution's impact on state structures and national identity is discussed in Martyn Lyons, 'Politics and Patois: The Linguistic Policy of the French Revolution', *AJFS* (1981); Clive Church, *Revolution and Red Tape: The French Ministerial Bureaucracy, 1770–1850* (1981); Peter Sahlins, *Boundaries: The Making of Modern France and Spain in the Pyrenees* (1989); and the special issue of *TM* (1973). The impact on the colonies and racial attitudes has received belated attention, from Carolyn Fick and Pierre Boulle in Frederick Krantz (ed.), *History from Below: Studies in Popular Protest and Popular Ideology in Honour of George Rudé* (1985); Robert Forster, 'Who is a Citizen? The Boundaries of 'La Patrie'', *FPS* (1989); Yves Benot, *La Révolution française et la fin des colonies* (1988); and James F. Searing *West African Slavery and Atlantic Commerce: The Senegal River Valley, 1770–1860* (1993).

The study of rural society in the nineteenth century has produced some outstanding social history, notably Maurice Agulhon, *The Republic in the Village: The People of the Var from the French Revolution to the Second Republic* (1982). Agulhon was also a major contributor to the best general survey, Georges Duby and Armand Wallon (eds), *Histoire de la France rurale*, vol. 3 (1976). There are detailed regional and political analyses in André Jardin and André-Jean Tudesq, *Restoration and Reaction, 1815–1848* (1983), though Tudesq's *Les grands notables en France (1840–1849): étude historique d'une psychologie sociale*, 2 vols. (1964) remains indispensable for the landed élite. Though ignoring politics, the insights gained from a sensible use of quantification are exemplified in James Lehning, *The Peasants of Marlhes: Economic Development and Family Organization in Nineteenth-Century France* (1980), and John Shaffer, *Family and Farm: Agrarian Change and Household Organization in the Loire Valley, 1500–1900* (1982). Both discuss the impact of the Revolution's inheritance laws on declining fertility rates, as does Etienne van der Walle in Robert Wheaton and Tamara Hareven (eds), *Family and Sexuality in French History* (1980). Rural cultures and their political dimensions are studied by contributors to Jacques Beauroy *et al.* (eds), *The Wolf and the Lamb: Popular Culture in France from the Old Regime to the Twentieth Century* (1977), and by Tessie Liu, *The Weaver's Knot: The Contradictions of Class Struggle and Family Solidarity in Western France, 1750–1914* (1994).

The case for social continuity in the countryside is put by Peter Jones, *Southern Massif Central*, and, less convincingly, by Eugen Weber, *Peasants into Frenchmen: The Modernization of Rural France, 1870–1914* (1976). Similarly, the emphasis on economic continuities before the 1860s in Roger Price, *The Modernization of Rural France: Communications Networks and Agricultural Market Structures in Nineteenth-Century France* (1983), and Hugh Clout, *The Land of France, 1815–1914* (1983) is challenged by Ted Margadant, 'Tradition and Modernity in Rural France during the Nineteenth Century', *JMH* (1984). A fine case-study of the rural exodus is Leslie Page Moch, *Paths to the City: Regional Migration in Nineteenth-Century France* (1983); seasonal migration is the subject of Abel Chatelain's exhaustive *Les Migrants temporaires en France de 1800 à 1914.* The best of the local studies have contributed to an understanding of the social history of politics in the nineteenth century: a fine example is John M. Merriman, *The Stones of Balazuc: A French Village in Time* (2002). Tamara L. Whited, *Forests and Politics in Modern France* (2000) is a pathbreaking exploration of the social history of the environment. Examples of social history focusing on the Second Empire are in Theodore Zeldin (ed.), *Conflicts in French Society: Anticlericalism, Education and Morals in the Nineteenth Century* (1970).

The twin processes of urbanization and industrialization have attracted a great deal of fine scholarship: there are good overviews by Georges Duby (ed.), *Histoire de la France urbaine*, vols 3–4 (1981–3); and Roger Magraw, *A History of the French Working Class*, 2 vols (1992). Outstanding local studies are John Merriman's engaging *The Red City: Limoges and the French Nineteenth Century* (1985) and *The Margins of City Life: Explorations on the French Urban Frontier, 1815–1851* (1991), and Elinor Accampo's innovative *Industrialization, Family Life, and Class Relations: Saint-Chamond, 1815–1914* (1989), to be considered in conjunction with Lehning's study of a nearby village, cited above. Other urban studies include Adeline Daumard, *Les Bourgeois de Paris au XIXe siècle* (1970); Ronald Aminzade, *Class, Politics and Early Industrial Capitalism: A Study of Mid-Nineteenth Century Toulouse* (1981); Christopher H. Johnson, *The Life and Death of Industrial Languedoc, 1700–1920: The Politics of Deindustrialization* (1995); William Reddy, *The Rise of Market Culture: The Textile Trade and French Society 1750–1900* (1984). Jacques Rancière's demanding *The Nights of Labor: The Workers' Dream in Nineteenth-Century France* (1989) challenges the importance imputed to the artisans' commitment to skilled trades, while seven workers' autobiographies are usefully collected in Mark Traugott (ed.), *The French Worker: Autobiographies from the Early Industrial Era* (1993). The lower middle-classes have been insightfully studied in Geoffrey Crossick and Heinz-Gerhard Haupt, *The Petite Bourgeoisie in Europe, 1780–1914: Enterprise, Family and Independence* (1995).

The writing of French history has until recently suffered from a failure to integrate colonial and metropolitan economics and politics. A useful and wide-ranging survey of colonialism is Robert Aldrich, *Greater France: A History of French Overseas Expansion* (1996). More specific studies are Aldrich, *The French Presence in the Pacific 1842–1940* (1990); John Ruedy, *Modern Algeria: The Origins and Development of a Nation* (1992); Martyn Lyons, *The Totem and the Tricolour: A Short History of New Caledonia since 1774* (1986); and Alice L. Conklin, *A Mission to Civilize: the Republican Idea of Empire in France and West Africa, 1895–1930* (1997).

John Merriman (ed.), *1830 in France* (1975) amounts to a revision from a national perspective of a Revolution formerly understood as Parisian and narrowly political; this is extended by Pamela M. Pilbeam, *The 1830 Revolution in France* (1991). Popular republican politics in Paris itself are evoked in Jill Harsin, *Barricades: The War of the Streets in Revolutionary Paris, 1830–1848* (2002). The roots of working-class radicalism are explored in Sewell, *Work and Revolution* and Robert Bezucha, *The Lyon Uprising of 1834: Social and Political*

Conflict in the Early July Monarchy (1974). The best introduction to the Second Republic is Maurice Agulhon, *The Republican Experiment, 1848–1852* (1983). Roger Price, *The French Second Republic: A Social History* (1972) is a detailed critique of Marx's classics, *The Class Struggles in France, 1848–1850,* and *The Eighteenth Brumaire of Louis Bonaparte*; Price also edited a fine collection of essays, *Revolution and Reaction: 1848 and the Second French Republic* (1975). On radical provincial movements and their repression, see Ted Margadant, *French Peasants in Revolt: The Insurrection of 1851* (1979); John Merriman, *The Agony of the Republic: The Repression of the Left in Revolutionary France, 1848–1851* (1978); Edward Berenson, *Populist Religion and Left-Wing Politics in France, 1830–1852* (1984); and Peter McPhee, *The Politics of Rural Life: Political Mobilization in the French Countryside, 1846–1852* (1992).

The Paris Commune and the founding of the Third Republic have long attracted detailed research; among the most helpful studies are Stewart Edwards, *The Paris Commune: 1871* (1971); Edith Thomas's classic *The Women Incendiaries* (1966); Sanford Elwitt, *The Making of the Third Republic: Class and Politics in France, 1868–1914* (1975); Robert Tombs, *The Paris Commune 1871* (1999) and Philip Nord, *The Republican Movement. Struggles for Democracy in Nineteenth-Century France* (1995). The only general survey of the provinces in 1870–1 remains Jeanne Gaillard, *Communes de province, commune de Paris, 1870–1871* (1971), although the struggle for symbolic legitimacy is superbly evoked by Agulhon, *Marianne into Battle: Republican Imagery and Symbolism in France, 1789–1880* (1981) and *Marianne au pouvoir: l'imagerie et la symbolique républicaines de 1880 à 1914* (1989). Episodes in the social history of politics are deftly explored by Michael Burns, *Rural Society and French politics: Boulangism and the Dreyfus Affair, 1886–1900* (1984); and Alain Corbin, *The Village of Cannibals: Rage and Murder in France, 1870* (1992). Leo Loubère, *Radicalism in Mediterranean France: Its Rise and Decline (1848–1914)* (1974) is a useful regional study.

Gérard Cholvy's *Être chrétien en France au XIXe siècle, 1790–1914* (1997) and Philippe Joutard (ed.) *Histoire de la France religieuse*, vol. 3, *Du roi Très Chrétien à la laïcité républicaine XVIIIe-XIXe siècle*, 2nd edn (Paris, 2001) are two outstanding surveys of the social history of religion in the nineteenth century. The religion of ordinary people is further illuminated by Alain Corbin, *Village Bells: Sound and Meaning in the 19th Century French Countryside* (1998); Thomas Kselman, *Death and the Afterlife in Modern France* (1993); Paula Hyman, *The Jews of Modern France* (1998); and Nicole Edelman, *Voyantes, guérisseuses et visionnaires en France, 1785–1914* (1995). There are some brilliant insights into the idea and practice of 'leisure' in Alain Corbin (ed.), *L'Avènement des loisirs 1850–1960* (Paris & Rome, 1995).

A fine overview of women's work is Louise Tilly and Joan Scott, *Women, Work and Family* (1978); specific areas of work are examined in Gay Gullickson, *Spinners and Weavers of Auffay: Rural Industry and the Sexual Division of Labor in a French Village, 1750–1850* (1986); Theresa McBride, *The Domestic Revolution: The Modernization of Household Service in England and France, 1820–1920* (1976); George Sussman, *Selling Mothers' Milk: The Wet-Nursing Business in France 1715–1914* (1982); Judith Coffin, *The Politics of Women's*

Work: The Paris Garment Trades, 1750–1915 (1996); and Victoria E. Thompson, *The Virtuous Marketplace: Women and Men, Money and Politics in Paris, 1830–1870* (2000). A superb exploration of attitudes to love and of village life in the 1860s is Gillian Tindall, *Célestine: Voices from a French Village* (1995). A fascinating and important argument is presented in Martine Segalen, *Love and Power in the Peasant Family: Rural France in the Nineteenth Century* (1983); this is one of a number of themes addressed in Michelle Perrot's succinct essay in Siân Reynolds (ed.), *Women, State, and Revolution: Essays on Power and Gender in Europe since 1789* (1987). Two important French collections are Jean-Paul Aron (ed.), *Misérable et glorieuse: la femme au XIXe siècle* (1980) and Christiane Dufrancatel *et al.* (eds), *L'Histoire sans qualités* (1979); one in English is Renate Bridenthal *et al.* (eds), *Becoming Visible: Women in European History*, 2nd edn (1987). An excellent overview, although focusing on urban France, is James McMillan, *France and Women 1789–1914: Gender, Society and Politics* (2000).

Increasing attention has been paid to the social history of the medical professions and their attempts to establish hegemony at the expense of popular practices and the Church. See Matthew Ramsey, *Professional and Popular Medicine in France, 1770–1830: The Social World of Medical Practice* (1988); William Coleman, *Death is a Social Disease: Public Health and Political Economy in Early Industrial France* (1982); Jan Goldstein, *Console and Classify: The French Psychiatric Profession in the Nineteenth Century* (1988); Robert Nye, *Crime, Madness and Politics in Modern France* (1984). The close links between professional discourse, idealized gender roles, and attitudes to sexuality and social order are explored by the contributors to Perrot (ed.), *From the Fires of Revolution to the Great War* (1990); Jill Harsin, *Policing Prostitution in Nineteenth-Century Paris* (1985); Alain Corbin, *Women for Hire: Prostitution and Sexuality in France after 1850* (1990), and *The Foul and the Fragrant: Odor and the French Social Imagination* (1986); Patricia O'Brien, *The Promise of Punishment: Prisons in Nineteenth-Century France* (1982); Angus McLaren, *Sexuality and Social Order: The Debate over the Fertility of Women and Workers in France, 1770–1920* (1983); Antony Copley, *Sexual Moralities in France, 1780–1980: New Ideas on the Family, Divorce and Homosexuality* (1989); Yannick Ripa, *Women and Madness: The Incarceration of Women in Nineteenth-Century France* (1990) and Jacques Donzelot, *The Policing of Families* (1980). Jeffrey Merrick and Bryant T. Ragan (eds), *Homosexuality in Modern France* (1996); and Jeffrey Merrick and Michael Sibalis (eds), *Homosexuality in French History and Culture* (2001), are uneven but important collections. All of these reflect in some way the influence of Michel Foucault, *The History of Sexuality* (1979) and *Discipline and Punish: The Birth of the Prison* (1977). Feminist responses to the constraints of gender stereotyping are clearly presented in Claire Moses, *French Feminism in the Nineteenth Century* (1984); very different were the women sensitively studied by Bonnie Smith, *Ladies of the Leisure Class: The Bourgeoises of Northern France in the Nineteenth Century* (1981). The presence of women in insurrections is usefully surveyed by David Barry, *Women and Political Insurgency. France in the Mid-Nineteenth Century* (1996).

The social history of children and government policies towards them is the focus of Colin Heywood, *Childhood in Nineteenth-Century France: Work, Health and Education among the 'Classes Populaires'* (1988); Katherine Lynch, *Family, Class, and Ideology in Early Industrial France: Social Policy and the Working-Class Family 1825–1848* (1988); and Rachel Fuchs, *Abandoned Childen: Foundlings and Child Welfare in Nineteenth-Century France* (1984). The sexual assault of children is studied by Georges Vigarello, *A History of Rape. Sexual Violence in France from the 16th to the 20th Century* (2001). Among an extensive literature on primary schooling, see François Furet and Jacques Ozouf, *Reading and Writing: Literacy in France from Calvin to Jules Ferry* (1982); Robert Gildea, *Education in Provincial France (1800–1914): A Study of Three Departments* (1983); Raymond Grew and Patrick Harrigan, *School, State, and Society. The Growth of Elementary Schooling in 19th-Century France: A Quantitative Analysis* (1991); Sharif Gemie, *Women and Schooling in France, 1815–1914: Gender, Authority, and Identity in the Female Schooling Sector* (1995); Laura Strumingher, *What were Little Girls and Boys Made Of? Primary Education in Rural France, 1830–1880* (1983) and Stephen L. Harp, *Learning to be Loyal: Primary Schooling and Nation-building in Alsace and Lorraine, 1850–1940* (1998).

Perhaps the most effective introduction to nineteenth-century society, and to the social history of ideas, is the literature generated in response to the social and political uncertainties of these decades. The novels of Stendhal, Flaubert, Balzac, Hugo and Zola are well known; of less renown or literary merit, but of real interest for the countryside, are Emile Guillaumin, *The Life of a Simple Man*; Eugène Le Roy, *Jacquou le Croquant*, and *Le moulin du Frau*; and *Le meunier d'Angibault* and *François le Champi* by George Sand. Among historical surveys of the social history of ideas, the most useful are Martyn Lyons, *Le Triomphe du livre: une histoire sociologique de la lecture dans la France du XIXe siècle* (1987) and *Readers and Society in Nineteenth-Century France: Workers, Women, Peasants* (2001). Painting is replaced in its social context, with revealing results, by Michael Marrinan, *Painting Politics for Louis-Philippe: Art and Ideology in Orléanist France, 1830–1848* (1988); Timothy Clark, *Image of the People: Gustave Courbet and the 1848 Revolution* (1973); and Robert Herbert, *Impressionism: Art, Leisure, and Parisian Society* (1988).

Index